Natural Resource Management for Sustainable Development in the Caribbean

Natural Resource Management for Sustainable Development in the Caribbean

Edited by

Ivan Goodbody

and

Elizabeth Thomas-Hope

Canoe Press
Barbados • Jamaica • Trinidad and Tobago

Canoe Press University of the West Indies
1A Aqueduct Flats Mona
Kingston 7 Jamaica

06 05 04 03 02 5 4 3 2 1

CATALOGUING IN PUBLICATION DATA

Natural resources management for sustainable development in
The Caribbean / edited by Ivan Goodbody and Elizabeth Thomas-Hope
p. cm.
Includes bibliographical references and index.

ISBN 13: 978-976-8125-76-7

1. Natural resources – Caribbean, English-speaking – Management. 2. Water resources development – Caribbean, English-speaking. 3. Aquatic resources – Caribbean, English-speaking – Management. 4. Sustainable development – Caribbean, English-speaking. 5. Agricultural resources – Caribbean, English-speaking – Management. 6. Forests and forestry – Caribbean, English-speaking – Management. 7. Coastal zone management – Caribbean, English-speaking. I. Goodbody, Ivan. II. Thomas-Hope, Elizabeth.

HC151.Z6N37 2002 333.7

Cover photograph of a fisherman's beach, Ocho Rios, Jamaica, by Elizabeth Thomas-Hope.

Cover design by Robert Harris.

Contents

Acknowledgements

We acknowledge with gratitude the assistance of the following persons who have given their time and expertise to read and comment upon different portions of the manuscript: Froylan Castaneda (Food and Agriculture Organization, Rome, Italy); Eleanor Jones (Environmental Solutions Ltd., Kingston, Jamaica); Robert Lancashire (Department of Chemistry, University of the West Indies, Mona, Jamaica); Gerald Lalor (Centre for Nuclear and Environmental Sciences, University of the West Indies, Mona, Jamaica); John Munro (International Centre for Living Aquatic Resources, Manila, Philippines and Perpignon, France); Robin Rattray (Centre for Nuclear and Environmental Sciences, University of the West Indies, Mona, Jamaica); Bruce Sewell (Forestry Commission, Scotland, U.K.); Kyran Thelan (Food and Agriculture Organization, Santiago, Chile); Terrence Thomas (former Executive Director, Environmental Foundation of Jamaica); and Michael White (hydrology consultant, Kingston, Jamaica).

We are also grateful for financial support in the preparation of the manuscript from the Canadian International Development Agency through the Canada/University of the West Indies (UWI) Programme, administered by the University Center for Environment and Development (UWICED).

Finally, the technical contribution of Therese Ferguson and Adonna Comrie of the Environmental Management Unit of the Department of Geography and Geology, UWI, Mona, is also gratefully acknowledged.

Introduction: Managing Nature as Resource

Elizabeth Thomas-Hope

Contents

The management of resources from nature, termed "natural resources", has been of growing concern throughout the world, particularly over the past half century, when their rapid destruction was brought to public attention by books such as Rachel Carson's *Silent Spring* (1962). This concern has been driven by the increasing awareness of the damage that is inflicted upon the environment through human use of nature as a resource. The damage occurs at local and global levels and is not only immediate in some of its effects but also persistent, even irreversible, in others. International anxieties culminated in the Earth Summit convened in Rio de Janeiro in 1994. All nations of the world were issued with a mandate to protect the environment for the benefit of present and future generations. The alarm, based upon worries for the future environments and, therefore, the lives and livelihoods of human beings, led to a series of explanations focusing in the first instance upon population and then widening into considerations of the very process of economic development.

The conflict between the interests of environmental preservation on the one hand and development based on contemporary models of economic growth on the other had to be resolved. In order to tackle some of the inherent contradictions the concept of what constitutes development came under scrutiny. The more radical view declared that a fundamental change in the criteria of development had to take place – that there needed to be a shift from criteria determined by direct or indirect extraction of value from nature to ones that were much less materialistic. This view was based upon the premise that such a process would ultimately lead to a connection of humans to their ecosystems, leading to spiritual enhancement and a new or renewed sense of place of humans on Earth. The more moderate view stated that development, in the existing sense of the term, would be possible, provided that there were checks on the damage inflicted on the environment by human activity, so that the resources that were the basis of modern development would not be thus destroyed. This led to international pleas for development that would endure, or would be sustainable.

Environmental protection, therefore, was incorporated into sustainable development strategies. It sometimes sits uneasily in this position; for though it is part of the solution, the thresholds of compromise are difficult to establish and are most certainly not universally agreed. The rejection of the Kyoto Agreement on Climate Change by the United States in 2001 shows once again the difficulties involved in international consensus building.

Nevertheless, environmental management is needed to proceed with the task of finding and implementing guidelines for the patterns of resource use that accompany development. What this really means is that environmental management is needed to manage people and their diverse and potentially damaging activities that take place, either within the context of ownership rights or of the use and misuse of shared resources – in particular, water and air. These include the range of formally institutionalized, as well as informal, activities.

How the objective of sustainable development may be achieved remains a major challenge. It clearly involves the management of human behaviour, but the terms of reference for such a mandate are complex. In order that these may be clarified over time and before time runs out, it is essential that the problem be addressed from every perspective. This should include the continued search for scientific evidence of damage sustained by nature due to human activity, the continued search for criteria to determine appropriate actions, and the mechanisms for achieving agreed behaviours in future.

RESOURCES FROM NATURE – ISSUES OF ETHICS AND GOVERNANCE

Nature is converted into a resource when it is ascribed value for human use or benefit. A resource, therefore, is inherently anthropogenic and to a greater or lesser extent represents nature appropriated by humans. Furthermore, value generates the urge to own. The value of a resource determines the cost of obtaining rights of access or ownership over it. In this way nature is converted into resource. This process, like that of the division of land into property and territory, may be convenient from the point of view of economic exchange but, as Low and Gleeson (1998: 19) remarked, "it is arbitrary from the point of view of environments".

Resources are owned, in the sense of being a possession over which rights are protected by law, even though in some parts of the world there are regulatory frameworks that constrain actions to accord with land use policies and, increasingly, environmental protection policies. Thus, management of human behaviour becomes necessary with respect to rights of ownership and use. History has shown that there is no universally agreed or practiced justice of people towards the environment. On the contrary, these relationships are usually motivated by selfishness. They become a measure of power and are used to enhance the wealth and opportunity of the powerful. Yet, where there is no clear delineation of ownership, as in the case of underground water and air, the result has reflected the all too familiar "tragedy of the commons". Everyone assumes a right to use but no one accepts any responsibilities to preserve the quality of these resources.

Even though it has become a widely held view in most societies that the preservation of the environment is good, the concept does not meet with agreement in terms of meaning, motives, and the nature of the ultimate good as the goal. There are at least two possible meanings behind the preservation of environment as a basis of environmental ethics: ethics for the use of the environment, which is a *technocentric* approach to environment, and ethics of the environment, an *ecocentric* approach to environment.

The "management ethic" of the West is based on the first meaning, in which the principles that check action or guide behaviour are based on market value and legal ownership. These provide guidelines as to what is right. From such a perspective, the environment is managed by whatever technology can be made available. The market value provides the check on overexploitation because it is evident that excessive use of resources will undermine this value over time. This is the fundamental principle of sustainable development.

The ecocentric approach to environment supports the idea of intrinsic value, based on the inherent worth of nature and all its elements. There are ethics that deal with people's relationships with people based on principles of human rights, but ethics that deal with nature and thus people's relationship with nature are limited. As yet there is no universal ethic concerning relationships of humans to animals, let alone to land, rocks, soil, minerals, plants, water, and air. The relationship with nature once it is deemed a "natural resource" is still largely economic, involving privileges, sometimes constraints, but not obligations. Yet the conqueror role is ultimately self-defeating.

A comprehensive "nature ethic", like a land ethic, "changes the role of *Homo sapiens* from conqueror of the land-community or environment to plain member and citizen of it" (Leopold, 1968: 204). The community must be involved to achieve this new role, but first, community has to be identified and understood so that its role can be operationalized. This process not only demands a new ethic but also new forms of governance relating to the management of nature as resource. The issues of resource management are not, therefore, solely or even primarily matters of organization and management procedures, as much as they are matters of ethics and governance.

Taking into consideration the fundamental ethical and political underpinnings of the management of resources derived from nature, the challenge lies in the development of mechanisms to reverse or, at the very least, prevent further negative impacts. While the debate continues over who should have the right of determining use, the scientist has an obligation to explore and explain the impact of humans upon the processes and transformations involved in the utilization of resources. But it is also critical that science should be used to measure the impact, assess the immediate consequences, and predict future risks of human actions. As Leopold defines it: "An ethic, ecologically, is a limitation on freedom of action in the struggle for existence. The complexity of co-operative mechanisms has increased with population density, and with the efficiency of tools" (Leopold, 1968: 204–205).

TYPES OF IMPACT OF THE HUMAN USE OF NATURE

Changes in nature occur without the intervention of human activity. However, these changes are considerably increased through human impact. Nor is human impact immediate: some types of impact are obvious in the short term, while other human impact only becomes evident much later. Some impact is only of local significance, while other impact has global consequences. There is a complex chain of actions and interactions that lead through direct and indirect ways to the effects upon ecosystems that cause depletion, contamination, or disturbance. Because these effects are potentially negative either in the short or long term, it is extremely important that human behaviour with respect to impact within ecosystems should be carefully monitored and managed.

The consequences of the impact that have to be averted are those that relate to the *depletion* or *exhaustion* of both nonliving and living (biotic) nature. There are possibilities that some of these – like air and water – can be cleansed and in that sense renewed; or it may be that they can be continuously used without altering their composition, as the power from the movement of wind or water is used without changing them. Other resources, like mineral deposits, once extracted and transformed, can never be returned to the state in which the initial resource value was derived. Thus, oil once used for fuel can never again be used for fuel, while waves or wind at any one place can continue to provide power to drive turbines indefinitely.

Other problems in the utilization or exploitation of the resource are derived from the *pollution* caused by the generation of waste. Land, air, and water are deliberately used as, or inadvertently become, the repositories of waste generated by the range of human activities and resource extraction. Some waste is degradable and decomposed by bacteria in the soil. Nevertheless, the transformation in the soil or water is not without its implications for their quality. In the air, waste particles are dispersed and may later settle elsewhere, thus creating additional impact. A further problem lies in the generation of waste that is not degradable or that is persistent and in particular that which is toxic or otherwise hazardous to ecosystems and humans.

Not all the human impact on the environment through the use of resources is caused by the extraction of too much value from, or the deposition of too much waste into, nature. A further form of impact is caused through environmental *disturbance* that leads to some form of disruption in the relationships within ecosystems. For example, the direct impact of clearing vegetation for residential purposes may well be managed so that the vegetation is not severely depleted. However, it could change the habitat of particular species of wildlife, which could in turn lead to other indirect effects upon the ecosystem. This is not necessarily harmful but it is usually impossible to predict whether or not at some future time it will have proved to be so. In the meantime, where risk to the environment either in the short- or long-term cannot be reliably assessed, the precautionary principle should prevail in guiding the management of resources.

The extent and nature of the effects of human activity upon the environment is determined by a combination of factors. Chief among these are the size and characteristics of the human population that is using a particular aspect or area of nature as resource, the characteristics of the economy, type of technology employed to exploit or otherwise harness nature, and forms and effectiveness of governance systems, including the institutional framework and other means of regulation. Humans, like all elements of ecosystems, demand space or territory, food, light, air, and water. They, like all elements, are in constant competition. The more intense or unregulated the competition between people the more intense is the struggle for access to, and control over, the natural resources. If this should result in a breakdown in the symbiotic nature of relationships within ecosystems or to a situation in which the carrying capacity of an ecosystem is exceeded in terms of its chemical, biological, or physical limits, then the impact will have a net negative effect. Thus, the size and spatial distribution of population and the types of systems of human use with respect to nature are fundamental issues in the forms and extent of impact.

The environment contains humans and human behaviours of all types. The prime objective of environmental management, therefore, must be to create and maintain a situation in which humans become as compatible with their environment as possible. What is possible depends on the disposition of people, together with the regulatory and management mechanisms that are established to maintain or improve the situation. The critical factor is people. People are variously concentrated into populations of differing size and composition. Composition here refers to demographic characteristics as well as economic activity and levels of sophistication of technological use.

POPULATION

People are major users of resources but, contrary to views that were current in the 1970s, population in terms of numbers is not a simple cause of damage to Earth (Ehrlich and Ehrlich, 1990; Commoner, 1971). Mere numbers of people do not determine the extent and type of use of resources that occur. The impact depends upon their demands for specific resources, how much, how they are extracted or otherwise used, and where the impact occurs. The types of technologies employed, the habits and expectations of societies and cultures, and the state of the economy are manifested in a wide range of producer and consumer activities. These include concentrations in use of vehicles, in numbers and types of industries, and in size of airports, all of which are competitors for space, high users of energy, and generators of waste. Therefore, the quality of lifestyle and resource use, rather than the quantity of people, matter most in the impact of populations upon the environment.

Urbanization that leads to ever-increasing levels of population density and of resource use also makes a difference. In the Caribbean the great majority of people are concentrated in urban areas and these are chiefly in the coastal zone. In 1995, 78 percent of Cuba's population was urban and estimated to become 80 percent by 2000. In Dominica, approximately 70 percent of the population lived in urban areas. In Trinidad and Tobago, over 72 percent were urban, in Jamaica some 56 percent, and in St Vincent and the Grenadines and Barbados approximately 50 percent were urban (United Nations, 1997). The greatest proportion of these urban populations is located in the capital towns – all of which are coastal.

The coastal locations of the vast majority of the Caribbean population has implications for the management of the coastal zone, which, in the case of small islands, represents a major part of the national territory. In small islands particularly, the ecological limits to such levels and characteristics of growth are immediate. Nor are these pressures necessarily all generated within the island itself. The distribution of sea-borne waste demonstrates the result of activities at the global level. Maritime traffic to the Caribbean has increased greatly in the 1990s. The ships, which chiefly comprise container vessels, other cargo vessels, and cruise ships, come from countries worldwide and dispose of waste from engine rooms, cargo holds, kitchens, and living quarters.

Other consequences of activities at a global scale relate to the indirect effects of gaseous emissions into the atmosphere and the rising temperatures that lead to the melting of icecaps. The resulting rise in sea levels relative to land now threaten the existence of some Pacific and Indian Ocean islands such as the Maldives. The coastal zone of Caribbean territories could be similarly threatened in the future. If sea levels rise significantly, the population of many Caribbean coastal settlements would be at risk, as would tourism and urban infrastructures. In addition, saline incursions of groundwater and losses of land area would occur. There are many other situations whereby the Caribbean is affected by actions occurring in other parts of the world. Island systems are open and, by virtue of their small size, highly sensitive to changes that take place at all levels of scale.

MANAGEMENT OF NATURAL RESOURCES

All resource use bears a cost to nature; the issue is whether it is a cost worth bearing and, if so, what the limits should be. This is what the management of resources from nature is all about: recognizing limits and developing capabilities to prevent those limits from being exceeded.

The management of the various elements and systems requires an understanding of all the components. In the case of the environment, the systems involved are multifaceted and complex, incorporating physical and biological elements, including human. Furthermore, it is invariably a complex set of natural elements, rather than a single element, that forms the resource. The same elements of nature in different combinations and configurations provide the varied resources for humankind as they are used in different ways and given value. For example, water is a resource for a range of human uses – direct human consumption, agriculture, recreation, and energy. Vegetation is a resource for direct human consumption, agriculture and agribusiness, tourism (through the amenity value of landscape and scenery), and also as a source of energy. The human use systems determine the combination of elements whereby nature is transformed into, and managed as, resource for human use and activity.

In addition to the physical elements, one has to take into account the demographic, socio-cultural, economic, and technological characteristics that condition human usage of the non-human elements. Account also has to be taken of the legislative and regulatory frameworks, which identify the parameters and apply the principles of usage of natural elements. It is only within this complex amalgam of considerations that the management of resources can be effectively addressed. It is within this total environment that the range of activities of human use systems occurs, decisions take place, and policies are developed. To manage natural resources it is necessary to understand not only a single part or parts of the physical and human environment of the particular resource, it is also necessary to understand them in relation to the whole.

An economic system, a socio-cultural system, a value system, an ecological system, a system of governance, all form parts or separate aspects of the whole. This is of itself challenging in terms of the operationalization of management and, at the same time, informative. For it is evident that if the objective is to bring about effective management, the various *systems* are merely *subsystems* of the whole. Every subsystem has its own boundaries and is linked in various ways to other subsystems. Further, the inputs of every subsystem into the whole become processed into new outputs – determined by the nature of the interaction with other subsystems. All elements of nature that enter the system – water, vegetation, aquatic life – the elements included in its volume, are inputs that will be processed or changed into outputs of the overall system. The system, therefore, must be viewed as more than the sum of its parts.

SCOPE AND ORGANIZATION OF THIS VOLUME

This book addresses the need for information about the human impact on the environment, with particular reference to the Caribbean region. The chapters that follow discuss the use and management implications of a range of resources. The scope of the work does not extend to a specific treatment of the population factor, nor to societal complexities that condition use and management of nature. However, each chapter does bring these matters into focus in the context of the issues and challenges involved in the sustainable management of the respective aspects and elements of nature under discussion.

This collection aims to introduce the reader to the major issues involved in the management of a number of resources of critical importance to Caribbean development. It begins with a chapter on the chemical components of the planetary environment. This outlines the origins of the planet Earth's environment, its composition, structure, and energy balance. A description of the cycles that are fundamental to the processes of physical change provides a background to the nature of the chemical composition and the transformations inherent in environmental change.

The following chapter is on water as a resource. It introduces the hydrologic cycle and the particular case of groundwater utilization in the Caribbean. Watershed planning and management are discussed and the implications for its development and range of uses outlined. The chapter concludes by raising the issues of the sustainability of water resources, water scarcity, and the problems of management for the continuing use of this resource in the future.

Chapters 3, 4, and 5 deal with living aquatic resources management (with a focus on fisheries), forestry, and agriculture, respectively. The characteristics and trends in fisheries management systems are outlined. The nature of Caribbean fisheries and the regulatory frameworks relating to management systems as well as fisheries in the context of the wider coastal zone, itself the topic of a later chapter (Chapter 8) are reviewed. Forestry, the topic of Chapter 4, emphasizes the close links between forest habitat and the particular biological diversity of the Caribbean region, along with the management of that diversity. The region's existing forest resources, as well as the demand and supply for specific forest products, are described and different forestry systems and their management discussed. Chapter 5 examines the sustainability of agriculture in the Caribbean in light of the challenges relating as much to changes in technology as to the liberalization of trade. The impact of agriculture on Caribbean environments is examined and alternative production systems suggested.

There is a shift in focus in the following three chapters. Chapters 6 and 7 discuss the use and management not of a single resource but of a number of resources, in the first case for the sustainable generation of energy, in the second, for recreation. Chapter 8 examines the use and management of the combined resources of the coastal zone. The close link between energy and development is highlighted in Chapter 6, as well as the close link between the generation of energy and the occurrence of severe levels of environmental damage. The histories of oil and nuclear energy are reviewed, including changes in the technological and political factors that have influenced their use and environmental impact. The "renewable" energy sources – moving water, solar radiation, wind, biomass, geothermal resources – are then described. These are discussed within the context of management issues, technological change, environmental impacts, and policy, to demonstrate the challenges and opportunities of energy sources for future Caribbean development. Attention turns to the recreational uses of nature in chapter 7. Various types of resource use are discussed, showing the range of impacts upon the environment and the importance of regulation.

The final chapter serves as a means of bringing together many of the issues already discussed in relation to the coastal zone, in addition to incorporating new considerations of mining, quarrying, and shipping. The principles of coastal zone management are therefore not focusing upon a single resource but upon the management of a number of resources within the wider ecological setting of the Caribbean coastal regions. To the issues of sustainable production and use are added those of resource accounting, population pressures, land use competition, waste management and pollution control, sanitation and public health, disaster management, and impact assessment.

The selection of resources from nature included here is not intended to be exhaustive, but rather reflects a selection of those that are of particular importance to sustainable development in the Caribbean. They also raise a number of critical issues in the debate over the management of resources from nature; a debate that is still ongoing and whose outcome will affect the environment in the Caribbean for generations to come.

REFERENCES AND FURTHER READING

Barker, D. and D. McGregor (eds.). 1995. *Environment and Development in the Caribbean: Geographical Perspectives*. The Press University of the West Indies, Mona, Jamaica.

Carson, R. 1962. *Silent Spring*. Houghton-Mifflin, New York.

Commoner, B. 1971. *The Closing Circle. Nature, Man and Technology.* Alfred A. Knopf, New York.

Ehrlich, P. and A. Ehrlich. 1990. *The Population Explosion*. Simon and Schuster, New York.

Gupta, A. and M. G. Asher. 1998. *Environment and the Developing World: Principles, Policies and Management*. John Wiley & Sons, New York.

Leopold, A. 1968. *A Sand County Almanac*, 2nd edition. Oxford University Press, Oxford.

Low, N. and B. Gleeson. 1998. *Justice, Society and Nature: An Exploration of Political Ecology.* Routledge, London.

Owen, L. and T. Unwin (eds.). 1997. *Environmental Management: Readings and Case Studies*. Blackwell, Oxford.

Redclift, M. and T. Benton (eds.). 1994. *Social Theory and the Global Environment* Routledge, London.

Thomas-Hope, E. 1996. *The Environmental Dilemma in Caribbean Context*. The Annual Grace, Kennedy Foundation Lecture. Institute of Jamaica Publications, Kingston, Jamaica.

Thomas-Hope, E. M. (ed.). 1998. *Solid Waste Management: Critical Issues for Developing Countries*. Canoe Press University of the West Indies, Mona, Jamaica.

United Nations. 1997. *The Statistical Yearbook for Latin America and the Caribbean*. United Nations, New York.

1

The Planetary Environment: A Chemical Perspective

Anthony Greenaway

Contents

INTRODUCTION

All materials in the universe – liquids, gases, and solids, living and dead – are comprised of chemicals. In the case of the gaseous oxygen in our atmosphere, a simple molecule comprises two oxygen atoms; in the case of a living biological cell, there exists a fascinating mixture of complex and simple chemicals, the mixture somehow giving life to the cell. Our environment is made of chemicals; nothing is chemical free. A knowledge of chemistry is therefore a prerequisite to an understanding of environmental processes.

Chemistry, according to the *New Shorter Oxford English Dictionary* (1993) is "the investigation of the substances of which matter is composed, and of the phenomena of combination and change which they display". The same source defines environment as "the set of circumstances, especially physical conditions, in which a person or community lives, works, develops etc., or a thing exists or operates"; alternatively, "the external conditions affecting the life of a plant or animal". Environmental is defined as "of or pertaining to the (physical) environment, concerned with the conservation of the environment".

Environmental chemistry can then be defined as the investigation of the substances of which the matter that affects the life and physical surroundings of a plant or animal is composed, and of the combination and change which they display. Such a definition seems to exclude the plant or animal from the investigation but, since all plants and animals are surrounded by other plants and animals, that need not be so. Pollutants, agents that damage the environment, and chemicals from natural sources are clearly included. Our understanding of the chemical processes that occur in the environment and the impact that they have on the physical conditions in which we live is very limited. In attempting to further our understanding we need to know the chemicals of which the environment is composed, the physical conditions (temperatures, pressures, etc.) under which they exist, and the processes that distribute them within our surroundings. To do this one must not only sample the materials that make up the surroundings and analyse them for their components but also investigate the constituent chemicals to understand how they interact, how they move within and between environmental spheres, and how changing environmental conditions affect them. Only then can the impacts of

1	2	3	4	5	6	7	8	9	10	11	12	13	14	15	16	17	18
1 H																	2 He
3 Li	4 Be											5 B	6 C	7 N	8 O	9 F	10 Ne
11 Na	12 Mg											13 Al	14 Si	15 P	16 S	17 Cl	18 Ar
19 K	20 Ca	21 Sc	22 Ti	23 V	24 Cr	25 Mn	26 Fe	27 Co	28 Ni	29 Cu	30 Zn	31 Ga	32 Ge	33 As	34 Se	35 Br	36 Kr
37 Rb	38 Sr	39 Y	40 Zr	41 Nb	42 Mo	43 Tc	44 Ru	45 Rh	46 Pd	47 Ag	48 Cd	49 In	50 Sn	51 Sb	52 Te	53 I	54 Xe
55 Cs	56 Ba	57 La	72 Hf	73 Ta	74 W	75 Re	76 Os	77 Ir	78 Pt	79 Au	80 Hg	81 Tl	82 Pb	83 Bi	84 Po	85 At	86 Rn
87 Fr	88 Ra	89 Ac	104 Rf	105 Ha	106												

Lanthanide Series	58 Ce	59 Pr	60 Nd	61 Pm	62 Sm	63 Eu	64 Gd	65 Tb	66 Dy	67 Ho	68 Er	69 Tm	70 Yb	71 Lu
Actinide Series	90 Th	91 Pa	92 U	93 Np	94 Pu	95 Am	96 Cm	97 Bk	98 Cf	99 Es	100 Fm	101 Md	102 No	103 Lr

FIGURE 1.1 The periodic table of the elements. Group numbers are given at the top of each column and atomic numbers above the symbol for each element.

these chemicals on conditions affecting the lives of plants or animals be understood.

It is not the intention of this chapter to cover the fundamentals of chemistry; readers are referred elsewhere for that (Harrison et al., 1991 is a good place to start). However, a knowledge of atoms, molecules, and ions, the chemical bond, molecular and ionic shapes and geometries, and chemical reactions are essential to the understanding of chemical change and so a brief overview of these topics follows.

CHEMICAL BONDS AND THE SHAPES OF MOLECULES AND IONS

The substances of which matter is composed are either the chemical elements or combinations of them. The basic units are the atoms. In the periodic table (Figure 1.1 and Table 1.1) the elements are organized according to their atomic structure. Atoms consist of nuclei (protons with positive charges and neutrons with no charge) and their surrounding negatively charged electrons. Atoms have no charge: the number of protons equals the number of electrons. The atomic number of an element is equal to the number of protons in the nucleus. Atomic masses increase as the number of protons and neutrons increases. Electrons are either held firmly by the protons and take no part in chemical reactions (core electrons) or are on the periphery of the atom (valence

TABLE 1.1 The Table of Elements

AN*	Symbol	Name	A.Wt**	AN*	Symbol	Name	A.Wt**
1	H	Hydrogen	1.0	43	Tc	Technetium	98.9
2	He	Helium	4.0	44	Ru	Ruthenium	101.1
3	Li	Lithium	6.9	45	Rh	Rhodium	102.9
4	Be	Beryllium	9.0	46	Pd	Palladium	106.4
5	B	Boron	10.8	47	Ag	Silver	107.9
6	C	Carbon	12.0	48	Cd	Cadmium	112.4
7	N	Nitrogen	14.0	49	In	Indium	114.8
8	O	Oxygen	16.0	50	Sn	Tin	118.9
9	F	Fluorine	19.0	51	Sb	Antimony	121.8
10	Ne	Neon	20.2	52	Te	Tellurium	127.6
11	Na	Sodium	23.0	53	I	Iodine	126.9
12	Mg	Magnesium	24.3	54	Xe	Xenon	131.3
13	Al	Aluminum	27.0	55	Cs	Cesium	132.9
14	Si	Silicon	28.1	56	Ba	Barium	137.3
15	P	Phosphorus	31.0	57	La	Lanthanum	138.9
16	S	Sulfur	32.1	58	Ce	Cerium	140.1
17	Cl	Chlorine	35.5	59	Pr	Praseodymium	140.9
18	Ar	Argon	39.9	60	Nd	Neodymium	144.2
19	K	Potassium	39.1	61	Pm	Promethium	145.0
20	Ca	Calcium	40.1	62	Sm	Samarium	150.4
21	Sc	Scandium	45.0	63	Eu	Europium	152.0
22	Ti	Titanium	47.9	64	Gd	Gadolinium	157.3
23	V	Vanadium	50.9	65	Tb	Terbium	158.9
24	Cr	Chromium	52.0	66	Dy	Dysprosium	162.5
25	Mn	Manganese	54.9	67	Ho	Holmium	164.9
26	Fe	Iron	55.8	68	Er	Erbium	167.3
27	Co	Cobalt	58.9	69	Tm	Thulium	168.9
28	Ni	Nickel	58.7	70	Yb	Ytterbium	173.0
29	Cu	Copper	63.5	71	Lu	Lutetium	175.0
30	Zn	Zinc	65.8	72	Hf	Hafnium	178.5
31	Ga	Gallium	69.7	73	Ta	Tantalum	180.9
32	Ge	Germanium	72.6	74	W	Tungsten	183.9
33	As	Arsenic	74.9	75	Re	Rhenium	186.2
34	Se	Selenium	79.0	76	Os	Osmium	190.2
35	Br	Bromine	79.9	77	Ir	Iridium	192.2
36	Kr	Krypton	83.8	78	Pt	Platinum	195.1
37	Rb	Rubidium	85.5	79	Au	Gold	197.0
38	Sr	Strontium	87.6	80	Hg	Mercury	200.1
39	Y	Yttrium	88.9	81	Tl	Thallium	204.4
40	Zr	Zirconium	91.2	82	Pb	Lead	207.2
41	Nb	Niobium	92.9	83	Bi	Bismuth	209.0
42	Mo	Molybdenum	95.9	84	Po	Polonium	209

TABLE 1.1 The Table of Elements (continued)

AN*	Symbol	Name	A.Wt**	AN*	Symbol	Name	A.Wt**
85	At	Astatine	210	96	Cm	Curium	247
86	Rn	Radon	222	97	Bk	Berkelium	247
87	Fr	Francium	223	98	Cf	Californium	251
88	Ra	Radium	226.0	99	Es	Einsteinium	254
89	Ac	Actinium	227.0	100	Fm	Fermium	257
90	Th	Thorium	232.0	101	Md	Mendelevium	258
91	Pa	Protactinium	231.0	102	No	Nobelium	259
92	U	Uranium	238.0	103	Lr	Lawrencium	260
93	Np	Neptunium	237.0	104	Rf	Rutherfordium	261
94	Pu	Plutonium	244	105	Ha	Hahnium	262
95	Am	Americium	243				

* Atomic Number
** Atomic Weight

electrons). Atoms react to gain, share, or lose valence electrons. Elements in the same group (column) of the periodic table (Figure 1.1) have the same number of valence electrons and thereby similar chemistries. Those in groups 1 and 2, the s block elements, have one and two electrons in the valence shell, respectively. The transition metals, or d block elements (groups 3 to 10) have up to ten valence electrons, while the metals of groups 11 and 12 behave in many ways like the s block elements. The elements of groups 13 to 18, the p block elements, have the group number minus ten valence electrons. The group 18 elements, the noble gases, are very unreactive: other elements tend to react to gain an electronic configuration of a noble gas. The lanthanides (atomic numbers 58 to 71) and actinides (atomic numbers 90 to 103), present on Earth in very low concentrations, have up to fourteen valence electrons.

Elements combine to form either ionic or covalent compounds (Figure 1.2). The structures of these compounds, even very large ones that may involve many elements (see Figures 1.3 and 1.13 to 1.17), are all based on either ionic or covalent linkages (bonds) between the constituent atoms. In ionic compounds, sodium chloride (NaCl) for example (Figure 1.2A), the elements involved have either lost or gained electrons to form cations (positively charged) and anions (negatively charged), respectively. In the solid state these ions pack like balls with the bigger ions (Cl^- in the case of NaCl) occupying what are called lattice sites and the smaller ions occupying lattice holes (Na^+ in NaCl is in an octahedral hole, it has six nearest Cl^- ions; notice that the Cl^- has six nearest neighbour Na^+ ions, hence the formula

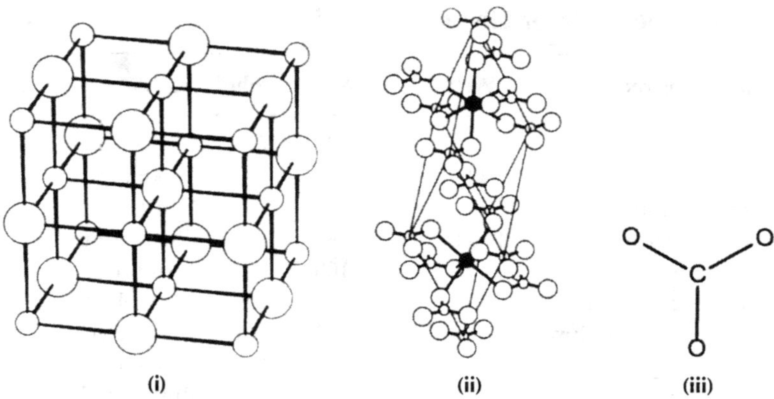

FIGURE 1.2A Ionic compounds. (i) Sodium chloride: (O) larger Cl^- anions on lattice sites; (o) smaller Na^+ cations in lattice holes. This unit cell, repeated in three dimensions, creates the crystal. (ii) Calcite, a form of calcium carbonate, $CaCO_3$: CO_3^{2-} anions on lattice sites; (•) Ca^{2+} cations in lattice holes. (iii) The CO_3^{2-} anion: a trigonal structure as a result of three areas of electron density around the central C. (Figures 2A(i) and 2A(ii) reproduced from Ladd, M. F. C. 1979. *Structure and Bonding in Solid State Chemistry.* Ellis Horwood, Chichester, U.K. With permission.)

NaCl). In the case of calcium carbonate ($CaCO_3$), Ca^{2+} is the cation and the carbonate (CO_3^{2-}) unit the anion. Within the CO_3^{2-} anion (Figure 1.2A), a complex anion, the linkages are covalent bonds. Such bonds are formed by sharing electrons. This occurs when neither element (carbon [C] and oxygen [O] in this case) has the ability to completely remove an electron or electrons from the other (as happened in Na^+ Cl^-, NaCl). Shared electrons are associated with both atoms and attracted to the protons of each nucleus. Electrons clearly repel each other but when they are involved in a bond the electron–nuclear attractions outweigh the electron–electron and nuclear–nuclear repulsions; the nuclei are bound together by the electrons. The carbonate anion has three areas of electron density around the central C atom (all bonds in this case), which results in the O atoms being arranged trigonally around the C atom, a planar anion. The cluster of elements has a net charge of minus two (Figure 1.2A).

The atoms in covalent (molecular) compounds like carbon dioxide and water (Figure 1.2B) are bound together by covalent bonds, with the resulting molecule having no formal charge. However, if the shared electrons spend more time closer to one element than the others, charge separation (a dipole) can develop. In carbon dioxide, for example, the O atoms attract the shared electrons to a greater extent than the carbon atom; oxygen is said to be more electronegative than the carbon. Thus, the two bonds have slightly negative ends at

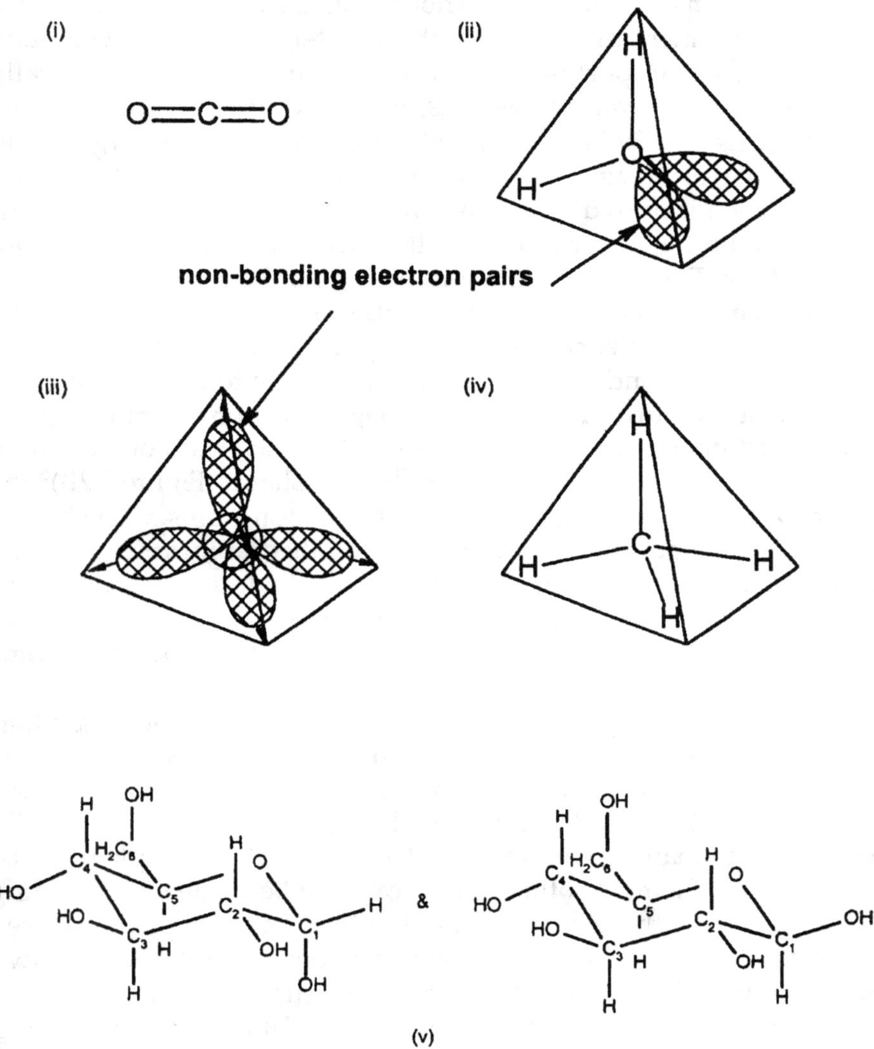

FIGURE 1.2B Covalent compounds. (i) Carbon dioxide, CO_2, a linear molecule with no dipole moment. (ii) Water, H_2O, a bent molecule with a permanent dipole moment and a structure based on four electron pairs around the central O. (iii) The tetrahedral shape based on four areas of electron density around a central atom. (iv) Methane, CH_4, a tetrahedral molecule with no dipole moment and a structure based on four areas of electron density around the central C. (v) Glucose, $C_6H_{12}O_6$. The two forms differ structurally at C_1. All the atoms except H have tetrahedral shapes.

the oxygen atoms and the carbon will be slightly positive. Because of the symmetry of the molecule, however, there is no net dipole. For the water molecule, H_2O (O is more electronegative than H) the charge distributions in the two bonds do not cancel; the molecule is not linear, it has a permanent dipole moment. In water this charge separation is particularly important. Water molecules are electrostatically attracted to other water molecules, the associations resulting in the high melting and boiling points of water, its relatively large liquid range, and in ice having a lower density than liquid water. The ability of many chemicals to dissolve in water depends on the charge distribution within the water molecule. If water did not have these properties, life on Earth, as we know it, would not be possible.

The shapes of molecules and complex ions are determined by the arrangement of valence and bonding electrons. Carbon has four valence electrons and normally shares these with four other electrons from the atoms surrounding it. These eight electrons form four pairs with directional properties. Methane (CH_4) then has four bonding pairs of electrons and hence a tetrahedral shape (Figure 1.2B); the electron pairs get as far apart as possible. Carbon atoms, when bound to four other atoms, always adopt this tetrahedral form; each C in a glucose molecule (Figure 1.2B) has a tetrahedral array of atoms around it. Notice also that the two forms of glucose: $C_6H_{12}O_6$ or $(CH_2O)_6$, a hydrate of carbon, a carbohydrate, contain the same atoms but the arrangement at C_1 is different.

When bound to fewer than four atoms, however, C adopts different geometries. Such C compounds are said to be unsaturated; alkenes, carboxylic acids, and aromatic compounds are examples (see Figures 1.14 to 1.17). Unsaturated linkages (or bonds) generally involve more than two electrons and are said to be multiple (double, triple) bonds. Elements other than C can also be involved in forming multiple bonds, the oxygen atoms in CO_3^{2-}, for example. However, most bonds are single bonds, two electrons shared between two nuclei. In water, the O has two bonding electron pairs (formed from one electron from each H and two from the O) and four other electrons, also paired; a total of four geometrically active electron pairs. Its shape is therefore also based on the tetrahedron but since there are only two Hs the molecule appears to be bent (Figure 1.2B). Shape and charge play very important roles in chemical reactions.

TYPES OF CHEMICAL REACTION

Interactions between chemicals that result in changes in the arrangements of atoms in molecules and ions (that is, chemical reactions) can be classified, in the main, as oxidation–reduction, acid–base, dissolution–precipitation, complexation, adsorption–desorption,

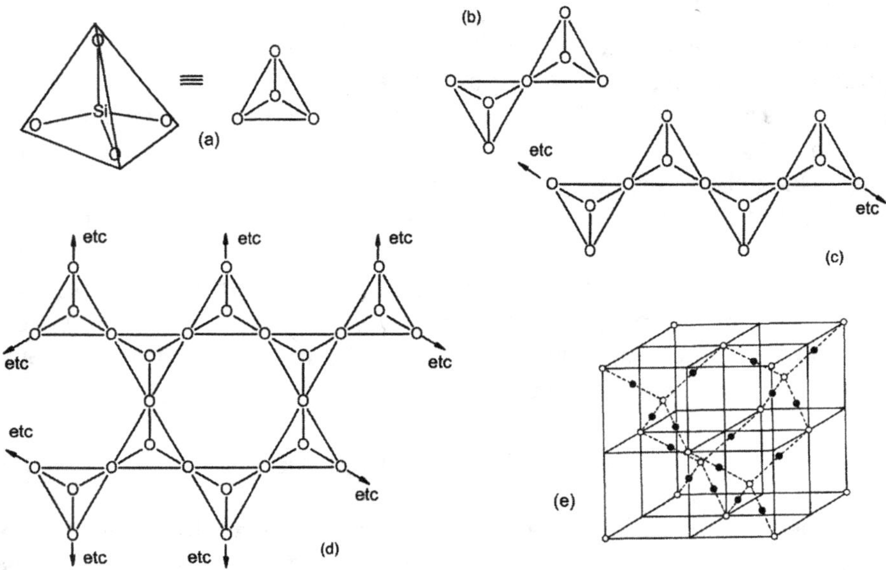

FIGURE 1.3 Silicates. (a) The SiO_4^{4-} tetrahedral unit found in the ionic olivines. (b) The $Si_2O_7^{6-}$ dimer. (c) A linear chain $(SiO_3^{2-})_n$, as found in pyroxenes. The constituent tetrahedra are covalently linked to form the chain structures. (d) A sheet $(Si_2O_5^{2-})_n$, as found in micas. (e) The unit cell of crystabolite, SiO_2, an infinite, three-dimensional solid. (o) Si^{4+}; (•) O^{2-}. In feldspars some of the Si^{4+} are replaced by Al^{3+} on the lattice sites. Other cations (Na^+, K^+, Ca^{2+}, etc.) balance the charge by occupying lattice holes. Note the linked SiO_4 tetrahedra. (Figure 1.3E from Addison, W. E. 1961. *Structural Principles in Inorganic Chemistry.* Longman, Green, London. With permission.)

and condensation–hydration reactions. Photochemical reactions involve the interactions between chemicals and light. Most reactions do not go completely from reactants to products but, rather, stop after a while to leave a mixture of products and reactants; reactions reach states of equilibrium, the positions of which can be expressed by equilibrium constants. We will be seeing many examples of these types of reaction and so need to consider them briefly.

Oxidation and reduction reactions involve the transfer of electrons from one chemical species to another. When it is oxidized, a species loses electrons; these are gained by the reduced species – oxidation and reduction go together. The elements are said to be in the zero oxidation state; they have been neither oxidized nor reduced. The oxide (O^{2-}) ion, as for example in silicate ions (SiO_4^{4-}; Figure 1.3), is in the minus two oxidation state, as the atom has gained two electrons. Si is in the plus four oxidation state; it has lost four electrons. The charge on the silicate ion is 4–, the sum of the charges on the atoms (4+ plus 4 × 2– = 4–). Carbon in CO_2 is in the plus four oxidation state (the highest oxidation state possible for C), whereas it is in the minus four state (the lowest possible) in CH_4. The maximum and minimum possible oxidation states for p block elements are related to their position in the periodic table (Figure 1.1; maximum = group number – 10; minimum = group number – 18). The situation is more complicated for the d block elements, the most common oxidation states being plus two or plus three for these metals. The s block elements become cations by losing the number of electrons equal to their group number (Na^+ and Ca^{2+} are examples). Very few elements exist in the natural environment in the zero oxidation state; S, Au, Pt, and the noble gases are some that do. Many, but not all, environmentally important oxidation reactions involve oxygen. For example in the photosynthesis reaction:

$$CO_2 + H_2O \rightarrow CH_2O + O_2 \qquad \textbf{(1)}$$

C has been reduced from the plus four oxidation state to the zero state (in CH_2O each hydrogen is in the plus one and the O is in the minus two oxidation state). This reaction will not happen in the absence of light.

Acid–base reactions generally involve the transfer of protons (hydrogen ions, H^+) from the acid to the base. For example, sulphuric acid (H_2SO_4) in water loses a proton to the water which, therefore, is the base in this reaction:

$$H_2SO_4 + H_2O \rightarrow HSO_4^- + H_3O^+ \qquad \textbf{(2)}$$

This reaction goes to completion and therefore sulphuric acid is a strong acid; it can give away one proton completely. The bisulphate ion (HSO_4^-) produced is also an acid:

$$HSO_4^- + H_2O \rightarrow SO_4^{2-} + H_3O^+ \qquad \textbf{(3)}$$

but, like most acids, it does not give up its proton completely to the water. Rather, an equilibrium is reached, the position of which is quantified by the equilibrium constant, K, where

$$K = \{[SO_4^{2-}]\,[H_3O^+]\}/[HSO_4^-]$$

Acids that behave in this manner are called weak acids. K is the ratio of the product of the concentrations of the resulting chemicals divided by the product of the concentrations of the reacting chemicals.

$[SO_4^{2-}]$ represents the concentration of the sulphate anion. These equilibrium expressions can become quite complicated as the stoichiometry of the reaction (the numbers in front of the reagents and products, all 1 in the above example) must also be considered. We will see examples of this later. The concentrations are the amounts of the species dissolved in the water and can usually be measured. The value of the above equilibrium constant is 1.02×10^{-2} molar (the units will be explained later), a small number, which means bisulphate (HSO_4^-) does not give up many of its protons to the water. The concentration of water does not appear in the equilibrium constant expression as its concentration will not change significantly under normal conditions (there is so much of it compared to the bisulphate that the amount of H_2O that goes to H_3O^+ is trivial compared to the amount of H_2O initially present).

The pH scale, a logarithmic scale, is usually used when expressing hydrogen ion concentrations since they can vary over many orders of magnitude; pH is the negative log (base 10) of the hydrogen ion concentration. pH 7 is neutral.

Dissolution and precipitation reactions are connected through equilibria. The dissolution of calcite, $CaCO_3(s)$ – the (s) implies solid – is described by the equation:

$$CaCO_3(s) \rightarrow Ca^{2+} + CO_3^{2-} \tag{4}$$

Its associated equilibrium constant

$$K = [Ca^{2+}]\,[CO_3^{2-}]$$

has a value of 4.5×10^{-9} mol^2 dm^{-6}. This number is very small, calcite is not very soluble. $[CaCO_3]$, the solid material, does not appear in the expression for much the same reason that $[H_2O]$ did not in the equilibrium constant expression for Equation 3. The precipitation of calcite, which involves the reaction between Ca^{2+} and CO_3^{2-} ions to produce $CaCO_3(s)$, is clearly the reverse of the above dissolution reaction and therefore need not be considered separately.

Complexation reactions involve the combination of metal ions with either anions or molecules and are similar, in some cases, to adsorption–desorption reactions. We will consider these in more detail when we study the environmental chemistry of C and lead (Pb). Photochemical (involving light) and condensation–hydration (involving water) reactions are particularly important in atmospheric

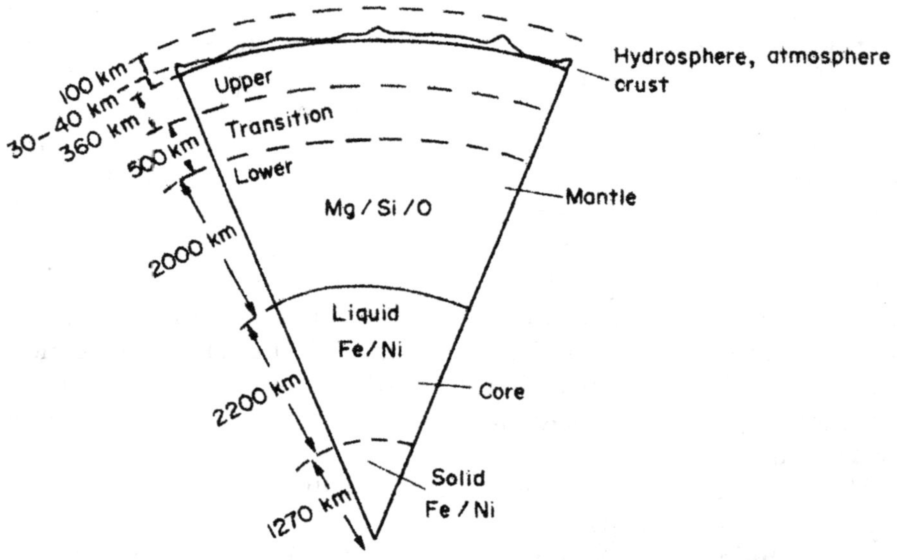

FIGURE 1.4 The structure of the Earth. (From Fergusson, J. E. 1982. *Inorganic Chemistry and the Earth. Chemical Resources, their Extraction, Use and Environmental Impact.* Pergamon Press, Oxford, U.K. With permission.)

and biochemical processes and so we will delay our consideration of them until later.

Most environmental matrices (air, soil, water, biological tissues) consist of many chemicals. Consider, for example, soils that contain minerals such as the oxides of iron, silicon, and aluminium, organic materials such as cellulose, proteins, and other complex products from the degradation of plant materials, water and air and species in them, and microbes. Many chemical changes will be occurring at the same time and the study of any of them within such a complex matrix becomes very difficult. In order to attempt to understand them, whether they are natural or as a result of human influence, we need to have a knowledge of the chemical composition of our environment and the various chemical reactions possible.

THE STRUCTURE AND COMPOSITION OF THE EARTH'S ENVIRONMENT

The structure of today's planet Earth is illustrated in Figure 1.4. The "big bang", postulated to have started the processes that led to its formation, occurred approximately ten to fifteen thousand million

TABLE 1.2 The Major Elemental Components of Environmental Matrices

Crust [a]	O	Si	Al	Fe	Ca	Mg	Na	K
(%)	45.6	27.3	8.36	6.22	4.66	2.76	2.27	1.84
Dry air [b]	N_2	O_2	Ar	CO_2	Ne	He	CH_4	Kr
(% or ppmv)	78.1%	20.9%	0.9%	360	18.2	5.2	1.6	1.1
Marine water [c]	Cl	Na	SO_4	Mg	Ca	K	HCO_3	Br
(ppm)	19344	10733	2712	1294	412	399	142	60
River water [c]	HCO_3	Ca	SiO_4	SO_4	Cl	Na	Mg	K
(ppm)	1.7	13.3	10.7	8.7	6.0	5.3	3.1	1.5
Reference plant [d]	C	O	H	N	K	Ca	S	E*
(% dw)	44.5	42.5	6.5	0.2	2.5	1.9	1.0	0.3
Reference man [e]	O	C	H	N	Ca	S	P	Na
(%)	63.0	19.0	9.3	5.1	1.4	0.64	0.63	0.26

* E implies P, Mg and Cl
[a] Miekle, 1979
[b] Brimblecombe, 1996
[c] Chester, 1993
[d] Markert, 1992
[e] Ochiai, 1977

years ago (Hawkins, 1988). Hydrogen and helium make up 99.8 percent of the present universe (Fergusson, 1982), the other chemical elements having been formed from them under conditions of extraordinarily high temperatures and pressures. While the elements of planet Earth number 103 (Figure 1.1), some do not occur naturally and only a few are in abundance (Table 1.2).

The formation of planet Earth is estimated to have started 4600 million years ago (Crystal, 1994). The oldest rock on the Earth's crust has been dated at 3800 million years and the oldest (known) fossil at 2600 million years (life therefore must have started earlier than that). The first appearance on earth of the *Homo* genus seems to have been about 3 million years ago, with the *sapiens* (modern) species existing for only the last 100,000 years. Dinosaurs existed between 200 and 50 million years ago and the last glacial maxima was 18,000 years ago (Table 1.3). Changes on the geological time scale are still occurring and the environmental changes of principal concern to us are occurring along with them.

TABLE 1.3 The Geological Time Scale

Eras	Approximate Age (years)	Subdivisions	Important Features
Quaternary	10,000–present	Holocene	
	2M–10,000	Pleistocene	Genus *Homo* emerges; last glacial maxima–18,000
Tertiary	5M–2M	Pliocene	Continents as at present
	24M–5M	Miocene	
	37M–24M	Oligocene	Grasses appear and forests diminish
	57M–37M	Eocene	Large tropical forests
	66M–57M	Paleocene	
Mesozoic	144M–66M	Cretaceous	
	208M–144M	Jurassic	Continents separated; Dinosaurs dominant
	245M–208M	Triassic	Continents start to separate; first mammals
Paleozoic	286M–245M	Permian	
	360M–286M	Carboniferous	Extensive forests
	408M–360M	Devonian	First insects and invertebrates on land
	438M–408M	Silurian	First plants on land
	505M–438M	Ordovician	
	570M–505M	Cambrian	
Precambrian			Earliest marine life–1000M
			Oldest fossil–2,600M
			Oldest rock–3800M
			Age of Earth–4600M
			Big bang–10,000M

THE ORIGINS OF OUR EARTH ENVIRONMENT

As the primitive Earth cooled from about 6000°C, the constituent chemical elements began to condense, react, and separate; the primary differentiation of the elements began (Fergusson, 1982). Iron and the more readily reduced metals (Ni, Au, and Pt, for example) settled to the core (Figure 1.4), silicates (Figure 1.3), predominantly of Fe(II) and Mg(II), crystallized as olivines and pyroxenes to form the mantle. The less dense feldspars (Figure 1.3e) were left floating on the surface to form the initial crust. These silicates contained many other elements within their lattices, either on lattice sites, where they can be considered to have replaced the normal occupant of the site (Al(III) for

Si(IV) for example), or in lattice holes. The primitive atmosphere consisted of the volatile elements that were unable to escape from the Earth's gravitational field (N_2, CO_2, H_2S, but not H_2 or He, which escaped). It contained no O_2; all of this element being associated, as oxide (O^{2-}), with the mantle and the crust. Water, which presently covers 70 percent of the Earth's surface, was formed by condensation from the atmosphere.

Following this primary differentiation the rocks at the surface underwent, and are still undergoing, secondary differentiation or weathering (Figure 1.5), modifications as a result of a wide variety of physical and chemical effects. Soluble ions, Na^+ and Ca^{2+} for example, are leached from the rocks by the slightly acidic waters (resulting from dissolved carbon dioxide, see later) that flow over them, the rate of leaching being enhanced by physical processes. These changes convert primary minerals (olivines, pyroxenes, feldspars, etc.) into secondary minerals (clays, oxides, and oxyhydroxides, etc.) and the dissolved species either accumulate in the oceans or are removed from the dissolved state by precipitation or adsorption onto particles.

The similarities between the chemical composition of cells and seawater suggest that life began in the oceans (Schlesinger, 1991). Only after this beginning did oxygen start to accumulate in the atmosphere; the photosynthetic formation of carbohydrates (CH_2O) and oxygen from inorganic carbon and water (Equation 1). Since their appearance, living organisms have been involved in the weathering process (Grant and Long, 1981; Manahan, 1994).

THE COMPOSITION AND STRUCTURE OF THE SPHERES OF OUR EARTH ENVIRONMENT

The major constituents of the environmental spheres are indicated in Table 1.2. There is considerable variability in the natural environment; these figures are averages or best estimates, they do not refer to any actual material. Different plants (or rocks, or animals, or rivers, etc.) will have significantly different compositions and thus the numbers given in Table 1.2 can only give an idea as to the likely concentrations to be encountered. Most materials also contain many other elements in trace amounts.

When considering concentrations one must be aware of the units involved. Chemicals react quantitatively according to the stoichiometry of balanced equations (elements and charges are equal on both sides; Equation 2 for example) and therefore the units used should be based on numbers of species (molecules, atoms, ions, radicals)

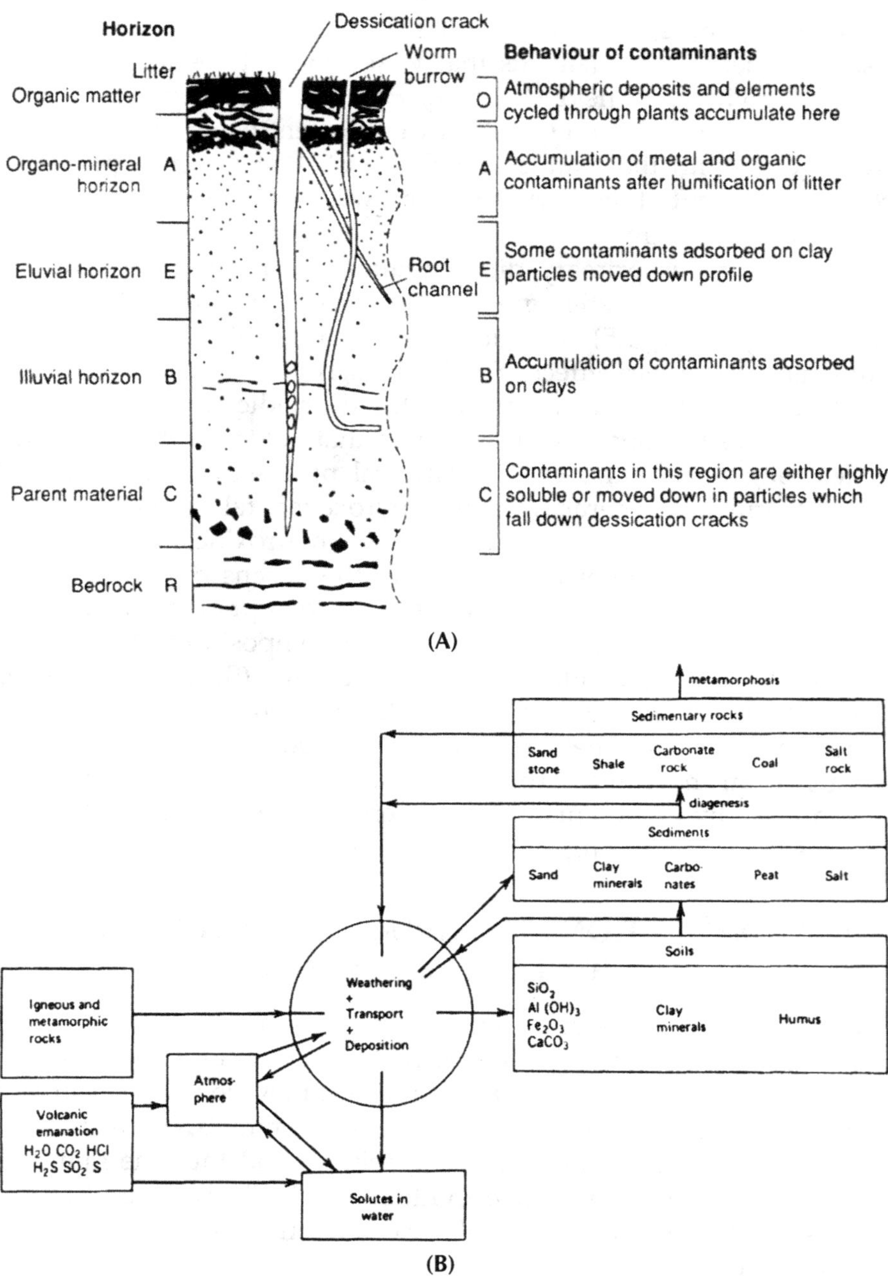

FIGURE 1.5 The weathering cycle and the production of soils. (A) A soil profile. (From Alloway, B.J. 1992. In *Understanding our Environment: An Introduction to Environmental Chemistry and Pollution*, pp. 137–164, edited by R. M. Harrison. Royal Society of Chemistry, Cambridge, U.K. With permission.) (B) The weathering cycle. (From Stumm, W. and J. J. Morgan. 1981. *Aquatic Chemistry: An Introduction Emphasizing Chemical Equilibria in Natural Waters*, 2nd edition. Wiley-Interscience, New York. With permission.)

whenever possible. The mole is the standard unit, representing 6.023×10^{23} molecules/ions/etc. (just as a dollar represents 100 cents). A mole of a chemical has a mass, in grams, given by the sum of the atomic weights of its constituent atoms; for example, a mole of H_2O weighs $2 \times 1 + 16 = 18$ grams (Table 1.1). This mass is called the relative molecular (or formula) mass (RMM). A litre of water, which weighs approximately 1000 grams, contains 1000/18 = 55.6 moles or 3.34×10^{25} molecules of water.

In aqueous solutions moles per litre (mol dm^{-3} or molar) is the preferred unit. Most environmental concentrations are in the milli ($\times 10^{-3}$), or micro ($\times 10^{-6}$) molar or lower ranges. Units based on mass (milligrams [parts per million, ppm] or micrograms [parts per billion, ppb]) per litre are also used. The concentrations of the chemicals in the atmosphere are expressed in units of volume or pressure as these can be related directly to the number of molecules and therefore to chemical reactivity. The unit ppm when referring to gases means millilitres of gas per 1000 litres of air and is frequently written as ppmv to ensure clarity.

In the biosphere and the lithosphere the mass of analyte per unit mass of matrix (soil, plant material, etc.) is normally used. Thus 1 ppm Pb in a soil refers to 1 milligram Pb per kilogram of soil. It is best to use the mass of the dry matrix rather than the wet mass, as water content is seldom stoichiometric.

A trace component implies that the component is present in less than 0.1 percent (0.1 part per hundred or 1000 ppm) by weight if a liquid or solid matrix is involved or by volume or pressure if a gas is involved.

The Biosphere

The biosphere, all plants and animals, is composed predominantly of C, H, and O, combined in biomolecules. Other major essential elements that play important roles in cellular functions and as structural materials are Na, Mg, K, and Ca (s block elements) and N, P, S, and Cl (p block elements). Trace elements that are often involved in enzymic activities include the transition metals Mn, Fe, Co, Ni, and Mo; the metals Cu and Zn; and the nonmetals B, Si, Se, and I (Holum, 1990). If plants and animals are deficient in any of these elements then their growth will, in some way, be impaired. The toxic elements of particular concern include Cd, Hg, As, and Pb. Most organisms are tolerant of these elements up to certain concentrations but at higher concentrations some biological function becomes impaired. Even essential elements can become toxic at high concentrations (Fergusson, 1990). Compounds can also be toxic – pesticides for example. The structures, reactions, and properties of biomolecules, and their toxicities, will be considered in greater depth when we consider the carbon and lead cycles.

The Lithosphere

Solid Earth can be divided into three regions: the core, the mantle, and the lithosphere (Figure 1.4). The lithosphere is the rigid outer portion of the Earth. While all of these regions are of importance on the geological time scale it is primarily the lithosphere, and in particular its upper portion, the crust, which is of concern when considering environmental change.

The crust consists predominantly of silicates (Figure 1.3) and oxides or carbonates of Al, Fe, Ti, Na, K, Ca, and Mg. These metals, with Si and O, make up 98.6 percent of the mass of the crust. All other elements are present only in trace amounts. Ore deposits (soil or rock that contains minerals in such quantity to make it economically viable to extract them) can lead to very high concentrations of elements in localized areas; for example the lead (galena, PbS) and bauxite deposits in Jamaica, the gold mines of Guyana, and manganese nodules on the ocean floors.

Soils, a component of the crust, are of vital importance to man's survival; they provide the base on which most terrestrial plant life, including our foods, grows (Cresser et al., 1993; Wild, 1993). Soils are the product of the weathering of rocks and biological litter. The weathering process is often apparent from a study of the soil profile; the variation of the components of the soil with depth (Figure 1.5A). The development of a clear profile will only occur if the soil, once produced, is not significantly eroded.

The many soil classification systems used (FitzPatrick, 1983) are based to varying extents on chemical composition, the climates under which the soils have been produced, and the sizes of the soil particles. The classification system based on climate is of chemical relevance; this system divides soils into two major categories, Pedocals and Pedalfers, the dividing line being 65 cm of rainfall per year. Pedocals are soils (ped) relatively rich in Ca. In dry conditions only the most soluble elements are removed by weathering. Under moist conditions temperature starts to play an important role. In the Arctic very little weathering occurs and silica-rich clays predominate. In warmer climates (as in the Caribbean) silica dissolves from the minerals and the resistate oxides of Fe and Al become prevalent. The bauxites of the tropical (present or past) regions represent soils that have been almost fully weathered.

The size distribution of the particles in a soil is also of importance. The divisions between gravel, sand, silt, and clay are set at 2 mm, 20 μm, and 2 μm, with a good agricultural soil (a loam) having 7 to 27 percent clay, 28 to 50 percent silt, and 0 to 52 percent sand. Porosity/water retention, air space, and physical stability are all partially determined by particle size. It is important to realize that the term *clay* here refers to particle size only, whereas clay minerals refer to chemical structures. Most clay minerals fall within the clay particle size, but not all particles in that size fraction have to be clay minerals.

The actual composition of a soil (at any stage in its development) depends on the source materials, the climate to which the source materials and their degradation products have been exposed, the terrain from which they have come and within which they are existing, and the composition of the aqueous solutions to which the parent rocks and weathered products are being exposed. The composition of the weathering solution depends in turn on what it has been exposed to: acids, organic materials, rocks, etc. The stabilities of the component parent and secondary rocks depend on the composition of the associated weathering solutions. This is illustrated in Figure 1.6 for the primary minerals K-feldspar and muscovite and the secondary minerals kaolinite and gibbsite. The composition of the weathering solution defines the axes.

Mineral stability regions are defined by the boundary lines within the axes. For example, at point A, within the region of stability for kaolinite, the silicic acid (H_4SiO_4) concentration is 1×10^{-4} mol dm^{-3} and the ratio of the potassium and hydrogen ion concentrations is 1000. If the ratio was to change to 10^6 (a change in pH from 5 to 8 while holding the potassium concentration constant would do that) K-feldspar would be the stable mineral. A change in the composition of the weathering solution will change the position of the equilibrium and the relative stabilities of the minerals involved.

Mineral stability diagrams such as this can be constructed by considering the reactions that convert one mineral to the other (Krauskopf and Bird, 1995), but must be used with caution. The equilibrium constants either refer to pure minerals and have been determined under laboratory conditions or are specific to a mineral of a particular composition. In the natural environment one seldom, if ever, encounters the pure minerals; they invariably have some degree of substitution in their lattices. Also, these diagrams do not

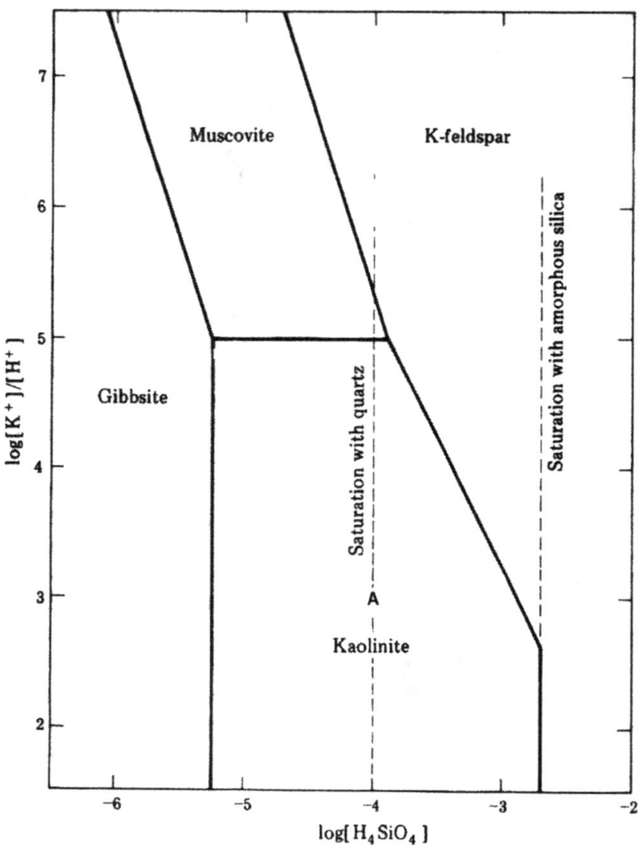

FIGURE 1.6 A mineral stability diagram. The chemical species on the axes are those found in the weathering solutions. The mineral stability regions are bound by the solid lines. (Adapted from Krauskopf, K.B. 1982.)

take into account the rates at which reactions occur. A reaction may be predicted to go under the weathering conditions prevailing but could be so slow as to be of no interest. Microbial activities also affect the rates considerably (Stumm and Morgan, 1981). Despite these limitations, diagrams such as these do give an initial idea as to the relative stabilities of minerals and to the probable direction of weathering reactions given the solution compositions.

Figure 1.5B indicates the overall progress of the weathering of inorganic materials. The soils initially produced contribute to the sediments in rivers, lakes, and the oceans, where they undergo further changes, particularly when buried (called diagenetic changes). Buried sediments, once under sufficient pressure, form sedimentary rocks and then metamorphic rocks and the weathering cycle closes.

The Hydrosphere

Marine waters make up 80 percent of the hydrosphere, with groundwaters, 19 percent, and ice, 1 percent, being the other major reservoirs. Rivers and lakes and the atmosphere hold only 0.002 and 0.0006 percent of the water, respectively (Stumm and Morgan, 1981).

Water, H_2O, as a result of its polar nature, is a good solvent for charged species such as Cl^-, Na^+, Ca^{2+}, HCO_3^-, and for polar species such as sugars and carboxylic and amino acids (Figures 1.2, 1.13, and 1.14). The dissolved species in marine and fresh waters (Table 1.2) are vastly different.

A very important, but highly variable, component of all water bodies is the suspended load. This consists of particles from soil erosion, particles produced *in situ* from precipitation of dissolved species and biota degradation, and road dusts, etc. Many of these particles will be colloidal, that is they are too small and highly charged to settle under normal gravitational forces. Such particles have two major effects: they decrease the depth of penetration of sunlight into the water body, and thereby decrease the extent of photosynthesis, and they are strongly adsorbing and accumulate most pollutants on their surfaces. These particles eventually become incorporated into the sediment. We will focus on this when considering the biogeochemical cycles of C and Pb.

Surface water and groundwater result from the percolation of rainwater through and over soils and rocks (Figure 1.7A). Their dissolved chemicals therefore reflect the leaching that has occurred during those processes. The ions of highest concentration are usually Ca^{2+} and HCO_3^-, reflecting a balance between their abundance and solubilities under normal weathering conditions. The concentrations of dissolved species vary considerably with flow rates. Rivers under high flow are dominated by surface runoff and have low total dissolved solids (TDS), as the water has had little contact with the ground over which it is flowing. Under low flow conditions the opposite will be true, groundwater runoff will dominate and high TDS prevail. Total suspended solids tend to be highest under high flow conditions due to the effects of erosion. When considering the chemistry of rivers it is important to determine both concentrations and flow rates; the amount of chemical passing a point (moles per hour) will be the product of the two. This is also important when considering industrial and domestic discharges into water bodies.

The chemical species dissolved or suspended in water will be continually undergoing chemical changes, frequently biologically

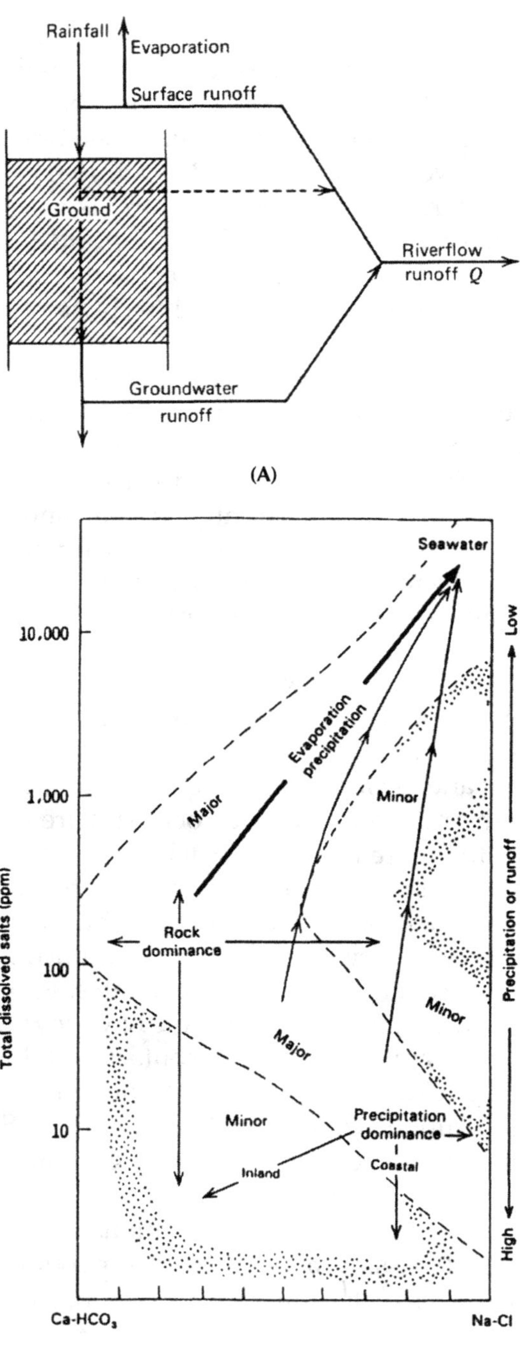

Rainfall
Evaporation
Surface runoff
Ground
Riverflow
runoff Q
Groundwater
runoff
(A)
Seawater
10,000
1,000
100
10
Total dissolved salts (ppm)
Evaporation precipitation
Major
Minor
Rock dominance
Minor
Major
Minor
Precipitation dominance
Inland
Coastal
Ca-HCO₃
Na-Cl
Low
Precipitation or runoff
High
(B)

FIGURE 1.7

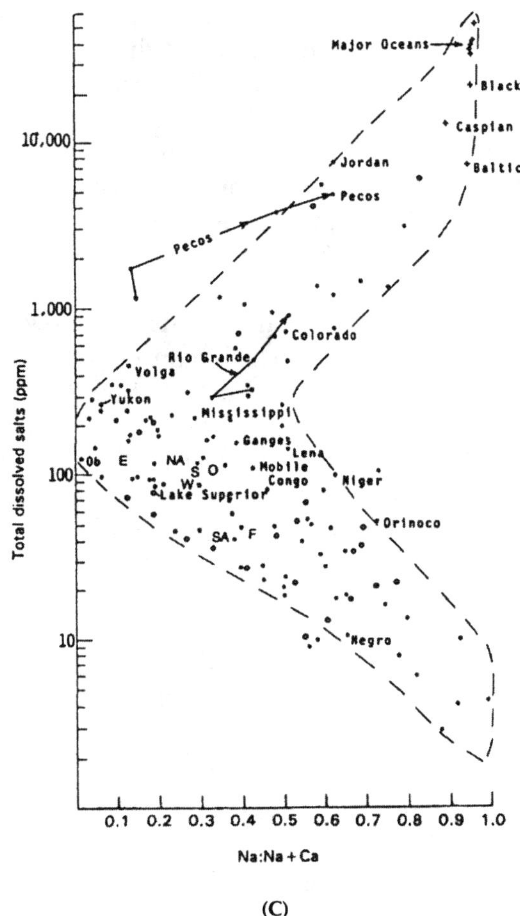

(C)

FIGURE 1.7 (continued) The composition of river waters. (A) The major sources to rivers. (From Stumm, W. and J. J. Morgan. 1981. *Aquatic Chemistry: An Introduction Emphasizing Chemical Equilibria in Natural Waters*, 2nd edition. Wiley-Interscience, New York. With permission.) (B) The processes controlling the chemistry of world surface waters. (From Gibbs, R. J. 1992. *Limnology and Oceanography* 37: 1338–1339. With permission.) (C) The variation of Na:Na+Ca as a function of total dissolved salts for major lakes and rivers. (From Gibbs, R. J. 1992. *Limnology and Oceanography* 37: 1338–1339. With permission.)

mediated, with many of the changes occurring at the marine–freshwater interface. In a global sense the rate at which chemical species reach the marine environment is equal to the rate at which they are removed and thus the composition of the marine environment on the geological time scale is at equilibrium. This is certainly not true, however, in coastal waters.

The water in the atmosphere comes from evaporation of water bodies on Earth and therefore mainly from the oceans. The evaporation process occurs in conjunction with the bursting of bubbles from the water–atmosphere interface and so some of the water entering the atmosphere carries with it chemicals of the water body from which it originated. This is evident from the composition of atmospheric water, which contains the same ions as marine waters, although in much smaller concentrations (Andrews et al., 1996). The concentrations of Na^+ and Cl^- in the oceans and the atmosphere are very different but the ratios of Na^+:Cl^- are essentially the same.

Figures 1.7B and 1.7C show the bulk compositions of some of the major world rivers and oceans and illustrate how the composition of a water body depends on its origins and the processes that it has undergone. The TDS reflects the amount of the dissolved chemical load, while the Na^+:{$Na^+ + Ca^{2+}$} ratio represents the dominant cations (Cl^- and HCO_3^- will be the corresponding dominant anions). When Ca^{2+} dominates (ratio close to zero), groundwaters with their high weathering load are the major sources of the water. When Na^+ dominates (ratio close to one) and the TDS load is low, rain is the major water source. At low TDS and intermediate ratios the compositions are a function of the relative amounts of rain- and groundwaters. At high TDS (>100 mg dm^{-3}) evaporation and precipitation are affecting concentrations.

The Atmosphere

The structure and composition of the atmosphere vary with height, as illustrated in Figure 1.8 (Fergusson, 1982). As the sun's energy enters the atmosphere it interacts with the chemicals there. Those interactions, in conjunction with physical processes, result in the separation of the atmosphere into the thermo-, meso-, strato-, and tropospheres (Wayne, 1993). Of the total mass of the atmosphere, 5.2×10^{18} kilograms (Brimblecombe, 1996), 99 percent is within 30 kilometres and 50 percent within 5.5 kilometres of the Earth's surface. The major gaseous components are N_2 (78.08 percent), O_2 (20.95 percent), and Ar (0.93 percent), with all others present in trace amounts only. These numbers refer to a dry atmosphere, as the amount of water, an important component, is very variable (1 to 3 percent; Wayne, 1993). Carbon dioxide, also somewhat variable, is present at concentrations of approximately 350 ppmv. The importance of these chemicals to the biosphere (excluding Ar) cannot go unnoticed. Indeed the composition of the atmosphere is determined, if one excludes pollutants, by biological processes. Oxygen, CO_2, and H_2O are linked by photosynthesis (Equation 1) and N_2,

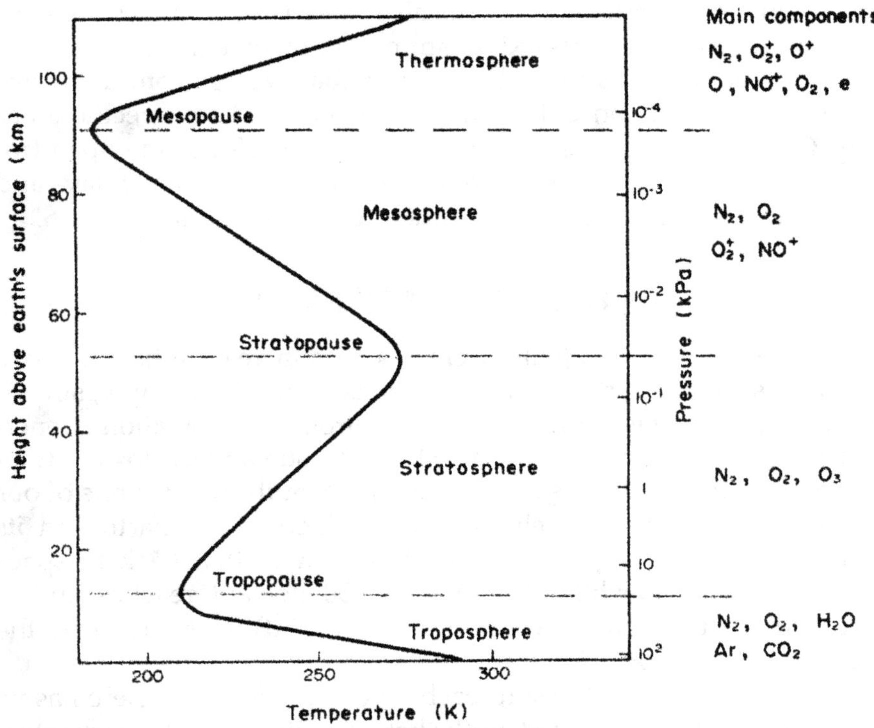

FIGURE 1.8 The structure and composition of the atmosphere. (From Fergusson, J. E. 1982. *Inorganic Chemistry and the Earth. Chemical Resources, Their Extraction, Use and Environmental Impact*. Pergamon Press, Oxford, U.K. With permission.)

although relatively unreactive, is incorporated into amino acids (see Figure 1.14) and other nitrogen-containing organic molecules (see Figure 1.15) via nitrogen-fixing enzymes.

The chemical processes that take place close to the Earth are somewhat different from those that take place in the upper troposphere. The unevenness of the Earth's surface including, at very low altitudes, the micro effects of buildings, leads to a general turbulence to heights of 0.5 to 2 kilometres during the day, somewhat less at night, and the identity of the so-called boundary layer (Wayne, 1993). Highly reactive species seldom enter the upper troposphere from this layer, either being incorporated onto or into particles, returning to the Earth's soils or waters or being chemically transformed into more stable species. The chemical composition of the boundary layer is also highly variable, depending on the sources and sinks of the chemicals. Urban areas tend to have higher concentrations of pollutants (oxides of sulphur and nitrogen, hydrocarbons, lead, etc.), while rural areas can have high concentrations of chemicals whose major sources are agricultural activities (nitrous oxide, ammonia, methane, etc.). The concentration variabilities are so high that global average concentrations are of little value; concentrations should be cited for specific areas only. Global distributions become more meaningful in the open troposphere where mixing processes are of the order of tens of days and comparable to, or less than, constituent chemical lifetimes.

THE EARTH'S ENERGY BALANCE

Whereas temperature initially decreases with increasing height above the Earth's surface, temperature inversions occur at the tropo-, strato-, and mesopauses (Figure 1.8). This results from a combination of energies reaching the upper atmosphere from the sun and the lower atmosphere from the Earth. The amount of energy at the outer limits of our atmosphere is approximately 1400 watts/metre^2. The Earth and its atmosphere reflect approximately 30 percent of that back to space unchanged (the Earth's albedo) while 50 percent reaches and is absorbed by the Earth. The balance (20 percent) is absorbed by the atmosphere (Clayton, 1995).

The radiation from the sun reaching our outer atmosphere has its maximum intensity at wavelengths between 250 and 800 nanometres (i.e., predominantly in the ultraviolet [UV] and visible regions of the spectrum; Figure 1.9A). This is representative of a perfectly emitting radiation source (frequently called a black body) at a temperature in the region of 5780 K (our sun). As the radiation passes into the thermosphere (Figure 1.8) the majority of the short wavelength ultraviolet energy (<190 nanometres) is absorbed by molecules, producing ions (the thermosphere is also called the ionosphere), atoms, and electrons. Interactions between the incoming radiation and the chemicals in the thermosphere are at a maximum at the outer edges of the thermosphere and drop to essentially zero at the mesopause as by then the effective radiation has been removed. The reactions evolve heat, the amount released decreasing with decreasing height and numbers of interactions, leading to the thermosphere being warmer at the top than the bottom (Figure 1.8).

Photochemical reactions (photon [hν]-initiated chemical change) become significant again in the stratosphere when the UV radiation of wavelengths less than 242 nanometres effect the dissociation of O_2 into oxygen atoms:

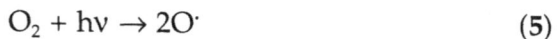

$$O_2 + h\nu \rightarrow 2O^{\cdot} \qquad (5)$$

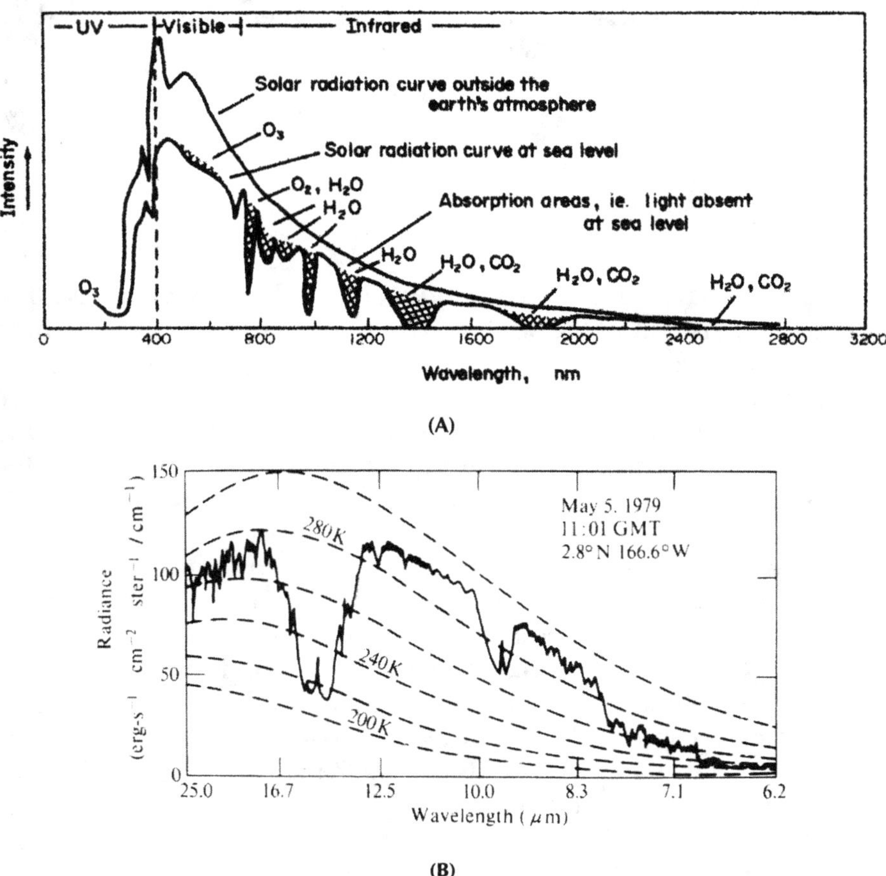

FIGURE 1.9 The Earth's energy balance. (A) Intensities and wavelengths of solar radiation reaching the outer atmosphere and the Earth's surface. The molecules cited absorb energy in the wavelength regions indicated, resulting in the intensity of the energy reaching the Earth's surface being less than that found outside of the Earth's atmosphere (see text). (From Fergusson, J. E. 1982. *Inorganic Chemistry and the Earth. Chemical Resources, Their Extraction, Use and Environmental Impact*. Pergamon Press, Oxford, U.K. With permission.) (B) Radiation from the Earth. The black body radiation lines (-----) indicate the intensities of the radiation emitted from an ideal blackbody at the cited temperatures. The actual radiation (—) from the earth detected at the upper edge of the atmosphere is less intense at certain wavelengths due to the absorption of the emitted energy by greenhouse gases. (From Hanel, R. A. et al. 1972. *Journal of Geophysical Research* 77: 2629–2641. With permission.)

These O atoms can then react with O_2 to produce ozone (O_3):

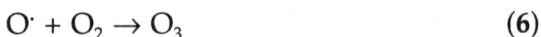

$$O^{\cdot} + O_2 \rightarrow O_3 \tag{6}$$

Ozone itself is dissociated back to dioxygen molecules and $O^{\cdot}$ atoms by radiation with wavelengths less than 340 nanometres:

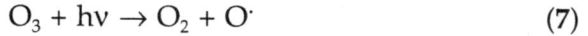

$$O_3 + h\nu \rightarrow O_2 + O^{\cdot} \tag{7}$$

The reaction

$$O_3 + O^{\cdot} \rightarrow 2O_2 \tag{8}$$

results in a balance between production and removal of O_3. The overall effect is that in the stratosphere the majority of the remaining UV radiation from the sun's incoming energy is removed via these photochemical reactions. As with the thermosphere, the stratosphere is warmed from above and we see a gradual cooling with decreasing height. Ozone clearly plays a very important role in this process, the process that protects biological materials from tissue-damaging UV radiation.

In the mesosphere the concentrations of O_2 are not high enough for photochemical reactions to produce any effective warming and so its temperature is controlled by the temperatures above and below it.

In the troposphere heating is from below. There is no UV radiation left to initiate photochemical reactions and effect the associated warming. In the troposphere H_2O and CO_2 and, to a lesser extent, trace components, such as nitrous oxide (N_2O), methane (CH_4), and in fact any non-homonuclear diatomic molecule (i.e., not N_2, O_2, for example), absorb infrared energy through the excitation of molecular vibrations. This further depletes, slightly, the energy that reaches the Earth's surface. Figure 1.9A shows the difference in the intensity of the incoming radiation at the top of the atmosphere and at the Earth's surface. At certain wavelengths the intensities drop to zero. The majority of energy reaching the Earth's surface is in the visible region of the spectrum.

As mentioned above, 48 percent of the energy from the sun is absorbed by the Earth. If the temperature of the Earth is to remain constant, that energy must be re-irradiated back to space. Using the principles of black body radiation (Wayne, 1993), the Earth's temperature would be 256 K (-17°C), far to cold too allow for life as we know it. A black body at 256 K radiates predominantly in the infrared region of the spectrum (the dotted lines in Figure 1.9B) and the energy of radiation is sufficient to excite molecular vibrations. Some of the infrared radiation leaving the Earth's surface is trapped in the atmosphere (consider the solid line in Figure 1.9B) and effects a warming of our environment to the average 288 K (15°C) that supports our life style. This is called the greenhouse effect.

Two very important global environmental concepts introduced in this explanation of the Earth's energy balance will be encountered several times during the remainder of our discussions: the stratospheric O_3 concentration and the greenhouse effect.

Stratospheric Ozone

Considerable concern has been expressed recently about the depletion of the stratospheric O_3 layer by pollutants from Earth. These pollutants, mainly N_2O and chlorofluorocarbons (CFCs: $CFCl_3$ or CFC11 and CF_2Cl_2 or CFC12, for example; molecules with structures based on the tetrahedral C atom, Figure 1.2B), are very unreactive and thus pass through the troposphere to the stratosphere unchanged. In the stratosphere the available UV radiation can effect the photochemical breaking of bonds and produce radicals (atoms or molecules with unpaired electrons, $R^{\cdot}$) which can alter the O_3 balance. The relevant equations are as follows:

For nitrous oxide

$$N_2O + h\nu \rightarrow N_2 + O^{\cdot} \tag{9}$$

$$N_2O + O^{\cdot} \rightarrow 2NO^{\cdot} \tag{10}$$

$$NO^{\cdot} + O_3 \rightarrow O_2 + NO_2 \tag{11}$$

$$NO_2 + O^{\cdot} \rightarrow NO^{\cdot} + O_2 \tag{12}$$

For CFCs

$$CFCl_3 + h\nu \rightarrow CFCl_2^{\cdot} + Cl^{\cdot} \tag{13}$$

$$CF_2Cl_2 + h\nu \rightarrow CF_2Cl^{\cdot} + Cl^{\cdot} \tag{14}$$

$$O_3 + Cl^{\cdot} \rightarrow O_2 + ClO^{\cdot} \tag{15}$$

$$ClO^{\cdot} + O^{\cdot} \rightarrow O_2 + Cl^{\cdot} \tag{16}$$

It can be seen from these reactions that the $NO^{\cdot}$ and $Cl^{\cdot}$ radicals are recycled and only the O_3 species is lost; the radicals catalyze the destruction of O_3, each can destroy several O_3 molecules. An understanding of the causes of the partial destruction of the stratospheric ozone layer becomes immediately apparent from a consideration of reactions 5 to 16. If the concentrations of these O_3 destroying radicals increase, then the rate of destruction of O_3 will exceed the rate of its production and the O_3 concentration will decrease. These radicals can increase in concentration if molecules capable of producing them upon exposure to high-energy radiation, and of sufficient chemical stability to be unreactive in the troposphere, are released from the Earth's surface. CFCs and nitrous oxide (N_2O) are such molecules. CFCs were in fact developed as refrigerants because of their lack of reactivity; the possibilities of reactions in the stratosphere were not considered.

A decrease in O_3 in the atmosphere will allow for an increase in the intensity of UV radiation reaching the Earth's surface, which in turn can lead to perturbations in cellular behaviour (cancer). Many other reactions also occur; recent models developed to estimate the impact of stratospheric O_3 depletion are complicated and the subject of continuing debate (Bridgeman, 1990).

The Greenhouse Effect

The greenhouse effect arises from the absorption by the atmosphere of radiation leaving the Earth's surface, the absorption effected by the excitation of molecular vibrations. The only effective vibrations are those that lead to a change in the asymmetry of charge in the molecule; an oscillating dipole must be present to allow the molecule to interact with the infrared radiation. Dioxygen and N_2 cannot do this and thus the gases of importance to the greenhouse effect are the atmosphere's trace components (H_2O, CO_2, CH_4, N_2O, CF_2Cl_2, etc.). Significant changes in their concentrations, as happened during the latter half of the twentieth century (Figure 1.10), can occur reasonably easily (to change the concentration of a major component requires huge amounts of the chemical). Polluting the atmosphere with these traces can lead to an alteration in the balance of the Earth's energy and could result in changes to the global climate (McBean, 1994; Clayton, 1995).

BIOGEOCHEMICAL CYCLES

We have divided our environment into the atmosphere, biosphere, lithosphere, and hydrosphere and considered some of their important chemical and physical characteristics. They are, however, not isolated from each other. When considering the behaviours of chemicals in the environment, all spheres and all forms of the elements (elemental speciation or the various chemicals that can contain that element) must be considered. Unless elements, in one form or other, are lost from the

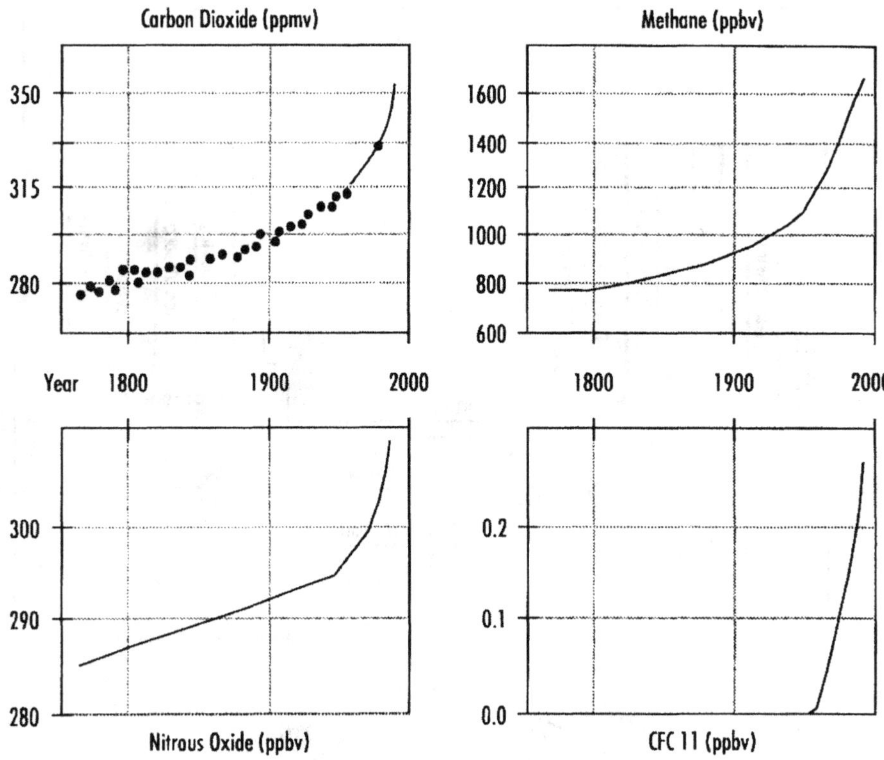

FIGURE 1.10 The variations in the concentrations of some greenhouse gases since 1800. (From Lorius, C. and H. Oeschger. 1994. *Ambio* 23: 30–36. With permission.)

Earth, matter on Earth must be conserved and elements therefore must cycle between and within the spheres; the cycles are referred to as biogeochemical cycles.

Biogeochemical cycles are normally represented diagrammatically by boxes for each of the spheres and arrows for fluxes between spheres. Figure 1.11A, which omits the biosphere in the interest of clarity, illustrates this and the important transportation processes within and between spheres. The major circulation patterns for the atmosphere and the oceans (Figures 1.11B and 1.11C) are linked and thus similar. Vertical transport must also be considered. Temperature inversions in the atmosphere (Figure 1.8) inhibit vertical mixing. In aquifers, where warmer waters float on the top of colder ones, unless there is turbulence, there will be little tendency for mixing across the temperature change (thermocline). Similarly fresh waters float on saline waters, the boundary being called the halocline; mixing across haloclines is slow.

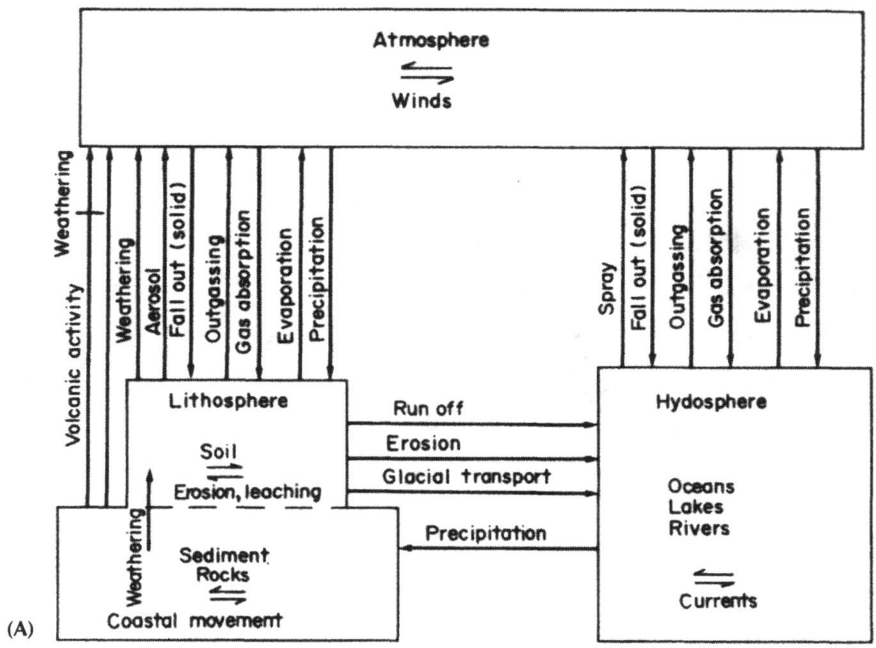

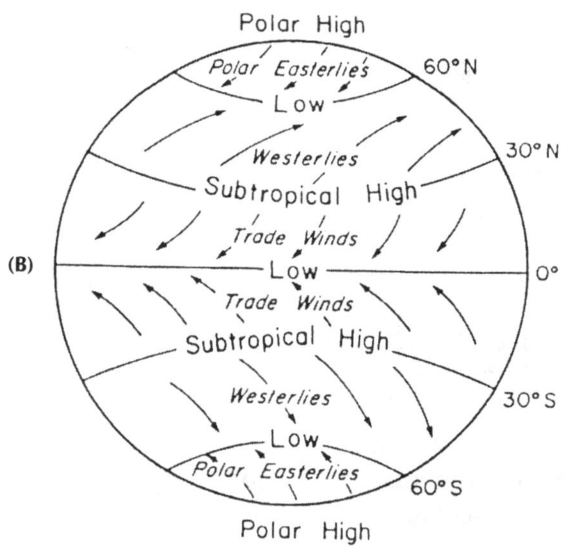

FIGURE 1.11 Global transport and circulation. (A) Transport processes in biogeochemical cycles. (From Fergusson, J. E. 1982. *Inorganic Chemistry and the Earth. Chemical Resources, Their Extraction, Use and Environmental Impact*. Pergamon Press, Oxford, U.K. With permission.) (B) Atmospheric circulation patterns. (From Chester, R. 1993. *Marine Geochemistry*. Chapman and Hall, London. With permission.) (C) Ocean surface currents. (From Stowe, K. S. 1979. *Ocean Science*. John Wiley & Sons, New York. With permission.)

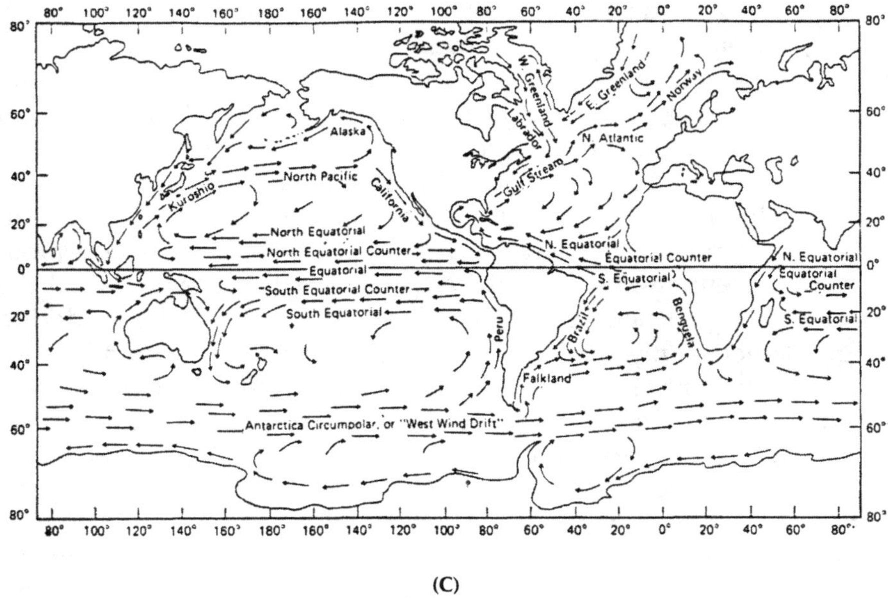

(C)

FIGURE 1.11 (continued)

It is normally assumed that on global scales the environment is at equilibrium and thus the net flux of a chemical from one sphere to another must be zero. If not, there would be an accumulation of that chemical in one of the spheres (which, in fact, is now happening as human activities impact upon the natural cycles). In order to quantify concentrations and fluxes many chemical analyses must be done in all the representative areas of the world and then averages taken. The analytical data must be accurate and extensive. Clearly there will be large uncertainties in the averages and when considering the balances one must bear this in mind.

The times that chemicals spend in spheres are normally represented by residence times (T_R) where T_R = [amount of chemical in the reservoir]/[the flux into (or out of) the reservoir]. This time represents the average time that a molecule will spend in the sphere if the sphere is well mixed and at equilibrium (flux in = flux out). A short residence time implies that the chemical species is highly reactive and will not be dispersed far from its source before it is chemically or physically changed. A long residence time means that the chemical will be widely dispersed throughout the sphere.

In constructing global biogeochemical cycles it is not reasonable to include chemicals whose residence times are short compared to the mixing times of the relevant sphere. Their concentrations will be highly variable and although global averages could be calculated such averages would grossly misrepresent the scope of their impacts. Residence times must be considered in conjunction with sphere mixing times and mixing processes. The larger population and land mass in the northern hemisphere and global ocean and atmosphere circulation patterns (Figure 1.11) also make averaging over the two hemispheres only relevant for chemicals with very long residence times. For chemicals with short residence times it is more instructive to consider variations of concentrations within the environmental spheres.

Global biogeochemical cycles are usually constructed considering single elements only. Chemicals and chemical change seldom involve only one element and thus to consider each element in isolation is a gross simplification of reality, but clearly the considerations would become complex very quickly if everything were to be included. Elemental biogeochemical cycles are a good place to start; attempting to balance them can lead to major omissions of data becoming quickly apparent. We will consider the C cycle in detail to illustrate the thinking processes that environmental scientists need to undertake and then the Pb, N, and P cycles will be overviewed.

The Carbon Biogeochemical Cycle

A biogeochemical cycle for carbon is given in Figure 1.12. This is probably one of the most complicated cycles, but also one of the most important. Carbon, through its inorganic $CO_3^{2-}/HCO_3^-/CO_2$ equilibria, its organic molecules like sugars (Figures 1.2B(v) and 1.13) and pesticides (see Figure 1.17), or its gaseous forms, plays a major role in most of the important environmental processes: the buffering of water bodies (the capacity for a water body to retain its pH when acids or bases are added to them), the structures and functions of biomolecules, and the greenhouse effect are familiar examples of the environmental importance of carbon.

By far the largest reservoir is the buried organic and inorganic carbon. As fluxes to these stores are small the residence times are large (420 and 330 million years, respectively). By far the largest fluxes in the cycle are those associated with the photosynthetic incorporation of CO_2 into plant materials and the related release of CO_2 during respiration (Table 1.4).

Carbon in the Atmosphere

The simplest part of the cycle is the atmospheric component. There are three major species (Table 1.4) to consider. Carbon dioxide, at an average

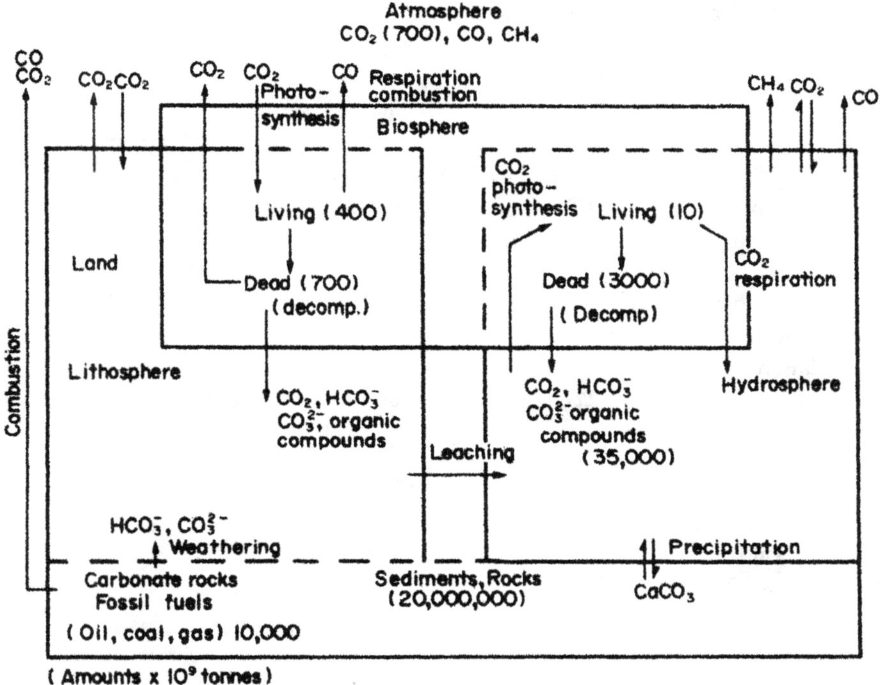

FIGURE 1.12 A biogeochemical cycle for carbon (from Fergusson, J. E. 1982. *Inorganic Chemistry and the Earth. Chemical Resources, Their Extraction, Use and Environmental Impact*. Pergamon Press, Oxford, U.K. With permission.)

concentration of 350 ppmv and with a total amount of 6.3×10^{16} moles is the most abundant. Its major sources are respiration and degradation (oxidation/burning) of carbohydrates ($CH_2O + O_2 \rightarrow CO_2 + H_2O$; the reverse of photosynthesis) from land (49 percent) and the oceans (48 percent). Anthropogenic sources account for only about 3 percent of the flux. The residence time for CO_2 is about 10 years. The average vertical atmospheric mixing time is approximately 80 days (Brimblecombe, 1996) and thus CO_2 released to the atmosphere has the potential to become mixed globally. The concentration of CO_2 has been gradually increasing throughout the last three centuries (Figure 1.10) after having been essentially constant since the previous glacial maximum (ca. 18000 BP, Street-Perrott, 1994). Monitoring of CO_2 began in the late 1950s with previous concentrations coming from the analyses of gas bubbles trapped in polar ice (Lorius and Oeschger, 1994). At present the atmospheric CO_2 concentration is increasing at about 2 ppmv per year and this is likely to have serious impacts on climate by promoting global warming (Moore and Braswell, 1995). Clearly, the increase implies that the cycle is not at equilibrium. Not only is it not at equilibrium, it is

TABLE 1.4 Carbon in the Atmosphere

Sources	Fluxes Pg C yr^{-1}	Sinks	Fluxes Pg C yr^{-1}
***Carbon Dioxide* (amount = 754 Pg; Pg = 10^{15} g)**			
Respiration, oceans	105	Photosynthesis, oceans	107
Respiration, land	55	Photosynthesis, land	113
Soils	54		
Fossil fuel burning	5.4		
Deforestation	1		
CO oxidation	0.7		
Total to CO_2 pool	**221.1**	**Total from CO_2 pool**	**220**
***Carbon Monoxide* (amount = 0.2 Pg)**			
Methane oxidation	0.37	Carbon dioxide	0.82
Natural hydrocarbons	0.25	Soils	0.11
Burning fossil fuels	0.19	Stratosphere	0.01
Forest fires & clearing	0.17		
Agricultural burning	0.11		
Hydrocarbons			
Wood as fuel	0.02		
Oceans	0.02		
Total to CO pool	**1.06**	**Total from CO pool**	**0.94**
***Methane* (amount = 0.0045 Pg)**			
Wetlands	0.12	Oxidation by OH to CO etc.	0.49
Rice paddies	0.11	Stratosphere	0.03
Microbial reduction	0.12	Soils	0.02
Water bodies	0.02		
Biomass burning	0.06		
Landfills	0.04		
Coal mining	0.04		
Natural gas	0.05		
Total to CH_4 pool	**0.56**	**Total from CH_4 pool**	**0.54**

Data from Bridgman, 1990; Schlesinger, 1991; Moore and Brasewall, 1995; Brimblecombe, 1996. Amounts and fluxes have considerable uncertainties and differ with data source and should not be considered to be highly accurate; the imbalances reflect this.

not balanced either; sources exceed sinks by about 2 picograms per year; the estimates of the fluxes must be in error. While it is thought that the terrestrial sink has been underestimated (Moore and Braswell, 1995; Mooney and Koch, 1994), much more research is needed before we attain a full understanding.

The concentration of methane (CH_4) has approximately doubled since the early 1800s, prior to which it was essentially constant (Figure 1.10). Its residence time (about 10 years) is long compared to global mixing times and so this greenhouse gas will also have an impact on global climate.

The principal source of CH_4 is microbially mediated reductive degradation of organic matter in marshes and rice growing areas and the intestines of higher animals (Brimblecombe, 1996):

$$CH_2O + 2H_2 \rightarrow CH_4 + H_2O \quad \textbf{(17)}$$

Fluxes from the oceans and volcanoes are usually minor in comparison.

The primary sink for CH_4 is oxidation to CO_2 through a series of photochemically initiated reactions (Brimblecombe, 1996). As for many tropospheric reactions, the first step involves the $OH^{\cdot}$ radical, formed by reaction of water with photochemically produced $O^{\cdot}$ atoms. Ozone, mixed into the troposphere from the stratosphere, is the main precursor of the $O^{\cdot}$ atoms (Equation 7; Wayne, 1993):

$$O^{\cdot} + H_2O \rightarrow 2OH^{\cdot} \quad \textbf{(18)}$$

The $OH^{\cdot}$ radical, with a residence time of the order of one second, through its reactions, produces many other highly reactive radicals. Among the short-lived chemicals produced from the oxidation of methane is formaldehyde, HCHO, a respiratory irritant that can reach relatively high concentrations in the atmospheres of polluted cities. Chemicals like this with short residence times are seldom included in global biogeochemical cycles.

The sources of carbon monoxide are approximately evenly divided between the oxidation of methane, the burning of fuels and anthropogenic hydrocarbons, the oxidation of natural hydrocarbons, and forest and agricultural clearing (Table 1.4). The residence time for CO is estimated to be about 2 months. However, for reactive species like CO such calculations are of limited value. Concentrations are higher in the boundary layer and, as expected for a chemical that has predominantly land-based sources, are highest in the northern hemisphere and over land. Concentrations of CO in urban areas with poor air circulation (parking buildings, tunnels, busy streets, etc.) can be as high as 25 ppmv, but are normally below 10 ppmv and average about 1 ppmv (Clarke, 1992). The short residence time implies that CO is of more concern locally than globally.

The hydroxide radical is the main reagent effecting the oxidation of CO:

$$CO + OH^{\cdot} \rightarrow CO_2 + H^{\cdot} \quad \textbf{(19)}$$

The hydrogen atom produced either reacts with O_2 to produce the peroxide radical, $HOO^{\cdot}$ or reacts with the peroxide radical to produce 2 $OH^{\cdot}$ radicals. The importance of radical reactions as oxidants will be illustrated when we consider photochemical smog.

There are many other C compounds present in the atmosphere at concentrations in the low ppbv. Plants and animals emit odours, pheromones, etc. (Brimblecombe, 1996) and human activities, such as cooking (Sievers et al., 1994), all contribute to the atmospheric soup.

Carbon in the Lithosphere and Biosphere

Essentially all the C on earth is tied up in the carbonate mineral (81 percent) and organic carbon (19 percent) reservoirs in sedimentary rocks (Figure 1.12). The natural fluxes to and from them are some of the smallest fluxes in the C cycle. The main anthropogenic environmental impact of this C is through the mining and subsequent burning of fossil fuels.

More than 99 percent of living biomass C is on land, with an average residence time of the order of 10 to 20 years. Living oceanic biomass C, on the other hand, is a small reservoir, with residence times of the order of 1 to 3 months. The non-living carbon compounds found on land and in aquifers result from the degradation of plant and animal litter and thus most C in the environment, including the inorganic carbonates, has at some time been incorporated in living materials.

Photosynthesis utilizing gaseous CO_2 (equation 1) or dissolved HCO_3^-:

$$HCO_3^- + H_2O + h\nu \rightarrow CH_2O + O_2 + OH^- \quad \textbf{(20)}$$

results in the fixing of C as carbohydrates. Biosynthetic pathways convert these into the wide variety of biomolecules that are essential to the functioning of cells. Subsequent biochemical reactions then produce a whole series of secondary metabolites that also have important biological functions (natural pesticides, pheromones, etc.).

A knowledge of biochemical reactions (Stryer, 1988) is important to the understanding of metabolic pathways and chemical toxicities

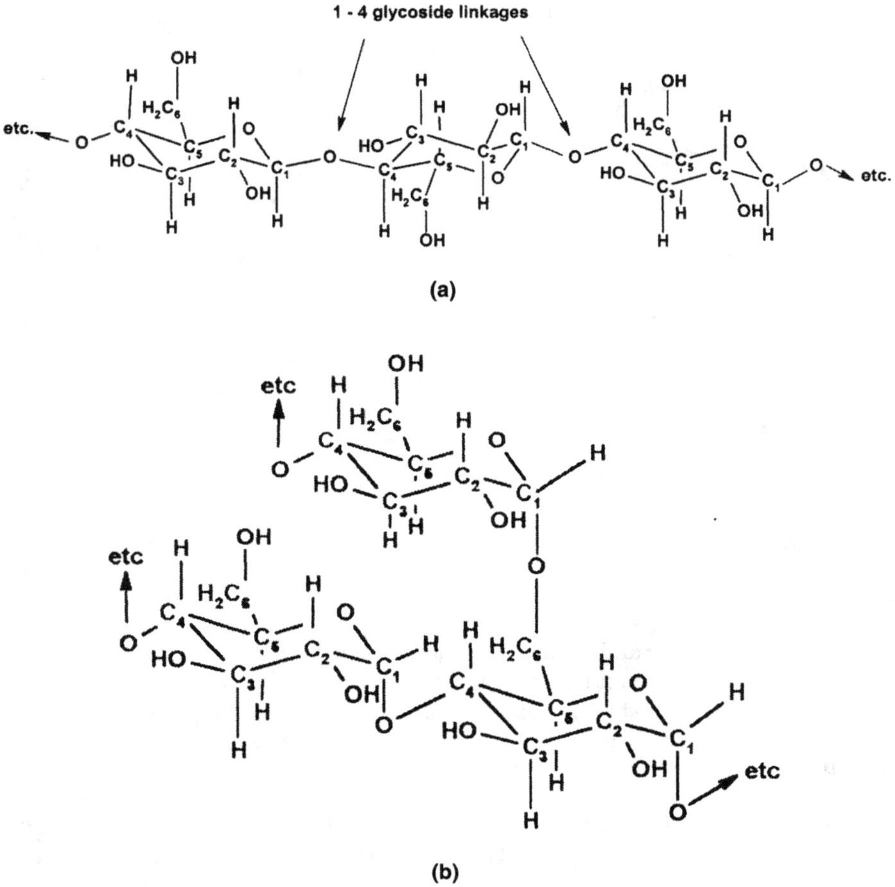

1 - 4 glycoside linkages

(a)

(b)

FIGURE 1.13 Polysaccharides. Polymers of monosaccharides (see Figure 1.2B). formed by condensation involving OH groups at the C_1, C_4, and/or C_6 positions. (A) Cellulose, a fibrous structural material. (B) A starch, structurally and chemically different from cellulose but consisting of similar monomers.

and thus to environmental chemistry, but is beyond the scope of our present discussion; we will limit ourselves to an overview of the types of biochemicals and then to their fates when they are external to the living systems. Most biomolecules are polymers made by the condensation (loss of water or dehydration) of smaller units, as for example the nucleic acids (see Figure 1.15).

The major biological C-containing compounds are carbohydrates (60 percent of the plant dry weight; Figure 1.13), proteins (10 percent), lipids (5 percent; Figures 1.14 and 1.15), and lignins (25 percent; Figure 1.16). The carbohydrates (Figure 1.13) are either food sources

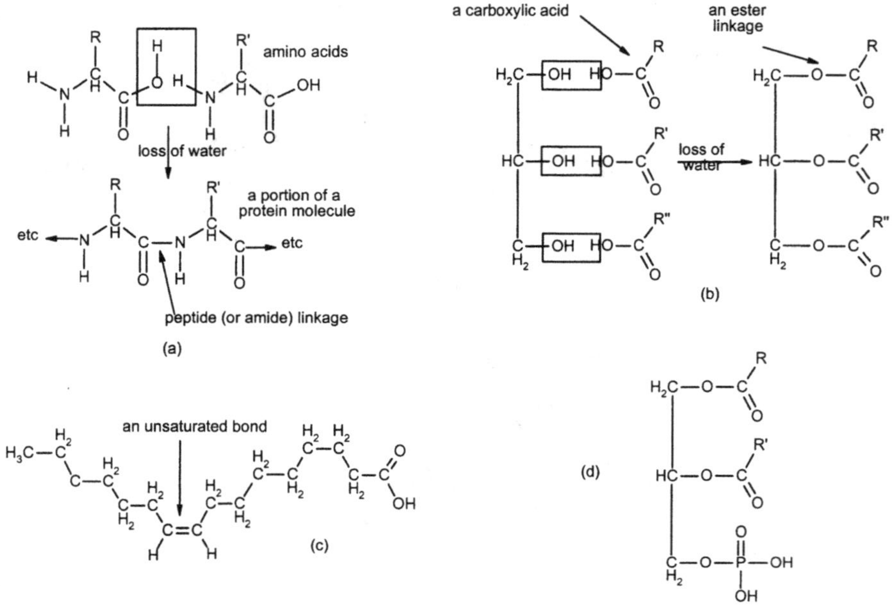

FIGURE 1.14 Proteins and lipids. (a) An amino acid (if R = CH_2SH the amino acid is cysteine, for example) and a protein, a polymer formed by condensation (loss of H_2O to form peptide linkages) of amino acids. (b) Glycerol and a glycerol trialkylate formed by condensation of glycerol with fatty acids. (c) A phospholipid. (d) An unsaturated fatty (long chain of C atoms) acid.

(sugars and starches) or structural materials (cellulose and hemicellulose). They have structures based on the polymerization (condensation) of monosaccharides (single unit sugars, Figure 1.2B). The differing chemical linkages between the monomeric units impart considerably different chemical properties to the resultant polymers. Starches hydrolyze (react with water) to produce shorter-chain polysaccharides which are used as foods, while cellulose fibres are extremely resistant to hydrolysis. The components of the polymers are similar, the structures are different.

Proteins are polymers of amino acids (Solomons, 1997). There are twenty-two different major amino acids involved in proteins, eight of which are essential to humans. The constituent amino acids are joined through peptide (amide) linkages (Figure 1.14). The sequencing of amino acids can be highly variable, leading to the many possible proteins. Of the three groups of biopolymers (polysaccharides, proteins, and nucleic acids), proteins have the most diverse functions: enzymes and hormones, muscles and tendons, skin and hair, haemoglobins, antibodies, and structural components of bones.

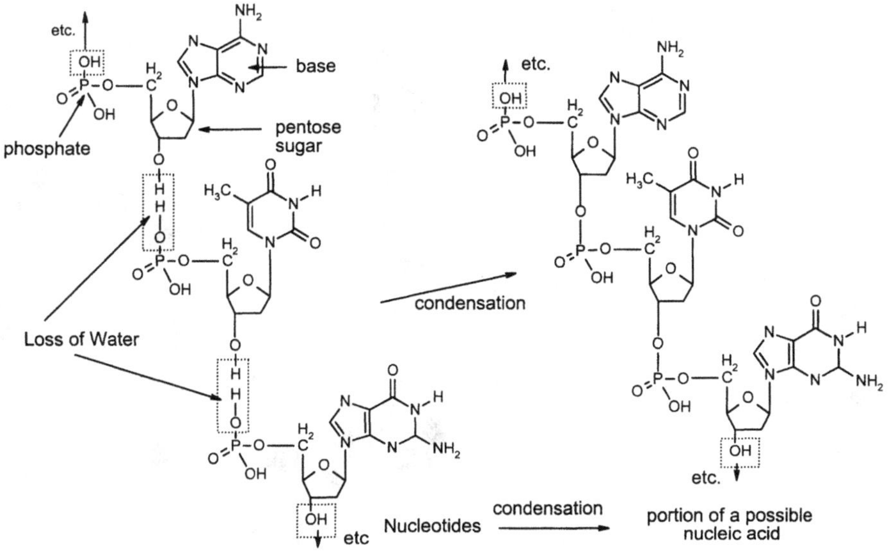

FIGURE 1.15 A nucleic acid and nucleotides. Nucleotides condense to form nucleic acids.

Lipids are molecules that can be extracted from plant and animal materials into nonpolar solvents (alkanes for example). They are further classified according to their reactions with aqueous sodium hydroxide (Holum, 1990). The largest group of chemicals that fall into the lipid definition are the oils, fats, and waxes, which are esters formed by dehydration reactions between alcohols, generally glycerol, and fatty (long C chains) organic acids (Figure 1.14b). Oils tend to be liquids with predominantly unsaturated fatty acid components, whereas fats are solids of predominantly saturated fatty acids. Waxes are esters formed from fatty acids and long-chain alcohols. Phospholipids, which are similar to the fats and waxes, contain phosphate groups. Steroids and terpenes also fall into the lipid category.

Nucleic acids are sugar-phosphate backbone biopolymers of nucleotides, where a nucleotide consists of a pentose sugar, a heterocyclic base (the ring contains C and other atoms), and a phosphate group (Figure 1.15). Adenosine triphosphate, ATP, has a structure similar to the nucleic acid nucleotides.

Lignins, found in the woody tissue of plants, are very resistant to weathering and thus provide a protective covering for the cellulose and other components of the woods. They are high-molecular-weight polymers based on derivatives of alkyl phenols (Figure 1.16). The six C atom rings in such structures are called aromatic rings; planar and

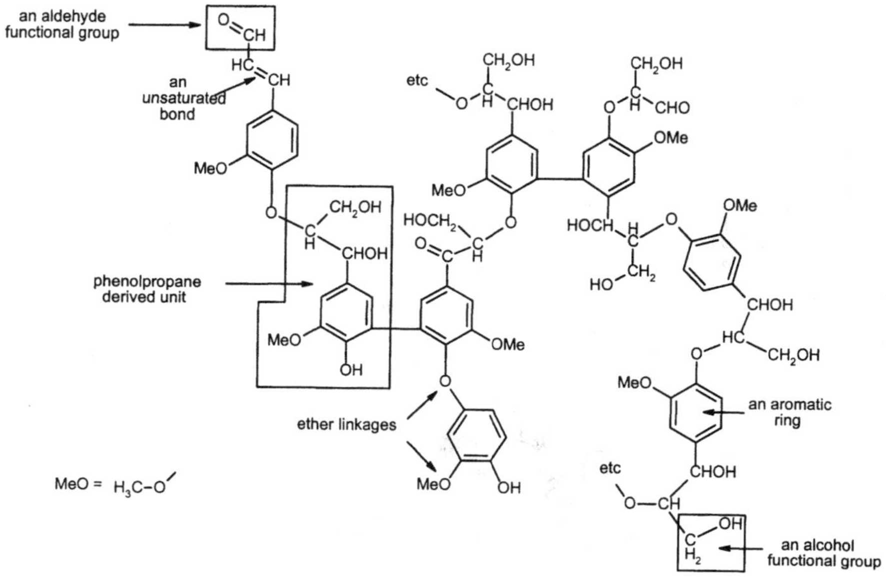

FIGURE 1.16 A possible structure for lignin. Based on the polymerization of the alkyl phenol units through, mainly, ether linkages. The many functional groups (alcohol, aldehyde, etc.) lead to surface reactivity.

unsaturated with some bonding electrons delocalized above and below the ring imparting considerable stability to these chemicals.

Thus, the biomolecules, initially produced by reduction of CO_2 (photosynthesis), consist predominantly of sugars, aromatic rings, aliphatic chains, and hydroxyl, acid, amine, and phospo functional groups and ether, ester, and peptide linkages. Upon the death of the plants and animals these chemicals become incorporated into the soils or water bodies upon or within which they grew. There they undergo degradation, generally microbially mediated, to release constituent organic molecules (amino acids, fatty acids, etc.) which can undergo further degradation (oxidization) to eventually produce CO_2. The organic species more resistant to weathering, particularly the aromatics, polymerize, possibly with incorporation of structural units from other types of biomolecules, to produce humic materials (Cresser et al., 1993). These semi- to nonbiological polymers become more and more resistant to weathering with age and play important roles in the fixing and transport of chemicals in the environment. Deep burial of organic carbon can lead to the eventual formation of peat, oils, coal, and natural gases, materials that contain predominantly carbon and hydrogen only (Krauskopf and Bird, 1995).

Humic materials (HM) constitute 80 to 90 percent of the carbon in soils (soil organic materials, SOM). HM is operationally divided into fulvic acids (extractable into base, soluble in acid and base), humic acids (extractable into base but insoluble in acid), and humin (insoluble). Since their formation depends on the organic materials available and the microbial activity involved in their production, no two "humic" molecules will be the same. Fulvic (and humic) acids therefore do not have definitive chemical formulae but rather are defined by their bulk chemical and physical properties (elemental composition, spectroscopic properties, complexing capacities/acidities, for example; Hayes, 1991). Some models have been proposed which give indications as to the structural units that may be expected to be present in humic materials (Buffle, 1990). Such models generally involve metals in addition to the structural units discussed above, as these polymers are capable of complexing metal ions, a reaction we will consider in more detail in the next section.

SOM is an important component of fertile soils, playing both chemical and physical roles. The non-living components of a typical soil will be, by weight, about 45 percent inorganic, 5 percent organic, 25 percent air, and 25 percent water, although clearly there exists considerable variability. In addition to the functional groups of the organic materials being very efficient at binding metal ions, as suggested above, they can also bind organic species, such as pesticides and other anthropogenic chemicals. Soil inorganic components are also involved in such reactions, but SOM is usually at least twice as efficient per unit mass (Harrison et al., 1991; Alloway, 1992). These binding reactions are generally reversible and are the same reactions that lead to soils being able to bind and release cations to and from soil water. The cation exchange capacity (CEC) is a measure of the number of cations that can be bound per kilogram of soil, and is an indicator of the ability of a soil to retain not only nutrients such as K^+, Ca^{2+}, and $Fe^{2+/3+}$ but also pollutants like Pb^{2+} and Cd^{2+}.

In addition to the natural organic materials in soils are the anthropogenic organics, such as pesticides, spilt oils, detergents, etc. Pesticides are of particular concern. They are used in agriculture for the control of insects and fungi. Although there is a strong move towards the use of biologically produced chemicals (extracts from plants), large amounts of a wide variety of synthetic materials (Chenier, 1986) are still widely applied (Figure 1.17 gives some examples). The majority are organic materials, although 50 years ago inorganics dominated pesticide sales.

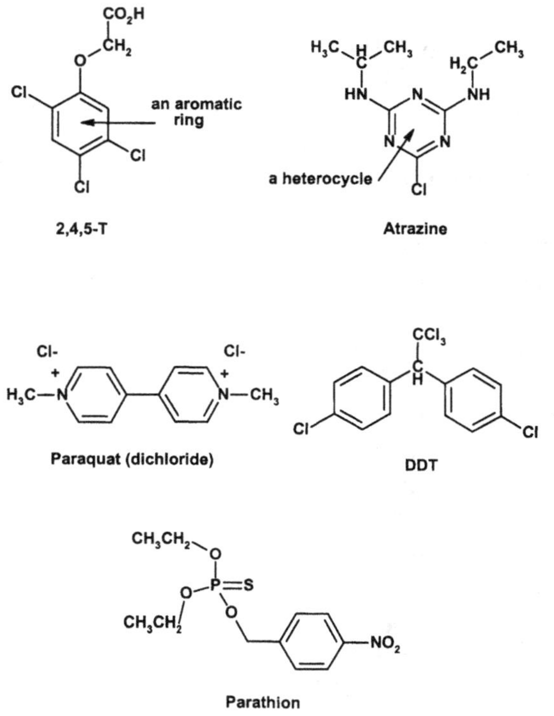

an aromatic ring

2,4,5-T

a heterocycle

Atrazine

Paraquat (dichloride)

DDT

Parathion

FIGURE 1.17 Some pesticides.

The biological activities of pesticides result from their functional groups and their structures or shapes. Some are transformed into biologically active materials after application (Somasundaram and Coats, 1991; Hassall, 1990). The primary degradation reactions (oxidation, photochemical, hydrolysis, and complexation/adsorption), again generally microbially assisted, usually result in innocuous products such as CO_2, H_2O, NH_3, mineral salts, and humic material components. Their dispersal through the environmental spheres depends on their solubilities and volatilities.

These materials, applied to control pests and enhance crop productivity, are especially important in tropical environments where pest numbers are great. However, they and many of their degradation products, are toxic – they are designed to be so. When incorporated into the soil and/or ground- or surface waters they become pollutants of concern. Often concentrations in the parts per trillion (nanograms [10^{-9} g] per kilogram) range or below are sufficient to be toxic to animals, including humans. It is only since the development of sophisticated analytical instrumentation and sampling and sample handling techniques that some of these species have been identified in the environmental spheres (Barcelo, 1991). These environmental poisons, of such economic importance to farmers, must be used with care if we are to avoid poisoning non-target species.

Carbon in the Hydrosphere

The concentrations of the various C species in the hydrosphere are in the millimolar or lower range. Total organic carbon seldom reaches more than 2 millimolar (Spitzy and Leenheer, 1991) with most of the biomolecule degradation compounds contributing to some extent. These compounds are important in that they coat particles and complex/adsorb metal ions, anions such as PO_4^{3-}, and pesticides and other organic pollutants.

Inorganic carbon (molecular CO_2 and the anions HCO_3^- and CO_3^{2-}) in the hydrosphere originates from the dissolution of carbonate minerals and atmospheric CO_2, or is produced *in situ* by biological respiration and organic degradation. Many marine organisms (algae and corals) use aragonite and calcite (both $CaCO_3$ but with slightly different arrangements of the ions in the lattices) for structural purposes. Upon death of the organisms these minerals become part of the sediment, joining other carbonates produced by precipitation. They are slightly soluble and thus form a source of inorganic C to the aquifers:

$$CaCO_3(s) \rightarrow Ca^{2+} + CO_3^{2-} \quad \textbf{(21)}$$

The solubility product, K_{sp}, is 4.47×10^{-9} mol^2 dm^{-6} (for calcite).

From the atmosphere gaseous $CO_2(g)$ can dissolve in water to give hydrated CO_2, the concentration of which depends on the partial pressure of CO_2 (P_{CO_2}) in the atmosphere:

$$CO_2(g) + H_2O \rightarrow H_2O{\cdot}CO_2 \quad \textbf{(22)}$$

The equilibrium constant for this equation, called Henry's law constant, equals 3.38×10^{-2} mol dm^{-3} atm^{-1} at 20°C. The CO_2 and CO_3^{2-} are linked through HCO_3^- according to the following acid–base equilibria (Andrews et al., 1996):

$$H_2O{\cdot}CO_2 + H_2O \rightarrow HCO_3^- + H_3O^+ \quad \textbf{(23)}$$

$$HCO_3^- + H_2O \rightarrow CO_3^{2-} + H_3O^+ \quad \textbf{(24)}$$

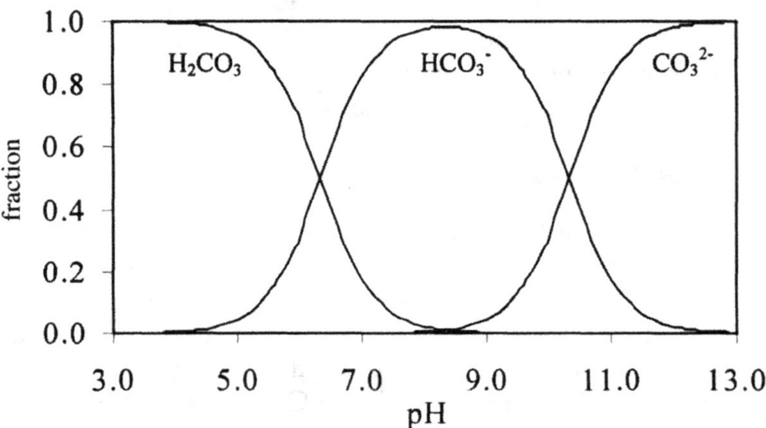

FIGURE 1.18 An inorganic carbon speciation diagram.

with equilibrium constants 4.5×10^{-7} mol dm^{-3} and 4.7×10^{-11} mol dm^{-3}, respectively.

The total inorganic carbon is therefore distributed among these three species (and more if the ionic strength increases and ion pairs such as $NaCO_3^-$ form; Stumm and Morgan, 1981). The fractions of the total inorganic C present as any one of these species as a function of pH, calculated from the above equilibrium expressions (Manahan, 1994), are illustrated in Figure 1.18. This plot shows that in acidic waters CO_2 is the dominant species, HCO_3^- becomes important at about pH 5 and dominates between pH 6.3 and 10.3, after which CO_3^{2-} is the dominant species. In natural water systems where the pH varies from about 6 to 8.5, inorganic C will be present predominantly as HCO_3^-. Diagrams such as these indicate qualitative change but do not indicate how much (concentration) of each species is present. The amounts can be quickly calculated if the sources of the species are known. If the water body is in contact with the atmosphere, the concentration of CO_2 in the water comes from Equation 22. Dissolved CO_2 is a weak acid and dissociates according to Equation 23 to produce an acidic solution. HCO_3^- is also a weak acid (Equation 24) but we will ignore that for the moment. If the atmosphere is the only source of CO_2, as for example for rainwater, then knowing the present concentration of atmospheric CO_2 to be 360 ppmv, a pH of 5.6 can be calculated by combining Equations 22 and 23. Referring to Figure 1.18 shows that at such a pH CO_3^{2-} is essentially absent and so ignoring Equation 24 was not unreasonable. This simple calculation shows that rainwater is naturally acidic.

If the water system is also in equilibrium with calcite then inorganic C can come from both the CO_2 in the atmosphere and by dissolution of the carbonate mineral (Equation 21). The principle of electroneutrality states that the sum of the positive charges on the cations in solution must equal the sum of the negative charges on the anions and therefore if the water body contains only the inorganic carbon species, Ca^{2+}, and H_2O dissociation products (generally a reasonable assumption for fresh waters overlying limestone), then

$$2[Ca^{2+}] + [H_3O^+] = 2[CO_3^{2-}] + [HCO_3^-] + [OH^-]$$

Using this and Equations 21 to 24 the concentrations of the various species can be calculated. Such calculations show that a water body in contact with limestone and the atmosphere will be basic (pH = 8.3) and have a total inorganic C concentration of about 1 millimolar (essentially all present as HCO_3^-). The hydroxide ion concentration, which determines the pH, is about 500 times lower than the HCO_3^- concentration. Bicarbonate is a weak base (the reverse of Equation 23) and thus the base content of the water is due almost exclusively to the bicarbonate ion.

While in most unpolluted waters, including marine waters, the inorganic C system dominates the base content, species such as silicates, borates, metal ions like Al^{3+} and Fe^{3+}, and organic acids, among others, have acid-base properties and thus can be involved. This base content is called the water's acid neutralizing capacity (ANC; the term alkalinity is also often used but strictly only refers to an inorganic carbon system; Kramer, 1981; Stumm and Morgan, 1981). An ANC value of 1 milliequivalent per litre is typical of many waters. ANC is determined by titrating the water with standard acid to a predetermined pH and is equivalent to the millimoles of acid required to neutralize a litre of the water. ANC gives a measure of the buffering capacity of the water body, that is the ability of the water to receive acid (or base) without a significant change in the pH of the water. This is achieved by the added acid (or base) reacting with chemical species in the water to effect neutralization. For example, with HCO_3^- in the water, added acid will result in a shift in the $CO_3^{2-}/HCO_3^-/CO_2$ equilibria but very little resulting change in pH. Clearly the more base present, the greater the buffering capacity. These concepts are important when considering the impact of acid rain on ecosystems; high buffering capacity waters can cope with acidic rainfall better than low capacity waters; most living species are very sensitive to changes in pH and thus its control by natural buffers is important.

Photosynthesis in water bodies occurs to the depths to which light penetrates. If it occurs fast enough so that equilibrium with the atmosphere is lost, as may occur under phytoplankton blooms, then the inorganic carbon in the water body starts to become depleted and the pH increases (Equation 20). For each millimole of bicarbonate used a millimole of hydroxide is produced and thus if the ANC is 1 milliequivalent per litre then 10^{-3} moles per litre of OH^- will be introduced to the water, and the pH will rise to about 11. Under normal circumstances CO_2 from the atmosphere would dissolve according to Equations 22 and 23 and effect the neutralization of this produced OH^-; the equilibria will shift to buffer the change. Only when the depletion of dissolved CO_2 is faster than the dissolution of atmospheric CO_2 can the rise in pH occur.

Transport of Carbon Between Spheres

The C biogeochemical cycle (Figure 1.12) indicates the fluxes of C within and between the spheres. We have already considered most of these processes but those that take place at the fresh–marine water interface need special consideration. These areas, estuaries, are particularly important, as they are frequently close to areas of high population and, in the tropics, near coral reefs. Fresh waters generally have low total dissolved solids, but frequently high total suspended solids and colloidal concentrations. Colloids are small particles (<45 microns) that do not settle under normal gravitational forces. These suspended solids are mixtures of inorganic oxides and oxyhydroxides of, predominantly, iron, aluminium, and manganese, organic materials such as humic acids and microbial organisms. They do not tend to coagulate, as they normally have charged surfaces and thus repel each other. The charges on the surfaces depend on the composition of the particle and the properties of the surrounding water (Stumm and Morgan, 1981). On the surfaces of metal oxyhydroxides are oxide and/or hydroxide groups that can undergo acid–base-type reactions:

$$\text{particle-OH} + H_2O \rightarrow \text{particle-O}^- + H_3O^+ \quad \textbf{(25)}$$

$$\text{particle-OH} + H_2O \rightarrow \text{particle-OH}_2^+ + OH^- \quad \textbf{(26)}$$

and thus the charge, positive or negative, will be pH dependent. Reactions with cations and anions can also generate surface charges:

$$\text{particle-O}^- + Pb^{2+} \rightarrow \text{particle-O-Pb}^+ \quad \textbf{(27)}$$

$$\text{particle-OH} + HPO_4^{2-} \rightarrow \text{particle-OPO}_3\text{OH}^- + OH^- \quad \textbf{(28)}$$

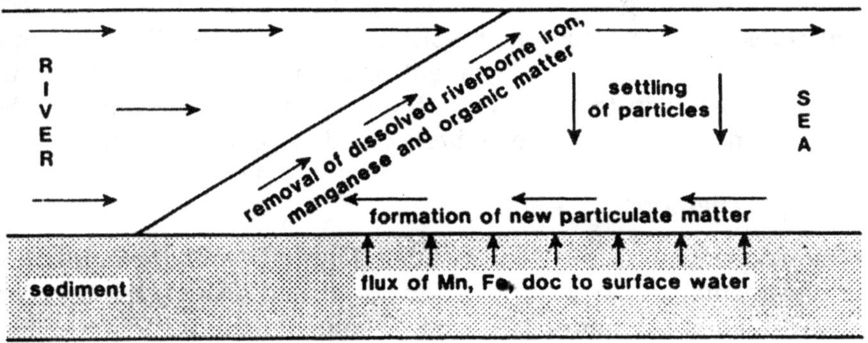

FIGURE 1.19 Particle processes at the fresh–marine water interface. (From Salomons, W. and U. Forstner. 1984. *Metals in the Hydrocycle*. Springer-Verlag, Berlin. With permission.)

These site-specific adsorptions, termed chemisorption, are the same types of reactions as those that lead to the cation exchange capacities of soils.

Large dissolved organic molecules, such as pesticides and humic materials, can also become associated with particles through simple electrostatic attractions arising either from direct ionic forces or from permanent or momentary dipoles. Such non-site-specific adsorptions, termed physisorption, generate organic-type surfaces that can undergo the chemisorption-type reactions. For example, the complexation of Pb by a carboxylic acid functional group:

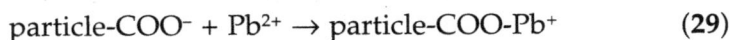

$$\text{particle-COO}^- + Pb^{2+} \rightarrow \text{particle-COO-Pb}^+ \qquad \textbf{(29)}$$

Thus, suspended solids in fresh waters have charged surfaces and organic and inorganic species of both natural and anthropogenic origin adsorb to them.

Waters in estuaries and the marine environment have high concentrations of dissolved solids that can effectively neutralize the surface charges on particles. Thus, when particles reach such water bodies they come closer together, coagulate, and start to settle. This coagulation process can lead to more of the readily adsorbed dissolved species becoming associated with the particles. There are several types of estuaries (Salomons and Forstner, 1984), the nature of which depends upon the relative flows of the fresh and saline waters (Figure 1.19). As the fresh water flows over the denser saline water the coagulated particles and their pollutant loadings start to settle from the halocline. Due to the flow out at the surface there must be a slight inward flow of the saline waters at depth and thus the settling particles and their pollutant loadings tend to accumulate in the sediment close to the freshwater source. Once buried they become exposed to a reducing environment and speciation changes occur which can result in the release of the pollutants to the aquifer. We will illustrate the possibilities when considering the Pb cycle.

The Biogeochemistry of Metals

Of the 105 elements in the periodic table (Figure 1.1), 83 are metals. For a few elements (Si, Ge, P, As, Sb, Se and Te, and also H) the division between metals and nonmetals is not absolute (Greenwood and Earnshaw, 1998).

Many metals are essential to biological processes and must be present in concentrations above a certain minimum for the plant or animal to function properly. Nonessential elements can usually be tolerated by plants and animals up to certain concentrations, but above those thresholds toxicities become apparent. Even essential elements can become toxic if their concentrations become elevated. Figure 1.20A illustrates the difference between plant and animal responses to toxic and essential elements, as measured by some growth factor relevant to the particular biological species. The level of tolerance varies considerably within and between biological species (Figure 1.20B) and from element to element. The biological activity of a particular metal often depends on its coexistence with other metals. For example, the biological functions of the essential elements Mo and Cu are impaired if their concentrations become unbalanced (Underwood, 1976). As should be apparent from our discussions, the environmental chemistry of one element cannot be isolated from that of others.

While each metal has its own chemistry, the types of reactions they undergo are similar: oxidation–reduction, complexation, adsorption–desorption, hydrolysis (acid–base), and precipitation–dissolution. The behaviour of metals in the environment will depend on their speciations just as was discussed for C. For example Cr is very toxic in the plus six oxidation state but environmentally rather unreactive in the plus three oxidation state. Mercury is at its most toxic when coordinated to organic molecules (Fergusson, 1990). Frequently the interconversion between metal species is fast on the analytical time scale and so the concentrations of the different species cannot be individually determined (Buffle, 1990).

Figure 1.20C schematically presents the species possibly present in an aquatic system. "Free" dissolved metal cations are hydrated by the polar water molecules (the partially negative O atoms being electrostatically attracted to the positive charge of the metal) and involved in acid–base equilibria in much the same way as inorganic carbon species:

$$\{Fe(H_2O)_6\}^{3+} + H_2O \rightarrow \{Fe(H_2O)_5(OH)\}^{2+} + H_3O^+ \qquad \textbf{(30)}$$

Such acid–base reactions are usually called hydrolysis reactions when metal ions are involved. Dissolved metals are also involved in equilibria with inorganic ions (CO_3^{2-} for example), organic molecules (either well defined, such as citric acid, or the highly variable fulvic acids), and particles with their various surfaces. They can also be incorporated into living organisms. While the chemical reactions of the hydrated metals and the metal ions coordinated to well-defined ligands are relatively straightforward, the interactions with surfaces and humic materials cannot be absolutely quantified. All of these interactions must be considered if a realistic understanding of the environmental chemistry of metals is to be achieved. However, since most environmental matrices consist of mixtures of materials, the quantitative expression of the behaviour of metals is not precise and is an area of very active research (Buffle, 1990, 1995).

We will illustrate the concepts behind the environmental chemistry of metals by considering the lead (Pb) biogeochemical cycle.

The Lead Cycle

A biogeochemical cycle for lead is shown in Figure 1.21. Lead is widely dispersed as a trace element in our environment. It occurs naturally in the minerals galena (PbS), cerussite ($PbCO_3$), and anglesite ($PbSO_4$), the latter two minerals generally forming as a result of natural weathering of galena. Lead also occurs substituted into the lattices of other sulphide minerals, in particular sphalerite (ZnS) and chalcopyrite ($CuFeS_2$) and in minerals containing metal ions of similar size. For Pb^{2+} that means in minerals containing K^+, Ca^{2+}, Sr^{2+}, and Ba^{2+}, but particularly Ca^{2+}.

World production of lead has been reasonably constant over the past few decades at about 4 million tonnes per year (Fergusson, 1990). Sixty percent of that is used in the production of anodes (Pb metal) and cathodes (a PbO paste on a Pb [91 percent]/Sb [9 percent] alloy grid) for lead-acid batteries. Of the remainder, 23 percent is used in the production of alloys, 4 percent in the production of tetraethyl and tetramethyl lead for use in petrol, and 13 percent as pigments (red, white, and yellow lead in paints).

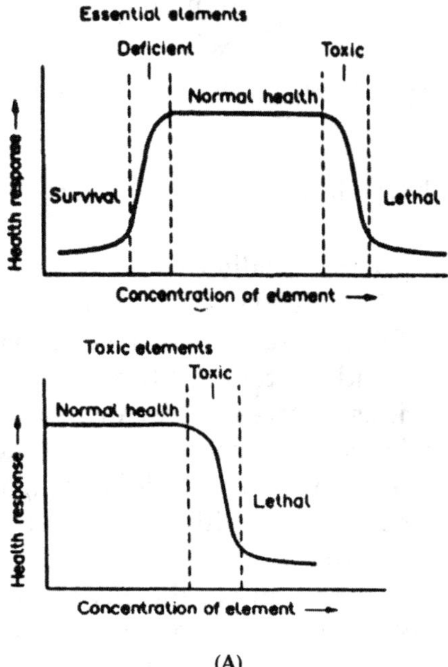

(A)

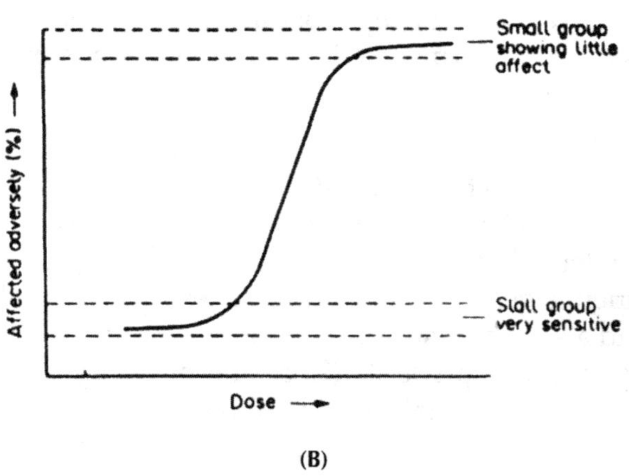

(B)

FIGURE 1.20 Metals in the environment. (A) The effects of essential and toxic elements on plant growth. (From Fergusson, J. E. 1990. *The Heavy Elements: Chemistry, Environmental Impact and Health Effects*. Pergamon Press, Oxford, U.K. With permission.) (B) The variable responses of biological species to toxic substances. (from Fergusson, J. E. 1990. *The Heavy Elements: Chemistry, Environmental Impact and Health Effects*. Pergamon Press, Oxford, U.K. With permission.) (C) Metal ion speciation in aquatic environments. (From Buffle, J. 1990. *Complexation Reactions in Aquatic Systems: An Analytical Approach*. Ellis Horwood, Chichester, U.K. With permission.)

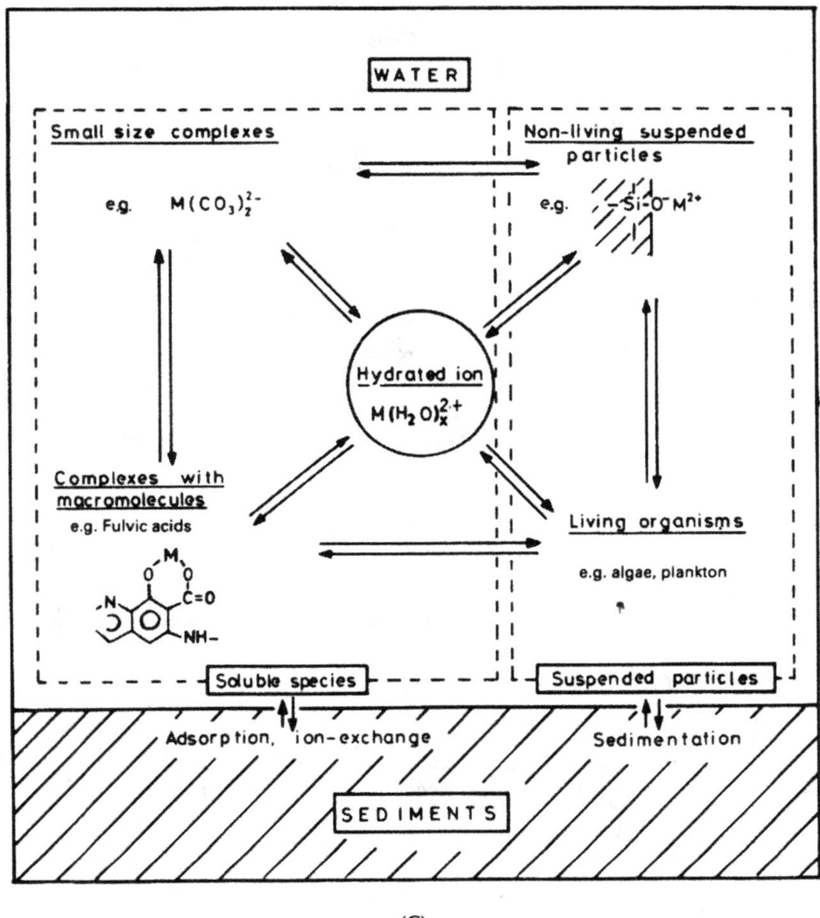

(C)

FIGURE 1.20 (continued)

The reliable determination of the concentrations of lead in environmental matrices has proven to be difficult. Fergusson (1990) notes that data collected prior to 1960 are of dubious quality and even some of the more recent data should be considered with caution; the contamination of samples during collection and handling is a serious problem. By comparing typical present-day concentrations with estimates of natural concentrations, he concludes that our environment is seriously polluted with lead.

There is no known essential biological function of lead. Most plants seem to be unaffected by concentrations of 0.1 to 10 ppm (dry weight), and grow successfully in contaminated soils and aquatic

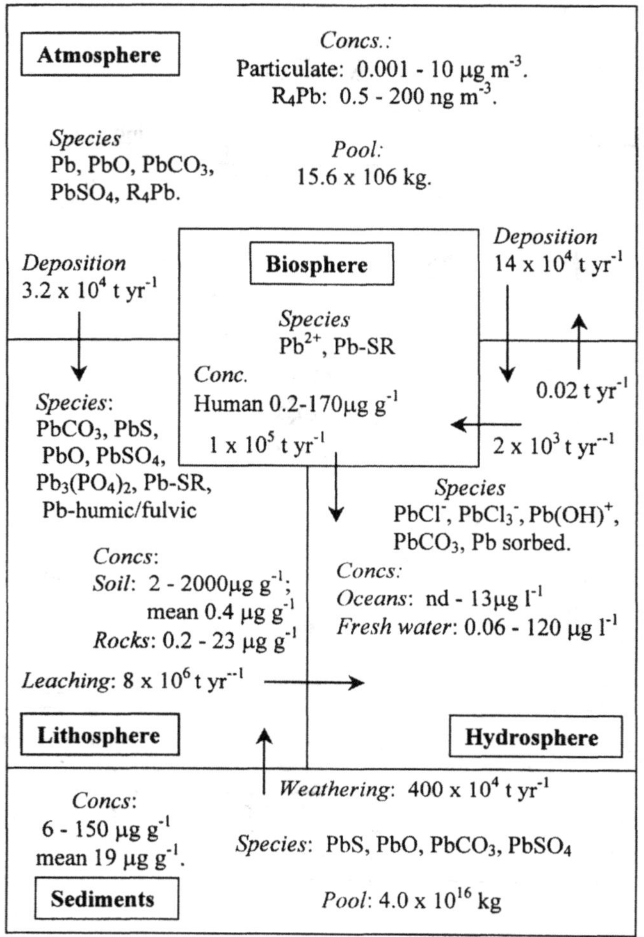

FIGURE 1.21 A biogeochemical cycle for lead. (Adapted from Fergusson, 1990.)

environments where they can accumulate lead to extremely high concentrations (up to 15000 ppm dw in lettuce leaves, for example; Kabata-Pendias and Pendias, 1984). Lead does not seem to be a serious toxin to plants. Adsorption from soils is minimal, probably because of the low availability of the lead in soils (liming, i.e., making the soil basic, is very effective at limiting the lead availability). Even where accumulation has been found it is only in the roots. Lead from atmospheric sources is readily adsorbed through the foliage, however.

Lead is a serious toxin to humans, particularly children (Fergusson, 1990). It has both physiological and neurological impacts and is thought to inhibit the activities of enzymes where S is important to their catalytic functions. Concentrations of 4 to 50 micrograms lead per decilitre of blood have been shown to be toxic to adults, although tolerances seem to vary considerably from person to person. In children tolerance levels are lower (10 to 20 micrograms lead per decilitre). Lead enters the body from food, water, and air at about 200 micrograms per day, 80 percent from food, 10 percent being adsorbed into body tissues (Harrison, 1992). Adsorption of lead from fine air particles entering the lungs can be as high as 50 percent. The majority (approximately 90 percent) of the adsorbed lead enters the bones, substituting for calcium (Ca). Lead therefore is a serious pollutant and reducing our exposure to it should be a social priority.

In freshwater environments lead is almost exclusively in the plus two oxidation state, with the free metal ion, Pb^{2+}, in equilibrium with the $PbCO_3$ ion pair and the $PbOH^+$ ion (Figure 1.22A), and precipitated lead carbonates (Figure 1.22B). These diagrams are comparable to the speciation diagrams for C (Figure 1.18) and minerals (Figure 1.6) and can be constructed similarly by considering complexation, reduction, hydrolysis, and precipitation reactions and their associated equilibrium constants (Krauskopf and Bird, 1995). Eh relates to oxidation–reduction reactions and ranges between -200 and +600 millivolts in the normal environment.

Organic ligands have not been considered in deriving the plots of Figure 1.22 but they do play a significant role in species distributions (Figure 1.20C). Fulvic acid (FA) concentrations in fresh waters are of the order of 0.1 to 2 millimolar (Spitzy and Leenheer, 1991). Lead will be involved in complexation reactions with them:

$$Pb^{2+} + FAH + H_2O \rightarrow PbFA^+ + H_3O^+ \qquad \textbf{(31)}$$

Such reactions usually involve the carboxylic acid functional groups but phenolic, alcoholic, and amine groups, among others, can also participate (Buffle, 1990).

The presence of particles compounds the problem (Tessier, 1992), as was suggested when we considered carbon (C) in marine waters. At pHs relevant to most natural waters and in the absence of other chemicals that can affect speciation, the bulk of pollutant metals will be adsorbed to Al and Fe oxyhydroxide and organic surfaces if they are present.

To consider all the possible equilibria mentioned above quantitatively requires computer programmes, many of which are available (Buffle, 1990). The distributions of the metals between the possible species have been calculated but due to the uncertainties associated with the equilibrium constants used and the considerable difficulties

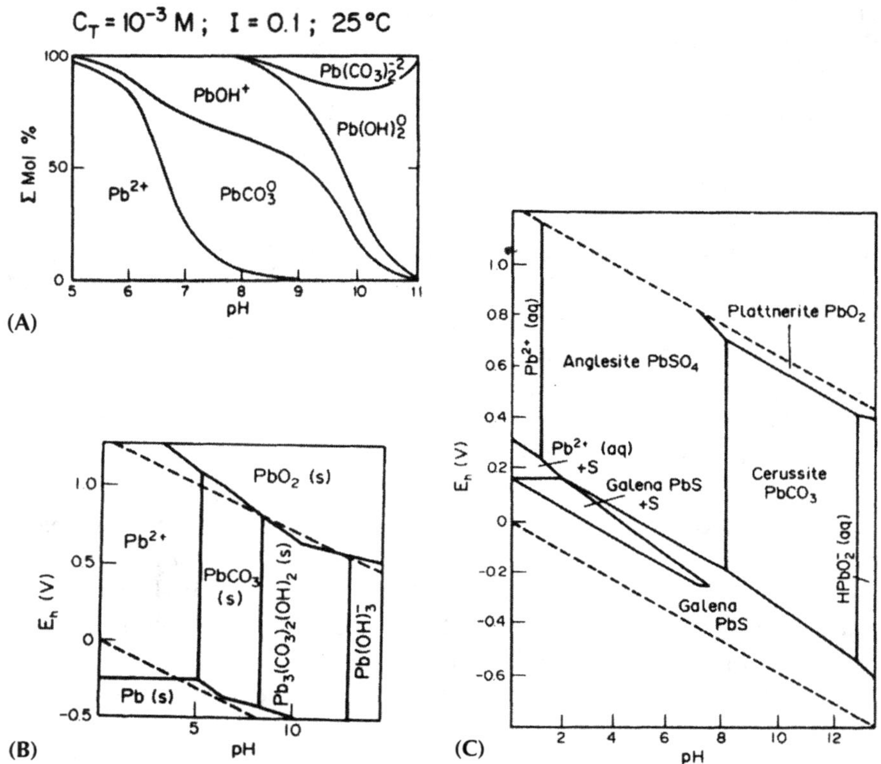

FIGURE 1.22 Lead speciation diagrams. (A) Dissolved Pb species: C_T, total Pb concentration mol. dm^{-3}; I, ionic strength. (From Stumm, W. and J. J. Morgan. 1981. *Aquatic Chemistry: An Introduction Emphasizing Chemical Equilibria in Natural Waters*, 2nd edition. Wiley-Interscience, New York. With permission.) (B) Lead speciation in the presence of lead minerals. (From Fergusson, J. E. 1990. *The Heavy Elements: Chemistry, Environmental Impact and Health Effects*. Pergamon Press, Oxford, U.K. With permission.) (C) Lead speciation in the presence of SO_4^{2-}. (From Fergusson, J. E. 1990. *The Heavy Elements: Chemistry, Environmental Impact and Health Effects*. Pergamon Press, Oxford, U.K. With permission.)

associated with experimentally testing the conclusions, the absolute numbers generated must be considered with caution. The development of these models and the experimental techniques to quantify species concentrations are areas of active research.

However, simplified calculations indicate the concentrations of Pb that we can expect to find in aquatic environments. In the absence of particulates, at typical HCO_3^- and fulvic acid concentrations of about 1 millimolar and a pH of 7, the concentration of total dissolved Pb will be at most about 4 micromolar. The hydrated Pb^{2+} (Figure 1.20C) will be at equilibrium with solid $PbCO_3$ (Manahan, 1994) and dissolved organic materials; 75 percent of the dissolved lead will be complexed. The presence of other metals that can complex with organics will further suppress the solubility of lead by tying the ligands up in complexes and therefore making them unavailable to react with Pb^{2+}. Ca^{2+}, which is present in millimolar concentrations, will reduce the amount of lead complexed to organics, and therefore the total amount dissolved, by a factor of about 3 (Manahan, 1994). Under normal environmental conditions then we should not expect to find dissolved lead concentrations in excess of about 1 to 2 micromolar, although there could be considerable amounts associated with the suspended particles.

When fresh waters reach the marine environment the lead speciation will change. There the sulphate concentration is 0.012 molar and the pH 8.2. $PbSO_4$ will become the predominant insoluble phase (Figure 1.22C) and the dissolved lead concentrations will be reduced even further. As we saw earlier, once they reach the saline environment particles are incorporated into the sediment and buried, carrying their pollutant load with them (Figure 1.19). Many other metals behave similarly.

In estuarine sediments the concentration of O_2 drops to zero within a few millimeters of the sediment surface (several meters in deep sea sediments; Andrews et al., 1996) as microbially assisted organic degradation continues. Once the O_2 has been depleted the electron sink (i.e., the oxidizing agent) becomes SO_4^{2-}, the concentrations of other oxidizing agents such as NO_3^-, Fe^{3+}, and Mn^{4+} being generally too low to be important. Sulphate reduction produces S^{2-} ions and is accompanied by the reduction of the oxides of Fe^{3+} and Mn^{4+}, which coat or constitute many sediments. Associated with this reduction, the pollutants adsorbed on the oxide surfaces will be released to the pore waters and undergo further reactions, possibly including incorporation into biological materials. At the interface between the oxidizing and reducing zones, the concentrations of dissolved species are likely to be highest (Figure 1.23; Shaw et al., 1994; Thamdrup et al., 1994). This tendency for iron and manganese to move between insoluble oxidized and soluble reduced forms under frequently encountered Eh and pH conditions makes their reactions highly relevant to environmental chemistry. It is also important to note the link between organic carbon, its oxidation in the environment, and the reactions of metals and other pollutants.

The S^{2-} ions produced under the reducing conditions, however, will effect the precipitation of many metals, including lead. The solubility product for PbS is a very small number and thus PbS is essentially insoluble. (pK_{sp} = 27.5. pK values are the negative logs (base

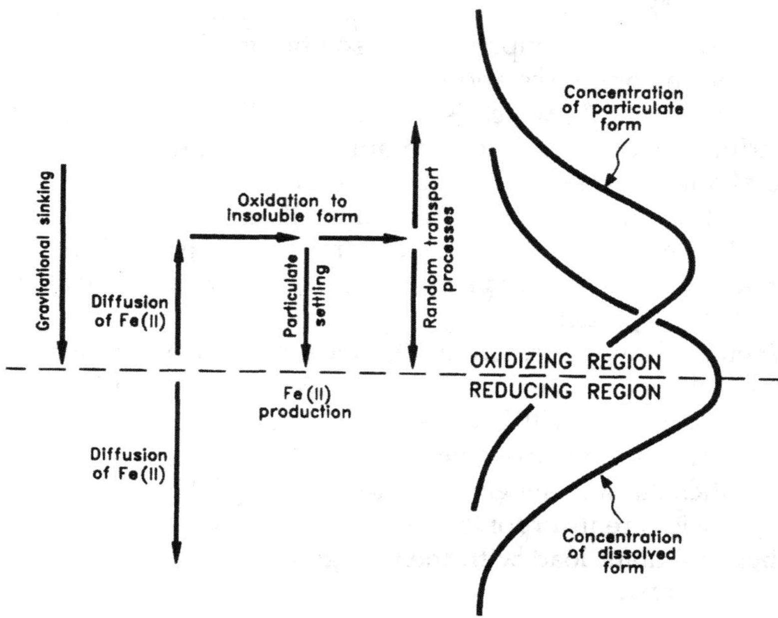

FIGURE 1.23 Iron equilibria at the water–sediment interface. The position of the oxidizing/reducing boundary varies depending on the nature of the ecosystem but generally is a few centimetres below the sediment–water interface. On reduction insoluble Fe(III) forms soluble Fe(II). Manganese(IV) and Mn(II) behave similarly. (From Davidson, W. and DeVitre, R. 1992. In *Environmental Particles*, Vol. 1, pp. 351–356, edited by J. Buffle and H. P. van Leeuwen. Lewis Publishers, Boca Raton, Florida. With permission.)

10) of the equilibrium constants K_{sp}; sp for solubility product. Large positive values imply very small equilibrium constants.) Any Pb^{2+} released from the sediment upon reduction of the surface oxides, or otherwise, will be reprecipitated as PbS. FeS and MnS have pK_{sp} values of 18.1 and 13.5, respectively. The solubilities for Cd and Zn sulphides are similar to that for Pb, while pK_{sp} for HgS is 52.7. CuS is of intermediate solubility. Thus, all these metals will be essentially completely incorporated into the sediment as sulphides.

Any pore water components that do not precipitate will migrate to the surface and be exposed to O_2. There, any Fe^{2+} or Mn^{2+} will be reoxidized and precipitate as oxyhydroxides and thus present active adsorbing surfaces to any dissolved species. For chemicals to escape the sediment the rate of flow will have to be such that the species do not have time to be readsorbed. The sediment acts as a trap to most chemicals although the activities of organisms can sometimes lead to pollutants bypassing the trap.

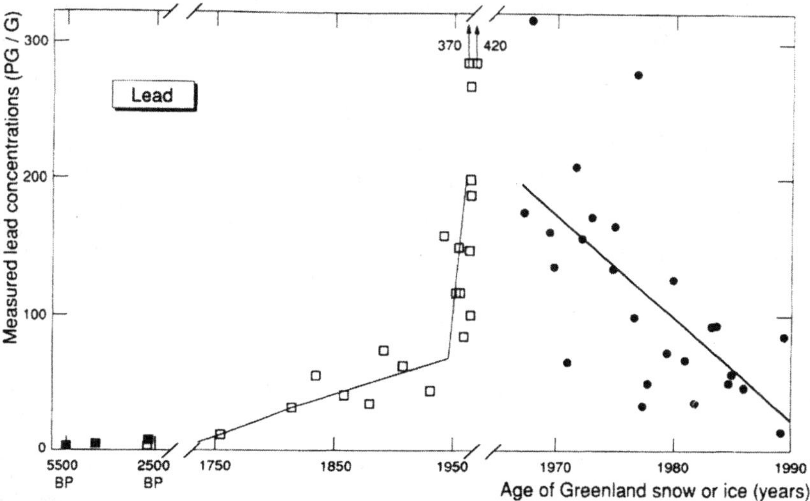

FIGURE 1.24 Lead in Greenland ice. The spike in the 1950s and its gradual reduction in size during the 1970s reflects the introduction and then gradual removal of Pb to and from petrol. (From Boutron, C. G. et al. 1991. *Nature (London)* 353: 153–154. With permission.)

A significant feature of the lead cycle is its atmospheric component. The natural flux to the atmosphere is zero but the anthropogenic flux is of the order of 400×10^9 grams per year. This has only been so for the last 45 years, since lead has been an additive to petrol. The residence time is only two weeks as the majority is quickly adsorbed onto particles or incorporated into water droplets and returned to the earth (37 percent) or the sea (63 percent) during rainfall events. A short residence time implies that the major concentrations will be close to the sources and as most sources are automobiles, and these are generally in cities, the atmospheric lead problem is predominantly an urban problem (Fergusson, 1990). The concentration of lead in rainwater in cities can be as high as 5 micromolar.

Evidence for the recent origin of the atmospheric lead problem comes from studies of the concentration of lead as a function of depth in Greenland ice (Figure 1.24). The significance of introducing lead to petrol in the 1950s, and then the banning of its use as such in many North American and European countries in the 1970s, is apparent. The diagram also illustrates the global nature of environmental issues. This lead pollution, clearly transported through the atmosphere, has its origins in countries some considerable distance from the Greenland ice. Thus, even though lead has a comparatively short residence time in the atmosphere, some has traveled a long way before being deposited.

Lead as tetraethyl- and tetramethyl-lead [$Pb(C_2H_5)_4$ and $Pb(CH_3)_4$] is added to petrol along with Pb scavengers 1,2-dibromoethane (DBE) and 1,2-dichloroethane (DCE) to enhance vehicular performance (Chenier, 1986). The additive is approximately 63 percent alkyllead, 26 percent DBE, 9 percent DCE, and 2 percent of a warning dye. Over the years the amount of Pb added has dropped in some countries (1 g dm^{-3} in 1970 to about 0.1 g dm^{-3} in 1985) although in Trinidad and Tobago (Chang-Yen et al., 1994), and probably in many other countries, 0.6 g dm^{-3} was still being used in 1994.

In the combustion engine the initial reaction is:

$$Pb(C_2H_5)_4 + 14O_2 \rightarrow PbO_2 + 8CO_2 + 10H_2O \qquad \textbf{(32)}$$

The PbO_2 produced acts as a catalyst in the burning of the hydrocarbon fuels (note that lead is in the plus four oxidation state in this insoluble oxide). In order to stop the accumulation of the PbO_2 in the cylinders of the engine the alkylhalide scavengers are added to effect its conversion to the volatile halides of Pb^{2+}:

$$C_2H_4Br_2 + PbO_2 + 2O_2 \rightarrow PbBr_2 + 2CO_2 + 2H_2O \qquad \textbf{(33)}$$

The actual halide that is emitted from the exhaust will depend on the composition of the fuel additive. In the atmosphere the halides become associated with particles and it has been shown that particulate bromine (Br) concentrations correlate with those of lead. Bromine can be used, with caution, as a probe for lead (Fergusson, 1990; Davis et al., 1994).

A feature of lead pollution that will not appear on a global cycle is localized contamination associated with lead-acid storage batteries. In many countries car batteries are recycled, the scrapping being done by both the original manufacturing companies and in small, generally uncontrolled, backyard industries. Studies in Jamaica (Matte et al., 1989) and in Trinidad and Tobago (Chang-Yen et al., 1994; Mohammed et al., 1994) highlight the seriousness of these practices. In the Jamaican study, lead concentrations in blood from adults working in the backyard battery repair shops had a geometric mean concentration of 32 micrograms per decilitre while children living in the yards averaged 110 micrograms per decilitre. Soils in the yards and dusts in the houses were considerably elevated over controls (factors of 700 for the soils and 20 for the dusts).

The Phosphorus and Nitrogen Cycles

Phosphorus and nitrogen are both essential micronutrients to all biological species. Phosphates are involved in cell membranes as phospholipids (Figure 1.14), in genetic materials DNA and RNA as phosphodiesters, in the energy transfer reagent ATP as phosphates (see Figure 1.15 for an indication of the structures involved), and in many essential intermediates in biochemical syntheses (Westheimer, 1987). Nitrogen is present in amino acids, proteins, and nucleic acids (Figures 1.14 to 1.15), porphyrins, and many metabolites.

Photosynthesis, a photochemical reduction reaction, involves the formation of organic molecules from CO_2 and H_2O to give primarily sugars (Figures 1.2B and 1.13). The involvement of enzymes and the presence of micronutrients at the later stages of the production results in the diverse biomolecules (see O'Neill, 1993, Roberts, 1993, and Stryer, 1988 for descriptions of photosynthesis).

Nitrogen and phosphorus are two of the micronutrients essential to the photosynthetic reaction, which, if they are included, becomes (Stumm and Morgan, 1981):

$$106CO_2 + 16NO_3^- + HPO_4^{2-} + 104H_2O + 18H_3O^+ \rightarrow \{C_{106}\,H_{263}\,O_{110}\,N_{16}\,P\} + 138O_2 \qquad \textbf{(34)}$$

Trace elements are also incorporated. Respiration or degradation of biological materials is the reverse of this reaction and thus both nutrients are depleted or generated together. There is considerable variability in the elemental composition between organisms and thus the N:P ratio of 16:1 is probably too precise. Goltermann and de Oude (1991) report that a reasonable mean algal composition is $C_5H_7NO_2P_{1/30}$ and thereby a totally different ratio. It is generally accepted that the factors that limit photosynthesis in the photic zone are the availability of nitrogen and phosphorus. Other trace elements are usually available in sufficient quantities. Essential nutrients are generally retained in terrestrial ecosystems via photosynthesis (primary production) and degradation cycling with nutrient losses from, and inputs to, such ecosystems being small compared to the stored amounts (Schlesinger, 1991). In waters rich in nutrients, such as sites of ocean water upwellings, productivity (of organic materials) is high. In waters with other sources of the nutrients, one or other becomes limiting to organic synthesis. These two nutrients are intimately linked in biomolecules and ecosystems and therefore their environmental chemistries are also linked. Their chemistries, however, are very different.

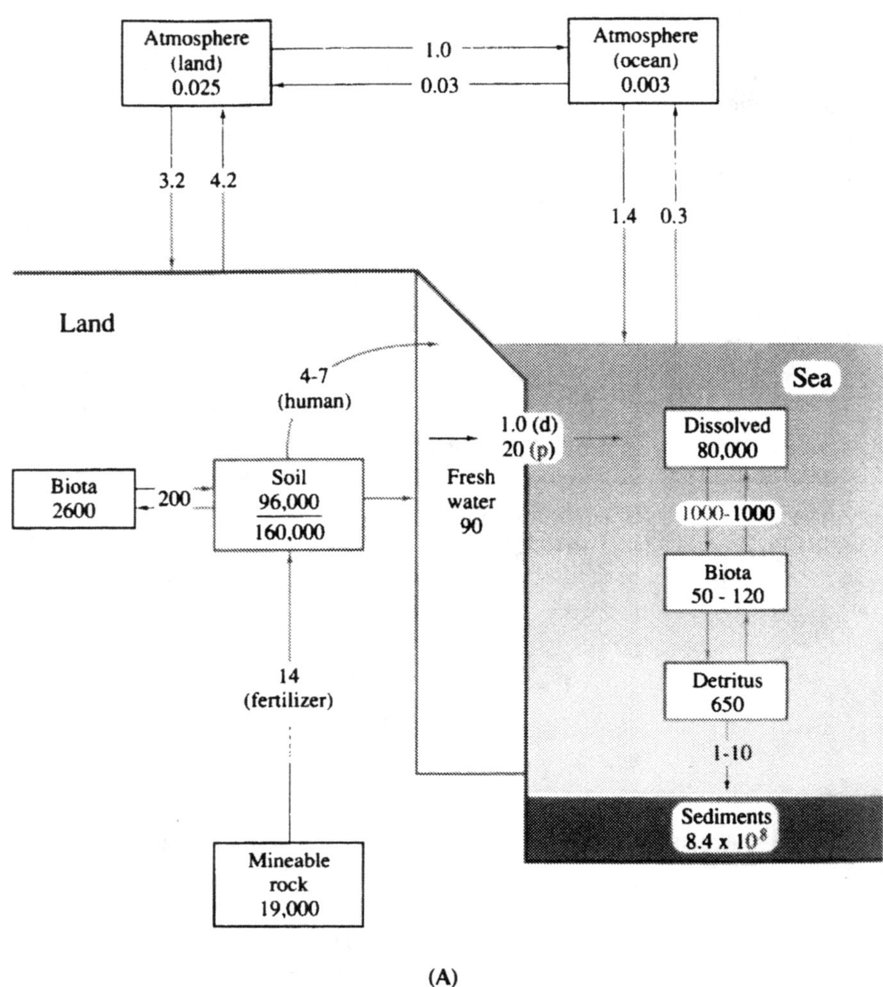

(A)

FIGURE 1.25 Environmental phosphorus. (A) A biogeochemical cycle for phosphorus. (From Schlesinger, W. H. 1991. *Biogeochemistry: An Analysis of Global Change.* Academic Press, London. With permission.) (B) A phosphate speciation diagram showing soil types and solubility ranges. (From Fergusson, J. E. 1982. *Inorganic Chemistry and the Earth. Chemical Resources, Their Extraction, Use and Environmental Impact.* Pergamon Press, Oxford, U.K. With permission.)

The Phosphorus Cycle

The phosphorus biogeochemical cycle (Figure 1.25A) is probably one of the simplest. There is essentially no atmospheric component and only the plus five oxidation state needs to be considered.

Phosphorus occurs in the lithosphere as calcium phosphates, primarily as hydroxy- and fluoroapatite, $Ca_5(PO_4)_3X$, where X is either

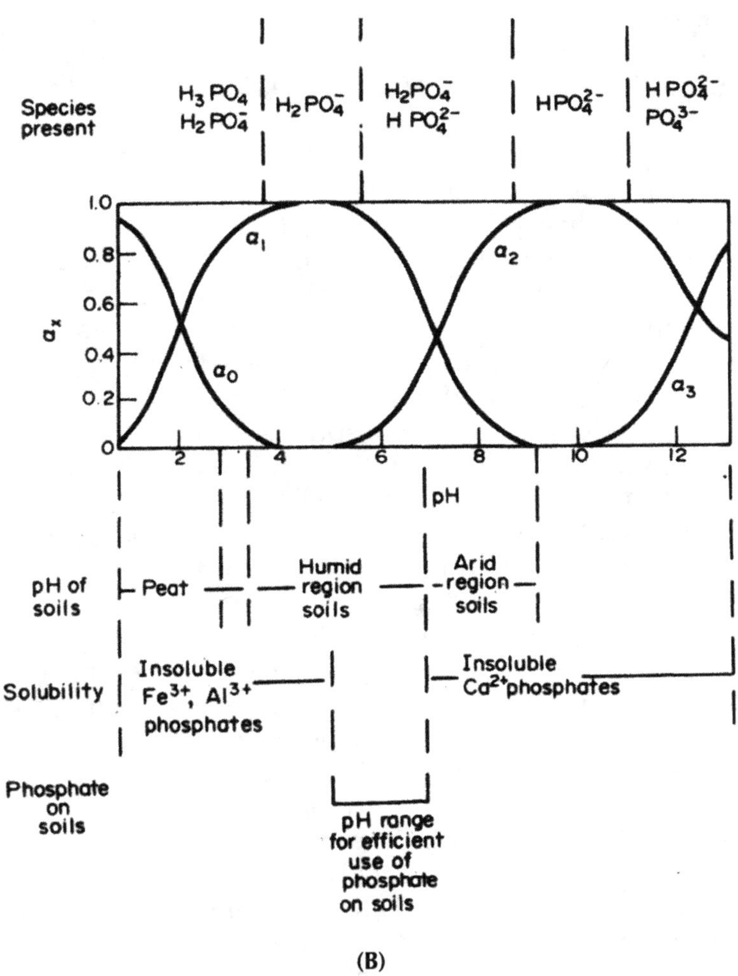

(B)

FIGURE 1.25 (continued)

OH^- or F^-. The huge mineable reserves are being depleted only slowly (0.1 percent per year) but still at rates seven times faster than natural weathering processes. Ninety percent of the mined phosphate rock is used to produce low purity phosphoric acid (H_3PO_4) or fertilizers (Childs, 1977):

$$Ca_5(PO_4)_3(OH) + 5H_2SO_4 \rightarrow 5CaSO_4 + 3H_3PO_4 + H_2O \quad (35)$$

$$2Ca_5(PO_4)_3(OH) + 7H_2SO_4 \rightarrow 7CaSO_4 + 3Ca(H_2PO_4)_2 + 2H_2O \quad (36)$$

$$2Ca_5(PO_4)_3(OH) + 14H_3PO_4 \rightarrow 10Ca(H_2PO_4)_2 + 2H_2O \quad (37)$$

The mixture of $7CaSO_4 + 3Ca(H_2PO_4)_2$ is single superphosphate. Triple superphosphate, $10Ca(H_2PO_4)_2$, is more effective per unit weight because of the absence of the $CaSO_4$. Ten percent of the mined phosphate is used to produce elemental P, 80 percent of which is converted to pure phosphoric acid for the food industry. The remaining 20 percent is used to produce specialty chemicals.

In the food industry phosphates are used as sequestering (complexing) agents to tie up metals and stop them from precipitating or reacting with food components (the black on the top of a ketchup bottle is a tannic acid complex of Fe; sequestering agents prevent its formation), as an additive to cola drinks where H_3PO_4 imparts a sour taste, and as a component of baking powder where phosphates act, once wet, as acids. The use of phosphates in detergents and water softeners also utilizes their ability to act as sequestering agents.

Polyphosphates, both linear or cyclic, are usually used for the sequestering agents. The linear polyphosphates, $Na_5P_3O_{10}$ for example, a sodium salt of a triphosphate, involve the tetrahedral PO_4^{3-} units linked through shared oxygens in much the same way as tetrahedral SiO_4^{4-} units link to produce silicates (Figure 1.3). In the cyclic species each tetrahedral PO_4^{3-} unit is linked to two others through O bridges. The phosphates used industrially are complex mixtures of linear and cyclic systems. Their use in water treatment is now limited to boiler waters; waters not generally released to the environment. These phosphates hydrolyze to orthophosphates (free tetrahedral PO_4^{3-} units), but slowly, and only become available to plants once hydrolyzed. Eighty percent of orthophosphate can be assimilated into plant material within 3 minutes if all other conditions are satisfactory.

We have already considered the biological functions of P (for example DNA and ATP); it plays major roles in our life styles and health. In a human, apatite forms 60 percent of bones, 70 percent of teeth (100 percent of enamel, fluoroapatite is much more resistant to erosion and thus the addition of F^- to toothpastes, salt, and water). Each adult human has about 3.5 kilograms of apatite and passes in urine about 3 to 4 grams PO_4^{3-} per day (in 1669 Brandt isolated P for the first time from urine; Greenwood and Earnshaw, 1998).

Phosphate availability in the aquatic environment, including pore waters, is limited to a very narrow pH range. The species distributions as a function of pH are shown in Figure 1.25B (compare the inorganic C speciation diagram, Figure 1.18). The concentrations of the phosphate species in the aqueous phase can be determined by considering the solubilities of the minerals likely to be in contact with the phosphate-containing waters. At pH 7, precipitation of PO_4^{3-} as apatite will result in a total dissolved phosphate concentration of about 1 micromolar. At pH 8, the concentration drops by about an order of magnitude and thus at pHs higher than about 7 phosphate is essentially unavailable to plants. Similar calculations based on the minerals variscite, $(AlPO_4)\cdot 2H_2O$, and strengite, $FePO_4\cdot 2H_2O$, show that phosphate will precipitate as either of these two minerals at pHs less than 5. In addition to these precipitation reactions phosphates are very effectively bound (adsorbed) to particles, both inorganic and organic (Froelich et al., 1982; Ingall and Jahnke, 1994). The concentrations of PO_4^{3-} in waters and pore waters will therefore be very small outside the pH 5 to 7 range. Such considerations suggest that the pH of the soil must be carefully controlled for effective use of phosphate fertilizers and that PO_4^{3-}, on entering the aqueous environment, will either be quickly assimilated by the biota or lost to the sediment. Under eutrophic conditions the reductive dissolution of the iron and manganese oxide particle surfaces can release adsorbed PO_4^{3-} to the dissolved phase.

The Nitrogen Cycle

Compared to the phosphorus cycle, the nitrogen cycle (Figure 1.26) is one of the most complicated. Not only are all spheres involved, but there are many oxidation states to be considered. The biological functions of nitrogen, which generally involve nitrogen in its most reduced form (minus three), are far more diverse than those of phosphorus. In addition to the problems of eutrophication, within which both phosphorus and nitrogen play major roles, N oxide gases in the atmosphere cause serious atmospheric pollution problems.

An immediately obvious difference between the nitrogen cycle and all others is that the atmosphere is the major reservoir, with almost 3×10^{20} moles of nitrogen atoms existing as the unreactive N_2. The next largest reservoir (0.6×10^{20} moles N) is organic nitrogen buried in sediment. The N_2 molecule has a very strong bond, too strong for the energy from the sun to break. The very low reactivity of N_2 is reflected in the long atmospheric residence time, 44 million years. The only fluxes from the N_2 reservoir are those that involve biological (Wild, 1993) and industrial (Andrews, 1982) nitrogen fixation or via lightning-induced reactions with O_2, all energy-demanding reactions. Although biological fixing exceeds industrial fixing by a factor of about 1.5, it is still a rare process, primarily limited to organisms associated with legumes (hence their importance in soil management). It occurs via microorganisms that use Mo- and Fe-containing enzymes (Schrauzer, 1977) to effect the reduction of the zero (N_2) to

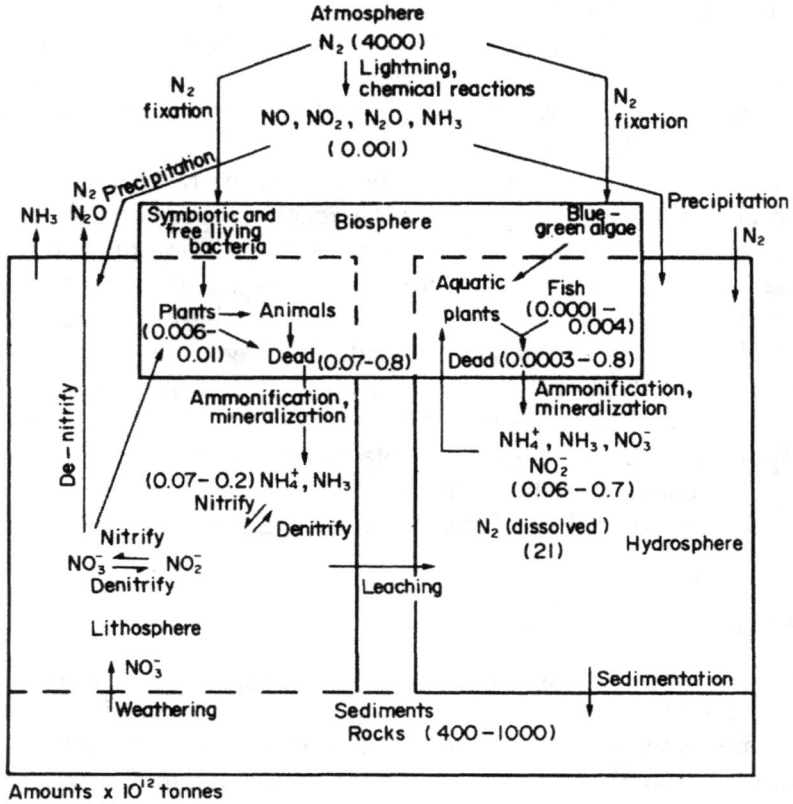

Atmosphere
N_2 (4000)
Lightning, chemical reactions
NO, NO_2, N_2O, NH_3
(0.001)
N_2 fixation
N_2 fixation
N_2 Precipitation
Precipitation
NH_3 N_2O
N_2
Symbiotic and free living bacteria
Biosphere
Blue-green algae
Plants → Animals
(0.006–0.01)
Dead (0.07-0.8)
Aquatic plants
Fish (0.0001–0.004)
Dead (0.0003–0.8)
Ammonification, mineralization
Ammonification, mineralization
NH_4^+, NH_3, NO_3^-
NO_2^-
(0.06–0.7)
(0.07–0.2) NH_4^+, NH_3
Nitrify
Denitrify
De-nitrify
Nitrify
NO_3^- ⇌ NO_2^-
Denitrify
N_2 (dissolved)
(21)
Hydrosphere
Leaching
Lithosphere
NO_3^-
Weathering
Sediments
Rocks (400–1000)
Sedimentation
Amounts x 10^{12} tonnes

(A)

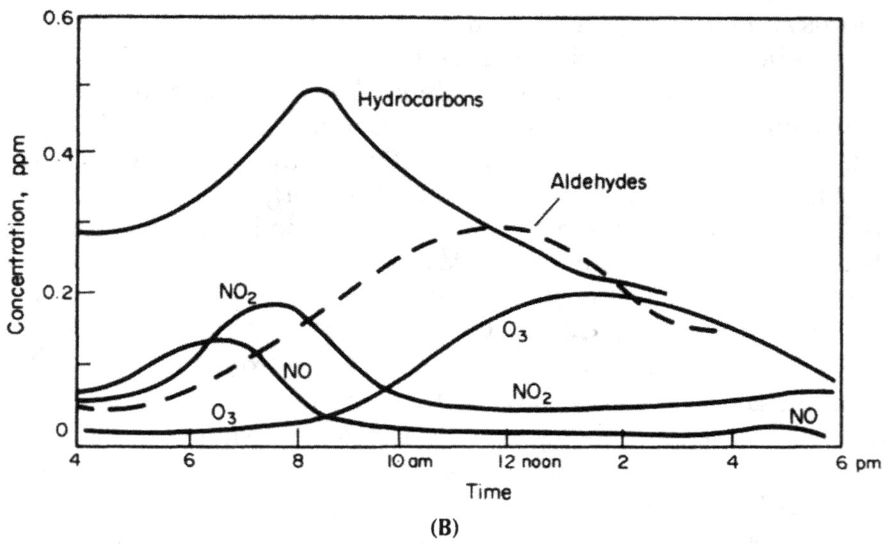

(B)

FIGURE 1.26

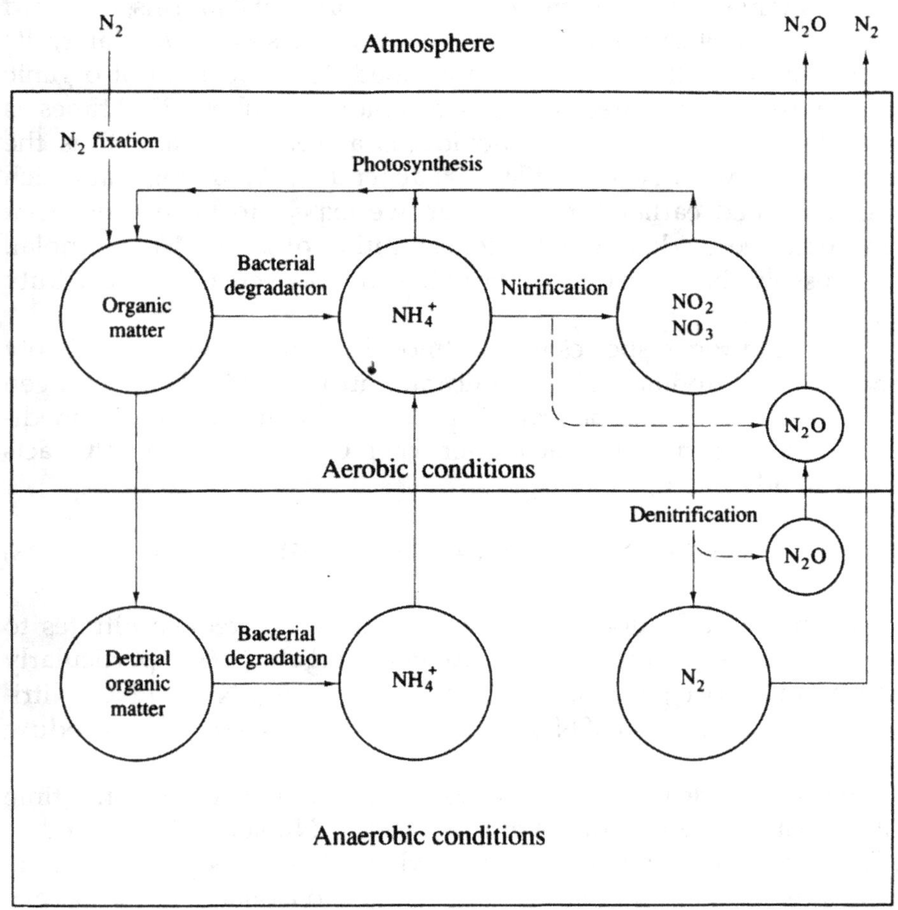

(C)

FIGURE 1.26 (continued) Environmental nitrogen. (A) A biogeochemical cycle for nitrogen. (From Fergusson, J. E. 1982. *Inorganic Chemistry and the Earth. Chemical Resources, Their Extraction, Use and Environmental Impact*. Pergamon Press, Oxford, U.K. With permission.) (B) The variation of important photochemical smog components with time of day. (From Fergusson, J. E. 1982. *Inorganic Chemistry and the Earth. Chemical Resources, Their Extraction, Use and Environmental Impact*. Pergamon Press, Oxford, U.K. With permission.) (C) Nitrification and denitrification processes. (From Schlesinger, W. H. 1991. *Biogeochemistry: An Analysis of Global Change*. Academic Press, London. With permission.)

the minus three (NH_3) oxidation state. Industrially, the reduction process involves the use of a catalyst and high temperatures and pressures. The NH_3 produced is used to make ammonium salts (predominantly $(NH_4)_2SO_4$, a fertilizer and NH_4NO_3, an explosive), urea ($CO(NH_2)_2$, a fertilizer), and nitric acid (HNO_3).

Ammonia (NH_3 and the protonated form NH_4^+) forms the third largest atmospheric reservoir of N (N_2O is the second, see later). Its major source is the microbially mediated decomposition of organic matter, particularly urea. This gaseous molecule, about 2500 times as soluble in water as carbon dioxide, is a weak base and thus the amount that will dissolve will be pH dependent. At pH 5.6, that which we calculated earlier for rainwater, we expect to have a nitrogen (minus three oxidation state) concentration of about 4 micromolar. The dissolution of NH_3 in water will lead to a decrease in the acidity of the water.

Of the nitrogen species in the atmosphere the oxides are probably the most environmentally significant. Nitrous oxide (N_2O, nitrogen in the plus one oxidation state) is produced by the microbially mediated degradation of organic matter when O_2 is limited and NO_3^- acts as the oxidizing agent:

$$CH_2O + NO_3^- \rightarrow CO_2 + \tfrac{1}{2}H_2O + OH^- + \tfrac{1}{2}N_2O \qquad \textbf{(38)}$$

Such denitrification processes (processes that reduce nitrates to gaseous nitrogen-containing compounds; Figure 1.26C), particularly important in rice growing areas, can also produce N_2 and NO. Nitrification (the oxidation of NH_3 to N-containing gases) can also produce N_2O and NO.

Nitrous oxide is very unreactive, as mirrored by its residence time of 12 years. Small amounts are reduced to N_2, some is oxidized to NO, some enters the stratosphere, where it is quickly depleted via reactions with ozone, but most is thought to dissolve in the oceans or be adsorbed by soils. A global balance has yet to be formulated. In the troposphere, as a greenhouse gas, it contributes to global warming and in the stratosphere it is involved in the depletion of the O_3 layer. Nitrous oxide is a significant trace component of the atmosphere and its concentration increased rapidly during the twentieth century (Figure 1.10).

Nitric oxide (NO, nitrogen in the plus two oxidation state) is the oxide of nitrogen with the largest flux to the atmosphere. Apart from organic degradation, it is produced from the burning of fossil fuels, the amount produced depending on the temperature of the burning process:

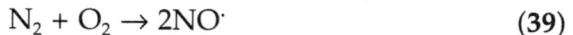

$$N_2 + O_2 \rightarrow 2NO^{\cdot} \qquad \textbf{(39)}$$

Automobiles produce the most NO when operating at an air to fuel ratio of 16:1, close to that required for maximum engine efficiency (Acres, 1990).

The biological production of NO is approximately ten times that of anthropogenic sources (Fergusson, 1982) but most anthropogenic production is in urban areas where fluxes can be very high. The nitrogen cycle suggests concentrations of NO (and NO_2) to be about 2 ppbv, but concentrations in urban areas can be as high as 840 ppbv with daily means of about 430 ppbv.

Nitric oxide and NO_2 (nitrogen dioxide, nitrogen in the plus four oxidation state) are often considered together as NOx as they have approximately the same atmospheric concentrations and residence times and both contribute significantly to urban smogs. Smogs are possible when there is a temperature inversion above the city and the city exists in a natural depression in the landscape, such conditions forming a partially closed reaction vessel. When there is a high input of NOx and hydrocarbons and there is sufficient sunlight to initiate photochemical reactions, smogs can follow. Chemical reactions of importance (Fergusson, 1982) include reactions of NOx with O_3 and $O^{\cdot}$, and photochemical reactions, which produce highly reactive free radicals and thus initiate a whole series of complicated reactions.

In the early morning, peak traffic produces the NO and hydrocarbons to start the process of smog development (Figure 1.26B). The oxidation of NO to NO_2 by O_3 (the oxidant) or $O^{\cdot}$ is followed by the photochemically initiated return of NO_2 to NO and the $O^{\cdot}$ radical with the associated production of O_3 and hydrocarbon-related free radicals. These species react with NO and NO_2 to produce nitrocompounds and aldehydes and effect the gradual depletion of the O_3 via assorted reactions. The process is not reinitiated during evening peak traffic as the light source is not present. The ozone concentration gradually drops. The chemical species in smogs are serious animal and plant toxins (Brimblecombe, 1996).

One of the other products from the NOx is nitric acid, a contributor to acid rain, although the major contributor is sulphuric acid (Galloway, 1995). Recall that natural rainwater in equilibrium with atmospheric CO_2 will have a pH of 5.6 and thus "acid" rain only refers to rainfall more acidic than this. The effects of acid rain (Clarke, 1992; Rodhe et al., 1995) include enhanced weathering of materials (soils, rocks, buildings, etc.) and the toxic effect that elevated hydrogen ion concentrations can have on plants and animals. Forests are particularly sensitive to acidic rainfall (Dixon and Wisniewski, 1995; Rodhe et al.,

1995). As noted earlier ammonia is somewhat effective in neutralizing acids to produce ammonium sulphates, chlorides, and nitrates (from sulphuric, hydrochloric, and nitric acids, respectively). The last two salts are reasonably volatile and thus can escape the water droplets and reform ammonia and the relevant acid. Also upon deposition to the soils, oxidation of the ammonium ion can lead to enhanced acidity:

$$(NH_4)_2SO_4 + 4O_2 \rightarrow H_2SO_4 + 2HNO_3 + 2H_2O \qquad \textbf{(40)}$$

The neutralization effect of ammonia can therefore be short lived.

It is beyond the scope of this presentation to consider all the reactions of N-containing species in soils and waters. Most of the reactions are microbially mediated oxidation and reduction reactions (Grant and Long, 1981; Manahan, 1994; Schlesinger, 1991).

Ammonia will be present predominantly as NH_4^+ (see above) due to its basic properties, and thus involved in the cation exchange capacities of soils. Its use as a fertilizer then is somewhat different from nitrates which, although charged, are only weakly held by clays and colloids (compare phosphates) and thus pass quickly through soils to aquifers. Under oxidizing conditions ammonia will be converted to nitrate via nitrite. Excess nitrate in aquifers can lead to phytoplankton blooms, provided other essential nutrients are also present. The pollution problems associated with nitrates have been well documented (Golterman and de Oude, 1991; Carpenter et al., 1998; Vitousek et al., 1997).

THE ROLE OF CHEMICAL ANALYSES IN ENVIRONMENTAL CHEMISTRY

An understanding of chemical behaviour and change in the environment can only be achieved if accurate, precise, and meaningful data are available. To ensure this, diligent application of the analytical process (Atkinson, 1982) is essential. This involves identifying the problem to be investigated, making hypotheses as to the nature of the problem, planning and conducting a series of experiments that will provide the data necessary to test the hypothesis, reporting the results, and finally deciding whether the problem has been adequately understood, and if not, starting again. All aspects of environmental studies that involve chemistry, whether they are base line data collection, the preparation of environmental impact assessments, investigations of pollution problems, or the basic understanding of chemical, biological, or geological processes, involve the collection of analytical data. Often the sample collection and chemical analyses will be contracted out to an analytical laboratory. In such cases it is vital that the laboratory manager is aware of the requirements of the data so that the correct analytical methods are applied; inappropriate methods produce meaningless data. The laboratory personnel should be involved in the planning.

Clearly, if the planning of the experiments is in error, then no matter what the quality of the data produced, the problem cannot be solved. For studies of processes occurring in actual environmental matrices (for example, pollution levels in a river, the impact of crop fertilizers on groundwaters) plans must be made to collect the relevant matrices (soils, pore waters, groundwaters, for example) and to conduct the relevant measurements accurately and with the appropriate precision. For laboratory-based studies (the determination of the ability of soil organic matter to bind metals, the release of PO_4^{3-} from polluted sediment, for example) the physical conditions (temperature, ionic strengths of solutions, for example) must be controlled.

For field-related studies it is essential to ensure that appropriate samples are collected and handled so as not to compromise their integrity. Sampling procedures for various matrices are generally well documented (Greenberg et al., 1992) and should be followed diligently. Sample treatment methods (filtration, addition of preservative chemicals, for example) have considerable impact on the subsequent analytical results and must be carried out carefully and be appropriate to the problem being investigated. For example, if eutrophication of coastal waters by phosphorus is being investigated then all forms of phosphorus (dissolved ortho-, hydrolyzable, organic, and particulate-bound phosphates) must be quantified and then the ease with which biological species can access these various forms must be assessed. If the pretreatment of the sample involves acidification in the field then the speciation of the phosphorus will change and thus trying to quantify the true speciation subsequently will be meaningless. Is this important? Decisions must be made prior to collecting the samples.

Samples must also be collected over all environmental forcing events (rainfall, industrial activity, the tourist season, for example) and the limitations of the sampling procedures realized from the start. If a coastal area is to be sampled it takes time to move from one sampling site to another. Will the wind have changed during the sampling exercise? If so can results for the different sites be compared? If not, how can the sampling plan be modified so that the question being asked can be adequately answered? This must all be thought through before sampling begins; it may also be necessary to modify plans once the reality of sample collection becomes apparent.

Once the required samples (experiments) have been collected (set up) the analytical work begins. Subsampling may be necessary and thus sample homogeneity must be ensured or allowed for. The method of analysis must be decided upon and carried out as defined. Preferably standard procedures (those that are accepted by respected organizations, such as the Association of Official Analytical Chemists, AOAC [1999], among others) should be used. If that is not possible a procedure may need to be developed and then it is essential that the chemist prove that the procedure allows for the determination of the analyte required. Considerable time and effort can be wasted if this is not done carefully (see Wangersky, 1993 and Sharp, 1997 for a recent example relating to the carbon cycle). It may be necessary to test the procedure on samples of known content but sometimes such standards are not available. The procedures chosen must be able to yield results of the required precision and be cost effective. Laboratory managers have the responsibility of producing accurate data (Skoog et al., 1996). They must be able to prove to their client, beyond all reasonable doubt, that the data coming out of the laboratory are correct. They must also be able to inform their clients of the uncertainties (precisions) associated with the data. Such uncertainties arise from the random errors of instruments, detection of colour changes, etc., and are unavoidable. Uncertainties in environmental data are not limited to laboratory uncertainties. Sampling is usually the least precise step (Keith, 1988).

All data must be interpreted with respect to their uncertainties. Statistical procedures are available for doing this (Miller and Miller, 1993; Taylor, 1987). Laboratories must report all concentrations with their associated uncertainties (for example 2.34 ± 0.03 mol dm^{-3}) and clients must insist that they do so. Reliable laboratories will be accredited by the appropriate national agency, involved in recommended quality assurance procedures, carrying out recommended quality control experiments and participating in interlaboratory calibration exercises. Their clients should make use of all their expertise and ensure that the services provided are appropriate to the problem being investigated. To do anything less is to compromise the study.

Laboratory managers must also ensure that all information relevant to the analyses carried out (sample identifications, analytical methods, quality control data, and instrument conditions, for example) are carefully documented, as this allows reinterpretation of data at later times when, possibly, a greater understanding of the problem has been achieved.

Chemical analyses play an important role in the preparation of environmental impact assessments (Ahmad and Sammy, 1985). The generation and use of a data base to predict the impact of the development on the environment will require a knowledge of all of the relevant environmental processes. Environmental chemists will seldom possess such knowledge and must combine their knowledge with those of other environmental scientists. Effective environmental management can only be achieved through interdisciplinary team efforts (Grant and Jickells, 1995).

CONCLUSION

There have been several unifying links throughout our considerations. One was the biological functions of elements and the necessary interactions between them; elements do not have biological functions in isolation. Another was the influence of the sun's radiation on chemicals at different heights in the atmosphere and the associated global issues of stratospheric ozone depletion, the greenhouse effect, and photochemically initiated smogs.

Central to our discussions has been the concept of speciation. Elements exist in a variety of species, each having different physical and chemical properties and potentially different effects on biological materials. The reactivity of chemicals is basic to these problems.

Chemicals emitted from the earth that are not removed by reactions in the troposphere (CFCs and N_2O, for example) can reach the stratosphere where the solar radiation is of sufficient energy to break bonds, produce radicals, and effect reactions not possible in the troposphere (Equations 9, 13, and 14). Such reactions have created an imbalance in the normal stratospheric reactions and led to a depletion of the stratospheric O_3 concentration. The removal of the ultraviolet light from the radiation that reaches the troposphere by the O_3 in the stratosphere allows these gases to reach the stratosphere before the photochemical reactions occur. The inertness of these gases led, at first consideration, to them being considered as environmentally friendly. Over time, this has been shown to be grossly in error and, given the long residence times of the gases, it will take a long time to get back to where we were.

Reactive chemicals are quickly removed from the atmosphere and this causes localized environmental problems. This is clearly illustrated in the smog problems where physical conditions can result in unusually high concentrations. Again, photochemical reactions are important but this time using light in the visible section of the solar radiation.

If chemicals have long life times, and anthropogenic activities lead to their build up in the atmosphere (CO_2, N_2O, and CH_4, among others; Figure 1.10), then the infrared radiation balance becomes disturbed. These trace species are able to adsorb infrared radiation through excitation of vibrations. This traps much of the energy leaving the Earth's surface and effects an increase in the global temperature. Again, however, it is not that simple. Particles in the atmosphere reflect light back into space and thus pollution of that nature will tend to decrease the global temperature. The two types of pollution are interrelated. The increase in CO_2 concentrations and an increase in global temperature will change the fluxes to and from the various reservoirs; which will dominate? It is predicted that the global temperature will increase by about 3°C by the year 2050 due to these effects (Lorius and Oeschger, 1994).

Environmental chemistry is intimately linked to other areas of environmental science. The concentrations of chemicals in environmental matrices do not necessarily give meaningful information about the status of the matrix: the concentrations may be low because the flow from the matrix is fast and thus the concentrations do not have time to build up. The biological impact of an element will depend on its speciation and thus meaningful information can only be obtained if speciations are determined. This is often a very difficult analytical task. To assess the impact of man's activities on a particular ecosystem involves the careful collection of an accurate data base that has resulted from thoughtful application of the analytical process. Predictions can then be made, but the actual impacts may deviate from these. Follow-up biological and chemical monitoring should therefore be effected to try to mediate any negative impacts.

We must, however, not be reluctant to make predictions from limited knowledge; our environment is fragile and to be inactive may lead to irreversible environmental degradation. While we strive for greater understanding, we must limit our activities to ensure that those of today do not limit our resources for tomorrow.

Our understanding of chemical processes in the environment is at an elementary stage. A definition of environmental chemistry, based on the wisdom of the *New Shorter Oxford English Dictionary* (1993) was attempted at the beginning of this chapter. The same source gives another definition of the environment as "a large artistic creation intended to be experienced with several senses while one is surrounded by it", and of chemistry as "the mysterious processes of change, imponderable interaction". These definitions should possibly be incorporated as they introduce the mystic associated with our limited understanding of how our environment works.

REFERENCES AND FURTHER READING

Acres, G. J. K. 1990. "Catalyst systems for emission control from motor vehicles". pp. 221–236, in R. M. Harrison, ed., *Pollution: Causes, Effects and Control*, 2nd edition. Royal Society of Chemistry, Cambridge, U.K.

Addison, W. E. 1961. *Structural Principles in Inorganic Chemistry.* Longman, Green and Co., London, England.

Ahmad, Y. J. and G. K. Sammy. 1985. *Guidelines to Environmental Impact Assessment in Developing Countries.* United Nations Environmental Programme, London.

Alloway, B. J. 1992. "Land contamination and reclamation". pp. 137–164, in R. M. Harrison, ed., *Understanding Our Environment: An Introduction to Environmental Chemistry and Pollution*, 2nd edition. Royal Society of Chemistry, Cambridge, U.K.

Andrews, S. P. S. 1982. "Modern process for the production of ammonia, nitric acid and ammonium nitrate". pp. 201–231, in R. Thompson, ed., *The Modern Inorganic Chemical Industry.* The Royal Chemical Society, London, U.K.

Andrews, J. E., P. Brimblecombe, T. D. Jickells, and P. S. Liss. 1996. *Introduction to Environmental Chemistry.* Blackwell Scientific, Oxford.

Association of Official Analytical Chemists (AOAC). 1999. *Official Methods of Analysis of the AOAC International*, 16th edition. P. Cunniff, ed. AOAC, Gaithersburg, Maryland.

Atkinson, G. F. 1982. "Introducing the analytical perspective". *Journal of Chemical Education* 59: 201–202.

Barcelo, D. 1991. "Occurrence, handling and chromatographic determination of pesticides in the aquatic environment: A review". *Analyst* 16: 681–689.

Boutron, C. F., U. Görlach, J. P. Candelone, M. A. Bolshov, and R. J. Delman. 1991. "Decrease in anthropogenic lead, cadmium and zinc in Greenland snows since the late 1960s". *Nature (London)* 353: 153–154.

Bridgeman, H. 1990. *Global Air Pollution: Problems for the 1990s.* John Wiley & Sons, Chichester, U.K.

Brimblecombe, P. 1996. *Air, Composition and Chemistry*, 2nd edition. Cambridge University Press, Cambridge, U.K.

Buffle, J. 1990. *Complexation Reactions in Aquatic Systems. An Analytical Approach.* Ellis Horwood, Chichester, U.K.

Buffle, J. 1995. "Biophysical environmental chemistry: A new frontier for chemistry". *Chemistry International* 17: 205–211.

Carpenter, S. R., N. E. Caraco, D. L. Correll, R. W. Howarth, A. N. Sharpley, and V. H. Smith. 1998. "Nonpoint pollution of surface waters with phosphorus and nitrogen". *Ecological Applications* 8: 559–568.

Chang-Yen, I., N. Pooransingh, and L. Boodlal. 1994. "Lead in air and roadside dust in Trinidad". p. 11, in B. E. Carby, ed., *Environmental Chemistry and Geochemistry in the Tropics: Abstracts of Geotrop94, an International Conference.* University of the West Indies, Kingston, Jamaica.

Chenier, P. J. 1986. *Survey of Industrial Chemistry.* Wiley Interscience, New York.

Chester, R. 1993. *Marine Geochemistry.* Chapman and Hall, London.

Childs, A. F. 1977. "Phosphorus, phosphoric acid and inorganic phosphates". pp. 375–402, in R. Thompson, ed., *The Modern Inorganic Chemicals Industry.* The Royal Society of Chemistry, London.

Clarke, A. G. 1992. "The atmosphere". pp. 5–51, in R. M. Harrison, ed., *Understanding Our Environment: An Introduction to Environmental Chemistry and Pollution,* 2nd edition. Royal Society of Chemistry, Cambridge, U.K..

Clayton, K. 1995. "The threat of global warming". pp. 110–130, in T. O'Riordan, ed., *Environmental Science for Environmental Management.* Longman, London.

Cresser, M., K. Killham, and T. Edwards. 1993. *Soil Chemistry and its Applications.* Cambridge University Press, Cambridge, U.K.

Crystal, D. (ed.). 1994. *The Cambridge Paperback Encyclopedia.* Cambridge University Press, Cambridge, U.K.

Davidson, W. and R. DeVitre. 1992. "Iron particles in fresh water". pp. 315–356, in J. Buffle and H. P. van Leeuwen, eds., *Environmental Particles,* Vol. 1. Lewis Publishers, Boca Raton, Florida.

Davis, M., C. Grant, A. Johnson, G. C. Lalor, and M. Vutchkov. 1994. "Suspended particles in the Jamaican atmosphere". p. 55, in B. E. Carby, ed., *Environmental Chemistry and Geochemistry in the Tropics: Abstracts of Geotrop94, an International Conference.* University of the West Indies, Kingston, Jamaica.

Dixon, R. K. and J. Wisniewski. 1995. "Global forest systems: An uncertain response to atmospheric pollutants and global climate change". *Water, Air, and Soil Pollution* 85: 101–110.

Fergusson, J. E. 1982. *Inorganic Chemistry and the Earth. Chemical Resources, Their Extraction, Use and Environmental Impact.* Pergamon Press, Oxford, U.K.

Fergusson, J. E. 1990. *The Heavy Elements: Chemistry, Environmental Impact and Health Effects.* Pergamon Press, Oxford, U.K.

FitzPatrick, E. A. 1983. *Soils. Their Formation, Classification and Distribution.* Longman, London.

Froelich, P. N., M. L. Bender, N. A. Luedtke, G. R. Heath, and T. De Vries. 1982. "The marine phosphorus cycle". *American Journal of Science* 282: 474–511.

Galloway, J. N. 1995. "Acid deposition: Perspectives in time and space". *Water, Air, and Soil Pollution* 85: 15–24.

Gibbs, R. J. 1992. "A reply to Comments of Eilers et al.". *Limnology and Oceanography* 37: 1338–1339.

Golterman, H. L. and N. T. de Oude. 1991. "Eutrophication of lakes and coastal seas". pp. 79–124, in O. Hutzinger, ed., *The Handbook of Environmental Chemistry,* Vol. 5A. Springer-Verlag, Berlin.

Grant, A. and T. Jickells. 1995. "Marine and estuarine pollution". pp. 263–282, in T. O'Riordan, ed., *Environmental Science for Environmental Management.* Longman, London.

Grant, W. D. and P. E. Long. 1981. *Environmental Microbiology.* Blackie & Sons, Glasgow, U.K.

Greenberg, A. E., L. S. Gesceri, and A. D. Eaton (eds.). 1992. *Standard Methods for Examination of Water and Waste Water,* 18th edition. American Public Health Association, American Water Works Association and Water Environmental Federation, Washington, D.C.

Greenwood, N. N. and A. Earnshaw. 1998. *Chemistry of the Elements,* 2nd edition. Pergamon Press, Oxford, U.K.

Hanel, R. A., B. J. Conrath, V. G. Kunde, C. Prabhakara, I. Revah, V. V. Salomonson, and G. Wolford. 1972. "The Nimbus 4 Infrared Spectroscopy Experiment. I. Thermal emission spectra". *Journal of Geophysical Research* 77: 2629–2641.

Harrison, R. M. 1992. "Integrative aspects of pollutant cycling". pp. 165–187, in R. M. Harrison, ed., *Understanding our Environment: An Introduction to Environmental Chemistry and Pollution,* 2nd edition. Royal Society of Chemistry, Cambridge, U.K.

Harrison, R. M., S. J. de Mora, S. Rapsomanikis, and W. R. Johnston. 1991. *Introductory Chemistry for the Environmental Sciences.* Cambridge University Press, Cambridge, U.K.

Hassall, K. A. 1990. *The Biochemistry and Uses of Pesticides. Structure, Metabolism, Mode of Actions and Uses in Crop Protection.* Macmillan, Houndsmill, U.K.

Hawkins, S. W. 1988. *A Brief History of Time.* Bantam Press, London.

Hayes, M. H. B. 1991. "Concepts of the origins, composition, and structures of humic substances". pp. 3–22, in W. S. Wilson, ed., *Advances in Soil Organic Matter Research: The Impact on Agriculture and the Environment.* The Royal Society of Chemistry, Cambridge, U.K.

Holum, J. R. 1990. *Fundamentals of General, Organic and Biological Chemistry,* 4th edition. John Wiley & Sons, New York.

Ingall, E. and R. Jahnke. 1994. "Evidence for enhanced phosphorus regeneration from marine sediments overlain by oxygen depleted waters". *Geochimica et Cosmochimica Acta* 58: 2571–2575.

Iribarne, J. V. and H. R. Cho. 1980. *Atmospheric Physics.* D. Reidel, Boston.

Kabata-Pendias, A. and H. Pendias. 1984. *Trace Elements in Soils and Plants.* CRC Press, Boca Raton, Florida.

Keith, L. H. 1988. *Principles of Environmental Sampling.* American Chemical Society, Washington, D.C.

Kramer, J. R. 1981. "Alkalinity and acidity". pp. 85–134, in R. A. Minear and L. W. Keith, ed., *Water Analysis,* Vol. 1, *Inorganic Species,* Part 1. Academic Press, New York.

Krauskopf, K. B. 1982. *Introduction to Geochemistry,* 2nd edition. MacGraw-Hill, New York.

Krauskopf, K. B. and D. K. Bird. 1995. *Introduction to Geochemistry,* 3rd edition. MacGraw-Hill, New York.

Ladd, M. F. C. 1979. *Structure and Bonding in Solid State Chemistry.* Ellis Horwood, Chichester, U.K.

Lorius, C. and H. Oeschger. 1994. "Paleo-perspectives: Reducing uncertainties in global change". *Ambio* 23: 30–36.

Manahan, S. E. 1994. *Environmental Chemistry,* 6th edition. Lewis Publishers, Boca Raton, Florida.

Markert, B. 1992. "Establishing of reference plant for inorganic characterization of different plant species by chemical fingerprinting". *Water, Air, and Soil Pollution* 64: 533–538.

Matte, T. D., J. P. Figueroa, S. Ostrowski, G. Burr, L. Jackson-Hunt, R. A. Keenlyside, and E. L. Baker. 1989. "Lead poisoning among household members exposed to lead-acid battery repair shops in Kingston, Jamaica". *International Journal of Epidemiology* 18: 874–881.

McBean, G. A. 1994. "Global change models: A physical perspective". *Ambio* 23: 13–18.

Mielke, J. E. 1979. "Composition of the Earth's crust and distribution of the elements. pp. 13–36, in F. R. Siegel, ed., *Review of Research on Modern Problems in Geochemistry.* UNESCO, Paris.

Miller, J. C. and J. N. Miller. 1993. *Statistics for Analytical Chemistry,* 3rd edition. Ellis Horwood, Chichester, U.K.

Mohammed, T., I. Chang-Yen, and J. Agard. 1994. "Lead pollution in east Trinidad resulting from lead recycling and smelting activities". p. 37, in B. E. Carby, ed., *Environmental Chemistry and Geochemistry in the Tropics: Abstracts of Geotrop94, an International Conference.* University of the West Indies, Kingston, Jamaica.

Mooney, H. A. and G. W. Koch. 1994. "The impact of rising CO_2 concentrations on the terrestrial biosphere". *Ambio* 23: 74–76.

Moore, B. and B. H. Braswell, Jr. 1995. "Planetary metabolism: Understanding the carbon cycle". *Ambio* 23: 4–12.

New Shorter Oxford English Dictionary. 1993. Clarendon Press, Oxford.

Ochiai, E.-I. 1977. *An Introduction to Bioinorganic Chemistry.* Allyn and Bacon, Boston.

O'Neill, P. 1993. *Environmental Chemistry,* 2nd edition, Chapman and Hall, London.

Roberts, M. B. V. 1993. *Biology: A Functional Approach.* Thomas Nelson and Sons, Walton on Thames, U.K.

Rodhe, H., P. Grennfelt, J.Wisniewski, C. Agren, G. Bengtsson, K. Johansson, P. Kauppi, V. Kucera, L. Rasmussen, L. Rosseland, L. Schotte, and G. Sellden. 1995. "Acid Reign '95? – Conference Summary Statement". *Water, Air, and Soil Pollution* 85: 1–14.

Salomons, W. and U. Forstner. 1984. *Metals in the Hydrocycle.* Springer-Verlag, Berlin.

Schlesinger, W. H. 1991. *Biogeochemistry. An Analysis of Global Change.* Academic Press, London

Schrauzer, G. N. 1977. "Molybdenum in biological nitrogen fixation". pp. 243–266, in W. R. Chappell and K. K. Petersen, eds., *Molybdenum in the Environment,* Vol. 1, *The Biology of Molybdenum.* Marcel Dekker, New York.

Sharp, J. H. 1997. "Marine dissolved organic carbon: Are the older values correct?" *Marine Chemistry* 56: 265–277.

Shaw, T. J., E. R. Sholkovitz, and G. Klinkhammer. 1994. "Redox dynamics in the Chesapeake Bay: The effect on sediment/water uranium exchange". *Geochimica et Cosmochimica Acta* 58: 2985–2995.

Sievers, R. E., K. Hansen, and B. Watkins. 1994. "Analysis of hour-to-hour changes in atmospheric aerosol composition in and near urban areas. p. 11, in B. E. Carby, ed., *Environmental Chemistry and Geochemistry in the Tropics: Abstracts of Geotrop94, an International Conference*. University of the West Indies, Kingston, Jamaica.

Skoog, D. A., D. M. West, and F. J. Holler. 1996. *Fundamentals of Analytical Chemistry*, 7th edition. Saunders College Publishing, Orlando, Florida.

Solomons, T. W. G. 1997. *Fundamentals of Organic Chemistry*, 5th edition. John Wiley & Sons, New York.

Somasundaram, L. and J. R. Coats. 1991. "Pesticide transformation products in the environment". pp. 2–9, in L. Somasundaram and J. R. Coats, ed., *Pesticide Transformation Products: Fate and Significance in the Environment*. American Chemical Society, Washington, D.C.

Spitzy, A. and J. Leenheer. 1991. "Dissolved organic carbon in rivers". pp. 213–227, in E. T. Degens, S. Kempe, and J. E. Richey, eds., *Biogeochemistry of Major World Rivers; SCOPE 42*. John Wiley & Sons, Chichester, U.K.

Stowe, K. S. 1979. *Ocean Science*. John Wiley & Sons, New York.

Street-Perrott, F. A. 1994. "Paleo-perspectives: Changes in terrestrial ecosystems. *Ambio* 23: 37–43.

Stryer, L. 1988. *Biochemistry*, 2nd edition. W. H. Freeman, San Francisco.

Stumm, W. and J. J. Morgan. 1981. *Aquatic Chemistry: An Introduction Emphasizing Chemical Equilibria in Natural Waters*, 2nd edition. Wiley-Interscience, New York.

Taylor, J. K. 1987. *Quality Assurance of Chemical Measurements*, Lewis Publishers, Boca Raton, Florida.

Tessier, A. 1992. "Sorption of trace elements on natural particles in oxic environments". pp. 425–454, in J. Buffle and H. P. van Leeuwen, eds., *Environmental Particles*. Lewis Publishers, Boca Raton, Florida.

Thamdrup, B., H. Fossing, and B. B. Jorgensen. 1994. "Manganese, iron and sulphur cycling in a coastal marine sediment, Aarhus Bay, Denmark. *Geochimica et Cosmochimica Acta* 58: 5115–5129.

Underwood, E. J. 1976. "Molybdenum in animal nutrition". pp. 9–32, in W. R. Chappell and K. K. Petersen, eds., *Molybdenum in the Environment*, Vol. 1, *The Biology of Molybdenum*. Marcel Dekker, New York.

Vitousek, P. M., J. D. Aber, R. W. Howarth, G. E. Likens, P. A. Matson, D. W. Schindler, W. H. Schlesinger, and D. G. Tilman. 1997. "Human alteration of the global nitrogen cycle: Sources and consequences". *Ecological Applications* 7: 737–750.

Wangersky, P. J. 1993. "Dissolved organic carbon methods: A critical review". *Marine Chemistry* 41: 61–74.

Wayne, R. P. 1993. *Chemistry of Atmospheres*, 2nd edition. Clarendon Press, Oxford, U.K.

Westheimer, F. H. 1987. "Why nature chose phosphates". *Science* 235: 1173–1178.

Wild, A. 1993. *Soils and the Environment: An Introduction.* Cambridge University Press, Cambridge, U.K.

2

Water Resources

Lester Forde

Contents

INTRODUCTION

Water is a unique natural resource, since it is essential for the survival of all forms of life. Like many other natural resources, the total amount of water in the world is constant and can neither be increased nor decreased. The conservation of water is therefore of the utmost importance.

A global total of 1400 million cubic kilometres of water covers about 70 percent of the Earth's surface. Of this total, only 3 percent is fresh. The majority of fresh water (87 percent) is locked up in glaciers and the polar ice caps or very deep under the Earth's surface. This means that a very small proportion of it, about 0.003 percent, is actually usable. Figure 2.1 is a diagrammatic representation of the distribution of water (Gleick, 1993). Nevertheless, there are over 40,000 cubic kilometres of fresh water available from the rivers of the world. This would be more than enough to meet present and future demands, the only problem being that water is not always available where it is needed and of the quality required.

The distribution of fresh water is so uneven that fifteen of the world's largest rivers carry one third of the global runoff. The Amazon alone carries 15 percent. In spite of its limited availability and its crucial role in human development, water is not treasured as it should be but, in fact, it is abused. For instance, water resources are polluted by industrial and domestic waste discharges, while irrigation water return threatens a significant number of water sources. In addition, these resources are exploited in many cases at a level beyond their renewable capacity. This attitude towards water may arise from the mistaken perception that, since so much of the Earth is covered by water, it is an abundant and never-ending resource.

Renewable fresh water is water that falls as precipitation, generally, either as rain or snow. Rainfall infiltrates the ground or runs off

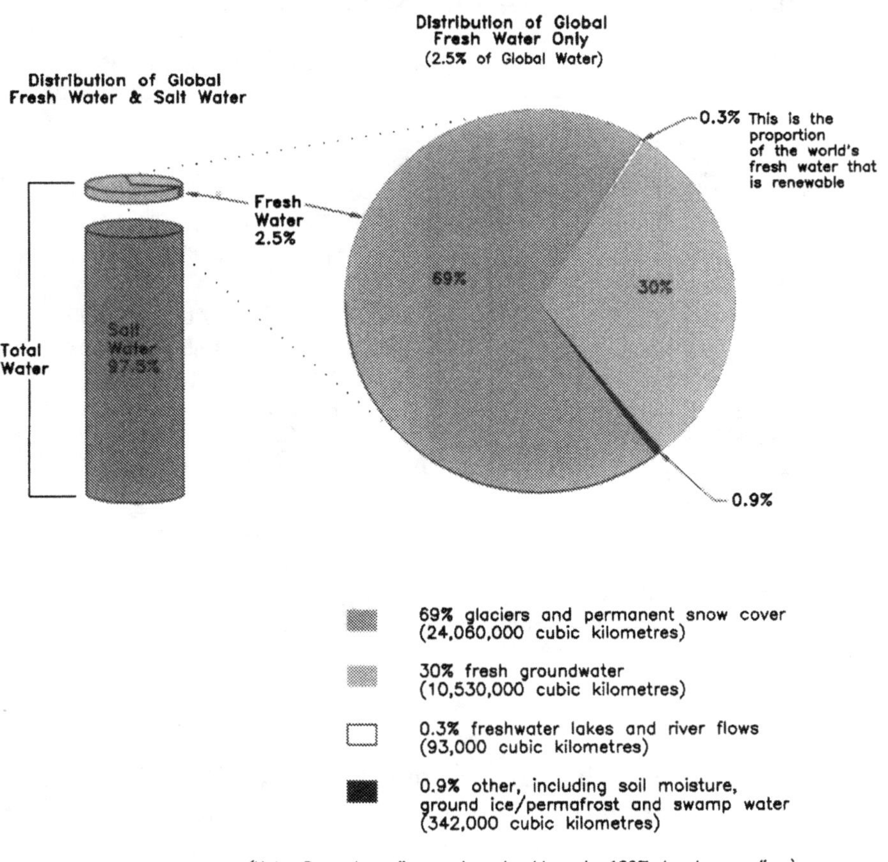

FIGURE 2.1 The world's water. (From Shiklomanov, I. 1993. "World fresh water resources". In P. H. Gleick, ed., *Water in Crisis: A Guide to the World's Fresh Water Resources*. Oxford University Press, New York. With permission.)

into rivers and lakes. Snow remains on the ground for a considerable time after the precipitation. When the temperature rises sufficiently for the snow to melt, the resultant water eventually flows into the sea, from where it returns to the atmosphere. In the Caribbean, precipitation occurs mainly in the form of rainfall. Table 2.1 lists the world's water supplies by location (Speidel et al., 1988).

THE HYDROLOGIC CYCLE

The interdependence and continuous movement of water between ocean, atmosphere, and land is called the hydrologic cycle. That is,

TABLE 2.1 The World's Water Supply (000 km³)

	Mean of Range[a]	Range of Values[b]
Total Volume	1,420,240	
Salt water (95.1%)	1,350,103	
Oceans	1,350,000	1,320,000–1,370,000
Inland seas	103	85.4–125.0
Fresh water (4.9%)	70,137	
Groundwater	48,000	7,000–330,000
Ice caps/glaciers	22,000	16,500–29,200
Soil moisture	49.7	16.5–150.0
Water in plants and animals	7.1	1–50
Lakes	67.1	30–150
Atmosphere	12.1	10.5–14.0
Rivers	1.47	1.02–2.12

[a] This mean is a geometric mean, which is the square root of the product of the high and low values given in the right-hand column.
[b] The numbers in this column are the highest and lowest values as noted in ten recent studies.

Source: Adapted from Speidel et al., 1988, p. 28.

fresh water is renewed by a giant solar distillation system. Liquid water is converted to vapour by a process called vaporization. This process requires heat and is driven by energy obtained from the sun. The water that evaporates from the oceans is transported by large moving air masses. When this moisture-bearing air is lifted to higher altitudes, it is cooled and, when it cools to its dewpoint temperature, the vapour condenses into water droplets that form fog or cloud. Condensation nuclei, the sites where the droplets develop, must be present. These droplets enlarge until their size is such that their falling speed is greater than the rate at which the air mass is rising. Precipitation is the final result of the growth of these droplets.

There are three main ways by which an air mass can be lifted. Orographic lifting, when air is forced up over the underlying terrain; frontal lifting, when an air mass is lifted up by a cooler air mass; and convective lifting, when moist air is heated from below as it passes over a warmer surface (the mechanism that causes thunderstorms). These processes may very often take place in conjunction with each other.

The hydrologic cycle is depicted diagrammatically in Figure 2.2. This simple figure cannot do justice to so complex a process, but it

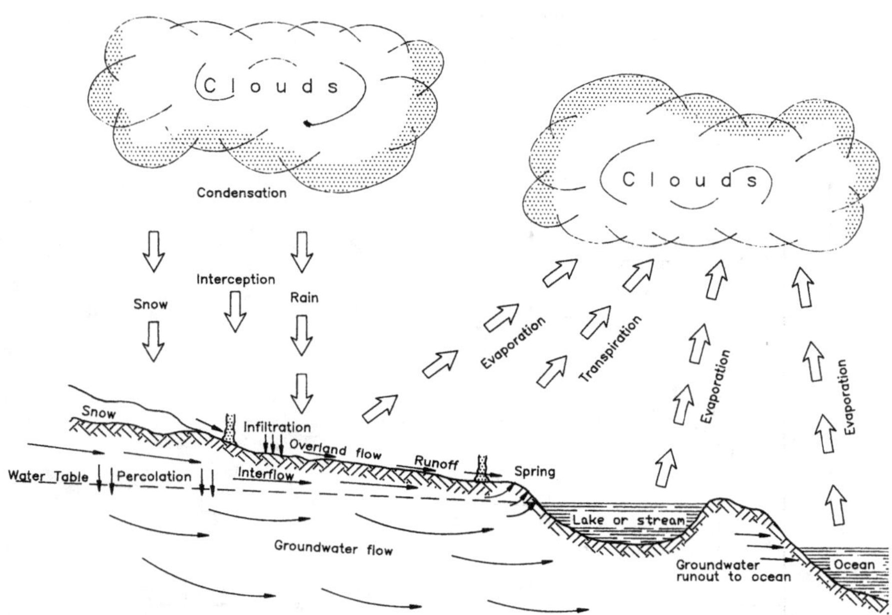

FIGURE 2.2 Schematic diagram of the hydrologic cycle.

does illustrate the flow-system concept of the hydrologic cycle. Although the illustration is one-dimensional, we should look at a watershed as a combination of both the surface drainage area and the underlying subsurface soils and geologic formations. Figure 2.3 is a representation of the process when a systems approach to hydrologic modelling is used (Freeze and Cherry, 1979). The hydrologic cycle is circulatory and is made up of a complicated array of water movements and transformations. When applied to any particular mass of water, the pattern may in fact be non-cyclic. It is more precise to envision a hydrologic sequence of events in which the different processes are interrelated and quantified. A cyclic order of events does occur but there is not a continuous mechanism through which the water cycle moves at some steady and constant rate.

Water vapour in the atmosphere condenses and produces precipitation, which can be in the form of rainfall or solid precipitation. Solid precipitation takes the form of snow, hail, sleet, and freezing rain. Rainfall runs into streams, whereas frozen precipitation may remain where it falls for a long time before the temperature rises enough to cause it to melt. When precipitation falls on land areas not all of it will reach the ground surface, since some will evaporate while falling and some will be caught by the vegetative cover or by buildings

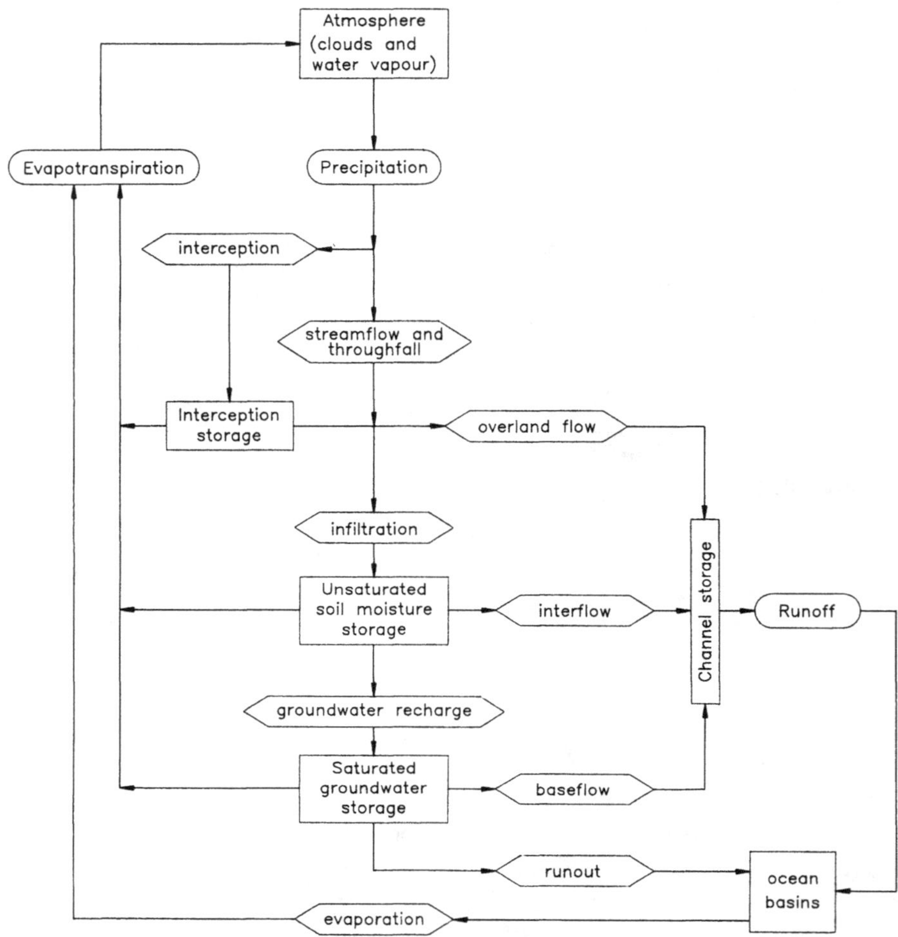

FIGURE 2.3 Systems representation of the hydrologic cycle.

and other structures. Interception of precipitation occurs when the moisture is evaporated back into the atmosphere. Precipitation that reaches the ground surface can follow one of three routes. First, the water can remain in the ground as surface storage, such as puddles, small pools, and surface moisture, which eventually evaporates into the atmosphere. Second, water may flow over the land surface as overland flow into depressions and channels, becoming surface runoff, such as into streams, rivers, or lakes. Evaporation will transfer the water from the streams, rivers, and lakes into the atmosphere. Surface runoff can also seep into the ground and move towards the groundwater or continue the surface flow, which finally ends up in the oceans.

The third route is by precipitation moving into the ground surface via infiltration to join the existing soil moisture. Soil moisture can return to the atmosphere by evaporation and transpiration from soil and vegetative surfaces. Moisture in the soil can also move by interflow towards stream channels or move downward via percolation to the groundwater. Groundwater can be held for long periods but it can be removed by upward capillary movement to the upper layers of the soil, where it is returned to the atmosphere by evaporation and transpiration. Groundwater may also be removed by groundwater seepage and flow into springs and surface streams or it can be discharged via runoff to the oceans.

Early on in the development of the science of hydrology, it was generally believed that continental evaporation was the principal source of moisture for continental precipitation. It is now known that evaporation from the oceans is the chief source of moisture for precipitation and probably no more than 10 percent of precipitation on continents is derived from the evaporation on the continents. It is also now known that about one fourth of the total precipitation that falls on continental areas is returned to the seas as direct runoff and underground flow. Table 2.2 defines some of the common hydrologic terms.

The components of the hydrologic cycle have also been examined from a quantitative point of view in order to assess the relative importance of the different parts. Table 2.3 presents data that look at water resources from such a point of view. This table is based on work by Nace (1971) and emphasizes that groundwater accounts for about two thirds of the freshwater resources of the world. When consideration of fresh water is limited to utilizable freshwater resources by removing that portion which is contained in ice caps and glaciers, then groundwater accounts for almost the total quantity. The superiority of groundwater in terms of volume, however, is attenuated by the average residence times of the different types of water. The life cycle of surface water circulation is about 1 year. Freeze and Cherry (1979) state that water in rivers has a turnover time of about 2 weeks.

Groundwater, however, moves very slowly and can remain underground for thousands of years. In fact, there are some experts who claim that because the life cycle of groundwater can be several hundred years, then on a human scale it is virtually a non-renewable resource. In global terms, groundwater is being consumed at a much higher rate than it is being replaced (Savenije, 1993).

THE HYDROLOGIC FRAMEWORK

The Hydrologic Basin

Throughout geological history, land has been shaped by water, with small streams joining to form rivers and eventually to form broad flood

TABLE 2.2 Common Terms of the Hydrologic Cycle

Evaporation:
As water is heated by the sun, its surface molecules become sufficiently energized to break free of the attractive force binding them together, and then evaporate and rise as invisible vapour in the atmosphere, collecting to form clouds.

Transpiration:
Water vapour is also emitted from plant leaves by a process called transpiration. Every day an actively growing plant *transpires* 5 to 10 times as much water as it can hold at once.

Condensation:
As water vapour rises, it cools and eventually *condenses*, usually on tiny particles of dust in the upper atmosphere. When it condenses it becomes a liquid again or turns directly into a solid (ice, hail or snow).

Precipitation:
Precipitation in the form of rain, snow and hail and comes from clouds. When clouds rise, they cool becoming so saturated with water that the water vapour is converted into rain, snow or hail depending on the temperature of the surrounding air.

Infiltration:
Some of the precipitation and snowmelt *infiltrates* joints and pores in soil and rocks. This water may flow laterally or move downwards.

Percolation:
Some of the water infiltrated into the soil can move downwards until it reaches the groundwater table.

Groundwater:
Groundwater fills the cracks and pore spaces in the soil. The water moves laterally as interflow. Depending on the geology, the groundwater can flow to support streams. It can also be discharged to springs or the ocean. Some groundwater is very old and may have been there for thousands of years.

Water Table:
The upper surface of the zone of saturation is called the water table. Where all the voids in the soil are filled with water.

Runoff:
Excessive rain or snowmelt can produce overland flow to creeks and ditches when the infiltrative capacity of the soil is exceeded. Runoff is the visible flow of water in rivers, creeks and lakes as the water stored in the basin drains out.

channels. There is some confusion in the terms used to describe those areas of water surplus from which streams flow, since usage is varied. Here, the terms *watershed, catchment area,* or *drainage basin* will be used for the area contributing to a watercourse. The terms *divide* or *watershed boundary* will be used for the perimeter defining the area. The term *watercourse* will be used to include all natural channels along which water flows either perennially or intermittently.

The watershed is defined as a unit of land on which all of the water that falls or that portion which is discharged from springs collects by gravity and runs off via a common outlet. That is, it is

TABLE 2.3 Estimate of the Water Balance of the World

Parameter	Surface Area $(km^2) \times 10^6$	Volume $(km^3) \times 10^6$	Volume (%)	Equivalent depth (m)[a]	Residence Time
Oceans and seas	361	1370	94	2500	~ 4000 years
Lakes and reservoirs	1.55	0.13	<0.01	0.25	~ 10 years
Swamps	<0.1	<0.01	<0.01	0.007	1–10 years
River channels	<0.1	<0.01	<0.01	0.003	~ 2 weeks
Soil moisture	130	0.07	<0.01	0.13	2 weeks–1 year
Groundwater	130	60	4	120	2 weeks–10,000 years
Icecaps and glaciers	17.8	30	2	60	10–1000 years
Atmospheric water	504	0.01	<0.01	0.025	~ 10 days
Biospheric water	<0.1	<0.01	<0.01	0.001	~ 1 week

[a] Computed as though storage were uniformly distributed over the entire surface of the Earth.

From Nace, 1971.

defined with respect to a given point where surface water discharge is measured as streamflow. The topographic divide or watershed perimeter follows the ridgelines between hydrologic units. On a topographic map it appears as an irregular closed traverse that is everywhere consistent with the land contour. There is also a groundwater catchment, which would be an area below the ground that drains into a single groundwater unit.

The drainage basin provides a suitable unit over which hydrological processes are integrated and over which fluvial geomorphic processes operate. Thus, it has become the unit for river basin planning by hydrologists, economists, and social scientists. In developing countries, population pressure results in large sections of the uplands of watersheds being deforested and converted into agricultural use. There has been significant literature on the impact in the tropics of upland forest use or conversion on soil erosion rates, sedimentation in streams and reservoirs, water quality in streams, peak stream discharges, and nutrient input in streams (Bonell et al., 1993). Deforestation increases soil erosion, which consequently affects the course and depth of rivers. The increase in the frequency and severity of floods that has been observed in many countries is partially as a result of deforestation of the upstream areas. This leads to siltation and a rise in the level of the riverbed.

In many countries, as a result of the pressures of human and livestock populations, the degradation of watersheds has recently accelerated. The natural causes of this acceleration are the geology and geomorphology of the region and the erosive action of rainfall. The human factors include the large and rapidly growing populations that are placing pressure on the land, which is a non-renewable resource, and on freshwater and forest resources, which are renewable but limited.

Surface Water

Streamflow is thought to represent the total catchment discharge and is ultimately that part of precipitation that is not lost to evaporation and transpiration. Streamflow is generally classified as either direct runoff or baseflow. Direct runoff is also called stormflow or quickflow. Baseflow is called delayed flow or groundwater flow. Baseflow is continuous in perennial streams but direct runoff is intermittent and occurs only as a direct response to specific rainfall or snowmelt events.

Streamflow is generated by processes that are identified in terms of the paths along which precipitation travels from its point of incidence to a catchment channel. Channel precipitation enters the stream directly or as throughfall to a stream and reaches the mouth of the catchment quickly. It is followed by overland flow, which occurs along surfaces that are relatively impermeable. Interflow occurs through the more permeable upper soil horizons and this also reaches streams. Finally, in the zone of saturation groundwater flow contributes to streamflow.

Overland flow and channel precipitation contribute to direct runoff. Groundwater flow is synonymous with baseflow. Interflow is usually associated with both delayed and quickflow. The relative importance of any individual streamflow-generating process depends on the physical parameters of the catchment and the cover characteristics of the vegetation. Other activities, such as mining and road building, also affect downstream areas. The increased runoff from the many roads that have been built also increases the volume that flows to the lower areas.

Groundwater

Nearly all terrestrial freshwater resources in liquid form are located underground and are called underground or subsurface water. The 10 million billion cubic metres of underground water represent more than a hundred times the amount contained in all of the lakes and rivers. It is less than the 28 million billion cubic metres contained in the ice masses on the Earth, but underground water is more evenly distributed on every continent when compared to surface water. Underground water is not stagnant, but flows very slowly and its mass when in motion makes a sizable contribution to the general circulation. Unlike surface water, underground water is not confined to only a few channels or depressions such as streams or lakes.

That portion of subsurface water in interconnected openings or interstices completely saturated with water is called groundwater. Groundwater can be found in the intergranular spaces between soil and rocks, or in the crevices or cracks in rocks. The water that fills these openings is found within 100 metres of the surface and represents most of the Earth's fresh water.

Groundwater flows slowly through water-bearing formations or aquifers at different rates based on the ease of transmission through the formations. Immediately below the surface, the pores in the soil contain both water and air in varying amounts. After rainfall, infiltrated water moves through this zone of aeration or vadose zone. Some moisture is held by capillary forces in the smaller pores or may be held by molecular attraction around soil particles. The water held in the upper layers of the zone of aeration is known as soil moisture.

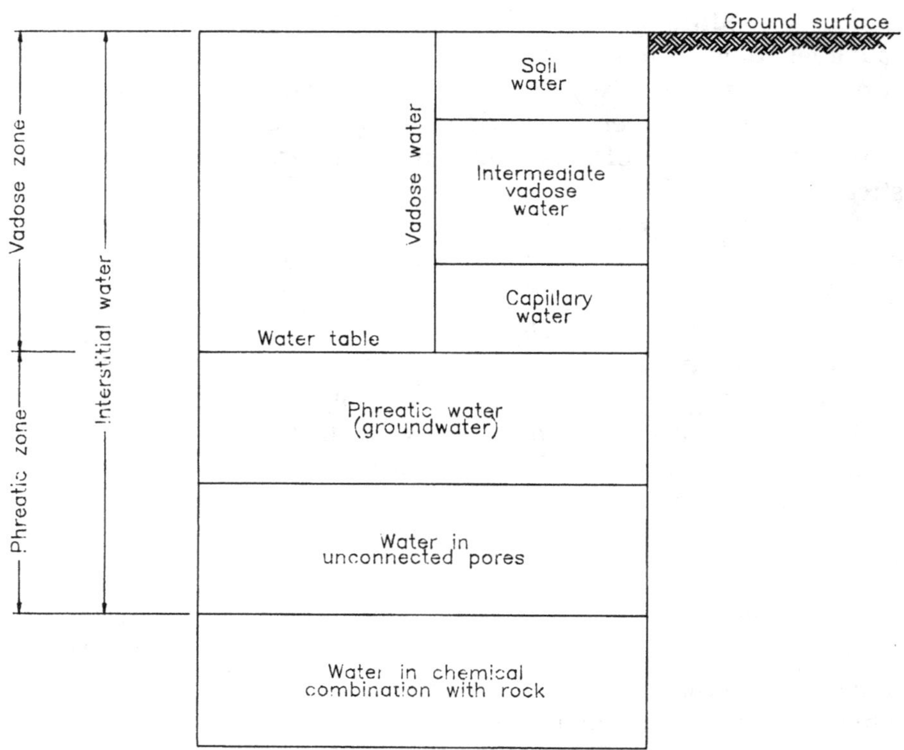

FIGURE 2.4 The groundwater profile.

The movement of water in the vadose zone is vital in the natural or artificial recharge of groundwater and in the loss of groundwater by evaporation either directly from the soil surface or via uptake by plants. So long as the retention capacity of the soil in the zone of aeration has been satisfied, water percolates downwards until it reaches regions where the pores of the soil or rock are completely filled with water. Water in this zone of saturation is called groundwater. The replenishment phenomenon of water moving downward is called recharge and the boundary between the vadose zone (formerly called the unsaturated zone) and the zone of saturation is the water table.

The capillary fringe is immediately above the water table and these pore spaces are completely filled with water that is held by capillary and molecular forces. Thus, the pressure of the water is less than atmospheric. A section illustrating the groundwater profile is shown in Figure 2.4. (For further reading on groundwater see Freeze and Cherry [1979] and Karamath [1989]).

Aquifers are geologic formations of sufficient lateral and vertical extent and of sufficient permeability to produce adequate and sustained flows of water to wells. Aquifers can be confined or unconfined. A confined or artesian aquifer is bounded above and below by relatively impermeable strata. Thus, the water pressure in the aquifer may be maintained above atmospheric pressure. An unconfined or water table aquifer, however, is bounded on the bottom by an impermeable layer and above by the water table or phreatic surface and the overlying vadose zone. Aquifers typically consist of sand and gravel layers and mixtures of alluvial or unconsolidated material such as sandstone. Consolidated material such as crystalline or sedimentary rocks must have fractures or large pores, such as the solution channels in limestone, in order to be considered as aquifers. Aquifers range in thickness from a few metres to several hundreds of metres and may extend laterally over millions of square kilometres. Unconfined and confined aquifers are the extremes of a spectrum of confinement conditions. The bottom layer may allow water loss to different degrees depending on its composition and structure (Driscoll, 1986).

WATER BALANCES

Water balance methodology is now well developed and is based on the principle of conservation of mass. For any three-dimensional section of the Earth, the total input equals the total output and if they are not equal, then the difference is accounted for by the change of storage within the section. This is sometimes referred to as the storage equation. Thus, a proper water balance involves the measurement of both storage and fluxes or rates of flow. When performing a water balance it is critical to define the hydrologic boundaries. If the supply source for the study area is a river only, then the boundaries should encompass the watershed area to the river. If, instead, there is a groundwater supply then the relevant portion of the groundwater basin must be included. Where both surface water and groundwater supply exist, it would be better if separate balances are prepared for each source. After a water balance is completed, it should, however, be recognized that the proportion of the resource that is available for use depends on several factors, such as time, place, technology, economics, and social and political considerations.

Surface Water Balance

In its general form, the water balance equation can be stated as:

$$\text{Inflow} - \text{outflow} \pm \text{change in storage} = 0 \tag{1}$$

When broken down into individual components the equation may be described as:

$$P + Q_{swi} + Q_{gwi} - ET - Q_{swo} - Q_{gwo} - \Delta S \pm \eta = 0 \quad (2)$$

where

P = precipitation
Q_{swi} = surface water
Q_{gwi} = groundwater inflow
} inflow, gain
ET = evapotranspiration
Q_{swo} = surface water outflow
Q_{gwo} = ground water outflow
} outflow, loss
ΔS = change in storage
η = a term that accounts for the error of estimation

When taken over a long period, during which precipitation-rich years are compensated by periods of drought, i.e., the change in storage of the groundwater reservoir equals the change in storage of the surface water reservoir, then the equation reduces to:

$$P = Q + ET \quad (3)$$

where

P = average annual precipitation
Q = the average annual runoff
ET = the average annual evapotranspiration

Groundwater Balance

The groundwater balance equation can be presented in a simplified form as:

$$\Delta S_G = Q_r - Q_d \quad (4)$$

where

ΔS_G = the change in groundwater storage
Q_r = the recharge to groundwater
Q_d = the discharge from groundwater

Recharge or discharge areas can be delineated depending on whether water in these areas is added to or removed from the zone of saturation. The main components of groundwater recharge are:

- Infiltration of a portion of precipitation at the ground surface
- Seepage into the ground through the banks and beds of surface water bodies, such as ditches, streams, rivers, lakes
- Groundwater leakage and inflow from adjacent aquicludes and aquifers
- Artificial recharge from irrigation, reservoirs, planned land spreading of water and injection wells

Groundwater discharge has as its main components:

- Evapotranspiration, in particular in those low areas where the water table is close to the ground surface
- Natural discharge as a result of flow from springs and seepage into surface water bodies
- Groundwater leakage and outflow through aquicludes and into adjacent aquifers
- Artificial abstraction

Storage changes in aquifers depend on the type of aquifer that is being considered. In unconfined aquifers, storage changes are not complicated and may be reflected directly in variation of the groundwater level. Levels rise when recharge exceeds discharge and levels fall when discharge exceeds recharge. Since recharge and discharge occur simultaneously in normal circumstances, then groundwater fluctuations reflect the net change of storage resulting from the two components interacting. Water table fluctuations tend to follow an arrhythmic seasonal pattern that is regular. High water tables are common during the rainy season in the Caribbean and low levels occur during the dry season. Short-term fluctuations also occur on a smaller scale as a result of other phenomena, both natural and man-made (for example, tidal movements in coastal areas). Sea level variations result in a train of sinusoidal waves being propagated inland from the ocean outcrops of an aquifer. The groundwater fluctuations are of lower amplitude and lag the tidal fluctuations.

Storage changes in confined aquifers are more complicated than in unconfined ones. The compressibility and elasticity of aquifers affect the relationship between changes in the piezometric level and changes in the groundwater level. Hydrologists have been able to determine that when water is pumped from a confined aquifer the grain structure is affected and the aquifer actually undergoes compression. Thus, comparatively small yields of water from a confined aquifer may be accompanied by large variations in piezometric levels when compared with the corresponding fluctuation in the water table in an unconfined aquifer. A variation in loading on a confined aquifer may also result in fluctuation of the piezometric surface. This type of variation may be caused by barometric pressure changes, tidal and gravitational loading, passage of a railway train, or an earthquake (Domenico, 1972). This compression of the aquifer as a result of groundwater abstraction may ultimately result in the subsidence of the overlying ground surfaces.

Groundwater Utilization in the Caribbean

In the Caribbean, there are several countries in which water supply is obtained from groundwater sources. In Trinidad, 28 percent of the total potable water supply is obtained from groundwater. The largest aquifers are sand and gravel alluvial fan types that outcrop at the base of the Northern Range and spread southwards to the central plains. Urbanization encroaching on the recharge areas has reduced the quantity of recharge, resulting in a general decline in groundwater levels (Forde, 1994). In Barbados and the Bahamas, all of the water supply is obtained from groundwater. However, unlike Trinidad and Tobago, the subsurface of both territories is comprised of coral-limestone. In fact, Barbados has reached the limit of its groundwater capability and the limited surface water potential will have to be explored if the country is not to embark on the more expensive desalination option (Forde, 1995).

In some areas of Barbados, over-pumping of the aquifer results in salt-water intrusion. Due to the widespread use of fertilizers and pesticides in the sugar cane industry, these chemicals are now present in detected quantities in the groundwater in Barbados. The Bahamas protects its groundwater by mandating that wastewater be injected into deep wells. This contrasts with the shallow subsurface disposal "suckaways" for septic tanks, which are common in Barbados and have contributed to contamination of some groundwater units.

WATERSHED PLANNING AND MANAGEMENT

The molecular structure of water results in its mobility, which is one of its most significant qualities. Throughout history, this mobility has allowed man to manipulate its use, in some cases with negative consequences. A water balance determination is only one of the factors that play a role in water resource planning. The information is necessary to determine the quantity of water that is available to all users. This quantification assists decision makers in making choices pertaining to:

- The allocation of water between various users
- The management of water resources so as to minimize the effects of allocation
- The design of water-related facilities
- The protection of the environment
- The development of the resource in a manner that conserves it

Dams

Precipitation is the process by which water replenishes the Earth. There are very few parts of Earth where precipitation is distributed evenly over time. In addition, the major mechanisms that result in condensation of the water vapour in clouds and the fact that the clouds themselves are transported by air currents result in significant areal variation in precipitation.

In order to store water during periods when precipitation is low, it was necessary for man to evolve coping strategies. For many years, the primary strategy has been to build dams across river valleys in order to impound water during periods of high flow and to release this water during periods of low precipitation. This dam building trend has been so excessive that there are few major rivers that do not have dams constructed across the river valley. Many of these dams have not performed as expected. The planners have forgotten that all hydrologic computations, such as yield, sediment load, etc., are estimates. Twice during the construction of the Kariba Dam the design flood was exceeded, with loss of life and serious economic cost. The Tarbela Dam in Pakistan ran into serious difficulties as a result of geotechnical problems that added significantly to the cost. Generally, developing countries do not have a sufficiently long period of hydrologic data collection to provide enough information for design purposes. Synthetic streamflows must therefore be generated. However, most models were developed in the developed countries and their applicability to the tropics is limited. Several items are critical if a dam is to work as expected. First, there must be a rigorous determination of the yield, the safe yield, and the yield during a year when precipitation is low.

In addition, the calculation of losses due to evapotranspiration, seepage, and leakage must be performed. The dead storage or the storage that is not usable, i.e., the level below the lowest drawoff pipe, must be taken into consideration. Sediment loads have been one of the major reasons that the expected life of dams has not been realized. The designer must provide storage volume for sediment and carry out sediment load determination. Finally, it makes no sense to construct a dam on a river and then allow activity on the watershed that negatively impacts on the facility. Puerto Rico, which does not control human activity on watersheds after the construction of dams, has experienced several instances where such changes have contributed to reduced flow and increased sediment loads.

Water Yield

Water yield is a drainage basin's total yield of liquid water during a specified period of time. This yield is equal to the difference between the gross precipitation and evapotranspiration, corrected for change in storage. The water yield from a catchment can be considered to be synonymous with total discharge but "yield' is used more in the sense of a harvest. Thus, it is usually applied to total volumes, depths, or average flow rates for months, seasons, and years. Even when the reference is to instantaneous phenomena, for instance, peak discharge rates, the focus is on average factors that influence yield. The seasonal variation in water yield usually conforms to a distinct pattern or flow regime, which is dominated by the interaction of rainfall, snowmelt, and evaporation. In the Caribbean, flow rates are highest in the rainy season and lowest during the dry season.

When designing a water resource project involving an impending reservoir, there are two important hydrological studies that must be performed: (1) the evaluation of the yield from the catchment area and (2) the choice of a flood design for the spillway of the dam. A definition of yield has been suggested by the Institute of Water Engineers as follows:

> The uniform rate at which water can be drawn from the reservoir throughout a dry period of specified severity without depleting the contents to such an extent that withdrawal at that rate is no longer feasible.

As populations grow in sophistication, their demand for high quality water grows. Small reservoirs cannot provide the regulation and efficient use of water resources as can be done with large ones. The main alternative to more large dams for water supply is further groundwater development or desalination. The former has certain environmental implications and the latter is uneconomical. These large dams can, if the proper studies are done, also be an excellent means of attenuating floods that cause damage. Thus, the building of large dams is still part of the future (Rao and Gosschalk, 1994). Unfortunately, the smaller islands of the Caribbean do not have many sites for very large dams because most river valleys are small with short distances to the sea.

China's Three Gorges Scheme on the Yangtze River, which is presently under construction, will be one of the largest ever built. The dam will be nearly 2 kilometres long and 100 metres high. The reservoir will stretch 600 kilometres upstream, which is the longest ever, and one million persons will have to be relocated to make way for it. The turbines of the hydroelectric power plant will generate 18,000 megawatts which is eight times that of the Aswan Dam on the Nile. This output is 50 percent more than that of the largest existing hydroelectric dam, Itaipu in Paraguay. The dam will take between 15 and 20 years to build and there is no final cost figure available at this time. However, it is feared that the floods experienced on the Yangtze will not be ameliorated if the dam is completed. Also, the area is seismically active and landslides are frequent. Only time will tell if Three Gorges will provide all of the benefits that are expected (Pearce, 1995).

WATER RESOURCES MANAGEMENT

The management of water resources is critically important. The term management implies the control of water by people as it passes through its natural cycle. For this management to be effective, equal attention must be paid to the optimization of economic, social, and environmental benefits. There must be a broad plan for the entire drainage area, whether the project is single or multipurpose. Integrated river basin development involves the coordination and the harmonization of the various project elements in relation to all of the reasonable possibilities of the basin. This notion of integration follows from the fact that the purposes of water management are interdependent and that water as a resource must be shared between different persons and groups.

The general purpose of river basin development, as far as its hydraulic aspects are concerned, is to improve the distribution and utilization of surface water. This control of water is usually concentrated on changing its distribution, both in time and space, with the aim of making it more useful or less harmful. While the focus has been on the management of surface water, the same process must be applied to groundwater. Groundwater is subject to pollution from both solid and liquid waste, while overpumping can result in saline water intrusion. Thus, there is also a need for detailed management studies for groundwater. The three key stages in the management process are assessment, planning, and implementation.

Integrated Water Resources Planning and Management

Given the complex linkage between physical, ecological, economic, and social issues, the task of integrating planning is a challenge because of the need to blend these disparate elements into a unifying whole.

Integrated water resources planning means that multiple objectives, multiple purposes, and multiple methods must be incorporated into a systems context in addition to linking water management to other sectors of the economy, such as energy, transport, and tourism. Multiple objectives involve social, economic, and environmental elements in any water resource plan. The objectives must be treated equally rather than considering, as has been the case in the past, social and environmental aims as secondary to economic objectives. Multiple purpose projects require that there should be a balanced consideration of a wide range of water use and management purposes. Withdrawal uses, such as domestic and industrial water supply; instream uses, such as navigation, hydroelectric power, fish and wildlife, and recreation; as well as problems such as flooding and pollution, must all be included. The planner must guard against the tendency to allow single-sector water development agencies to take too narrow a focus. Environmental purposes, such as habitat maintenance, should not be neglected.

Multiple means is the strategy whereby a combination of methods is used to achieve the objectives set out in the plan. For example, the means should not be narrowly defined as the physical facilities needed to solve water problems but also the other management options, such as adjusting to water shortages or to floods.

The planning paradigm of multiple objectives, purposes, and means has to be included in the country's national planning process if full integration is to be achieved. Other national issues, such as population growth, economic and social development, international trade, and the country's energy, agricultural, transport, and infrastructure sectors also have to be included.

Integrated water resources management has been advanced as one of the mechanisms to ensure that water resources are developed in a rational manner. There are three issues that are interrelated (Hufschmidt and Tejwani, 1993):

- The natural water resource system, which includes the hydrologic cycle and "the hydrologic continuum", such as soil, biota, and the atmosphere (Leopold, 1990).
- The human activity system, comprising those activities of people that affect or are affected by the natural water

resource system. These are the "demand side" issues for water, such as irrigation, hydroelectric power, fisheries, and recreation.

- The water resources management system, which consists of those interrelationships that attempt to harmonize the supply and demand side so that the objectives of society are realized.

At the United Nations Conference on Environment and Development in Rio de Janeiro in 1992, a blueprint for survival on planet Earth, called Agenda 21, was developed by the world's leaders. The key principles for integrated water management cited in Agenda 21 were as follows:

- Water is a scarce resource and should be treated as a social and economic good.
- Water should be managed by those who use it most and all those who have an interest in its allocation and use – particularly women – should be involved in decision making.
- Water should be managed within a comprehensive framework, taking into account its impact on all aspects of social and economic development.

Although integrated water resources management has been talked about and there have been demonstrated benefits, there are many projects that have failed. That is, in spite of the technological packages available, there have been failures that have led to a loss in credibility of the concept.

Institutionalization of the Integration Process

Several factors have been identified for successful integrated water resource management to be institutionalized.

- Awareness. The linkages between activity on the upstream watershed and factors that reduce the productive base downstream must be recognized.
- Institutional arrangements. A successful water resource management programme depends upon institutional arrangements. Land tenure and ownership have been identified as key issues, whether the land is government- or privately owned or subject to common use. Generally, on the upper watershed there is the occurrence of all three.

Improper arrangements result in the exploitation of the land in such a manner that there are negative impacts.

- Problems with plan implementation. The responsible agencies have encountered problems in implementing soil conservation and watershed management programmes. Since actual land use decisions are in the hands of the watershed residents, who are generally rural farmers, they must be convinced that the programme is in their interest and that there are benefits to be obtained.
- Implementation tools. The ways of installing and operating water management measures are referred to as the implementation tools. They are closely related to the institutional arrangements. Implementation tools include legal arrangements, monetary incentives or disincentives, technical assistance, education, and research and investment.
- Organizational aspects. Watershed management programmes are generally entrusted to forestry departments. If the project is on agricultural lands, then agricultural departments are the lead agency. In Nepal and Pakistan, a separate soil conservation or watershed management department has been created to do this, with some success. A separate independent authority can be created, as in Pakistan's Water and Power Development Authority or the Philippines' National Power Corporation and National Irrigation Administration.
- Operational issues. Watershed management programmes whose major focus is on conservation provide long-term benefits. In the short term, farmers living in the watershed will not change their practices unless they understand how these changes will benefit them directly or immediately. Thus, there is a need to balance the conservation versus production conflict.
- Research and demonstration. There is a need for more research in the Caribbean and, generally, throughout the developing world.
- Training. Appropriately trained personnel is required at all levels. Generally, the persons in the top positions are university trained but the sub-professionals are not properly trained. Large numbers of suitably trained people will be required to implement successful integrated water resources management.

Since the supply of water is fixed and the demand for its use is rapidly increasing, it is necessary to embark on sustainable watershed management and practice. Water management problems are complex and the issues differ in their contextual setting. However, the main challenge is to achieve sustainability in providing the water needed for expanding populations and economies in the region. Since the policy will encompass both current and future needs, it must not only have a long-term planning horizon but should be adaptable to the changing needs.

There have been examples of excessive development planning due to over-estimates in forecasting. Although irrigated agriculture is frequently identified with such excesses, one study in England and Wales determined losses of 23.7 percent in water mains. Improvement in efficiency is a key factor in water management. A successful model of integrating a national agricultural policy and a national master plan for water can be found in Malaysia (Mather and Applegreen, 1993).

DEVELOPMENT AND USE OF WATER

The major uses of water can be classified as either in-stream or off-stream use. In-stream use is further subdivided into flow use or on-site use. Flow uses are dependent on the existence of freely running water. Included in this type of use are maintenance of fish populations and other habitat, hydroelectric power generation, and waste dilution and removal. On-site uses are those that occur when water in a stream, lake, or reservoir is used directly, for example, for recreation, navigation, and as a source of supply for off-stream use. The major off-stream uses of water are for agriculture (mostly irrigation), industry (mainly for steam generation in thermoelectric power plants), and domestic uses. Domestic uses may either be through individual supplies or through municipal systems.

Agriculture

Agricultural activity consumes by far the greatest quantity of fresh water, with most of the water being used for irrigation. About 80 percent of available water is used by agriculture, but the efficiency of water use is less than 30 percent (Clarke and Dembner, 1992). In low-income countries, agricultural water use can be as high as 90 percent of the total available supply. The use of receding floodwater as a form of natural irrigation has been practiced in the Nile Valley since about

5000 BC. In this method, crops were sown as the floodwaters receded. Hygroscopic and capillary soil moisture and the high water table permitted plants to grow and mature during long periods without rains.

As agricultural production expanded there were two major types of agriculture practiced: rain-fed and irrigated agriculture. Rain-fed agriculture supplies two thirds of the world's available crops. As the name implies, rain-fed agriculture depends on the quantity and reliability of rainfall. When the rains are late or not sufficient, the crop yields are reduced, since the water requirements of the crop are not met. Although nothing can be done to increase rainfall there are many techniques for making better use of the rainfall that does fall. Over the last four decades, the growth in food production to meet the population explosion has come from the expansion of the area under irrigated agriculture. Irrigated land is twice as productive as rain-fed crop land and the Food and Agriculture Organization (FAO) estimates that one sixth of the world's crop land that is irrigated produces about one third of the world's food (Clarke and Dembner, 1992).

In addition to the fact that only a small percentage of the irrigated water reaches the crops, there is also the problem that excessive water application to cropland results in waterlogged soils and this leads to salinization. Salinization is caused when irrigated land is not properly drained to take away excess water and as a result of evaporation there is a cumulative buildup of salt in the surface soil. In order to reverse this, the soil must be leached out by applying more water and draining it away. According to data collected by the FAO, about 10 to 15 percent of irrigated land in the world has been degraded by salinization. This figure could be much higher in individual countries, with the estimated amount in the U.S. being 27 percent. Good irrigation management requires that all irrigated lands should be drained from the start. There are wide expanses of white salt deposits in many parts of the developing countries caused by salinization. Even in the U.S., the irrigation return water to the Colorado River is so saline that the water must be demineralized by downstream farmers before it can be used on crops. Israel has dealt with the problem of more efficient water use for irrigation by pioneering drip irrigation and low-pressure systems. It has also developed crop varieties that are tolerant of water with higher salinity levels.

Industry

Industry uses less water than agriculture but the return flows from industry are much more polluted. Water is necessary for all industrial activity. Industrial water use is generally not highly consumptive and in the developed countries can account for more than 50 percent of all water withdrawals. Most of the water is used for cooling and cleaning. The water that is returned to the source is polluted with by-products of the manufacturing process. As an example of the problem with industrial return flow, some chemicals, such as methylmercury, which was used as a fungicide in the pulp and paper industry, heavy metals, and complex organic compounds, are returned to the withdrawal source and can lead to serious ecosystem damage. The large volume of water used for cooling purposes is returned to the source at elevated temperatures and thermal pollution is the result. As a result of the higher temperature, the ability of water to hold oxygen decreases and this can alter the ecology of the stream, since organisms can generally survive only within very narrow ranges of variation in temperature and dissolved oxygen.

Domestic Use

Researchers have stated that domestic water accounts for only 6 percent of the total freshwater consumption (Clarke and Dembner, 1992). It has been demonstrated that improved water supply is an important factor in reducing diseases and, when coupled with other health factors, can lead to lower mortality and morbidity in the developing countries. Such an improvement is a very necessary precondition for economic development. A considerable number of working hours are lost in developing countries as a result of poor water supply and sanitation. This loss can cripple a country in terms of the productivity expansion that is required for economic growth.

In the developed countries, the standard of service that is accepted is the provision of an individual supply of water in unlimited quantity, of acceptable quality, with a high level of reliability, for each residence. This is not possible in developing countries where the costs for providing new supplies have become prohibitive. Consequently, the concept of an acceptable minimum level of service to the greatest number of people is preferred to a situation where only a few would get good service and many would get none at all.

Domestic water as a direct consumer commodity operates as a basic component of welfare. Adequate domestic water supply is also an important input into the development process, since the ability of a country to support economic activity is related to the adequacy of its water supply. Cities, in particular, depend on domestic water supply for their daily activities and growth. Most water supply improvement in the developing countries has been in the urban areas. However, the success of agriculture in rural areas is dependent on an adequate supply of domestic water to the workers involved in this activity and also to the industry itself for agro-processing. This is the only way to sustain productivity and to reduce the attractiveness of urban centres as places for rural inhabitants to go to because amenities such as water are available there.

Water as Habitat

In addition to its other beneficial uses, which usually depend on human intervention, water functions as an important part of the ecosystem. An aquatic ecosystem is a group of interacting organisms that are dependent on one another and the water environment for nutrients and shelter. Added to the familiar examples, such as rivers and lakes, other aquatic ecosystems include sites such as floodplain marshes that are flooded with water for only a portion of the year.

A variety of life forms is usually found in aquatic ecosystems. The fauna includes bacteria, fungi, protozoans, snails, worms, and insect larvae. Flora, such as free-floating microscopic plants and large rooted plants like cattails, bulrushes, reeds, and grasses, is also present. Larger animals, such as fish, amphibians, reptiles, and birds, are common. The communities are diverse and the species distribution depends on habitat conditions that are unique to the particular type of ecosystem. Many rivers, for example, are oxygen-rich and fast flowing when compared to lakes, thus the species that are adapted to riverine conditions are very rare or may be absent from the quiescent lake waters. Fisheries contribute to human welfare directly as a source of food. About 10 to 15 percent of the total world catch of fish comes from fresh water, but in Africa 25 percent of animal protein comes from fish and this could be as high as 70 percent in some places. Aquaculture in fresh water is still growing as a major contributor to inland fisheries.

Wetlands are those lands that are saturated by surface or near-surface waters for long enough periods to promote the development of hydrophytic vegetation. In these areas, the water may be static or flowing and can range from fresh to brackish or salt. Wetlands can purify polluted water, act as buffers against floods, provide recreation, and protect against coastal erosion during high seas. Wetlands depend on large inflows of fresh water, which are evaporated or are discharged to the sea. Wetlands are often relatively large and Africa has about twenty-five wetlands which are larger than 100,000 hectares, with a total area of more than 30 million hectares (Clarke, 1994). Food, shelter, and water, which are important requirements for life, abound in wetlands. Hence, wetlands are either permanent or periodic homes to many species of animals.

Fresh Water from Sea Water

Desalination of sea water is becoming an important source of fresh water. In some countries, it is either the dominant or the only source of fresh water. Theoretically, desalination is sustainable in that there is so much salt water available. Dabbagh et al. (1993) state that in 1991 about 15.5 million cubic metres of fresh water were produced through desalination. This quantity is about one thousandth of the total fresh water that is used worldwide, according to data provided by Gleick (1993). Of the total, 7.7×10^6 m^3 per day or 49.7 percent of this desalinated water was produced by the six Arab states that make up the Gulf Cooperation Council. In this region of the world, the options for supplying fresh water are either by desalination or long distance conveyance of fresh water. Examples of the latter are Libya's artificial river, 1900 kilometres long, and Egypt's conveyance of water from the Nile to the Sinai Peninsula.

The two main types of desalination processes are distillation and membrane methods. There are two important distillation methods: multistage flash distillation (MSF) and multieffect distillation (MED). Both methods involve the evaporation of water from sea water and its condensation back into fresh water, leaving dissolved substances in the waste brine. The two major membrane processes are reverse osmosis (RO) and electrodialysis (ED). In RO, a pressure that is greater than the osmotic pressure of the feed water is applied to the feed water side of a semipermeable membrane, resulting in a flow of fresh water through the membrane. In ED, the feed water flows through a stack of membranes to which an electric voltage is applied. Ions migrate to the charged electrodes so that in the alternate spaces between the membranes there is an ion-depleted product and a concentrated reject brine stream. This method is used only for small volumes and for low to medium brackish water that must be pretreated carefully.

Desalination is an expensive way to provide fresh water but it is the only acceptable option for several of the Gulf states. In these places, where the MSF method is used to produce fresh water, this and electricity can be produced simultaneously by utilizing the waste heat from electricity generation to provide the source of heat for the distillation process. The point is that desalination is driven by the combustion of fossil fuels. Thus, there is a downside in terms of air pollution risk and the contribution of air emissions to global climate change. It has been determined by Dabbagh and Al-Saggabi (1990) that the 15.5×10^6 m^3 per day of water produced by desalination costs U.S.$ 4.09 billion per year. Unit costs for desalination in Qatar, Kuwait, and Bahrain range between U.S.$ 0.95 and 2.2 per cubic metre. This compares with $0.24/$m^3$ for Singapore, which imports water via pipelines and Tunisia, Mexico, Zimbabwe, Ghana, Malaysia, Madagascar, and the Philippines where the cost ranges between $0.08 and $0.20/$m^3$ (Dabbagh and Al-Saggabi, 1990). Thus, for the foreseeable future, desalination will be affordable only to the very wealthy nations of the world.

Due to the high costs, most of the Gulf states that are oil producers heavily subsidize the cost of desalinated water to their citizens. These high costs are comparable to the cost of the long distance conveyance of water and compare favourably in ecological and economic terms with the depletion of fossil groundwater.

During the 1991 Gulf War, Iraqi troops dismantled desalination plants in Kuwait. The oil spills that resulted from the sabotage of oil wells fouled the Persian Gulf and damaged desalination sites in Saudi Arabia. This demonstrates the vulnerability of desalination facilities.

Desalination using solar stills is another option. They are relatively easy to build and operate but the unit costs are high. This technology would be suitable for providing an individual source of supply in an area with considerable amounts of sunshine.

Water and Conflict

Disputes about the allocation and use of water can become very contentious and emotional and may involve a single country, a region, or a large portion of a continent. The transboundary nature of river basins also raises serious geopolitical questions. In Africa, the Nile River is shared by nine countries and the Niger River is shared by ten. An example of the complicated geopolitics of water is provided by the Zambezi River and its tributaries. These form the fourth largest river basin in Africa and drain 1.4 million square kilometres. The river stretches 3000 kilometres from its source in the Central African Plateau to the Indian Ocean. The river provides water for people in eight countries and 70 percent of the population of Malawi, Zambia, and Zimbabwe lives in the river basin. At present, there are no major conflicts in the utilization of the water within the river system but this will change as the countries in the basin develop their socioeconomic plans and place demands on the rivers (Mather and Applegreen, 1993).

TABLE 2.4 The World's Largest River Drainage Basins

Rank (by Drainage Basin)	Drainage Basin (1000 km²)	Discharge Rate (m³/s)
1. Amazon	6,150	175,000
2. Congo	3,822	39,000
3. Mississippi Missouri	3,222	17,270
4. Plata-Parana-Grande	3,100	22,900
5. Nile	2,802	3,000
6. Yenisey	2,619	18,000
7. Lena	2,478	16,100
8. Ob-Irtysh	2,470	10,200
9. Niger	2,092	5,700
10. Amur	2,050	9,800
11. Yangtze	1,827	32,190
12. Mackenzie	1,764	9,910

From Showers, V., 1973.

Table 2.4 lists the twelve largest river drainage basins in the world (Showers, 1973). Across the globe there are 200 river systems that are shared by two or more countries. There are also many major aquifers that extend across national borders. One school of thought postulates that future major international conflicts will arise out of disagreements over the sharing of water resources. An extreme example of the uneven distribution of water is the Congo–Zaire basin, which has less than 10 percent of Africa's population but more than 50 percent of its water.

Another area where potential conflict with respect to water resources may occur is in the Middle East, particularly over the waters of the Euphrates and Jordan rivers. The latter is shared between Israel and the Palestinians. Although Israel has a very efficient water use programme, since 1975 this country's demand exceeds the sustainable annual yield of its sources. Israel withdraws 90 percent of its groundwater and 25 percent of its surface water from Palestinian land. Israel also very strictly controls water use on the West Bank. However, Israeli settlers using better technology are able to drill much deeper wells, thus allowing them to obtain more water than their Palestinian neighbours.

Jordan has been severely affected since the 1967 war when Israel gained control of the headwaters of the Jordan River. With a 1990 annual per capita water availability of 308 cubic metres, Jordan already exploits all of its available water resources. Water shortages are now endemic and this has been recently exacerbated by Jordan's provision of refuge for thousands of migrant workers and refugees from the Gulf War. Consequently, a key element of the Arab–Israeli peace accord is the resolution of the potential for conflict with respect to the use of water resources.

Recognizing that transboundary river basin management is a key strategy of water resources management, UNESCO's International Hydrological Programme (IHP) has recommended that transboundary river basin management cannot be imposed but should come from the neighbouring states by peaceful negotiations, with the assistance, if needed, of international organizations (Van Dam and Wessel, 1993).

WATERSHED PROCESSES AND THEIR IMPACT ON WATER RESOURCES

Most watersheds have varying degrees of vegetative cover. In the Caribbean, most are covered with forests and there is agricultural activity in watersheds in many of the islands. Since these forests play an important role in water supply availability for domestic, industrial, and agricultural uses, some understanding of these watershed processes, in particular forest hydrology, is important. Similarly, activity on the watershed, whether planned logging or unplanned slash and burn agriculture, seriously impacts on water quantity and quality.

Forest Hydrology

In the tropics, whenever there are floods or landslides after a heavy rainfall event, deforestation and logging are held responsible. Similarly, droughts and low streamflow are also usually attributed to the same factors. The natural hydrologic cycle in a tropical forest is represented in Figure 2.5. Rain falling on the forest reaches the ground by three routes:

1. Between 5 and 25 percent reaches the forest floor by direct throughfall by falling through openings in the canopy without touching leaves or stems
2. 1 to 2 percent flows down the tree trunk as stem flow
3. The remainder of the rain strikes the vegetation

Of the rain striking the vegetation the largest proportion reaches the ground as drip from the canopy. However, 10 to 25 percent of all

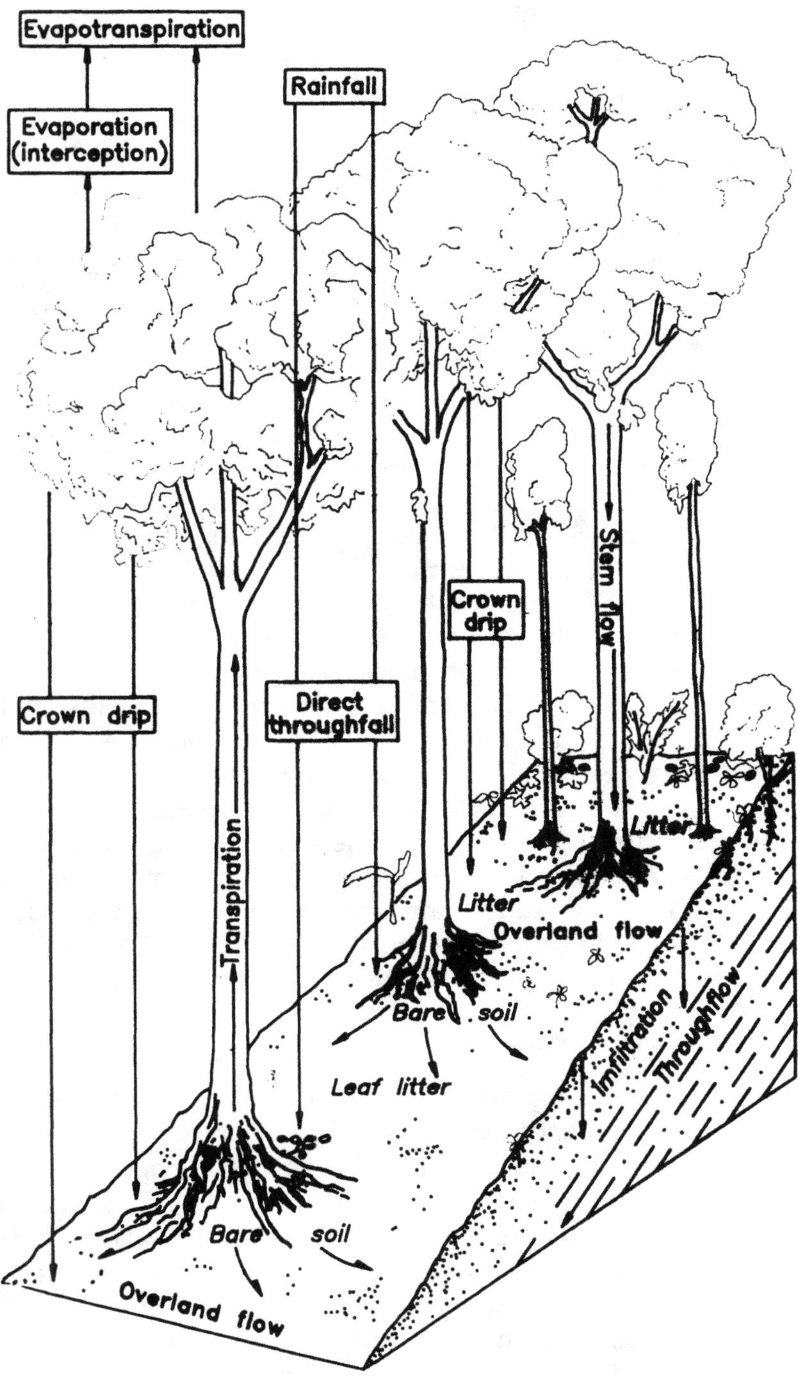

FIGURE 2.5 The hydrological cycle for a forested ecosystem.

of the rain falling onto the forest is intercepted by the leaf canopy and never reaches the ground, since it is evaporated back into the atmosphere. The total amount of water that reaches the forest floor via throughfall, drip, and stem flow is called net precipitation. The litter on the soil is important in preventing splash erosion from the rain that falls from the canopy. While it has been a popular belief that the canopies of tropical forests break the force of the incoming rain, in fact, they tend to increase it, since the raindrops on the trees coalesce, forming a film of water on the leaves, which produces drops that are larger than the original ones.

The ground vegetation in most tropical forests is sparse as a result of low levels of light. The litter layer absorbs the enhanced erosive power of the raindrops falling from the canopy. Forest soils are rich in organic matter with a high degree of faunal activity, which helps to maintain soil structure, porosity, and infiltration rates. The leaf litter protects against overland flow and erosion. Thus, the greatest proportion of the rain that reaches the forest infiltrates the soil.

There is some surface runoff from forest soils when rain falls onto soil that is already saturated. Loss of water from tropical forests occurs by two major pathways. Water can be lost through uptake by the trees and transpiration from the canopy. The amount of water lost by this route is high. So long as water is available, this could be as high as 1000 millimetres per year. That is, a large portion of the soil moisture is pumped back into the atmosphere by the forest trees. The other way that water can be lost is when the soil moisture drains downwards and encounters an impermeable layer and flows laterally as throughflow. This is a steady drain from the soil to the streams in the drainage network and accounts for the baseflow or the flow in the dry season which is found in streams.

Impact of Logging on Water Yield

Logging leads to varying degrees of disturbance of the soil and litter. The degree of disturbance depends on the system used to extract the trees. The forest floor is particularly vulnerable to damage and most of the roots are concentrated in the top 30 centimetres of soil. Access roads are cut into the forest to facilitate tree removal and these also contribute to the impact. Bruijnzeel and Critchley (1994) state that for every tree removed, a second tree is destroyed and a third is damaged beyond recovery. However, no matter how carefully the logging is carried out, there is a threshold of damage that is unavoidable. The repeated passage of heavy equipment and logs over the extraction roads results in compaction of the soil and a significant reduction in the porosity and water intake capacity of the soil. The situation is worse where there is clay.

The two researchers concluded that compaction creates problems by hampering the establishment of seedlings, since the forest floor is the seed bank from which new trees germinate. Root penetration is also reduced and the leaf litter is washed off the surface during rain.

Logging creates gaps in the forest canopy. As a result of these gaps, evapotranspiration is reduced temporarily because the trees are no longer there to pump water into the atmosphere and more rainfall reaches the soil through the gaps since less rain is intercepted by the canopy. Both of these factors increase the level of soil moisture in the gaps although there is a higher evaporative loss in the cleared areas. Bruijnzeel and Crichley (1994) report that so long as logging is limited to less than 10 percent of the area, the extra net rainfall and reduced evapotranspiration will result in increased water yield. If logging is intense and the soil disturbance is high, there will be increased water yield mainly in the form of rapid throughflow and overland flow, thus increasing the storm flow component of the streamflow.

The same report cites research in the Malaysian Peninsula that confirms that water yield is increased by logging, with the majority of the increase arising from increased baseflow. A popular perception is that logging causes flooding. However, it should be remembered that floods are a natural consequence in areas with heavy rainfall. Since logging results in the soil becoming wetter than it was previously, the additional rain that falls rapidly enters the drainage network. Consequently, more water reaches the stream network after a rainfall event.

Both erosion and sediment yields are increased after logging. This is a consequence of the removal of the leaf litter and the root mat, which protect against erosion. Splash erosion, the process by which particles of soil are detached and transported by the energy of raindrops on the soil surface, and sheet erosion, which is the transport downslope by overland flow of these detached particles, are not important in undisturbed forests. However, when the soil has been made bare and compacted by heavy machinery, then substantial amounts of sediment may be produced. In steep areas, during high rainfall, mass wasting of the soil can occur and result in landslips and bank erosion. All of this eroded material is not transported directly to the stream network but the particles may be stored temporarily lower down on the slope. The few data that exist on the extent in the increase in erosion and sediment yield as a result of logging in tropical forests are of limited scope.

Data collected by Bruijnzeel and Critchley (1994) indicate that after logging, the sediment yields may increase by two to ten times from road construction alone. Where heavy machinery is used to extract the trees, the figure can increase to twenty times. These roads and compacted tracks can become a lasting source of runoff and sediment to the streams. There are mitigation measures that may be undertaken to reduce the adverse effects of logging on streamflow. Activities should be carried out away from the drainage channels that could transport sediments downstream. Buffer strips along the sides of the streams are particularly effective in protecting the stream from disturbance, thus reducing bank erosion. These buffer strips will also filter out eroded material from the overland flow and result in reduced sediment losses. It should be recognized that buffer strips are not a panacea and should not replace the proper planning of logging operations (Bruijnzeel and Critchley, 1994).

Forest exploitation is often accused of causing substantial reductions in rainfall but it cannot be substantiated that such a relatively small reduction in evapotranspiration could cause these effects. For additional information on the relationship between forests and water regimes, see Chapter 4.

Flood and Drought

Floods and droughts are examples of extreme hydrologic events whose study is of great significance because of their socio-economic consequences. A flood is a relatively high flow that causes the river to overtop the banks in any reach of the stream. As a result of this overtopping, the water spreads over the floodplain and causes serious damage to crops, livestock, and property, and can also cause the loss of human life. In the tropics, floods are the result of rainfall events. The events may be a single large-scale event, such as rainfall produced by cyclone, hurricane, or typhoon conditions, or may be the result of small-scale and short-duration thunderstorms that are locally intense (Gladwell and Sim, 1993).

In the temperate zones, flooding may be caused by spring snowmelt, either from a larger than usual snowpack, ice jams on the river, or rapid spring thaw conditions that accelerate the volume of water carried to the streams. As long as precipitation exceeds the infiltrative capacity of the soil then runoff will occur. The runoff is channeled to the various tributaries and eventually into the main streams.

Modification of the land surface by constructing buildings and roads results in instantaneous runoff since there is no soil surface to infiltrate. This reduction in the time of concentration for the basin or the time that it takes a particle of water to flow from the top of the watershed to the mouth of the basin can result in flash flooding. Sometimes this occurs less than half an hour after the beginning of a tropical downpour.

Squatter settlements on hillsides, as is the case in Venezuela or in gullies in most Caribbean islands, exacerbate the problem of runoff. In addition, the dumping of solid waste into natural watercourses impedes the flow of water, thus leading to flooding, even when the quantity of water is not large. The flood plains in the tropics are heavily populated and it is estimated that 75 percent of the flood plains in these areas have been settled. In some cases, there is little choice in terms of where to live, as is the situation in Bangladesh. There, the flood of 1991 at the time of monsoonal storms resulted in a heavy loss of life.

The Great Flood of 1993 on the Upper Mississippi River and the Lower Missouri River Basins was an extreme event. Unlike typical flooding events that occur in the spring, this flood occurred in the summer. At Hannibal, Missouri, the Mississippi River remained above the flood stage for more than 6 months. There are many dams on these river systems but these were not enough to store all of the runoff and levees were also breached in several areas. This flood was estimated to be greater than the 100-year flood – an extreme event that occurs, on average, once in every 100 years (U.S. Army Corps of Engineers, 1994). In addition to the marooned people and livestock, major highways, bridges, and rail lines were damaged and closed for long periods. Navigation on the Mississippi River, which is a major transportation artery in the mid-western U.S., was closed down for 52 days. Water and wastewater facilities in many cities and smaller communities were shut down for long periods and people had to rely on bottled water as their only source of drinking water.

This flood occurrence demonstrates that the two common methods of flood control, structural measures, such as dams and levees, and non-structural measures, as represented by flood plain zoning, failed. The hydrologic record is the main source of information on the incidence of floods and the utilization of the floodplain. Planners can only guess, at best, about the hydrologic data and make assumptions about the probability of occurrence of a particular event. In fact, the levees along many parts of the Mississippi were constructed based on the experience of previous floods up to as late as 1973 and were expected to withstand the 25- or 50-year flood. Estimated damage totalled about $15 to $20 billion. Nature demonstrated that it is not subject to the probability rules when major flooding occurred again in 1994 in the mid-western U.S.

Many of the squatter settlements in developing countries are located on hillsides. Thus, flooding results in heavy loss of life from mudslides triggered by the excessive rainfall as well as the floodwaters. The precariously perched and structurally unsound buildings are destroyed very easily when the land is eroded. In several instances, in both Brazil and Venezuela, neighbourhoods have been covered completely by mudslides after torrential rain.

Most of the research on hydrologic extremes has focused on flood phenomena as compared to droughts, and the literature on floods is several times larger than the literature on droughts. This may be because rapid disasters are more frequently studied and draw more attention from the public and the media. One of the major problems with analysing droughts is determining when they have occurred, because drought occurrence is the interaction between hydrometeorological factors and the intended use of water. As far as the meteorologist is concerned, drought is below normal precipitation in a region. For the person involved in agricultural activity, a drought is soil moisture deficit during the growing season. The hydrologist defines drought as below normal streamflow (United Nations Environment Programme, 1992). Agricultural drought or soil moisture deficit depends on both the crop type and meteorological conditions. As far as hydrologic drought is concerned, much depends on the intended uses of water. If the area is one where there is a large storage capacity, then a short period of below normal streamflow will be insignificant. However, where the drought is of long duration but low in intensity, that is, a long period of below average streamflow, then it will be significant to those uses that depend on storage, such as operating multipurpose impounding reservoirs.

In analysing drought phenomena, one must distinguish between the cause of drought and the soil moisture or streamflow, which is the impact of drought. Water resource planners are more interested in impacts. Another important factor is the truncation level, which distinguishes drought from other events in the hydrologic record. All flows lower than the truncation level are considered as drought or low-flow periods. Droughts and floods are the opposite ends of the water surplus/deficit scale.

The social and economic results from droughts are also quite different from those of floods. The consequences of droughts are so widespread and interwoven that an assessment of damage is impossible. This contrasts with the generally short-term inconvenience of floods (Schultz et al., 1973). In the future, because of continued pressure on limited water supplies, drought problems will become even more urgent. Aspects of conservation, development, and control will be critical elements in any mitigation strategy.

The development of stochastic models in hydrology has significantly impacted drought analysis, since this allows designers to generate synthetic streamflows, which are as severe or more severe than the historic record. Such information permits water resource planners to have a broader predictive capability and thus have a better handle on the less well known of the two hydrologic extremes.

WATER QUALITY

Questions about the quality of water have engaged people's attention for many years. Over the centuries, humankind has polluted nearly every source of water, except those that are inaccessible. These areas too are becoming more rare since winds can transport pollutants over long distances and deposit them in remote areas such as Antarctica or the Arctic.

In 1977, the World Meteorological Organization (WMO), UNESCO, and the World Health Organization set up the Global Environment Monitoring System (GEMS), with the aim of developing a global water quality monitoring network. Since 1988, data were assessed and the report concluded that sewage, nutrients, toxic metals, and industrial and agricultural chemicals were the major pollutants. Water pollution was spread over both developing and developed countries. Deforestation and wetlands destruction were cited as the major contributors to increased sediments in water (United Nations Environment Programme, 1992). Pollution is said to occur when the quality of water is impaired for any of its potential uses. Water quality is defined in terms of the chemical, physical, and biological constituents in water. The water quality of surface water sources such as rivers and lakes changes with the seasons and geographic location and these changes take place whether or not pollution occurs. Thus, there is not a single criterion for water quality. Water that is suitable for drinking can be used for irrigation but irrigation water does not generally meet drinking water quality guidelines.

Factors Affecting Water Quality

The factors affecting water quality are varied. Substances present in the air, for example dust and gases such as nitrogen and sulphur oxides, are entrapped or dissolved in rain as it falls. Rain that reaches the surface can either infiltrate the soil or flow on the surface as runoff. Soil that contains soluble substances, such as limestone, or some rocks, such as ore bodies, will have high concentrations of metals. Consequently, water flowing over or through the soil will dissolve some of these substances. Generally, surface water sources have a higher concentration of particulate matter (suspended solids) and groundwater contains dissolved substances from the very long period of time that groundwater remains in contact with the soil.

These natural sources of pollutants are compounded by man's activities. Logging tends to increase sediment loads in streams, while mining increases both the sediment load and the amount of dissolved metals in the runoff. In addition to these natural sources of pollutants, industrial activity, agriculture, and urban wastewater disposal also contribute significant pollution loads to both surface water and groundwater. There are some chemicals used and produced by industry, which, when present in very small concentrations, significantly contaminate water sources.

Domestic wastewater treatment, either by central sewage treatment facilities or individual on-site systems, discharges significant pollution loads to both surface water and groundwater. For example, sewage treatment plants in the New Jersey/New York area discharge billions of gallons of treated sewage into the Long Island Sound and into several major rivers in the area. The City of Chicago discharges its treated wastewater to Lake Michigan. In rural areas and in unsewered urban areas, septic tanks release millions of gallons of partially treated wastewater into the soil. The wastewater originating from many homes contains different household chemicals that are used on a regular basis and are not removed in the treatment process in the septic tanks before the effluent is discharged into the soil.

Farming increases the concentration of suspended sediments, pesticides, and nutrients from fertilizers found in water. Agricultural runoff is diffuse and is referred to as non-point source pollution runoff, as compared to an end of pipe discharge such as that from a wastewater treatment plant or factory, which is called a point source. Non-point sources have been identified as some of the major contributors to pollution loads in streams and other surface sources. A manure pile for example or an area where empty containers for agricultural chemicals are stockpiled can be a continuing source of pollution to both surface water and groundwater. (See also chapter 7.)

Another significant source of non-point pollution is runoff from urban areas. This will contain debris that litters the streets, oil from vehicles, asbestos fibres from brake linings, materials that have been spilled and, in the temperate regions of the world, salt used for road de-icing.

Toxic chemicals are a special category of pollutants. These substances either degrade very slowly or cannot be broken down at all. When these chemicals enter water they are toxic to plants, animals, and human life, even when they are present in very minute amounts. The irony of the situation is that the qualities that make these chemicals desirable, that is, their toxicity and persistence, are the same characteristics that make them so harmful to the environment.

Groundwater contamination escaped our attention for many years because we have always subscribed to the myth that groundwater quality was implicitly better than that of surface water. The natural quality of groundwater differs from surface water in the following ways:

- The quality, temperature, and other parameters are less variable over time
- The range of groundwater parameters encountered in nature is much larger than for surface water. For example, the total dissolved solids can range from as low as 25 mg/l to as high as 300,000 mg/l for saline groundwater in the Plains of North America
- Groundwater tends to be harder and more saline than surface water
- Groundwater is usually free of disease-causing microorganisms as a result of the filtering action in the aquifer formation and the long residence times underground

Generally, groundwater is not as easily contaminated as surface water. However, once groundwater is contaminated, it is much more difficult to institute remedial measures, due to its relative inaccessibility.

Recent research on sources of groundwater contamination found that landfills, underground storage tanks (gasoline, etc.), and industrial waste disposal sites are significant contributors to groundwater pollution. In Jamaica, sodium contamination of groundwater by bauxite-alumina plants has affected a 20 km^2 area and threatened the domestic wells that supply the town of Mandeville (Fernandez, 1991).

WATER RESOURCE MANAGEMENT AND SUSTAINABILITY

Over recent decades, it has become evident that the balance sheet between the depletion and replenishment of environmental resources at the local and global levels has shown a cumulative decline. The challenge has been to determine how to stop this decline. The Report of the World Commission on the Environment and Development in 1987 referred to sustainable development as the type of development that ensures that the needs of the present are met without compromising the ability of future generations to meet their own needs (Bruntland et al., 1987). The issue of intergenerational responsibility is central to the concept of sustainability.

Definition of Water Resource Sustainability

The term sustainability, although much debated, has always been implicit in the objectives of resource managers. Farmers, foresters, fisheries managers, and water resource planners have always worked with the concept of sustained yield management. Their task has been to determine how much of a renewable resource, such as wood, fish, and water, can be reliably utilized in a particular region now and in the foreseeable future. They have been involved in the practical management of these renewable resources and their associated environments so as to achieve maximum sustained yields (Loucks, 1994).

It may be better to replace the term sustainability with "development for sustainable use". The International Conference on Water and the Environment (ICWE) in 1992 made the following assessment of the current situation:

> Scarcity and misuse of freshwater pose a serious and growing threat to sustainable development and protection of the environment. Human health and welfare, food security, industrial development and ecosystems on which they depend are all at risk, unless water and land resources are managed more effectively in the present decade and beyond than they have been in the past. (ICWE Secretariat, 1992)

When the concept of sustainability, as defined by the Bruntland Commission, is applied to water resources there are three distinct interpretations:

- As a physical concept for the single resource water only
- As a physical concept for a group of resources in a watershed or river basin
- As a socio-physical-economic-ecological concept

The first definition of the concept is too narrow, since a significant proportion of fresh water in some areas is non-renewable groundwater, which, once it has been depleted, would not be replenished for centuries. The concept also does not address the quality of the water and its temporal and spatial distribution, but looks only at quantity. The second interpretation of the concept is also too narrow, as it limits itself to sustaining quality over time and space within the watershed context. The third way of looking at the concept helps us to define sustainable water resources management as activities that ensure that the value of the services provided by a given water resource system will satisfy the present needs of society without compromising the ability of the system to satisfy those of future generations. These needs include domestic, agricultural, industrial, and recreational use, as well as ecosystems maintenance.

Early on in the development of water resources management the scope was very narrow and projects tended to focus on individual water use activities. Single purpose development grew out of development that was undertaken by private parties or by local government for domestic water supply. Multipurpose projects, utilizing a more comprehensive approach, were further steps taken. This was encouraged by technology that afforded the building of large dams for multipurpose uses. There has been opposition to these large projects as a result of their environmental impact. The further development in project planning which does not require that the project be large, as must be the case in a multipurpose project, is the idea of the coordinated management of water resources within a basin-wide framework.

This focus on basin-wide water development places emphasis on the basin as a physiographic unit for water resources planning and management. With this came the addition of constraints on the developmental process. A major one of these constraints is the added consideration of natural environmental amenities. As a result of these changes in the development process, water resources development has now become a central component of comprehensive regional development (Cox, 1987).

Water Scarcity

In each major area of water use, namely agriculture, industry, and domestic use, demand has increased rapidly. At the same time, water tables are being lowered rapidly, lakes are shrinking, and wetlands are being lost. Worldwide per capita water availability is a third lower at present than in 1970 and there is an increasing number of countries in which the population cannot be sustained by the available water.

A country is considered to be water-stressed when annual supplies of water total 1000 to 1700 cubic metres per person. The country is considered to be water scarce when the figure drops below 1000 cubic metres. When there is water scarcity, the lack of water begins to hamper economic development and human health and well being. This concept of water stress was developed by the internationally acclaimed Swedish hydrologist Malin Falkenmark. Israeli water planners would challenge this, since they have had to sustain development with less than 500 cubic metres per capita per year. Based on this index, by 1990 there were twenty-eight countries with populations totaling 335 million that experienced water stress or scarcity. It is estimated that by 2025, between forty-six and fifty-two countries will fall into these categories and the number of people affected could be in the range of 2.8 to 3.3 billion (Engleman and LeRoy, 1993). Fifteen of the twenty nations that are classified as being water scarce have a combined total of 113 million persons, which, it is estimated, could grow to 1.08 billion by 2025. With respect to island nations, Cape Verde and Barbados are running short of fresh water, the latter largely as a result of tourism developments.

Overuse of groundwater is now endemic in parts of China, India, Mexico, Thailand, the western U.S., North Africa, and the Middle East. The worst case of unsustainable groundwater use involves "fossil groundwater", which are aquifers holding water for hundreds or thousands of years that receive little replenishment from rainfall. These aquifers, like oil reserves, are essentially non-renewable. Saudi Arabia is now mining fossil groundwater to meet 75 percent of its water needs. The situation was exacerbated by the government's encouragement of wheat growing in that country. The country's wheat farmers receive payments that are four times the world's market price for the commodity. It is estimated that Saudi Arabia's groundwater will be depleted in 55 years at the present abstraction rates (Technical Centre of Agriculture and Rural Cooperation, 1995).

Libya is also depleting its fossil groundwater with projections to abstract more in order to grow food that it now imports. This agricultural expansion is Libya's response to the perceived threat to its food security. Table 2.5 is a list of those countries in which water use exceeds 100 percent of renewable water supplies. The Ogallala Aquifer, cited by Engleman and Le Roy as one of the largest in the world, underlies several states in the U.S. On the northwestern corner of Texas, the exploitation of this groundwater has reduced it by one fourth (Falkenmark, 1988). In Beijing, water tables have been dropping 1 to 2 metres a year and a third of all wells are now dry. Consequently, pumps must be set deeper so as to abstract the water from greater depths. Thus, both water and energy are being used unsustainably. In Mexico City, groundwater abstraction exceeds recharge by 50 to 80 percent and, as a result, groundwater levels have fallen and the aquifer has compacted. The resulting land subsidence has led to damage to many buildings, including the famous Metropolitan

TABLE 2.5 Countries in which Water Use Exceeds 100 Percent of their Renewable Water Supplies, with Population Doubling Times

Country	Water Withdrawals as a Percentage of Renewable Water Supplies, Late 1980s	Years Required for Population to Double at Current Rate of Natural Increase[a]
Libya	374%	20.4
Qatar	174%	33.0
United Arab Emirates	140%	24.8
Yemen	135%	21.7
Jordan	110%	19.3
Israel	110%	46.2
Saudi Arabia	106%	21.7
Kuwait	>100%	23.1
Bahrain	>100%	28.9

[a] Excludes rates of migratory flows, which are significant in some of these countries.

Sources: Adapted from Peter H. Gleick, "Water and Conflict", 1993; Population Reference Bureau, 1993 World Population Data Sheet.

Cathedral (Clarke, 1994). Bangkok, Thailand, and Jakarta in Indonesia are also experiencing land subsidence as a result of overpumping of groundwater.

Several of the larger dam building projects have not turned out to be the solution that they were intended to be because the reservoirs have silted up more quickly than expected. The Akosombo Dam flooded 5 percent of Ghana when it was completed in 1966. Lake Volta, which was created behind the dam, trapped so much of the silt from the Volta River that the capacity of the reservoir has been seriously reduced. In addition this silt, which was formerly carried to the mouth of the river in neighbouring Togo, is no longer there to protect against coastal erosion (Technical Centre of Agriculture and Rural Cooperation, 1995). Many of the dams that were constructed in Brazil when the interior was opened up are grim testimonies to sedimentation. Some of the reservoirs silted up in less than 10 years. The surrounding rainforest had been cleared for expansion of agricultural land. Of course, it should have been expected that laying bare the forest soil would have resulted in excessive erosion and rapid transport to streams in the high rainfall tropical rainforests. Dams are usually built with a theoretical life span of 50 years. However, sedimentation in Morocco's El Kansera dam caused it to become inoperative in less than 30 years. A similar problem took place in Algeria, when dams on the Fodda Wadi and Mebtouh

Wadi were silted up and the embankment had to be raised or a new dam constructed (Braun, 1994).

There is now a virtual water crisis in the countries of the South. All of the easily available sources of water have been developed and the unit costs of new sources are very high (Biswas, 1993). These countries are also grappling with young populations that are growing at a very rapid rate so that, with a one to one relationship between population and water requirements, a substantial increase in population will increase water requirements. This will be exacerbated by any rise in the standard of living, since this leads to an increase in per capita water consumption. These growing populations will also tend to contaminate and pollute freshwater resources at an increasing rate, with wastewater, agricultural chemicals, and industrial wastes.

Imports of surface water is another problem for several countries. Water flowing across the borders of another country makes some nations very vulnerable to actions over which they have little control. Egypt depends on the Nile for most of its water but the Blue and White Nile Rivers originate in other countries and pass through seven countries before joining in Sudan and then flowing into Egypt. Ethiopia, the source of the Blue Nile, is considering developing sections of the watershed, while Kenya and Tanzania plan to use Lake Victoria. Burundi, Tanzania, and Uganda are developing the Kajera River, which supplies water to Lake Victoria (Postel, 1996). Transportation of water across boundaries is not limited to developing countries. For instance, the Netherlands depends on water from outside its borders.

The Guneydogu Anadolu Project (GAP) in Turkey will harness the waters of two historically important rivers, the Tigris and Euphrates, and benefit Turkey, Syria, and Iraq. The project was initiated by Turkey without World Bank funding, since the bank insisted that a treaty on the utilization of the waters must be signed by all three countries prior to the bank providing funding for the project. Turkey obtained funding from a consortium of private financiers at a rate of 15 to 20 percent, more than if the funds had come from the World Bank. Turkey regards the project as essential for the economic development of the neglected Anatolia region. The twenty-two dams will provide hydroelectric power and water to irrigate three million hectares of land. Turkey has signed a protocol with Syria to guarantee water to that country, and Syria and Iraq have agreed on how to share the water that passes from Syria to Iraq. This project is an example of how, although political tensions may exist, transboundary transfers of water can take place (Bagis, 1993).

WATER RESOURCE MANAGEMENT: PROBLEMS AND ISSUES IN THE TROPICS

Several management problems have been identified with respect to water resources in the tropics:

- Projects are not completed on time and there are serious cost overruns
- Outputs are not achieved
- No economic feasibility studies are performed for many projects
- There is too much focus on the physical without any emphasis on management issues
- Poor operation and inadequate maintenance results in rapid deterioration of the physical infrastructure

To address these shortcomings, it is recommended that international financial agencies should encourage a more rigorous and comprehensive approach to the planning and implementation of all water resources projects (McCauley and van Beek, 1993).

Demand Analysis and Management

When analysts speak of "demand" for water they are typically referring to the use of water as a commodity or a factor of production in agriculture, industry, or household activities. This demand function for various uses of water is an essential element of information for planning. When the perception that water is a freely available resource is coupled with the fact that supply and demand are cyclic functions, then the problem is all the more complex. The demand or supply function is the functional relationship between various prices of water and the quantities used or supplied at those prices (Chaturvedi, 1987).

Water is a limited although renewable resource. Thus, there is a need for long-term planning for its utilization. It is not enough to rely on past trends because the technological, economic, and environmental conditions are all changing. In order to predict future requirements, it is necessary to carry out an exercise in technological and economic planning both within the water sector and also taking into account multisectorial and cross-sectorial issues.

One interesting area of demand management is being practiced in Israel and the western U.S. In both cases, persons who own rights to water can trade them freely to the highest bidder. These "water markets" are being touted as a promising tool for water management

(Simpson, 1994). In the case of California, there has been a significant reduction in the amount of water used for irrigation when farmers were able to sell these "water futures", either permanently or on an annual basis, as it were, to a willing buyer. Israel has combined this with an aggressive programme of wastewater reuse, thus making more fresh water available for other uses.

Options for a Sustainable Future

Sustainability with respect to water resources requires the following priority action:

- Placing issues related to the freshwater requirements of the developing countries on the international agenda. This will include special access to funding to deal with water resources issues, for both studies and implementation.
- Making water conservation and water demand management integral aspects of water resources management. Mustafa Tolba, former executive director of the United Nations Environment Programme, has stated that the next major revolution will occur when politicians demanded efficiency in the use of irrigation water. Since agriculture accounts for the largest consumption of water, it has been estimated that if agricultural demand is reduced by 10 percent, then the clock on water stress would be turned back by about 30 years.
- Demand management in terms of domestic and industrial water use is also critical. With respect to domestic water supply, this means that water audits must become as common as a financial audit for most water utilities. Audits will help to reduce unaccounted for water. Quantities lost as a result of leakage, waste, and illegal connections should be reduced to no more than 25 percent of water produced. In most developing countries this figure is 40 to 50 percent. Reduction of industrial use could involve plant process engineers reviewing their water use and developing strategies for recycle and reuse. It may also require a change in the manufacturing process. Demand management should be a mandatory component of the detailed plans for any water project.
- Reducing quick-fix solutions that are being offered to the South. Privatization is not a panacea for water problems in the South. A range of solutions needs to be considered to deal with the proper management of water resources.

- Managing basins that straddle political entities. Where water is shared by two or more countries, the situation is much more critical. Strategies must be developed to prevent hostilities between countries over water resources. These basins must be developed so as to optimize benefits for the different countries that share the resource.
- Managing the use of irrigation water. The belief in the Third World that farmers have a right to water at no cost to themselves encourages excess utilization of water resources. Subsidies for water should be tailored to the farmers' ability to pay and a close look must be taken at what types of crops are grown. Evidence shows that changes to different types of cash crops may be one solution. Another way to manage irrigation water is to organize the farms into irrigation districts or some other cooperatively organized structure that will be responsible for both allocating and scheduling water deliveries to individual farms.
- Encouraging wastewater reuse for irrigation purposes. Reuse would provide additional sources of water, and the nutrients contained in the effluent and organic matter would improve the condition of the soil. This would have the additional advantage of reducing effluent discharge to surface water or the sea. In order to increase wastewater reuse, it will be necessary for education programmes to be designed to assist in reducing the serious cultural bias that exists in many societies against using wastewater effluent.

CONCLUSION

The future for water resources in developing countries does not appear optimistic. It is estimated that by the year 2000 there will be at least eight cities in the developing world with populations greater than ten million persons. Included in the list are Sao Paulo, Calcutta, Bombay, and Jakarta. The people of these cities will have to be provided with water supply for domestic purposes and water to grow food, and the wastewater generated will have to be disposed of in such a manner as not to pollute the existing sources. In rural areas, water is continually undervalued and this does not promote efficient use of the resource. While a market approach may never be adopted with respect to irrigation water, at least it should be priced at a level which fosters proper use (Savenije, 1993). In order to manage water resources properly, many inputs will be needed. Information is a key issue. Too many decisions affecting water resources are made without basic information. The hydrological network and database of many developing countries needs to be improved.

With respect to water resources, we are no longer living on the surplus but have started to deplete the capital. If sustainable development is to be a reality, humankind needs to dramatically change its approach to the use of water resources.

REFERENCES AND FURTHER READING

Bagis, A. I. 1993. "The Euphrates and Tigris watercourse systems: Conflict or cooperation?" *Turkish Review of Middle East Studies* Annual no. 7, Istanbul, Turkey.

Biswas, A. K. 1993. "Crisis in the South". *UNESCO Courier* (May).

Bonell, M., M. Hufschmidt, and J. S. Gladwell (eds.). 1993. *Hydrology and Water Management in the Humid Tropics*. Cambridge University Press, Cambridge, U.K.

Braun, A. 1994. "The megaproject of Mesopotamia". *Ceres, FAO Review* 26, no. 2.

Bruijnzeel, L. A. and W. R. S. Critchley. 1994. *Environmental Impacts of Logging Moist Tropical Forests*. IHP Humid Tropics Programme Series no. 7. UNESCO, Amsterdam.

Brundtland, G. H. et al. 1987. *Our Common Future, Report of the World Commission on the Environment and Development*. Oxford University Press, Oxford, U.K.

Chaturvedi, M. C. 1987. *Water Resources Systems Planning and Management*. Tata McGraw-Hill, New Delhi, India.

Clarke, R. 1994. *Water for Life*. Food and Agriculture Organization, Rome.

Clarke, R. and S. A. Dembner. 1992. *Safeguarding the World's Water*. UNEP Environment Brief no. 6, United Nations Environment Programme, Nairobi, Kenya.

Cox, W. E. (ed.). 1987. *The Role of Water in Socio-Economic Development*. International Hydrological Programme (IHP) Report. UNESCO, Paris.

Dabbagh, T. et al. 1993. *Desalination: The Neglected Option*. Kuwait Economic Development Fund, Kuwait.

Dabbagh, T. A. and A. Al-Saggabi. 1990. *The Exorbitant Cost of Water in Africa: Contributing Factors*. All-Africa Water Supply and Sanitation Conference, Abidjan, Cote d'Ivoire.

Dixon, J. A. and L. A. Fallon. 1989. "The concept of sustainability: Origins, extensions and usefulness for policy". *Society and Natural Resources* 2, no 2.

Domenico, P. A. 1972. *Concepts and Models in Groundwater Hydrology*. McGraw-Hill, New York.

Driscoll, F. G. 1986. *Groundwater and Wells*. Johnson Division, St. Paul, Minnesota.

Engleman, R. and P. Le Roy. 1993. *Sustaining Water: Population and the Future of Renewable Water Supplies*. Population and Environment Programme. Population Action International, Washington, D.C.

Falkenmark, M. 1988. *Sustainable Development as Seen from a Water Resources Perspective*. Stockholm Studies in Water Resources Management, no. 1. Stockholm, Sweden.

Fernandez, B. 1991. "Caustic waste contamination of Karsitic limestone aquifers in two areas of Jamaica". Report for the Underground Water Authority, Kingston, Jamica.

Forde, L. H. 1994. "Groundwater management in Trinidad and Tobago". University of Mauritius/CSC Workshop on Groundwater Modelling, 13–18 June, Reduit, Mauritius.

Forde, L. H. 1995. "Sustainable water resources management. The case of Barbados". University of the West Indies, Centre for Environment and Development/CSC Workshop on Water Resources Problems in Small Island Developing States, August 1995, Bridgetown, Barbados.

Freeze, R. A. and J. A. Cherry. 1979. *Groundwater*. Prentice Hall, Englewood Cliffs, New Jersey.

Gladwell, J. S. and L. K. Sim. 1993. *Tropical Cities: Managing their Water*. IHP Humid Tropics Programme Series no. 4. UNESCO, Paris.

Gleick, P. H. (ed.). 1993. *Water in Crisis: A Guide to the World's Freshwater Resources*. Oxford University Press, New York.

Goldman, D. 1985. *Stochastic Analysis of Drought Phenomena*. Hydrologic Engineering Centre, U.S. Army Corps of Engineers, Davis, California.

Hufschmidt, M. M. 1993. "Water policies for sustainable development". In A. K. Biswas and M. Abu-Zeid, eds., *Water for Sustainable Development in the 21st Century*. Oxford University Press, Oxford, U.K.

Hufschmidt, M. M. and K. G. Tejwani. 1993. *Integrated Water Resources Management: Meeting the Sustainability Challenge*. IHP Humid Tropics Programme Series no. 5. UNESCO, Paris.

ICWE Secretariat. 1992. International Conference on Water and the Environment. Keynote Paper, Dublin, Ireland. WMO, Geneva, Switzerland.

Karamath, K. R. 1989. *Hydrology*. Tata McGraw-Hill, New Delhi, India.

Leopold, L. B. 1990. "Ethos, equity and water resources". *Environment* 32, no. 2.

Linsley, R. K., Jr. et al. 1988. *Hydrology for Engineers*, 3rd edition. McGraw-Hill, New York.

Loucks, P. 1994. *Water Resources Management, Focusing on Sustainability*. IHP, UNESCO, Paris.

Mather, T. H. and B. Applegreen. 1993. *Policies, Strategies and Planning for Integrated Rural Water Management*. Proceedings of the Food and Agriculture Organization Technical Consultation on Integrated Rural Water Management, 15–19 March, 1993. Food and Agriculture Organization, Rome.

Mcauley, D. S. and E. Van Beek. 1993. "Water Resource Management Workshop". In M. Bonnel et al., eds., *Hydrology and Water Management in the Humid Tropics*. Cambridge University Press, Cambridge, U.K.

Nace, R. L. (ed.). 1971. *Scientific Framework of World Water Balance*. Technical Paper Hydrology, 7. UNESCO, Paris.

Pearce, F. 1995. "The biggest dam in the world". *New Scientist* (28 January).

Postel, S. 1993. "Running dry". *UNESCO Courier* (May).

Postel, S. 1996. "Sharing the rivers". *People and the Planet* 5, no. 3.

Rao, K. V. and E. M. Gosschalk. 1994. "The case for impounding reservoirs: An engineer's viewpoint". *International Journal on Hydropower and Dams* 1, no. 6.

Savenije, H. H. G. 1993. "A framework for analysis to enhance efficiency in agriculture and urban water use". *Proceedings of Technical Consultation on Integrated Rural Water Management*, 15–19 March. Food and Agricultural Organization, Rome.

Schultz, E. F. et al. (eds.). 1973. *Floods and droughts. Proceedings of 2nd International Symposium on Hydrology.* Water Resources Publications, Fort Callairs, Colorado.

Showers, V. 1973. *The World in Figures*. John Wiley & Sons, Toronto, Canada.

Simpson, L. D. 1994. "Are 'Water Markets' a Viable Option?" *Finance and Development* 31, no. 2.

Speidel, D. H. et al. (eds.). 1988. *Perspectives on Water: Uses and Abuses*. Oxford University Press, Oxford, U.K.

Technical Centre of Agriculture and Rural Cooperation. 1995. "Water, the limiting resource". *SPORE* bimonthly bulletin of CTA, Wageningen, The Netherlands.

United Nations Environment Programme. 1992. *Freshwater Pollution*. UNEP/GEMS Environment Library no. 6, Nairobi, Kenya.

U.S. Army Corps of Engineers. 1994. *The Great Flood of 1993. Post-Flood Report, Upper Mississippi River and Lower Missouri River Basins*. U.S. Army Corps of Engineers, Chicago.

Van Dam, J. C. and J. Wessel (eds.). 1993. "Transboundary river basin management and sustainable development". *Proceedings of Lustrum Symposium*. IHP UNESCO, Paris.

3

Living Aquatic Resource Management

Robin Mahon

Contents

INTRODUCTION

Caribbean fishery resources are generally either fully or overexploited. Therefore, the main task for fishery managers will be to rebuild them and to establish management systems that will permit the sustained harvest of yields at levels that will provide the optimal return to society without compromising the harvesting options of future generations. Offshore fisheries for large pelagic fishes may be an exception in which there is scope for expansion. The standard assessment model-based approach to fisheries which has predominated in the past has not been effective. In fact, it has been fraught with uncertainty. More importantly, we have probably overestimated our ability to control fisheries, particularly when the approach taken is not accepted by the majority of users. For resources whose value merits substantial investment in research, efforts to quantify uncertainty and risks may lead to better management advice. For other resources, whose values do not justify such expenditure, the emphasis must be on making the best use of available information and taking action based on a combination of technical information and common sense. For all resources, fishery managers must involve the interested parties and develop approaches that are agreed upon by all. Ultimately, living aquatic resource management must be carried out within the broader contexts of ecosystem management and integrated coastal and marine area management.

THE NATURE OF THE MANAGEMENT SYSTEM

Living aquatic resource management involves a complex interplay of biological, sociological, anthropological, economic, and political factors. These components interact at local, national, and international levels. This chapter deals largely with the management of exploited living aquatic resources (fisheries) but also considers the non-consumptive use of aquatic resources for recreation, education, and conservation of biodiversity; aspects that are also dealt with in other chapters. This chapter takes the approach of introducing readers to the main concepts involved in living aquatic resource management, particularly the newer ones and those that relate to the Caribbean region, and of referring readers to the key literature available for fuller treatment of the topics discussed.

One attempt to summarize the multidisciplinary, multi-institutional nature of living aquatic resource management and to recognize its many components is shown in Figure 3.1. It is the framework for this chapter and should be seen only as a basis for discussion. The sequence on the left is common to many activities, beginning with strategy formulation and moving through data acquisition and analysis to implementation. The remainder of the figure illustrates the fact that fishery management is not so much about managing resources, as about managing of the people who exploit them.

The management sequence is implemented primarily by the entities within the box entitled "Fisheries Management System" which includes both government institutions and the fishing industry. The industry participants, all of whom play an important role and must interact with the government, range from large-scale commercial fishing and processing companies to individual small-scale fishers. A wide variety of information, biological, economic, and social, is required as input to the fishery management decision making process. The result should be a fisheries management plan (FMP) that is essentially a contract between

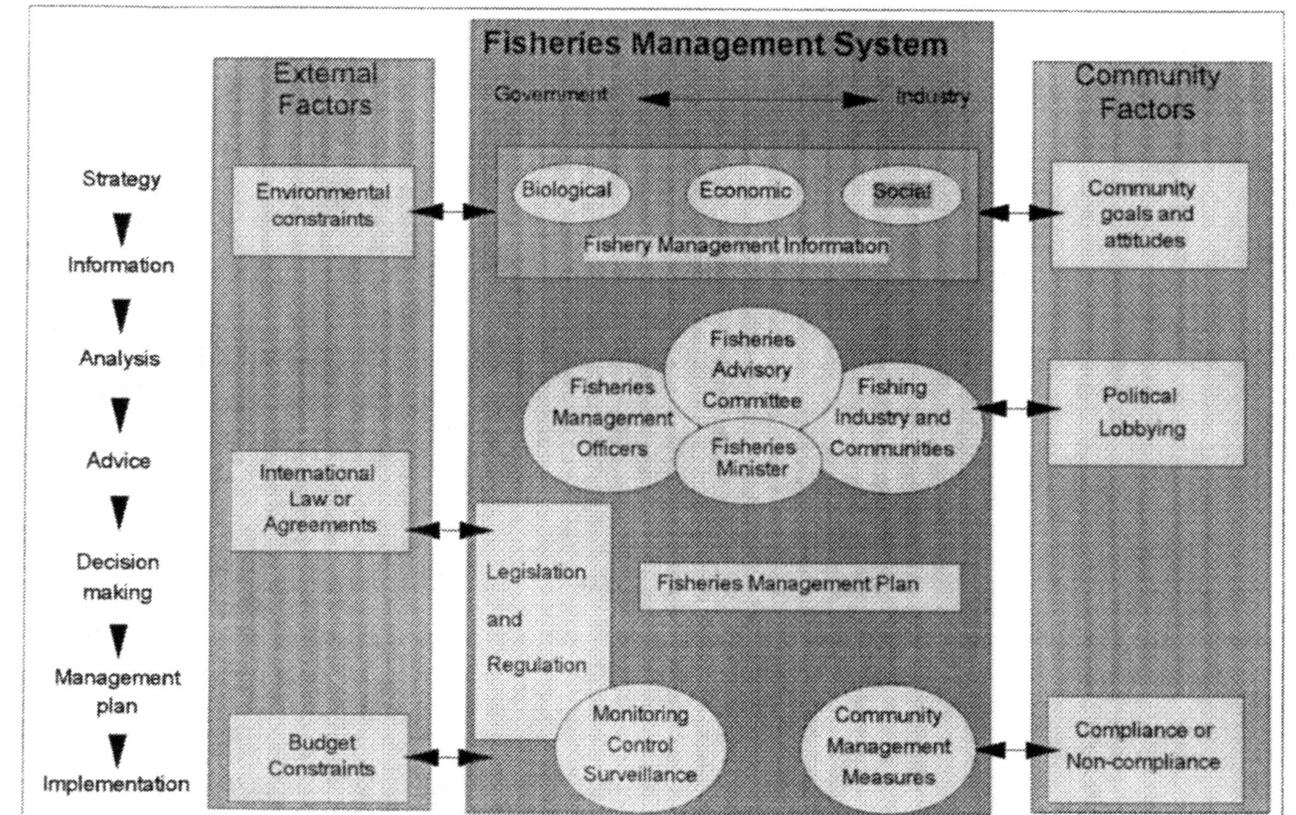

FIGURE 3.1 A view of fisheries management systems indicating the process and interplay of components (after CFRAMP, 1995).

the government and the interested parties. The FMP is based on legislation and regulation, and leads to government-based monitoring, control, and surveillance of fisheries, or to community-based management measures. These components are considered in greater detail later in the chapter.

The fishery management system is also subject to external factors, such as the effects of the environment, the context of various international laws and agreements, and, by no means least, financial constraints related to the national economy and the national budget for fisheries management. Also of considerable influence are community factors, such as the goals and attitudes of individuals in fishing communities and in the community at large, and the political lobbying of various interest groups that are not part of the fishing industry but have concerns about the health of the fisheries system. Together, they significantly influence the extent to which the fishing industry is inclined to participate in the fishery management process.

What is it about fisheries that requires, or results in, such a complex system of management? To answer this, it is useful to look briefly at the historical development of attitudes and approaches toward fisheries resources and fisheries management.

Trends in Fishery Management

In the late 1800s, even though fishery yields were observed to fluctuate considerably, the resources of the ocean were thought to be so vast as to be virtually inexhaustible. By the early 1900s, however, it had become apparent that fish stocks were being impacted by fisheries, and scientists began to develop a theory of exploited fish stocks based on population dynamics. This approach to fisheries was described by Beverton and Holt in 1957, in *On the Dynamics of Exploited Fish Populations*, which dominated fishery science for several decades until scientists in the late 1970s and 1980s began to pay more attention to the interactions among species and what are referred to as multispecies approaches to fisheries management. Owing to the complexity of the marine ecosystem and species interactions, multispecies approaches prove to be very difficult and single-species population dynamics continues to play a major role in fishery management. Most recently, the complexity has led fishery scientists to take a more holistic approach to fishery management. This is best reflected in a rapidly developing body of literature on "large marine ecosystems" studies, which attempt to take into account all aspects of the ecosystem in which the exploited resources live (Sherman et al., 1993).

Concurrent with the above changes in the perception of fishery management, world fishery landings have grown steadily from about four million metric tons in 1900 to about 97 million metric tons in 1990 (about 15 percent comes from inland waters). An historical review of world catches and of the current distribution of catches among the regions of the world is provided by the Food and Agriculture Organization (FAO, 1994). The steady increase in landings has disguised a sequence of events in which many of the world's largest conventional fishery resources (demersal and pelagic) have been overexploited, only to be replaced by lower value resources such as small pelagics and by nontraditional species such as invertebrates. Recent trends suggest that we may be approaching the limits of the fishery production capacity of the world's oceans.

Fisheries management, as it has been practiced in the past, is widely perceived as having failed. In addition to the dramatic decline of major stocks such as the Peruvian anchovy, the North Sea herring, and, most recently, the northern cod in the northwest Atlantic, overfishing of smaller stocks has been widespread. Some examples relevant to the Caribbean are reef fishes, conchs, blue marlin, and bluefin tuna. Although there have been problems with the technical basis for management, for example, failure to embrace uncertainty or to address multispecies/ecosystem concerns, problems of implementation appear to be more significant (Hilborn and Walters, 1992). Notably, the failure to restrict access and thus avert the "Tragedy of the Commons" is the primary cause of overfishing (FAO, 1993a).

The unsatisfactory performance of fishery science and management procedures to date and the likelihood that we are approaching the limits of marine fishery production call for a significant change in the global approach to management of fisheries (Ludwig et al., 1993; FAO, 1993a). A new era for fishery management, one of rehabilitation and husbandry of resources for sustainable production, is needed. While scientists and conservationists have been promoting this approach for several decades, it has only been incorporated into the political agenda within the past few years. This is due largely to the 1992 United Nations Conference on Environment and Development (UNCED) which produced Agenda 21 (United Nations, 1992) the manifesto of follow-up actions needed which was adopted by the majority of coastal nations.

There have been several fishery-specific and related follow-up activities to UNCED. Issues of concern to small island developing states (SIDS) were addressed at the Global Conference for Sustainable Development of Small Island Developing States (held in Barbados in

1994). Among coastal states, SIDS have a particularly high stake in marine management since their ratio of marine to land area or population is significantly higher than for mainland states (Mahon, 1996b). Two areas of focus by the United Nations are the development of a Code of Conduct for Responsible Fishing (FAO, 1995a) and the development of guidelines for the management of straddling stocks and highly migratory stocks, as outlined in the United Nations agreement for the conservation and management of straddling fish stocks and highly migratory fish stocks (United Nations, 1995). Both of these include adaptation of the precautionary approach (Principle 15 of the Rio Declaration on Environment and Development; United Nations, 1992) to fisheries (FAO, 1996).

The initiatives described above, the apparent increased receptivity by the political directorate to new ideas about fisheries management and marine resource conservation, and the availability of the United Nations Convention on the Law of the Sea (UNCLOS; United Nations, 1983) as a framework for change, are positive signs that mankind is willing to learn from experience and enter a new era.

THEORETICAL BASES OF LIVING AQUATIC RESOURCE MANAGEMENT

Ultimately, the sustainable use of any living resource depends on the conservation of the resource and of its ecosystem. This is well recognized in the UNCLOS and elaborated upon in Agenda 21. The scientific basis for conservation includes all aspects of population and ecosystem ecology, a more in-depth discussion of which may be found in basic ecology texts. Here, the reader is introduced to some of the key concepts that relate to exploited populations and their ecosystems.

Single-Species Population Models

Fishery scientists refer to the population units that they manage as *stocks*. A population unit is a group of interbreeding individuals of the same species. Ideally, management should deal with populations, but in some cases, the extent of interbreeding between subpopulations is sufficiently low that each can be managed separately, and is referred to as a stock. In reality, stocks may be defined for management purposes without a full knowledge of the extent of interbreeding with other stocks, simply because the information is not available, or for practical reasons, for example, part of the stock lies outside the jurisdiction of the management authority. In such cases the management authority must allow for the resulting uncertainty.

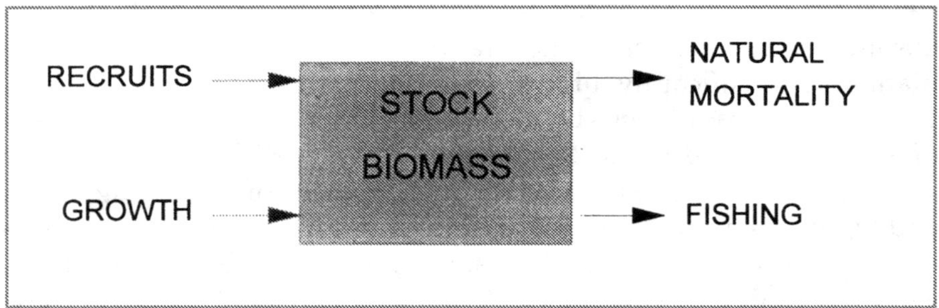

FIGURE 3.2 The simple box model of an exploited fish stock showing the factors that tend to reduce and increase stock biomass (after Ricker, 1975).

Fishery management usually relies on quantitative population models. The simplest conceptual population model is the box model of Ricker (1975; Figure 3.2). The *stock biomass*, its wet weight, usually measured in metric tons (mt) (1 mt = 1000 kg), is increased by the *growth* of existing individuals and by reproduction, which results in the *recruitment** of new individuals to the stock. It is decreased by deaths that may be due to natural causes, *natural mortality*, or to fishing, *fishing mortality*. The biomass reduction due to fishing mortality is referred to as the *yield*. Immigration and emigration are also causes of local biomass change but if the stock has been properly defined, they should not affect overall stock biomass.

When the rates of change of biomass, growth, recruitment, and mortality are described mathematically, the above conceptual model becomes a mathematical model. As previously mentioned, fishery scientists have placed considerable emphasis on developing quantitative models and on methods for measuring the various rates, the study of *fish population dynamics*. The use of these models to describe exploited populations and to predict the yields that can be harvested from them is the process of *fish stock assessment*. Detailed technical treatment of the models and methods used in fish stock assessment can be found in standard fisheries texts (for example, Ricker, 1975; Gulland, 1983; Clark, 1985; Hilborn and Walters, 1992). An overview is provided here of concepts and terminology.

The relationship that describes how fishing mortality (F) results in yield (Y) from a stock with biomass (B) is fundamental to most fishery models:

---

* Fishery scientists also refer to recruitment of individuals to the fishery of fishing gear. These individuals will have been in the stock for some time, but will be just becoming available to the fishing gear.

$$Y = FB$$

The fishing mortality is the result of fishing effort (f), such that:

$$F = fq$$

where q is the catchability constant.

Fishing effort is an important concept in fisheries. The units of measurement of fishing effort will vary from fishery to fishery and could include time spent fishing, number of times a particular gear is used, number of hooks fished, and length of net set. For a given type of fishery, effort units may vary in precision, for example in a trawl fishery effort may be measured in days fished, hours fished, trawl sets made, or distance towed. The catch per unit of effort (CPUE) or catch rate, as it is sometimes termed, is assumed to be directly proportional to the stock biomass:

$$CPUE = qB$$

Consequently, CPUE is frequently used as an index of stock biomass in fishery analysis. The monitoring of catch and effort is fundamental to fishery management. Even if no population analysis is carried out, catch and effort data are essential in order to determine if there are changes in stock biomass.

The simplest population model used in fisheries is based on the logistic or sigmoid population growth curve shown in Figure 3.3a. The rate of growth, which equals the rate of biomass production, of a population that grows according to the sigmoid curve is lowest at high and low biomass levels and highest at intermediate levels. The unfished biomass of the population fluctuates around a carrying capacity that is determined by the productivity of the environment, predators, and competitors.

As a fishery develops, and the fishing effort removes biomass, the stock biomass shifts to a new equilibrium at which the amount that can be removed in a given time equals the amount that can be produced. The relationship between fishing effort and the equilibrium amounts that can be removed each year is described by a parabola (Figure 3.3b). These amounts are referred to as the *surplus production*, and the models as *surplus* or *general production models*, of which there are several variations. These models do not treat growth, recruitment, and natural mortality separately. They deal with the combined effect of these variables on population production.

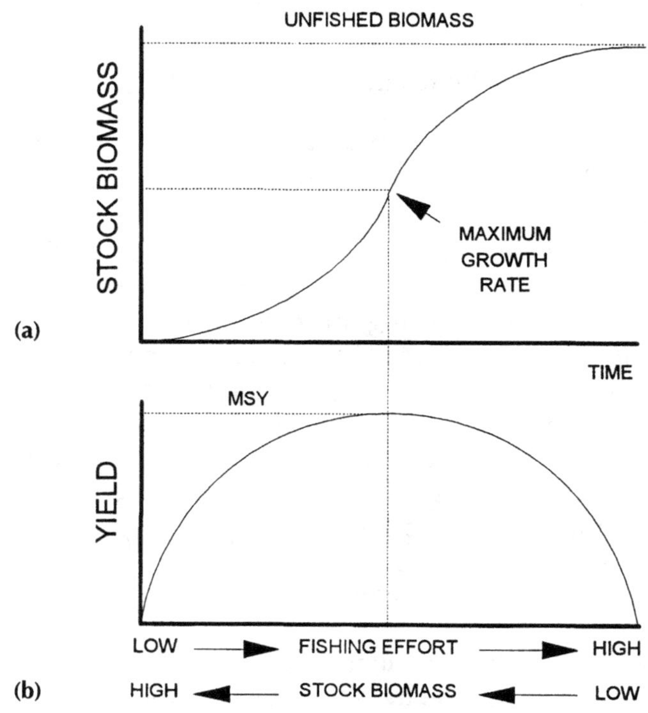

FIGURE 3.3 (a) The logistic population growth curve, and (b) the resulting general or surplus production model of an exploited population.

The point at which production, and thus potential yield, is highest is called the *maximum sustainable yield* or MSY. This has been a target of fishery management for many decades. One definition of overfishing is when the effort is greater than, and thus the stock biomass is less than, that which produces MSY. Managers now realize that because biological production fluctuates, mainly due to environmental variability, it is impossible to take the equilibrium MSY from a stock, year after year, without severely depleting the stock biomass. It is also important to note that high amounts of catches in the early stages of development of a new fishery include the removal of existing biomass as well as annual production and are therefore not sustainable.

Models that specifically consider growth, mortality, and recruitment factors are called *analytical* or *dynamic pool models*. When fish stocks consist of individuals of several ages, these variables are usually modelled on an age-specific basis using *age-structured models*. Each age group or age class is referred to as a *cohort*, which moves through the population increasing in individual size due to growth and decreasing in numbers due to mortality. Growth and mortality interact in such a way that the cohort biomass increases (growth greater than mortality) to a maximum, then decreases (mortality greater than growth) until all individuals have died. The age or mean fish size at which the cohort biomass is maximal would be the point at which the greatest yield can be taken from that cohort (if all individuals could be harvested at once). If the fishery catches fish that are on average younger or smaller then *growth overfishing* is said to take place, and a reduction in fishing mortality can be expected to result in an increase in the yield from a given number of recruits. The analysis of natural mortality, fishing mortality, and growth to determine the optimal age or size of capture for the cohorts of a stock is called *yield-per-recruit* (Y/R) analysis.

Yield-per-recruit analysis is aimed at optimizing yield in relation to growth and mortality. However, it does not consider the maturity schedule of the fishes. If few individuals have matured and reproduced by the age or size which the Y/R analysis indicates is optimal for harvesting, then maximizing Y/R may deplete the biomass of mature individuals in the stock, the *spawning stock biomass*, below the point at which the stock can replenish itself. This is called *recruitment overfishing*. One approach to preventing recruitment overfishing has been to examine relationships between stock biomass and the amount of recruitment produced by that biomass, *stock recruitment analysis*. A theoretical stock recruitment relationship is shown in Figure 3.4. In reality, stock recruitment analysis has been found to have limited application (primarily for salmon) and the recent emphasis has been on defining appropriate levels of spawning stock biomass based on other criteria (Goodyear, 1993; Mace and Sissenwine, 1993). A spawning stock biomass of 30 to 40 percent, the unfished level, is now gaining acceptance as a minimum.

Multispecies and Ecosystem Considerations

A multispecies fishery is one in which several species are caught together by the same fishing operation. The need for multispecies and ecosystem perspectives in fishery management has been frequently noted (Mercer, 1982; Sugihara et al., 1984). There is a focus on three types of interactions:

Technical interactions – The technical problem of managing sets of species that are harvested together, regardless of whether there are any biological interactions among them;

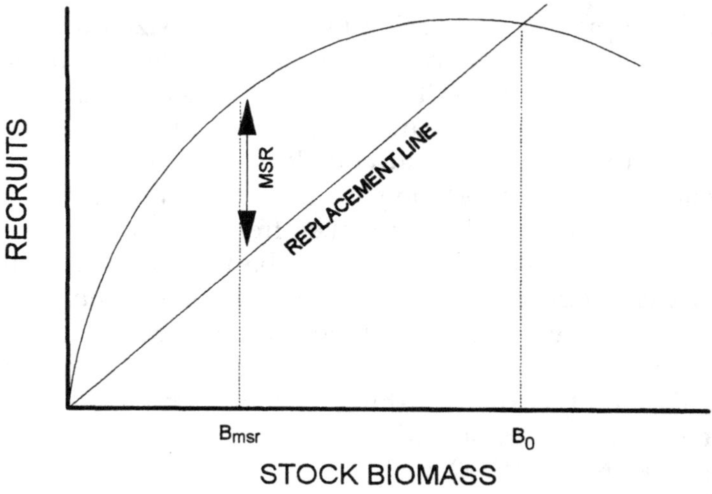

FIGURE 3.4 A stock-recruitment relationship showing the unfished equilibrium B_O, and the maximum surplus recruitment MSR, which is the point at which the difference between replacement biomass and recruitment is greatest.

Species interactions – Primarily the effect of predation and competition on the population responses of the species for which management advice is being provided;

Ecosystem interactions* – The effect that the reduction of biomass of exploited species may have on the other organisms or habitats in the ecosystem of which they are a part.

Fisheries scientists have recognized the potential impacts of these relationships on the probability of success of management based on single-species models, and have devoted considerable effort over the past two decades to developing practicable solutions to these problems. Formal incorporation of these considerations into management advice, however, has been difficult to achieve.

Technical Interactions

The major problem with harvesting several species from an assemblage using a single unselective type of gear, such as a trawl or fish trap, is that the species will have different life history characteristics and, consequently, different responses to exploitation. Thus, some species will be overexploited and others underexploited.

---

* Clearly, species interactions play a leading role in ecosystem responses to exploitation. Nonetheless, the latter two categories are intended to distinguish between population level and ecosystem level phenomena.

There is increasing concern about the direct physical effect of fishing activities on marine habitats (EEC, 1994). For example, trawling and dredging directly affect benthic habitats and communities. Therefore, based on the rate of regeneration of the community, it may be desirable to limit fishing to a level at which the total area trawled in any year does not exceed some proportion of the total trawlable area.

The direct effects of fishing on non-target species are also of concern (EEC, 1994). Sea birds, turtles, and mammals are primary examples of the casualties in such an approach to fishing. In the case of turtles, incidental catches are limited by the use of turtle excluder devices (TEDs). However, these increase fishing costs (Gibbons-Fly et al., 1994). Another notable example is the tuna purse seine-dolphin interaction in the east-central Pacific in which concern over the capture of dolphins in tuna purse seines has dramatically affected tuna fishing practices and management procedures.

Species Interactions

The UNCLOS (United Nations, 1983) considers the potential impact that fishing one resource may have on others. These kinds of impacts are likely to be most pronounced for species that are competitors, predators, or prey of the target species, or are taken as bycatch. The explicit recognition and quantification of these types of interaction has not been common in fishery management. The information requirements generally go beyond the level of knowledge presently available for most marine ecosystems, though there are various instances in which interactions of coexisting species are considered.

Predator-prey situations have long been of concern to fishery scientists (Clepper, 1979). Pauly (1979) emphasizes the trade-offs in attempting to exploit both predator and prey. In some situations management has provided for the food requirements of a predator when the prey is harvested, for example capelin management off eastern Canada (Shelton et al., 1993) and Norway (Norwegian Ministry of Foreign Affairs, 1993).

More formal, model-based approaches of taking species interactions into account have included attempts to link single-species models together by including terms for the interactions, notably predation. The multispecies models for the North Sea are notable examples. These models incorporate the trade-offs between exploiters of different ecosystem components but are extremely data intensive. At the present time, there are few systems for which the data for this type of approach are available.

An alternative approach to dealing with the effect of species interactions on yield from an assemblage of coexisting species is to combine them into a single analysis which assumes that the behaviour of the combined biomass will be similar to that of a single species. This approach has been used to estimate MSY for coral reef fisheries in which there are too many species to attempt single species analyses (Medley et al., 1993).

Ecosystem Interactions

Another area of concern regarding the sustainability of fishery production is that the significant reduction of biomass of several, possibly keystone, species from an ecosystem will bring about changes in the system which may be precipitous and possibly irreversible. Many ecosystems have exhibited significant changes in response to exploitation, although this has often been confounded with environmental changes and with pollution. Notable examples are the demersal assemblages off the north-eastern U.S. and in the Gulf of Thailand (Saila, 1993). Similarly, several studies have noted the effects of fishing on the species composition of coral reef fish assemblages (Medley et al., 1993).

Concern about ecosystem responses to exploitation extends beyond the effects on fisheries outputs to include aspects of overall ecosystem health, stability, and biodiversity (United Nations, 1993, Chapter 17; Norse, 1993; Gimbel, 1994). In attempting to encompass these concerns, Sherman (1994) takes a broad ecological view of the sustainability of biomass yields from marine ecosystems. He promotes the use of the large marine ecosystem (LME) concept as a context for management of renewable resources. In this context, management decisions would have to be viewed in the light of their expected impacts on the entire ecosystem. He cites several LMEs in which an holistic approach to management is being attempted (the Yellow Sea, Benguela Current, Great Barrier Reef, North-west Australian Shelf, and Antarctic marine ecosystems) or is being developed (the Black Sea, Barents Sea, North Sea, and North California Current ecosystems; see Sherman et al., 1993 for basic descriptions of these systems).

For the most part, initiatives towards ecosystem level management are at the stage at which efforts are being made to develop conceptual reference points or guidelines and define the research and monitoring needed to address the major questions (Holling, 1993; Apollonio, 1994; Sherman, 1994). Indeed, there are significant challenges involved in providing descriptions of ecosystem health, even without reference to the impacts of exploitation (GESAMP, 1994). Converting these conceptual approaches into quantitative models that can be used

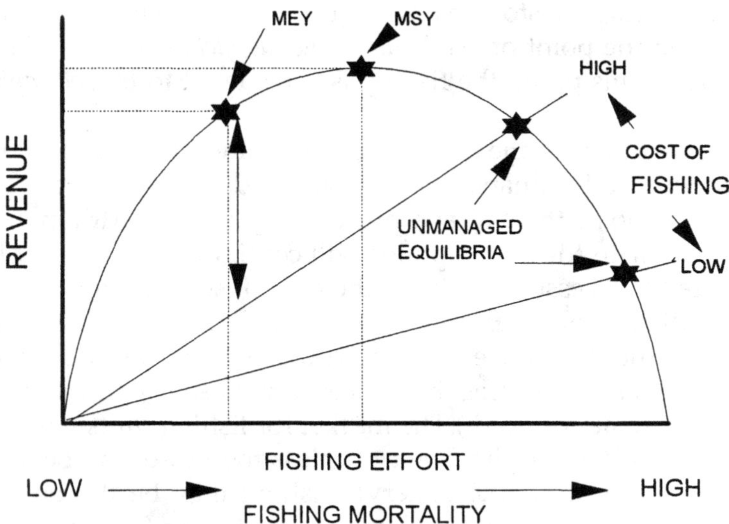

FIGURE 3.5 The bioeconomic model of fisheries, based on the surplus production model (Figure 3.3), showing key points on the curve.

routinely in support of management decisions will take time and negotiation (Norse, 1993).

There are also a number of institutional issues that must be addressed. At both national and international levels many of the important components of ecosystems cut across issues of health, trade, tourism, transportation, *inter alia*, and are beyond the current terms of reference of institutions charged with marine resource management. Nonetheless, as these concepts evolve towards applicability, they can still provide a context within which fishery managers can attempt to understand the effects of their decisions on the systems they are managing (Apollonio, 1994).

The Bioeconomic Model

The surplus production model described above was expanded to include economic aspects of fisheries (Gordon, 1954). In the bioeconomic model yield in weight on the y-axis is replaced by revenue in currency units (Figure 3.5). If the value of fish does not vary with the total yield, then the yield and revenue curves have the same shape. Otherwise, they differ in shape, with the peak being flattened when the value is inversely related to supply. The total cost of fishing is shown as a linear function of effort, that is, the cost per unit effort is constant. The total profitability of the fishery is the difference between the cost line and the revenue curve. Profit is maximized at a somewhat lower fishing effort (higher stock biomass) than that which produces MSY. This is called the point of *maximum economic yield* (MEY). At levels of effort beyond this point, the fishery is considered to be *overcapitalized* (Clark, 1985).

The point at which the cost and revenue lines intersect is the point towards which all unmanaged fisheries tend, the *unmanaged equilibrium*. At this point the average profitability is zero. Although those fishing units with the best captains will continue to be profitable and to upgrade their vessels and gear, the overall scenario for the fishery is usually dismal. New fishing units are seldom inclined to enter the fishery, and those that are already in the fishery may be unable to leave. (Many fishing vessels have been purchased with loans. These units must also be serviced.) The market for fishing units will usually be poor at this stage in the fishery (unless the vessel can be adapted to another more profitable fishery). Fishing may be the only, or at least the best, available employment opportunity for those already involved in the fishery. This is frequently the case in communities that rely heavily on fishing, such as the outport communities of Newfoundland and Norway.

When the cost of fishing is low, as is frequently the case in subsistence and small-scale fisheries, the biomass level at which the unmanaged equilibrium occurs may be too low for the resource to sustain itself and it may decline precipitously. When this happens, the fishery is said to have collapsed.

The Development Sequence of a Fishery

The typical sequence of events for a fishery is consistent with the bioeconomic model (Figure 3.6). During the growth phase, catches include not only the surplus yield, but also some of the existing stock biomass, creating the impression that the resource is abundant. This leads to overcapitalization. The elimination of fishing effort, whether by management or for economic reasons, usually lags behind the collapse. Severe economic hardship results and the rehabilitation of the fishery takes place under more stringent management.

Environmental variability can play a significant role in the collapse of a fishery. Unfished stocks vary in abundance through time due to environmental variability. This natural variability tends to increase when biomass is reduced by fishing. Unless fishing effort is reduced during periods of low abundance, the catches may be a relatively high proportion of the biomass, thus inducing further variability and leading ultimately to stock collapse.

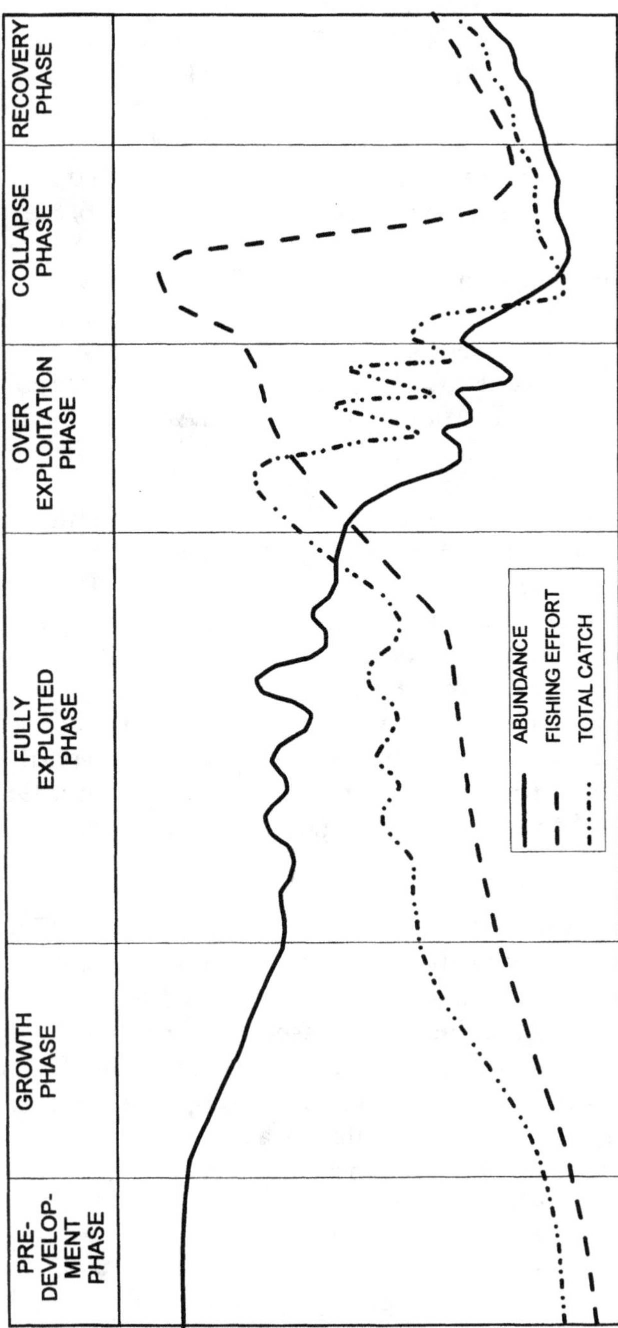

FIGURE 3.6 The usual phases of development of a fishery, with environmental fluctuations (after Csirke and Sharpe, 1984). Overexploitation and collapse are the result of failure to recognize the potential sustainable yield of the resource and/or to prevent overcapitalization.

AN OVERVIEW OF CARIBBEAN FISHERIES

The wider Caribbean area includes the Caribbean Sea, the Gulf of Mexico, the north-east coast of South America, and the south-eastern Atlantic coast of the U.S. This is also the area referred to as the West Central Atlantic (WCA) by FAO. They also refer to it as their Fishery Statistical Area 31 of the West Central Atlantic Fishery Commission (WECAFC). Although there are no current comprehensive reviews of Caribbean fisheries there are two older ones (Klima, 1976; Stevenson, 1981) and some recent ones, which relate to particular areas or resource types (Mahon, 1990; Oxenford, 1991; Sturm, 1991; FAO, 1993b; Mahon, 1996a). This section provides an overview of the fisheries of this region, in the context of world fisheries.

The oceanography of the Caribbean region is highly variable both spatially and temporally. The north coast of South America and the Gulf of Mexico are dominated by the effects of three of the largest river systems in the world: the Amazon, Orinoco, and Mississippi Rivers (Muller-Karger, 1993). Most Caribbean islands are more influenced by the nutrient-poor North Equatorial Current which enters the Caribbean Sea through the passages between the Lesser Antilles. Those islands with appreciable shelf area exhibit significant coral reef development. From Isla Margarita west to Mexico, the continental shelf is also extensively occupied by coral reefs at shallow depths. Seagrass beds and mangroves are also common coastal habitats. In the south-east, seasonal and interannual climatic variability are determined by the north–south migration of the intertropical convergence zone (Hastenrath, 1988).

The fisheries of the Caribbean region are based upon a diverse array of resources. The fisheries of greatest importance are for offshore pelagics, reef fishes, lobster, conch, shrimps, continental shelf demersal fishes, deep slope and bank fishes, and coastal pelagics. There are a variety of less important fisheries, such as for marine mammals, sea turtles, sea urchins, and seaweeds. These fishery types vary widely in terms of their exploitation, the vessel and gear used, and the approach taken to their development and management. The importance of these fisheries also varies widely among the countries of the region (Table 3.1). Although quantitative assessments of status and importance are not available for most fisheries, Table 3.1 provides a qualitative evaluation from several sources (Mahon, 1987; Southeast Fisheries Science Center, 1993; FAO, 1993b).

The WCA does not support any of the world's major fisheries. In fact, it contributed only 1.8 percent of total world fishery landings in 1990. Nonetheless, the fisheries are economically important to the countries (Table 3.2). After increasing, over 15 years, to a high of 2.6 million mt in 1984, landings in the WCA have decreased steadily to 1.7 million mt in 1992 (FAO, 1994; Figure 3.7a). Most of this decline has been due to three U.S. fisheries: the Gulf menhaden, the American oyster, and the calico scallop, which constituted 60 percent of landings from the area in 1984, but only 35 percent of landings in 1992. Total landings from the remaining finfish fisheries of the region (excluding menhaden) were relatively stable at an average of about 620,000 mt from 1982 to 1989 but increased to an average of about 715,000 mt for 1990 through 1992. During this period, reported landings of sharks and rays, other pelagics, snappers, king and Spanish mackerel, and unidentified fishes have increased, while other finfishes have remained stable or have decreased slightly.

In general, shelf resources (lobster, conch, reef fish, shrimps) are either fully exploited or already overexploited, particularly near the shore (FAO, 1993b, 1994). Optimizing the returns from these resources will require careful husbandry and management. Offshore resources, mainly tunas and swordfish, appear to hold some potential for development.

The Harvesting Subsector

The terms subsistence, artisanal, small-scale commercial, large-scale commercial, and industrial are frequently used in describing fisheries, but are seldom clearly defined. The following definitions serve as a guide to their interpretation but will not apply precisely in all cases.

Subsistence: fishing for consumption, and possibly for barter, by self and family using simple, nonmechanized gear.

Artisanal: this term is most often used when fish are caught for sale. It is based mainly on the use of simple, often traditional, gear, usually constructed by the fisher.

Small-scale commercial: usually refers to the size of the boat and operation. The catch is primarily for sale. The vessel is usually owner-operated and uses mechanized, relatively modern, often commercially produced, gear. Boats are usually in the range of 8 to 15 m.

Large-scale commercial: as above, but usually the vessel is company-owned and in the 15 m size range.

Industrial: also refers to large-scale commercial fishing but sometimes specifically refers to the capture of fish for processing into fish meal.

TABLE 3.1 The Relative Importance of Various Fisheries to Caribbean Countries and their State of Exploitation

	Fishery Type									
Caribbean State	Lobster	Conch	Reef fish	Slope/ Bank	Large Pelagic	Flying-fish	Coastal Pelagic	Shrimp	Ground-fish	Coastal Demersal
Antigua/Barbuda	√√√	√√	√√√	√	√		√			
	f	o	f	u	u		f			
Bahamas	√√√	√√	√	√	√					
	f	f	u	u	u					
Barbados	√		√	√√	√√√	√√√	√			
	f		f	f	u	u	f			
Belize	√√√	√√√	√√	√	√			√√		
	f	o	u	u	u		uk	f		
British Virgin Islands	√√	√√	√√	√	√		√			
	o	o	f	u	u		u			
Dominica	√	√	√√	√√	√√√	√	√			
	o	o	o	u	u	u	f			
Dominican Republic	√√	√√	√√√	√	√		√	√√		
	o	o	o	u	u		uk	o		
Grenada	√√	√√	√√	√	√√√	√	√√			
	o	o	o	u	u	u	f			
Guyana				√√	√		√	√√√	√√	√√
				f	u		u	o	o	uk
Haiti	√√	√√	√√√	√	√		√√	√		
	o	o	o	u	u		f	o		

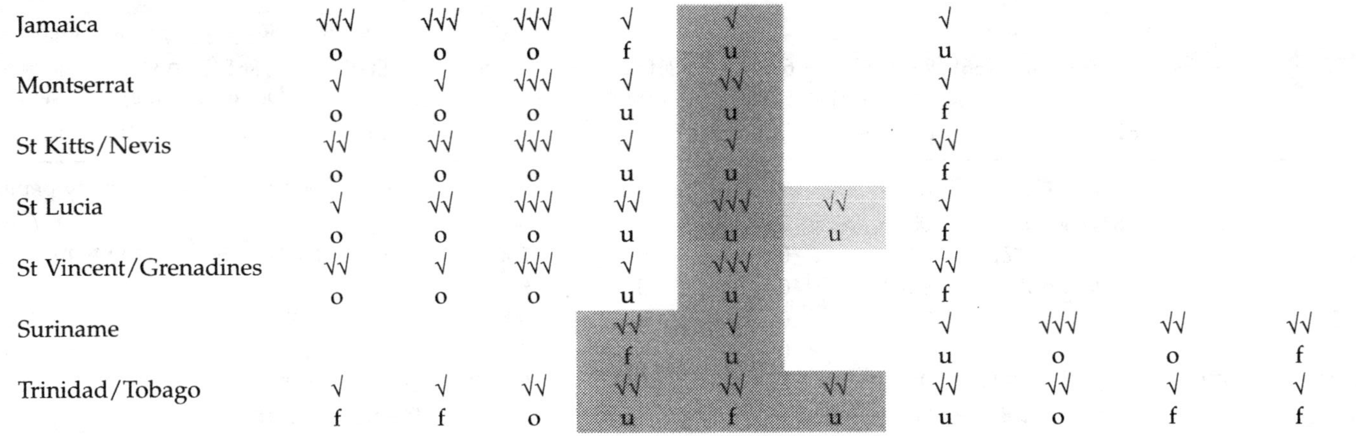

Jamaica	√√√	√√√	√√√	√	√		√			
	o	o	o	f	u		u			
Montserrat	√	√	√√√	√	√√		√			
	o	o	o	u	u		f			
St Kitts/Nevis	√√	√√	√√√	√	√		√√			
	o	o	o	u	u		f			
St Lucia	√	√√	√√√	√√	√√√	√√	√			
	o	o	o	u	u	u	f			
St Vincent/Grenadines	√√	√	√√√	√	√√√		√√			
	o	o	o	u	u		f			
Suriname				√√	√		√	√√√	√√	√√
				f	u		u	o	o	f
Trinidad/Tobago	√	√	√√	√√	√√	√√	√√	√√	√	√
	f	f	o	u	f	u	u	o	f	f

Note: See text for description of each fishery type. Illegal foreign fishing is indicated by shading.

Key: √√√ = extremely important; √√ = important; √ = significant; f = fully exploited; o = overexploited; u = underexploited; uk = unknown.

Illegal foreign fishing: [dark shading] Extensive problem [light shading] Problem in certain areas

1. The indication that large pelagics are underexploited means that the country is not taking a share that would be expected on the basis of the size of its EEZ. If all countries develop the relevant capacity to exploit, the resources will certainly become overfished.
2. Resource status is based largely on circumstantial evidence.

TABLE 3.2 The Social and Economic Value of Fisheries in Selected Caribbean Countries

	Employment		Vessels			Landings				
Caribbean State	Fishers	Secondary	Artisanal	Small commercial	Large commercial	Quantity (mt)	Value (mil. US$)	% GDP	Exports (mil. U.S.$)	Imports (mil. U.S.$)
Antigua & Barbuda	569		140	57	0	[4]890	[4]0.3	[3]1.9		[5]1.4
Bahamas	2,500	200		255		[2]4,295	[2]40.0	[9]4.5	[2]36.3	[8]0.3
Barbados	1,600	1,200	180	500		[3]9,100	17.0			[11]2.4
Belize	2,300		450	450	1	[1]636	[1]5.0	[3]2.2	[1]4.8	
British Virgin Islands	276		120	15	0	[3]836	1.7	[3]2.2		
Dominica	1,103	?	630	4	0	[2]711	1.4	[3]2		[4]0.95
Dominican Republic	8,000	2,000	[5]2,760	35	0	[6]9,530	19.2		[7]1.6	[7]8.5
Grenada	1,749	120	600	25	1	[1]2,111	[1]2.9	[3]1.7	[2]1.3	[2]1.4
Guyana	4,500	5,500	900	500	120	40,000		[3]8.3		0
Haiti	10,000	[5]3,500				[6]7,500	8.1	1.2	[7]0.6	[7]18.1
Jamaica	12,000	24,000	2,000	20	15	[8]10,500	[8]15.5	0.9	[8]1.3	[8]17.2
Montserrat	174	?	62	8	0	[5]115		[3]0.4		
St Kitts & Nevis	650	?	409	5	0	[3]1,500		[3]1.7		[8]0.6
St Lucia	2,100	?	483	5	0	[1]1,115	[2]1.7	[3]0.9		[4]1.4
St Vincent & Grenadines	6,000	1,020	393	10	0	[1]1,222	[1]2.2	[3]0.2	[2]0.2	[3]0.6
Suriname	2,550	?	100	100	150	9,800	22.2	[10]3.8	[10]25.4	0.1
Trinidad & Tobago	7,300	4,400	1,350	20	14	[7]3,200	[7]8.2	0.3	[7]2.0	[7]9.4

Note: OECS country data taken from *Fisheries Statistical Digest*, Number 1, OECS Fisheries Unit, St. Vincent, 1993.
Bahamas data taken from Department of Fisheries Annual Report 1992, Statistical Abstract.
Superscripts: 1983 = 11, 1984 = 10, 1985 = 9, 1986 = 8, 1987 = 7, 1988 = 6, 1989 = 5, 1990 = 4, 1991 = 3, 1992 = 2, 1993 = 1.
Other data from FAO Fishing Profiles.

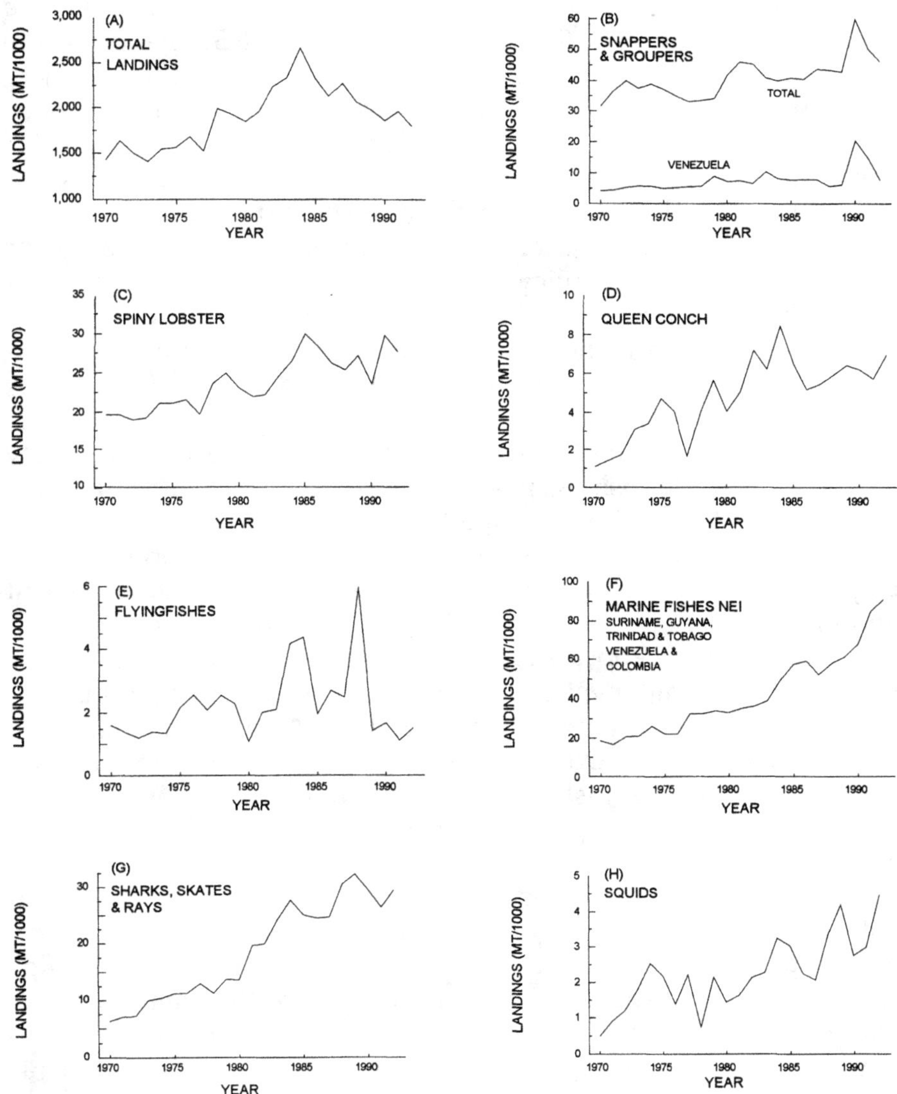

FIGURE 3.7 Trends in landings of some of the major resource types in the west central Atlantic.

Fish are harvested using a wide variety of gear. A review of gear and fishing methods is beyond the scope of this chapter. An overview of gear and methods typically used in Caribbean fisheries is provided by Mahon and Mahon (1990). A fuller review of fishing methods is provided by von Brandt (1985).

The harvesting of fishery resources in Caribbean countries is primarily artisanal, or small-scale, using open, outboard powered vessels 5 to 12 m in length (Table 3.2). The most notable exceptions are the shrimp and groundfish fisheries off Guyana and Suriname, where trawlers in the 20 to 30 m size range are used, and the tuna fishery of Venezuela, which uses large (less than 20 m) lines and purse seiners. In some countries there has been a recent trend towards mid-size vessels in the 12 to 15 m range, particularly for large pelagics, deep slope fishes, and lobster and conch on offshore banks.

The appropriate scale of vessel is one of the main issues for fishery development policy makers to address. This will differ among fishery types. Encouraging or permitting the introduction of mid-size vessels in inshore areas can lead to user conflicts. If artisanal fishers are displaced, the socio-economic impacts in rural areas can be severe.

Many fishers are part-time and make their living from a variety of activities besides fishing, particularly where fish resources are seasonal. This is termed multioccupationality or occupational multiplicity. This socio-economic aspect of fisheries, which has only recently begun to receive attention through studies such as those of Espeut and Grant (1990), has substantial implications for management and development. If, as appears to be the case in many rural areas, fishing is an essential component of a complex mix of activities for a family, then regulation of fishing by limiting access to only some areas or times of year may be extremely disruptive to fishing communities. When displaced from fishing such individuals are not available for full-time alternative employment, contrary to what managers often assume.

Another frequently overlooked problem arising out of multioccupationality occurs when development initiatives make loans available to fishers to acquire larger boats and better gear. The investment often requires that the fishers fish full-time to service the loan. This may disrupt patterns of multiple activities that are essential to the traditional mode of existence. In those cases where resources are available only occasionally, perhaps seasonally, full-time fishing may not be feasible. Development initiatives must take these factors into account and should consider potential negative impacts of encouraging higher capital investment by such individuals.

Fishery Resource Types

The major fishery resource types of the Caribbean region are described below. Identification keys by Fischer (1978) and Cervignón et al. (1993) also provide notes on the biology of, and fisheries for, the species.

Shallow Reef Fishes

Throughout the tropics, reef fishes in shallow coral reef habitats support significant fisheries (Russ, 1991). In the Caribbean, trap and line fisheries for these fishes are among the most socio-economically important. They are artisanal or small-scale. The fishermen are typically part-time and often have low levels of income. The fish are generally landed at a large number of small landing sites and are often an important source of protein for rural communities. Reef fish resources are considered to be overexploited throughout the Caribbean region, with the possible exception of a few countries with large areas of coral reef on their shelves (for example, the Bahamas, Belize, and possibly Antigua and Barbuda). The evidence for overexploitation is the low catch per trap, the small size of fish, and the scarcity of the largest, most valuable, species. Rehabilitated and properly managed, reef fish resources are those most likely to provide a continuous, stable yield that is easily accessible with minimum investment in fishing gear (Sale, 1991; Munro, 1983; Huntsman et al., 1982).

In general, knowledge of the status of reef fish stocks is very poor, even in the U.S., where it is limited to a few key species (FAO, 1994; Southeast Fisheries Science Center, 1993). In countries where the fisheries are primarily small-scale and artisanal, data on landings are inaccurate because of the widely dispersed nature of the fishery. The problem is exacerbated by the nature of the fishery, which harvests a large number of species and uses a variety of gears (traps, spears, hand lines, and trammel nets) for which estimation of fishing effort is difficult.

A serious problem related to the overexploitation of reef fishes, here and elsewhere in the tropics, is the extreme vulnerability of spawning aggregations to fishing. This problem is most well known for groupers but appears to be a concern for other families of reef fishes as well (Auil-Marshalleck, 1993). Ciguatera poisoning continues to be an impediment to the effective utilization of reef fish resources in the northern Lesser Antilles and Puerto Rico.

Deep Slope and Bank Fishes

There are important fisheries for deep-water snappers, groupers, and associated species throughout tropical and subtropical regions of the world (Polovina and Ralston, 1987; Dalzell and Preston, 1992). In the Caribbean, commercially important stocks of snappers, groupers, and associated species are found in deep water along the slopes at the edges of island platforms, on deep banks, and along the edge of the continental shelf off Guyana and Suriname. These species are high-priced and are primarily exported or sold to restaurants. They are harvested with lines or traps. Although there are reports of local depletion in various islands, particularly of known spawning aggregations, there is little quantitative information on the state of exploitation of these resources. Landing of these species from the entire WCA has shown a steady increase from 1970 to the present.

The landings of snapper and grouper by Venezuela, the country most active in this fishery, have increased steadily throughout the past two decades but are probably underestimated because much of the catch is taken off the Guyana-Brazil shelf and landed in other Caribbean countries. A major peak in landings for 1990, believed to be due to changes in the port of landing and to the increased reporting of the catch, raises concerns as to the accuracy of earlier reported landings (Figure 3.7b).

There are preliminary survey estimates for the slope of the continental shelf off Guyana, Suriname, and Trinidad and Tobago by the RV *Fridtjof Nansen* (Institute of Marine Research, 1989). These are biomass estimates and, since the area is heavily fished by snapper boats from Venezuela (up to 150 off Suriname alone), there is no way to relate this biomass to potential yield without a more detailed study of the fishery. For other areas, there are only rough yield estimates, which have been based on observed yields per unit drop-off multiplied by the length of the drop-off (FAO, 1993b). These can provide guidelines for development and, for the Eastern Caribbean islands, suggest that a small increase in exploitation can be accommodated.

There is probably scope for expansion of these fisheries in many countries and thus a need for policy decisions regarding the mix of commercial versus small-scale fishing that would be desirable. However, deep slope and bank habitats are small in area relative to shelves and open ocean. Thus, the total abundance of these resources will be relatively small and they will be particularly susceptible to overexploitation.

Spiny Lobster

The spiny lobster supports valuable fisheries throughout the tropics (Phillips et al., 1994). In the Caribbean, lobster (*Panulirus* spp., mainly *P. argus*, the Caribbean spiny lobster) is a high-priced resource distributed in coral reef and associated habitats. Lobsters are caught by divers, lobster traps (for example, in Belize) and, frequently, in fish traps with reef fish. Most are either exported as frozen tails or sold locally to hotels and restaurants for tourist consumption. In the Bahamas the value of lobster exports for 1992 was U.S.$ 35 million. Lobsters are considered to be fully or overexploited throughout the Caribbean. Possible exceptions are some offshore banks. The situation is worse on the south shelf of Jamaica and in the Eastern Caribbean islands, where shelf areas are small.

Total spiny lobster landings in the region increased in 1991 and 1992 after a decline since 1985 (Figure 3.7c). This is due mainly to increases in landings in the two countries with the highest landings, the Bahamas and Cuba. Landings from the heavily overexploited U.S. lobster fishery were stable over the last decade but decreased by about 30 percent in 1992 due to a reduction in fishing effort.

If properly managed, lobster stocks should recover and provide valuable sustainable yields. This species has the potential to earn foreign exchange as an export and through the tourist industry. For Eastern Caribbean islands, rough estimates of potential yield indicate a potential export value of U.S.$ 3.8 million. If this catch were retailed locally in restaurants the value would be about U.S.$ 14 million (Mahon, 1990).

Conch

The queen conch, *Strombus gigas*, is a large marine snail found only in the Caribbean region. Conch, like lobster, is a high-priced resource which is either exported or sold to hotels and restaurants for tourist consumption. Conch is usually harvested by divers. In Haiti, tangle nets are also used. Conch occurs in specific, easily identifiable habitats with limited distribution and is therefore even more susceptible to overexploitation than lobster. Except in the Bahamas, this resource is considered to be fully or overexploited throughout the region, with areas of severe local depletion. Appeldoorn and Rodríguez (1994) and the Caribbean Fisheries Management Council (CFMC, 1995) provide reviews of conch biology and fisheries in the Caribbean.

Overall landings of conch in the WECAFC region steadily increased until 1985, then declined and now appear to be levelling off (Figure 3.7d). Some unexploited conch stocks probably exist on offshore banks in relatively deep water, 25 to 30 m. On Pedro Bank, south of Jamaica, where commercial harvesting began in 1990, estimated landings have been about 1800 mt, but are not reported (Mahon et al., 1999). In most areas, intensive fishing has depleted conch populations to the point of forcing permanent (in the case of the U.S., Mexico, and Bermuda) or temporary (in the case of Cuba) closure of the fisheries (Berg et al., 1992a, 1992b). Reseeding programmes to rebuild conch stocks have been tried in many countries but have not been proven to enhance fishery yields (Stoner, 1999).

With proper management, conch stocks should also recover and provide valuable sustainable yields. Rough estimates of potential yield from the Lesser Antilles indicate a total export value of U.S.$ 5 million and a restaurant retail value of about U.S.$ 40 million (Mahon, 1990). Stocks in Cuba seem to have recovered quickly after a temporary closure of the fishery and stocks in the U.S. are steadily increasing after many years of fishing closure. In Bermuda, however, in spite of more than 10 years of protection, stocks have not recovered from overfishing.

Large Pelagic Fishes

Large pelagic fishes, primarily tunas, support substantial commercial fisheries throughout the world's oceans but the majority of catches are taken in tropical and subtropical waters (Longhurst and Pauly, 1987). Large pelagic resources are considered to hold the greatest potential for fishery development in Caribbean countries, particularly in the eastern Caribbean. Most countries are increasing, or intend to increase, their effort in these fisheries. Several species (tunas, billfishes, dolphin, wahoo, kingfish, and sharks) are exploited on the same fishing trips by trolling from boats ranging from canoes to launches. Recently, small-commercial longliners (12 to 15 m) have been acquired by several islands. The stocks of several species (tunas, billfish, and swordfish) are widely distributed in the Atlantic Ocean. Although these species are assessed by the International Commission for the Conservation of Atlantic Tunas (ICCAT) (see below), the status of the stocks is poorly known in the Western Atlantic where the data base is weak.

According to ICCAT assessments, the potential for expansion of offshore pelagics varies considerably among species. The major stocks are considered to be fully exploited (yellowfin tuna, bigeye tuna, and albacore) or overexploited (bluefin tuna, swordfish, blue marlin, and white marlin)(ICCAT, 1995). There is little or no information on the status and potential of other species, such as blackfin tuna, dolphinfish, little tuna, wahoo, and king mackerel, outside of U.S. waters. The most up to date information on large pelagics is contained in the annual reports of ICCAT (for example, ICCAT, 1995).

Fisheries for offshore pelagics have already expanded within the region throughout the 1980s. This was due primarily to purse seine and longline fishing for tunas by Venezuela and swordfish fishing by U.S. longline vessels. In the mid 1980s, many of the Venezuelan vessels shifted their area of operation from the WCA to the eastern

Pacific. Recent fluctuations in tuna landings from the WCA are primarily caused by the movement of the vessels between these areas. From 1982 through 1990, the U.S. swordfish longline fleet expanded its operations into the south-east Caribbean as far as the north coast of South America. The effort by artisanal and small commercial fisheries for offshore pelagics also increased through this period, particularly in the Eastern Caribbean islands (Mahon, 1996a).

The stocks of many species (yellowfin tuna, billfishes, and swordfish) extend outside the area and are migratory. In both groups management will require close collaboration among countries within and outside the region, as specified by the United Nations agreement relating to the conservation and management of straddling fish stocks and highly migratory fish stocks (United Nations, 1995). The stocks of several other species (dolphinfish, wahoo, and blackfin tuna) are probably more local in distribution. These also come under the auspices of ICCAT but they have received virtually no attention, owing to the emphasis on large tunas, billfish, and swordfish and also to the lack of data. These stocks are shared among the countries of the wider Caribbean. Therefore, the management measures implemented by Caribbean countries alone could probably have a significant impact on their status and sustained yield but will also require collaboration among countries.

As fisheries expand offshore to catch pelagics, new problems arise. For example, migratory fish are often only present in the waters of any country for a few months of the year. So, to keep fishing boats working all year, they must either follow the fish from one exclusive economic zone (EEZ) to another or switch to fishing other kinds of resources when the migratory species are absent.

However, as previously mentioned, the fish living at the bottom of the sea, to which they might switch, are already overfished. In most countries, the only resources for which there is potential for expansion are the bottom-living fishes in the deep waters down the slope of the island or continental shelf. These fishes are mainly snappers which are commercially valuable but which are also easily overfished. Therefore, in order to avoid overfishing them, management will need to strike a delicate balance between the expansion of fleets for pelagic fishing and those allowed to fish the deep-water snappers during the off season.

By far, the most significant problem regarding the expansion of fleets into offshore areas is that the pelagic fishes that they will be targeting are already being extensively exploited by distant water fishing nations, such as Japan, Korea, and Taiwan and also by large commercial vessels of countries within the region, both on the High

Seas to the east of the region and within the EEZs of Caribbean countries (Singh-Renton and Mahon, 1996).

The ultimate question concerns the fraction of the potential yield that is already being taken over by distant-water and regional fisheries. If current catches are already at, or close to, the maximum sustainable yield, then the problem is to decide how the countries of the Caribbean will be able to access the share of the resource that their EEZs entitle them to without the resource becoming overfished.

Coastal Pelagic Fishes

In the Caribbean, the term coastal pelagics refers mainly to jacks, robins, and ballyhoo (*Caranx* spp., *Decapterus* spp., and *Hemirhamphus* spp.), although small tunas are sometimes caught. These species are fished primarily using seine nets and vary greatly in importance among the islands, ranging from about 30 percent of the catch in Grenada to less than 1 percent in Barbados. Although several islands report declining catches of coastal pelagics, neither the extent of the decline nor the species involved is documented. There is very little information on the distribution or migration of these species.

The term coastal pelagics is sometimes also used for large pelagic fishes which are found primarily on island or continental shelves and which are caught by trolling, for example, dolphinfish, blackfin tuna, and *Scomberomorus* spp. (Goodbody, 1986; Southeast Fisheries Science Center, 1993). Around Trinidad the fishery for coastal pelagics targets the mackerels, *Scomberomorus* spp., using gillnets. About 1200 mt per year are landed and the resource is believed to be fully exploited. Similar resources occur in unknown quantities in the waters off Guyana and Suriname and are probably underexploited.

Small Pelagic Fishes

Small shoaling pelagics, primarily clupeoids (sardines, pilchards, and anchovies), support some of the largest commercial fisheries in the world (Csirke, 1988). The Peruvian anchovy is the best known of these, having yielded a substantial percentage of the world's landings before its dramatic collapse in the 1970s.

In the wider Caribbean region, the major fisheries for small pelagics are those for menhaden off the eastern U.S. and the Gulf of Mexico (Southeast Fisheries Science Center, 1993). In most countries, there are small-scale fisheries for near-shore shoaling clupeids for bait and food (Goodbody, 1986). Acoustic surveys by RV *Fridtjof Nansen* indicate that there are substantial stocks of small pelagics off the north coast of South America, from Suriname to Colombia. These consist primarily of clupeids, engraulids, and carangids and are virtually unexploited, except by Venezuela in the Isla Margarita area (Institute of Marine Research, 1989).

In the southern Lesser Antilles, the fourwing flyingfish is the single most important small pelagic. The countries that fish them probably share a common stock. Therefore, the fate of the resource and hence the fishery could depend largely on management measures implemented by these countries.

There was a trend of increased landings throughout the 1980s owing to the rapid expansion of the fleet and the area fished. The fishing fleet in Barbados expanded rapidly and total landings of flyingfish more than doubled during this period. Recently, landings have declined due to a fishing agreement that has reduced effort in the principal fishing area off Tobago (Figure 3.7e). Despite considerable fluctuations in abundance, there are no indications that the resource is overexploited (Oxenford et al., 1993).

A regional flyingfish assessment programme, the Eastern Caribbean Flyingfish Project, has conducted preliminary analyses of the resource and its fishery to determine appropriate exploitation rates for the stock (Oxenford et al., 1993). The analyses suggest that owing to their short lifespan (they are annual) and considerable interannual variability in abundance, traditional deterministic stock-recruitment assessment methods will not be applicable to flyingfish. Instead, an approach that attempts to evaluate the risks of, and returns from, various fishing options was recommended.

Shrimps

Penaeid prawns (shrimps) are one of the most valuable resources of the tropics, particularly in areas where there are coastal mangroves and wide shallow shelves (Garcia, 1988). The Guyanas-Brazil shelf area and the northern Gulf of Mexico are two of the major penaeid shrimp fishing areas of the world. The shrimp are fished primarily by an industrial fleet of trawlers (25 to 30 m). The total landings for the former area are about 20,000 mt per year, of which most is landed by Brazil, French Guiana, Guyana, Suriname, and Trinidad and Tobago. There are also artisanal coastal fisheries for shrimps in the Guyanas-Brazil area. Other small, localized marine shrimp fisheries occur in the coastal waters of many of the larger Caribbean islands (Cuba, the Dominican Republic, and Jamaica) and mainland countries such as Venezuela, Nicaragua, and Belize. The shrimp fishery of the Guyanas-Brazil area has been thoroughly documented (FAO, 1995b; CFRAMP, 1996).

Shrimp from Guyana, Suriname, Trinidad and Tobago, and Belize is exported and earns significant foreign exchange in these countries. One of the primary problems with the shrimp industry in Suriname and Guyana is foreign ownership. In Suriname only 10 to 15 percent of the U.S.$ 21 million per year earned by the fishery is retained by the country. With domestic ownership, the percentage would be expected to increase to about 40 to 50 percent.

Groundfish

Trawling fisheries for demersal species (groundfish) occur on all continental shelves. The fisheries for cod, haddock, and flatfishes of the north Atlantic are some of the most studied in the world. Although temperate demersal stocks are among the most productive in the world, tropical shelves also support significant trawl fisheries (Longhurst and Pauly, 1987; Pauly, 1988).

On the continental shelf off Guyana and Suriname and in the Gulf of Mexico, demersal finfishes are a considerable resource, much of which are caught as bycatch in the shrimp fisheries. Most are discarded, constituting a global problem in shrimp fisheries (Alverson et al., 1994). In Guyana, regulations require that some of the bycatch be landed. Fisheries specifically targeting demersal fishes other than coral reef fishes are found primarily on the north-eastern continental shelf of South America, in the Gulf of Mexico, and off the south-eastern U.S. In the waters of the U.S., recreational fisheries take about half of the catch consumed by humans, mainly drums (sciaenids). Although the long-term potential yields of most U.S. stocks of coastal demersals are unknown, all their stocks are considered to be overexploited (Southeast Fisheries Science Center, 1993). Off South America, the catch is more diverse; catfishes and sciaenids are important. Inshore, small-scale fisheries take a large component of the landed catch.

Recently, some trawlers have been specializing in demersal finfish off Suriname and Guyana. The drums, croakers, and snappers that comprise most of the finfish catch are valuable export species. Recent surveys by the RV *Fridtjof Nansen* estimated the potential yield of these stocks at about 40,000 mt for Guyana, 16,000 mt for Suriname, and 13,000 mt for Trinidad and Tobago. Landings in Guyana are at or near the estimated potential yield. Those in Suriname and Trinidad and Tobago are below the estimated potential yield. However, the amount of fish discarded by shrimp trawlers is unknown and may account for most of the potential yield.

The landings that are reported as unidentified marine fishes by the countries along the north coast of South America have increased steadily over the past 20 years (Figure 3.7f). The recent estimates of potential yield in this area by the RV *Fridtjof Nansen* suggest that some of these resources are likely to be overexploited. A more precise breakdown of the catch is required in order for there to be a valid comparison of current yield with the survey estimates.

Coastal Demersal

The small-scale inshore fisheries off the north-east coast of South America catch significant quantities of coastal demersal finfish, using gillnets and longlines from open and decked wood vessels 10 to 15 m in length. The catches consist mainly of sciaenids (sea trouts and drums: three major species) and ariids (catfishes: three major species). The status of this multispecies resource is not well known. Neither the RV *Fridtjof Nansen* survey nor others distinguishes between the inshore demersal stocks and the groundfish stocks exploited by the offshore trawlers (Institute of Marine Research, 1989). A recent assessment of these resources in Suriname suggests that they are at or near full exploitation (Suriname Fisheries Department, 1993).

Miscellaneous

There is a variety of fishery resources that support small but valuable fisheries (for example, sea urchins, sharks, black coral, and whelks) and there is scope for the development of these in some areas. For example, sea urchins are a valuable resource that is unexploited in several countries. Fisheries for this resource must be cautiously developed, as experience in Barbados has shown that it can easily be overexploited.

Sharks, skates, and rays are caught throughout the region. Landings appear to be levelling after a steep increase between 1977 and 1985 (Figure 3.7g). They are caught primarily in continental shelf areas influenced by river outflow. Their potential yield in most areas is unknown, but their low fertility or slow growth makes them particularly susceptible to overfishing. In the waters of the U.S., coastal species are fully to overexploited (Southeast Fisheries Science Center, 1993). Pelagic and demersal sharks are not well distinguished in the reported landings. Both the U.S. National Marine Fisheries Service and ICCAT are increasing efforts at collecting information on shark landings, with a view to better management of shark stocks.

Octopus fisheries occur in only a few locations, most notably on Campeche Bank in Mexico and in Venezuela, despite a much wider distribution. Landings by Mexico have increased steadily over the period of record, doubling in 5 years (1989 to1993) to over 16,000 mt.

Squid landings, primarily by Venezuela, are variable but continue to increase steadily (Figure 3.7h). Reported landings of 2800 tonnes (t) by Korea for the first time in 1992 suggest that there is potential for squid fisheries in the WCA region. This resource deserves investigation, for both human consumption and as a bait for large pelagic and sport fisheries.

Post-Harvest Handling of the Catch

The loss of catch due to inappropriate post-harvest handling procedures is a substantial, though largely unquantified, problem in small-scale fisheries in the Caribbean. The use of ice for fish storage at sea is an important factor in reducing spoilage. Availability of ice is a problem in many landing areas. Shore-based facilities for unloading, storing, and retailing fish also play an important role in reducing post-harvest loss due to spoilage. Modern landing facilities with jetties, ice, cold storage, fuel, water, and storage lockers for fishers exist at several sites throughout Caribbean countries. These complexes usually have been constructed with foreign aid. In many instances they are operated as cooperatives. The impact of these facilities varies widely. The Japanese-built fish complex in Kingstown, St Vincent and the Grenadines is an example of a complex that has brought about a significant increase in fish landings and the quality of fish available to consumers. There are several contrasting examples of facilities that operate well below capacity and are used only occasionally by fishers when there are gluts of fish. The reasons they have failed to meet expectations include inappropriate site selection, bad management, failure of the contractor to complete construction, lack of operating capital, and instability in the supply of fish.

Smaller-scale developments, such as slipways, ice machines, lockers, and sheds, have often been undertaken at landing sites. The success of such initiatives is also highly variable. The probability of success appears to be increased significantly by prior consultation with fishers and fish vendors. Similar small-scale improvements to landing facilities are required at many landing sites throughout Caribbean countries.

In Caribbean countries, processing is restricted largely to the gutting and dressing or trimming of seafood for export, either as fresh or frozen products. Shrimps are sorted by size, frozen, and exported with the heads on or off. Lobster tails are exported frozen in the shell, and conch is exported trimmed and frozen. There is a limited degree of further processing in several countries. Some examples are the smoking of fish in Guyana, Suriname, St Vincent, and Trinidad; fileting and vacuum packing of flyingfish in Tobago and Barbados; boiling and shrink-wrapping of lobster in Belize; and canning of conch chowder in the Bahamas.

Distribution and Marketing of the Catch

The marketing of fishery products must be considered at local, regional, and international levels, as was done in a group of studies carried out for the Organization of Eastern Caribbean States (Wolfe, 1990; Farmer and Associates, 1990; Charles and Neverson, 1990). Export outside of the region is targeted primarily at North America. Arrangements are usually made directly with importers in the respective countries. Prices and packaging requirements are cross checked among buyers to ensure that they are reasonable and correct.

Most producers find that it is easier to export outside the region than within it. There is no central marketing information service available for seafood products within the Caribbean. Therefore, arrangements must be made through the numerous importers in the various countries, each of whom requires relatively small amounts of the product. Furthermore, facilities for the storage and shipping of iced or frozen seafood products among Caribbean countries are inadequate in most countries.

The standards required of seafood processors exporting to the U.S., Canada, Japan, and European Commission countries have recently been upgraded. These countries have adopted a consistent set of requirements based on the Hazard Analysis and Critical Control Point (HACCP) system of quality control, which emphasizes preventative measures (Huss, 1994). As of the beginning of 1995, processors wishing to export to the above countries must be certified as to their compliance with HACCP requirements. The costs to processors of upgrading to comply with the new standards may be significant in terms of technology (testing facilities), equipment (air conditioning, replacement of surfaces), and expertise. However, long-term benefits of adopting the HACCP system may be considerable, through reduction of the amounts of product that must be discarded, and of the duration of plant down-time due to contamination. Although driven by export market requirements, these improvements will also benefit seafood consumers nationally and within the region.

At the national level, there is often inadequate distribution of fish. There can be gluts in one area and demand in another only a few miles or hours drive away. In many countries, entrepreneurs with vans, motorcycles, and bicycles distribute fish, often without ice. A typical distribution pathway is shown in Figure 3.8. However, for

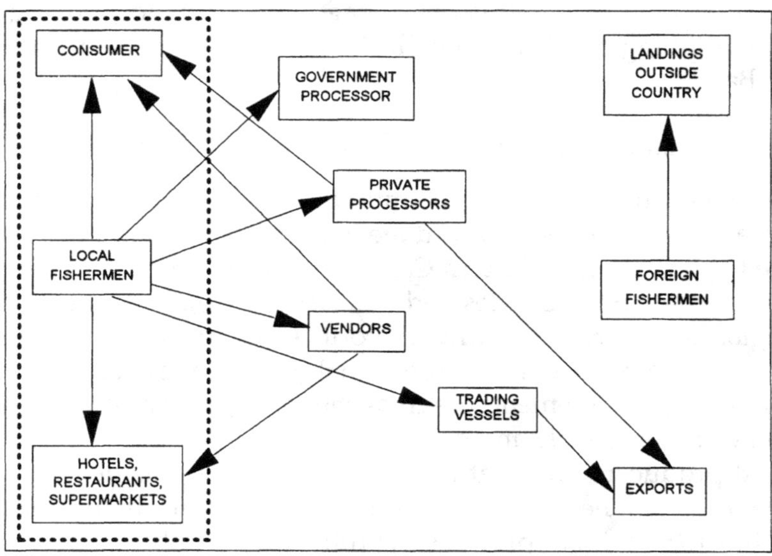

FIGURE 3.8 An example of the distribution pathways that typically occur for a small-scale Caribbean fishery.

many fisheries the pathway may consist only of the subcomponent enclosed in the dotted line.

Improvements in landing facilities, described above, have often been complemented by improved marketing facilities at the same site. At the least, these improvements will include the provision of ice, water, cutting tables, and retailing stands, often in open, covered areas. In several countries, donors have provided combined fish landing, processing, and retailing facilities at a larger scale. These are generally referred to as fishery complexes and may include jetties, enclosed processing areas, freezers, and cold storage. These types of facilities can be found throughout the Caribbean.

DEVELOPMENT AND MANAGEMENT

Management Objectives and Reference Points

Development and management are complementary activities. Development should include management at the earliest stages. There are currently few fisheries for which development will take the form of increased exploitation of an underexploited resource. It will mainly take the following forms: the improved economic efficiency of harvesting, reduction of post-harvest losses, better and safer working conditions for

TABLE 3.3 Some Possible Management Objectives for Fisheries

Conserve fish stocks	Prevent waste of fish
Maintain healthy ecosystem	Improve quality of fish
Maximize catches	Maintain low consumer price
Stabilize stock levels	Increase cost-effectiveness
Stabilize catch rates	Reduce overcapacity
Provide employment	Develop underutilized stocks
Increase fisher's incomes	Increase fish exports
Reduce conflicts	Provide government revenue
Protect sports fisheries	

Data from Clark, 1985.

fishers, and efforts to increase the value added component of fishery products, *inter alia.*

Successful development and management require well thought out plans with clearly stated objectives. The plan is essentially a contract between the managers and the interested parties. Various terms have been used to describe the interested parties (for example, participants and stakeholders) but what is clear is that this group must include everyone with a valid interest in the resource: fishers, processors, conservationists, nonexploitative users such as SCUBA divers, and consumers. The need to involve the interested parties in the development and implementation of the plan has become evident and accepted in recent years with the failure of "top-down" management in many fisheries. "Top-down" refers to the process whereby the government makes unilateral decisions about management and imposes them on the fishing industry.

Fishery management aims for more than a simple maximization of yield. Other objectives take into account foreign exchange, employment, contribution to disadvantaged rural areas, profit, *inter alia* (Table 3.3). Several of these objectives are clearly in conflict with one another. For example, profitability is usually maximized at a lower total catch than the maximum that the stock can yield (Figure 3.5) and the interests of sport fishers, who target predatory species, are in conflict with those of commercial fishermen, who usually exploit the prey of those predators.

A lack of clearly defined management objectives has been identified as one of the main impediments to the establishment of, and adherence to, management targets or reference points (Smith et al.,

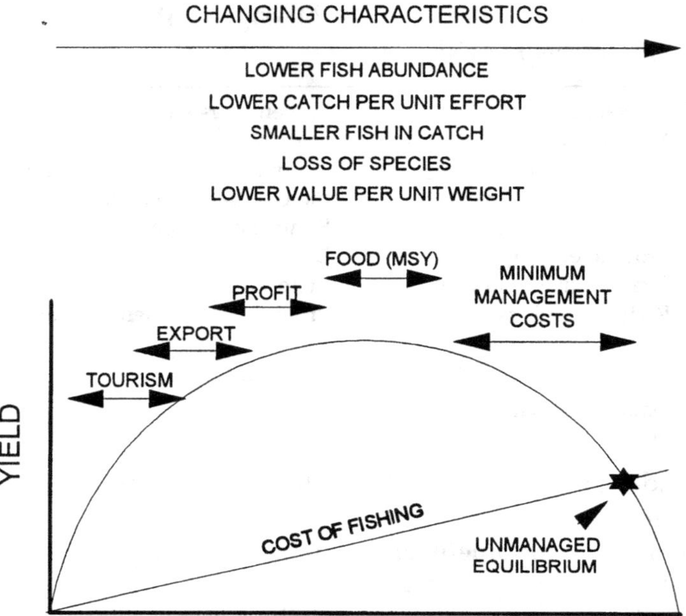

FIGURE 3.9 The relationship between management systems, the surplus production model and some fish assemblage/population characteristics which are of concern to interested parties.

1993). Each of the possible societal objectives in managing a fishery will frequently correspond to the interests of a particular user group. Since all objectives cannot be met at the same time, the stakeholders in a fishery need to agree on the management objectives for the fishery and to make compromises in doing so. To participate effectively in the decision making process, users must understand the relationships among the objectives and the characteristics of the fishery in order to appreciate the trade-offs among the various possible objectives, even if only in relative terms, such as catch rates, fish sizes, or species caught.

A theoretical illustration of the relationships among various fishery management objectives, the state of exploitation of the resource, its characteristics, and those of the catch is shown in Figure 3.9. The example is based on the bioeconomic adaptation of the surplus production model described previously, and on the changes that are known to take place in fish communities or populations as exploitation increases. The example uses reef fishes, a multispecies resource, to exemplify its point but any single-species resource can be used.

The concept of an overall objective that incorporates all of the important considerations for a fishery was termed optimal sustainable yield and was initially defined as the yield level that takes account of "economic, social and biological values . . . rather than being limited to maximizing net profits or maximizing sustainable yield" (Wallace, 1975). This is intuitively satisfactory but no model was proposed from which a corresponding level of fishing could be estimated.

Thus far, there are very few instances in which multiple objectives have been formally incorporated into a fishery management strategy. One approach to determining the optimum yield for a fishery is based on multi-attribute utility analysis (Healey, 1984). It depends on reaching an agreement among participants on the weighting that should be given to various conflicting objectives. It appears to be a reasonable way of making agreed decisions when there are multiple objectives involved. However, there are few instances in which a multicriterion approach to decision making has been applied in fisheries management. Two cases are the Yucatan Shelf octopus fishery (Diaz-de Leon and Seijo, 1992) and a chinook salmon fishery in Alaska (Merritt and Criddle, 1993).

In order to proceed from an agreed set of management objectives for a fishery to an operational management plan, the objectives must be stated in terms of agreed *reference points* on quantifiable *reference variables*. These points may be defined as targets or limits (Caddy and Mahon, 1995). Reference variables are usually derived from biological or economic models considered to adequately represent the behaviour of the resource or fishery. Some examples of reference variables are fishing mortality, catch, stock biomass, profit margin, total revenue, and fishing effort.

A *target reference point* may be derived from the above models as a point on a reference variable that is an optimum in mathematical terms (maximum sustainable yield, maximum economic yield) or may simply be any agreed upon value believed to represent the desired state of the fishery or population. Such agreed reference points may be arbitrary. Similarly, *limit reference points* are agreed points either derived from models or are arbitrary points on reference variables beyond which the fishery is not allowed to go.

It is worth noting that all of the model-based reference points and the status of stocks relative to these reference points are only known approximately, often with considerable uncertainty. Thus, as described in Appendix 3, there are risks associated with the use of these reference points and managers should consider the risks in their decision making.

Data and Information Requirements

Data and information on a fishery are essential for proper management. Systems for the collection, management, analysis, and reporting of data and information should be provided for in the management plan. Biological, economic, and social data are required for a complete picture of the fishery (Figure 3.1). The design and implementation of data collection systems in situations of limited budget and manpower have been widely discussed (Stevenson et al., 1982; Caddy and Bazigos, 1986). There are specific applications to Caribbean situations (e.g., Mahon and Rosenberg, 1988; Fanning, 1992; CFRAMP, 1993a).

At a very minimum, knowledge of the amount and type of fishing capacity and active effort are required for management. The distinction between capacity (total available effort) and active effort is an important one, since unregulated capacity may quickly become active effort under favourable economic circumstances. Next in importance is information on the amount of catch, preferably by species and type of gear, so that trends in the amount of catch and catch per unit effort can be derived as indicators of changes in the exploited stocks. Other information may be acquired depending on the funds available and the management approach that will be taken. Before information is collected, it should be clear how it will be used in managing the fishery.

A complete review of the types of information that can be collected from a fishery and how they may be used is beyond the scope of this chapter. Stevenson et al. (1982) provide a practical overview. For biological assessment, details such as the size of fish caught and their age and reproductive condition may be required. Information on fishing practices and community organization is valuable as a basis for evaluating the feasibility of management options, particularly co-management. Information on prices and costs of fishing are necessary in order to determine the value of the fishery sector, to determine appropriate budgetary allocations to management, and to provide advice to investors on the most economically feasible options for harvesting (e.g., Barbados Development Bank, 1993).

Given the uncertainty associated with the interpretation of resource assessment models, the narrow focus on collecting the data required to use these models, which has often predominated in the past, may be inadequate. A broad understanding of the fishery appears to be necessary for interpretation of the results of the models (Hilborn and Walters, 1992). For example, thematic mapping has been found to be a useful means of summarizing fishery information as a basis for management (Butler et al., 1986).

Traditional Knowledge

Top-down management has largely ignored traditional knowledge as a source of information. It is now widely recognized that fishers often have detailed knowledge of the resources that they harvest and may have traditional management systems (Johannes, 1978; Ruddle, 1994). With proper interview techniques and cross validation, it is possible to extract useful information that may otherwise take a researcher many years and considerable expense to acquire. This knowledge appears to be most extensive in communities with a long and close association with the sea, as is the case in the Pacific Islands, where the acquisition of this information was pioneered (Johannes, 1981). The South Pacific Commission (SPC) recognizes the value of traditional knowledge through its Traditional Marine Resource Management and Knowledge Special Interest Group within its Pacific Islands Marine Resources Information System (PIMRIS). In contrast, in the Caribbean, there appears to be a valuable accumulation of knowledge that has seldom been tapped.

Resource Assessment

Resource assessment is the process that provides information on the status of a resource. This information is used to determine whether the resource is over- or underexploited and the management action that should be taken. The technical reference points that are used in quantitative stock assessment are based largely on biometric or econometric models, and hence on mathematics, and can be difficult to assimilate for the nontechnical reader. The basic concepts and models have already been described, and references provided for fuller treatment of the topic.

Although analytical models incorporating growth and mortality rates, and age at first capture, are widely used in the fisheries of developed countries, the data required to estimate current age-structure of the fish population are either not available for many small or tropical stocks or are labour and technology intensive. Where assessments have been carried out, many of them still depend on low precision approaches using sparse or inaccurate data, making management by target reference points problematic and precautionary approaches to avoiding stock collapse mandatory. Although resource assessment can be highly technical, useful assessments may also be based on relatively simple criteria, such as catch per unit effort, the mean size of fish in the catch, and, in the case of multispecies fisheries, the species composition of the catch.

In those cases where the application of detailed stock assessment methodology is cost effective and where there are funds to carry out the work, training in the analytical skills that are required can be a constraint. FAO and the International Center for Living Aquatic Resources Management (ICLARM) are two organizations that have developed a programme of short-term training for stock assessment scientists in developing countries. They provide courses based on manuals by Sparre et al. (1989a, 1989b) and have developed a stock assessment software package that includes most of the standard analyses (Gayanilo et al., 1994).

Owing to the technical difficulty and cost of age determination for many tropical species, there has been a recent emphasis in assessment of tropical fisheries on methodology that uses length data. Gulland and Rosenberg (1992) provide a readable overview of the pros and cons of these methods, all of which are included in the above software.

Management Measures

Control Measures

Once the objectives of the fishery and reference variables and points are defined and agreed upon, the means by which the fishery will be controlled must be devised. Various tools are available for the regulation of fisheries and these have frequently been reviewed (Sissenwine and Kirkley, 1982; FAO, 1983; Beddington and Rettig, 1984). Hilborn and Walters (1992) provide an excellent analysis of the efficacy of the various approaches and discuss the reasons why many of them fail to prevent overexploitation.

Management may attempt to control either inputs (number of vessels, types of gear) or outputs (catches, fish sizes). Some of the commonly used methods are summarized in Table 3.4. Managers may attempt to control reference variables directly or indirectly. For example, if the reference variable is fishing effort measured in number of fish traps hauled per season, the number of trap hauls permitted may be regulated directly. However, the number of hauls may be more difficult to monitor and enforce than the number of vessels allowed to fish. The number of hauls is indirectly related to the fishing effort because the number of traps or the days fished may vary. Gear regulations, closed areas, or seasons will be even less direct controls on inputs.

Monitoring, Control, and Surveillance (MCS)

Effective monitoring, control, and surveillance (MCS) is essential to successful fishery management. The problem can be viewed in two parts. The first is the surveillance and enforcement of regulations for local fishers. This is usually effected by fishery officers, the coast guard, police, and other security officers ashore. One of the common reasons for the failure of fishery controls to prevent overfishing is that it is not feasible to implement the monitoring requirements with the resources available. Many countries lack the capability for extensive enforcement of fishery regulations. Widely scattered, small-scale rural fisheries are particularly difficult to monitor and regulations are usually ignored. This has led to the recent upsurge of interest in community-based or co-management, which will be discussed below under institutional arrangements. In the Caribbean, the alternative exists of establishing special enforcement units but this may not be sustainable except for the most valuable resources.

The responsibility for the enforcement of fishery regulations usually lies with agencies that are also responsible for enforcing other laws (for example, those relating to narcotics smuggling, immigration, and criminal violations). In comparison to these, fisheries violations may be perceived as insignificant. Even when domestic violations are taken to court they may not be given priority (Towle et al., 1991). Part of the solution lies in educating the agencies with responsibility for enforcement as to the need for, and potential benefits of, fisheries enforcement.

The second aspect of MCS is aimed at curtailing illegal foreign fishing. This usually requires seagoing capability and is often the mandate of the coast guard. Seagoing capability is minimal in most small or less developed Caribbean countries. Problems with illegal foreign fishing vary among countries and resource types (Table 3.1). For most countries with 200 mile EEZs, except OECS countries where the OECS Fishery Unit has an ongoing programme of surveillance and enforcement, illegal foreign fishing for large pelagics is essentially unaddressed. In Suriname, Guyana, and Trinidad and Tobago, deep slope resources are fished extensively by snapper boats from neighbouring countries. A variety of more localized problems occur wherever there is easy access to the EEZ of one country from the fishing communities of another.

One of the difficulties in evaluating the potential for cost recovery from fines and forfeitures is a lack of quantitative information on the types and numbers of vessels actually present in the EEZs of Caribbean countries. Fishers could be involved in programmes to acquire information on the presence of foreign vessels in national waters.

Parks and Protected Areas

Marine parks and protected areas are gaining in favour as a means of reducing the impact of exploitation on living aquatic resources. There is clear evidence that fish populations in protected areas recover within

TABLE 3.4 An Overview of the Main Methods Used for Control of Fisheries

Method[a]	Aim/Effect	Comments
Licensing, limited entry (ID)	Licensing is the only way to directly limit the number of participants in the fishery.	Licenses can be used as a means for recovering some revenue from the fisheries. Licensing alone is seldom enough to control the amount of fishing effort.
Effort limits (ID)	Direct limits to the number of units of effort, e.g., hours fished, traps pulled, or trawl sets.	Limiting effort in this way is more direct, but fishers usually find ways of getting around effort limits by increasing aspects of effort that are not limited, i.e., larger traps or larger boats.
Closed season (II)	Aimed at protecting a specific part of the stock known to occur in or at a particular place or time; usually spawning or young fish. May also be used to control total effort by eliminating fishing from a particular area of the stock or period of the year.	When used as a means of controlling total effort, fishing usually increases in the open area and at the open time of the year. Thus, reduction of effort is not directly proportional to the closed season or the closed area. Closed seasons are easier to monitor than closed areas, unless the latter are very large.
Closed area (II)		
Gear restrictions (II)	These usually aim to control the size or species of fish caught, e.g., by regulating the mesh size used in nets or traps.	Although the relationship between gear and size of fish caught is imprecise, gear restrictions can be monitored by inspection ashore.
Catch quotas, total allowable catch (TAC) (OD)	Quotas directly limit the amount of fish taken from the stock to that corresponding to the target reference point. TAC is the simplest form of catch quota.	Catch quotas will vary with the abundance of the resource and must thus be re-estimated at regular intervals. This requires substantial amounts of detailed data. Regulation by catch quotas also requires that fish landings be monitored on a real-time basis so that the fishery can be closed by the catch when the quota has been taken. A single TAC often results in a race for the quota and consequently, over-capitalization.
Industry quotas (ID)	The TAC is divided up among participants in the fishery.	Individual fishing companies can manage the way in which they take their share in order to optimize their economic return. The equitable distribution of quotas among participants is usually difficult and contentious.

TABLE 3.4 An Overview of the Main Methods Used for Control of Fisheries (continued)

Method[a]	Aim/Effect	Comments
Individual transferrable quotas (ITQs) (OD)	A form of industry quota in which the quotas may be transferred, sold, or traded.	ITQs facilitate the operation of normal market effects in the fishing industry. More efficient companies can buy quotas and so increase their share of the resource. A basic proportion of ITQs are given out on a long-term basis so that companies may plan their operations. Remaining quotas are distributed or sold each year with the amount becoming available being dependent on the abundance of the resource. May lead to monopolies.
Size limits (OD)	Directly limits the size of fish landed in order to reduce growth over-fishing and to ensure that immature individuals are not caught.	Shore-based monitoring of size limits will often lead to discarding of smaller sizes at sea. Because discarded individuals usually die, this defeats the purpose of the regulation.
Taxes or tariffs (OI)	Taxation on the fish landed is one means of reducing the amount of fish caught.	Increases the cost of fishing and thus shifts the cost and revenue equilibrium to the left (Figure 3.5).

[a] I/O = input/output control; D/I = direct/indirect control.

a few years and reach levels that are substantially higher than those in adjacent fished areas (Roberts and Polunin, 1991). As such, they can provide areas in which tourism and recreational activities can take place while fisheries continue elsewhere. Protected areas are also cited as enhancing fisheries in adjacent areas through emigration of adult biomass into fished areas and through enhanced recruitment in fished areas. The recruitment is assumed to be due to the additional spawning biomass in the protected area. These effects, particularly enhanced recruitment, although plausible, are not well documented (Roberts and Polunin, 1993; Rowley, 1994).

There are many marine parks and protected areas throughout the Caribbean (Organization of American States, 1988). Some, such as the Hol Chan Reserve in Belize, are well-known tourist attractions that have provided alternative employment for fishers. Others remain protected only in name, due to the lack of funds to establish effective management and cost recovery systems.

Adaptive Management

The concept of adaptive management was proposed by Walters (1986) as an alternative to model-based assessment and management. He considered the most effective approach to be to implement measures and monitor the effects of, and undertake, further management based on the response. He suggested that in some cases an experimental approach be used to probe the response of the system to exploitation in order to learn more about it. Such experimentation, though risky, may be appropriate in situations where there are several small stocks with relatively short regeneration times, so that the cost of learning will be low relative to the potential value of the knowledge gained (for example, local sea urchin stocks). In situations where funds and expertise for resource assessment are limited, as in most Caribbean countries, the approach of implementing reasonable management measures and monitoring the response of stocks to those measures may be the most effective use of funds.

The Legislative Basis of Fishery Management

Effective legislation is fundamental to successful fishery management. In most countries there is a Fisheries Act, which empowers the Fisheries minister to establish the fisheries regulations required to manage fisheries. Various other acts, usually pertaining to coastal conservation, may also be relevant to fisheries management.

The United Nations Convention on the Law of the Sea (UNCLOS)

Many countries have already updated, or are in the process of updating, their legislation on the basis of the UNCLOS (United Nations, 1983). UNCLOS is a key reference point for discussion on national and international fisheries management.

The UNCLOS refers extensively to the exclusive economic zone (EEZ), which is an ocean area over which a country has jurisdiction for all living (mainly fisheries) and nonliving (oil, manganese, sand) resources. EEZs are generally bounded by a line that is 200 miles from the country's shore. If the distance between two countries is less than 400 miles, the equidistant principle is used, and a boundary is established.

All countries in the Caribbean have declared their EEZs but many are still in the process of negotiating boundaries with their neighbours. For example, Venezuela claims that Aves Island is entitled to a 200 mile EEZ but this claim is not recognized by the neighbouring countries that are members of the Organization of Eastern Caribbean States (OECS). Such disagreements are ultimately referred to the World Court in The Hague, Netherlands. Marine space located beyond the EEZs is called the High Seas. In the Caribbean region, the EEZs encompass nearly the entire ocean space, leaving only two tiny sections of High Seas in the Gulf of Mexico (Figure 3.10).

This new economic division of the ocean gives Caribbean countries considerable rights to the resources within their waters. However, along with these rights there are also substantial responsibilities to manage them properly.

> In the exclusive economic zone, the Coastal State has . . . sovereign rights for the purpose of exploring and exploiting, conserving and managing the natural resources, whether living or non-living . . . (UNCLOS, Article 56, United Nations, 1983)

Articles 61 to 64 of the UNCLOS provide criteria for managing a stock within a single EEZ. To conserve the living resources,

> The Coastal State shall determine the allowable catch of the living resources in its exclusive economic zone . . . taking into account the best scientific evidence available to it, shall ensure through proper conservation and management measures that the maintenance of the living resources in the exclusive economic zone is not endangered by over-exploitation, . . . shall also . . . maintain or restore populations of harvested species at levels which can produce the maximum sustainable yield [and] shall take into consideration the effects on species associated with or dependent upon harvested species. (Article 61)

This means that the coastal state is responsible for the conservation and management of the various resources in its EEZ. In order to do so, it must develop the technical capability needed and allocate the necessary funds. The state must also put in place an effective management system, including national legislation, regulations, surveillance, and enforcement and must pay special attention to rebuilding measures required for overexploited resources. Furthermore, it should not permit fisheries to lead to the destruction or endangerment of unfished species that co-occur with the fished species or are part of the same food chain.

To utilize the living resources,

> The Coastal State shall promote the objective of optimum utilization of the living resources in the exclusive economic zone, . . . shall determine its capacity to harvest the living resources of the exclusive economic zone . . . Where the Coastal State does not have the capacity to harvest the entire allowable catch, it shall, . . . give other States access to the surplus of the allowable catch. (Article 62)

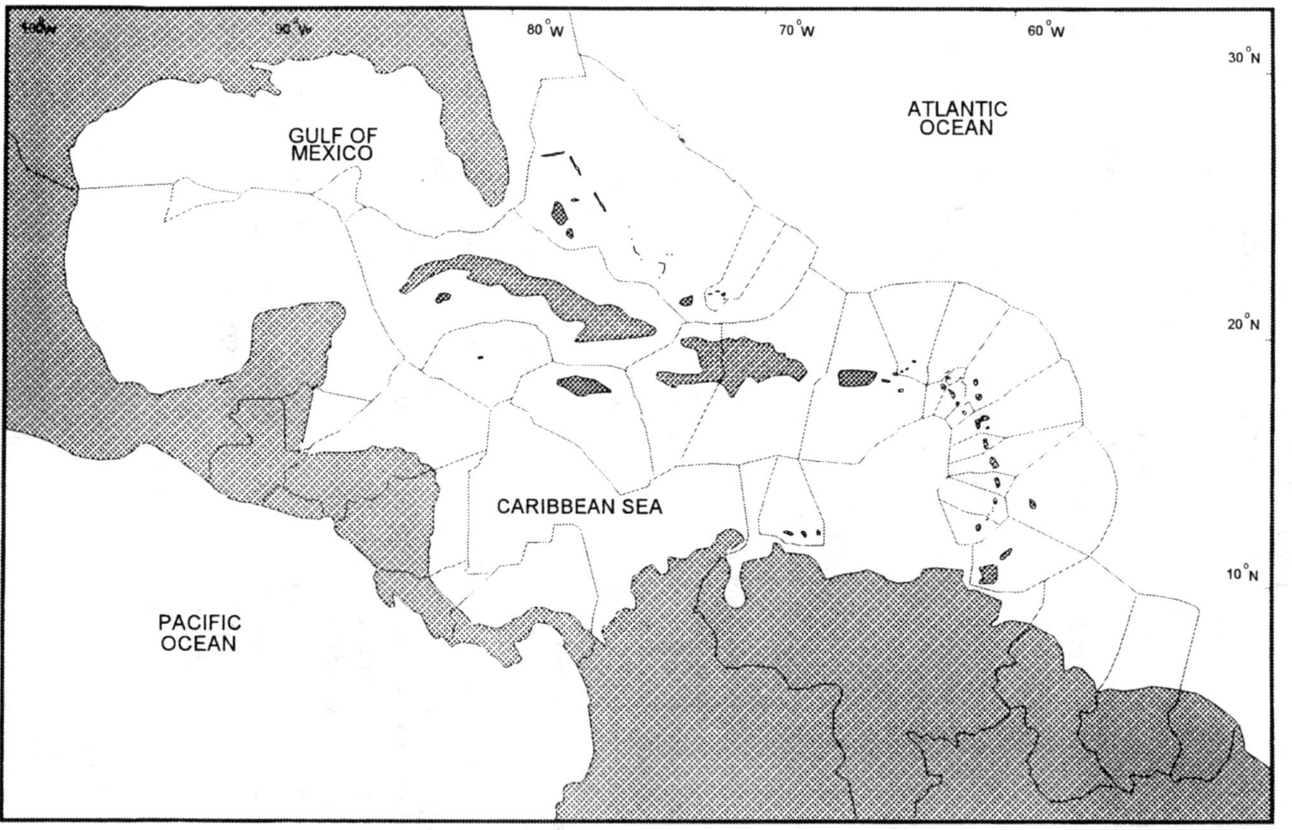

FIGURE 3.10 The exclusive economic zones of Caribbean countries.

Operationally, several coastal states have already declared that even though they may not be taking the entire potential catch, not doing so is a deliberate strategy to ensure the future health of the stock, thus there is no surplus for other states to access. Article 62 of the UNCLOS also gives coastal states the right to determine the extent and type of fishing activities in their waters and to monitor them.

Under the UNCLOS, fishery management of those fish stocks that extend beyond the EEZ of a single country involves additional responsibility (Hayashi, 1993). Stocks that occur in two or more EEZs are referred to as *shared stocks*. Those that also occur in the High Seas are called *straddling* and *highly migratory stocks*, while those that occur out on the High Seas are *High Seas stocks*. The most important shared, straddling, and highly migratory resources are the large pelagic fishes.

The rights and responsibilities of coastal states in regard to straddling stocks and highly migratory stocks have been elaborated in detail in a UN agreement relating to the conservation and management of such stocks (United Nations, 1995). The implications of this agreement for Caribbean countries are primarily in relation to pelagic fish stocks. Although these are already fully exploited, mainly by countries outside the Caribbean, the UN agreement includes special considerations for developing countries, which could be used to increase the share of these resources available to Caribbean countries (Mahon, 1996a).

Under UNCLOS Article 63, shared and straddling stocks are treated together. In both cases the states concerned, whether coastal or distant water fishing nations, should seek "either directly or through appropriate regional or subregional organizations", to agree upon the measures necessary for their conservation and development. Article 64 deals with highly migratory species, where again, "the Coastal State and other States whose nationals fish in the region" are urged to "cooperate directly or through appropriate international organizations with a view to ensuring conservation and promoting the objective of optimal utilization of such species . . . both within and beyond the exclusive economic zone". Under both of these last mentioned articles, there is the overall objective of conserving for optimal utilization.

With regard to the High Seas, the UNCLOS states that

> All States have the right for their nationals to engage in fishing on the high seas (Article 116)

> All States have the duty to take, or to co-operate with other States in taking, such measures for their respective nationals as may be necessary for the conservation of the living resources of the high seas. (Article 117)

and that

> States shall co-operate with each other in the conservation and management of living resources in the areas of the high seas. (Article 117)

Thus, there is great emphasis on the need for international cooperation in management of all resources other than those in a single EEZ. Sharing of information is a cornerstone of cooperation, and

> Available scientific information, catch and fishing effort statistics, and other data relevant to the conservation of fish stocks shall be contributed and exchanged on a regular basis through competent international organizations, whether subregional, regional or global, where appropriate and with participation by all States concerned . . . In regions for which no appropriate international organization exists, the Coastal State and other States whose nationals harvest these species in the region shall co-operate to establish such an organization and participate in its work. (Article 117)

At the national level, the legislative basis for fishery management in most Caribbean countries is, at least, adequate and usually good. Up-to-date legislation has been prepared with FAO assistance and passed for OECS countries and Barbados. Suriname, Guyana, and the Bahamas are in the process of passing legislation prepared with FAO assistance. The OECS-harmonized legislation that has been enacted in all OECS countries provides a good example of fisheries legislation. The reader should review the Fisheries Act of Saint Vincent and the Grenadines in order to appreciate its scope.

In brief, the Fisheries Act addresses the following issues:

- Promotion of fisheries
- The need for a fisheries management and development plan
- The need for a fisheries advisory committee
- Foreign access and licenses
- Local licensing fees and conditions
- Processing and handling of fish
- Establishment of management areas
- Research
- Registration of vessels and associated requirements
- Enforcement of regulations and laws
- Types of regulations which may be made

Institutional Requirements

Fisheries management must deal with stocks that vary considerably in geographical distribution from highly localized, within an EEZ, to widely distributed across several EEZs and the High Seas. Thus, the institutional arrangements for management and the interested parties will differ considerably (Table 3.5). Note that it is the level of representation rather than the type of interested party that varies among geographical stock categories.

National

At the national level in Caribbean countries, as elsewhere in the world, the management of capture fisheries is the mandate of a government fisheries department. Ultimately, this is necessary because fishery resources are a public asset that must be managed by government for the national benefit. Fisheries departments in Caribbean countries vary widely in staffing and in the level of training of their staff (Mahon and Boyce, 1992). The number and capability of staff determine the capacity of a country to manage its fisheries.

The list of subject areas covered by national legislation in the previous section indicates the range of activities that must be addressed by a fisheries department. Small fisheries departments will seldom have the expertise or numbers of staff to address these areas adequately. Consequently, the structure and function of small fisheries departments must be carefully planned and human resource development programmes must be geared towards the need for individual staff members to cope with several different subject areas.

Alternatives to in-house expertise in small fisheries departments are to approach problems on a project basis using outside expertise, and to share expertise within the region (World Bank/UNDP/CEC/FAO, 1992). The development of proposals and management of projects can be a significant activity in a small fishery department. Thus, training in project management may be an essential asset for most professional staff. The OECS and CARICOM Fisheries Units in St Vincent and the Grenadines and Belize are two examples of efforts to share expertise and experience at the regional level.

One of the weakest areas in fisheries departments is in fishery assessment. It is probably unrealistic to expect that in the foreseeable future many fisheries departments will be able to develop significant resource assessment capability. In the long term, as management produces benefits, and as better information enables fisheries departments

TABLE 3.5 Examples of Possible Fishery Management Organizations and Interested Parties for Different Geographical Categories of Resources

Geographical Category of Resource	Fisheries Management Organization	Possible Interested Parties
High Seas stocks (occurring entirely or largely on the High Seas)	Multinational fishery organization Joint standing commission (agreements between coastal and DW nations)	Government departments for coastal and DW states National representatives of industry and fishers International conservation NGOs
Straddling and highly migratory stocks (distributed or migrating across EEZ boundaries and onto the High Seas)		
Shared stocks (distributed or migrating across two or more EEZs)	Bi(multi)lateral agreement Joint standing commission	Government departments for coastal states Industry representatives Fisher and sportfisher associations National conservation NGOs
National stocks (widely distributed throughout the EEZ and exploited by several communities or companies)	The minister of fisheries, National FMO and its advisory bodies Multisectoral organization (e.g., a national CZM organization)	National government departments (e.g., fisheries, environment, tourism, physical planning) Provincial, prefectural, state government departments (for federated states) Commercial and sport fishers and associations National or regional conservation NGOs
Local stocks (circumscribed distribution and exploited by one or a few communities)	Community-based fisheries and/or multisectoral committees (e.g. a CZM committee)	Regional/municipal government departments Individual fishers or community representatives, sportsfishers, Local, or local chapters of, conservation NGOs

DW = distant water; NGO = non-governmental organizations; EEZ = exclusive economic zone; FMO = fishery management organization; CZM = coastal zone management.

to document the value of fisheries, national governments will probably increase the resources allocated to fishery management.

At the national level, the mechanism for fisheries management decision making is critical for successful management; the lack of political will to regulate users is a common cause of failure. Fishers inevitably suffer genuine short-term hardship due to regulations and the political directorate will often favour their short-term needs over the long-term sustainability of the resource. One solution may be to formalize the advisory and decision making process so that inputs from fishers are incorporated, long-term versus short-term benefits are documented, and it is more difficult for the political directorate to ignore the advice.

The fisheries advisory committee (FAC) can play a central role in this process. The membership of the FAC should include representatives of all interested parties. The FAC should review all aspects of fishery development and management and advise the minister responsible for fisheries. The fishery department provides the technical information for the FAC. Ideally, in a well-managed system, most of the issues pertaining to fisheries will be addressed by a fishery management plan, which the FAC will review at regular intervals. This should keep ad hoc and emergency decision making to a minimum.

Because most of the issues to be addressed by the FAC will usually be routine and very specific to fisheries, it may be advisable to have a two-tiered advisory decision making process, such as recommended for Bermuda by Towle et al. (1991). In this system, the FAC is a subsidiary to a Marine and Coastal Environmental Advisory Committee (MCEAC) and includes primarily representation from the fisheries department and the fishing industry. The MCEAC includes wider representation for interested parties, such as conservation groups, the tourism authority, the port authority, the health department, etc., and advises on a wider range of topics. They also review the activities of the FAC.

International

As stated, the UNCLOS requires that in regions where no appropriate international organization exists, the fishing countries cooperate to establish such an organization and participate in its work. Where only a few countries are involved, this can be achieved through bilateral or multilateral agreements. For example, Trinidad and Tobago, Grenada, Barbados, St Lucia, Dominica, and Martinique could cooperatively manage flyingfish on the basis of a multilateral agreement.

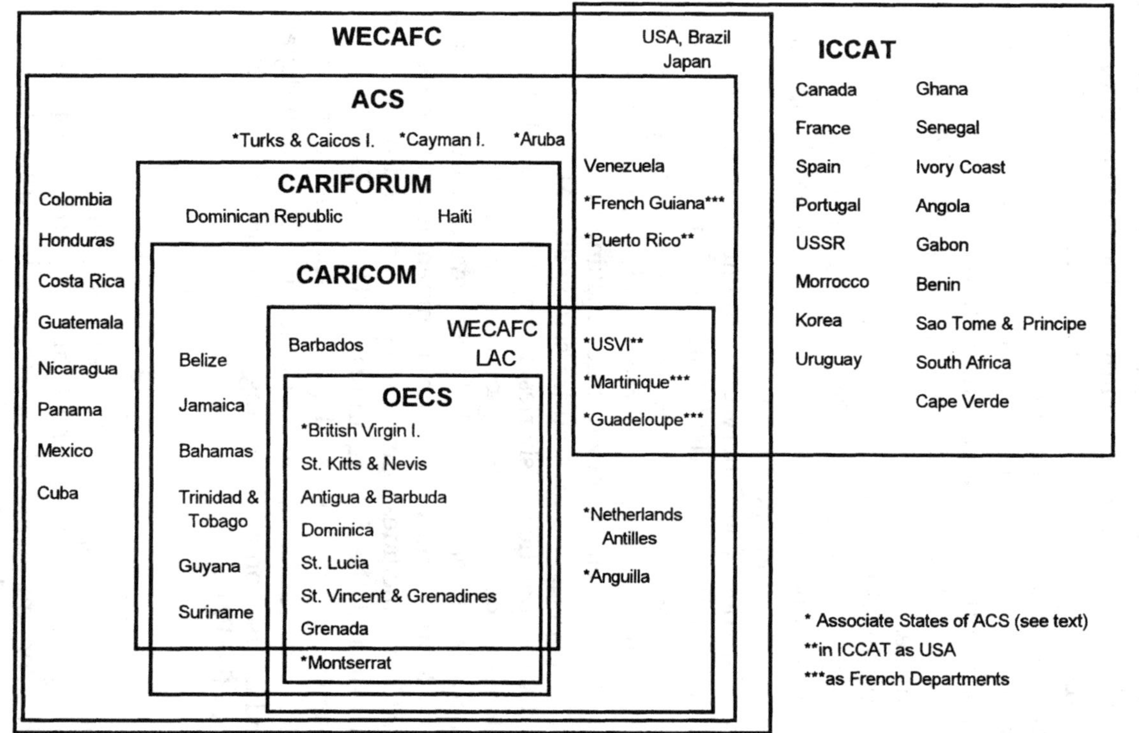

FIGURE 3.11 The membership of regional and international organizations with responsibility for fisheries management and development in the wider Caribbean (WECAFC = FAO West Central Atlantic Fishery Commission; ACS = Association of Caribbean States; CARICOM = Caribbean Community and Common Market; OECS = Organization of Eastern Caribbean States; LAC = Lesser Antilles Committee; ICCAT = International Commission for the Conservation of Atlantic Tunas).

When stocks extend more widely (for example, throughout the Caribbean region and on to the High Seas) there will be the need to involve many countries in their management. In such cases, regional or international organizations will be required. There are several international organizations that have an interest in fisheries and development in the Caribbean (Figure 3.11). Some of these organizations could play a role in fisheries management of shared, straddling, or highly migratory stocks but will need strengthening (Mahon, 1996a).

The OECS and CARICOM are already addressing fisheries issues and can represent the interests of their member states collectively. However, because their member states are interspersed with numerous other non-member countries, their ability to undertake international fisheries management without referring to non-member countries is limited to relatively small geographical areas. Newly emerging organizations such as CARIFORUM and the Association of Caribbean States (ACS) provide more complete geographical coverage but the extent to which their mandates include cooperative management of fisheries remains to be defined.

The West Central Atlantic Fisheries Commission (WECAFC) of the Food and Agriculture Organization (FAO) includes all the countries of the wider Caribbean region. Since its inception in 1975, WECAFC has been primarily a forum for the exchange of technical information among fisheries personnel. There has been no attempt to use WECAFC for fishery management decision making as has been the case in FAO commissions in other parts of the world. Now that the UNCLOS has become operational, WECAFC could be enhanced so that it can assume a more significant coordinating and decision making role.

The most active international organization relevant to the Caribbean is the International Commission for the Conservation of Atlantic Tunas (ICCAT). With headquarters in Madrid, ICCAT's mandate is the conservation and management of all tuna and tuna-like species in the entire Atlantic, including the Caribbean and Mediterranean Seas. Each year, scientists from member countries meet to assess the major tuna resources and advise the Commission on management measures. However, until recently, membership has included only those countries with large commercial fisheries. Thus, Venezuela, the U.S., Brazil, and Cuba (now resigned from ICCAT) have been the only Caribbean countries participating in ICCAT and there is very little attention to the details of pelagic fishery resources within the Caribbean region.

Although CARICOM and Mexico have recently sent observers to ICCAT meetings in order to become more informed about the management of these resources, these and other Caribbean countries will have to increase their membership, either individually or collectively, and become more involved before they can have a significant impact on ICCAT decisions. Readers interested in the activities of ICCAT can refer to the most recent annual reports (ICCAT, 1995).

Research and Development Institutions

The lack of a focal point for fisheries management development within the Caribbean makes it difficult for researchers and managers to obtain a comprehensive picture of related activities in the region. However, there are several institutions within the wider Caribbean that carry out training, research, and project implementation related to fisheries management and development (Freon et al., 1991; Mahon and Bateson, 1992). These include several university centres (the Marine Science Centre, University of the West Indies (UWI), Jamaica, the Marine Resource and Environmental Management Programme, MAREMP, UWI, Barbados); college departments (University College of Belize, College of the U.S. Virgin Islands, St. Croix); university-related laboratories (UWI Discovery Bay Marine Laboratory, Jamaica, Bellairs Research Institute, Barbados); government institutes (Institute of Marine Affairs, Trinidad and Tobago); non-governmental organizations (CANARI, St Lucia, Caribbean Conservation Association, Barbados, Island Resources Foundation, St Thomas); and international organizations (UN Environmental Programme, Caribbean Environmental Programme, Jamaica, UNESCO, IOCARIBE, Colombia).

There are also several international organizations the activities of which should also be monitored by fisheries researchers and managers. These include non-governmental organizations, such as the International Center for Living Aquatic Resources Management (ICLARM), the Philippines; regional governmental organizations, such as the South Pacific Forum Fisheries Agency, the Solomon Islands; and long-term programmes such as the FAO Bay of Bengal and South West Indian Ocean Programmes.

Much of the transfer of expertise and technology to the fisheries community of the Caribbean has been through bilateral development assistance from northern temperate countries. Whereas some of the approaches and techniques for management and assessment are adaptable, many are not, or have been adopted without adaptation. Caribbean fisheries would benefit from an increase in interaction with other tropical areas of the world with similar fisheries and similar problems. For example, involvement in the recent initiative on tuna interactions in the Pacific Ocean would have provided Caribbean fishery personnel with useful insights into the management and development of large pelagic fisheries (Shomura et al., 1991a, 1991b). Increased south–south cooperation could include liaison with institutions such as ICLARM, the Forum Fisheries Agency, and the various fishery commissions in the eastern Atlantic and Indian and Pacific Oceans.

Co-Management

The top-down approach to management has seldom worked, particularly among small-scale fishers who are widely dispersed in remote areas where enforcement is difficult. Recently, approaches that involve fishers and the fishing industry in management decision making (co-management) and confer some form of property rights have been considered as more likely to succeed (World Bank/UNDP/CEC/FAO, 1992). Thus, there has been an increased emphasis on acquiring information about the social and economic conditions of fishers and fishing communities (for example, Indo-Pacific Fishery Commission, 1994).

Throughout the world there is a trend in fisheries management towards the inclusion of all users in the management process. Formal mechanisms for the input of users are now included in the management process in many countries (the Fishery Management Councils of the U.S., the newly established Fisheries Resources Conservation Commission (FRCC) of Atlantic Canada). The fisheries advisory committees required by legislation in some Caribbean countries are an explicit attempt to incorporate the inputs of users into management decision making.

One requirement for the continued successful evolution of these trends is that the process of assessing fisheries and providing management advice based on management reference points be made more understandable to nontechnical interested parties so that they can participate meaningfully in the decision making process. There are extension activities in most Caribbean countries but these are generally oriented toward a unidirectional flow of technical information from fisheries departments to fishers rather than toward a dialogue.

In many instances the trend extends to the point of vesting the responsibility for management in the users. This requires that the users be adequately organized to undertake the task. Fisher organizations, cooperatives, and associations are the most likely candidates to assume the role of management with technical assistance from government or non-governmental organizations (Hannesson and

Kurien, 1988; Jentoft, 1989). Fisher cooperatives and associations are common throughout the Caribbean but their levels of organization vary a great deal. The most successful cooperatives are those of Belize and Guyana, where they manage the full range of operations from the supply of fishing gear and ice to processing and marketing the catch. Many cooperatives, however, exist only to purchase fuel and gear wholesale and would need to be strengthened and better organized before they could undertake any significant management responsibility (Jentoft and Sandersen, 1993).

These approaches are new to fishery managers in Caribbean countries, where there are only a few instances of community participation in fishery management, such as the Discovery Bay reef fish fishery, Jamaica (van Barneveld et al., 1999) and sea urchin management in St Lucia (Smith and Berkes, 1991). Nonetheless, the staff of fisheries departments are aware of and interested in applying these approaches wherever they may be applicable.

Environmental Linkages and Integrated Coastal Zone Management

There is a close link between fisheries and the environment. In extreme cases, fishery products may be inedible due to contamination by pollutants. Fishery production systems also suffer from the direct effect of habitat degradation. Nearshore fisheries are most at risk. Coastal habitats, notably seagrasses, mangroves, and coral reefs are frequently destroyed or impacted by development for non-fishery uses. Apart from the loss of adult habitat, near shore habitats are often important nursery areas for species that live in other habitats as adults (Clark, 1992).

Coastal wetlands (mangroves and salt marshes) may also serve as buffers between terrestrial and marine ecosystems by absorbing pollutants or reducing the rate at which they are released into the sea. The extent of destruction of coastal wetlands throughout the Caribbean is largely undocumented but dredging and filling have been carried out for coastal development since the earliest settlements. These practices continue in the Caribbean, at a time when many developed countries are undertaking multimillion dollar habitat restoration programmes (National Research Council, 1992).

The interface between fisheries and environmental concerns will be most effectively addressed in the context of integrated coastal zone management (ICZM) (Clark, 1992). ICZM can also provide the context for resolution of previously mentioned conflicts between fisheries and other sectors that use the coastal zone, including tourism, transportation, housing, and industry. The need for inclusion of fisheries in ICZM is explicit in the FAO Code of Conduct for Responsible Fishing.

Relationships Among Harvesting, Processing, and Marketing Subsectors

Since most fishing resources are now, or soon will be, fully exploited, it is appropriate to focus on optimization of returns from the catch. Attention to post-harvest handling, processing, and marketing of fish can increase the returns, both in terms of total amount and monetary value, from the current catch. These are primarily developmental issues, a detailed analysis of which is beyond the scope of this chapter. However, virtually all development actions have implications for management, inasmuch as they change the context within which management takes place.

There is a need for ongoing technical assistance in all countries in the areas of fish handling practices required to reduce post-harvest losses and appropriate scale and technology for fish landing facilities. Developments in this area will affect the data and information collection process. For example, fishes that are landed gutted and without heads will require conversion factors for estimates of whole weight. Estimation of total weights of fish landed in ice in containers will require a change in sampling practices.

Processing can play an important role in fishery development by increasing the value of the landed catch and, in the case of seasonal fisheries, by making products available over an extended period. However, it can also create an increased demand for fishery products, which may in turn lead to an increase in fishing effort. When the resources are already overexploited, this will lead to a reduction in total landings and a net loss in revenue from the fishery. Thus, as should be the case for harvesting capacity, the development of processing capacity should be matched to the potential sustainable yield of the resource. Managers and developers should consider whether increased processing capacity is likely to increase fishing pressure on the resource beyond sustainable levels before permitting and facilitating investment in processing.

In situations where the amounts of fish landed are limited by the existing markets, marketing and shipping initiatives can affect the movement of investment funds and thus of fishing effort into and out of the harvesting sector. For example, the opening of a new market to fishers by establishing a shipping facility that will allow the export of fish to markets that were previously unavailable may lead to overexploitation of the resource. Even in a regulated fishery, currently licensed fishers may increase their efforts by fishing more gear (unless the amount is limited) or by fishing longer hours. New markets may also bring pressure from new investors seeking to enter the fishery with new and usually more efficient equipment. Unless the management objectives and limits are very clear and well based, these pressures may be very difficult to resist because in the short term they bring new jobs and opportunities to earn foreign exchange.

CONCLUSIONS AND FUTURE DIRECTIONS

It is now clear that in the Caribbean, many of the fisheries management practices in the past have not been effective. There has probably been too much reliance on technical models to describe the status of the fisheries. It has now been discovered that, for many reasons, the outputs from these models are fraught with uncertainty. More importantly, there has probably been an overestimation of our local ability to control fisheries, particularly when the regime is not accepted by the majority of users. Hopefully, lessons learned from the past will lead to the new era of fisheries management discussed in the introduction (Rosenberg et al., 1993).

In developing ideas for change, it will be wise to take note of and adopt, where possible, principles for effective management based on global experience with natural resource management (Ludwig et al., 1993) as follows: include human motivation and responses as part of the system to be studied and managed; act before scientific consensus is achieved; rely on scientists to recognize problems but not to solve them; question claims of sustainability; and confront uncertainty. A fuller discussion of these concepts, and the relative roles of science and application in sustainable management of renewable resources is provided by the Ecological Society of America Forum on Science and Sustainability (Levin, 1993).

There has to be a balance between taking action now, with the best available information, as required by the UNCLOS, and the acquisition of new information for improved decision making in the future. For valuable resources that merit substantial investment in research, efforts to quantify uncertainty and estimate risks may lead to better management advice. For other resources, where value does not justify such expenditure, the emphasis must be on making the best use of available information and taking action based on a combination of technical information and common sense. For all resources, fishery managers must emphasize the involvement of interested parties and seek to develop approaches that are agreed upon. These will best be implemented in a structured framework within which all parties know their role and prescribed action, once agreed upon, follows automatically (as in the case of a legal system) without the possibility of being affected by political interests.

In most Caribbean fisheries, there is more fishing effort than is required for optimal return from the resource, whether this is measured in biological or economic terms. Thus, the task of achieving optimal returns from the fishery resources will be largely one of reducing fishing effort and allowing the resources to increase to levels where they can provide their full potential. Rebuilding overexploited resources will be more difficult than preventing overexploitation in the first place, as may still be possible in the case of fishing for large pelagics. This is because stock rehabilitation requires either displacing those who have invested in or depend on fishing or waiting for them to retire from the fishery. Either way, a clear policy and accepted plan of action will be required in order to achieve resource rehabilitation.

The cost of management, particularly monitoring and enforcement, will always be sufficiently high so that a top-down approach is likely to fail. The emphasis of co-management seen throughout the world must, wherever applicable, be adapted and tried in the Caribbean (Chakalall et al., 1998). This may range from full control of a resource by a community or organization, as may be possible for some coastal resources with limited distribution, to participation in the process of planning for development and management, which may be all that is practicable for wide-ranging resources requiring international collaboration.

Ultimately, living aquatic resource management must be set within a broader context of coastal and marine area management. Fisheries must be included in the newly emerging practice of integrated coastal zone management if conflicts in area and extent of impact on marine resources are to be minimized.

Clearly, the management and development of living aquatic resources would benefit from a variety of additional technical and scientific information. Wherever possible, activities to acquire the necessary information should be undertaken. However, for the many small-scale fisheries that are typical of the Caribbean, the application of approaches that were developed for large-scale temperate fisheries may not be affordable (Mahon, 1997). Furthermore, experience suggests that many of the problems that have occurred are due to inadequate institutional arrangements and a tendency to delay action until better information is available. The present reality throughout the Caribbean, one of limited expertise and funds for acquisition of technical information, dictates that management must proceed without all the desired information and that institutional arrangements that address this reality must be put in place.

REFERENCES AND FURTHER READING

Alverson, D. L., M. H. Freeberg, S. A. Murawski, and J. G. Pope. 1994. "A global assessment of fisheries bycatch and discards". FAO Fisheries Technical Paper no. 339. Food and Agriculture Organization, Rome.

Apollonio, S. 1994. "The use of ecosystem characteristics in fisheries management". *Reviews in Fisheries Science* 2, no. 2: 157–180.

Appeldoorn, R. S. and B. Rodríquez (eds.). 1994. *Queen Conch Biology Fishery and Mariculture*. Fundacion Cientifica Los Roques, Caracas, Venezuela.

Auil-Marshalleck, S. 1993. "A review of the occurrence of fish spawning aggregations in the Caribbean and the implications for fisheries management". CARICOM Fisheries Resource Assessment and Management Program, LPRSF Assessment SSW/WP/24. Ms. CFRAMP, Belize.

Barbados Development Bank. 1993. *The Feasibility of Developing Longline Fisheries in Barbados*. Technical Report, Barbados Development Bank, Bridgetown, Barbados.

Beddington, J. R. and R. B. Rettig. 1984. *Approaches to the Regulation of Fishing Effort*. FAO Fisheries Technical Paper no. 243. Food and Agriculture Organization, Rome.

Berg, C. J., Jr., F. Couper, K. Nisbet, and J. Ward. 1992a. "Stock assessment of queen conch, *Strombus gigas*, and harbor conch, *S. costatus*, in Bermuda". *Proceedings of the Gulf and Caribbean Fisheries Institute* 41: 433–438.

Berg, C. J., Jr., R. Glazer, J. Carr, J. Kreiger, and S. Acton. 1992b. "Status of queen conch, *Strombus gigas*, in Florida waters". *Proceedings of the Gulf and Caribbean Fisheries Institute* 41: 439–443.

Beverton, R. J .H. and M. A. Holt. 1957. *On the Dynamics of Exploited Fish Populations*. Ministry of Agriculture, Fisheries and Food, Fishery Investigations Series 2, Volume 19. Her Majesty's Stationery Office, London.

Butler, M. J. A., C. LeBlanc, J. A. Belbin, and J. L. MacNeill. 1986. *Marine Resource Mapping: An Introductory Manual*. FAO Fisheries Technical Paper, no. 274. Food and Agriculture Organization, Rome.

Caddy, J. F. and G. P. Bazigos. 1986. *Practical Guidelines for Statistical Monitoring of Fisheries in Manpower Limited Situations*. FAO Fisheries Technical Paper, no. 257. Food and Agriculture Organization, Rome.

Caddy, J. F. and R. Mahon. 1995. *Reference Points for Fisheries Management*. FAO Fisheries Technical Paper, no. 347. Food and Agriculture Organization, Rome.

Cervignón, F., R. Cipriani, W. Fischer, L. Garibaldi, M. Henrickx, A. J. Lemus, R. Márquez, J. M. Poutiers, G. Robaina and B. Rodríguez. 1993. *Field Guide to the Commercial Marine and Brackish-Water Resources of the Northern Coast of South America*. Food and Agriculture Organization, Rome.

CFRAMP (CARICOM Fisheries Resource Assessment and Management Program). 1993a. "Report of the sub-project specification workshop for data and information systems and licensing and registration systems". CARICOM Fisheries Research Document, no. 11. CFRAMP, Belize.

CFRAMP (CARICOM Fisheries Resource Assessment and Management Program). 1993b. "Sub-project initiation mission report for: large pelagic, reef and deep-slope fishes assessments". CARICOM Fisheries Research Document, no. 10. CFRAMP, Belize.

CFRAMP (CARICOM Fisheries Resource Assessment and Management Program). 1995. "CARICOM Fisheries Newsnet". *CFRAMP Newsletter* 2, no. 1: 1–2.

CFRAMP (CARICOM Fisheries Resource Assessment and Management Program). 1996. "Report of the joint meeting of the CFRAMP shrimp and groundfish sub-project specification workshop and fourth WECAFC ad hoc shrimp and groundfish working group of the Guiana-Brazil shelf". Unpublished report, CFRAMP, Belize.

CFMC (Caribbean Fisheries Management Council). 1995. *Fisheries Management Plan for Conch,* Strombus gigas. Caribbean Fisheries Management Council, Puerto Rico.

Chakalall, B. 1992. "Fisheries management in the Lesser Antilles". *Proceedings of the Gulf and Caribbean Fisheries Institute* 42: 294–330.

Chakalall, B., R. Mahon, and P. McConney. 1998. "Current issues in fisheries governance in the Caribbean Community (CARICOM)". *Marine Policy* 22: 29–44.

Charles, D. O. and S. A. Neverson. 1990. "Report of the Eastern Caribbean seafood marketing strategy project", volume 2. OECS Fish Marketing Studies. Organization of Eastern Caribbean States, Fisheries Unit, St Vincent.

Charlier, P. 1993. "Fisheries information system in Suriname preliminary analysis of first year's results and guidelines for fisheries management". Suriname Fisheries Report, no. 2.

Clark, C. W. 1985. *Bioeconomic Modelling and Fisheries Management.* John Wiley & Sons, New York.

Clark, J. R. 1992. *Integrated Management of Coastal Zones.* FAO Fisheries Technical Paper, no. 327. Food and Agriculture Organization, Rome.

Clepper, H. (ed.).1979. *Predator-Prey Systems in Fisheries Management.* Sport Fishing Institute, Washington, D.C.

Csirke, J. 1988. "Small shoaling pelagic fish stocks". pp. 271–302, in: J. A. Gulland, ed., *Fish Population Dynamics,* 2nd edition. John Wiley & Sons, New York.

Csirke, J. and G. D. Sharpe. 1984. "Reports of the expert consultation to examine changes in abundance and species composition of neritic fish resources", volume 1. FAO Fisheries Report, no. 291. Food and Agriculture Organization, Rome.

Dalzell, P. and G. L. Preston. 1992. *Deep Reef Slope Fishery Resources of the South Pacific, a Summary and Analysis of the Dropline Fishing Survey Data Generated by the Activities of the SPC Fisheries Programme Between 1974 and 1988.* South Pacific Commission, Noumea, New Caledonia.

Diaz-de-Leon, A. and J. C. Seijo. 1992. "A multi-criteria non-linear optimization model for the control and management of a tropical fishery". *Marine Resource Economics* 7: 23–40.

EEC (European Economic Community). 1994. "Report on the meeting on the data base for evaluation of biological impact of fisheries". Commission Staff Working Paper. Charlottenlund, Denmark (May).

Espeut, P. and S. Grant. 1990. *An Economic and Social Analysis of Small-Scale Fisheries in Jamaica*. University of the West Indies, Institute of Social and Economic Research, Mona, Jamaica.

Fanning, P. L. 1992. "Sub-project initiation mission report for fisheries data and information systems licensing and registration systems". CARICOM Fisheries Research Document, no. 3. CARICOM Fisheries Resource Assessment and Management Program, Belize.

Farmer & Associates Ltd. 1990. Report of the Eastern Caribbean seafood marketing strategy project", volume 3. OECS Fish Marketing Studies, Survey of North American Markets. Organization of Eastern Caribbean States, Fisheries Unit, St Vincent.

FAO (Food and Agriculture Organization). 1983. "Report of the expert consultation on the regulation of fishing effort (fish mortality)". FAO Fisheries Report, no. 289. Food and Agriculture Organization, Rome.

FAO (Food and Agriculture Organization). 1993a. "Marine fisheries and the Law of the Sea: A decade of change". FAO Fisheries Circular, no. 853. Food and Agriculture Organization, Rome.

FAO (Food and Agriculture Organization). 1993b. *Marine Fishery Resources of the Antilles*. FAO Fisheries Technical Paper, no, 326. Food and Agriculture Organization, Rome.

FAO (Food and Agriculture Organization). 1993c. "Western Central Atlantic Fishery Commission. Technical consultation on sustainable fisheries development in the WECAFC area". FAO Fisheries Report, no. 503. Food and Agriculture Organization, Rome.

FAO (Food and Agriculture Organization). 1994. *Review of the State of World Marine Fishery Resources*. FAO Fisheries Technical Paper, no. 335. Food and Agriculture Organization, Rome.

FAO (Food and Agriculture Organization). 1995a. *Code of Conduct for Responsible Fisheries*. Food and Agriculture Organization, Rome.

FAO (Food and Agriculture Organization). 1995b. "Western Central Atlantic Fishery Commission. Report of the third workshop on the biological and economical modelling of the shrimp resources on the Guyana-Brazil shelf". FAO Fisheries Report, no. 526. Food and Agriculture Organization, Rome.

FAO (Food and Agriculture Organization). 1996. "Precautionary approach to capture fisheries and species introductions". FAO Technical Guidelines for Responsible Fisheries, no. 2. Food and Agriculture Organization, Rome.

Fischer, W. (ed.). 1978. *FAO Species Identification Sheets for Fishery Purposes. West Central Atlantic*, volumes 1–6. Food and Agriculture Organization, Rome.

Freon, P., B. Gobert, and R. Mahon. 1991. "La recherche halieutique et les pecheries artisanales dans la Caraibe insulaire". pp. 195–222, in J.-R. Durand, J. Lemoalle, and J. Weber, eds., *La Recherche Face a la Peche Artisanale*. International Symposium, ORSTOM-IFREMER, Montpellier, France, July 3–7.

Garcia, S. 1988. "Tropical penaeid prawns". pp. 219–249, in: J. A. Gulland, ed., *Fish Population Dynamics*, 2nd edition. John Wiley & Sons, New York.

Garcia, S. M. 1994. "Precautionary principle: Its implications in capture fisheries management". *Ocean and Coastal Management* 22: 99–125.

Gayanilo, F. C., Jr., P. Sparre, and D. Pauly. 1994. *The FAO-ICLARM Stock Assessment Tools (FiSAT) User's Guide*. FAO Computerized Information Series (Fisheries), no. 6. Food and Agriculture Organization, Rome.

Gibbons-Fly, W., C. Oravetz, and W. Seidel. 1994. "Public law 101–162, for the international conservation of sea turtles: a status report". In B. A. Schroeder and B. E. Witherington, eds., *Proceedings of the Thirteenth Annual Symposium on Sea Turtle Biology and Conservation*. Jekyll Island, Georgia, February. NOAA Technical Memorandum NMFS-SEFSC-341. U.S. Department of Commerce, Washington, D.C.

GESAMP – IMO/FAO/UNESCO – IOC/WMO/WHO/IAEA/UN/UNEP. 1994. Joint Group of Experts on the Scientific Aspects of Marine Environmental Protection (GESAMP): Report of the twenty-fourth session. New York, 21-25 March, Rep. Stud. GESAMP no. 53.

Gimbel, K. L. 1994. *Limiting Access to Marine Fisheries: Keeping the Focus on Conservation*. Center for Marine Conservation and World Wildlife Fund U.S., Washington, D.C.

Goodbody, I. (ed.). 1986. *Coastal Pelagic Fishery Resources in the Caribbean*, parts I, II, and III. Research Report No. 7. University of the West Indies, Zoology Department, Mona, Jamaica.

Goodyear, C. P. 1993. "Spawning stock biomass per recruit in fisheries management: Foundation and current use. pp. 67–82, in S. J. Smith, J. J. Hunt, and D. Rivard, eds., *Risk Evaluation and Biological Reference Points for Fisheries Management*. Canadian Special Publication of Fisheries and Aquatic Science, no. 120. National Research Council of Canada, Ottawa.

Gordon, H. S. 1954. "Economic theory of a common-property resource: The fishery". *Journal of Political Economics* 62: 124–142.

Gulland, J. A. 1983. *Fish Stock Assessment: A Manual of Basic Methods*. John Wiley & Sons, New York.

Gulland, J. A. 1988. *Fish Population Dynamics*, 2nd edition. John Wiley & Sons, New York.

Gulland, J. A. and A. A. Rosenberg. 1992. *A Review of Length-Based Approaches to Assessing Fish Stocks*. FAO Fisheries Technical Paper, no. 323. Food and Agriculture Organization, Rome.

Hannesson, R. and J. Kurien. 1988. *Studies on the Role of Fishermen's Organisations in Fisheries Management*. FAO Fisheries Technical Paper, no. 300. Food and Agriculture Organization, Rome.

Hardin, G. 1968. "The tragedy of the commons". *Science* 162: 1243–1248.

Hastenrath, S. 1988. *Climate and Circulation of the Tropics*. D. Reidel Publishing, Boston, Massachusetts.

Hayashi, M. 1993. "The management of transboundary fish stocks under the LOS convention". *International Journal of Marine and Coastal Law* 8, no. 2: 245–261.

Healey, M. C. 1984. "Multiattribute analysis and the concept of optimum yield". *Canadian Journal of Fisheries and Aquatic Science* 41: 1393–1406.

Hilborn, R. and C. J. Walters. 1992. *Quantitative Fisheries Stock Assessment: Choice, Dynamics and Uncertainty.* Chapman and Hall, New York.

Holling, C. S. 1993. "Investing in research for sustainability". *Ecological Applications* 3, no. 4: 552–555.

Huntsman, G. R., W. R. Nicholson, and W. W. Fox, Jr., eds. 1982. *The Biological Bases for Reef Fishery Management.* NOAA Technical Memorandum, NMFS-SEFC-80. U.S. Department of Commerce, Washington, D.C.

Huss, H. H. 1994. *Assurance of Seafood Quality.* FAO Fisheries Technical Paper, no. 334. Food and Agriculture Organization, Rome.

ICCAT (International Commission for Atlantic Tunas). 1995. *Report for Biennial Period, 1994–1995,* part 1 (1994). ICCAT, Madrid, Spain.

Indo-Pacific Fishery Commission. 1994. *Proceeding of the Symposium on Socio-economic Issues in Coastal Fisheries Management.* Bankok, Thailand, 23–26 November 1993. RAPA Publication 1994/8.

Institute of Marine Research. 1989. *Surveys of the Fish Resources in the Shelf Areas Between Suriname and Colombia.* NORAD/UNDP/FAO Programme, GLO\82\001. Institute of Marine Research, Bergen, Norway.

Jentoft, S. 1989. "Fisheries co-management: Delegating government responsibility to fishermen's organizations". *Marine Policy* (April): 137–154.

Jentoft, S., and H. T. Sandersen. 1993. *Co-management in Tropical Fisheries: The Case of St Vincent and the Grenadines.* Nordland Research Institute, Norway.

Johannes, R. E. 1978. "Traditional marine conservation methods in Oceania and their demise". *Annual Review of Ecological Systems* 9: 349–364.

Johannes, R. E. 1981. "Working with fishermen to improve coastal tropical fisheries and resource management". *Bulletin of Marine Science* 31: 673–680.

Johannes, R. J. 1981. *Words of the Lagoon: Fishing and Marine Lore in the Palau District of Micronesia.* University of California Press, Los Angeles.

Klima, E. 1976. *A Review of the Fishery Resources in the Western Central Atlantic. International Project for the Development of Fisheries in the Western Central Atlantic (WECAF).* WECAF Studies, no. 3. Food and Agriculture Organization, Rome.

Koslow, J. A., K. Aiken, S. Auil, and A. Clemetson. 1994. "Catch and effort analysis for the reef fisheries of Jamaica and Belize". *U.S. Fishery Bulletin* 92: 737–747.

Kruse, G., D. M. Eggers, R. J. Marasco, C. Pautzke, and T. J. Quinn II, eds. 1993. *Proceedings of the International Symposium on Management Strategies for Exploited Fish Populations.* Alaska Sea Grant College Program, Report no. 93-02, University of Alaska, Fairbanks.

Levin, S. A. (ed.). 1993. "Science and sustainability". *Ecological Applications* 3, no. 4: 545–589.

Longhurst, A. R. and D. Pauly. 1987. *Ecology of Tropical Oceans.* Academic Press, New York.

Lluch-Belda, D., R. J. M. Crawford, T. Kawaski, A. D. MacCall, R. H. Parrish, R. A. Schwartzlose, and P. E. Smith. 1992. "World-wide fluctuations of sardine and anchovy stocks: The regime problem". *South African Marine Science* 8: 195–205.

Ludwig, D., R. Hilborn, and C. Walters. 1993. "Uncertainty, resource exploitation, and conservation: Lessons from history". *Science* 260: 36–37.

Mace, P. M. and M. P. Sissenwine. 1993. "How much spawning per recruit is enough?" pp. 101–118, in S. J. Smith, J. J. Hunt, and D. Rivard, eds., *Risk Evaluation and Biological Reference Points for Fisheries Management*. Canadian Special Publication of Fisheries and Aquatic Science, no. 120. National Research Council of Canada, Ottawa.

Mahon, R. (ed.). 1987. "Report and proceedings of the expert consultation on shared fishery resources of the Lesser Antilles". FAO Fisheries Report, no. 383. Food and Agriculture Organization, Rome.

Mahon, R. 1990. *Fishery Management Options for Lesser Antilles Countries*. FAO Fisheries Technical Paper, no. 313. Food and Agriculture Organization, Rome.

Mahon, R. 1996a. "Fisheries of small island states and their oceanographic research and information needs". In G. Maul, ed., *Small Islands: Marine Science and Sustainable Development*. American Geophysical Union, Washington, D.C.

Mahon, R. 1996. *Fisheries and Research for Tunas and Tuna-like Species in the Western Central Atlantic: Implications of the International Agreement on Conservation and Management of Straddling Fish Stocks and Highly Migratory Fish Stocks*. FAO Fisheries Technical Paper, no. 357. Food and Agriculture Organization, Rome.

Mahon, R. 1997. "Does fisheries science serve the needs of managers of small stocks in developing countries?" *Canadian Journal of Fisheries and Aquatic Science* 54: 2207–2213.

Mahon, R. and R. Bateson. 1992. "Report of the CFRAMP baseline survey on the role of regional institutions in fisheries research and management". CARICOM Fisheries Research Document, no. 3. CARICOM Fisheries Resource Assessment and Management Program, Belize.

Mahon, R. and S. L. Boyce. 1992. "CARICOM Fisheries Resource Assessment and Management Program baseline survey of fisheries division in participating countries". CARICOM Fisheries Research Document, no. 5. CARICOM Fisheries Resource Assessment and Management Program, Belize.

Mahon, R., and A. A. Rosenberg (eds.). 1988. "Fishery data collection systems for eastern Caribbean islands". OECS Fishery Report, no. 2. Organization of Eastern Caribbean States, Fisheries Unit, St Vincent.

Mahon, R., G. A. Kong, and K. A. Aiken. 1999. "The status of the conch fishery on the shelf and banks off the south coast of Jamaica". *Proceedings of the Gulf and Caribbean Fisheries Institute* 45: 955–971.

Mahon, R., F. Murphy, P. Murray, J. Rennie, and S. Willoughby. 1990. "Temporal variability of catch and effort in pelagic fisheries in Barbados, Grenada, St Lucia and St Vincent: With particular reference to the problem of low catches in 1989". FAO FI: TCP/RLA/8963 Field Document, no. 2. Food and Agriculture Organization, Rome.

Mahon, S. and R. Mahon. 1990. *OECS Island Fisheries: An Overview for Students and Fishermen.* Food and Agriculture Organization, Rome.

Marcille, J. M. and J. F. Caddy. 1987. "Tuna resources of the Lesser Antilles, present state of fishing and prospects for development". *Proceedings of the Gulf and Caribbean Fisheries Institute* 38: 620–654.

Medley, P.A., G. Gaudian, and S. Wells. 1993. "Coral reef fisheries stock assessment". *Reviews in Fish Biology and Fisheries* 3: 242–285.

Mercer, M. (ed.). 1982. *Multi-Species Approaches to Fisheries Management Advice.* Canadian Special Publication of Fisheries and Aquatic Science. National Research Council of Canada, Ottawa.

Merritt, M. F. and K. R. Criddle. 1993. "Evaluation of the analytic hierarchy process for aiding management decisions in recreational fisheries: A case study of the chinook salmon fishery in the Kenai River, Alaska". pp. 683–703, in G. Kruse, D. M. Eggers, R. J. Marasco, C. Pautzke, and T. J. Quinn II, eds., *Proceedings of the International Symposium on Management Strategies for Exploited Fish Populations.* Alaska Sea Grant College Program Report, no. 93-02, University of Alaska, Fairbanks.

Muller-Karger, F. E. 1993. "River discharge variability including satellite-observed plume-dispersal". pp. 162–192, in G. A. Maul, ed., *Climatic Change in the Intra American Sea.* Edward-Arnold, New York.

Munro, J. L. (ed.). 1983. *Caribbean Coral Reef Fishery Resources.* ICLARM Studies and Reviews, no. 7.

Myers, R. A., A. A. Rosenberg, P. M. Mace, N. Barrowman, and V. R. Restrepo. 1994. "In search of thresholds for recruitment overfishing". *ICES Journal of Marine Science* 51: 191–205.

NAFO (North Atlantic Fisheries Organization). 1991. *Special Session on Management under Uncertainty.* NAFO Science Council Studies, no. 16. North Atlantic Fisheries Organization, Dartmouth, California.

National Research Council. 1992. *Restoration of Aquatic Ecosystems, Science, Technology and Public Policy.* National Academy Press, Washington, D.C.

Norse, E. A. 1993. *Global Marine Biological Diversity, A Strategy for Building Conservation into Decision Making.* Island Press, Washington, D.C.

Norwegian Ministry of Foreign Affairs. 1993. *Norwegian Management of Marine Resources.* UDA 247. Norwegian Ministry of Foreign Affairs, Oslo.

Organization of American States. 1988. *Inventory of Caribbean Marine and Coastal Protected Areas.* Organization of American States/U.S. National Park Service, Washington, D.C.

Oxenford, H. A. 1991. "Management of marine resources for sustainable development in the Caribbean". pp. 120–126, in E. A. Moore and J. Rudder, eds., *Sustainable Development for the Caribbean.* Centre for Resource Management and Environmental Studies (CERMES), University of the West Indies, Cave Hill, Barbados.

Oxenford, H. A., R. Mahon, and W. Hunte (eds.). 1993. "The Eastern Caribbean flyingfish project". OECS Fishery Report, no. 9. Organization of Eastern Caribbean States, Fisheries Unit, St Vincent.

Pauly, D. 1979. *Theory and Management of Tropical Multi-Species Stocks: A Review, with Emphasis on the Southeast Asian Demersal Fisheries*. ICLARM Studies and Reviews, no. 1.

Pauly, D. 1988. "Fisheries research and the demersal fisheries of Southeast Asia".pp. 329–348, in J. A. Gulland, ed., *Fish Population Dynamics*, 2nd edition. John Wiley & Sons, New York.

Phillips, B. F., J. S. Cobb, and J. Kittaka. 1994. *Spiny Lobster Management*. Fishing News Books, Oxford, U.K.

Polovina, J. J. and S. Ralston (eds.). 1987. *Tropical Snappers and Groupers, Biology and Fisheries Management*. Westview Press, Boulder, Colorado.

Ricker, W. E. 1975. *Computation and Interpretation of Biological Statistics of Fish Populations*, Bulletin 191. Department of the Environment Fisheries and Marine Service, Ottawa, Canada.

Roberts, C. M. and N. V. C. Polunin. 1991. "Are marine reserves effective in management of reef fisheries?" *Reviews in Fish Biology and Fish*. 1: 65–89.

Roberts, C. M. and N. V. C. Polunin. 1993. "Marine reserves: Simple solutions to managing complex fisheries?" *Ambio* 22, no. 6: 363–368.

Rosenberg, A. A. and V. R. Restrepo. 1993. "The eloquent shrug: Expressing uncertainty and risk in stock assessment". International Council for the Exploration of the Sea CM.D12, Session 10.

Rosenberg, A. A., M. J. Fogarty, M. P. Sissenwine, J. R. Beddington, and J. G. Shepherd. 1993. "Achieving sustainable use of renewable resources". *Science* 262: 828–829.

Rowley, R. J. 1994. "Marine reserves in fisheries management". *Aquatic Conservation: Marine and Freshwater Ecosystems* 4: 233–254.

Ruddle, K. 1994. "A guide to the literature on traditional community-based fishery management in the Asia-Pacific tropics". FAO Fisheries Circular, no. 869. Food and Agriculture Organization, Rome.

Russ, G. R. 1991. "Coral reef fisheries: Effects and yields". pp. 601–635, in P. F. Sale, ed., *The Ecology of Fishes on Coral Reefs*. Academic Press, San Diego, California.

Saila, S. B. 1993. "The use of multivariate trend analysis to provide preliminary multi-species management advice". pp. 493–506, in G. Kruse, D. M. Eggers, R. J. Marasco, C. Pautzke, and T. J. Quinn II, eds., *Proceedings of the International Symposium on Management Strategies for Exploited Fish Populations*. Alaska Sea Grant College Program Report, no. 93-02. University of Alaska, Fairbanks.

Sale, P. (ed.). 1991. *The Ecology of Fishes on Coral Reefs*. Academic Press, San Diego, California.

Southeast Fisheries Science Center. 1993. *Status of Fishery Resources off the Southeastern United States for 1992*. NOAA Technical Memorandum. National Marine Fisheries Service-Southeast Fisheries Science Center, Miami, Florida.

Shelton, P. A., J. E. Carscadden, and J. M. Hoenig. 1993. "Risk evaluation of the 10% harvest rate procedure for capelin in NAFO Division 3L". pp. 193–202, in S. J. Smith, J. J. Hunt, and D. Rivard, eds., *Risk Evaluation and Biological Reference Points for Fisheries Management*. Canadian Special Publication of Fisheries and Aquatic Science, no. 120. National Research Council of Canada, Ottawa.

Sherman, K. 1994. "Sustainability, biomass yields, and health of coastal ecosystems: An ecological perspective". *Marine Ecology Progress Series* 112: 277–301.

Sherman, K., L. M. Alexander, and B. D. Gold (eds.). 1993. *Large Marine Ecosystems: Stress, Mitigation, and Sustainability.* AAAS Press, Washington.

Shomura, R. S., J. Majkowski, and S. Langi (eds.). 1991. *Interactions of Pacific Tuna Fisheries*, volume 1. *Summary Report and Papers on Interaction.* FAO Fisheries Technical Paper, no. 336/1. Food and Agriculture Organization, Rome.

Shomura, R. S., J. Majkowski, and S. Langi (eds.). 1991. *Interactions of Pacific Tuna Fisheries*, volume 2. *Papers on Biology and Fisheries.* FAO Fisheries Technical Paper, no. 336/2. Food and Agriculture Organization, Rome.

Sissenwine, M. P. and J. E. Kirkley. 1982. "Fishery management techniques". *Marine Policy* (January): 43–57.

Singh-Renton, S. and R. Mahon. 1996. "Catch, effort and CPUE trends for offshore pelagic fisheries in and adjacent to the exclusive economic zones (EEZS) of several CARICOM states". CARICOM Fishery Report, no. 1. CARICOM Fisheries Unit, Belize City.

Smith, A. H. and F. Berkes. 1991. "Solutions to the `tragedy of the commons': Sea-urchin management in St. Lucia, West Indies". *Environmental Conservation*, 18, no. 2: 131–136.

Smith, G. B. 1988. "Abundance and potential yield of groupers (Serranidae), snappers (Lutjanidae) and grunts (Haemulidae) on the Little and Great Bahama Banks". FAO Fisheries Report, no. 376 (Suppl.), pp. 84–105. Food and Agriculture Organization, Rome.

Smith, S. J., J. J. Hunt and D. Rivard. 1993. *Risk Evaluation and Biological Reference Points for Fisheries Management*. Canadian Special Publication of Fisheries and Aquatic Science, no. 120. National Research Council of Canada, Ottawa.

Sparre, P., Ursin, E., and Venema, S. C. 1989a. *Introduction to Tropical Fish Stock Assessment*, Part 1. *Manual.* FAO Fisheries Technical Paper, no. 306/1. Food and Agriculture Organization, Rome.

Sparre, P., Ursin, E., and Venema, S. C. 1989b. *Introduction to Tropical Fish Stock Assessment*, Part 2. *Exercises.* FAO Fisheries Technical Paper, no. 306/2. Food and Agriculture Organization, Rome.

Stevenson, D. K. 1981. *A Review of the Marine Resources of the Western Central Atlantic Fisheries Commission (WECAFC) Region.* FAO Fisheries Technical Paper, no. 211. Food and Agriculture Organization, Rome.

Stevenson, D., R. Pollnac, and P. Logan. 1982. *A Guide for the Small-Scale Fishery Administrator: Information from the Harvest Sector.* International Center for Marine Resource Development (ICMRO), Kingston, Rhode Island.

Stoner, A. W. 1999. "Queen conch stock enhancement, the need for an integrated approach". *Proceedings of the Gulf and Caribbean Fisheries Institute* 45: 922–925.

Sturm, M. G. de L. 1991. "The living resources of the Caribbean Sea and adjacent regions". *Caribbean Marine Studies* 2, nos. 1 and 2: 18–44.

Sugihara, G., S. Garcia, J. A. Gulland, J. H. Lawton, H. Maske, R. T. Paine, T. Platt, E. Rachor, B. J. Rothschild, E. A. Ursin, and B. F. K. Zeitzschel. 1984. "Ecosystems dynamics, group report". pp. 131–153, in R. M. May, ed., *Exploitation of Marine Communities*. Springer-Verlag, New York.

Suriname Fisheries. 1993. Report of the National Workshop on Fisheries Information System. Suriname Fisheries Department, Paramaribo, Suriname.

Techniques for Biological Assessment in Fisheries Management. Report of the Workshop Jülich, July 17-24, 1991. Berichte ans der Ökologischen Forschung, Forschungszentrum Jülich GmbH, 9.

Towle, E., R. Carney, and R. Mahon. 1991. "Report of the Commission of Inquiry into the Future of Fisheries Management and the Future of the Marine Environment in Bermuda". Government of Bermuda Printing Office, Hamilton, Bermuda.

United Nations. 1983. The Law of the Sea. Official text of the United Nations Convention on the Law of the Sea with Annexes and Tables. United Nations, New York.

United Nations. 1992. Agenda 21: programme of action for sustainable development. Final text of Agreements Negotiated by Governments at the United Nations Conference on Environmental Development (UNCED), 3–14 June 1992, Rio de Janeiro, Brazil.

United Nations. 1995. Agreement for the implementation of the provisions of the United Nations Convention on the Law of the Sea of 10 December 1982 relating to the conservation and management of straddling fish stocks and highly migratory fish stocks. United Nations Conference on Straddling Fish Stocks and Highly Migratory Fish Stocks, Sixth Session, New York, 24 July–4 August 1995, A/CONF.164/37.

van Barneveld, W., Z. Sary, J. Woodley, M. Miller, and M. Picou-Gill. 1999. "Towards the co-operative management of fishing in Discovery Bay, Jamaica: The role of the fisheries improvement project". *Proceedings of the Gulf and Caribbean Fisheries Institute* 44: 195–210.

von Brandt, A. 1985. *Fish Catching Methods of the World*. Fishing News Books, Oxford, U.K.

Wallace, D. H. 1975. "Keynote address". pp. 5–8, in P. M. Roedel, ed., *Optimal Sustainable Yield as a Concept in Fisheries Management*. Special Publication no. 9. American Fisheries Society, Washington, D.C.

Walters, C. J. 1986. *Adaptive Management of Renewable Resources*. McGraw-Hill, New York.

Willmann, R. and S. M. Garcia. 1985. *A Bio-Economic Model of Sequential Artisanal and Industrial Shrimp Fisheries*. FAO Fisheries Technical Paper, no. 270. Food and Agriculture Organization, Rome.

Wolfe, A. 1990. "Report of the Eastern Caribbean seafood marketing strategy project", volume 4. OECS Fish Marketing Studies Survey of U.K. Markets. Organization of Eastern Caribbean States, Fisheries Unit, St Vincent.

Wolf, R. S. and W. F. Rathjen. 1974. "The UNDP/FAO Caribbean Fishery Development Project (1965–1971): A summary". *Marine Fisheries Review* 39, no. 9: 1–8.

World Bank, United Nations Development Program, Commission of European Communities, Food and Agriculture Organisation. 1992. *A Study of International Fisheries Research*. World Bank, Washington, D.C.

APPENDICES

Appendix 1:
The "Tragedy of the Commons"

Few people who are not involved in fishing view themselves as part-owners of the resource. In most countries, the fish of the ocean are a "common property" resource, which means that they belong to everybody. This has resulted in "open access" to the resource by anyone who wants to fish and has inevitably led to overfishing. Even when the people who are doing the overfishing know that it's happening, there is no incentive for any one of them to do anything about it, unless all the others are going to do so too.

This problem was first recognized for common grazing lands in English villages and has been termed the "Tragedy of the Commons" (Hardin, 1968). It sets fisheries apart from most other kinds of resources which can be owned by the exploiter and has led to the conclusion that government must manage the resource on behalf of the owners.

Appendix 2:
Earth Summit - Agenda 21

Chapter 17: Protection of the oceans, all kinds of seas, including enclosed and semi-enclosed seas, and coastal areas and the protection, rational use and development of their living resources.

In Chapter 17 on the oceans, States committed themselves to:

- Integrated management and sustainable development of coastal areas and the marine environment under their national jurisdiction;
- Prevent, reduce and control degradation of the marine environment so as to maintain and improve its life-support and productive capacities (in accordance with the provisions of the United Nations Convention on the Law of the Sea on protection and preservation of the marine environment);
- Conservation and sustainable use of marine living resources on the High Seas;
- The principal that coastal States, particularly developing countries and states whose economies are overwhelmingly dependent on the exploitation of the marine living resources of their exclusive economic zones, should obtain the full social and economic benefits from sustainable utilization of

marine living resources within their exclusive economic zones and other areas under national jurisdiction;
- To improve the understanding of the marine environment and its role on global processes (in accordance with provisions of the United Nations Convention on the Law of the Sea on marine scientific research);
- To promote institutional arrangements necessary to support the implementation of the programme areas in this chapter [...] (at national, subregional, regional and global levels, as appropriate;..);
- Addressing the problems of sustainable development of small island developing States.

(United Nations 1992)

Appendix 3: Risk and Uncertainty in Fisheries Management

Uncertainty and risk are related but different aspects of fishery management. Uncertainty reflects the probability that a particular estimate or piece of advice may be incorrect. Risk is the potential cost, in terms of societal benefits, of adopting the estimate or advice should it turn out to be inaccurate. When management decisions are to be based on quantitative estimates from fishery assessment models, it is desirable that the uncertainty be quantified, and used to calculate the probability of achieving the desired target and/or of incurring undesirable events.

The process of communicating uncertainty to decision makers is in its early developmental stages and presents substantial challenges to fishery technicians and managers. Likewise, fishery managers and participants are only just developing means of objectively evaluating the potential costs of these events and defining acceptable levels of risk based on the probabilities.

While the inclusion of estimates of risk and uncertainty in management advice has been rare in the past, some failures in management of well-studied stocks in recent years have brought this issue to the scientific forefront, and several workshops have focused on the issue of risk in fisheries management (see, for example, *Techniques for Biological Assessment in Fisheries Management*; NAFO, 1991; Smith et al., 1993; Kruse et al., 1993).

There are several sources of uncertainty in the fishery management process (Rosenberg and Restrepo, 1993):

- Measurement error is the error in the observed quantities such as the catch or biological parameters;
- Process error is the underlying stochasticity in the population dynamics such as the variability in recruitment;
- Model error is the misspecification of model structure;
- Estimation error can result from any of the above uncertainties and is the inaccuracy and imprecision in abundance or fishing mortality rate;
- Implementation error results from variability in the resulting implementation of a management policy, i.e., inability to exactly achieve a target harvest strategy.

4

Managing Forest Resources

William S. Chalmers

Contents

OVERVIEW

The region's most valuable natural resource is considered to be its diverse forests. Forest resources are defined in this chapter in three categories, natural forest, secondary forest, and plantation forest. Existing resources and ownership patterns are considered, with emphasis on Guyana, Jamaica, and Trinidad and Tobago. Exploitation and sales systems are reviewed and some data given on imports of timber. The merit of import substitution is discussed. The operations of the Barama Plywood Company in Guyana, the largest forest industry project in the region, are outlined. Established with a commitment to operate on a fully sustainable basis, this project could serve as a forestry development model for other Caribbean countries.

Direct and indirect benefits from the forest are reviewed. The traditional role, as a source of timber and a wide range of minor forest products, is in jeopardy because of overexploitation and the clearing of large areas of forest for a variety of reasons. The other benefits from a permanent forest cover, such as soil and watershed protection, conservation of biological diversity, nature tourism, and other recreational facilities are discussed. The reasons for the destruction of forests, the impact of this on environmental degradation, and its long-term negative impact on sustainable development are considered. The adverse effects of overexploitation of forests are recognized and some examples cited.

The close links between forest habitat and the region's unique biological diversity are stressed. Examples are given of other threats to this biodiversity, including professional plant and animal collectors who export much material on an international scale for commercial gain. The lack of basic data on many aspects of Caribbean biodiversity is recognized – a shortage of ecologists is a handicap in tackling this problem. The challenges of managing tropical forest on the basis of sustainable development are recognized and the means of achieving this are outlined.

Forest management is one of a range of overlapping disciplines considered. In the final analysis forest management can be relied upon to achieve predetermined, clearly defined, objectives in terms of the production of raw material and environmental protection but only to the extent to which forestry departments are given the means to do the job. Attention is drawn to the Food and Agriculture Organization Tropical Forestry Action Programme (FAO/TFAP) and to the national forestry action plans it has stimulated in the region. This commitment by governments must be backed up by an appropriate forest policy supported by the necessary legislative instruments and a level of staffing and funding commensurate with the urgency and size of the forestry development programme in each country. In making the case for government funding it is stressed that the role and value of forestry in the national economy has been undervalued in the past, particularly because of the failure to evaluate the costs that accrue as a result of indiscriminate destruction of protective forest cover. The formulation and implementation of a relevant national forest strategy is explained and emphasis is given to the need for major reforestation and agroforestry programmes to remedy critically degraded environments throughout the region, particularly watersheds. The procedures and activities involved in establishing and managing forest plantations are considered. The limited results to date from mature teak and pine plantations in Trinidad and Tobago are reviewed and it is concluded that plantation forests have a major role to play, not only in rehabilitating widespread environmental degradation but also in terms of social and economic development. It is emphasized that private landowners can play an important role in this respect but some form of financial or tax incentive may be required to secure their involvement. Subregional and regional collaboration in a range of activities will be essential to achieve the optimum development of the region's forest resources.

INTRODUCTION

The diverse forests of the Caribbean are the region's most valuable natural resource. This is not only because they can be managed effectively, in perpetuity, with the objective of obtaining a sustained yield of valuable raw material, but also because they are critically important in preventing environmental degradation and significant (though greatly undervalued) in their economic and social aspects. The purpose of this chapter is to justify that statement. To do so it is necessary to consider a range of disciplines that constitute forest science. However, in the general context of managing the region's forest resources and remedying the destruction and neglect of these resources over the past century, it is useful to consider first a number of background issues and concepts related to the existing forest resources, forest conservation, and sustainable development.

Initially, a brief overview is given of existing forest resources, of past and current methods of exploitation and the reasons for the widespread forest destruction so prevalent throughout much of the Caribbean today. As this account unfolds there emerges a picture of interrelationships and interactions among forest cover, land ownership, land use patterns, the conservation of forest ecosystems, water, wildlife, and the supplying of timber, fuelwood, and a wide range of minor forest products – relationships that in some areas have disintegrated at great cost to the environment and society as a whole.

This threat was recognized during the colonial era and in some of the larger Caribbean countries small forestry departments were established to check the decline. A range of forest management practices was introduced, including plantation forestry. In describing these initiatives, and in considering the enormous efforts that are currently required to reverse the process of environmental disintegration, attention is focused on a range of scientific disciplines and some of the formal mechanisms that are being put in place to undertake this task. The most recent and comprehensive initiative is the FAO/TFAP. The wide-ranging disciplines and issues that are addressed in that programme and considered in this chapter are summarized below:

- Exploitation of forest resources, utilization of timber and minor forest products
- Forest ownership and land use practices
- Forests and the environment – soil conservation, watershed management, and amenity
- Conservation of natural forest ecosystems
- Biological diversity, wildlife conservation and management, national parks, and nature tourism
- Forest policy and national forestry strategy
- Forest legislation relating to ownership, access, exploitation, and fees
- Reforestation – plantation and agroforestry systems
- Protection of forest resources from fire, pathogens, and pests
- Forest economics – valuation of the direct and indirect benefits derived from forests; funding for forest development
- Forest management for sustained yield and habitat conservation
- Forest research
- Institutional and regional/subregional issues
- Training requirements

EXISTING FOREST RESOURCES

The existing forest resources in the region can be classified for simplicity into three broad categories: natural forest (NF), secondary forest (SF), and plantation forest (PF). The NF has a range of ecotypes. Each consists of large numbers of different tree species of varying age and size, with a varied lower canopy of shrubs, climbers, and herbs growing in diverse ecological combinations depending on geology, soil, water relations, elevation, and climate. Secondary forest is usually derived from NF that has been so heavily overexploited that the original forest type has changed beyond recognition, is of no commercial value, and is left unmanaged. Forest cleared for agriculture and subsequently abandoned may start regenerating through a number of pioneer species, which are usually of no commercial value. Such areas can be classed as SF, as would large areas of "ruinate" in Jamaica. Ruinate is the Jamaican term used to describe the varied herbaceous shrubby and woody formations arising on forest land cleared and abandoned or otherwise modified by man. Plantation forest involves the replanting of cleared former forest land or the clearance of degraded SF of no commercial value to provide protective cover or a commercial crop. The reforestation process has usually involved the planting of a single species of commercial importance but, occasionally, a mixture of two or more species has been used. Non-indigenous, so-called exotic species, have often been favoured because of their faster rate of growth and shorter rotation age. Plantation forest is costly to establish, maintain, and manage but has the advantage of producing a uniform crop of the desired species, with intermediate and final crop yields that can be forecast in advance. The techniques and economics of PF are considered in more detail later.

In global terms, the forest areas of the Caribbean island states are minute yet, where they survive, the NFs are a most important renewable natural resource, containing a unique biological diversity and providing unequalled environmental protection, especially in mountainous conditions. In the immediate future PF also has an indispensable role to play, not only in the rehabilitation of severely degraded environments, but also in making a significant contribution to the economic and social development of each country.

Forest Area

The first comprehensive assessment of the forest resources in the Caribbean was compiled in connection with the regional forestry study

TABLE 4.1 Land and Forest Areas in the Region

County	Total Land Area (TLA) km²	All Woodlands Area 1,000 ha	% of TLA	Commercial Forests Area 1,000 ha	Vol/ha m³	Tot Vol 1,000 m³
Antigua & Barbuda	430	25	58	4	80	320
Anguilla	77	5.5	71	—	—	—
Bahamas	13,878	1,180	75	180	45	8,100
Barbados	431	5	11	4	80	320
Belize	22,663	2,201.5	96	1,784	24	42,816
British Virgin Islands	153	3.3	21	0.5	100	500
Dominica	790	55	70	39	200	7,800
Grenada	344	7	20	5.5	100	550
Guyana	214,970	16,446.5	77	14,000	130	1,820,000
Jamaica	11,424	491.3	43	92	110	10,120
Montserrat	101	3.5	35	2.5	90	200
St Kitts	268	11	41	4.5	120	540
St Lucia	617	37.3	60	8	190	1,520
St Vincent	390	17.5	45	10.5	120	1,260
Trinidad & Tobago	5,128	299	58	202	83	16,766
Turks & Caicos	500	40	80	2.5	45	112
Total	272,164	20,828.4	—	16,339	—	1,910,924

Data from CDB, 1984.

(RFSS) organized in 1983 by the Caribbean Development Bank (CDB) to include its sixteen member countries. The RFSS final report (CDB, 1984) contained a summary of the forest area in each country, which is given in Table 4.1. This demonstrates a peculiar feature of Caribbean forestry in that two countries, Guyana (85.7 percent) and Belize (10.9 percent), between them share 96.6 percent of the region's commercially exploitable forests. This is of significance especially in terms of Guyana's role in helping CARICOM countries to meet their sawn timber and wood panel needs, from within the region, in the near future.

In most countries there has been no national forest inventory that would provide basic information on forest types, species, number, size, and standing volumes of marketable and non-marketable species. A national forest inventory would also provide data on other factors that would assist in determining how much of the total forest area was unsuitable for commercial exploitation, such as mountainous terrain, inaccessibility, native reservations, watershed, wildlife conservation needs, national parks, and any other ecological or environmental considerations. Normally such areas should be clearly designated and legally constituted as protected areas in which exploitation is forbidden.

For example, in Belize, Dominica, and Jamaica, mountainous topography significantly reduces the area of forest suitable for commercial exploitation. In Belize, forest on slopes in excess of 25 degrees is declared as protected and exploitation is prohibited, thus reducing the exploitable area from 262,000 to 167,900 hectares (ha); while another estimate reduces it to 96,500 ha. In Jamaica the commercial area of hardwood forest is estimated to be only 20,000 ha out of a total of 77,000 ha. With hindsight it is easy to criticize what may now appear to be optimistic RFSS estimates. However, the report drew attention to the lack of accurate forest statistics in the Caribbean and the difficulty in trying to collate and interpret data, so much of which was based on estimates.

Unfortunately, the situation has changed little, as indicated in Table 4.2, which provides some miscellaneous forest statistics prepared in connection with more recent studies related to the FAO Tropical Forestry Action Plan (TFAP). The data, mainly for 1988–1989, indicate the extent of PF in the region and provide some incomplete data on the volume of timber cut locally for sawn lumber and energy purposes. These data also include the volume and value of imports of logs and sawn wood.

Forest Ownership

Land ownership, in particular the extent to which forest land is state or privately owned, is of great significance in the future development of forestry and in related environmental issues. In most countries in the region, the state is the principal landowner and controls the largest forest area. This is mainly on steeper land at higher elevations, since the lower, flatter lands were systematically cleared for the cultivation of traditional colonial export crops, such as sugar, citrus, coconuts, cocoa, coffee, and bananas. Unfortunately in recent years the lucrative banana market has led to the clearance of more NF at higher elevations on steep slopes.

In some countries, the more valuable areas of NF, in terms of environmental protection and commercial value, have been legally proclaimed as forest reserve, with control over access and exploitation given to the local forestry authority, which may also implement varying levels of forest management. There is correspondingly less control

TABLE 4.2 Forestry Statistics for some CARICOM Countries

Country	Total	Forest Area (ha)			Fuelwood/charcoal cu m/yr	*Timber* volume cu m	*Supports* value $ million	Local sawlogs cu m/yr
		NF	PF	SF				
Antigua/Barbuda	5,600	5,600	Negligible	—	8,400	8,500	No data	Negligible
Barbados	70	30	Negligible	—	Nil	No data	BD $27.6	Negligible
Belize	2.085 mil	2.046 mill	3,900	—	No data	Nil	Nil	61,100
Dominica	57,000	47,000	100	10,000	No data	No data	EC $6.3	3,290
Grenada	9,406	4,100	166	5,300	20,000	19,500	EC $31.5	2,500
Guyana	16.5 mil	16.5 mill	Negligible	—	10,000	Nil	Nil	240,000
Jamaica	267,000	—	—	—	725,441	No data	No data	37,000
Montserrat	3,500	2,500	20	1,000	5,000	No data	EC 2.0	Negligible
St Kitts/Nevis	11,000	3,005	Negligible	5,700	No data	No data	No data	Negligible
St Lucia	37,310	7,750	260	—	50,000	No data	EC $8.6	1,000
St Vincent	13,000	4,320	120	8,600	35,000	9,560	EC $7.2	1,000
Trinidad & Tobago	287,835	237,430	15,245	10,500	No data	34,650	TT $27.2	48,000

Data from Chalmers, 1990.

TABLE 4.3 Forest Ownership in Jamaica (Area: '000 ha)

Forest Type	Public	Private	Total
NF	61	16	77
SF[1]	34	135	169
PF	19	2	21
Total	114	153	267

Data from FAO, 1990a.

and forest management in other non-reserved state forests where, although exploitation is usually permitted, access is likely to be more difficult. In Trinidad and Tobago, which maintains a very experienced and broad-based forestry operation, approximately 51 percent of the total land area (TLA) is under forest, of which 28 percent is forest reserve, 21 percent other state forest, and 2 percent privately owned.

Swabey (1945) described a different situation in Jamaica where the area of farm lands and rural holdings was approximately 80 percent of the TLA. Within those holdings private woodlands covered approximately 125,100 ha (12 percent of TLA) of which 33,600 ha were used for livestock grazing. State owned forest reserves and protected areas totalled only 94,370 ha (9.1 percent of TLA). The Jamaica National Forestry Action Plan report (FAO, 1990a) does not give such a detailed breakdown but estimates the area of forest with commercial potential as 267,000 ha (24.1 percent of TLA), broken down as shown in Table 4.3. It is clear that Jamaica presents a more complex situation in terms of land and forest ownership and this has implications for the development of a major reforestation programme for environmental rehabilitation.

Unfortunately, in the Caribbean, the boundaries of privately owned forest are often inadequately designated and not well documented, and it is difficult to give an accurate picture of the area of private forest in the region as a whole. Such forest is rarely subject to any form of management and there is virtually no information on the volume of timber they produce. In Belize and Guyana, the countries with the largest area of NF, the state is by far the largest owner. In Belize, 46.7 percent of the TLA is covered by two forest types, 34.7 percent being broadleaf and 12.0 percent carrying coniferous forest types that produce the pine timber of commerce.

In Guyana the NF covers 16.5 million ha, about 76.6 percent of the TLA, of which 9.1 million ha are classified as state forest. This is under the control of the Guyana Forestry Commission (GFC) which operates under two Acts of Parliament.

Forest Types

About 95.5 percent of the forest vegetation in the Caribbean consists of various types of mixed broadleaf forest. The remainder is natural pine (*Pinus*) forest that, in the countries within this purview, is restricted to the Bahamas and Belize. Beard (1946, 1949) gives a detailed description of the climax vegetation formations in the Caribbean based on his ecological studies in Trinidad and Tobago and the Leeward and Windward Islands. Climate, especially rainfall, elevation, and soil type are the principal site factors influencing the development of different direct types. The main forest types are climax tropical rainforest with a number of species-specific associations, tropical semideciduous forest, mangrove, palm forest, dittoral dry woodlands, and cactus shrub. At the highest elevations elfin woodland is common; this can be described as dwarf forest. Few of these forest types are commercially exploitable but it is in our interest to ensure all are conserved for future generations.

Demand and Supply

The RFSS prepared statistics on the annual demand and supply for wood and wood products in the region during the early 1980s. The estimates given in Tables 4.4 and 4.5 demonstrate the gap between the annual demand of 533,000 cubic metres (m^3) and local supply of 193,000 m^3 – a deficit of 64 percent. Of the local supply Guyana was producing nearly 50 percent and Belize, Jamaica, and Trinidad about 15 percent each. The more recent (1988–1989) data in Table 4.2 indicate an increase in local production to about 392,000 m^3, with the contribution from Trinidad and Tobago and Jamaica falling to 12.2 percent and 9.4 percent, respectively. Guyana's share increased to 61.2 percent, and Belize remained almost unchanged at 15.6 percent.

These statistics demonstrate the challenge the region faces in attempting to achieve self-sufficiency in timber and other wood products. The Tropical Forestry Action Programmes (TFAP) in several Caribbean countries has laid the foundation for meeting that challenge. Table 4.6 indicates how Trinidad and Tobago planned to develop its forest resources. In the 1990s its annual planting programme had declined to 252 ha, compared with 630 ha in the 1970s.

In Guyana, the GFC made two assumptions based on historical yield data in calculating the sustainable timber production capacity

TABLE 4.4 Annual Demand for Wood and Wood Products in the Region

Country	Poles Piles m^3	Lumber		Panels		Total
		Conifers m^3	Non-conifer m^3	Plywood Veneer m^3	Other wood Products m^3	
Bahamas	1,600	54,000	—	10,000	5,000	70,600
Barbados	100	1,000	—	12,000	10,000	23,100
Guyana	1,600	—	30,000	500	800	32,900
Jamaica	2,700	54,400	26,000	14,000	4,000	101,100
Trinidad & Tobago	2,000	152,300	68,000	28,500	5,200	256,000
Other Countries	1,000	17,300	16,000	10,000	5,000	49,300
Total	9,000	279,000	140,000	75,000	30,000	533,000

Data from CDB, 1984.

TABLE 4.5 Annual Production of Wood and Wood Products in the Region

Country	Poles Piles m^3	Lumber		Plywood m^3	Other wood Products m^3	Total
		Conifers m^3	Non-conifer m^3			
Belize	—	15,000	10,000	—	—	25,000
Guyana	7,000	—	88,000	2,500	1,000	98,500
Jamaica	—	10,000	14,000	—	5,000	29,000
Trinidad & Tobago	500	—	30,000	—	1,000	31,500
Other Countries	500	—	8,000	—	500	9,000
Total	8,000	25,000	150,000	2,500	7,500	193,000

Data from CDB, 1984.

TABLE 4.6 Trinidad and Tobago Forestry Development – Targets (ha) for 1992–1997

Type	1992/93	1993/94	1994/95	1995/96	1996/97	Total
Teak	200	200	250	250	300	1200
Mixed hardwoods	200	200	250	250	400	1300
Pine	100	100	100	100	100	500
Agroforestry – livestock	25	100	100	100	100	425
Watershed rehabilitation	50	100	200	300	500	1150
Private Forestry	100	200	400	500	500	1700
Total	700	1000	1400	1600	2000	6700

Data from Chalmers and Faizool, 1992.

of its forests: an actual availability for exploitation of 75 percent of the area of state forest and an average growth increment in the forest of 1 m^3 per hectare per year. On this basis, the productive potential of the state forests was calculated to be approximately 6.8 million m^3 per year. Production was expected to expand rapidly to 1 million m^3 within 2 years, giving an expected export value in excess of U.S.$ 100 million. Actual production figures show that these expectations did not materialize. The export value of Guyana's forest products in 1998 was U.S.$ 38,830,000 and the annual forest cover change between 1999 and 2000 was estimated as –48,644 ha, representing –3 percent change per year (FAO, 2001).

The current rate of exploitation in Guyana is low by international standards, though with efficient control and management greater volumes could be harvested for export within the Caribbean without impairing the long-term integrity of the forests. The main danger would be excessive demands for the most popular species, greenheart (*Ocotea rodiei*) and wallaba (*Eperua falcata*), and this would have to be monitored.

Apart from Belize and Guyana regional timber production is not substantial. Reliable data on the annual yield from NF and PF is not readily available in most countries. The Jamaica NFAP report estimates the national annual roundwood requirements (at 1988 consumption levels) to be 866,000 m^3. It is remarkable that 84 percent of the total is to meet energy needs, 49 percent for charcoal, and 35 percent for firewood, in a situation where it is calculated that charcoal provides 37 percent of all household energy. The trend is increasing but the report indicates clearly that this level of wood consumption cannot be sustained much longer from existing forest resources. Much of the fuelwood is cut from private forest which is so poor in terms

TABLE 4.7 Annual Volume (m^3) of Timber Harvested in Trinidad and Tobago from NF and PF

		PF		
Period	**NF**	**Teak**	**Pine**	**Total**
1955–1980 (annual av.)	85,700	—	—	—
1984–1989 (annual av.)	43,730	—	—	—
1988	45,167	41,310	17,200	58,510
1989	62,054	45,580	7,300	52,880
1990	—	42,460	18,900	61,360

Data from Chalmers and Faizool, 1992.

of tree stocking and soil fertility that the entire area could not sustain the annual yield levels required, which are in excess of 4 m^3 per ha.

In the context of the regional development process it should be noted that all the island states are major importers of wood and a wide range of manufactured wood products, mostly from hard currency countries, although the bulk of their requirements could be met from Guyana. However, in the long term, it is reasonable to anticipate that most of these countries could become self-sufficient in timber from their own forest resources if the state and private sector demonstrate a firm commitment and make the investment required to undertake the major plantation programme that is urgently needed in any event on environmental grounds.

Jamaica and Trinidad and Tobago have made a considerable investment in the on-going establishment of PF over the past 40 years. Jamaica has 21,000 ha, mainly of *Pinus* spp. and *Eucalyptus* spp. and Trinidad and Tobago has 16,000 ha, mainly of *Pinus caribaea*, *Tectona grandis*, and mixed hardwoods.

The statistics in Table 4.7, comparing the annual volumes of timber harvested in Trinidad and Tobago from NF and pine and teak plantations, provide good evidence that PF can be managed in the region on a sustainable basis to give yields comparable or better than NF. The major risk to date has come from hurricane damage, as demonstrated in Jamaica in 1988 with Hurricane Gilbert, when the pine plantations suffered extensively. There is little the forester can do about this except to avoid planting on exposed sites in high risk locations and, where possible, choose species that tend to be deep rooting. The experience gained to date with these species will be invaluable to the region in tackling the major reforestation challenges that lie ahead.

The size of the available forest resource has influenced the methods of exploitation. The complexity of many tropical forest ecosystems frequently limits the number of commercially attractive species available at a particular time, and exerts a negative impact on the cost effectiveness of locating, felling, and extracting the trees to be logged. In Guyana, the allocation of cutting rights is in accordance with the Forest Act, which makes provision for the following: long-term, exclusive cutting rights under a Timber Sales Agreement, medium term, exclusive cutting rights as a Wood Cutting Lease, and annual non-exclusive cutting rights as a State Forest Permission. Each type of agreement clearly defines the conditions under which the trees are harvested. These restrictions are designed to prevent overexploitation and illegal logging, which could otherwise have a negative impact on future sustainability of the commercially important species and the forest as a whole, in addition to impairing soil fertility and the wildlife habitat.

An excellent example of managing forest resources on the basis of sustained yield and making optimal use of a previously underutilized forest type can be seen in Guyana. A combination of entrepreneurial flair and government initiative led to the establishment of the Barama Plywood Company whose plywood factory, commissioned in 1993, is by far the largest forest industry project established in the Caribbean. The South Korean/Malaysian company has a 25-year concession on 1.6 million ha of forest in the relatively depressed North-West District. The lowland forest type in this area has not been exploited very intensively in the past and the two predominant species of baromalli (*Calostemma commune* and *C. fragrans*) were under-exploited. Under the terms of the Concession Agreement the company undertakes to observe stated objectives of sustainable development and the principal means of achieving this will be by the implementation of an agreed Forest Management Plan approved by the Guyana Forestry Commission. Under this plan a selective felling system will be used and exploitation will be restricted to a small number of trees per hectare, with a minimum diameter of 35 centimetres at a height of 1.3 metres above ground, once every 25 years. The annual logging plan has to be approved in advance and detailed inventories will be undertaken of the main logging areas both before and after exploitation. This information will be enhanced by comprehensive data (diameter, stem form, crown size, crown height, timber height) collected from every tree in a number of permanent sample plots, established at random throughout the concession area, which will be measured at regular intervals over its life. Under the Forest Management Plan appropriate areas will be reserved to set up gene banks and to facilitate research into biological diversity. If the results of research indicate a need to change either the current logging strategy or intensity in order to maintain sustainability, these changes will be incorporated into a revised Forest Management Plan. It should be stressed that all Amerindian Lands are excluded from the Barama concession.

Plywood is a high value-added commodity aimed primarily at the export market, but Caribbean countries could benefit from this development and save much foreign exchange. One of the major risks in such capital intensive projects is the risk of overexploitation, but the implications of this are not really in the long-term interests of the Barama Company. In the final analysis the company has formally accepted that its over-riding responsibility is to achieve sustained yields without compromising the ecological integrity of this very large forest area, rather than exploit it to harvest the maximum possible commercial volume of timber. All of the appropriate safeguards to achieve this objective have been recognized and if they are implemented, the outcome, by 2018, should be a model of sustainable forest development and environmental management.

DIRECT AND INDIRECT BENEFITS OF FORESTRY

Timber and Minor Forest Products

Foresters have long recognized and managed NF as a valuable, multipurpose, renewable natural resource providing many direct and indirect benefits, as illustrated in Figure 4.1. Indigenous broadleaf species, also known as the "hardwoods" of the timber trade, are the major component of most forest types, and are among the most versatile of raw materials. Many are exploited commercially throughout the region for use in various forms: sawn timber, transmission poles, fence posts, firewood/charcoal, and sliced or peeled for the manufacture of plywood. The NF is also the source of a considerable range of much used minor forest products (MFP), derived from a variety of trees, shrubs, and vines to provide handicraft materials, herbal remedies and bush teas, as well as edible fruits, nuts, and drinks. An indication of the range of these MFP in Trinidad and Tobago is given in Table 4.8. Many of these species occur and are used in other countries in the region and they have been well documented (Williams and Williams, 1941; Ayensu, 1978; Honeychurch, 1986).

Although some sources believe the value and future potential of MFP is exaggerated, they are a valuable part of local culture and an

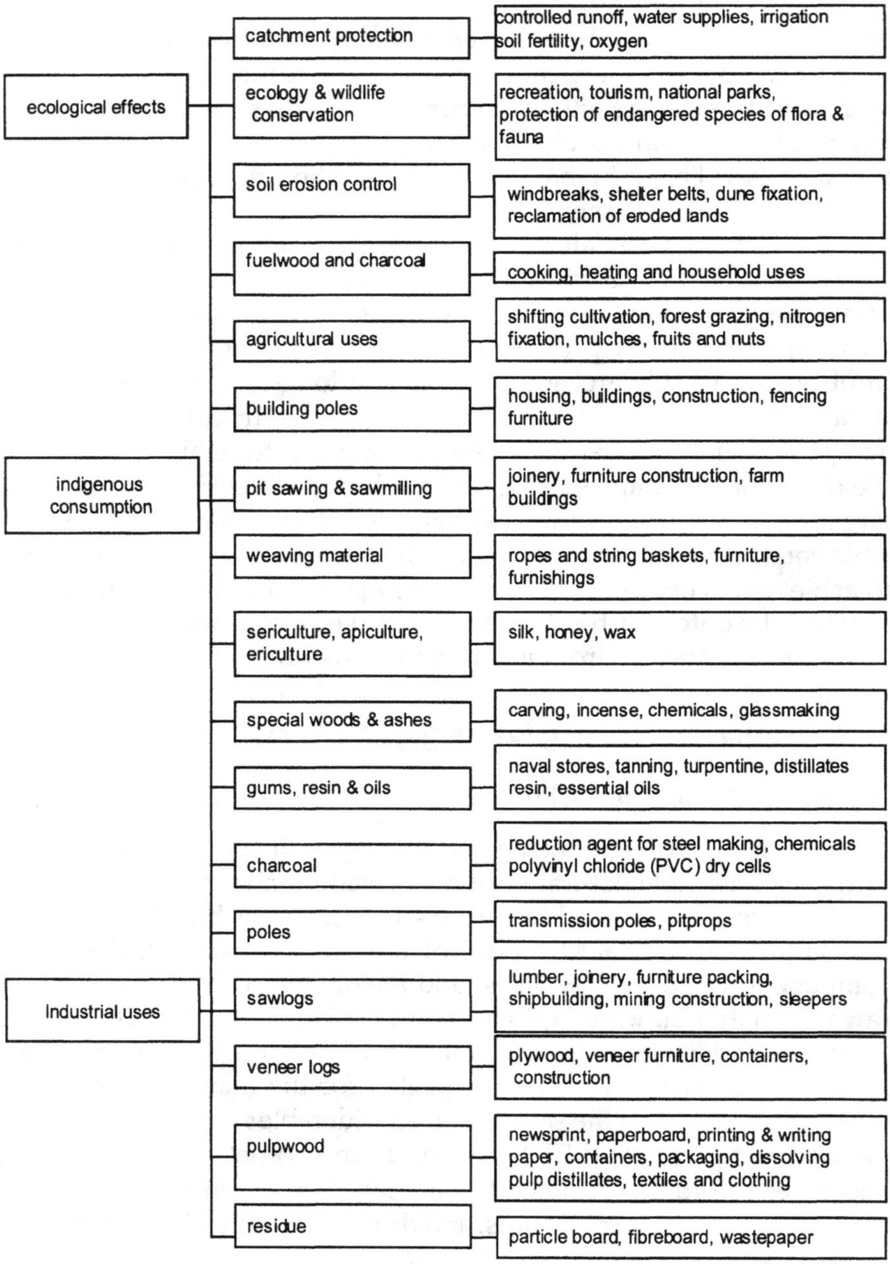

Category	Use	Products / functions
ecological effects	catchment protection	controlled runoff, water supplies, irrigation soil fertility, oxygen
	ecology & wildlife conservation	recreation, tourism, national parks, protection of endangered species of flora & fauna
	soil erosion control	windbreaks, shelter belts, dune fixation, reclamation of eroded lands
indigenous consumption	fuelwood and charcoal	cooking, heating and household uses
	agricultural uses	shifting cultivation, forest grazing, nitrogen fixation, mulches, fruits and nuts
	building poles	housing, buildings, construction, fencing furniture
	pit sawing & sawmilling	joinery, furniture construction, farm buildings
	weaving material	ropes and string baskets, furniture, furnishings
	sericulture, apiculture, ericulture	silk, honey, wax
	special woods & ashes	carving, incense, chemicals, glassmaking
Industrial uses	gums, resin & oils	naval stores, tanning, turpentine, distillates resin, essential oils
	charcoal	reduction agent for steel making, chemicals polyvinyl chloride (PVC) dry cells
	poles	transmission poles, pitprops
	sawlogs	lumber, joinery, furniture packing, shipbuilding, mining construction, sleepers
	veneer logs	plywood, veneer furniture, containers, construction
	pulpwood	newsprint, paperboard, printing & writing paper, containers, packaging, dissolving pulp distillates, textiles and clothing
	residue	particle board, fibreboard, wastepaper

FIGURE 4.1 The role of forests. (From World Bank, 1979 Forestry Sector Policy.)

additional argument in favour of conserving existing NF to ensure their continuing regeneration and allow for the extension of their use. This may be further justified in the light of research being undertaken at the University of the West Indies into the chemical and biological

TABLE 4.8 List of Minor Products from the Forests of Trinidad and Tobago

Common Name	Botanical Name	Part Used	Purpose
A. Trees			
Balata	*Manikara bidentata*	fruit; latex	edible; gum
Balsa	*Ochroma pyramidale*	seed floss	stuffing pillows
Bay rum	*Amomis caryophyllata*	leaves	bay rum of commerce
Black mangrove	*Avicennia nitida*	heartwood	contains lapachol
Black sage	*Cordia cylindrostachya*	leaves	medicinal
Bois bande	*{Parinari campestris*	bark	aphrodisiac properties
	{Roupala montana		
Calabash	*Crescentia cujete*	fruit	ornaments
Chenet	*Melicocca bijuga*	fruit	edible
Cherry Guava	*Eugenia floribunda*	fruit	preserves
Crappo	*Carapa guianensis*	seeds	medicinal oil
Fat Pork	*Chrysobolanus icaco*	fruit	edible
Fustic	*Chlorophora tinctoria*	wood	khaki dye
Hog Plum	*Spondias monbin*	fruit	jellies; preserves
Incense	*Protium guianense*	bark exudate	incense smell on burning
Jumbie bead	*Erythrina spp.*	dried seeds	necklaces
Mahoe	*Sterculia caribaea*	bark	cordage
Obi	*Trichilia trinitensis*	wood	cutlass handles
Penny Piece	*Lucuma multiflora*	fruit	edible
Pois Doux	*Inga spp*	fruit	edible
Quassia, Bitter Ash	*Quassia amara*	wood, leaves	medicine, insecticide
Red mangrove	*Rhizophora spp*	bark	tanning material
Rokoo jab	*Ryania speciosa*	stem, branch	insecticide properties
Sandbox	*Hura crepitans*	fruit	ornamental
Seaside grape	*Coccoloba uvifera*	fruit	edible/astringent
Silk Cotton	*Ceiba pentandra*	seed floss	stuffing pillows
Tirite	*Ischnosiphon arouma*	leaves, stem	handicrafts
Tree fern	*Cyathea spp*	stem	horticulture
B. Palms			
Anare	*Geonoma vaga*	stem	walking sticks
Cabbage palm	*Roystonea olerace*	leaf bud	edible
Camwell	*Desmoncus major*	stem	basket making
Carat	*Sabal mauritiiformis*	leaves	thatching
Cocorite	*Maximiliana caribaea*	leaves, kernel	thatching/edible palm oil
Gri-Gri	*Bactris cuesa*	fruit	edible
Gru-Gru	*Acrocomia aculsata*	fruit & kernel	edible
		leaf bud	edible
		trunk	walking sticks
Mamoo	*Calamus rotang*	leaves	handicraft
Manac	*Euterpe oleracea*	leaf bud	edible
Roseau	*Bactris major*	stem	thatching
Timite	*Manicaria saccifera*	leaves	thatching

TABLE 4.8 List of Minor Products from the Forests of Trinidad and Tobago (continued)

Common Name	Botanical Name	Part Used	Purpose
C. Vines, Shrubs and Herbs			
Bamboo	*Bambusa vulgaris* Gramineae		vases, baskets, waiters, tables, blinds, trinket boxes
Bow-string hemp	*Sansevieria thyrsiflora* Liliaceae		fibre plaited or woven for ropes, hats, bags, slippers
Cachibou	*Calathea discolor* Marantaceae		water-proof baskets
Khus Khus	*Vetiveria zizanoides* Gramineae		floor & table mats, hats, bags, coasters, blinds, waiters
Screw Pine	*Pandanus* spp Pandaceae		woven & plaited for hats, bags, mats, waiters, coasters, baskets, slippers
Sisal	*Agave sisalana* Amaryllidaceae		fibre for ropes, twine, bags, mats and hats
Supple Jack	*Paullinia pinnata* Sapindaceae		Fish poison, baskets, chairs, walking sticks

Data from Chalmers, 1981.

activity of some of these species. It is unfortunate that no attempt has been made to place a monetary value on this component of the NF – a deficiency that should be remedied as part of a wider project into fostering their greater use.

Other Benefits from Forests

The indirect benefits to society in a broad environmental sense are numerous, invariably taken for granted and not generally attributed to the forest. They are summarized below:

- Conserving soil fertility and moisture
- Preventing soil erosion
- Protecting water catchment areas
- Preventing flooding and landslides
- Conservation of biological diversity and genetic resources
- Amelioration of microclimate
- Positive role in the carbon cycle

- Forest recreation and nature tourism
- Hunting for wild game
- Amenity and aesthetic values

As with MFP there has been no attempt in the Caribbean to quantify the value of these indirect benefits in monetary terms – a value that should be added to the value of the timber and MFP to arrive at the true overall value of multipurpose NF to society. Such quantification is not an easy exercise but one component of the overall assessment must be related directly to the costs incurred by society as a result of the increasing widespread and indiscriminate destruction of NF and SF over the past 40 to 50 years. A number of negative consequences follow in regular sequence as soon as the forest is destroyed, frequently accelerated by the indiscriminate use of fire to clear the land. Once the erosion process starts the loss of soil humus, moisture, and fertility proceeds apace and if the site has been cleared for shifting agriculture there is a rapid decline in crop production and within 2 or 3 years the site is abandoned and the cycle is repeated in a new location.

The soil loss from sheet and gully erosion results in the silting up of streams, rivers, and reservoirs and ultimately impacts on coastal estuaries and coral reefs. There is a dual impact on water supply and quality, since with the clearance of NF in many water catchment areas there is excessive run-off and reduced water absorption and the storage capacity of reservoirs is being constantly reduced. Sheng (1986) reports that the capacity of Hermitage Reservoir in Jamaica was reduced by 47 percent within 30 years of its completion and he quotes soil loss rates on steep slopes in excess of 40 tons per acre.

Cox and Embree (1990) stress that water resources management has to be a critical element in the sustainable development process within the region. The inseparable linkage between forest cover and water supply and quality is not disputed, yet the annually recurring problems of alternative periods of severe drought and damaging floods are common throughout the region. Indeed, the situation is deteriorating in most countries because the destruction of forests in water catchment areas is continuing and the present level of forest conservation and management cannot compensate for the accumulated impact of more than 50 years of malpractice and neglect. The water supply situation, which is already critical in several countries, is likely to deteriorate unless there is an immediate and very substantial reforestation programme in key watersheds. An unavoidable issue is the cost, and who will pay the bill. At least part of the cost should be reflected in increased charges for water use and should be indicated as such on the consumer's bill. Unfortunately, many consumers in the region are not connected to the mains and do not receive a bill. The level of such a forestry watershed surcharge should be determined after consultation with the government ministries responsible for forestry and water. The reader is referred to Chapter 2 for a further discussion of forest hydrology and the impact of forestry activity (for example, logging) on water regimes.

Nature Tourism

The issue of biological diversity is considered later but it must be recognized that although there is a wide range of forest ecosystems that it is important be conserved, with minimal interference, for scientific research, many of the same areas are of interest to an increasing number of local and foreign amateur field naturalists. Indeed, there are so many that nature tourism and ecotourism have become significant money earners in several Caribbean countries and have been formally recognized by the Caribbean Tourism Organisation. In this respect, forests have a major role to play in providing different forms of recreation for the dedicated naturalist and for the ordinary citizen. The richness of their forest wildlife and the spectacular nature of the forest vegetation have led several countries to establish national forest parks or similar special areas for their protection and conservation and to facilitate organized access by the public. These facilities are now so popular that wildlife and forest recreation are an integral part of the multiple-use concept of forest management throughout the region, and provide for a wide range of activities by local and overseas tourists, such as birdwatching, fishing, hunting, hiking, camping, and nature trails.

Some wildlife habitats have become major tourist attractions, for example, the nesting grounds of the scarlet ibis (*Eudocimus ruber*) in the Caroni Swamp National Park in Trinidad. Although guides may be employed by tourists, with few exceptions access to most of the facilities is free and there is undoubtedly a strong case to introduce a modest charge to assist in meeting administrative and management costs. The possibility of adverse effects through overuse has to be monitored. In the 1980s, the Caroni Swamp National park attracted over 5000 visitors annually; although this may not be an excessive number taken over a year, a negative impact on the site or the bird population could arise from excessive numbers of boats and visitors during intensive peak holiday periods.

One section of the community that appears to underutilize the region's unique forest and wildlife resources is the formal education sector. A few informative books and scientific articles have been written on the region's forests, national parks, and wildlife but little use is made of these unique biological science "laboratories" for school or community educational trips and natural history projects. Perhaps the real deficiency lies in the various school curricula and an inadequate public relations thrust by the various forestry and wildlife authorities.

Forestry has a useful role to play in another area of environmental management which all too often gets very low priority – the provision of amenities and the enhancement of industrial sites, disused gravel pits, waste disposal, and similar sites. Trees can contribute appreciably to reducing noise levels and to climate regulation in terms of their impact on temperature, shade, and wind. Amenity planting along major and minor roads helps to reduce the glare from the sun and some of the most attractive flowering trees, such as the pink poui (*Tabebuia rosea*) and *Cassia* species grow quickly and have excellent timbers.

FOREST DESTRUCTION AND OVEREXPLOITATION

From the aspect of environmental management the Caribbean starts with some natural disadvantages: mountainous terrain, friable soils (some very sandy and gravelly), a propensity for hurricanes, as well as other periods of exceptionally strong winds and destructively heavy rains alternating with severe dry seasons and drought conditions, which greatly increase the frequency and severity of bush fires. It is well established that NF withstands all these hazards remarkably well, whereas many agricultural crops do not. The exposed soils suffer severely as a result.

There are few precise data on the current rate of destruction of NF and SF in the region. The RFSS (CDB, 1984) gave an estimate of 1 to 2 percent per decade for the entire region, equivalent to 30,000 ha per year, but this could be an underestimate. The Jamaica NFAP (FAO, 1990a) report estimated that the average rate of deforestation for all forest lands was 3.3 percent per year, and concluded with the stark statement that unless immediate steps were taken to halt the process the country would be denuded of its forests within 30 years! In this respect, Sheng (1986) emphasizes the impact of the many thousands of small farmers in Jamaica who clear and cultivate steep slopes to produce various subsistence crops. These farmers do not take any measures to conserve the soil, even though the steeper slopes are frequently in areas of highest rainfall.

The principal reason for the destruction of so much NF and SF in the Caribbean is the agriculture practiced by unemployed, landless shifting cultivators, attempting to provide food for themselves and eke out a living by growing a range of short-term cash crops, usually as squatters on state or private lands, which are cleared and burned indiscriminately. In most countries the impact is exacerbated by adverse site and climate conditions. The persistent burning is particularly damaging because it destroys the top layer of soil humus, as well as the soil structure, and encourages a grass succession which is itself a fire hazard.

The underlying causes of this situation are usually attributed to very high unemployment levels, poverty, increasing population pressure, inadequate land available to peasant farmers, while much of what is available is too steep and unsuitable for such farming. Although these reasons are valid to some extent, in most countries in the region it must be acknowledged that the general level of environmental degradation is much worse than it ought to be for several reasons: a marked decline in the application of soil conservation measures and a totally inadequate response to control irregular practices and to take prompt remedial action – which in many instances requires reforestation. In some instances forest has been cleared to facilitate the implementation of some state or private project designed to enhance social and economic development, but all too often such projects have been undertaken with inadequate planning and in the absence of any independent environmental impact assessment (EIA).

Although the destruction of NF and SF is the major cause of environmental degradation in the Caribbean there is reason for concern in some countries about the extent of overexploitation in some NF and the potentially very damaging impact this could have in the long term on the composition of the forest, the maintenance of a sustained yield of the commercially important species, the soil status, and the general forest habitat. In this respect, it is informative to review experience in the Trinidad mora (*Mora excelsa*) forests, which has been well documented as a result of research by Bell (1971).

Mora is the most abundant timber tree in the country. Beard (1946) assessed the area of mora to be about 37,000 ha or about 17 percent of the remaining NF. It is a dominant, gregarious species occurring in two main locations, in the south-east, where it covers about 22,000 ha, and in the north-east, about 11,000 ha. Commercial exploitation of mora was not very significant until the 1920s but by the 1950s the local market depended heavily on the species and over the period 1961 to 1970 the average annual volume cut was 22,430 m^3 or 20 percent of the total volume of all species harvested. In 1987 the volume of mora cut was 14,340 m^3, equivalent to 26 percent of the total volume harvested.

Bell describes the history of exploitation of the north-east mora forests, which initially consisted of haphazardly "creaming off" the largest mora trees over large areas. In 1953 the principal objectives of management were changed to encourage the natural regeneration of mixed hardwoods to replace the mora and, to facilitate this change, exploitation was restricted to prescribed blocks of forest each year. Because the natural regeneration of other species was so poor it was decided from 1958 on to clear a fixed area each year and replant it with pine (*Pinus caribaea*). It is interesting to note that because of the very large number of timber licensees wishing to exploit the increased demand for the species a system of rationing had to be introduced. Bell indicated that as a result of overexploitation in two of the forest reserves in the north-east mora forest there was no virgin forest left, and that out of a total of 5000 ha in those reserves 4600 ha had been devastated as a result of overexploitation and the fires that tend to follow such treatment. Bell was also critical of the decision to clear mora and replace it with pine, particularly since the planting of pine was not keeping pace with the clearing of mora, which became an unproductive fire hazard. Bell's study demonstrated quite convincingly that mora forest could be managed successfully to give a sustained yield at commercially acceptable levels but he stressed that strict supervision of exploitation was essential and that royalty rates should be kept under regular review.

A few years ago a similar problem occurred in Guyana with the overexploitation of the wallaba (*Eperua falcata*) forests where this species is dominant and is in great demand internationally for transmission poles. Here again, overexploitation resulted in a rapid deterioration of the poor white sandy soil and a virtual total failure of the natural regeneration. In the past, large areas of former wallaba forests have been written off but the Forest Authority now exercises much closer supervision of the exploitation to ensure that excessive numbers of trees are not removed at any one time or at too frequent an interval.

The critical factor in both these examples is the rapid negative impact of destroying the permanent closed forest canopy formed by the overlapping tree crowns in the various strata in the NF. A feature of many rainforest soils is their low content of plant nutrients combined with a remarkable fertility which is due to the incorporation in the top layer of the nutrient-rich organic matter derived from the prolific leaf litter. However, once the crown canopy is permanently destroyed this rich humic layer is rapidly destroyed by the sun or by bush fires and the unique nutrient cycle is broken, with detrimental effects on any subsequent tree growth and the long-term fertility of the soil.

A number of research studies have been undertaken recently in the Blue Mountains of Jamaica by McDonald and Healey (2000a, 2000b), into various aspects of the problems arising from SF clearance, for example: soil erosion, soil deterioration, and the evaluation of indigenous tree species and naturalized provenances of *Calliandra calothyrsus* for reforestation and agroforestry. It is significant that foreign universities seem to be taking the lead in this type of research. Without in any way denigrating their efforts it would be preferable if donor funding could be directed to institutions/forestry departments within the region to undertake such research on a collaborative basis.

FOREST ECOLOGY AND BIOLOGICAL DIVERSITY

The climax vegetation that covered considerable areas of the Caribbean before the arrival of the first inhabitants was mainly luxuriant tropical forest. This varied in extent, type, and species composition depending on a number of factors, such as soil, terrain, elevation, rainfall, and temperature. These forests provided a range of habitats associated with diverse animal populations, which formed complex ecological systems reflecting the evolutionary process of aeons. The wide range of existing forest ecosystems comprises the principal habitats for much of the biological diversity in the region. In one of the earliest warnings of the irreversible threats to global biodiversity, Erenfeld (1970) stressed the importance of retaining natural forest ecosystems at all costs and emphasized that the science of ecology is the foundation for the conservation of both forests and biodiversity. Unfortunately, for many years ecology, and especially forest ecology, was ignored in the Caribbean as a science of importance and, until a recent upsurge of interest in conservation ecology, much of the significant research was undertaken a long time ago. These early studies demonstrated that many of the Caribbean islands have a very special ecological significance as a result of a combination of factors: geographical isolation, geology, small size, and mountainous topography. These factors have given rise to an unusually high level of endemism amongst the fauna and flora of the region. That is, there exists certain plant and animal species that are adapted and restricted to specific habitats and ecosystems and are not found in any other island. Beard (1949) reported 25 percent endemism among the species he recorded during his forest ecology research in the Leeward and Windward Islands. In Jamaica, Adams (1972) indicates that 30 percent of its approximately 3000 species of flowering plants are reported as unique, while Tanner (1986) reported that in the montane forests of the Blue Mountains and Port Royal Mountains approximately 41 percent of the tree species are endemic and floristically different from other montane forests in the Caribbean. Trinidad is of special interest because of its historical geological connection with the South American mainland and because its forests have been so well documented by the pioneer dendrology and ecology studies of Marshall (1939) and Beard (1946). Similar forest ecology studies were undertaken in Guyana by Fanshawe (1952) and in Jamaica by Asprey and Robbins (1953). A useful introduction to the ecology of the flora and fauna of the Caribbean is provided by Bacon (1978).

In terms of specific ecosystems, Bacon (1989) indicates that little attention has been given to the wet forested ecosystems which are such an important feature of low lying coastal areas throughout the Caribbean. Bacon distinguishes *swamps*, which are wetlands dominated by trees, and *marshes*, which are wetlands dominated by herbaceous plants. In the forest context then we can distinguish *mangal*, which is a saline swamp dominated by mangrove trees, *swamp forest*, which is a freshwater swamp dominated by other trees, such as *Pterocarpus*, and *palm swamp forest*, which is a freshwater swamp dominated by palms. The general lack of ecological data also extends to the fauna, although studies in the Trinidad Nariva Swamp by Bacon (1989) indicate the considerable faunal diversity that can exist in such habitats, with more than 600 aquatic and nonaquatic species being recorded. Interestingly, it appears that it is the water status of such habitats, rather than vegetative cover, that has a dominant role in the distribution of fauna, except for the essentially arboreal species, such as bats, birds, and monkeys. Insects are a rarely mentioned component of biodiversity even though they may be of considerable social significance. Biting insects are common in the Nariva Swamp fauna, which includes 84 species of mosquito. Although the fauna of swamp forest formations is not distinctly habitat specific the studies in the Nariva Swamp indicate the value of extending such investigations to other islands.

From a forestry aspect very little is known of the productive capacity of the swamp forests. Although they contain at least a dozen species of commercial importance which are harvested regularly, they

TABLE 4.9 Animal Species in Guyana and Species under Threat

	Families	Species	Appendix II
Birds	69	720	117
Mammals	32	232	26
Reptiles	11	42	22

Data from Pilgrim, 1994.

have never been subject to any form of forest management, possibly because of the limited access for long periods during the wet season. Unfortunately they are becoming increasingly exposed to human interference for commercial agricultural purposes, particularly rice cultivation. During extended dry periods they are also susceptible to bush fires which are particularly destructive since regular burning favours the regeneration of herbaceous plants at the expense of the traditional forest species.

Bacon (1989) gives a summary of the fauna of Trinidad and Tobago which, in spite of its small size, has the following range of vertebrate species: 26 frogs, 24 lizards, 36 snakes, 32 mammals, and 58 bats. The bird population has also been intensively studied and well documented, with at least 350 species recorded. It is this type of diversity, added to other more typical tourist attractions, that makes the country increasingly popular as a base for nature tourism.

Guyana is also attempting to develop a similar ecotourism market to benefit from its considerable forest and wildlife resources. Table 4.9 shows a summary from Pilgrim (1994) indicating its diverse resources. The Convention on International Trade in Endangered Species (CITES) Appendix II column indicates the species believed to be threatened, although there is little detailed information on population size for many of the species.

For over 50 years Guyana has been exporting wildlife internationally, with 114 species designated as "commercially exportable", including birds, mammals, reptiles, amphibians, and arthropods. Since 1987, annual export quotas have been imposed on all species on the list and between December 1992 and November 1994 there was a complete embargo on the export of wildlife. The export earnings from this trade in 1992 amounted to G$ 30 million, some of which was channelled back into the national programme of wildlife conservation.

Assessment of Biological Diversity

The investigations of biodiversity should not be confined solely to NF. Over the past 50 to 60 years, Jamaica and Trinidad and Tobago have established quite considerable areas of single-species PF, mainly coniferous species of the genus *Pinus*, usually *P. caribaea*, and a number of broadleaf species: *Eucalyptus* species and Blue Mahoe (*Hibiscus elatus*) in Jamaica and teak (*Tectona grandis*) in Trinidad. Over the past 20 years several other countries have taken a positive step in establishing small commercial plantations using valuable indigenous broadleaf species, such as cedar (*Cedrela mexicana*), mahogany (*Swietenia* spp.), and cypre (*Cordia alliodora*), usually as a single species and occasionally in mixture. In these areas, and in the much larger areas of SF, there is virtually no information on changes in biodiversity. Due to this scarcity of information, data collected by a study team from the University of Newcastle on bird populations at sites near Hardwar Gap in the Blue Mountains of Jamaica are of interest (Thomson and Bretting, 1986). Comparing NF and Caribbean pine plantations it was found that the total number of birds using the mature pine plantation was 53 percent less than in NF and that only slightly more than 50 percent of the native mountain forest bird species were recorded in the pine. Similarly, Goodbody (1994) has shown that on a degraded hillside at 1,220 metres in the Port Royal Mountains indigenous forest species of bird retreated into pockets of natural forest in preference to living in *Pinus* or *Eucalyptus* plantations. These studies are significant because of the enormous programme of reforestation that has to be undertaken throughout the region as an essential component of the national programmes of environmental rehabilitation. The issue of wildlife and biodiversity cannot be divorced from this exercise. Wildlife is an integral part of the forest habitat and of the forest multiple-use concept and a typical example of this interrelationship is demonstrated by Tanner (1986), who found that the seed of most trees in montane forest in Jamaica is dispersed by birds.

A constantly recurring theme in the current discussion on regional biodiversity is the chronic lack of reliable data on issues such as species populations, breeding populations, current rate and reasons for loss of different species, habitat pollution and its impact on specific populations, the impact of overexploitation in the forest, and the impact of hunters and professional plant and animal collectors. With a few exceptions (for example, birds) there is a lack of recent detailed national inventories of fauna and, in some cases, of flora also. Nor is there a comprehensive, up to date picture either of the overall ecology or of a range of critical habitats. Nevertheless, a number of specific ecosystems and individual species (for example, parrots) and habitats have been identified as being under threat.

Johnson et al. (1988) report on an assessment of biodiversity and forests in seven island states in the Eastern Caribbean and provide a useful list of references. For each country they indicate those species considered to be under threat, including various land turtles, mountain chicken, frigate birds, parrots, waterfowl, and wading birds. In reviewing the reasons for the threat to the region's biological diversity the report shares some views in common with other observers, which are, in summary:

- Impact of economic and social development
- Overexploitation and destruction of natural resources for short-term commercial gain
- Unplanned agricultural expansion and shifting cultivation
- Development planning undertaken without or with inadequate environmental impact assessments (EIAs)
- Hunting and trapping wildlife for meat and for the pet market
- Inadequate legislation and legal constraints to control abuse
- Inadequate staff and funds to enforce existing legislation/regulations
- Deficiencies in formal school curricula
- Inadequate adult education and public relations activities
- Poverty, unemployment, and shortage of land for peasant farming

Conservation of Wildlife

The region's biodiversity, especially in wildlife, is particularly at risk from unscrupulous hunters and collectors. In several countries in the region forest hunting for sport and food is an extremely popular activity. For example, in Jamaica and Trinidad and Tobago, there is legislation to protect game species from overexploitation but such legislation can only serve its purpose if there are adequate staff and support facilities on the ground to enforce its provisions. Unfortunately, this is not the case. Cooper and Bacon (1981) reviewed the hunting of wildlife in Trinidad and Tobago and indicated that in 1975 approximately 3500 hunting permits were issued. The number of wildlife game licences issued in 1999/2000 had risen to 9379, bringing in revenue of TT$ 187,580. Cooper and Bacon (1981) reported that some protected animals were hunted for food and that the ocelot (*Felis pardalis*), hunted for its skin, was probably extinct. At the same time, they warned that other vertebrate species would be under similar threat unless the excesses of the hunting fraternity were controlled and wildlife protection and management were given much greater attention.

In Jamaica, where only birds may be hunted, the Wildlife Protection Act specifies the species that may be hunted and gives protection to all others. It also makes provision for the control of the length of the hunting season (usually from August to October), the number of days in each week on which hunting may take place, and the number of birds (bag limit) that may be shot by any hunter in a single day. In spite of these regulations and in spite of improved surveillance and monitoring, protected species such as the ring-tailed pigeon (*Columba caribea*) continue to be under pressure from hunters. Two species of parrot in Jamaica, the yellow-billed parrot (*Amazona collaria*) and the black-billed parrot (*Amazona agilis*) are also threatened by habitat disturbance and by collectors for the live animal trade. However, a public awareness programme by the Natural Resources Conservation Authority (NRCA) and prosecution of some offenders is helping to curb the collection of live birds (Goodbody, personal communication).

In Guyana, there is concern about the increased pressure on some game species, for example, labba (*Agouti paca*), deer (*Mazama* spp.), iguana (*Iguana iguana*), and capybara (*Hydochaeris hydrochaeris*), as a result of increased hunting for the domestic market and for the restaurant trade. There is also concern about the impact on forest wildlife if sports hunting becomes a popular component of the ecotourism thrust. Of particular significance is the possible dilemma the country faces in its thrust for economic development, which inevitably involves increased access into the interior and exploitation of, or within, the NF. The opening in Guyana in 1993 of the Barama plywood factory is a classic example and the company and the government should be complimented on the measures formally agreed upon, not only to ensure the maintenance of a sustained yield from the forest in the concession area, but also to monitor and conserve the biological diversity and undertake research in this area. Barama has prepared a useful information package on all aspects of its Guyana operations and this is available on request from the company in Georgetown. However, in the Guyana context, as in most other countries in the region, there are two overriding concerns with respect to conserving biodiversity. The existing legislation is inadequate to cope with the needs and increasing pressures, and the current revision process would benefit from some regional collaboration, for example, to deal with the transhipment of wildlife smuggled out of Guyana to North America via a second Caribbean country. The second general concern is the totally inadequate level of funding and staffing devoted to wildlife management and research throughout the region.

Although the commercial exploitation and export of wild animals receives the most criticism, there is an equally determined cadre of professional plant collectors operating throughout the region, exporting the rarer species of a number of families that are under threat, including the Bromeliaceae, Cactaceae, and Orchidaceae. Most of these species are protected under the Convention on International Trade in Endangered Species (CITES) to which most countries in the region are a party. The manner in which different countries give protection to these plants, particularly orchids, differs from country to country. For instance, in Costa Rica all orchids are state property and no collecting is permitted at all. In Suriname, visitors may obtain a permit to export a small number of orchids but must do so in collaboration with a local dealer. In Belize, specimens may only be collected in the company of a local guide who has responsibility for regulating the activity. In Jamaica, a new policy framework has been established to protect endangered species. Again, there is inadequate monitoring on the ground and unscrupulous collectors are only likely to be detected by particularly vigilant plant protection and customs officers at points of departure.

The protection and conservation of the region's wildlife is inextricably tied to its forest habitats. The concept of forest conservation is to ensure the growth and survival of forest ecosystems which may or may not be under some form of controlled exploitation or subject to some other threat. Conservation should not be confused with preservation, although in some instances it may be necessary to restrict or prohibit any form of exploitation in the interest of conserving a rare or sensitive forest ecosystem that otherwise might be at risk. Trinidad and Tobago is a good example of a country with comprehensive legislation under the aegis of the Forest Authority to protect both forests and wildlife. In addition, Trinidad and Tobago has provided further protection through the legal establishment of special habitat sites in the form of 13 wildlife sanctuaries covering 16,480 ha and 11 more specialized nature reserves covering 610 ha. Because of their close interdependence it is advisable that the responsibility for the conservation and management of all aspects of a country's biological diversity be linked, institutionally and organizationally, with the operational authority responsible for forests. In a situation where this does not happen, as in some countries in the region, it is essential that there is close consultation among all the agencies involved.

It is necessary to make a distinction between the scientific demands of the conservation of biological diversity and genetic resources, and the more generalized natural history activities related to much of the same basic populations in forest habitats throughout the region. The biodiversity programme is a strictly scientific programme with specific needs in terms of staff and funding. A key requirement is to specify the priority research programme and the precise forest sites needed for ecological and other scientific studies. In this respect attention is drawn to stimulating papers by Corlett (1988) and Westoby (1984). Based on his studies in the rainforests of Bukit Timah in the Pacific, Corlett suggested that very large areas of forest are not required to sustain forest ecosystems and maintain biological diversity. Westoby challenges some of the traditional views on the complexity and fragility of forest ecosystems. It would be worthwhile testing their theories in some island states in the Caribbean, where, if applicable, they could bring distinct savings to the forest and biodiversity research budget and make the implementation of intensive research in these fields a reality instead of wishful thinking.

There is no lack of documentation stressing the importance of biological diversity within the region. In recent years there has been a number of informative conferences, seminars, and workshops drawing attention to a range of critical issues. The 4th Annual Meeting of the Caribbean Foresters Association (CFA, 1989) had as its theme the subject of wildlife management in the Caribbean and the proceedings, while emphasizing wildlife conservation concepts, expressed concern over the increasing pressures being exerted on wildlife resources throughout the region. However, equal concern must be expressed that this continues to happen in spite of the efforts and funding from innumerable national, regional, and international organizations that have been engaged in conservation activities in the region for many years. In terms of effective environmental management there is an unnecessary duplication of effort, with funding spread too thinly across too many organizations, resulting in an undesirable counterproductive bureaucracy and a mountain of documentation, much of which says little that is original. This may appear harsh criticism of organizations whose dedication and commitment is clear. Nevertheless, the real challenge is for such organizations to ensure that most of their available manpower and funding is spent in the field as opposed to office bureaucracy and meaningless paperwork.

What action can be taken to conserve the region's invaluable biodiversity? The most important decision will be made when the comprehensive 20-year NFAPs, now completed for at least 12 Caribbean countries, are formally approved and funded, because a priority project in each is the conservation and sustainable development of existing NF. Related projects involving the conservation of biodiversity are also included. Included among these projects is the concept of wildlife farming – the breeding in captivity of a range of wildlife species, particularly those on the endangered list and those subject to being hunted for wildmeat. With the systematic release of young adults into the wild, populations could begin to achieve normality. Such projects undertaken by keen amateur naturalists or non-governmental organizations (NGOs) could be encouraged by appropriate subsidies when animals are bred specifically for release into the wild, possibly as a component of a community forest project. As with many other indirect benefits derived to a large extent from NF there has been no attempt within the region to quantify in dollar terms the value to society of the various benefits derived from this biodiversity, so much of which is taken for granted. Such an exercise should be undertaken as part of an overall research programme in which gifted amateur naturalists and relevant organizations should be encouraged to play an active role.

Finally, there is scope within the Caribbean for the "debt-for-nature swap" concept, as a means of assisting poorer developing countries in tackling their environmental problems. This has had a mixed reception internationally and a more effective and less controversial approach in the Caribbean region could be direct funding, through regional and international development agencies, to finance the various NFAPs mentioned previously.

An important outcome of the 1992 United Nations Conference on Environment and Development (UNCED) was agreement on the establishment of a convention on biological diversity. UNCED recognized the vital role of forests in conserving biodiversity and the serious threat posed by their continuing widespread destruction. The specific requirements needed to ensure that the conservation of biological diversity receives adequate attention from a forestry perspective are summarized as follows:

- Biodiversity must be accepted as a fundamental element of the National Forest Policy and accepted by governments as a priority that must be addressed in all land use planning activities
- The identification, description, formal recognition, and designation of sites of special biological interest must receive urgent attention

- The implementation of appropriate activities designed to assist the conservation of diversity through local, regional, and international actions, e.g., national policies, legislation, regulations, international treaties, educational programmes, and public relations programmes designed to increase public awareness of the vital role of forests
- The active encouragement of inputs by NGOs and community groups with incentives where deemed appropriate
- The implementation of forest management plans designed to favour the conservation of existing biodiversity
- The assessment and, where necessary, improvement of the capacity of existing forest administrations to monitor forest ecosystem conservation priorities
- The enforcement of effective regular consultations between forest administrations and other departments and agencies involved in any other aspect of the conservation of biodiversity including local, regional, and international NGOs and funding agencies

The Iwokrama International Rain Forest Programme

In recognition of the importance of tropical rain forests and the need to understand them and the linkages that exist among their various elements, including the indigenous peoples who live there as a part of the natural systems, the government of Guyana has set aside an area of 360,000 ha of rain forest to be used by the international community for research on the sustainable management of rain forests. The site contains a variety of ecological conditions and natural resources, as well as high levels of biological diversity. In the neighbouring area live Amerindian communities whose traditional livelihood depends on the forest. The decision to set aside this site was announced at a meeting of Commonwealth Heads of Government in 1989 and expressly stated that the programme of work would be carried out under the auspices of the British Commonwealth. An Interim Board of Trustees was set up and an operational plan for the first 5 years prepared (Kerr, 1993). The mission statement of this programme was:

> To promote the conservation and the sustainable and equitable use of tropical rain forests in a manner that will lead to lasting economic and social benefits to the people of Guyana and to the world in general, by undertaking research, training, and the dissemination of technologies.

Five core programmes were recognized in the 5-year plan — three central programmes:

- Sustainable management of forests
- Conservation and utilization of biodiversity
- Sustainable human development

and two cross-cutting programmes:

- Forest research (interpreted in the broadest sense)
- Information and communication

MANAGEMENT OF FORESTS FOR SUSTAINED YIELD

Forests and Sustainable Development

Over the past 30 years, as the environmental lobby has become a more powerful force, much literature has been generated at the international level on the concepts of conservation and, more recently, sustainable development (SD) to combat the increasing abuse of the global environment. New ideas, and the refinements of old ones, have appeared regularly as the debate has expanded. Little was achieved on the ground but the fundamental role of forests was slowly being recognized in the international dialogue. The World Commission on Environment and Development, appointed in 1983 by the UN General Assembly, stressed the fundamental importance of SD, which its final report (Bruntland, 1987) defined as "development that meets the needs of the present without compromising the ability of future generations to meet their own needs." In this context it stressed the importance of conserving and enhancing the Earth's natural resources.

The UN Conference on Environment and Development (UNCED), which was convened in 1992, gave unprecedented attention to forestry, the widespread destruction of forests, and the need for sustainable forestry development. Although the developing countries rejected a proposal for an international convention on forests, the conference reached agreement on a non-legally binding statement of principles for a global consensus on the management, conservation, and sustainable development of all types of forest. At the same time, it recognized the sovereign rights of individual countries to utilize the products of their forests according to their own environment and development policies. A number of other far-reaching decisions pertaining to forestry were taken at UNCED 1992, which resulted in positive steps being taken at the international, regional, and national levels. The responses and specific actions within the forestry sector have been collated and reviewed by Maini (1995) and Grayson (1995). It is clear that the role of forests is now receiving considerable attention in the deliberations of the conventions on biodiversity, climate change, desertification, and trade in endangered species (CITES).

To encourage the implementation of the recommendations from UNCED, Agenda 21 was prepared as an action plan for the year 2000 and beyond, with proposals for conserving forests and biological diversity and combating deforestation. The final element in this monumental effort for global self-preservation was the establishment of the United Nations Commission on Sustainable Development to monitor progress and identify problems in the implementation of Agenda 21.

Freezailah (1993) presents a controversial view of conservation and environmental management from the perspective of supporting the commercial exploitation of natural forests in the tropics, maintaining that the apparent conflict with sustainable development arises from a too literal interpretation of sustainable development as defined by the Bruntland Commission. He may be taking an extreme view in insisting that the type of natural regeneration that occurs following traditional methods of exploitation in natural tropical forests may compromise the needs of future generations. Nevertheless, he insists that commercial exploitation of tropical forests and the concepts of conservation and sustainability can be harmonized in practice.

Forest Policy

The starting point in the process of managing the region's forests to achieve a sustained yield must be the unequivocal commitment to the forestry sector by the state. This should be demonstrated by the adoption of an unambiguous, comprehensive forest policy designed to cover a wide range of environmental issues and the traditional activities falling within the forestry sector on state and private lands. An effective forest policy must be formulated in such a way as to ensure:

- That enough government-owned forest is kept in appropriate places to ensure that the community gains from its indirect benefits (protection for agricultural crops, preservation of water supplies, prevention of soil erosion and flooding) and from its direct benefits (timber, fuelwood, and other minor forest produce)

- That these forests are harvested and managed in such a way as to provide a permanent supply of timber and other products, with a view to achieving self-sufficiency in timber supplies
- That the forestry operations of private landowners are monitored, encouraged, and assisted where possible
- That forest-based industries are encouraged and assisted where possible
- That the conservation and management of forests on watersheds receive high priority
- That denuded areas and degraded SF are reforested without delay to allow the environmental protection and increased productivity of the site with agroforestry given priority where feasible
- That forests are managed as multi-purpose resources to facilitate and promote the conservation and management of biodiversity
- That forest recreation and ecotourism facilities are developed through the creation and management of national parks, wildlife sanctuaries, and similar facilities, encouraging individual and community involvement
- That organized research is carried out in relevant branches of tropical forestry
- That staff at all levels receive appropriate education and training to fit them for their work
- That young persons and the general public are made aware of the benefits and value of scientific forestry through the active promotion of community forestry projects

Forest Legislation

To be effective, the forest policy must be supported by appropriate legislation, normally acts of Parliament. Comprehensive legislation must be drafted in such a way as to ensure that all aspects of the policy can be implemented effectively. It must take into account issues such as boundaries, access, trespass, conditions controlling the exploitation of timber and other forest products, licensing procedures and fees, and land use issues, including watershed management, wildlife conservation, hunting, national parks, and protection of the forest from fire, pathogens, and pests. Such legislation should give the forestry service authority to discharge its wide-ranging responsibilities effectively and efficiently with a minimum of bureaucracy. This can only be done if the state provides adequate funding, staffing, support services, and an organizational/administrative structure commensurate with the size of the country, as well as the extent of the forest and other biological resources to be managed.

At the national level the forest service should be responsible primarily for the preparation of a national forestry strategy. This should be formulated in consultation with related groups, namely, agriculturalists, water resource managers, land-use planners, workers in the timber trade, including sawmillers and loggers, private land owners, hunters, naturalists, rural community groups, and any other NGOs with a genuine interest in the conservation and sustainable use of the nation's forest resources. For day to day administrative and forest management purposes the forest resources should be divided into a number of geographic regions normally large enough to be managed by an experienced professional forestry officer. These staff members will be responsible for implementing the details of the national forestry strategy.

Forest Management

Forest management has been described as the application of science, technology, and economics to a forest for the achievement of predetermined, clearly defined objectives. Indeed, the management of forests to ensure a sustained yield is a very old and fundamental concept of forest science. However, sustainable development (SD), in the sense defined by the Bruntland Commission, poses a dilemma for the tropical forester when taking into account the following: the management of NF with its complex ecosystems, containing many different tree species; forests that have been perpetuated through a process of natural regeneration that cannot be readily manipulated and for which market demands are changing but increasing, while the forest area is declining.

Freezailah (1993) suggests that foresters must be pragmatic in interpreting the Bruntland prescriptions on SD and recommends that the immediate priority in the forest policy of most tropical countries must be conserving the existing NF, with its invaluable biological diversity and genetic resources, maintaining the existing ecological balance, and taking urgent action to stem widespread environmental degradation by implementing major reforestation and agroforestry programmes. In other words, he suggests that SD is a means of attaining such goals and not itself the primary goal. With the generally deteriorating condition of the region's NF, its degraded environment, and the uncertainty over much of its biodiversity, Freezailah's strategy seems appropriate for the Caribbean.

To facilitate the routine management of the typical operational forestry unit, a comprehensive management plan, known as the working plan, is prepared, usually to cover a period of 10 years, with provision for review after 5 years. It contains detailed background information on the forest, including the following factors: history, geology, soils, climate, forest type, previous management, rate of growth, volume production, previous exploitation, expenditure, and income. Detailed prescriptions are prepared for future management of the existing forest and for any other activities in the working plan area (for example, reforestation, wildlife management, forest recreation, and forest research). These prescriptions are designed to achieve the goals set out in the national forest strategy. Due to the very long periods involved in the growth cycle of trees in NF and PF, all planning and management decisions have to be made with great care, should have a degree of flexibility, and should be subject to regular review. The success of any forest management proposal depends largely on the accuracy of the data on which decisions concerning a range of forestry disciplines have to be based. All too often in the region this basic data is nonexistent or incomplete. This is also true of the limited research undertaken to ascertain the most appropriate silvicultural and management systems needed in different forest types so that a commercially exploitable yield of the species will be sustained. Because of the complex ecology and the very large numbers of species in different strata of the NF it requires a good knowledge of the dendrology, ecology, and growth rates of individual species and the forest as a whole. This will enable the forester to determine the most appropriate silvicultural and forest management systems to adopt for each forest type under different site and climatic conditions in order to achieve a sustained yield for the range of timber species in demand by the commercial market.

To overcome the lack of basic data, one or two countries have implemented a national forest inventory using aerial photography and/or satellite technology backed up by a statistically designed series of permanent and temporary sample plots distributed over the whole growing area. These are representative of the various types of localities and normal growing conditions and cover the range of existing age classes. Individual trees are marked for future reference and the following data are usually collected: total height, utilizable height, girth or diameter (at 1.3 metres above ground) and bark thickness. Using well-established forest mensuration techniques this type of data is used to prepare two standard tools of forest management – volume tables and yield tables. Volume tables provide, in tabular form, the average volumes of trees based on their height and girth or diameter. A yield table is a tabular statement that gives data on the course of development of an even-aged plantation from a certain minimum age (usually 5 or 10 years) up to the maximum rotation age, at periodic intervals (usually 5 years). Once compiled a yield table can provide information on the standing volume or volume increment, the likely intermediate and final crop yields of a plantation, the site quality of any particular locality based on the yield compared with other sites, the choice of species and the method of treatment and optimum rotation for any particular site. Good examples of this type of technical information exist in Trinidad with the yield tables for teak and pine prepared by Miller (1969a, 1969b) and the volume tables for the 26 principal indigenous hardwood species prepared in conjunction with the inventory of the indigenous forests completed in 1979.

Outside Belize and Guyana there is probably little accessible NF in the Caribbean that has not been subject to exploitation, or overexploitation, at regular intervals. It is this type of forest that has to be conserved, enhanced, and managed on a sustainable basis as a matter of urgency. In attempting to do this, the production of timber cannot be isolated from economic considerations and the maintenance of soil fertility and biological diversity. In practical terms, how can such forest be managed to ensure a sustained yield? Initially, from an administrative aspect, there should be a system in place to authorize, regulate, and monitor all types of exploitation of sawlogs, fuelwood, and any other forest produce, to fix charges, and to collect revenue. This will be through some form of licensing system, tied in with removal permits to allow harvested material to be transported from the forest. Outside the forest this system should be supported by a monitoring of conversion points, such as sawmills, to prevent or limit illegal felling.

Yield Regulation

In forestry terms, sustained yield represents the regular forest harvest, with an approximate balance being maintained between the net growth and the volume harvested. Fundamental aspects of any forest management system are yield regulation, that is, determining the volume of timber to be harvested from a forest at any one time, and the felling cycle, namely, the frequency at which such exploitation may take place. In NF, with a range of marketable and non-marketable species of different ages and sizes occupying different strata in the forest canopy, yield regulation is more complex than in a single-species plantation. Success in implementing any particular silvicultural and management system depends very much on the experience of the forest manager. The techniques to be applied will depend on the area of the forest, the forest type, and the composition and condition of the standing crop. It should be stressed that the capital with which the forester works is the soil and its fertility can only be maintained or enhanced by a judicious manipulation of the standing crop.

From previous records, or from a fresh inventory of the forest, the volume of the standing crop and its current rate of growth are determined and the volume to be harvested decided upon. This assessment cannot be very precise and in practice it is preferable to err on the low side. There are several options in obtaining the volume required. One can exploit a larger area at longer intervals, or a smaller area more intensively or at shorter intervals. Because of the relatively small size of the Caribbean forests outside Guyana and Belize there is little choice in these matters and the felling cycle will rarely be less than 10 years. In any system there is normally a minimum diameter below which trees cannot be cut. This precaution exists, in the short term, to safeguard future harvests and, in the long term, to ensure that there are mature seed trees to provide for natural regeneration of the original forest type.

Once the volume to be removed has been fixed, individual trees are marked for removal with a number of objectives in view: providing the required number of trees of marketable species, opening up the tree canopy to stimulate the growth of other marketable species and young regeneration, and the removal of any dead, diseased, or damaged trees. In making this selection it is tempting to confine attention to the principal marketable species but in practice it is preferable to try and maintain the composition and structure of the original forest type while encouraging the growth and regeneration of as many different marketable species as possible. Care has to be taken in the timing, actual felling, and extraction of the harvested material to minimize damage to the standing crop, the soil, and extraction routes by heavy duty vehicles and other equipment.

In many of the badly degraded areas of the NF in the Caribbean in which the principal marketable species have been consistently overexploited there may be no alternative but to resort at the outset to some form of enrichment planting in attempting to restore the original forest type. In this system seed or plants of the desired mixture of species are established through the forest or in cleared strips 20 to 25 metres apart. Regular maintenance is essential to ensure the introduced material is not suppressed by weed species or lianes. In this system there may be a role for the landless shifting cultivator to grow some one-off short-term crops or for community forest projects.

Once such silvicultural and management systems are implemented it is essential that a monitoring system is established to assess survival and growth at regular intervals, normally 3 to 5 years. This is done by means of a series of permanent sample plots marked in the forest in which individual trees are measured to provide data for the calculation of volume and rate of growth. The economics of implementing these systems must also be monitored with a view to determining means of reducing costs but also as an input in the process of determining a realistic fee to be charged for the material to be harvested from these forests in the future.

PLANTATION FORESTRY AND AGROFORESTRY SYSTEMS

The widespread destruction of NF, including that in many critical water catchment areas, the considerable areas of degraded SF, the substantial areas of abandoned, idle former agricultural land, and the many acres subjected to squatting and shifting cultivation combine to produce an unacceptable level of environmental degradation. The most effective means of reversing this situation and permanently rehabilitating a devastated environment would be through a very large-scale reforestation programme involving a range of plantation projects having at their core a major agroforestry thrust. Such projects would be designed to protect the environment and, where appropriate, produce a sustained yield of timber, combined with the production of other crops and fruits with a livestock component where sites and conditions permit. The economic issues involved are considered later, but even if all the financial resources required were made available this would not be an easy task. As Lundgren (1980) stresses, it is essential that foresters recognize the fragile, debilitated physical and biological environments involved and ensure that the selection of species and the silvicultural and forest management systems adopted are appropriate in the short and long term. Such decisions must benefit from a thorough review of previous experience – local, regional, and, where appropriate, international.

It is significant that there is concern throughout the region about the general decline in agriculture and it is essential that agriculturists, foresters, and land use planners take the initiative and collaborate closely to develop strategies that will accelerate the process of environmental rehabilitation. In addition, these strategies should not only prevent any further decline in the productive capacity of the land, but also stimulate a significant increase in production of timber, food, and livestock on state and private lands. In most countries the first priority should be watershed rehabilitation, but because of the urgent need to solve one of the root causes of forest destruction, landless shifting cultivators, the development of appropriate agroforestry techniques, including livestock, should also receive high priority in most PF projects. The planning process must ensure that all the infrastructural needs are in place (for example, forest nursery facilities, transport, surveys, mapping, and access roads).

The successful establishment of plantations in a cost effective manner is a complex process requiring meticulous planning and timing, starting with the selection of the planting sites and the preparation of a detailed assessment of the site factors: soil type, pH, nutrient status, drainage, and microclimate. On the basis of this assessment a decision will be made as to the actual species or mixture of species to be planted, at which stage market requirements have to be taken into consideration. The greatest demand in most countries is for sawn timber for use in the construction, furniture, and other related industries. At present sawn timber is mainly imported, at considerable cost, from North America in the form of coniferous softwood timber. Much of this could be substituted eventually by planting an increased area of *Pinus caribaea* or other suitable pine species, and by increasing the use of appropriate indigenous hardwood species grown in NF and PF. Alternatively, a greater volume of sawn hardwood timber could be imported from Guyana. In either case, a considerable saving in foreign exchange could be effected.

Some environmental lobbyists in the region have expressed concern about the adverse effects of large areas of single-species plantations, of species such as eucalyptus, pine, and teak, on soil and biodiversity, as well as their susceptibility to diseases, pests, and fire. There is some justification for such concern although, apart from teak in Trinidad, there is little documented research data to confirm it. Nevertheless, there is now sufficient local experience of a wide range of exotic species to establish mixed plantations. These should eventually include at least 50 percent indigenous hardwoods. Both mixed plantations and agroforestry systems should include occasional groups of the feed trees known to sustain the local fauna. The ultimate aim in the development of new PF systems should be to move away from single-species plantations that are clear-felled at rotation age, to a mixed, unevenly aged forest, propagated by natural regeneration, which would never be clear-felled, providing a permanent tree canopy to protect the soil, a sustained yield of commercial timber, and a habitat that becomes increasingly amenable to wildlife.

Having determined the various species required for the national planting programme the method of propagation has to be decided. In most cases this will be by seedlings and good quality seed of the most suitable variety should be obtained, normally at least 18 months before the proposed planting date. Trinidad and Tobago developed a tree improvement programme for its pine and teak plantations and where such seed is available it should be used within the region. The onus is then on the nursery to produce good quality, vigorous planting stock. This is essential to ensure a high establishment rate and good early growth. The nursery must be aware of any special requirements some species may have. For instance, *Pinus caribaea* has an obligate mycorrhiza without which its growth would be inferior, so this has to be introduced into the potting soil mixture used to raise the seedlings. The type of planting material used, such as potted seedlings, bare root plants, stump plants, or seed sown directly, will depend on the species, site conditions, and cost factors.

Preparation of the planting site is equally important, and it may be necessary to clear the site of excessive vegetation, improve internal drainage, and, on steep slopes, introduce some erosion control measures. The final pre-planting decisions concern tree spacing and planting pattern, which may be affected by the site conditions and the species used. On fairly flat sites square spacing would be normal but on steep slopes rectangular spacing, with closer spacing within the rows along the contours and wider spacing between the rows would be normal. Very branchy species would be planted more closely in order that self-pruning can avoid very costly manual pruning. Very close spacing may be used if site conditions demand early canopy closure to ensure soil protection or the control of excessive weed growth. The timing of planting is also critical and ideally should take place at the start of the wet season to ensure the maximum period of growth. Conversely, delayed planting can seriously jeopardize the survival of the plantation and its future long-term success.

Maintenance and Thinning

During the first 4 to 5 years most plantations require regular maintenance to control excessive weed growth, since this could easily suppress and kill the young tree seedlings. The major threat, however, is from frequent bush fires during long, severe dry seasons. Eyre (1987) stresses the accumulative adverse effect of late dry season burning on the destruction of soil humus and soil structure, particularly where this is a regular occurrence spreading from cane fires. If pronounced dry seasons are prevalent, it is unwise not to clear protective fire traces and during peak risk periods fire patrols may be necessary. Large plantations in high risk areas could justify the cost of the construction of a fire-inspection tower to ensure early detection and control of bush fires. One major disadvantage of plantations, particularly of an exotic single species, is their susceptibility to pests and diseases, which may be difficult to control and adversely affect final crop yields. Such outbreaks rarely occur in NF and this is another argument in favour of mixed plantations and a greater use of fast-growing indigenous species wherever possible.

The close initial spacing in PF results in a greater number of trees per hectare than can grow to optimum commercial size. An important task of forest management is to decide how many trees should be removed and how frequently such thinning operations should be carried out. These decisions have a far reaching effect on the plantation, silviculturally and economically, particularly if it is not possible to sell small sized early thinnings. Delayed thinnings can result in a slow down in growth and a reduction of total volume production, but with some species there can be a further loss in volume production because after a delayed thinning, in teak for instance, growth stagnates and is slow to restart. There is evidence in some countries that thinning cycles are behind schedule. This can only be detrimental to the crop and wasteful of the scarce resources invested in PF.

The term rotation is used in forest management to specify the number of years, specified in the working plan, between the establishment of a plantation and the felling of the final crop. Fixing the rotation age is also critical in terms of its influence on the volume of timber to be harvested and the overall profitability of the plantation. However, because of the very long periods involved in the production of timber crops, the fixing of rotation age is flexible and has to be subject to review in the light of growth data obtained from sample plots, possible projections of these data, and market influences. Foresters have defined several types of rotation but in making this important decision forest management has to consider a number of issues, namely, the objectives of management, the silvicultural needs of the species, market demands, and timber prices. The final decision will normally be based on a combination of silvicultural and economic considerations but the latter should not be to the detriment of the long-term productivity of the site. Initial spacing, thinning schedules, and rotation age are closely interrelated and because of the very long-term nature of investment in PF it is essential that forest management make well-informed decisions. This can best be done with the assistance of reliable yield tables for the species concerned and any country without them should start to collect the relevant data for this purpose.

One of the attractions of PF was the expectation of large volumes of a uniform crop of a particular species in a much shorter period than was possible from much slower growing trees in NF. In Trinidad, the rotation for teak and pine was originally designated as 60 and 40 years, respectively, at which ages the plantations would be clear-felled and the cycle repeated. In fact, because of the better than anticipated growth rates, the rotation ages were reduced to 50 and 30 years, respectively, and satisfactory final crops of both species have been harvested at these ages. The planting policy has been reviewed and confirmed with the exception that on the worst quality sites both species would be replaced by a mixture of local hardwoods. One other commendable proviso was that any teak plantations falling within a designated wildlife sanctuary would be replaced by mixed hardwoods to enhance the habitat for wildlife. There could also be greater selectivity within individual planting sites, with pine being planted just below and on top of poor quality ridge top sites and teak being planted on the better quality lower slopes and valley bottoms, in order to obtain the optimum volume production from the site and from each species.

In spite of its outstanding quality and an exceptionally high commercial value on the international market, teak poses environmental problems in Trinidad because of its deciduous habit. The trees drop all their very large leaves promptly at the end of the wet season and in the dry season they rapidly produce a highly inflammable litter layer throughout large areas of contiguous plantations, causing a major fire hazard. In fact, most teak plantations suffer regular burning followed by varying intensities of soil erosion during the first rains of the wet season. In spite of the intensity of such fires very few teak trees are killed but they may suffer damage at the base of the trunk. The full extent of the damage is not revealed until the logs eventually go on the sawbench when fire damage and butt rot may jointly reduce the value of the most valuable butt log. Fire protection is essential if teak is to be grown on a commercial scale but this adds to the overall cost of production.

However, another property of teak could possibly be used to lessen both the fire and soil erosion hazards. This is its ability to coppice, that is, to regrow vigorously from the base of the trunk after being cut down. The NFAP recommended that after the final thinning, between 20 and 30 years, the most vigorous coppice stems should be marked for retention and serve as the new crop after the normal harvest at 50 years, so that there would be no clear felling at that harvest. After that felling operation the natural regeneration of useful indigenous hardwoods should be encouraged, or hardwoods should be planted, to move away gradually from pure stands of rather "environmentally unfriendly" teak. It has also been advocated that the introduction of some agroforestry practices would be feasible at this stage.

Agroforestry Systems

Agroforestry has an important role to play in the major reforestation programme that is integral to the task of rehabilitation and the future management of the environment throughout the Caribbean. The combined technologies of agriculture and forestry have a role to play in enhancing crop yields and profitability of existing farms of all sizes by crop diversification (including a livestock dimension) and in the task of rehabilitating the considerable areas of SF and degraded agricultural land abandoned by owners and shifting cultivators alike. The shifting cultivator knows that if he clears NF he will obtain better yields than from exhausted ruinate or eroded hill land elsewhere. In most countries this situation is aggravated by the cultivator's lack of land and the unavailability of good land to lease on a long- or short-term basis. Inevitably, this vicious cycle has been perpetuated at considerable cost to the environment and society. This problem will not disappear automatically with the introduction of some new agroforestry systems. However, there are benefits to be gained from having a permanent cover of leguminous forest trees on steep slopes previously subject to constant erosion, and from increasing the scope in terms of choice of crops, scale of operation, versatility of crop and livestock mixtures, longer rotations, and much better overall yields. These benefits may even be sufficient inducement for private land owners, the local community, and the state to enter into agreement with the shifting cultivators on a crop sharing, rather than an expensive rental, basis. With so much at stake some form of incentive scheme might be introduced, possibly through the vigorous promotion of community forest projects.

An area that requires urgent attention from policy makers and legislators relates to private land holding and the forests on such land. In several countries in the region traditional plantation crops such as cocoa, coffee, coconuts, and citrus once covered considerable areas, frequently on the better quality soils. Originally, under first class intensive management, it was common to find several quality hardwood species planted extensively throughout such properties as shade trees and windbreaks. In Trinidad, species such as cedar (*Cedrela mexicana*), cypre (*Cordia alliodora*), Honduras mahogany (*Swietenia macrophylla*), and pink poui (*Tabebuia rosea*) were in such demand by the furniture trade that they paid prices six times the royalty charged by government and this induced more planting of these species. From the mid-1960s onwards there was a marked decline in the area of such agricultural crops and a reduction in the volume of timber harvested from private lands in Trinidad, from 26 percent of the total volume of timber cut in 1972 to 7.8 percent in 1987. There is no accurate information on the area of such private lands under NF or under abandoned plantation crops, a deficiency that should be corrected. It is unacceptable that such land should be left idle and unproductive when the capacity to produce considerable quantities of first class timber has been well established. Incentives should be introduced to encourage landowners in the establishment of forest crops, using agroforestry systems wherever possible. In the case of reluctant landowners some more stringent measures may have to be devised and implemented in the national interest.

One neglected element of Caribbean agriculture that can be fully exploited in most agroforestry projects is the superb collection of West Indian fruits, many of which are unknown to the vast majority of tourists. Cooper and Bacon (1981) provide a comprehensive list of 55 species of cultivated and forest fruit species that are common throughout the Caribbean and can be used for many purposes, such as the manufacture of ice-cream, juice, jams, sauces, and jellies, as well as stewed, candied, and pickled fruit. Additional attractions are the ease with which many can be grown and the fact that some fruit year round. Their taste and culinary attractiveness could facilitate the development of an export market, for example, for guava (*Psidium guajaba*), hog plum (*Spondias mombin*), Jamaica plum (*S. purpurea*), pomerac (*Eugenia malaccensis*), and tamarind (*Tamarindus indica*).

Although the Caribbean Agricultural Research and Development Institute (CARDI) and the University of the West Indies (UWI) have undertaken some agroforestry research there has been no significant commercial developments in this area. All the FAO/NFAP country reports have recognized its importance and included agroforestry projects, but these will require some effective support services if they are to succeed in the long term. The shifting cultivators and small farmers must be involved in dealing with extremely adverse site conditions and they will need the services of experienced agriculture and forestry extension services staff who have expertise in soil conservation measures. There is certainly a role for community forest and cooperative projects but past experience has shown that such groups have difficulty in functioning, or even surviving, without some professional management inputs. If the agroforestry venture is to succeed there has to be organized assistance in the marketing of the entire variety of commodities to a range of outlets, from the local market to supermarket chains, tourist hotels, and the tourists themselves.

Agroforestry can also play a practical role in solving a worsening environmental disaster in some Windward Islands caused by the fragile economies and an inevitable dependence on the substantial, regular revenue from the export of bananas. This is resulting in increased areas of NF at higher elevations and on steep slopes being cleared for banana cultivation. There should be a total ban on the clearance of any further NF for banana cultivation and the existing banana plantations on unsuitable sites should be converted gradually, through appropriate agroforestry initiatives, back to a permanent forest cover. The implementation of such a policy requires urgent investigation in terms of the agroforestry options and the cost implications for the banana farmers.

The International Timber Trade Organisation (ITTO), a commodity organization established in 1988, has prepared a useful set of guidelines for the sustainable management of natural tropical forests (ITTO, 1990) to provide an international yardstick against which the sustainability of various management practices can be measured. It has also issued similar guidelines for planted tropical forest and for the conservation of biodiversity in tropical production forests.

Fuelwood Needs

The demand for firewood and charcoal is growing in several countries and is responsible for damage to some ecosystems, with far reaching consequences for example, in mangrove forests. It is resulting in general environmental degradation where SF is being heavily overexploited for fuelwood. The situation is most acute in Jamaica, where it has been reported (FAO, 1990a) that 84 percent of the total roundwood consumption (866,000 m^3 in 1988) is used for charcoal production (49 percent) and firewood (35 percent). The situation is compounded in Jamaica where, as a result of foreign exchange constraints, the government's stated energy policy is to reduce the dependence on imported petroleum products and develop local energy resources, including charcoal. The NFAP report emphasizes the largely unrecognized social, economic, and environmental dimensions of the current situation in which it is estimated that the fuelwood industry employs 10,000 full- and part-time charcoal producers exploiting forests on state and private lands to their limit. In the general vicinity of Kingston it is estimated that 40,000 ha of SF have been severely degraded and 40,000 ha moderately degraded. If further environmental damage is to be avoided a substantial programme of fuelwood plantations needs to be established as a matter of urgency. Such plantations have been successful in Africa and Asia where fast growing leguminous species planted at very close spacing have yielded between 5 and 20 m^3 per hectare per year over a 5-year rotation.

There are several benefits of such plantations, especially if leguminous species are used. They are often pioneer species, which seed early and prolifically, colonizing and tolerating the degraded conditions on freshly abandoned or burned land. At very close spacing they are capable of rapid growth with minimal inputs. They are often able to tolerate quite severe drought conditions and several species are capable of coppice regrowth when cut. Their nitrogen fixing properties are a major bonus at no cost to the farmer or forester and several species have components that are edible by humans and livestock. Jamaica has undertaken some work in this area and has established plantations of *Acacia auriculi-formis*, *Cassia siamea*, and *Leucaena leucocephala*, all of which are legumes. For reasons that are not clear, the initiative has not been a success. There is a strong case for this work to receive priority, and in Jamaica and elsewhere perhaps, consideration should be given to introducing an incentive scheme to encourage the establishment of energy plantations on private lands or as community forest projects.

Among the leguminous species that have achieved spectacular growth elsewhere in the tropics are *Acacia mangium*, *Albizzia lebbek*, *Calliandra callothyrus*, and *Sesbania grandiflora*, some of which have already been introduced to the region. There is a need to give greater recognition to the family Leguminoseae for the very beneficial and practical role it can play in achieving sustainability and enhancement of the environment. Although the single-species fuelwood plantation has not been challenged on environmental grounds it would be useful to know the outcome when two or more such fast-growing species are grown in mixture. Jamaica is also undertaking research into improving charcoal production and usage methods through better kiln or cookstove design.

Some Economic Considerations

With major reforestation and agroforestry programmes being essential in most countries two questions arise: Does the region have the expertise and techniques to undertake such programmes? If so, what will they cost and will they be cost effective? In some countries the answer to the first question is a qualified, "Yes"; but overall the region does not have sufficient trained foresters to tackle the programmes needed. The second question has to be addressed. Gane (1969), in the first study of its kind in the region, made a detailed investigation of the economics of growing teak and pine in comparison with exploitation of the NF. His conclusions with respect to the economic profitability of both species were gloomy, but it should be stressed that his assessment, made 30 years ago, when the oldest pine plantations were barely 12 years old, was based on lower royalty rates, longer rotations, and lower timber volumes than is the case at present.

The critical factor was the high cost of establishment and Gane drew attention to some contributory factors, such as the high cost and low output of the "task" system of undertaking most fieldwork; the high cost of building forest roads needed for access, maintenance, fire protection, and extraction of the thinnings and final crop; and the relatively high cost of transport. Jointly, these accounted for a disproportionate amount of the potential receipts.

In 1984 the RFSS (CDB, 1984) estimated the cost of establishing PF to be U.S.$ 2000 per hectare. These costs covered the various operations described earlier and, on the assumption of average yields of 10 m^3 per hectare per year for hardwood species and 15 m^3 per hectare per year for pine, and a rotation age of 40 years for each species, the real rates of interest on the investment were approximately 6.5 percent for pine and 7.5 percent for hardwood species. While indicating that these were comparable to rates earned by many industrial projects the report stressed the long pay back period and the risk of crop damage or loss over that period from pests, diseases, fire, and natural disasters, such as hurricanes.

More recent studies by the Trinidad and Tobago Forestry Division quoted in the NFAP Report (Chalmers and Faizool, 1992) indicated that the teak plantations were achieving forecast yields on schedule and that the world market price for teak had exceeded original forecasts, with the result that on medium quality sites teak should earn a real rate of interest of over 8 percent. Table 4.7 compares the annual volume of timber harvested from teak and pine plantations and the NF from 1955 to 1990. The situation with pine is more problematic, even though yields are higher than originally forecast. This is because, unlike teak, it is proving difficult to find a market for the thinnings and because of the stiff market competition from cheap imported pine lumber from Central and North America. Although *Pinus caribaea* has an important role to play in reforesting degraded sites with sandy/gravelly soils, current experience indicates a review of existing silviculture and management practices in order to make the species more attractive in environmental and economic terms, particularly if the private land owner is to be encouraged into PF. It should be stressed that these calculations have been based on the traditional methods of economic analysis and the time is now overdue for economists in the region to update this type of analysis to take into account the criticisms expressed by Goodland and Ledec (1987), particularly with respect to taking into account the quantification of the numerous important indirect benefits derived from PF.

REVISION OF NATIONAL ECONOMIC STRATEGIES

A major deficiency in Caribbean forestry has been a lack of any significant economic data or detailed analysis relating to the quantification of the overall value of the direct and indirect benefits accruing from a country's NF and PF resources. This deficiency has been highlighted recently by the realization that the forester's traditional argument for additional funding, on ecological and environmental grounds, has failed to sway finance ministers to produce the funding needed for forestry development throughout the region. An alternative approach must produce irrefutable economic evidence, not only that the financial benefits to be derived from a vibrant broad-based forestry sector include sustained, managed exploitation of the NF and a vigorous PF programme, but also that there is an unacceptably high cost, in social and economic terms, of continuing to neglect forestry and incur widespread and rapidly increasing environmental degradation. Such an analysis will take into account the following: the revenue obtained directly from the sale of timber and any other produce from the forest; an assessment of the value of the sawn timber and wood products imported and of how much of this material could be grown locally or imported from Guyana and the likely savings thereby; the potential earnings and the scope for import substitution through a vigorous agroforestry programme including livestock; and the scope for creating employment through a vigorous reforestation programme in relation to environmental rehabilitation.

At present, governments do not receive a reasonable fee for timber and other forest produce. Evolving a realistic method for fixing and reviewing such fees at reasonable intervals must be a priority in developing economic strategies within the forestry sector. Similarly, the revenue earned directly from activities related to wildlife, nature tourism, hunting, and other forest recreation is not very great but some value has to be placed on the pleasure factor and an assessment made of the amenity value of these activities. The three major indirect benefits derived from the forest are the conservation of soil, water, and biodiversity and appropriate techniques have to be applied in the Caribbean to evaluate and quantify the role of the forest in these areas. In the final analysis the most accurate estimate must include the real cost to the country when the forest is destroyed and its protective role is lost, with corresponding damage to agricultural crops, the loss of soil, and decline in crop yields; damage to roads, bridges, and reservoirs by floods and landslides; impairment of the coastal marine environment; shortage of water; and the negative impact on the carbon cycle. The information gained from this all-embracing assessment of the value of the direct and indirect benefits from our forests should always be taken into account in the course of updating traditional economic analysis of forestry and forestry related projects. At present this type of data is not available in the Caribbean to influence the economic planning and political decision making processes.

The range of forest uses and functions addressed in a study to determine the total economic value of the Mexican forest estate (estimated at U.S.$ 4 billion) have been described (Adger et al., 1994), in which they included, *inter alia*, the value of the carbon sequestration benefits from NF and PF, potential pharmaceutical uses of a range of forest species, and the negative costs of improving water supply and quality following the deforestation of watersheds. In fact, they discovered that the largest proportion of economic value came from the functional values of hydrological and carbon cycling.

Cox and Embree (1990) suggest there is an indisputable case for redefining economic development at national levels using criteria that will ensure the sustainable development of the country's natural resources. Any failure or delay in accepting this challenge will result in exacerbating the existing, costly process of environmental degradation. On the same subject Muthoo (1990) advocates that there should be radical changes in government accounting procedures to reflect not only the value of the country's natural resources but the negative impact of environmental degradation and the depletion of its renewable natural resources – the severity in both cases being concomitant and reflecting in large part the level of destruction of the ever-declining forest resources. Some countries, notably France, have started to incorporate "environmental accounting" in their national accounts and the time is long overdue for Caribbean countries to adopt similar procedures without delay. Muthoo also suggests that the costs and benefits should be shared equitably among all users of environmental assets and he focuses attention on the long-standing dilemma faced by forestry administrators in many developing countries: an acute awareness of the inexorable process of environmental degradation linked with the steady irreparable depletion of a unique natural resource, yet governments persistently fail to provide the funds to halt and remedy the crisis. The problem is demonstrated vividly by Trinidad and Tobago's experience. In 1984 the Forestry Division's budget reached a peak of TT$ 38.7 million but by 1989 this had been reduced to TT$ 14.4 million. In most countries in the region the budget allocation for forestry is totally inadequate for the performance of essential wide-ranging responsibilities. In order to release the financial constraints on sustainable development in the forestry sector new innovative asset management and reinvestment policies must be put in place.

CONCLUSION

In his presidential address to the 1987 CDB Annual Board of Governors meeting, William Demas, an eminent Caribbean economist, urged regional governments to tackle forest conservation and the development of forestry with a greater sense of urgency. He went on to stress the importance of import substitution in relation to food but his arguments in this respect apply equally to timber and wood products, namely that, though this may result in somewhat higher prices, the increased cost would almost certainly be greatly exceeded by the benefits from a stronger more diversified economy, a long-term structural improvement in the balance of payments, and expanded productive employment opportunities.

Through a major forestry and agroforestry development programme throughout the Caribbean several objectives could be achieved simultaneously – increased production of food and wood, multiple improvements to the environment, the maintenance of the region's biological diversity, and a considerable increase in employment. The overall benefits to the economy, the environment, and society as a whole, are too great to be ignored any longer. Forestry development, as embodied in the region's National Forestry Action Programmes, must be given the highest priority in national and regional development programmes throughout the Caribbean.

REFERENCES AND FURTHER READING

Adams, C. D. 1972. *Flowering Plants in Jamaica*. University of the West Indies, St Augustine, Trinidad and Tobago.

Adger, A., K. Brown, R. Cervigni, and D. Moran. 1994. "Towards estimating total economic value of forests in Mexico". CSERGE Working Paper GEC 94-21. University of East Anglia, Norwich, U.K.

Asprey, G. F. and R. G. Robbins. 1953. "The vegetation of Jamaica". *Ecological Monographs* 23: 359–412.

Ayensu, E. S. 1978. *Medicinal Plants of the West Indies*. Smithsonian Institution, Washington, D.C.

Bacon, P. R. 1978. *Flora and Fauna of the Caribbean. An Introduction to the Ecology of the West Indies*. Key Caribbean Publication, Port of Spain, Trinidad and Tobago.

Bacon, P. R. 1989. "Ecology and management of swamp forests in the Guianas and Caribbean region". In A. E. Lugo, M. Brinson, and S. Brown, eds., *Forested Wetlands Ecosystems of the World*, volume 15. Elsevier, New York.

Beard, J. S. 1944. "Climax vegetation in tropical America". *Ecology* 25: 127–158.

Beard, J. S. 1946. "The natural vegetation of Trinidad". *Oxford Forestry Memoirs* 20.

Beard, J. S. 1949. "The natural vegetation of the Windward and Leeward Islands". *Oxford Forestry Memoirs* 21.

Bell, T. I. W. 1969. "An investigation into aspects of management of the mora (*Mora excelsa*) forests of Trinidad with special reference to the Matura Forest Reserve". Ph.D. thesis, University of the West Indies, St Augustine, Trinidad and Tobago.

Bell, T. I. W. 1971. "Management of the Trinidad mora forests with special reference to the Matura Forest Reserve". Government of Trinidad and Tobago Forestry Division.

Bruntland, G. H. 1987. *Our Common Future. World Commission on Environment and Development*. Oxford University Press, Oxford, U.K.

Caribbean Conservation Island Resources Foundation. 1991. *Environmental Agenda for the 1990's – A Synthesis of the Eastern Caribbean Country Environmental Profile Series*. U.S. Agency for International Development, Washingon, D.C.

CDB (Caribbean Development Bank). 1984. *Regional Forestry Sector Study (RFSS)*. Caribbean Development Bank, Bridgetown, Barbados.

CFA (Caribbean Foresters Association). 1989. *Proceedings of the 4th Meeting of Caribbean Foresters Association*. Institute of Tropical Forestry, Rio Piedras, Puerto Rico.

CFC (Commonwealth Forestry Conference). 1980. *Report of the 11th Commonwealth Forestry Conference. Proceedings, Committee Reports, Recommendations*. CFC, St Augustine, Trinidad and Tobago.

Chalmers, W. S. 1981. "Forests". pp. 78–105, in St G. C. Cooper and P. R. Bacon, eds., *The Natural Resources of Trinidad and Tobago*. Edward Arnold, London.

Chalmers, W. S. 1990. "Natural resources management in the Caribbean region: Forestry issues with particular reference to CARICOM countries participating in the FAO Tropical Forestry Action Programme". In J. Cox and C. Embree, eds., *Sustainable Development in the Caribbean*. Report on Regional Conference on Public Policy Implications of Sustainable Development in the Caribbean, Jamaica 1990. Institute for Research on Public Policy, Halifax, Nova Scotia.

Chalmers, W. S. 1992. "Preparation of Tropical Forestry Action Programmes for nine CARICOM countries. Project findings and recommendations". FAO CP/RLA/098/UK. Terminal report. Food and Agriculture Organization, Bridgetown, Barbados.

Chalmers, W. S. and S. Faizool. 1992. "Trinidad and Tobago National Forestry Action Programme – Report of the Country Mission Team". GCP/RLA/098/UK. Food and Agriculture Organization/CARICOM TFAP, Port of Spain, Trinidad and Tobago.

Cooper, St G. C. and P. R. Bacon (eds.). 1981. *The Natural Resources of Trinidad and Tobago*. Edward Arnold, London.

Corlett, R. T. 1988. "Bukit Timah: The history and significance of a small rain-forest reserve". *Environmental Conservation* 15, no. 1: 37–43.

Cox, J. and C. Embree (eds.). 1990. *Sustainable Development in the Caribbean*. Report on Regional Conference on Public Policy Implications of Sustainable Development in the Caribbean, Jamaica 1990. Institute for Research on Public Policy, Halifax, Nova Scotia.

Erenfeld, D. W. 1970. *Biological Conservation*. Holt, Rinehart & Winston, New York.

Evans, J. 1982. *Plantation Forestry in the Tropics*. Clarendon Press, Oxford, U.K.

Eyre, L. A. 1987. "Fire in the tropical environment". *Jamaica Journal* 20, no. 1: 10–16.

Fanshawe, D. B. 1952. *The Vegetation of British Guiana (A Preliminary Review)*. Institute Paper 29. Imperial Forestry Institute, Oxford.

FAO (Food and Agriculture Organization). 1957. *Tropical Silviculture*, volume 2. Food and Agriculture Organization, Rome.

FAO (Food and Agriculture Organization). 1990a. *National Forestry Action Plan – Jamaica*. Government of Jamaica, UNDP, FAO, Kingston, Jamaica.

FAO (Food and Agriculture Organization). 1990b. "FAO/CARICOM Tropical Forestry Action Programme for 9 CARICOM countries (Antigua/Barbuda, Barbados, Dominica, Grenada, Monterrat, St Kitts/Nevis, St Lucia, St Vincent and the Grenadines, Trinidad and Tobago)". Report on preparatory mission. Food and Agriculture Organization, Bridgetown, Barbados.

FAO (Food and Agriculture Organization). 1991. "Sustainable agriculture and rural development (SARD)". Paper presented to a conference on Agriculture and the Environment, s-Hertogenbosch, The Netherlands, April.

FAO (Food and Agriculture Organization). 1992a. "Forest resources management in small island countries". Paper presented to Inter-Regional Conference of Small Island Countries on Sustainable Development and Environment in Agriculture, Forestry and Fisheries. Santiago, Chile, April 28–30.

FAO (Food and Agriculture Organization). 1992b. "Forest resources and forestry development". Executive summary of a paper presented to an FAO Consultation on Sustainable Development and Environment in Agriculture, Forestry and Fisheries Sector in Latin America and the Caribbean. FAO Regional Office for Latin America and the Caribbean, Santiago.

FAO (Food and Agriculture Organization). 2001. www.fao.org/forestry.

Figueroa Colon, J.C. (ed.). 1986. "Management of the forests of tropical America: Prospects and technologies". Conference proceedings. Institute of Tropical Forestry, Southern Experimental Station and University of Puerto Rico.

Freezailah, B. C. Y. 1993. "Sustainability and Tropical Forests. 14th Commonwealth Forestry Conference, Kuala Lumpur 1993". *Commonwealth Forestry Review* 72, no. 4: 226–232.

Gane, M. 1969. *Priorities in Planning: Cost Benefit Methodology and Simulation with Special Reference to Forestry and Economic Development in Trinidad.* no. 43. Commonwealth Forestry Institute, Paper no. 43, University of Oxford, Oxford, U.K.

German Bundestag. 1990. "Protecting the tropical forests. A high priority international task". 2nd Report of the Enquete Commission (Preventive Measures to Protect the Earth's Atmosphere) of the 11th German Bundestag.

Glasgow, J. (ed.). 1989. "Environmental education: Global concern Caribbean focus". *Caribbean Journal of Education* 16, nos. 1 and 2.

Goodbody, I. 1994. "Avian refuges". *Jamaica Journal* 25, no. 2: 55–60.

Goodland, R. J. A. and G. Ledec. 1987. "Neo-classical economics and the principles of sustainable development". *Ecology Modelling* 38: 19–46.

Government of Trinidad and Tobago. 1980. *Forestry in Trinidad and Tobago. A Select Bibliography.* Government of Trinidad and Tobago Forestry Division, Port of Spain.

Grayson, A. J. (ed.). 1995. *The World's Forests: International Initiatives since Rio.* Commonwealth Forestry Association, Oxford in association with the U.K. Department for International Development.

Grayson, A. J. and W. B. Maynard (eds.). 1997. *The World's Forests – Rio + 5: International Initiatives Towards Sustainable Development.* Commonwealth Forestry Association.

Gregerson, H., S. Draper, and D. Elz (eds.). 1989. *People and Trees. The Role of Social Forestry in Sustainable Development.* World Bank Economic Development Institute, Washington, D.C.

Grut, M. 1989. "Economics of managing the African rainforest". Paper presented at the 13th Commonwealth Forestry Conference. New Zealand, September.

Honeychurch, P. N. 1986. *Caribbean Wild Plants and Their Uses.* Macmillan, London.

IDB (Inter-American Development Bank). 1990. "Our own agenda". Report of the Latin America and Caribbean Commission on Development and Environment. IDB/UNDP, Washington, D.C.

ITTO (International Timber Trade Organisation). 1990. "The ITTO guidelines for the sustainable management of natural tropical forests". ITTO, International Organisations Centre, Yokohama, Japan.

Johnson, M. S. and H. L. Blackett. 1990. *Bibliography of Forestry in CARICOM Countries of the Eastern Caribbean.* Natural Resources Institute, Chatham, U.K.

Johnson, N., A. deGeorges, I. Jackson, K. Talbott, and R. Teyland. 1988. "Biological diversity and tropical forest assessment for the Eastern Caribbean". CIDE/WRI for U.S. Agency for International Development, Regional Development Office, Barbados.

Kerr, B. 1993. "Iwokrama: The Commonwealth Rainforest Programme in Guyana". *Commonwealth Forestry Review* 72, no. 4.

Lamprecht, H. 1989. *Silviculture in the Tropics.* Institute of Silviculture, University of Gottingden, GTZ Tech. Coop, Federal Republic of Germany.

Loveless, A. R. 1960. "The vegetation of Antigua, West Indies". *Journal of Ecology* 48: 495–527.

Lugo, A. E. and L. B. Ford (eds.). 1987. *Forest Recreation in the Caribbean Islands.* Proceedings of the 3rd Meeting of Caribbean Foresters, Guadeloupe, 1986. Institute of Tropical Forestry, Puerto Rico.

Lugo, A. E., M. Brinson, and S. Brown (eds.). 1989. *Forested Wetlands Ecosystems of the World,* volume 15. Elsevier, New York.

Lundgren, B. 1980. "Global deforestation, its causes and suggested remedies". *Agroforestry Systems* 3: 91–95.

Maini, J. S. 1995. "The international dialogue on forests: A preliminary assessment". pp. 1–4, in A. J. Grayson, ed., *The World's Forests: International Initiatives since Rio.* Commonwealth Forestry Association, Oxford in association with the U. K. Department for International Development.

Managing Global Genetic Resources – Forest Trees. 1991. National Academy Press, Washington, D.C.

Marshall, R. C. 1939. *Silviculture of the Trees of Trinidad and Tobago.* Oxford University Press, Oxford, U.K.

McDonald, M. A. and J. R. Healey. 2000a. "Nutrient cycling in secondary forests in the Blue Mountains of Jamaica". *Forest Ecology and Management* 139: 257–278.

McDonald, M. A. and J. R. Healey. 2000b. "Variations and phenotypic correlation of growth attributes of Calliandra calothyrsus in the Blue Mountains of Jamaica". *Agroforestry Systems* 50: 293–314.

McGaughey, S.E. and H. M. Gregersen (eds.). 1983. "Forest based development in Latin America. An analysis of investment opportunities and financing needs". Report of a regional conference. Inter-American Development Bank, Washington, D.C.

Miller, A. D. S. 1969a. "Provisional yield tables for *Pinus caribaea* (var. *hondurensis*) in Trinidad". Government of Trinidad and Tobago Forestry Division, St Augustine.

Miller, A. D. S. 1969b. "Provisional yield tables for teak in Trinidad." Government of Trinidad and Tobago Forestry Division, St Augustine.

Muthoo, M. K. 1990. "Economic considerations and environmental policy implications in the management of renewable natural resources". *Unasylva FAO Quarterly Journal* 41.

National Academy of Sciences. 1979. *Tropical Legumes: Resources for the Future.* National Academy of Sciences, Washington, D.C.

Pilgrim, K. 1994. "The biodiversity of the Linden/Lethem Road, Guyana". Ministry of Agriculture Wildlife Services Division, Georgetown, Guyana.

Poore, D. et al. 1989. *No Timber without Trees – Sustainability in the Tropical Forest. A Study for the International Tropical Timber Organisation (ITTO).* Earthscan Publications, London.

Ramdial, B. S. 1975. "The social and economic importance of the Caroni Swamp in Trinidad and Tobago". Ph.D. thesis, University of Michigan, Lansing.

Reay, J. and J. Steward (eds.). 1988. *Science Applied in the Caribbean.* Macmillan, London.

Richards, P. W. 1952. *The Tropical Rain Forest.* Cambridge University Press, Cambridge, U.K.

Sheng, T. C. 1986. "Forest land use and conservation". pp. 100–106, in D. A. Thomson, P. K. Bretting, and M. Humphreys, eds., *Forests of Jamaica.* Papers presented to Caribbean Regional Seminar. Jamaica Society of Scientists and Technologists, Kingston, Jamaica.

Stehlé, H. 1945. "Forest types of the Caribbean". *Caribbean Forester* 6 (Suppl.): 273–408.

Swabey, C. 1945. "Forestry in Jamaica". *Forestry Bulletin* no. 1. Kingston, Jamaica, Government Printing Office.

Tanner, E. V. J. 1986. "Forests of the Blue Mountains and the Port Royal Mountains of Jamaica". Paper presented to Caribbean Regional Seminar. Jamaica Society of Scientists and Technologists, Kingston, Jamaica.

Thomson, D. A., P. K. Bretting, and M. Humphreys (eds.). 1986. *Forests of Jamaica.* Paper presented to Caribbean Regional Seminar. Jamaica Society of Scientists and Technologists, Kingston, Jamaica.

Wadsworth, F. H. 1997. *Forest Production for Tropical America.* U.S. Department of Agriculture, Forest Service, Agriculture Handbook 710, Washington, D.C.

Westoby, M. 1984. *Constructive Ecology: How to Build and Repair Ecosystems.* AES Working paper 1/84. Griffith University, Brisbane, Australia.

Williams, R. O., Jr. and R. O. Williams. 1941. *Useful and Ornamental Plants of Trinidad and Tobago,* 4th edition, rev. Government Printing Office, Trinidad and Tobago.

5

Sustainable Development of Caribbean Agriculture

Carlisle A. Pemberton, Lawrence A. Wilson, Garry W. Garcia, and A. Khan

Contents

INTRODUCTION

The objective of this chapter is to utilize a conceptual framework to analyze the sustainability of agriculture in the Caribbean. Based on this, technological alternatives and socio-economic strategies will be proposed that could contribute to the sustainable development of agriculture in the Caribbean.

The concept of sustainable agriculture envisages the use of technologies in agriculture that would not only lead to improved incomes and welfare in the community, but would also improve, or at least preserve, the natural resources of all ecosystems in the community. A major issue arising out of the concept of agricultural sustainability is whether the introduced, man-made, intensive systems of crop cultivation and livestock husbandry, as they exist today, can be continued in perpetuity. In other words, whether or not these open agro-ecosystems can substitute for the closed, stable, natural systems that they replaced.

With respect to the socio-economic dimension of agricultural sustainability, there is increasing demand for food by regional and global populations, which requires greater utilization of resources for end products used for human consumption. In both developed and developing countries, economic growth has afforded an increased demand for food, often leading to an escalation of problems of environmental degradation, for example, pollution. On the other hand, there is the existence of poverty, which itself leads to agricultural practices by low resource farmers that may be detrimental to the environment. Therefore, sustainable agricultural development must not only maintain productivity at existing levels, but must also diversify and expand the production base to meet rapidly increasing human needs. This must be achieved while, at the same time, conserving and replacing the natural resources used to effect such production increases.

To discuss the sustainability of Caribbean agriculture requires a conceptual framework that would describe the factors that affect the sustainability of agriculture and utilize these factors to provide an assessment. Such a framework has been provided by Smyth and Dumanski (1993) in *An International Framework for Evaluating Sustainable Land Management* (FESLM). In this approach, sustainable agriculture may be defined as follows.

TABLE 5.1 The FESLM Classification System

	Class	Confidence Limits (years)
Sustainable	1. Sustainable in the long term	>25
	2. Sustainable in the medium term	15–25
	3. Sustainable in the short term	7–15
Unsustainable	4. Slightly unsustainable	5–7
	5. Moderately unsustainable	2–5
	6. Highly unsustainable	<2

From Smyth and Dumanski, 1993.

Sustainable agriculture combines technologies, policies, and activities aimed at integrating socio-economic principles with environmental concerns so as to simultaneously:

- Maintain or enhance production/services (*productivity*)
- Reduce the level of potential risk (*security*)
- Protect the potential of natural resources and prevent degradation of soil and water quality (*protection*)
- Be economically viable (*viability*)
- Be socially acceptable (*acceptability*)

The five objectives – productivity, security, protection, viability, and acceptability – in this approach are taken as the basic pillars of sustainability. FESLM proposes class distinctions for sustainability, in the sense that a particular agricultural practice can be classified on the basis of its effect on the five basic pillars. This classification is given in Table 5.1.

If an agricultural system fails to meet at least one of the pillars of sustainability within 6 years then, according to Table 5.1, it may be classified as slightly unsustainable. Classification of an agricultural system as slightly unsustainable of course does not necessarily mean that it will cease to exist after 6 years. What it does mean, however, is that within 6 years, the system will fail to contribute meaningfully to some aspect of the sustainable development of the environment (human, biotic, and physical) in which it exists. In other words, it will not meet one of the "pillars" of sustainability.

According to Smyth and Dumanski (1993):

> It will be apparent also that, in many parts of the world, there are active land use (management) systems which should be placed in Class 6 . . . since they

> palpably fail to meet some or all of the "pillar" requirements (e.g., they generate an economic loss or a conservation disaster) but which, for a variety of reasons, not all bad, are expected to continue for more than two years. Whether continuation reflects artificial subsidy, irresponsibility, indifference, or a lack of any identified alternative, [such] classification . . . should draw desirable attention to a serious situation.

Based on its classification and its definition of a sustainable agricultural system, therefore, the FESLM approach allows for the assessment of an agricultural system or the comparison of alternative agricultural practices. The key requirement of the approach is the identification of *evaluation factors*, which are independent variables with a known effect on *sustainability*, which is the dependent variable. Only factors that have an effect on sustainability qualify as evaluation factors. Therefore, to be useful as an evaluation factor, the factor must vary with the alternative agricultural practices and its effect on sustainability must be measurable. Diagnostic criteria are used to measure the variation in the evaluation factor and indicators and thresholds are used to assess the impact of different levels of the evaluation factors on the sustainability of the system.

SUSTAINABILITY ISSUES ASSOCIATED WITH AGRICULTURE

Agriculture contributes to the welfare of communities through the provision principally of food, fibre, and firewood, which not only provide the sustenance of life, but also allow humans to ward off pests and diseases. In addition, agriculture contributes to economies, especially those of developing countries, through:

- Its earnings of foreign exchange
- Its employment of a large proportion of the labor force
- The provision of (investible) surpluses, which are often invested in other sectors (for example, industrial and service sectors), which then become the "engines" of economic growth
- The production of primary products for the manufacturing sector
- The creation of demand for goods and services from other sectors of the economy (internal linkages such as transport)

Agriculture can also be *the* "engine" for economic growth and thus make a direct contribution to improved incomes of developing countries. In this regard, Chile represents a recent and important example (Valdes et al., 1991).

Notwithstanding the contribution of agriculture to welfare and improved incomes, the sector is often viewed as a major activity causing the degradation of natural resources. This view is based on the severe pollution problems associated with agricultural production. These problems will now be discussed under the headings of the main source of pollutants: pesticides, fertilizers, livestock, and irrigation, and are also summarized in Table 5.2.

Pesticides

During the early phases of the Green Revolution, farmers were often encouraged to use pesticides as an insurance against pests. Many governments also promoted pesticide use by subsidizing, explicitly or implicitly, pesticide prices. At the same time though, farmers were not aware of the hazards involved with the overuse or inappropriate use of pesticides. These factors have led to pesticide contamination of waters, food, and the environment, as well as the atmosphere.

Pinstrup-Andersen and Pandya-Lorch (1994) have stated that long-term use of broad-spectrum or nonselective pesticides has led to buildup of resistance in target species and, as a result, over 1600 insect species have developed significant resistance to pesticides. Added to this, over 100 weeds have developed resistance to herbicides and approximately 150 plant pathogens have shown resistance to fungicides. The long-term effect is that a number of common pests have become resistant, to the point that they are virtually uncontrollable by conventional insecticides. Another impact of these pesticides is that they attack non-target organisms and lead to the emergence of secondary pests by destroying their natural enemies.

Excessive use of pesticides, accompanied by their indiscriminate application, has resulted in the contamination of soils and the pollution of water sources. In areas of the U.S., Western Europe, and Japan, a number of pesticides have been found in wells and in rainfall and fogs, and herbicides have been detected in drinking waters obtained from surface waters and aquifers. This chemical contamination of water sources occurs mainly through run-off and leaching into groundwater. Besides contaminating the water supply, these chemical residues also destroy aquatic flora and fauna. These chemicals may remain for years in the soil, as they are degraded slowly, and can destroy many soil organisms.

Pesticides can also be detrimental to man if pesticide poisoning occurs. This has been a serious problem in developing countries and has been the result of improper pesticide handling and prolonged exposure. The effects of such exposure have led to the development

TABLE 5.2 The Principal Pollution Problems Caused by Agriculture

Agricultural Practices	Impact on the Environment
Contamination of Water	
Pesticides	Contamination of rainfall, surface water, and ground water, causing harm to wildlife and exceeding standards for drinking water
Nitrites	Methaemoglobinaemia in infants; possible cause of cancers
Nitrates, phosphates	Algal growth and eutrophication causing taste problems, surface water obstruction, fish kills, coral reef destruction, and illness due to algal toxins
Organic livestock wastes	Algal growth, plus deoxygenation of water and fish kills
Silage effluents	Deoxygenation of water and fish kills nuisance
Processing wastes from plantation crops (rubber, oil palm)	Deoxygenation of water and fish kills nuisance
Contamination of Food and Fodder	
Pesticides	Pesticide residue in foods
Nitrites	Increased nitrates in foods; methaemoglobinaemia in livestock
Contamination of Farm and Natural Environment	
Pesticides	Harm to humans; nuisance
Nitrates	Harm to plant communities
Ammonia from livestock and paddy fields	Disruption of plant communities; possible role in tree deaths
Metals from livestock wastes	Raised metal content in soils
Pathogens from livestock wastes	Harm to human and livestock health
Contamination of Atmosphere	
Ammonia from livestock; manures and paddy fields	Odour nuisance; plays role in acid rain production
Nitrous oxide from fertilizers	Plays role in ozone layer depletion and global climatic warming
Methane from livestock and paddy rice	Plays role in global climatic warming
Indoor Contamination	
Ammonia, hydrogen sulphide from livestock wastes	Harm to farm workers and animal health, odour nuisance
Nitrogen dioxide from silage in silos	Harm to farm worker health

From Petry, 1995.

of chronic diseases that have also been passed on to infants through breast-feeding. These chemicals are also a hazard to wildlife. The major causes of unintentional pesticide poisoning have been unsafe techniques for transporting, storing, labelling, applying, and disposing of the pesticides. Some of these problems may actually be the result of ignorance of the hazards associated with the chemicals.

Fertilizers

Fertilizers are used to replace nutrients in the soil that are removed by crops and to stimulate agricultural production. Organic manures may also be used for the same purposes but in many developing countries, where shortages of animal wastes and crop residues are prevalent, chemical fertilization is necessary to support intensive agriculture. Fertilizers can be used as a means to correct damage caused by soil erosion by creating an environment suitable for plant cover. Fertilizers can also be used to protect existing soil organic matter.

However, like pesticides, fertilizers, through excessive use, can pollute groundwater by leaching out of its nutrients. These nutrients are ordinarily not harmful, since they are usually found in small quantities but if they are leached out and reach sufficiently high levels, they become harmful to man. The nutrient of particular importance in this regard is nitrogen in its nitrate form, which can be reduced to nitrites that are harmful.

The leaching out of nitrates from the soil may be due to the imbalance in fertilizer composition, untimely application, and improper application methods. The pollution of the surface water mainly takes place through eutrophication, which is the accumulation of nutrients, primarily through erosion. Balanced application of the essential nutrients provides maximum benefits with a minimum of environmental degradation (Pinstrup-Andersen and Pandya-Lorch, 1994).

Livestock

Most of the world's rangelands have deteriorated and are losing productivity, often because of overstocking of livestock. Where homogeneous herds, above the carrying capacity of rangelands, selectively graze preferred grasses, this results in the exposure of the soils to the agents of erosion and compaction of the bare soil. The effects on these rangelands include decreases in water percolation, intensified soil erosion, declines of water tables, and replacement of nutritious and palatable species by hardy, less nutritious species (FAO, 1995).

In the effort to increase grasslands, farmers have converted large forested areas to extensive pastures. Poor management and inadequate fertilization have resulted in many converted soils losing nutrients through leaching, lands becoming invaded by weeds and, within a few years, productivity of the lands declining, to the extent that pastures are left abandoned (FAO, 1995).

Livestock wastes also pose a serious problem to the environment, when the livestock is intensively reared. Animal organic wastes are used as fertilizers and are an adequate source of nutrients in many instances. However, the use of these wastes can have negative effects as well. These wastes can enter the water supply through the groundwater, by leaching, or into nearby streams or river courses via runoffs and cause algal growth, water deoxygenation, and the destruction of the natural habitats.

Irrigation

Irrigation, in many cases, has proven to be quite successful but in some instances it can disturb the ecological balance and lead to waterlogging and salinization of the irrigated lands. In the case of waterlogging, irrigation may make water constantly available to plants throughout the year, more than can be handled by evapotranspiration, which may lead to a rise in the water table and eventual waterlogging. With respect to salinization, irrigation can result in the deposition of salts on the surface of the soil and in the sub-soil, especially in arid and semi-arid areas. This can result in the abandonment of otherwise arable lands.

Waterlogging and salinization, problems associated with irrigated land, can be minimized or even prevented by reducing over-watering and seepage from canals, improving drainage to lower the high water-table and establishing improved and adequate water management practices.

The chapter now turns to an overview of Caribbean agriculture before discussing the contribution of agriculture to the Caribbean economy and society and the environmental problems associated with it.

OVERVIEW OF CARIBBEAN AGRICULTURE

This chapter stresses perspectives of sustainable agriculture in the states of the Caribbean Economic Community (CARICOM), which include the Caribbean islands of the British Commonwealth and the mainland states of Belize, Guyana, and Suriname.

Variations in the natural flora of the Caribbean are due chiefly to differences of climate, altitude, and soils. The main plant formations are rainforest, semi-evergreen forests, and deciduous seasonal forests. Variations in soil conditions also lead to edaphic plant formations, such as savannahs and pine forests. The natural fauna still remains to be extensively explored and described (Ahmad et al., 1991).

Agriculture has been a major productive activity in the Caribbean region for at least 500 years. The following have been the main types of agricultural activities:

- Export crop production (sugar cane, bananas, citrus, cocoa, coffee, coconuts, spices, rice)
- Domestic food crop production (rice, maize, tropical root crops and legumes, vegetables, and fruit and food trees)
- Animal production (poultry, pigs, beef and dairy cattle, goats, and sheep)

The land use pattern has been determined principally by historical metropolitan demand for tropical, export crop commodities, rather than by the characteristics of climate, soils, and natural vegetation. Moreover, the agriculture that has resulted largely remains a dualistic system including:

1. Large, well capitalized farms that:
   - Have advanced technologies
   - Produce monocropped perennial or ratoon crops
   - Are located on flat lands
   - Have highly fertile soils
   - Are capable of producing commodities for distant export markets
2. Small, undercapitalized farms that:
   - Have low input technologies
   - Produce multiple cropped, annual, arable crops
   - Are located on sloping lands
   - Are located on fragile soils of low capability
   - Are capable of producing crop and livestock commodities for the local food market.

THE IMPACT OF AGRICULTURE ON THE CARIBBEAN ENVIRONMENT

As indicated earlier, the FESLM approach is used to discuss the sustainability of Caribbean agriculture. In this discussion, focus will be on the major export crops of sugar cane and bananas and the major domestic crops, which include root crops and vegetables and livestock production. The framework for this assessment is provided in Table 5.3 and is organized according to soil, air, water, biological, and human resources.

Soil

Nitrogen, phosphorus, and potassium are the three major nutrients in soil that are required in relatively large amounts by plants. Both ammonium sulphate (growing salt) and urea are the forms of nitrogen used and the levels of nitrogen applied are considered highly unsustainable (Table 5.3). This is because of the very high usage of nitrogen in banana and vegetable production, as well as in sugar cane production. High usage of nitrogen fertilizer in the Caribbean results in high nitrogen loss from the soil, by leaching and run-off (Deare et al., 1992). Such nitrogen loss is also considered highly unsustainable. Nitrogen loss through run-off contributes to eutrophication in Caribbean coastal waters.

The high use of potassium fertilizer in the production of bananas (approximately 1200 kilograms per hectare (kg/ha) as the recommended application; WINBAN, 1993a) and vegetables leads to its classification as a moderately unsustainable practice. Its use is also high in sugar cane and some root crop production. Phosphorus fertilization is considered slightly unsustainable because this fertilizer is used at much lower levels (331 kg/ha) in bananas but at fairly high rates in vegetable production (622 kg/ha). However, its use is low in sugar cane and root crop production.

Irrigation use in Caribbean agriculture is low. Thus, problems of salinization and waterlogging associated with irrigation are not generally encountered in the Caribbean. Only 1.4 percent of banana farmers in the Windward Islands reported irrigation use (WINBAN, 1993b), while only 5 percent of cane farmers in Trinidad and Tobago reported using irrigation (Pemberton et al., 1988). Lawrence (1992) reports that the irrigated acreage in Jamaica is 35,200 hectares, which represents about 19 percent of the total arable acreage of Jamaica. The Sugar Association of the Caribbean *Hand Book 1961–1993* (1994) reported that irrigation was not practised by sugar companies in Trinidad and Tobago, Belize, and St Kitts and Nevis. For Barbados, the *Hand Book* reported that irrigation in sugar cane production was limited to only a few farms, while for Jamaica it reported that 22,000 hectares comprised the southern irrigated cane-growing region of the island. For Guyana, where the greater part of sugar cane cultivation is below the high tide levels, the *Hand Book* reported that, during dry periods, irrigation is carried out by flooding through gravity flow in the low elevation levels and pumping in the higher fields.

Cropping on steep slopes in the Caribbean is a highly unsustainable practice (Table 5.3) yet indications are that up to 18 percent of the bananas in the Windward Islands are grown on slopes exceeding 20 degrees (WINBAN, 1993b). Sugar cane and vegetables are usually grown on less steep slopes or on undulating plains and these crops are less associated with soil erosion. Root crops, however, tend to be grown on a wide range of slopes and they are associated with substantial soil erosion. Due to the limitations of arable land, especially in the Leeward Islands, marginal lands, sometimes located on hilly slopes, are used for grazing. These lands, which are already unsuitable for agricultural crop production, are made even more so by livestock overgrazing them, leaving the soil exposed and promoting soil erosion.

The problems of soil compaction in Caribbean agriculture are largely associated with the harvesting of sugar cane. Georges et al. (1985), for example, report declines in early regrowth of sugar cane when mechanical harvesters are used. However, the effects of soil compaction on regrowth tended to disappear after 8 to 10 months of regrowth, allowing cane yields and sugar yields to be unrelated to soil compaction. Soil compaction is not normally associated with other forms of cropping activities in the Caribbean.

Soil pollution is also a hazard as a result of agriculture. In banana production in the Windward Islands, for example, heavy use of pesticides to control soil-borne pathogens has adversely affected the broad spectrum of soil fauna, including useful species, such as earthworms and other organisms involved in the carbon and nitrogen cycles. This retards the recycling of nutrients, requiring increasing use of fertilizers, which simply adds to the chemical load of the environment, with all of the associated hazards (Ahmad et al., 1991).

Water

A major impact on water resources caused by agriculture in the Caribbean is pollution of the environment caused by agricultural chemicals, chiefly pesticides, and suspended sediments from soil erosion. Where there is a high concentration of pesticides, both surface water and groundwater become contaminated. This is particularly critical in territories with a porous limestone base and shallow overlying soil and where groundwater is important for domestic and agricultural use, such as in Barbados, the Bahamas, and the Cayman Islands. Pollution is also found in rivers and streams. Overall, the situation with regard

TABLE 5.3 Evaluation of the Impact of Caribbean Agriculture on Resources in the Caribbean Environment

Resource	Evaluation Factor	Diagnostic Criteria	Unit	Class 1	Class 2	Class 3	Class 4	Class 5	Class 6
Soil	Nitrogen fertilizer	N Applied	kg/ha						x
	Phosphorus fertilizer	P Applied	kg/ha				x		
	Potassium fertilizer	K Applied	kg/ha					x	
	Excess of salts	N Loss	kg/ha						x
		Irrigation use	% farmers	x					
	Soil loss	% on slope >30⁰	t /ha/year						x
		% on slope > 20⁰	t /ha/year					x	
		% on slope >10⁰	t /ha/year				x		
		% on slope <10⁰	t /ha/year			x			
	Soil compaction	Bulk density	g/cm^3	x					
Water	Pesticide toxicity	Pesticide detected in animal tissue	ppb				x		
	River pollution	Waste seen	Complaints		x				
Air	Aerial spraying	Human health	Complaints				x		
	Factory emissions	Human health	Complaints			x			
	Fires	Human health	Complaints			x			
	Livestock wastes	Odours	Complaints				x		

				1	2	3	4	5	6
Biological									
Forest	Forest loss	Farmers reporting	% Land						x
	Pesticide toxicity	Wildlife	ppb		x				
Other	Biodiversity	Pure stand crops	%		x				
	Pesticides	Biodiversity					x		
Human									
Health	Pesticide toxicity	Herbicide use	Oral LD_{50}						x
		Insecticide use	Oral LD_{50}			x			
		Fungicide/ nematicide use	Oral LD_{50}						x
	Food provided	Population malnourished	%	x					
Economic	Gross domestic product (GDP)	Contribution	%		x				
	Competitiveness	Subsidy received	$/year				x		
	Risk	Wind damage	% Land susceptible			x			
	Foreign exchange earnings	Exports	% Total exports	x					
Social	Literacy	% Illiterate	%				x		
	% Male		%		x				
	% Female		%		x				
	Mean age of farmers		years				x		

Note: For an explanation of Classes 1 to 6, see Table 5.1.

to water pollution in the Caribbean is considered to be slightly unsustainable (Table 5.3).

In Trinidad, relatively large volumes of pesticides are used in vegetable and sugar cane production, particularly by Caroni (1975) Limited, the state-owned sugar company, which applies its chemicals aerially. Many of its lands are also positioned near the Gulf of Paria coastal zone and, through transport by wind and water, these pesticides are a potential source of coastal fish contamination and could well have other direct impacts on coastal communities. For example, Siung-Chang (1990) reports that an analysis of water, sediment, and mussel tissues collected from the Caroni Swamp during 1979 showed the presence of organochlorine pesticides.

The pollution of rivers and streams by waste materials, for example, blue diothene (plastic) and cardboard boxes, is a common occurrence in the banana producing countries of the Caribbean. When carried down to the sea, diothene sleeves from the banana industry can kill animals such as turtles, due to their being mistakenly ingested as food, and can also smother and kill corals if they come to rest on reefs. Effluents from sugar factories are also major pollutants of nearby rivers and streams. By increasing the biological oxygen demand (BOD) of the water, these organic wastes may cause fish kills in the river or make the water along a significant length of the water course unusable for other purposes. Other types of cropping activities are not major contributors to this type of pollution. However, livestock wastes in the Caribbean, especially from poultry and pigs, are generally inadequately disposed of. In many instances, these wastes are washed into nearby rivers or waterways. The end result is sedimentation in water courses, foul odours, destruction of the water habitat, and the general pollution of the water, making it inadequate as a drinking source.

Air

Aerial spraying represents the major unsustainable practice associated with the air resource (Table 5.3). This practice is common in sugar cane and banana production and is used, in some cases, in rice production. In Guyana, it has been reported that shortages of men who spray have necessitated the use of aircraft for application of triazines (herbicides) where the blocking system provides relatively large and consolidated areas of crop land. Aerial application also has the advantage of providing better drain-corner control of weeds and uniformity of application of the chemical.

Associated with aerial spraying are concerns for human health and loss of biodiversity. Ash emissions from sugar factories pose major health concerns during harvesting periods. There are also concerns about the effects of smoke from fires, associated with land clearing, on human health. As mentioned in the previous paragraph, inadequate disposal of livestock wastes is a major cause of air pollution in the form of foul odours.

Forests

Perhaps the most significant ecological impact of agriculture on the environment is the clearing of forests for crop cultivation (Table 5.3). Such forest clearing has been most extensive on the flat to gently sloping islands of the Caribbean, as in Antigua, Barbados, and St Kitts, for the purposes of sugar cane cultivation. For example, in Barbados, all the forests were cleared over a 39-year period from 1627 to 1666 more than 300 years ago. For Trinidad and Tobago, Pemberton (1995) reports that extensive clearing of forests took place to facilitate the expansion of agricultural production despite the early institution of forest conservation measures. She concludes:

> Tobago's Forest Reserve was established as far back as 1764 and the colony of Trinidad and Tobago had a workable forest policy and a Forestry Department by 1901. It is noteworthy that this Department preceded the Department of Agriculture, which was set up in 1908. Yet problems of the choice between economic growth and natural resource conservation have plagued the history of the forests in this country. (pp. 165–166)

Thus, although statistics (Table 5.4) show forest cover as a percentage of vegetative cover in the region of 40 to 55 percent in the island states, a high proportion of these forests is secondary.

Forest clearing, however, has taken place at different rates in CARICOM states. For example, in the continental states of Belize and Guyana, forests still occupy more than 90 percent of the vegetative cover (Table 5.4). In the more developed island states of Bahamas, Barbados, Jamaica, and Trinidad and Tobago, they occupy about 54 percent of the vegetative cover, while in the Organization of Eastern Caribbean States (OECS), forests account for only 40 percent of vegetative cover.

Some of the most deleterious effects of forest clearing, particularly on hillsides include:

- Extensive soil erosion (especially in Haiti and Jamaica)
- Major catastrophic landslides
- Flooding of coastal plains

TABLE 5.4 Land Use in the Caribbean in '000 hectares (% of total)

States	Total Vegetative Cover	Forest Lands	Pasture Lands	Permanent Crop Lands	Arable Crop Lands
Continental states	19,237	17,408	1,278	27	524
	(100)	(90.5)	(6.6)	(0.1)	(2.7)
More developed island states[a]	1,351	731	205	110	305
	(100)	(54.1)	(15.2)	(8.1)	(22.6)
OECS states[b]	178	72	19	45	42
	(100)	(40.4)	(10.7)	(25.3)	(23.6)
Total CARICOM	20,766	18,211	1,502	182	871
	(100)	(87.7)	(7.2)	(0.9)	(4.2)

[a] Barbados, Trinidad and Tobago, and Jamaica.
[b] Organization of Eastern Caribbean States.

From Economic Commission for Latin America and the Caribbean, 1993.

Other Natural Resources

Agriculture also has important effects on resources considered valuable to the tourism industry. This is caused by pollution of coastal waters from land-based suspended sediments, originating from improper land use. In this process, beaches have become polluted and less attractive to tourists. Also, some suspended materials are injurious to the growth and survival of off-shore coral reefs, which are major attractions to visitors. Urgent research is necessary to determine the extent of these impacts.

Through the various effects of agriculture, biodiversity in flora and fauna is slowly but steadily being reduced. The Caribbean shares biological diversity with the Amazon region on the one hand and Central America on the other and, as such, it is a rich and strategic area biologically (Ahmad et al., 1991). However, many endemic and indigenous species are threatened or have already been lost, not only through the effects of agriculture but also as a result of other development activities.

Human Health

Several factors associated with agricultural production, which affect human health, have already been discussed. In addition, in Table 5.3, pesticide toxicity is identified as a highly unsustainable agricultural practice. Many pesticides in use are highly toxic and in CARICOM states they are often associated with suicides. Many farmers have shown definite signs of pesticide toxicity but research in the Caribbean has been limited. Stored animal wastes attract pests and pathogens and are a major public health hazard. In addition, inadequate feeding operations, especially in poultry and pig production, attract rodents, which are another major public health hazard.

Agriculture has contributed, however, to improving the health status of the population of CARICOM states by the provision of food. In Table 5.3, this provision of food is considered a highly sustainable feature of agriculture. McIntosh (1992) and Sinha (1995) reported a general increase in per capita energy and protein availability per day during the period 1961–1963 to 1986–1988, with all CARICOM countries having levels above those recommended. Thus, protein-energy malnutrition has declined substantially in CARICOM states during the last 25 years and few countries have serious problems of malnutrition. While food availability has been above the recommended levels for all countries, household access has not been universally satisfied. The existence of protein-energy malnutrition within pockets of certain socio-economic groups side by side with obesity points to a maldistribution of available food supplies. Inequity in the distribution of income is undoubtedly a critical factor in the maldistribution of food supplies. McIntosh (1992) and Sinha (1995) thus concluded that, in general, the nutrient availability profile in CARICOM states was good, though they also stated that there was room for improvement in the quality of the diets and food distribution.

Economic Impact

In addition to its contribution to food security, agriculture, particularly the traditional export crops, is a significant earner of foreign exchange. This is exemplified in Table 5.5, which gives the ratio of agricultural exports to total export for CARICOM states. This ratio for Guyana and Belize is very high, ranging between 44 percent and 73 percent, and also very high for the Windward Islands (Grenada, Dominica, St Lucia, and St Vincent), in the range of 55 percent to 84 percent. For both Barbados and Jamaica the ratios range from 22 percent to 31 percent, and range from 3 percent to 13 percent for Trinidad and Tobago, Antigua, Suriname, and the Bahamas.

However, this foreign exchange earning capacity of agriculture is highly dependent on preferential marketing arrangements whereby Caribbean exports receive prices substantially higher than world market prices. In some countries, for example Trinidad and Tobago, further support to the agricultural sector is provided by the state in the form of support prices. The combined effects of preferential marketing

TABLE 5.5 Agricultural Exports as a Percentage of Total Exports ($U.S. '00,000)

State	1991			1992			1993		
	Total Exports	Agric. Exports	%	Total Exports	Agric. Exports	%	Total Exports	Agric. Exports	%
MDCs[a]									
Bahamas	15,951	900	6	14,700	885	6	13,000	653	5
Barbados	2,045	515	25	1,961	614	31	1,809	524	29
Guyana	2,800	1,513	54	3,817	1,932	51	4,155	1,834	44
Jamaica	11,452	2,529	22	10,536	2,478	23	10,445	2,582	25
Trinidad and Tobago	19,826	1,179	6	18,666	1,173	6	16,722	1,309	7
LDCs[b]									
Antigua and Barbuda	354	17	4	525	16	3	550	19	3
Belize	1,232	846	69	1,405	1,023	73	1,322	950	72
Dominica	542	369	68	574	352	61	501	290	58
Grenada	232	156	67	200	122	61	204	119	58
Montserrat	16	—	—	17	—	—	29	—	—
St Kitts and Nevis	296	118	40	331	154	46	330	129	39
St Lucia	1,008	709	70	1,139	803	70	1,071	588	55
St Vincent	784	656	84	774	620	80	835	604	72
Suriname	3,459	369	11	3,410	452	13	2,900	389	13
Total	59,217	9,876	17	58,055	10,624	18	53,872	9,990	18

[a] MDC, medium developed country.
[b] LDC, less developed country.

Unpublished data from the Inter-American Institute for Cooperation in Agriculture (1991–1994).

arrangements and subsidies cause the competitiveness of Caribbean agriculture to be slightly unsustainable (Table 5.3).

In general, the contribution of agriculture to gross domestic product (GDP) is considered a highly sustainable feature of the sector. This contribution to GDP varies among CARICOM countries (Table 5.6). For Guyana, Belize, Dominica, St Vincent, and Suriname, the data indicate that the contribution of the agricultural sector to GDP is significant, ranging from 13 percent to 40 percent of GDP. In comparison, the sector's contribution to GDP ranged from 10 percent to 13 percent in St Lucia and Grenada and contributed less than 10 percent in the other Caribbean

TABLE 5.6 Agricultural Sector Contribution (%) to GDP, 1991–1994

Country	1991	1992	1993	1994
MDCs[a]				
Bahamas	3.4	2.9	N/A	N/A
Barbados	5.6	6.1	5.7	5.1
Guyana	29	28.8	38.3	36.2
Jamaica	6.2	6.9	7.4	8
Trinidad and Tobago	2.5	2.4	2.3	2.1
LDCs[b]				
Antigua and Barbuda	4	4.1	4.1	3.7
Belize	18.9	19.5	13.1	19.1
Dominica	25.7	24.5	23.5	22.2
Grenada	13.1	11.3	10.6	10.2
Montserrat	6.7	6.9	6.8	6
St Kitts and Nevis	3.3	3.9	5.6	5.8
St Lucia	13.1	13.3	10.8	9.9
St Vincent	16.5	18.6	14.2	11.7
Suriname	12.1	14.2	22.8	14

[a] MDC, medium developed country.
[b] LDC, less developed country.

Unpublished data from the Inter-American Institute for Cooperation in Agriculture (1991–1994).

member states. In general, contribution to GDP from agriculture is considered as a moderately sustainable feature of the sector. Agriculture continues to be an important source of employment in CARICOM states and plays a critical role in the economic survival of rural communities.

There is an additional economic factor affecting the sustainability of the agricultural sector: risk. One important cause of risk is wind damage and its incidence is stated in Table 5.3 as the major risk criterion for assessing agricultural sustainability. In general, the island states and Belize are more susceptible to wind damage, especially hurricane damage, than the other continental states and, overall, agriculture is considered to be sustainable with respect to this factor.

Social Factors

The social factors identified as affecting the sustainability of Caribbean agriculture are literacy, gender, and the mean age of farmers. In general, fairly high rates of literacy have been reported among Caribbean farmers (WINBAN, 1993b), although the levels of functional literacy may in fact be much lower than the reported literacy rates. There is some doubt whether Caribbean farmers are sufficiently equipped to handle technological developments that may characterize agriculture in the future. Therefore, Caribbean agriculture is considered to be slightly unsustainable with regard to the factor of literacy. With respect to the participation of both genders in agriculture, surveys generally report that approximately 20 percent of the farmers are female (WINBAN, 1993b; Pemberton et al., 1988). This situation is considered moderately sustainable. Finally, concerns have been raised about the advanced age of farmers in the Caribbean, and the lack of young recruits into farming (Pemberton, 1985). Caribbean agriculture is considered slightly unsustainable with regard to this factor.

Overall Assessment

In general, Caribbean agriculture has to be considered unsustainable because of the use of high levels of fertilizers, farming on steep slopes, its effect on human health and biodiversity, and the level of literacy and the advanced age of the farming population. In addition, even though the sector makes a valuable contribution to CARICOM economies, especially with respect to export earnings, its dependence on preferential markets and state subsidies, in some cases, renders it unsustainable with regard to its competitiveness.

It must be borne in mind, however, that agriculture in the Caribbean is very diverse, and thus there must be considerable differences in the sustainability of the different agricultural systems. For example, cocoa production systems, especially in Trinidad and Tobago, are maintained in a mainly forest type ecosystem, and Pemberton et al. (1995) reported that 88 percent of coconut farmers in Trinidad and Tobago did not use any manufactured chemical inputs. Much research remains to be done, however, to quantify the costs and benefits of agriculture to natural resources, including human resources, and the differences in sustainability of Caribbean agricultural systems.

SUSTAINABILITY CHALLENGES FOR CARIBBEAN AGRICULTURE

In their paper introducing the "2020 Vision for Food, Agriculture and the Environment" project of the International Food Policy Research Institute (IFPRI), Pinstrup-Andersen and Pandya-Lorch (1994) referred to three challenges facing global agriculture:

> As we look toward 2020 and beyond, the world must confront three central, intertwined challenges: alleviating widespread poverty, meeting current and future food needs, and managing the natural resource base to assure sustainability. Compounding the difficulty of meeting these challenges is the expected addition of almost 100 million people to the world's population every year for the next 30 years, and the limited availability of new land for cultivation in much of the world.
>
> Agricultural intensification – production of more food on land already under cultivation – is the key to effectively addressing all three challenges. Increased food production will have to come from increased yields. (p. 1)

If the forms of agriculture used to achieve these increased yields are to be sustainable, they must be based on sound agronomic principles but they must also embrace understanding of the constraints and interactions of all other dimensions of sustainable land management. As yields increase, production risks will have to be controlled to ensure more reliable cash flow and permit confident planning. Soil resources will need to be controlled and water pollution cannot be tolerated. Production systems will have to be flexible, diversified, and developed on a broad genetic base to ensure the possibility of rapid response to changing conditions. Land management practices, in large measure, control processes of land degradation. The efficiency of these practices will largely govern the sustainability of a given land use. However, institutional, political, social, and economic pressures and structures can cause or exacerbate environmental problems.

The Caribbean, and CARICOM states in particular, will have to face the same three global challenges. An additional challenge for Caribbean agriculture is to ensure that the principles and concepts of sustainable land management become entrenched not only in rural populations but in the policy arena as well. For example, some major changes in systems of national accounting may be required to ensure that the loss of options for the future, consequent upon depreciation of natural resources – loss of a nation's true "wealth" – are properly recognized. Procedures of national accounting, for example, that mistakenly assume that natural resources are so abundant that they have no marginal value, may have to be seen as being unacceptable.

Technical and scientific advances will be instrumental in the Caribbean in the transition to sustainable agriculture. These advances will need to be tailored to local environmental conditions. In this context, there is much that can be learned from indigenous knowledge systems in the formulation of sustainable agricultural practices. Care also has to be taken to avoid agricultural systems that result in the wholesale disruption of social and cultural norms, since they generally lead to the loss of indigenous knowledge and thus the loss of vital information on the sustainability of the natural resource base.

There are normally a variety of alternative agricultural production systems and these systems, since they involve different transformations of natural and manufactured inputs into commodities, are characterized by different levels of agricultural sustainability. Another challenge to Caribbean agriculture is to develop measures to assess the sustainability of the alternative systems so that the best ones can be chosen for particular target situations.

Attention now turns to some of the alternative agricultural production systems that have potential for the sustainable development of Caribbean agriculture. Then some socio-economic approaches to improve the sustainability of Caribbean agriculture are presented.

ALTERNATIVE PRODUCTION SYSTEMS TOWARDS SUSTAINABLE CARIBBEAN AGRICULTURE

A number of unsustainable factors in Caribbean agriculture have been identified. The following will focus on systems and practices that have been proposed, which can counteract or eliminate the major unsustainable factors.

Green manuring and organic mulches: Green manuring refers to the growing of legumes and other plants in order to fix nitrogen and then incorporate them into the soil for the following crop. Organic mulches refer to crop residues, which are placed or left on the surface of the soil. Davis (1991) reviewed the beneficial effects on various soils of green manures and organic mulches. These, he stated, include moisture retention, weed control, moderating soil temperature, and increased availability of nutrients, especially phosphorus and potassium. In his study in Jamaica, Davis found highly significant differences between mulched and unmulched plots for a number of parameters, including the total and marketable yields of vegetables.

Conservation tillage: These are systems of minimum tillage or no tillage, in which the seed is placed directly into the soil with little or no preparatory cultivation. This reduces the amount of soil disturbance and so lessens run-off and loss of sediments and nutrients.

Intercropping: This is the growing of two or more crops simultaneously on the same piece of land. Benefits arise because crops exploit different resources or mutually interact with one another. If one crop is a legume, it may provide nutrients for the other. The interactions may also serve to control pests and weeds. Intercropping systems have been a feature of traditional small-scale (peasant) production in the Caribbean. However, monocultural systems have been extensively adopted, especially in export crop production. (For further information on intercropping see Stinner and Blair, 1990).

Alley cropping: Alley cropping involves the intercropping of food crops within hedgerows of woody species, usually of leguminous or multipurpose trees. This system has been found to reduce soil erosion and run-off, resulting in improved soil water and nutrient use. Kang et al. (1988) reported higher maize yields with alley cropping with leucaena hedgerows in trials carried out in Ibadan, Nigeria. Hauser (1988) reported higher concentrations of calcium, magnesium, and inorganic nitrogen in the soil solution in unfertilized alley cropping systems. Wilson (1992) also reported that:

> alley cropping appears [as] the most efficient method of exploiting the many attributes of Leucaena. Not only will it [leucaena] aid conservation, but it can be a major renewable source of wood that can be used as stakes, poles and fuel, possibly the most attractive aspect in countries that can no longer afford fossil fuel energy. The high protein leaves are good animal feed, which can be exploited in alley farming which is alley cropping with ruminant animal components. (p. 221)

Rotation: This involves the growing of two or more crops in sequence on the same piece of land. Benefits are similar to those arising from intercropping. Gumbs (1987) reported that rotation also improves soil structure and reduces erosion.

Agroforestry: This is a form of intercropping in which annual herbaceous crops are grown with perennial trees or shrubs interspersed among them. The deeper- rooted trees can often exploit water and nutrients not available to the herbs. The trees may also provide shade and mulch, while the ground cover of herbs reduces weeds and prevents erosion. Andreatta (1992) has provided an interesting description of an agroforestry project in Green Park, Jamaica.

Silvipasture: This is similar to agroforestry and involves combining trees with grassland and other fodder species on which livestock graze. The mixture of browse, grass, and herbs often supports mixed livestock.

Biological control: This involves the use of natural enemies, parasitoids or predators, to control pests. If the pest is exotic, these enemies may be imported from the country of origin of the pest. If the pest is indigenous, various techniques are used to augment the numbers of the existing natural enemies.

Integrated pest management: This refers to the use of all appropriate techniques of controlling pests in an integrated manner that enhances rather than destroys natural controls. If pesticides are part of the programme, they are used sparingly and selectively so as not to interfere with natural enemies (FAO, 1995). (For further information on integrated pest management see Henneberry et al., 1991; Luna and House, 1990; Petry, 1995; and Walmsley, 1994.)

Integrated livestock/fish farming systems: An example of this system is the intensive culture of ducks and fish (e.g., tilapia) in the same pond. In this system, the waste from the ducks nourishes plant and animal life, which the fish utilize. It is calculated that 600 ducks stocked on a 0.5 hectare pond have the potential to produce up to 600 kg of tilapia, 280 kg of carp, and 4680 kg of duck meat in 100 days (University of the West Indies, 1993).

Biodigesters: Conway and Gavett (1991) have reported that a promising biomass energy option is the use of animal waste:

> By fermenting, animal waste in an anaerobic digester, the waste is broken down into methane, carbon dioxide, water and fibre. The methane can be burned to produce hot water or space heat, or used in an internal combustion engine to produce shaft power, or electricity . . . In addition to producing energy, the digester produces a powdery substance that contains all the nitrogen, potassium, and phosphate that was in the original manure. But the nitrogen is converted into a form more readily usable by crops, thereby making this an excellent fertilizer. (p. 136)

SOCIO-ECONOMIC STRATEGIES

Trade Liberalization

Trade liberalization can improve agricultural sustainability by removing distortions in the markets for agricultural commodities and, thus, improving the competitiveness of agriculture. It is argued that trade liberalization may result in the cessation of the production of commodities unsuited to the natural, physical and social environments. The cushion of trade protection allows the expansion of production of unsuitable commodities, which may require the use of techniques and inputs to change the natural environment, and which may cause severe degradation of natural resources.

Even though such trade protection may result in farmers producing the commodities profitably (in a private as opposed to a social sense), this profitability is based on a country's ability to continue transfers to the farmers, either in the form of higher prices to consumers or direct subsidy payments by the state. If this ability to pay on the part of the state is lost and trade protection is ended, then severe adjustments can become necessary within the farming community. However, these adjustments should result in the long-term improvement of the quality of life and health of those involved in agriculture.

Trade liberalization can therefore be supported because of its benefits to agricultural sustainability. Short-term measures may be necessary, however, to lessen the burden of adjustment, especially on lower income groups within developing countries. For further discussion on the role of trade liberalization the reader is referred to Pearce (1993).

Promotion of Economic Growth

Another approach to improved agricultural sustainability lies in the promotion of economic growth. New income generated from economic growth can provide the wherewithal to design new policies and projects to offset the negative consequences from unsustainable features of agriculture. Economic growth should occur, not only through the incorporation of natural and physical resources into the production function but also through science and technology.

Improvement of Human Capital in Agriculture

Investment in human capital is a key factor in the advancement of science and technology and hence is a key factor in economic growth and agricultural sustainability. With particular regard to improving agricultural sustainability, an important area for the improvement of human capital is in the education of farmers, especially to raise the productivity of their systems. Such improvements in productivity are necessary for Caribbean farmers to lower their cost so that their production becomes internationally competitive in an environment of trade liberalization. The *Evaluation Report of the Caribbean Agricultural Extension Project* (Alkin et al., 1989) proposed several measures that can be taken to improve the productivity of Caribbean farmers. Their recommendations were:

- Training in farm management for extension officers
- Identification of target farms that can be used to demonstrate the benefits of specific types of technology to other farmers
- Analysis of enterprise data to determine the changes in technology or management practices that have been most effective in increasing farm income
- Initiation of whole-farm planning with target farm families

CONCLUSION

The objective of this chapter was to discuss the sustainable development of agriculture in the Caribbean, with particular reference to CARICOM. It may be concluded that agriculture in CARICOM states is unsustainable in at least five respects: the high level of fertilizer use, especially in vegetables and bananas; the utilization of steep slopes, causing severe erosion; heavy reliance on highly toxic pesticides, with effects on human health and biodiversity; and the advanced age and levels of literacy of the farming population. Several alternative production systems were discussed which have potential for improving the sustainability of CARICOM agriculture. Also, a number of socio-economic strategies were suggested.

In order that the alternative production systems might contribute to improving the sustainability of Caribbean agriculture, they must be adopted by farmers. For such adoption to take place, it is necessary for these systems to be tested in the Caribbean environment and also for information on suitable systems to be communicated to farmers. Research, development, and extension, therefore, have crucial roles to play in the process of devising and implementing systems to improve the sustainability of Caribbean agriculture.

Turning to the socio-economic strategies, these require a re-orientation of the role of the state in agriculture and institutional adjustments. No longer should the role of the state be to support uncompetitive agricultural production, which tends to degrade natural resources. Instead, the state should focus on the promotion of sustained economic growth by encouraging productive economic activity in the agricultural sector as well as in other sectors.

States should also concentrate activity on the alleviation of poverty. Poverty associated with population pressures, land constraints, and lack of appropriate production technology to intensify agriculture, is a major source of environmental degradation, as it forces people to use available natural resources in unsustainable ways to survive. Alleviation of poverty can be achieved through agricultural intensification that generates income and employment in both farm and off-farm activities.

Among the priority areas that CARICOM identified for the development of the region were (CARICOM Secretariat, 1995):

- Agricultural production and diversification
- Environmental protection
- Employment creation

- Human resource development
- Export promotion and external market penetration

Successful realization of the objectives of agricultural production and diversification will require major technological and marketing initiatives. Moreover, such initiatives must also include dimensions of environmental protection and employment creation to satisfy regional aspirations. Therefore, collaborative efforts are necessary among scientists, technologists, the farm and agribusiness communities, and officials in governmental organizations, so that the appropriate strategic initiatives can be formulated for sustainable development of Caribbean agriculture.

REFERENCES AND FURTHER READING

Ahmad, N., G. W. Garcia, C. A. Pemberton, G. V. Pollard, and L. A. Wilson. 1991. "Perspectives on sustainable agricultural development in the Caribbean: Theory and practice". In A. Moore and J. Rudder, eds., *Sustainable Development for the Caribbean: The Role of UWI*. University of the West Indies, Cave Hill, Barbados.

Alkin, M. C., M. Andrews, H. Manhertz, G. Robinson-Lewis, and J. West (eds.). 1989. *Evaluation Report of the Caribbean Agricultural Extension Project Phase II*. U.S. Agency for International Development, Bridgetown, Barbados.

Andreatta, S. 1992. "A sociological analysis for silvo-pastoral management systems among Jamaican small farmers: A case study of Green Park". Proceedings of the Second Annual Conference of JSAS. *JAGRIST, The Bulletin of the Jamaican Society for Agricultural Sciences* 4.

Canter, L. W. 1986. *Environmental Impacts of Agricultural Production Activities*. Lewis Publishers, Chelsea, Michigan.

CARICOM Secretariat. 1995. "The role of resource mobilization in the Caribbean community". *CARICOM Perspectives* 65: 71–74.

Conway, R. and E. Gavett. 1991. "Interagency alternative fuels research". In *Agriculture and the Environment. The 1991 Year Book of Agriculture*. U.S. Government Printing Office, Washington, D.C.

Davis, M. S. 1991. "A study of the soil characteristics as developed in a grass mulch system of vegetable cultivation in Jamaica". Proceedings of the Second Annual Conference of JSAS. *JAGRIST The Bulletin of the Jamaican Society for Agricultural Sciences* 3: 5 – 8.

Deare, F. M., N. Ahmad, and T. U. Ferguson. 1992. "Soil losses from a flatland soil". In *Sixth Annual Seminar on Agricultural Research*. NIHERST, Port-of-Spain, Trinidad and Tobago.

Dixon, J. A., L. F. Scura, R. A. Carpenter, and P. B. Sherman. 1994. *Economic Analysis of Environmental Impacts*. Earthscan Publications, London.

Economic Commission for Latin America and the Caribbean. 1993. *Agricultural Statistics – Caribbean Countries,* volumes 10 and 11. UN Economic Commission for Latin America and the Caribbean, New York.

FAO (Food and Agricultural Organization). 1986. "Report on natural resources for food and agriculture in Latin America and the Caribbean". *FAO Environment and Energy* no. 8.

FAO (Food and Agriculture Organization). 1995. *Sustainability Issues in Agricultural and Rural Development Policies: Training Materials for Agricultural Planning,* Document 38/1, edited by F. Petry. Food and Agriculture Organization, Rome, Italy.

Georges, J. E. W., M. S. Mohammed, and W. Harvey. 1985. "Effect on soil water content and compactive effort on soil compaction and sugar cane regrowth". *Proceedings of the West Indies Sugar Technologists Congress* 22: 635–653.

Girvan, N. P. and D. A. Simmons. 1991. *Caribbean Ecology and Economics.* Caribbean Conservation Association.

Gumbs, F. A. 1987. *Soil and Water Conservation Methods for the Caribbean.* University of the West Indies Department of Agricultural Extension, St Augustine, Trinidad.

Hall, R. A. 1994. "Insect pathologies in integrated pest management for the Caribbean". pp. 149–161, in D. Walmsley, ed., *Integrated Pest Management: New Strategies for the Caribbean Farmer.* CTA Seminar Proceedings. CTA, Wageningen, The Netherlands.

Hauser, S. 1988. "Water and nutrient dynamics in alley cropping". In *Resource and Crop Management Program Annual Report 1988.* International Institute of Tropical Agriculture, Ibadan, Nigeria.

Henneberry, T. J., E. H. Glass, R. G. Gilbert, E. G. King, Jr., R. W. Miller, and C. J. Whitten. 1991. "Integrated pest management – a sustainable technology". pp. 150–159, in *Agriculture and the Environment. The 1991 Yearbook of Agriculture.* U.S. Government Printing Office, Washington, D.C.

IICA (Inter-American Institute for Cooperation in Agriculture). 1991–1994. "Review of the performance of the agricultural sector in CARICOM member states for the period 1991–1994". Unpublished report.

Kang, B. T., D. Fawunmi, and J. Mareck. 1988. "Performance of three maize and cowpea cultivars alley cropped with various combinations of *Acioa barterii* and *Leucaena leucocephla*". In *Resource and Crop Management Program Annual Report 1988.* International Institute of Tropical Agriculture, Ibadan, Nigeria.

Lal, R., D. J. Eckert, N. R. Fausey, and W. M. Edwards. 1990. "Conservation tillage in sustainable agriculture". pp. 203–225, in C. A. Edwards, R. Lal, P. Madden, R. H. Miller, and G. House, eds., *Sustainable Agricultural Systems.* Soil and Water Conservation Society, Ankeny, Iowa.

Lawrence, M. S. 1992. "Water resources planning and management in Jamaica". Proceedings of the Second Annual Conference of JSAS. *JAGRIST The Bulletin of the Jamaican for Agricultural Sciences* 4.

Luna, J. M. and G. J. House. 1990. "Pest management in sustainable agricultural systems". pp. 157–173, in C. A. Edwards, R. Lal, P. Madden, R. H. Miller, and G. House, eds., *Sustainable Agricultural Systems*. Soil and Water Conservation Society, Ankeny, Iowa.

McIntosh, C. 1992. "Report of the Caribbean Network for Integrated Rural Development (CNIRD)". Task Force on Food Security and Nutrition, St Augustine, Trinidad.

Pantin, D. (ed.). *Planning For Sustainable Development in the Caribbean: Implications for Research and Training*. Workshop Proceedings, McGill University, Montreal, University of the West Indies, St Augustine, Trinidad.

Pantin, D. 1994. *The Economics of Sustainable Development in Small Caribbean Islands*. University of the West Indies Centre for Environment and Development, Jamaica and University of the West Indies Department of Economics, St Augustine, Trinidad.

Parker, C. F. 1990. "Role of animals in sustainable agriculture". pp. 238–245, in C. A. Edwards, R. Lal, P. Madden, R. H. Miller, and G. House, eds., *Sustainable Agricultural Systems*. Soil and Water Conservation Society, Ankeny, Iowa.

Pearce, D. (ed.). 1993. *Blueprint 3. Measuring Sustainable Development*. Earthscan Publications, London.

Pemberton, C. A. 1985. "Economic behaviour of peasants in Tobago". In P. I. Gomes, ed., *Rural Development in the Caribbean*. C. Hurst and Company, London.

Pemberton, C. A., S. Ragbir, and S. Ramjit. 1988. "Report of a cost of production survey of sugar cane farmers in Trinidad and Tobago". University of the West Indies Farm Management Information Systems Project, Department of Agricultural Economics and Farm Management, St Augustine, Trinidad.

Pemberton, C. A., E. L. Harris, and V. Lall. 1995. "Organic farming in the coconut industry of Trinidad and Tobago". In C. A. Pemberton, ed., *Sustainable Agriculture and Economic Development in the Caribbean: Proceedings of the Twenty-first West Indies Agricultural Economics Conference*. Caribbean Agro-Economic Society, University of the West Indies Department of Agricultural Economics and Farm Management, St Augustine, Trinidad.

Pemberton, R. A. 1995. "The quest for a pattern of sustainable development: The genesis of a forest policy in the Colony of Trinidad and Tobago 1890–1950". In C. A. Pemberton, ed., *Sustainable Agriculture and Economic Development in the Caribbean: Proceedings of the Twenty-first West Indies Agricultural Economics Conference*. Caribbean Agro-Economic Society, University of the West Indies Department of Agricultural Economics and Farm Management, St Augustine, Trinidad.

Petry, F. 1995. "Sustainable agriculture and rural development". pp. 2.1–2.30, in F. Petry, ed., *Sustainability Issues in Agricultural and Rural Development Policies*. Training Materials for Agricultural Planning 38/1. Food and Agriculture Organization, Rome, Italy.

Pinstrup-Andersen, P. and R. Pandya-Lorch. 1994. *Alleviating Poverty, Intensifying Agriculture, and Effectively Managing Natural Resources*. Food, Agriculture, and the Environment, Discussion Paper 1. International Food Policy Research Institute (IFPRI), Washington, D.C.

Sinha, D. P. 1995. "Food, nutrition and health in the Caribbean: A time for re-examination". Caribbean Food and Nutrition Institute, Kingston, Jamaica.

Siung-Chang, A. 1990. "Principal river basins and aquatic systems in Trinidad and Tobago: Impacts of pesticides used in agriculture on ground waters, rivers and river basins, estuaries and coastal lagoons". Paper presented to Regional Seminar on Impacts on Agricultural Uses on Pollution of Aquatic Systems. Puerto Morelos, Quintana Roo, Mexico.

Smith, D. 1995. "Science, development and the environment". *Proceedings of the Caribbean Academy of Sciences* 6: 159–176.

Smyth, A. J. and J. Dumanski. 1993. *FESLM: An International Framework for Evaluating Sustainable Land Management*. Food and Agriculture Organization, Land and Water Development Division, Rome, Italy.

Stinner, B. R. and J. M. Blair. 1990. "Ecological and agronomic characteristics of innovative cropping systems". pp. 123–140, in C. A. Edwards, R. Lal, P. Madden, R. H. Miller, and G. House, eds., *Sustainable Agricultural Systems*. Soil and Water Conservation Society, Ankeny, Iowa.

Sugar Association of the Caribbean. 1994. *Hand Book 1961–1993*. Sugar Association of the Caribbean, Sugar Technologists Committee, Angelus Press Ltd., Belize.

University of the West Indies. 1993. "The integrated duck/fish farming system". *Extension Newsletter* 24, no. 3: 8–9. University of the West Indies, Department of Agricultural Extension, St Augustine, Trinidad.

Valdes, A., H. Hurtado, and E. Muchnik. 1991. "Chile". pp. 100–143, in *The Political Economy of Agricultural Pricing Policy*, volume 1, *Latin America*. The Johns Hopkins University Press, London.

Walmsley, D. (ed.). 1994. *Integrated Pest Management – New Strategies for the Caribbean Farmer.* CTA Seminar Proceedings. CTA, Wageningen, The Netherlands.

West, J. G. 1989. "More productive farmers". pp. 1–19, in M. C. Alkin, M. Andrews, H. Manhertz, G. Robinson-Lewis, and J. West, eds., *Evaluation Report of the Caribbean Agricultural Extension Project Phase II*. U.S. Agency for International Development, Bridgetown, Barbados.

Wilson, G. F. 1992. "Leucaena and alley cropping". In T. U. Ferguson and G. W. Garcia, eds., *Leucaena in Agricultural Development: Proceedings of the 1st International Conference on Leucaena*. Port-of-Spain, Trinidad and Tobago.

WINBAN (Windward Islands Banana Growers Association). 1993a. *Banana Growers' Manual: A Guide to Successful Banana Production in the Windward Islands*, 4th edition. Windward Islands Banana Growers Association, Research and Development Division, Castries, St Lucia.

WINBAN (Windward Islands Banana Growers Association). 1993b. "Report of the Productivity Constraints Phase I". Unpublished report, Windward Islands Banana Growers Association, Research and Development Division, Castries, St Lucia.

6

Energy and Sustainable Development

Raymond M. Wright

Contents

INTRODUCTION

The production and use of energy can be viewed as causing more environmental damage than any other single economic activity. For this reason, the role of energy in global climate change is an important topic of study today. There is new interest in renewable energy applications, and in encouraging their accelerated development. This is because they are more environmentally benign than fossil fuels.

During this decade, nearly U.S.$1 trillion will be spent to meet new electricity-generating needs. Energy technologies are among the most critical technologies for sustainable development. The generation and use of energy are responsible for a significant portion of most forms of pollution – air, land, and water. Hence, sustainable development may be unattainable without new energy technologies. Electrical power generated from renewables is 5 percent of present electricity generation worldwide, a figure that could nearly be doubled by the year 2040. When traditional biomass and large-scale hydropower are included, total renewable energy resources contribute about 18 percent of mankind's energy use today. However, one should not be overly optimistic that fossil fuels can be readily replaced. It will take great strides in technology innovation and changing economics for renewables to become the world's primary energy source.

A major barrier to increasing the use of renewables is the large investment that has already been made in the various fossil fuels, in their processing, and in the equipment installed to use them. Thus, a shift from current patterns of energy provision and use will have to overcome the barriers and inertia that currently exist (Jefferson, 1994). One has to recognize the present economic advantages of the fossil fuels that are generally readily available, and the difficulties, when making economic analyses, of costing and pricing externalities such as environmental effects.

Financing new renewable energy projects is also difficult, particularly in poorer economies or even in more vibrant economies, which, for varying reasons, are unable to attract the necessary domestic or external funds. For this reason, some developing countries suggest that under the UN Framework Convention on Climate Change, technology and funding to which they are committed should be provided by the developed countries (Houghton, 1994).

Renewable energy technologies that are immediately relevant include hydropower, modern biomass, wind, active solar (thermal and photovoltaic [PV]), passive solar (low energy architecture), ocean thermal energy conversion (OTEC), tidal power, wave energy, and geothermal energy. Some of these technologies, such as large hydropower and modern biomass, can have adverse environmental impacts. Modern biomass, for example, is a potential threat to biodiversity because it replaces natural forests by monoculture energy forests. Also, there is a risk of competing for agricultural land and the need for maintaining and improving soil quality in biomass production.

Table 6.1 shows important characteristics of new renewable energy resources. Wind power, biomass, hydropower, geothermal energy, and some solar technologies are the energy sources that are most economic at present. As market applications of renewable energy become more diverse and the technologies are more widely demonstrated to the public, these technologies, with reducing costs, may well become justifiable on economic criteria alone. Then we will see an example of an approach to solving environmental issues that creates a positive economic benefit in the energy sector. Already there is a body of thought that solar power is a reservoir of energy that will be an important addition to the future global economy (Scheer, 2001).

HISTORY OF THE OIL INDUSTRY

Oil seepages were tapped in Mesopotamia as early as 3000 BC, and the Romans used bitumen for its pharmaceutical value. Although the use of petroleum had a long history in the Middle East, there was no direct transmission of that knowledge to the west.

In the 1850s the use of kerosene became popular in Europe and North America. Before this time, the Vienna lamp, which had a glass chimney and no smoke or smell, was commonly used. With this inexpensive lamp that could satisfactorily burn kerosene, George Bissell and his fellow shareholders in the Pennsylvania Rock Oil Company in the U.S. tried to discover a new source for the raw material, for which there was an established refining process. They wanted to find "rock oil" cheaply and in abundance. Digging for oil would not do it. Perhaps drilling, known then as salt boring, which had been developed more than 1500 years earlier in China, would do it. The essential insight of Bissell and his fellow investors was to adapt the salt-boring technique directly to oil. They hired "Colonel" Edwin Drake to arrange the drilling of the first well in Pennsylvania. Drake found a driller, a blacksmith named William Smith, who undertook the drilling. On a Saturday afternoon, August 27, 1859, at 69 feet the drill dropped into a crevice in the ground and oil was found in Titusville. Drake's discovery would ultimately bequeath mobility and power to the global population, play a central role in the rise and fall

TABLE 6.1 Some Important Characteristics of New Renewable Energy Sources

		Solar	Wind	Geothermal	Biomass	Ocean	Small Hydro
Resource	Magnitude	Extremely large	Large	Large	Very large	Very large	Large
	Distribution	Worldwide	Coastal, mountains, plains	Volcanic areas and faults	Worldwide	Coastal, tropical	Worldwide mountains
	Variation	Daily, seasonal, weather-dependent	Highly variable	Constant	Climate-dependent	Seasonal, diurnal	Seasonal
	Intensity	Low 1 kW/m^2 peak	Low average 0.8 MW/km^2	Low average Up to 600°C	Moderate to low	Low	Moderate low
Technology	Options	Low to high temp. thermal systems, photovoltaics, passive systems, bioconversion	Horizontal and vertical-axis wind turbines, wind pumps, sail power	Steam and binary thermodynamic flow turbines, geopressured magma	Combustion, fermentation, gasification, liquefaction	Low temp. thermodynamic cycles, mechanical wave oscillators, tidal dams	Low to high head turbines and dams
	Status	Developmental, some commercial (photovoltaics)	Many commercial, some developmental	Many commercial, some developmental	Some commercial, more developmental	Developmental	Mostly commercial

	Capacity factor	<25% without storage, intermediate	Variable most 15–30%	High, base load	As needed with short-term storage	Intermittent to base load	Intermittent to base load
	Key improvements	Materials, cost efficiency, resource data	Materials, cost design, siting, resource data	Exploration, extraction, hot dry rock use	Technology, agriculture and forestry management	Technology, materials, and cost	Turbines cost, design, resource data
Environmental characteristics		Very clean; no emissions; some visual impact, local climate, PV manufacturing contributes pollutants	Very clean; no emissions, visual impact, noise, bird mortality	Clean dissolved gases, brine disposal	Clean; impacts on fauna and flora, toxic residues	Very clean; no emissions, impact on local aquatic environment, visual impact	Very clean, no emissions, impact on local aquatic environment, land use

of nations and empires, and become a major element in the transformation of human society.

At the end of the nineteenth century, the demand for artificial light was met mainly by kerosene, gas, and candles. Then Thomas Edison, having already developed the mimeograph, the phonograph, storage batteries, and motion pictures, in 1879 developed the heat-resistant, incandescent light bulb. He applied himself to commercializing his invention and, in the process, the electric generation industry emerged. The new technology was quickly transferred to Europe and the rest of the world.

As the illumination market was slipping away there arrived another – the motor car. Entrepreneurial investors soon entered the picture. One such was Henry Ford, who resigned as chief engineer of Edison Illuminating Company in Detroit to manufacture a gasoline-powered vehicle named after himself – the Ford.

On January 10, 1901, in Beaumont, Texas, the first real oil gusher, called Spindletop, was found and the Texas oil boom began. The Shell Company from England acquired an interest in the Spindletop find and thus became the second largest oil company in the world, behind Standard Oil. Shell later amalgamated with Royal Dutch, which had production facilities in Burma, Borneo, and Sumatra. Ultimately, they controlled more than half of Russian and Far Eastern oil exports. By the 1940s a number of large companies had emerged in addition to Shell and Standard Oil of New Jersey (now Exxon), which came from the break-up of the Standard Oil Trust in 1911. Among them were Phillips, Mobil, Amoco, Sun, Atlantic Richfield, Union, and Texaco.

By this time also, Mexico had become a major producer and its state oil company, PEMEX, was born after a long battle between government and oil companies over the stability of agreements and the question of sovereignty and ownership. The expropriation of foreign companies took place on March 18, 1938 and was the centrepiece of the Mexican Revolution.

However, it was in the East, not the West, that the collision between politics and petroleum was most dramatic. Before World War I Russian oil had been one of the most important elements in the world market but it was now in the hands of a new communist government of the Soviet Union. Major events in international oil were to take place in the Middle East. Oil was discovered in Kuwait on February 23, 1938 and in Saudi Arabia in March of the same year. Saudi Arabia was on the road to fortune. This set off efforts to obtain concessions by the Iraq Petroleum Company (of Britain) and by German, Italian, and Japanese interests (Yergin, 1991). War and politics over oil continued during the period 1941 to 1945. In late 1943, U.S. geologist Everette DeGolyer arrived in Saudi Arabia and introduced geophysics into oil exploration there. His expertise signalled large finds in that country, which was destined to become the world's largest producer.

In the 1950s and 1960s a battle for production intensified between Iran and Saudi Arabia. In the years between 1957 and 1970 Iranian production grew faster than Saudi output. Consumers around the world welcomed cheap oil from Venezuela and the Middle East. The government of the U.S. put a stop to cheap oil imports in order to prevent the undercutting of the domestic industry. Import quotas were imposed. Thus, prices were higher in the U.S. than they would have been without protection. In 1968, the price of oil at the wellhead in the U.S. was $2.94 per barrel, some 60 percent more than Middle East crudes fetched on the east coast of the U.S.

Total world energy consumption tripled between 1949 and 1972. In Europe it increased fifteen times during that period, and in Japan over 100 times. This surge in oil use was due to rising incomes and rapid economic growth. Oil became cheaper than coal, and cheap oil encouraged consumption.

THE ORGANIZATION OF PETROLEUM EXPORTING COUNTRIES

On September 14, 1960, at a meeting in Baghdad, the large oil exporting nations established the Organization of Petroleum Exporting Countries (OPEC), to confront the pricing strategies of the international oil companies. Its intention was to protect the price of oil by regulating production. The five founding members (Iran, Iraq, Kuwait, Saudi Arabia, and Venezuela) then controlled 80 percent of the world's oil reserves.

Almost as soon as OPEC was formed its member countries lost their grip on world oil exports as new oil producers developed. While most of the new producing countries eventually became members of OPEC, they first entered the world market as competitors. Libya, for example, where small independent units produced most of the oil, flooded Europe with cheap oil.

In 1973, OPEC virtually instigated the onset of a new international economic order by raising oil prices significantly, thereby redistributing economic and political power. The member countries of OPEC now had an important say in the foreign policies of some of the most powerful countries in the world. The international oil market saw significant changes in the period from 1973 to 1994, partly as a result of OPEC's ability to manipulate production. Before 1973 oil price forecasting was not really necessary, because price changes were measured in cents, not dollars. The situation changed dramatically in October 1973.

The momentum leading to the price increases of October 1973 was spurred by Libya's success in obtaining higher prices and taxes from the foreign oil companies operating there in 1970. This set the stage for the important Teheran Agreement of February 1971. The Teheran negotiations improved the collective bargaining power of OPEC. Further price increases came in January 1972 and June 1973 as a way of compensating oil producing countries for the devaluation of the U.S. dollar.

In 1973, OPEC viewed the oil market as increasingly tight and the oil producing OPEC countries were pressured to produce more crude oil. Further, inflation was eroding sales revenues. In October 1973, OPEC members began negotiations to obtain an increase in price, with a twofold justification: first, that the increase would compensate for inflation, and second, that it would allow them to extract a portion of the oil companies' increasing profits. When the oil companies no longer cooperated in the negotiations, OPEC unilaterally raised the posted price of oil by U.S.$ 2.00 per barrel. At the same time, Arab oil producing states imposed an embargo on oil exports to the U.S. and the Netherlands because of their support for Israel during the ongoing Arab–Israeli conflict. In addition, Arab producers reduced production by 20 percent and promised further reductions until the U.S. changed its position. The market shortages forced prices upwards as private companies and oil-deficient countries competed for supplies. By December 1973, the posted price of oil was raised to $11.65 per barrel. By January 1974, the posted price of oil had increased by 300 percent above pre-1973 prices and a new plateau of high oil prices had been reached.

In September 1980, OPEC reached agreement on an official price in which marker crude was set at $30 per barrel. Soon after this price agreement was reached the oil market experienced another supply disruption with the starting of the Iran–Iraq War. The decline in oil output was offset by increased production in other OPEC countries and by gradual reduction in demand due to conservation in the oil-deficient countries. The OPEC marker crude price was raised to $34 per barrel in January 1982, when the spot market price was approximately $36 per barrel.

Growth in non-OPEC production, draw-down of stockpiles, lower economic growth, and demand reduction by oil-deficient countries resulted in softer market conditions between 1982 and 1983. However, OPEC was able to maintain its marker crude price until March 1983 by lower output. For example, OPEC production in 1979 was 31 million barrels per day (b/d) compared with 17 million b/d in 1983. In March 1983, OPEC decreased its official price to $29 per barrel, set an output limit of 17.5 million b/d and gave a quota to each member. Saudi Arabia was not given a quota, however, but left to determine its own production level. As a result, it became the "swing" producer, keeping a desired price by balancing supply and demand.

Increasing non-OPEC production, coupled with lack of demand recovery, led to a new agreement on production ceilings on October 30, 1984. Production was to be cut by 1.5 million b/d, making the new output ceiling 16 million b/d. Production limits were not adhered to by OPEC members and this led to large cuts in Saudi Arabia's production during 1985. Tiring of its role as "swing" producer, Saudi Arabia abandoned it and, in November 1985, increased its output from 2.3 million to 4.2 million b/d. Another production rise to 6.4 million b/d was made by Saudi Arabia in August 1986. A soft market, in tandem with a significant increase in output, brought about a dramatic decline in oil prices in July 1986. The price even fell lower than $10 per barrel.

Oil prices experienced a modest rebound in August 1986 due to a return to the OPEC production ceiling set in 1983 and assisted by increased demand attributable to economic growth. The new price for marker crude was $18 per barrel. The outcome of the 1986 price war was a decrease in the price of crude oil to approximately $9.00 in 1987. In real terms, this price was lower than it had been in 1974. Thus, the declining trend in real oil prices over the period from 1980 to 1987 was steep and made alternative energy sources less competitive during the mid-1980s (Wright, 1991).

Four times during the period from 1973 to 2001, OPEC, and in particular the volatile politics of the Gulf region, had a powerful effect on the oil market. Oil and politics have been linked in the Middle East so that political and strategic considerations have often intruded into the world of oil. The former concessionary system of exploration and production gave oil companies excessive power over production and pricing, which eventually led to confrontations with host governments. The dissolution of the system in the 1970s left the producer governments with the impression that the exercise of sovereignty was all-important and that market forces were of little significance.

Oil prices, which have been relatively low from 1983 to the present, have caused a major contraction in the oil industry. As a consequence, emphasis is now being placed on increased exploration and production, especially in the Western Hemisphere. This will help to adjust

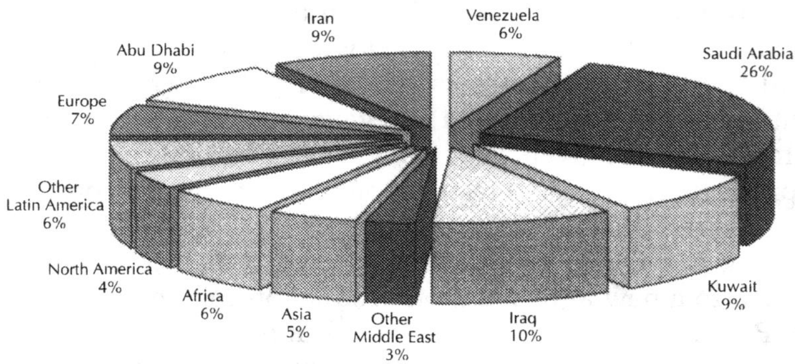

FIGURE 6.1 World proven oil reserves, at the end of 1999; total = 1 trillion barrels.

the present imbalance whereby nearly 70 percent of world oil reserves are located in the Middle East.

The energy needs of the world will continue to be met in part by oil well into the twenty-first century. However, over the next decade OPEC may continue to have difficulty in reaching its price objectives because the need to agree on fixed outputs may be outweighed by the incentive to secretly produce beyond agreed ceilings. Also, there is the lack of stringent enforcement mechanisms, and the simple fact that about 60 percent of the world's crude oil production is now outside of OPEC (Figure 6.1).

Energy substitutes for oil will help to restrain future increases. Large-scale substitutes include coal, heavy oil, tar sands, and nuclear power. Small-scale alternatives include wind and solar energy generation and biomass.

Figure 6.1 gives proven world oil reserves at the end of 1999. OPEC's share of world oil production is expected to rise because of lower output in the U.S. North Sea production that should peak in about 5 years. The fact that production has been significantly reduced in the former Soviet Union because of lack of investment, slow national decision making, and the inability to move the oil to market because pipelines have to pass through neighbouring countries is also a factor in OPEC's expected increased production.

OPEC envisages that over a period of 25 years production from its twelve member states will double to around 50 million barrels per day. This may be optimistic given the many imponderables that impact on oil production and prices.

There is likely to be a firming of oil prices in the first decade of this century due to increased demand, especially from the Asia-Pacific region. Of course, there will be fluctuations influenced by political swings and, at worst, outright war. Energy conservation will help in restraining future oil price increases, although by the year 2020 the nonrenewable nature of oil may initiate gradual price increases.

Since 1973 the oil industry has embraced, then abandoned, a number of strategies. Two examples are the diversification away from energy from the mid-1970s to the mid-1980s and the adoption of a preference for North America when making upstream investments (exploration and production). Neither strategy proved to be a satisfactory approach and both have been reversed. The industry had difficulty costing developments, including what would seem obvious ones like the fall in demand during the 1970s, leaving the oil industry with a large surplus capacity. These examples show that the industry has not always been able to understand and predict the market.

Boopsingh (1990) gives an overview of the issues involved in oil and gas pricing, taxation, and licencing systems. The management of petroleum resources by the public and private sector is critical to national development. His thesis identifies the growing globalization of the petroleum industry and the internationalization of finance.

HEAVY OIL AND TAR SANDS

Heavy oil reserves and tar sands resources are being exploited in California, U.S. and Alberta, Canada. Commercial production has been on stream for two decades. The Orinoco belt in Venezuela houses some 1.2 trillion barrels of heavy oil but economic reserves are not high at present, because production costs are too high compared to product prices. High production costs compared to product prices also hold for the world's oil shale resources. In contrast, synthetic oils are presently economically producable from Canadian tar sands. Increased capacity of the Syncrude integrated oil sands mining project has increased synthetic crude reserves to over two billion barrels. In all cases, as product prices increase relative to production costs, recoverable reserves will expand. Thus, Orinoco's heavy oils will become important substitute resources for conventional crude if the price of crude oil should increase significantly in the future. So, both heavy oil and tar sands will be constraining factors for crude oil prices in the longer term. In the Caribbean, only Venezuela, Trinidad, and Colombia have important volumes of heavy oil.

Orimulsion, a new fuel from Venezuela, is now commercially available. Derived from bitumen and extra-heavy oils in the Orinoco Basin, it has to be emulsified with approximately 30 percent water. Outside of Venezuela, the fuel is now being burned by utility companies in the U.S., Canada, and the U.K. There is, however, an environmental disadvantage to orimulsion because of the high sulphur content (3 percent) which, on a heat basis, is 50 percent worse than a similar 3 percent sulphur content in heavy fuel oil, and up to three times worse than low-sulphur coal (Wright, 1991).

COAL

Coal ranks second to petroleum as an important energy resource. World reserves of recoverable coal amount to 1150 billion tons or the equivalent of 4.4 trillion barrels of oil. The largest reserves of coal are in the U.S., Russia, and China. In terms of heating value, coal has consistently remained the least expensive fuel. However, coal is a major provider of the greenhouse gas carbon dioxide when burnt as fuel. Furthermore, approximately 50 percent of the sulphur dioxide released into the atmosphere by human activity comes from the combustion of coal. For this reason, costly emission controls have been put on the use of coal as a fuel. At the same time, the environmental standards to be met by coal combustion are becoming more stringent.

The conventional method of producing electricity from coal is to burn pulverized coal in a boiler and use the heat to vaporize water in steam tubes. The steam drives a turbine that converts energy into electricity using a generator. The transformation of coal into gas is now an attractive commercial option. The gas, a mixture of hydrogen and carbon, contains lesser amounts of hydrogen sulphide, methane, and carbon dioxide. The hydrogen sulphide is nearly all removed by commercially available processes before the gas is burned. The gas then powers a combined cycle; the pressurized gases drive a turbine, while vapour from the combustion chamber runs a conventional steam turbine. Efficiency claims for coal-to-gas conversion systems is about 42 percent, with electricity being generated at approximately U.S. 4.85 cents per kilowatt-hour (kWh), depending on location.

There are no commercial bituminous coal deposits in Caribbean countries but there are deposits of the lower grades of coal – lignite and peat. The deposits of lignite identified in the Chapelton Formation of the Tertiary Yellow Limestone Group of central Jamaica seem to have little possibility for commercial exploitation. The lignite seams are thin, reaching a maximum of 1.5 metres, with low calorific value. Moreover, there are problems in strip mining such thin deposits because large amounts of land would need to be disturbed.

Peat deposits have been identified in Jamaica in the Negril and Black River Morasses. The extractable energy from Negril peat could possibly drive a 60-megawatt (MW) plant for 23 years. However, the Black River peat resources are lesser in quality and do not have as attractive a potential for energy generation as does the Negril peat. There are important environmental considerations at Negril related to the following factors:

- Adverse effects of air emissions of dust, sulphur oxide, and nitrogen oxide gases. These are expected to produce ground level concentrations in excess of U.S. Environmental Protection Agency standards.
- Possible pollution of the Negril Lake by flocculents in the return water.
- Possible interference with coral reef growth from turbid water discharged into the sea.
- Soil and groundwater contamination from fly ash amounting to approximately 64,000 tonnes per annum. The ash would have a high alkali content and pH.

It is likely that peat mining for electricity generation will not take place at Negril because of environmental considerations although smaller quantities of peat can be extracted for briquetting without adverse effects at Negril. Peat briquettes may be used for home and commercial barbecuing of meats as a replacement for charcoal.

NUCLEAR POWER

Although nuclear power has been used successfully in countries such as France, where it provides approximately 70 percent of domestic electricity, there have been significant doubts about nuclear risk issues and safety measures in the industry. Furthermore, there have been a number of nuclear accidents. These have been well documented by May (1990), who presents a comprehensive account of both civil and military nuclear accidents occurring up to 1989.

The Three Mile Island (U.S.) and Chernobyl (former Soviet Union) accidents are the most serious recent nuclear accidents. The Three Mile Island accident did not cause any significant harm to the population, whereas the Chernobyl accident was a disastrous event resulting from a faulty core design with a positive temperature coefficient of reactivity and control systems that were disconnected as a result of human error.

The International Atomic Energy Agency (IAEA) has been active in taking corrective action since the occurrence of these accidents in order to improve reactor safety worldwide. There have been numerous cancellations of orders for nuclear reactors in the second half of the 1980s, a period also marked by the abandonment of some reactors under construction or operating. One example of this was that of the Shoreham reactor belonging to the Long Island Lighting Company, where operations were terminated in 1989 (McCallion, 1995).

Presently, there are 431 nuclear reactors worldwide that provide 335 gigawatts of power. In addition, 64 power reactors are being planned in 16 countries. The growing concern with global warming and acid rain is forcing the scientific and energy community to take a second look at nuclear power. Nuclear power is presently the only major available known non-fossil fuel resource that can sustainably close the gap in the near future between primary energy supply and demand.

Within the next two decades the capital cost of most of the nuclear power plants will have been paid for. This will make them the most competitive and cleanest source of large-scale electricity. What is ideally expected is that new generations of reactors with inherent safety features, high efficiency, and competitive costs will be developed and operated. Such reactors include the direct cycle gas-turbine modular helium-cooled reactor, the IFR breeder reactor, and advanced water-cooled reactors (Simnad, 1996). There is now a more positive outlook on nuclear power because of developments that have occurred in recent years, such as more effective enforcement of quality control rules and regulations, the use of standardized designs for nuclear facilities, the development of passively safe reactor designs, and improved training of personnel and management in the nuclear industry. It seems that nuclear power, which is compatible with sustainable development, will continue to contribute in the future to our expanding energy needs. In fact, nuclear power is the only source of energy that could economically give optimal value to Jamaican bauxite by allowing smelting to aluminium within the country.

As small nuclear plants become more efficient and are constructed economically, for example in modules of 350 to 400 MW, this source of power could be considered an option for a number of the larger Caribbean countries. Cuba already has a 490 MW nuclear plant where construction was halted, primarily for safety considerations. The initial plan was to add another 490 MW module later.

FUTURE ENERGY SUPPLY

The present global energy mix is likely to change significantly during the next century as a result of several factors. First, comparative scarcity due either to political or resource constraints may increase the relative price of oil. Second, the cost of reducing environmental degradation will alter the present weighting in the cost competition among fuels. Third, the fear of global climate change will encourage a shift from carbon-based fuels to non-fossil alternatives. An energy resource perspective of the next century involves speculation on future energy demand and likely economic energy supply alternatives, as well as possible changes in energy systems and technologies. The expectations of the future are shaped and directly affected by the long time periods required to develop new or improved energy technologies and to install them commercially. Long-term projections are by nature speculative and rely on present knowledge and experience, yet they allow the recognition of trends and possible outcomes and so help to guide present plans, projects, and strategies.

In the context of the timescale of the next century, an obvious question is whether the cumulative effect of the gradual depletion of carbon-based energy resources will result in a global constraint on energy systems, especially on the future supply of liquid fuel for transport. Present technology, however, points to the potentially large-scale convertibility of all fossil fuels to liquid or gas forms. In this way, a global source of liquid fuel could be derived from the large known world coal reserves. The rising cost of oil will bring into competition known higher-cost sources, such as coal conversion, tar sands, and oil shale.

It is unlikely that a serious worldwide shortage of fuels will develop during the next century because of the depletion of coal, oil, and gas. The main uncertainties arise from the constantly changing economic competition among the various fuel sources and the effects of environmental factors that induce increased costs because of the need to reduce the creation of undesirable effluents from fuel use.

A fact to be borne in mind is that the real resource cost of energy is lower today than at the start of the twentieth century, while the world's population has tripled and its economic output increased by an order of magnitude. This shows that technology and economic incentives have historically overcome perceived resource limitations. Nonetheless, it is likely that the real costs of primary energy from conventional oil and gas sources will increase. This is because the average cost of exploration and development of new oil fields has risen steadily. At some increasing price level, unconventional oil sources will become competitive but they will require large capital investments. For instance, at an oil price of $35 per barrel, large high-cost oil resources such as tar sands become economically viable. Oil shales and tar sands are in sufficient reserves to provide the liquid fuel requirements of the next century but need much higher capital investment for the same flow rates. If this happens it will change the character of the liquid fuel production industry.

Coal is the most abundant fossil fuel, representing about 85 percent of all known conventional fossil resources. It can be converted to both liquid and gaseous hydrocarbons. The production of complex hydrocarbons by coal conversion has been deployed commercially worldwide. All such coal conversion plants burn coal in the presence of an oxidant and water vapour, leading to decomposition of the steam and reaction with the hot coal to produce syngas (carbon monoxide and hydrogen), the ratio of each component depending on the system parameters.

Subsequent treatment can be applied to produce a spectrum of hydrocarbon mixtures and hydrogen. The production of methane or liquid fuel thereafter is a well-established engineering process. Since 1985, a plant in New Zealand has demonstrated the feasibility of converting methane into gasolene with a zeolite process. The Sasol plant in South Africa has been producing liquid fuel from indigenous coal for more than two decades. The true costs would be competitive with oil at $25 per barrel. Large natural gas reserves in some remote areas have encouraged investment in on-site conversion of natural gas to liquid fuel, so as to be able to ship the product to a distant market. Hence, it is obvious that if the price of oil becomes sufficiently high, conversion of coal to liquid fuel will become of interest to the energy industry (Starr et al., 1992).

The use of coal conversion to gas for generating electricity has been demonstrated with the 100-MW integrated gasification combined cycle (IGCC) power plant of Southern California Edison. It is the cleanest coal-fueled technique available. A more advanced integrated gasification humid air turbine cycle (IGHAT) has been proposed. This eliminates the steam bottoming cycle by using the residual heat in a modified combustion turbine. These advanced cycles are important steps for improving the efficiency of coal use. Presently, a modern commercial coal station has an efficiency of about 34 percent. The coal conversion IGCC has an efficiency of 38 percent, and the IGHAT has an efficiency of approximately 41 percent. The advanced cycles have a higher capital cost but with continuing development they may become competitive, especially for environmental reasons.

A significant improvement in the efficiency of fossil fuel generation will come from the development of the fuel cell (World Energy

Council, 1994). The molten carbonate fuel cell is the present focus of developmental work. An electrochemical process is used to move from hydrogen and oxygen in gas to electricity. The hydrogen is derived from natural gas by a process called reforming, while the oxygen is available from the air. As long as gas and air are supplied, conversion to electricity continues without interruption. Thus, fuel cells need no recharging. In principle, the fuel cell directly replaces the combustion turbines in the integrated cycles described before. It would raise the efficiency of the two cycles to 46 and 55 percent, respectively. Commercialization of the fuel cell would eventually decrease the electricity component of the global demand for coal to approximately 65 percent of that needed for present plant practice, thus reducing atmospheric carbon emissions.

IS RENEWABLE ENERGY IMPORTANT?

Increasing concerns about greenhouse gases, global warming, and acid rain will make oil and coal less acceptable for long-term use. International agreements are being worked out to deal legally with these environmental matters. Moreover, because oil and coal supplies are depleting resources, there needs to be emphasis over the long term on energy alternatives, even if the environmental issues are resolved. While these questions are being raised about fossil fuels, new and renewable sources of energy are beginning to see some degree of maturity and, in many instances, now compete in economic terms with conventional sources. If the trend is accelerated, probably as much as 25 percent of the world's electricity production could come from renewable sources by the year 2025. It is also noticeable that the increased use of renewables also tends to come in tandem with aggressive conservation measures. Certainly, renewables have an increasingly important role to play in the energy mix of nearly all countries, and oil-deficient Caribbean countries in particular.

The importance of renewables and non-fossil fuel sources in future global energy use is directly dependent on their economic competitiveness. This group includes solar, wind, biomass, geothermal, hydropower, and nuclear sources of energy. Only hydropower and nuclear energy are important contributors today, with hydropower providing about 20 percent of global electricity and nuclear energy about 16 percent. There are limitations to the potential contributions of the renewable and non-fossil sources. The energy input to manufacture the renewables and their high initial capital costs are major issues. This question of net energy output, that is, output less the

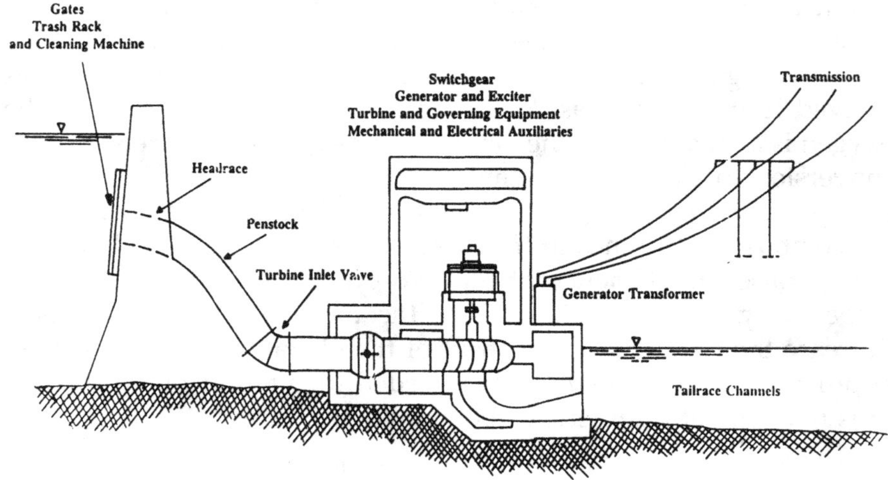

FIGURE 6.2 Schematic representation of a hydropower installation. (Adapted from Wright, 1996.)

energy input from other resources needed for their manufacture, is especially pertinent to biomass, where the energy input for their growth (for instance fertilizer and water) and processing are substantial. It is yet to be determined if the competitive lifetime cost per unit of delivered end-use energy is high.

The economics of hydropower and nuclear power are the best understood of all the renewables. They both need approximately the same capital investment per plant (per MW), about twice that of a coal-fired unit. When compared to coal, hydropower has no fuel cost and low maintenance and operating costs. Nuclear energy has a low fuel cost and high maintenance and operating costs. In the highly industrialized countries, nuclear power is now generally competitive with coal. Global growth of hydropower could be increased by four times the current level before it reaches the upper limit. However, both technologies are constrained by environmental issues. Figure 6.2 shows the schematics of a hydropower installation. Hydropower expansion requires flooding large areas and changing river flows. Nuclear power installations have a lesser environmental impact but are restrained by public concerns about the risk of accidental release of radioactivity from either the reactor or used fuel. For this reason, engineering developments have concentrated on ways to reduce the likelihood of accidents. When comparative evaluations of the risks to public health, safety, and environment are considered, nuclear power seems to be a better choice than coal at the present time.

Biomass is more difficult to analyse. In the developing world the true cost of biomass is not easy to assess because the sources are non-commercial (wood, agricultural wastes, animal dung) and, in most cases, require no capital, only labour. The labour time used for collection is high.

The use of commercial biomass fuel production through managed agriculture and forestry has been studied. Ethanol production from sugar cane in Brazil is a demonstration of commercial biomass utilization. Its success is questionable. For the production of net energy, Brazilian ethanol has been assessed as ranging from marginal to providing about 20 percent more energy than it consumes (Goldenberg et al., 1993). The tropics are the optimal areas for production of biomass through managed forestry. Also, managed forestry has a positive environmental impact. As reduction of carbon emissions becomes a global priority, managed biomass production is highly weighted because it sequesters or recirculates atmospheric carbon. Perhaps managed forestry should be used to sequester carbon rather than as a fuel because of its uncertain net energy contribution.

Solar and wind sources, although of low efficiency, have the potential to provide a significant proportion of future world energy needs. The major barrier is overcoming their intermittent nature with energy storage and expanded collectors. Unless a low cost electricity storage device is developed, the large-scale participation of solar and wind sources will be limited to about 10 percent of the net work capacity of fossil-based electricity systems.

It has been suggested that solar electricity be used to dissociate water for the production of hydrogen as a transportation fuel. This would achieve an ideal system of energy storage, no carbon emissions or pollutants, and an external primary energy resource. Although scientifically sound, there are practical economic and technological barriers. Many billions of cubic feet of pure hydrogen are being produced presently by the world's oil refineries at a fraction of the cost of electrolytic hydrogen. Further, there is indication that a transition from conventional energy systems to hydrogen-based systems will be of practical interest. Current developments suggest that economic and technical constraints will be removed, making the obvious merits of hydrogen combustion producing only water as a by-product a tantalizing concept. We will describe briefly some relevant renewable energy technologies – hydropower, solar thermal, PVs, wind, biomass, geothermal and fuel cells.

TABLE 6.2 Hydroelectric Plants Installed in Jamaica

Plant Location	Year Put in Service	Installed (MW)
Upper White River	1945	3.8
Lower White River	1952	4.9
Roaring River	1949	3.8
Rio Bueno A	1949	2.5
Maggotty Falls	1966	6.3
Constant Spring	1989	0.8
Rams Horn	1989	0.6
Rio Bueno River	1989	1.1
TOTAL		23.8

Data from Wright, 1996.

Hydropower

A number of Caribbean countries such as Guyana, Dominica, and Jamaica, have hydropower resources. Plants capable of generating some 23.8 MW of power are presently installed in Jamaica (Table 6.2) and there is the potential for about another 100 MW (Table 6.3).

The principle of hydropower is quite simple. Water flowing at Q cubic metres (cumec) per second and falling through a vertical height of h metres will lose energy at a rate of $Qhpg$ joules per second (Js), where p is the density of water, approximately 1000 kg^{-3} and g is 9.81 ms^{-2}. When the water is passed through a suitable turbine most of this energy can be converted into electricity. As an example, Q = 3 cumecs over a head of $h = 5$ m would produce about 15,000 Js^{-1}. In a hydropower system this would produce about 105,000 Js^{-1} or 105 kilowatt (kW). These figures imply a conversion efficiency of approximately 70 percent.

Resource systems should take into account energy losses. In a real system water will lose energy as a result of frictional drag and the turbulence as it flows in channels and through pipes, and the effective head will thus be less than the actual head.

Hydropower installations can be classified in different ways: by the effective head of water, whether low, medium, or high heads; the capacity, that is, the rated output; the type of turbine used (Figure 6.3); or the location and type of dam or reservoir.

Conventional hydropower schemes, such as high head, low flow Turgo and Pelton impulse machines, and the reaction machines that operate at low and medium heads, such as the cross flow Francis and Kaplan designs, are well known and operate in ranges indicated on Figure 6.4.

TABLE 6.3 Potential Hydropower Schemes, Jamaica (not Including Schemes less than 0.8 MW)

Hydropower Scheme	Installed Capacity (MW)
Back Rio Grande (BRG)	50.5
BRG Upper (Incremental)	6.0
Rio Grande	4.4
Great River	8.0
Laughlands Great River	5.3
Rio Cobre	1.0
Negro River (two schemes)	1.9 (1 + 0.9)
Yallahs River	2.6
Wild Cane River	2.5
Morgans River	2.3
Green River	1.4
Spanish River	2.3
Dry River	0.8
Martha Brae River	5.4
Swift River	2.8
TOTAL	97.0

Data from Wright, 1996.

Environmental impacts from hydropower generation can be grouped in three main categories:

- Hydrological effects on water flows, groundwater, water supply, and irrigation needs
- Ecological effects on plants and animals, as well as the land itself
- Social implications for landowners and the displacement of persons

There is still little agreement on how to translate environmental gains into the economic data that are used in comparing options. One issue of pertinence is the costing of long-term compensation for people who have been displaced or had their productivity adversely affected by new hydroelectric installations.

Due to the high capital costs of hydropower schemes, they are sensitive to the high interest rate regime of recent years in Caribbean countries. For this reason, it is paradoxical that, on close analysis, hydropower schemes look favourable in retrospect but uncertain in prospect. However, hydropower compares unfavourably with fuel-consuming

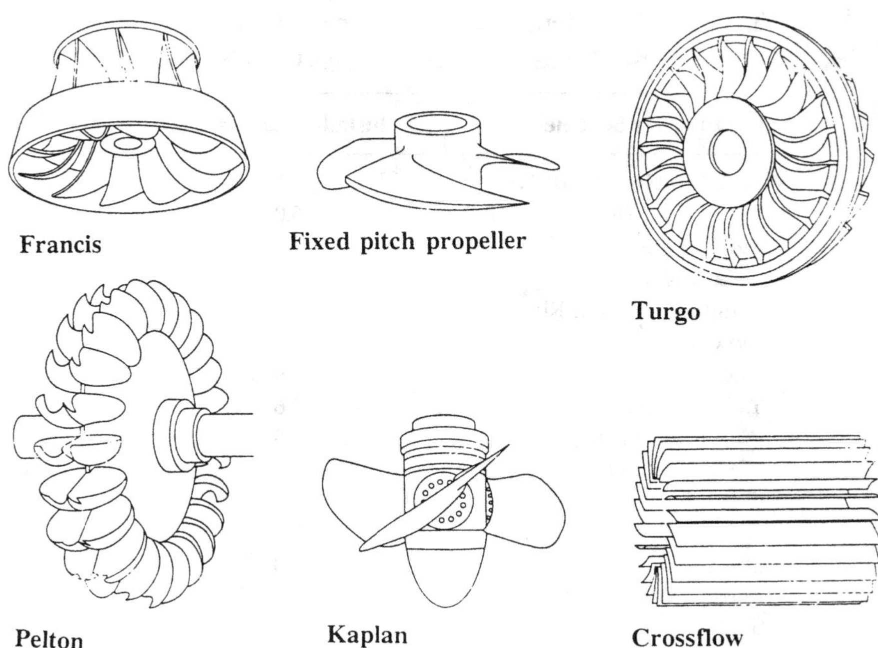

FIGURE 6.3 Types of turbine configurations. (Adapted from Ramage, 1996.)

alternatives which have costs that are more evenly spread over the life of the plant.

From an investor's viewpoint, the fact that the hydropower plant will be producing power in the year 2050, long after the capital is paid for, is of little immediate interest. However, it will interest future generations when they realize that a significant portion of the conventional energy resources have been used up.

Solar Thermal Energy

Solar thermal systems vary from passive approaches, such as daylighting, to active systems, such as solar water heaters, parabolic trough and dish concentrator systems, solar ponds, and central receiver systems. These systems are reviewed by Wright (1996).

The 10-MW Solar One system at Barstow, California is an example of a central receiver system. It uses a field of tracking heliostats, which reflect the sun's rays onto a boiler atop a central tower. Temperatures rise to over 500°C and the systems use molten rock salt or high-temperature synthetic oils. Rock salt is a preferred heat transfer medium because of its high thermal capacity and conductivity. The hot salt is used to produce high-temperature steam that drives a turbine.

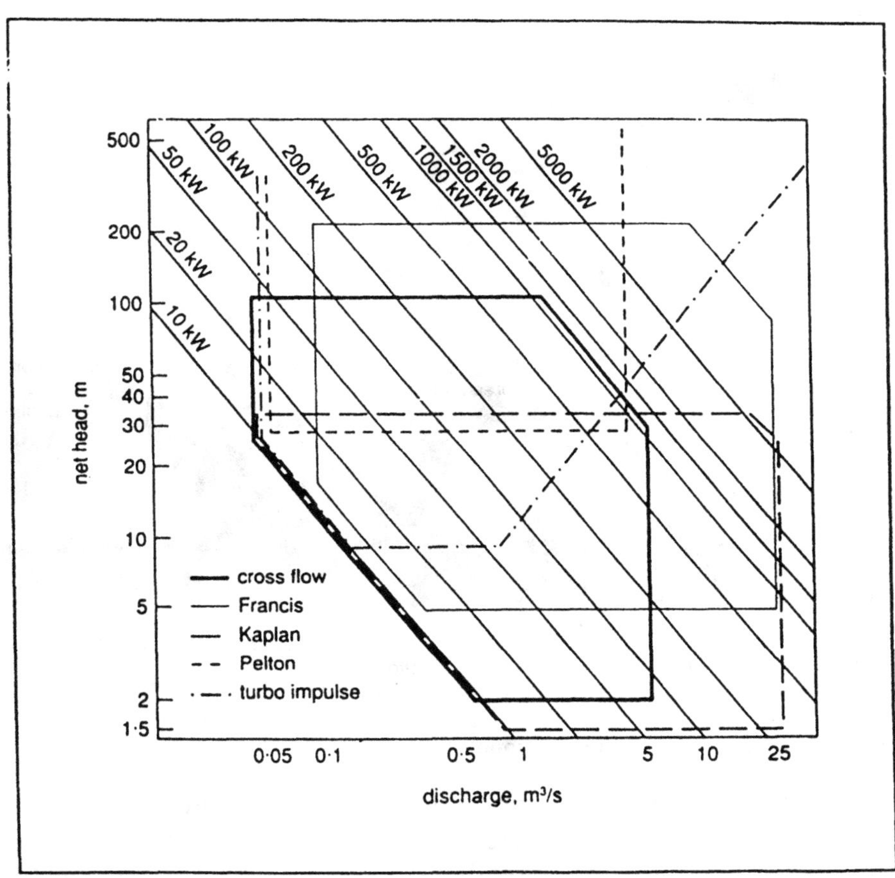

FIGURE 6.4 Net head plotted against flow rate for hydropower turbines.

The Luz International parabolic trough concentrator systems operated uneconomically, in the Mojave Desert, California. The collectors heated synthetic oil to 390°C, which then produced high-temperature steam through a heat exchanger. Efficiencies of about 14 percent were possible, on par with PV systems. All operations presently using the parabolic trough system are having financial difficulties. The parabolic dish concentrator systems put the engine itself at the focus of a mirror. Both Stirling and small steam engines have been used. At present, only developmental experiments exist in Germany and Spain.

Solar ponds use a salt pond as a type of flat plate collector (Figure 6.5). If the pond has a proper gradient with fresh water at the top and salt water at the bottom, solar energy is absorbed on the bottom of the pond. (The salt water at the bottom is heavier than the

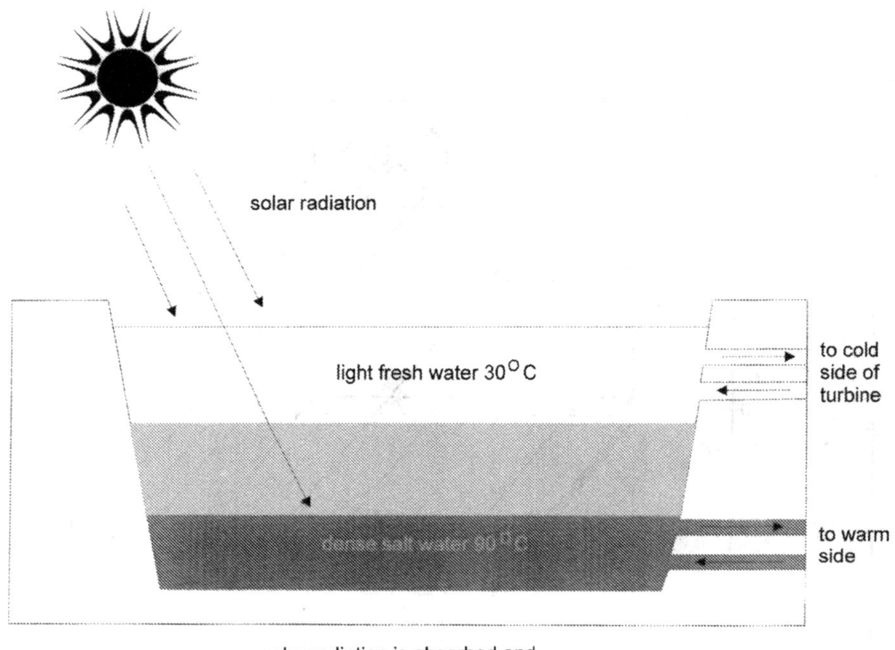

FIGURE 6.5 Schematic of a solar pond.

fresh water on top so it cannot rise.) The fresh water acts as an insulating blanket and the bottom temperatures can reach more than 90°C, a temperature high enough to operate a vapour cycle engine. However, the low temperatures mean low conversion efficiencies, less than 2 percent. Large quantities of water are needed to maintain the salt gradient. Commercial systems have been attempted in Israel, Saudi Arabia, and the U.S.

About 3500 solar water heaters (Figure 6.6) have been installed in Jamaica and 34,000 have been installed in Barbados, in a market stimulated by fiscal incentives. The most popular unit is about 250 litres (60 gallons) in size. Increase in the market size in all Caribbean countries could be stimulated by economic incentives and by regulations making it mandatory to have solar water heaters installed in new housing and commercial developments. Perhaps this could begin with all new government buildings. There is also a need to provide working capital for solar water heater loans to consumers as well as manufacturing and inventory finance to suppliers.

Solar stills could be used to provide all or most of the distilled water used in Jamaican industry. They produce small volumes at a

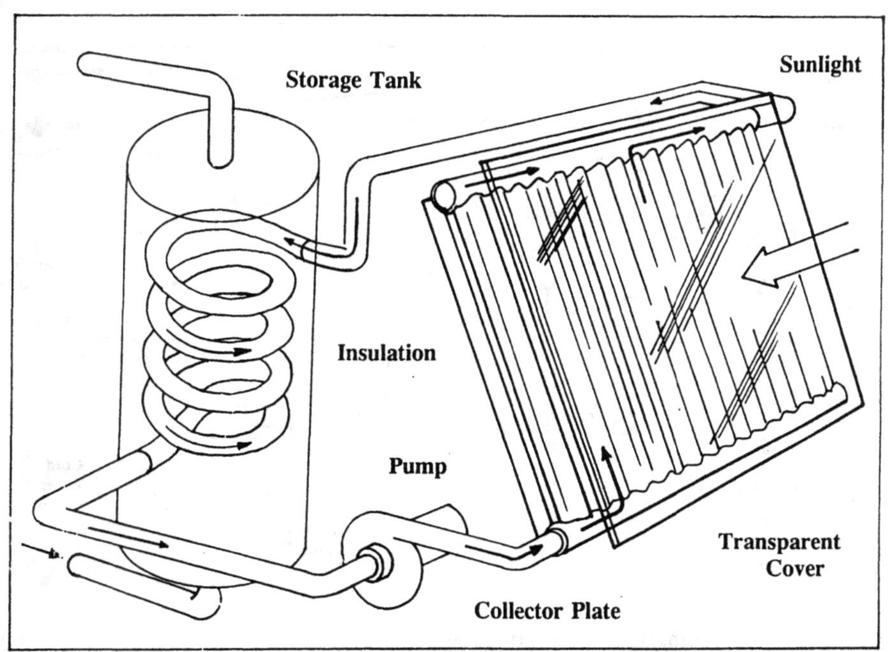

FIGURE 6.6 Flat plate solar collector.

rate of about 3 to 6 litres per square metre per day. Solar crop dryers have an important application in food preservation and lumber drying, throughout the Caribbean (Headley, 1995).

Ocean thermal energy conversion (OTEC) is a relatively new solar thermal technology that is currently being tested for commercial use as a renewable energy source. The OTEC energy generation system is dependent on the temperature difference that exists between warm surface waters and cold deep-ocean waters. A temperature difference of at least 20°C is a prerequisite for a viable OTEC operation. This condition is likely to be more available in tropical and subtropical seas.

In the tropics, there is a significant temperature difference between surface and deep water, the latter also being rich in nutrients such as nitrates and phosphates. If the warm and cold water (20°C difference) are brought together, a turbine can be operated to generate electricity by OTEC. There are two methods of generating such energy. The "closed cycle" system uses a working fluid, such as ammonia or freon, which evaporates in a heat exchanger through which warm water passes. Vapour is produced at high pressure and this is used to drive a turbine that generates electricity. The exhaust vapour from the turbine

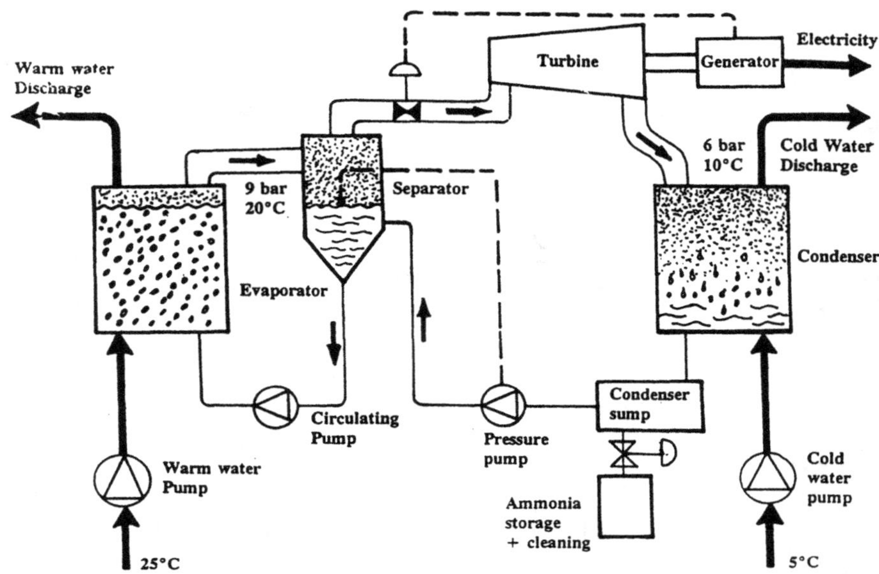

FIGURES 6.7 Schematic of a closed-cycle ocean thermal energy conversion (OTEC) system.

is condensed back into liquid in a heat exchanger through which cold water passes (Figure 6.7).

"Open cycle" OTEC uses sea water as the working fluid, the sea water being flash evaporated under a partial vacuum. The low-pressure steam is passed through an extremely large turbine that produces energy (Figure 6.8). Spent vapour is cooled in a condenser and because the condensate is not returned directly to an evaporator it is called open-cycle. Powerful vacuum pumps not only maintain the vacuum required to make the warm sea water flash evaporate but remove much of the large quantities of gases dissolved in the sea water. Desalinized water is a by-product of closed-cycle OTEC, whereas aquaculture and air-conditioning are ancillary products of both closed-cycle and open-cycle OTEC, both of which utilize cold, deep water.

Although OTEC has been demonstrated experimentally to be a sound technology for producing positive net electric power, certain design and economic uncertainties have hindered its commercial development so far. Further, the problem of financing huge OTEC power installations is complicated by the fact that lending institutions need to be convinced that OTEC is a well-proven technology and that the operation of any OTEC plant is economically viable. Evidence has

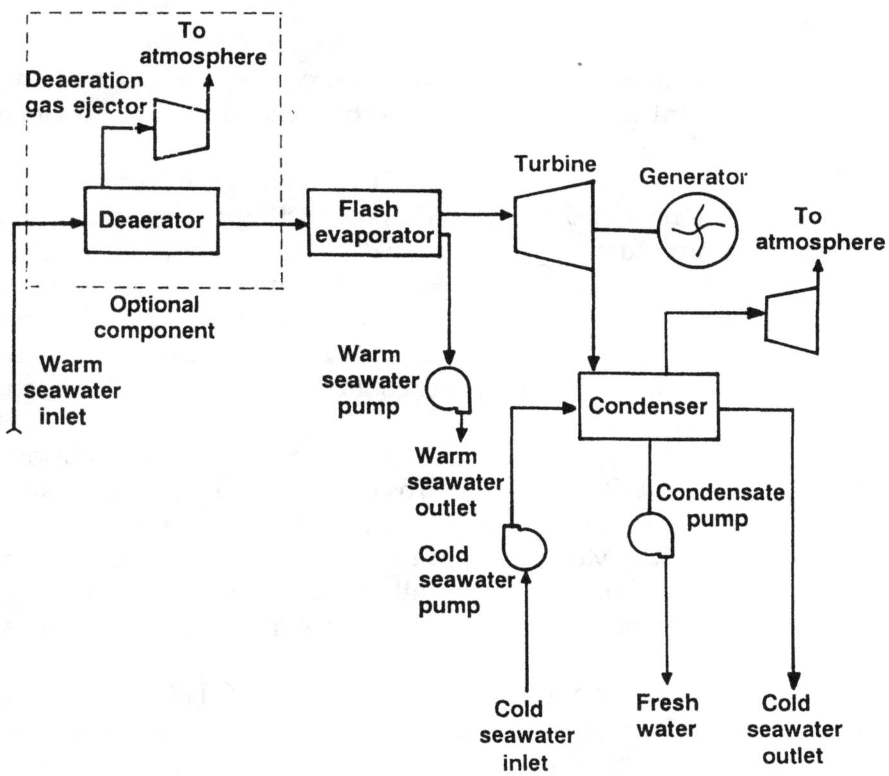

FIGURE 6.8 Principle of an open-cycle ocean thermal energy conversion (OTEC) system.

accumulated over the past 5 years to show that the economic viability of an OTEC plant can be significantly improved if, in addition to producing electricity, by-products of OTEC can also be profitably utilized. There is a general realization among those working on OTEC technology that the time is right to go ahead with a small pilot plant at a commercial scale which would provide sufficient operational information to plan, design, and finance large-scale commercial OTEC plants. The size of this early commercial pilot plant would vary between 2 MW and 10 MW.

One of the key components of an OTEC system is a continuous supply of cold sea water pumped up from ocean depths. These deep-ocean waters not only have low temperatures, but are also rich in nutrients and are more or less sterile. However, the installation of a cold-water pipeline to pump the water up represents a significant technical challenge, and, depending upon the coastal underwater topography, length and diameter of piping required, flow rates, and pumping power needed, it can become the most expensive component of any OTEC system. There are some problems in laying the pipeline and there are also high costs in servicing and maintaining the pipeline over time. The pipe should be made from polyethylene and be relatively light.

The greatest advance made in OTEC technology in recent years has been in the heat exchangers. Whereas costly titanium was used in the past, aluminium can now be used instead without any significant corrosion or bio-fouling problems. Titanium costs about $26 per kilogram, whereas aluminium costs approximately $2 per kilogram at the ingot stage. Thus, important cost savings can be realized without loss of performance of the heat exchanger (Tanner, 1995; Lennard, 1995).

A number of Caribbean islands have the bathymetric conditions suitable for OTEC technology – Andros Island, Antigua, Aruba, Bahamas, Cayman, Cuba, Curaçao, Dominica, Grenada, Guadeloupe, Jamaica, Martinique, Montserrat, St Lucia, Turks and Caicos Islands, and the U.S. Virgin Islands, among others. A 5-MW OTEC plant will require approximately 3 to 4 hectares of land area and 100 metres of ocean frontage.

One of the most important components of an OTEC system is a continuous supply of cold sea water pumped up from ocean depths. These ocean waters not only have low temperatures but they are also rich in nutrients. Compared to warm surface water, inorganic nitrate-nitrite values in deep cold water are 190 times higher, phosphate values 15 times higher, and silicate values 25 times higher. Aquaculturists have long viewed such waters as a valuable resource that can be utilized for growing a mix of aquatic animals and plants. This ability of the OTEC system to provide flexible, accurate, and consistent temperature control, high volume flow rates, and sea water that is relatively free of biological and chemical contaminants, can be translated into a saleable aquaculture product.

In some geographical locations, in addition to power generation and aquaculture, OTEC can be used to provide fresh and potable water, air conditioning, and specialized agriculture using drip irrigation. If there is a local need for these by-products the economics of an OTEC power plant operation can be significantly improved.

Although the upcoming deep cold water becomes warmer as it passes through the power generating section of the OTEC plant, it is still too cold for most aquaculture applications. Approximately 1 gallon of fresh water can be produced per degree of temperature rise, for each 1000 gallons of cold sea water flowing through the heat exchanger. Hence, a 5-degree rise in the temperature of the exhaust from the OTEC plant, which would leave the cold water at a temperature suitable for aquaculture activities, could produce 5 gallons of fresh water for every 1000 gallons of sea water passing through the heat exchangers.

The deep, cold water that is pumped up could provide effective and relatively inexpensive air conditioning after it has gone through the OTEC power plant. If sited near a town the cold water could be used for "district air conditioning" in much the same way as "district heating" in Sweden. The cold water, put through a heat exchanger, could offset approximately 20 times the electrical energy that an OTEC plant actually produces. Hence, theoretically, a 1-MW plant could, in a suitable location, handle up to 20 MW of air conditioning load. In practice it is likely to be less.

Commercial OTEC plants will have some negative effects on the marine environment. Construction facilities may disrupt the seabed, temporarily destroying marine ecosystems, and maintenance routines to reduce bio-fouling may increase the level of toxic substances. If ammonia, freon, or some other environmentally hazardous working fluid were to be spilled accidentally from a closed-cycle OTEC plant the environmental effect on fish life in the immediate surroundings could be serious.

On the positive side, OTEC facilities release no additional heat and little carbon dioxide when compared with similar-sized conventional fossil-fueled power plants. Open-cycle OTEC produces more carbon dioxide than closed-cycle OTEC, yet the immediate carbon dioxide release from an open-cycle OTEC plant would be approximately 15 to 20 times smaller than the emission from a similar-sized fossil fuel power plant. Further, the release of carbon dioxide could be ameliorated if the discharge water is used for mariculture or other secondary operations.

Most of the developmental work on OTEC has been directed to the production of energy. However, plans for an early commercial OTEC plant may be better implemented with freshwater production in conjunction with energy generation. The high throughput rate (450 m^3 per second for a 100-MW open cycle plant) allows fresh water to be generated at rates comparable to municipal requirements (Tanner, 1995). In areas where fresh water is at a premium, such as some Pacific and Caribbean islands, OTEC-generated fresh water can be cheaper than that generated by other means such as reverse osmosis. Malta is a classic example of the potential application of OTEC technology for supplying fresh water. At present, the major portion of Malta's fresh water is desalinated at the country's five plants, which consume some 15 percent of the country's electricity production and makes it the most expensive water in the Mediterranean area (Tanner, 1995).

Present problems and constraints on OTEC are that:

- Investors and governments are conservative in their approach and often unwilling to invest in technology that has no proven track record.
- OTEC has high capital costs, particularly in the large turbines, heat exchangers, and pipes. However, these costs are rapidly being engineered downwards and will further improve as OTEC technology expands.
- OTEC does have competition from other conventional energy forms that are lower in cost at present. This cost differential will be reduced as fossil fuel prices increase and OTEC costs decrease. At the same time, it is competing with other renewable energy sources (such as wind) that are more competitive. OTEC has a specific market niche (tropical islands lacking fresh water) in which it will become economically feasible.
- OTEC has geographic limitations because near-shore sites require an appropriate slope of the ocean floor and a temperature difference of 20°C to be operationally effective. Floating systems offshore will enhance the versatility of OTEC.

In essence, OTEC technology needs cost reduction, particularly in pipe construction and installation. When OTEC becomes a carefully planned part of national energy policies that incorporate energy, environmental, and economic issues, the technology will grow. Its time should come during the first two decades of this century.

Photovoltaic Energy

Photovoltaics (PVs) are solar cell devices that absorb light and convert it into electricity through the use of semiconducting materials (Figure 6.9). If an electric field exists within the semiconductor, the negative electrons and positive holes move in opposite directions, and this electrical charge separation results in the creation of a voltage. It is the only technology that does not convert renewable resource energy into mechanical energy to generate electricity. Discounted electricity production costs show PVs to be more expensive than oil, probably until the year 2015. Its application has proven technically useful in both large-scale utility networks and remote locations where other fuel

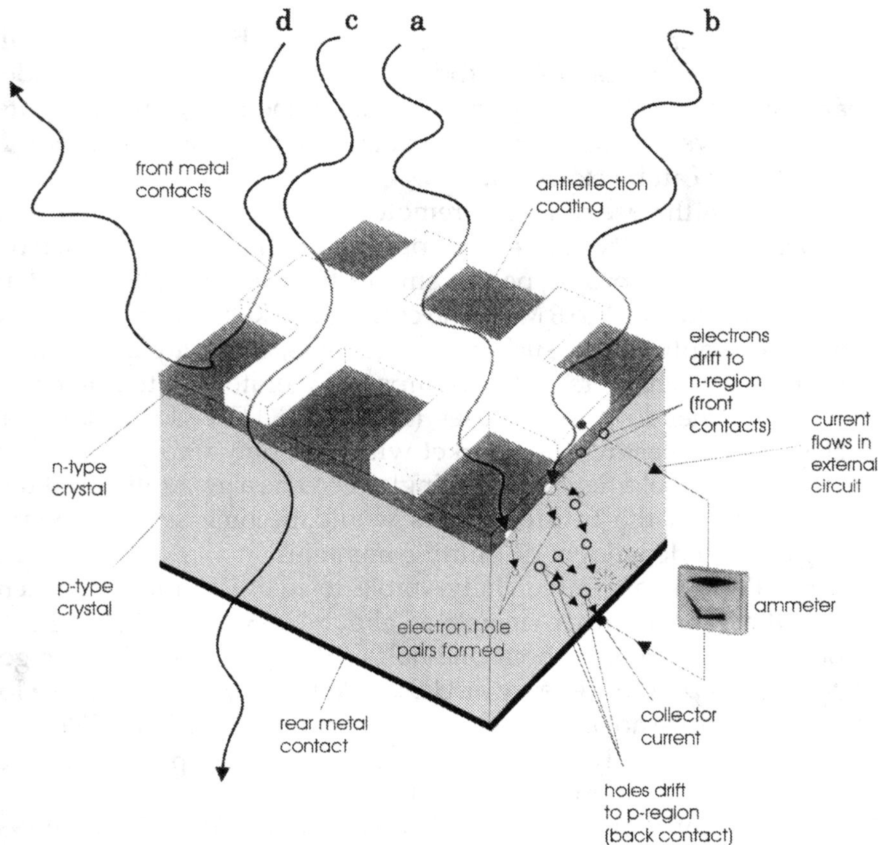

FIGURE 6.9 A solar cell is a wafer of p-type silicon with a thin layer of n-type silicon on one side. A photon of light penetrating the cell near the junction of the two types of crystal will encounter a silicon atom (**a**). It dislodges one of the electrons, leaving a hole. The energy needed to promote the electron into the conduction band is known as the bandgap. The electron so promoted tends to migrate into the layer of n-type silicon, and the hole tends to migrate into the layer of p-type silicon. The electron will then travel to a current collector on the front surface of the cell, generating an electric current in the external circuit. It then reappears in the layer of p-type silicon, where it may recombine with waiting holes. When a photon with an amount of energy greater than the bandwidth strikes a silicon atom (**b**), it will again give rise to an electron-hole pair, and the excess energy is converted into heat. If the amount of energy in a photon is less than the bandwidth it will pass through the cell (**c**), so that it surrenders virtually no energy along the way. Some photons are also reflected from the front surface of the cell even with an antiflective coating (**d**).

sources are restricted. In addition, during the past decade, PV cell efficiencies have increased from 5 to as much as 30 percent.

Rapid deployment of PV technology in the user market is not expected. Those working on this energy-producing technology will have to transfer it from the laboratory to the production line and build consumer confidence in PVs. Today, the PV industry remains a dedicated yet relatively small part of the total energy production enterprise. However, markets are now expanding and gradual growth for the industry can be expected.

Although the use of PVs in remote applications has been increasing over time, utility-connected applications have been restricted to test facilities and prototype systems in the western U.S., and have been of the order of 1 to 6 MW. The current marketing trend is towards consumer applications, such as street lamps, walkway lights, calculators, battery chargers, water pumps, refrigerators, cathodic protection, and other low power uses (Figure 6.4). The U.S., Japan, and Germany are meeting this market with thin-film amorphous silicon technology. Should flexible PV shingles become a generally used roofing material in the future, houses would become self-sufficient in energy and independent of utility companies.

It will become commercially viable to manufacture PV systems when they can produce energy at about U.S.$ 0.12/kWh. The PV module will represent about one-half of this cost. The ultimate goal is for PVs to produce energy at U.S.$ 0.06 to 0.09/kWh. At these low prices, which are not expected to take effect until after 2010, PVs could competitively supply electricity needs, at least in part, in tropical countries such as those in the Caribbean.

The international market for PVs was approximately 85 MW in 1996. PV modules are constructed from several solar cells. The modules vary in size but are generally about 1 square metre and deliver no more than 60 to 150 watts at that size. The modules are arranged in ways that can track the sun's movement so as to maximize their performance.

There are two requirements for a solar cell: (1) a large semiconductor diode capable of collecting as much light as possible and (2) electrical contacts on each of the diodes; one side should collect the incident light.

The simplest way to establish an electrical field is by joining two dissimilar semiconductors to create a p-n junction. The electrical field at the junction attracts electrons from the p-side and forces them to the negative side (n-side), thus making it negatively charged. At the same time holes from the n-side are forced to the p-side (positive side), making this positively charged. This electric field creates a voltage. The electrical current is transmitted to an external load via the metal contacts on the p and the n layers.

The primary criterion for choosing a solar cell material is its energy gap. The voltage generated by a cell is a fraction (known as the energy factor) of its energy gap. Hence, the larger the energy gap the higher the voltage (Hill, 1995). A semiconductor will absorb light only if the photon energy is more than the energy gap of the semiconductor. In respect of the sun, which has its energy spread over a wide range of photon energy (colours), the greater the energy gap the smaller the amount of sunlight that can be absorbed, and thus the lower the current. Therefore, there is an optimum energy gap for a solar cell at which the sum of current and voltage is a maximum. The optimum value is about 1.4 electric volts (eV) (Hill, 1995). A number of semiconductors are close to the optimum gap, including silicon, gallium arsenide, indium phosphide, and cadmium telluride. Copper indium diselenide, amorphous silicon, and alloys of these materials are also close to the optimum.

Sunlight has a maximum power of 1000 watts per square meter (W/m^2), so solar cells must cover a large area in order to collect significant amounts of power. The large area should be available at as low a cost as possible and the cells should be manufactured by low-cost methods. Although the latest monocrystalline silicon PV modules are fairly efficient, they are expensive. This is because they are manufactured by the Czochralski process, which is slow and laborious as well as energy intensive. Another reason is that until about 1993 solar cells were made from highly pure "electronic-grade" polycrystalline silicon. However, PV cells are now made from less pure "solar-grade" silicon with only a small decrease in conversion efficiency.

Silicon is the most researched element and, as a result, much development has taken place for the electronic industry. Silicon cells are used as silicon ribbon cells, polycrystalline silicon cells, polycrystalline thin-film silicon cells, and amorphous silicon.

Silicon ribbon cells are produced from a polycrystalline or single crystal silicon melted and made into a thin "ribbon" of monocrystalline silicon by a process known as "edge-defined, film-fed growth." This technology, developed by Mobil Solar in the U.S., is now used by a German group in the electric utility business.

Polycrystalline silicon consists mainly of small grains of monocrystalline silicon. Usually the molten polycrystalline silicon is cast into ingots, which are cut by fine wire saws into thin square wafers and made into complete cells, in the same manner as monocrystalline cells. The wafers are doped p-type during growth, and the p-n junction is formed by introducing thin layers of donors on one surface by diffusion from a gas or paste in a furnace (Hill, 1995).

Silicon reflects about 30 percent of the incident light and this must be reduced to less than 5 percent using, among other techniques, antireflective coatings. Although polycrystalline PV cells are easier and cheaper to manufacture than monocrystalline counterparts, the light generated charge carriers (electrons and holes) can recombine at the boundaries between the grains within polycrystalline silicon before they cross the junction and contribute to the power output of the cell. This recombination is prevented by hydrogen treatment and by reducing the concentration of impurities that support recombination. Surfaces act as recombination centres and are inactivated by growing an oxide layer on the surface. Polycrystalline cells now in commercial production have efficiencies of approximately 10 to 12 percent.

Polycrystalline "thin-film" silicon cells are typically between 0.001 and 0.002 millimetres thick, compared with 0.3 millimetres for a typical "thick-film" silicon cell. Since the manufacturing techniques are less costly than making ("growing") single cells they have much potential for low-cost, high-volume production. Polycrystalline thin films, deposited on ceramic substrates, form the bases of PV cells with efficiencies as high as 15 percent.

Silicon can also be made into a less structured form called amorphous silicon (a-Si) in which the silicon atoms are less ordered than in the crystalline form. Solar cells using a-Si have a different type of junction between the p- and n-type material. A so-called "p-i-n" junction is usually formed, consisting of a very thin layer of p-type a-Si on top, followed by a thicker "intrinsic" layer of undoped a-Si and then an extremely thin layer of n-type a-Si. Amorphous silicon cells are cheaper to produce and better light absorbers than crystalline silicon. The manufacturing process requires less energy and it can be deposited on a wide variety of substitutes, including glass and plastics and steel. However, efficiencies are low (7 to 8 percent), and degrades with exposure to sunlight.

Gallium arsenide cells have high light absorption coefficients and are better light absorbers, so they have high efficiencies. They are much more expensive than silicon cells though, largely because gallium and arsenic are not common materials. Thus, gallium arsenide PV cells are used in specialized high technology applications.

Copper indium silenenide (CIS) cells have production efficiencies of 10 percent and do not suffer from the performance degradation observed in a-Si modules. Indium is an expensive material but the quantities needed are small. Also, parts of the CIS manufacturing process require the use of hydrogen selenide gas, which is highly toxic.

Cadmium telluride (CdTe) is another compound semiconductor used for thin-film PV cells. The bandgap of CdTe is close to the optimum and efficiencies are around 10 percent. Screen printing technologies can be used to effect low-cost production at small scale. Electroplating or a vacuum deposition process can be used for CdTe cells, thus lowering cost. Again, there are environmental effects because cadmium in the manufacturing, use, and disposal processes is highly toxic.

The standard PV module is usually a collection of 36 cells, each 10×10 cm, connected in series, mechanically supported and protected from corrosion. The outer surface of the module is normally iron-tempered glass. The low iron content enhances the transparency of the glass. Tempered glass has impact resistance and glass is a cheap waterproof material. The protective backing for the cells may be glass, plastic, or metal. Plastic foil is most common, combining lightness, low cost, and high thermal conductivity, ensuring that cell temperatures do not rise too high in operation. The wafer cells are then encapsulated in a compound that is transparent, ultraviolet (UV) resistant, and allows for thermal expansion. This laminate usually consists of glass/glass or fibre/plastic foil. Modules in production today have expected lifetimes of over 30 years based on accelerated life testing. In 2000, the average international price for a silicon wafer PV module in bulk orders was approximately U.S.$ 4.0/peak watts (Wp). Prices should reach $3 to 3.5/Wp by the year 2006.

PV systems cannot run without sunlight. Sunlight is a diffuse fuel source, hence, PV systems are energy limited and, with the present state of technology, are probably not the best choice for applications with high power requirements, such as air conditioning – especially if they are needed at night. Battery storage is required for night use, increasing system cost and complexity. In addition, there is a high initial cost. To address this, some sort of financing is required to spread the high capital cost of PV systems out over the life of the system and make them more accessible to potential users. Also, batteries need regular maintenance and eventual replacement. Some training is also useful to safely operate a complete PV system.

PV modules produce direct current (DC) electricity only, so an inverter must be added to the system to run alternating current (AC) devices. Although this adds to the total system cost, it enables the use of more readily available and cheaper AC appliances. There is also an issue of vulnerability. The modular characteristic that allows easy expansion of PV systems also leaves them vulnerable to theft and vandalism. Although PV field applications require a large land area (0.8 km^2 per 100 MW), grass and other low-lying growth remain largely undisturbed, so that small livestock can graze in PV fields.

Silicon does not pose an environmental health hazard on disposal. This is not necessarily the case with other heavy metals such as cadmium telluride, cadmium sulphide, gallium arsenide, and copper indium diselenide, which can be hazardous if the solar cell arrays are burnt, producing poisons (arsenic) or toxic gases. Cadmium, for example, is poisonous and possibly carcinogenic. It is a health risk both at the production and disposal phases and thus good factory management is essential.

The present PV market has three major segments – consumer products, remote power, and utility generation. Although the consumer market was once dominated by calculators and watches, battery chargers and security lights are growing rapidly and have now become the largest part of this market. Utility companies are investigating the technology both for possible future use as well as to learn how it interacts with their systems. One approach is for utility companies to sell or lease small systems for remote cabins and homes. The remote power sector is by far the largest market today used to power vaccine refrigerators in health clinics, pump and disinfect water, provide lighting, and power communication systems. French Polynesia alone has over 2500 individual PV power systems. An important segment of the Caribbean market consists of providing backup power for computer systems and protection from blackouts on grid-line electricity. More than 200 PV systems are presently installed in Jamaica for practical and demonstrative purposes.

One high-cost component of the PV system at present is storage batteries because of their high initial cost and short lifetime (3 to 5 years). The cost mainly affects remote systems. Utility grid-attached systems for peak power, or PV systems used with existing hydropower schemes in a hybrid arrangement, are usually not in need of storage. In remote areas, hybrid PV-diesel generator systems (Figure 6.10) typically will cost less than a stand-alone PV system for loads ranging from 6 to 250 kWh/day. Also, a PV-diesel hybrid will have a lower operating cost than a primary diesel electric generator.

Building-integrated PV systems will be an important part of future construction. There is potential for incorporating PV modules into shading devices, rainscreen overcladding, wall cladding, and roof systems. High rise residential units and conventional housing also offer generating potential, although the lack of an appropriate load match in the case of housing means that PV-clad buildings in this category would have to export the bulk of electricity to the distribution networks. Building-integrated PV installations are not likely to be a retrofit option. In any event, it appears that conventional cladding is

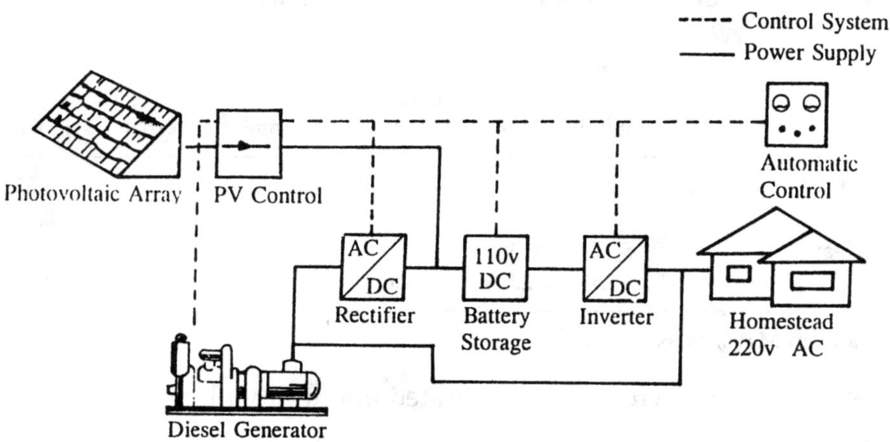

FIGURE 6.10 Hybrid photovoltaic and diesel system.

likely to remain a cheaper option than PV cladding at least until 2010 when there will be significant reductions in unit costs (Abbate, 1996, 2001).

The next decade promises rapid increases in growth for PVs as the utility power market comes into economic reach. The successful future use of PVs in electricity grid operations seems certain and awaits only the required cost reduction in solar collectors to be economical.

Wind Energy

Wind power is a renewable energy resource that has become widely recognized during this decade. If expectations are met, windpower could provide as much as 2.5 percent of the world's electricity and 10 percent of the electricity in some Caribbean countries by the year 2020 (Wright, 2001).

Wind has been used for over 3000 years for the pumping of water, the milling of grain, and other mechanical power applications. Water pumping is the principal use of wind turbines today, although the use of wind power as a way of generating electricity on a large scale is attracting interest. Wind turbines are the modern counterpart of windmills and are also called wind generators or aerogenerators.

Like other renewable energy resources, wind power provides a better energy balance, more local investment and employment, and less reliance on imports than other forms of energy. Wind power is becoming more attractive worldwide as environmental externality costs, including those penalizing fossil fuel emissions and nuclear

TABLE 6.4 Comparative Cost of Electricity Generation (EU cents/kWh)

	Capital	Fuel	Operation & Maintenance	Total	External	Full Cost
Wind (7.5 m/s site)	5.2	0	1.6	6.8	0.05	6.85
Coal	2.0	2.8	0.7	5.5	2.5	8.0
Nuclear	5.1	1.9	1.3	8.3	2.5	10.8
Gas	0.25	2.8	0.6	3.65	0.95	4.6

Data from Mays, 1996.

safety risks, are increasingly integrated into utility planning accounting systems.

The cost of wind energy-generating equipment fell sharply in the 1990s and the technology also improved in reliability. Today, at good sites, if external costs are considered, wind is more economical than coal and nuclear energy but costs more than gas (Table 6.4).

Wind energy has the advantages of being widespread and non-depletable. No heat, air, or water pollution is produced when wind power is converted to energy. In contrast to thermal plants (coal, nuclear, fuel oil), it does not require water for the production of electricity. Its disadvantages are the low density of the energy and the wind's variability. The low density means that the initial cost of wind turbines is relatively high. If on-site storage is needed, then the initial cost can double.

In the early part of this century small windmills were used for water pumping and electric power generation. Between 1930 and 1950 a few (10 to 20 MW) experimental, wind-powered electric systems were built in Europe and North America. By the second half of the 1950s, however, electric wind generators were displaced by inexpensive, centralized oil and coal electric power generation. When a 300 percent increase in world oil prices occurred between 1973 and 1974 wind turbines were again envisioned as an alternative source of energy. Since that time research and development of wind energy by government and industry has resulted in the emergence of the modern wind energy industry.

The progress in harnessing wind energy over the past 10 years suggests that a gradual shift to alternative energy will become feasible. Wind power has developed rapidly, both in terms of cost effectiveness and technical performance. While traditional energy costs have been rising, wind energy costs have been declining. Larger and more efficient manufacturing, advances in technology, and improved experience with wind turbines have contributed to this trend. Meanwhile, as the number of systems in operation has grown, the cost of maintaining the systems has fallen significantly. Wind technology is already the least costly source of renewable energy, ahead of PVs and solar thermal, and could become the most economic new source of electricity during this decade. At advantageous sites, wind power costs are presently competitive with power from conventional sources such as coal and oil.

Wind energy provides other economic benefits, such as greatly reduced environmental impact, reduced dependence on fossil fuels, and flexibility in electric power planning as a result of the simplicity and modularity of wind turbines. Another socio-economic benefit is its compatibility with other land uses, such as animal rearing and agriculture. Policy makers are realizing that these benefits have value and should be considered when calculating energy costs. According to a 1989 report by the California Energy Commission, which concluded that the selection of energy technologies should be based on societal benefits and costs, wind power had one of the lowest societal costs (Taylor, 1996).

As the technology improved, the cost of energy from properly maintained 250- to 500-kW wind turbines fell from U.S.$ 0.90/kWh in 1973 to less than U.S.$ 0.10/kWh in 1995. A wind turbine is economically feasible only if its overall earnings exceed its overall costs within the lifetime of the system. The time at which earnings equal costs is called the payback period. The relatively large initial cost means that this period could be a number of years. Of course, a short payback is preferable and a payback of 5 to 7 years is acceptable. Longer paybacks should be viewed with caution.

The energy available from wind is its kinetic energy and is equal to half the mass, m, of the air times the square of its velocity, V. Thus, kinetic energy = $\frac{1}{2} mV^2$.

Power is the rate at which energy is used or converted and can be expressed as energy per unit of time, for instance, as joules per second (Js^{-1}). The standard unit of power is the watt (W) and one watt equals one joule per second, that is, $1 \text{ W} = 1 \text{ Js}^{-1}$.

Energy per unit of time is equal to power, so the power in the wind can also be expressed as:

power, P (watts) = kinetic energy per second (joules per second).

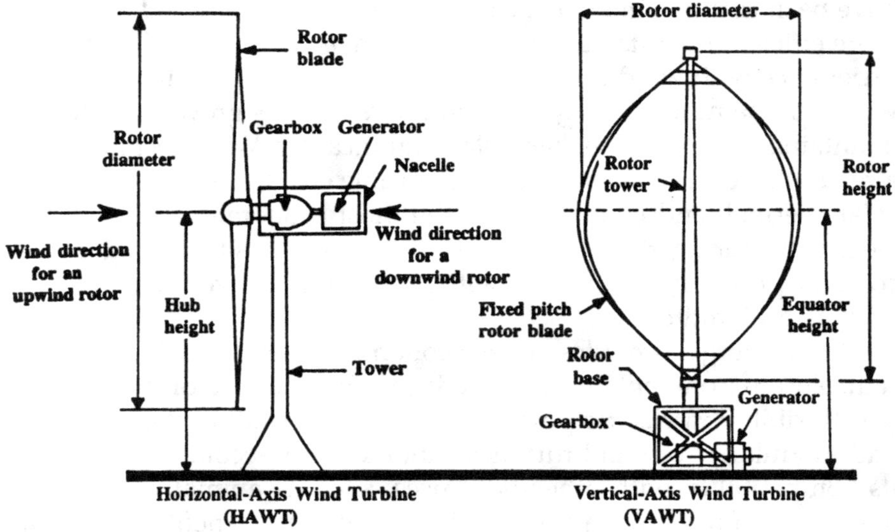

FIGURE 6.11 Schematic overview of wind turbine components.

Two major relationships may be calculated showing that the power in the wind is proportional to the cube of the velocity of the wind, and the area through which the wind is passing.

The power contained in the wind is not the amount of power that can be extracted by a wind turbine, because of losses incurred in the energy conversion process. There are two basic configurations for wind turbines: horizontal axis turbines and vertical axis turbines (Figure 6.11). At present, the horizontal axis turbines are more competitive. They range in size from small turbines producing a few tens of watts to turbines as large as 1.6 MW.

In order to interact with as much as possible of the wind passing through the rotor swept area, wind turbines have one to many blades, although two- and three-bladed machines are most popular. The blades of a multi-blade machine interact with all of the wind at low tip speed ratios, whereas the blades of two- or three-bladed low-solidity turbines have to travel faster to interact with as much of the wind as possible passing through. Theoretically, the more blades a wind turbine rotor carries, the more efficient it should be, but large numbers of blades tend to interfere with each other, so multi-bladed, high-solidity wind turbines are usually of lesser overall efficiency than low-solidity turbines. Three-bladed rotors are usually the most energy efficient; two-bladed and one-bladed rotors are slightly less efficient.

Torque is important in wind turbine applications. Torque is the moment about the centre of rotation due to the driving force presented by the wind to the rotor blades. Torque is measured in newton-metres (Nm). For a given amount of power, the higher the angular velocity, the lower the torque. Conversely, the lower the angular velocity, the higher the torque. Pumps used with wind turbines applied to water pumping need a high starting torque for proper functioning. Thus, multi-bladed turbines are used for water pumping because their low tip speed ratios produce high torque characteristics.

Conventional electrical generators operate at speeds much greater than wind turbine rotors and so require some form of adaptive gearing when used with wind turbines. Low-solidity wind turbines operate at higher tip speed ratios, so they do not require as high a gear ratio to match rotor speed to that of the generator. For this reason, low-solidity wind turbines are better suited to electricity generation than multi-bladed high-solidity turbines.

The complexity of wind turbine aerodynamics is quite daunting when analysing unsteady and three-dimensional effects and a full discussion is outside the scope of this text. Suffice it to say that there are two major physical forces, "drag" and "lift." Drag forces are those forces experienced by an object in an air stream that are in line with the direction of the air stream. Objects designed to minimize the drag forces experienced in an air stream are described as streamlined because the airflow around them follows smooth, stream-like lines. Lift forces are those experienced by an object in an air stream that are perpendicular to the direction of the air stream. These are the forces that allow an aeroplane to lift off the ground and fly. Lift forces acting on a flat plate air stream are at a zero angle to the flat surface of the plate. When the *angle of attack* is small (at low angles relative to the direction of the air stream), a low pressure area is created on the "downstream" or "leeward" side of the plate as a result of an increase in the air velocity on that side. In this situation there is a direct relationship between air speed and pressure: the faster the airflow, the lower the pressure (Taylor, 1996). This is known as the *Bernoulli effect*. The lift force then acts as a "pulling" force on the object in a direction normal to the airflow. Lift forces are the principal forces that operate a wind turbine.

The energy produced is proportional to the swept area of the turbine and is proportional to the cube of the wind speed. Momentum theory can be applied to show that there is a limit to how much of the free stream energy can be extracted. Flow through the rotor must be maintained and so there will be some energy left in the airflow which cannot be extracted (Infield, 1995). This theoretical limit, called the Betz limit, is 16/27 (59.3 percent). The relative wind angle ϕ is the angle that the relative wind makes with the blade (at a particular point with local radius r along the blade) and is measured from the plane of rotation (Taylor, 1996). The angle of attack, α, at this point on the blade can be measured against the relative angle, ϕ. The blade pitch angle (β) is then equal to the relative wind angle minus the angle of attack.

At any position along the blade of a wind turbine the force generated locally depends on the angle of incidence μ of the relative airflow onto the blade. The rotor rotates only in a plane at right angles to the undisturbed wind, so the driving force at a point on the blade is that component of the aerofoil lift force that acts on the plane of rotation. This is given by the product of the lift force, L, and the sine of the relative wind angle, ϕ (that is $L \sin \phi$) (Figure 6.12). The drag force in the rotor plane at this point is the product of the drag force, D, and the cosine of the relative wind angle ϕ (that is $D \cos \phi$). The relative wind angle ϕ varies along the blade, and an optimum blade pitch angle is important.

Rotor speed must be adjusted in proportion to the instantaneous wind speed. So, wind turbines that are operated in this way have to rotate at variable speed. However, many large wind turbines rotate at a fixed speed.

The development of wind energy requires sites with suitable wind resources. A confident estimate of the annual mean wind speed is of paramount importance. It is appropriate for measurements to be made at the site for more than 1 year and, if possible, at the hub height of the intended turbine. There should also be corroboration with wind speeds recorded at nearby meteorological stations, as well as those extrapolated from long-term meteorological data. For most sites, a probability function, known as the Weibull distribution, is used to analyse the data. This is a non-symmetric function because wind speeds can attain high values, for instance, during storms. The shape of the distribution is determined mathematically by the scale parameter, denoted c, and the shape parameter k. These two numbers contain all the information required to describe the strength of the wind and its variation during the year. Figure 6.13 shows the frequency distribution of measured wind speeds and the fitted function. A Weibull distribution can be used to calculate the energy that may be derived from a turbine yearly on a site for which the two parameters c and k are known.

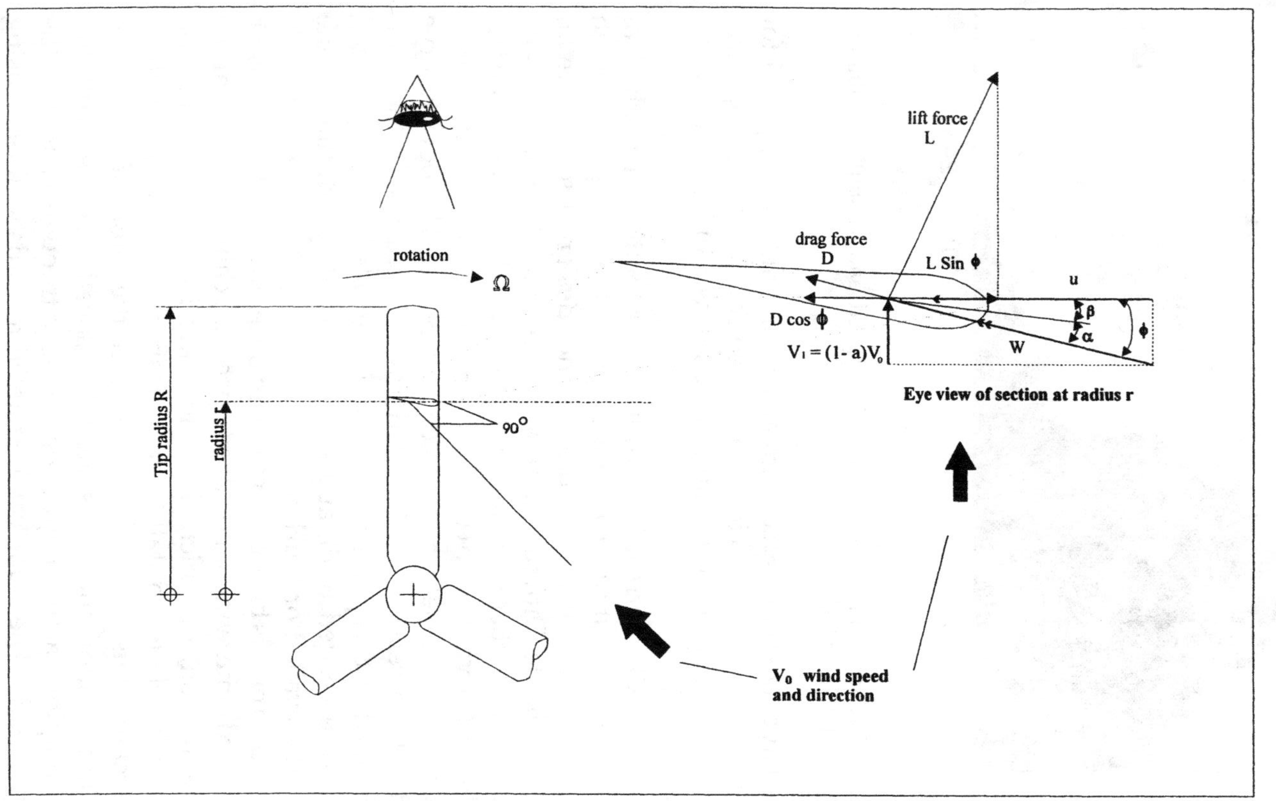

FIGURE 6.12 Vector diagram showing a section through a moving horizontal axis blade. The drag force, **D**, at the point shown is acting in line with the direction of the relative wind, **W**, and the lift force, **L**, is acting at 90 degrees to it. (Adapted from Taylor, 1996.)

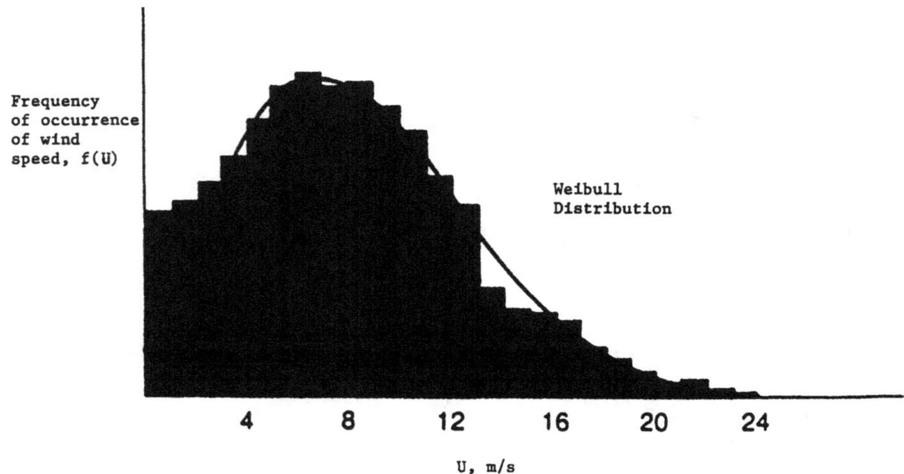

FIGURE 6.13 Frequency of occurrence of wind speed and Weibull distribution. (Adapted from Infield, 1995.)

Annual average wind speeds greater than 5 m/s are required for small wind turbines. Less wind is required for mechanical applications such as water pumping. Large wind farms require wind speeds of at least 6 m/s.

One feature all wind turbines must incorporate is a method of limiting the power output from the rotor in high winds. Since high winds occur infrequently, structures are not designed to capture all the energy available. Different approaches are in use to control power. At very low speeds there is insufficient energy in the wind to operate the turbine. At a value between 3 and 5 m/s, known as the cut-in wind speed, the turbine begins to generate power. The power curve will gradually increase until the rated power is reached at the rated wind speed. After this point the power is controlled so that the rated power is not exceeded until, at a specified wind speed, the turbine operation is curtailed or "furled."

Usually the rotor is brought to a halt in order to avoid the excessive loads from extreme winds. For fixed speed machines control can be by stall regulation, in which the blades are fixed and the natural tendency of the blades to stall (thereby losing power) as the angle of attack increases is used (Infield, 1995). Since the rotor speed is fixed, this will occur automatically as the wind speed increases. Another approach employs active regulation, usually through changing the pitch of the blade. The blade can be moved towards stall (increasing β) or towards feather (reducing β) as seen in Figure 6.12.

The difficulties in predicting stall and in designing stall regulated rotors have meant that the larger turbines in use today are usually pitch regulated. Because a feedback system is used in the control, power can be limited to the intended rated value. Research into rotor aerodynamics is leading to improved understanding of the stall process (Infield, 1995). This will allow more confident design of large stall regulated wind turbines in the future. Improvements in the understanding of the interaction between aerodynamics and rotor dynamics will lead to lighter and more flexible rotor designs. Consequently, the cost of wind turbines will be gradually reduced.

Most wind turbines providing power to the grid operate at fixed speed using an induction generator. Such 415-V three-phase generators are connected to the grid through suitable transformers. In some circumstances they can be connected directly online or via back-to-back thyristors configured to allow a soft start facility. Some static compensation is included in the connection to decrease the demand on the grid for reactive power supply, which would otherwise become a cost to the wind turbine operator. Wind farms (groups of wind turbines) are most effective when connected to strong sections of the high-voltage grid line. Single machines can be connected to the 11 kilovolts (kV) distribution network. Usually, no technical difficulties are encountered in integrating into the grid. It is suggested that at least 10 percent wind energy penetrations can be accommodated without problems.

However, at a local level, integration problems become more important as significant amounts of wind power are installed in a particular region. Depending on the fault level of the network at a particular point, if the installed wind capacity is too high, unacceptable voltage fluctuations may occur. Rapid fluctuations in the power output due to wind turbulence or wind turbines coming off line will create voltage flicker. Power electronic interfaces are being used more and more to assist in reducing the impact of wind turbines on the grid.

As mentioned earlier some wind turbines operate at variable speed (Figure 6.14). This is done through electronic (AC/DC/AC) variable speed drives. A synchronous generator is usually used with a rectifier or the turbine side of the DC link, and line commutated thyristor inverters on the grid side of the system. However, thyristor inverters introduce harmonic distortion, which requires filtering. Further, they make reactive power demands on the grid. More efficient high-frequency self-commutated inverters will be used increasingly on the grid side of the system link as their costs are reduced. The use

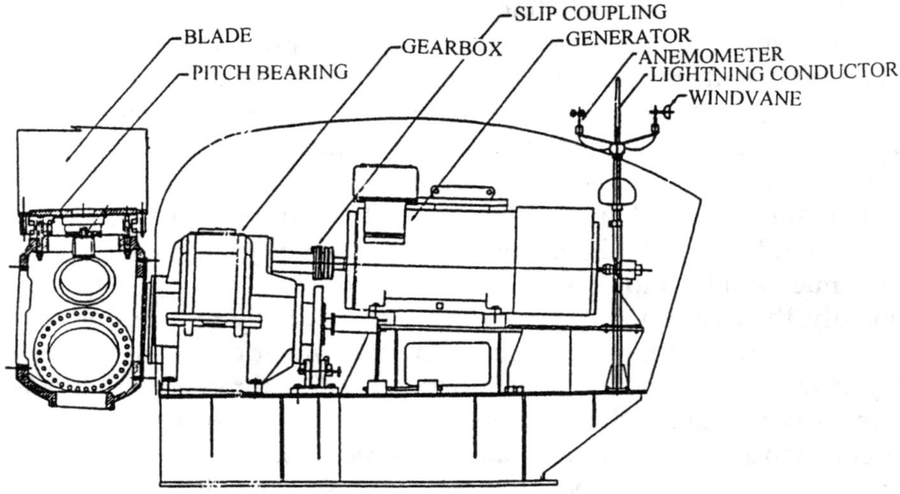

FIGURE 6.14 Schematic overview of wind turbine components.

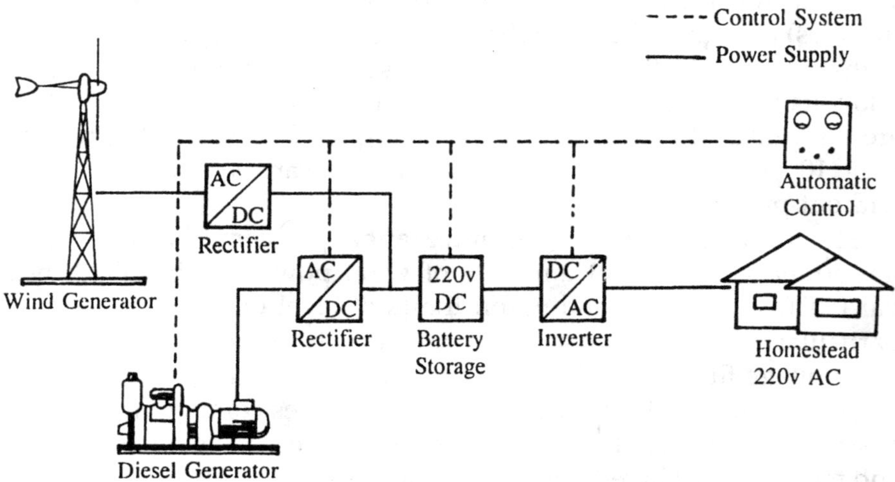

FIGURE 6.15 Hybrid wind-diesel generation system.

of power electronic interfaces will allow for greater use of direct drive and the elimination of the gearbox. Presently, in nearly all turbines a generator is used to take the electrical generator up to a nominal speed of 1500 revolutions per minute (RPM).

In order to ensure continuous power availability hybrid systems have been recommended (Figure 6.15). These combine windpower with diesel generators. In wind–diesel configurations, wind turbines are coupled to the diesel generators on a common electric grid, to displace part of the fuel. The benefits of such a combination of power sources outweigh the disadvantages characteristic of the individual power sources. A windpower–diesel hybrid typically will have significantly lower operating costs than a primary diesel electric generator. State-of-the-art intelligent microprocessor-based controllers are now making such systems easy to arrange. Stand-alone wind power systems will only provide power when the wind is blowing. Thus, the power output is variable, unless a storage system is available. Also, a hybrid system with a diesel generator makes storage unnecessary.

Wind energy is a partial solution to environmental problems created by other power-generating technologies. For example, in 1993, California's wind power plants offset the emission of more than 2.8 billion pounds of carbon dioxide from relatively clean-burning gas-fired power plants. These same wind power plants offset 16 million pounds of nitrogen oxide, sulphur dioxide, and particulates which would have been emitted from California's oil-fired power plants. Also wind energy generation has no adverse effect on water supply.

Once installed, wind turbines have little or no impact on ground-based flora or fauna. Impacts on humans include interference with electromagnetic signals, aeroacoustic noise generation, and visual pollution. All of these require careful attention to project design as well as siting clusters of machines away from highly populated areas. Regulation of noise level is under consideration in some countries. The most recent Danish regulation recommends a 45-decibel (dB) level at a 200-m distance from the nearest dweller (Tavares, 1995). In residential areas a noise level of only 40 dB is permitted. At present, there are no standard maximum permitted noise levels specifically for wind turbines in any Caribbean country. For wind farms, with say 30 turbines of 300 kW each, 45 dB at 500 metres distance is acceptable. Table 6.5 shows the noise level of different activities compared with wind turbines.

Wind turbines are also a potential electromagnetic interference source. Telecommunication interference can occur and so plant locations should avoid microwave transmission paths, keeping a 5-km clearance from radio stations and airports (Tavares, 1995). Safety for people and property is an environmental concern in wind farm installation. Blades and nacelle structures can fail, so people and property should have proper clearance. In Denmark, regulations forbid roads and buildings to be sited at less than 90 metres plus 2.7 times the rotor diameter from the nearest turbine of a wind farm.

A primary impact of wind turbines is visual. This is exacerbated by the need to site wind farms in the windiest areas, usually exposed

TABLE 6.5 Noise from Various Activities Compared with Wind Turbines

Source	Noise Level in dB(A)[a]
Threshold of pain	140
Jet aircraft at 250 m	105
Pneumatic drill at 7 m	95
Truck moving at 48 km h^{-1} (30 mph) at 100 m	65
Busy general office	60
Car moving at 64 km h^{-1} (40 mph)	55
Wind farm at 350 m	35–45
Quiet bedroom	20
Rural night-time background	20–40
Threshold of hearing	0

[a] dB(A) decibels (acoustically weighted).

Data from Department of the Environment, 1993.

high areas, which often have a natural beauty. Perhaps wind farms should not be sited within nature reserves and other protected areas or special areas of conservation (Weightman, 1995).

Biomass

Biomass may be defined as any organic substance other than oil, natural gas, and coal. Primarily plant matter, it accounts for about 15 percent of world energy use and 38 percent of energy use in developing countries.

Biomass, mainly in the form of agricultural and industrial waste, burned to fuel conventional steam turbines to produce electricity, has been in use for many years. Biomass is often regarded as "non-polluting", despite the large emission of carbon dioxide and other pollutants, because the amount of carbon dioxide emitted in the combustion process equals the amount absorbed from the atmosphere during the growth of plants and photosynthesis of atmospheric carbon dioxide.

Large quantities of wood are consumed each year in the Caribbean, mainly burnt as charcoal and used in cooking. Wood remains the fuel most used for cooking in rural situations. However, if we continue using wood for charcoal at the present rate, without replenishment, many island states will be deforested in a manner similar to Haiti.

Growing biomass for energy in an environmentally sensitive manner can provide a livelihood for farmers and pay for restoration of land. A common example of biomass conversion into electricity in Jamaica is the burning of bagasse, the leftover residue of sugar cane, in a conventional steam boiler plant. Likewise, the residues of growing corn, rice, and other field products provide a large mass of material suitable for electricity production. Ethanol from sugar cane can be used as an octane enhancer in gasolene.

Biomass electricity generating plants have tended to be small because of the dispersed nature of the feedstock. Also, low-pressure boilers have low efficiencies, in the range of 10 to 18 percent. As a result, biomass plants have relied on low or zero cost of the biomass fuel to be operated economically. With the advent of biomass-integrated gasifiers/gas turbines, the unit cost of electricity production will decline in the future, bringing it down to approximately U.S.$ 0.05 per kilowatt hour for the cost of generation, in 1993 dollars. When other external costs are taken into account, the actual costs will be higher. These costs include financing, interest during construction, and profit if constructed by the private sector. Typically, a privately owned biomass facility must charge about U.S.$ 0.07 per kilowatt hour to be minimally profitable.

Biomass also has a problem of seasonality. A large quantity of biomass matter may be available in agricultural communities during the season following harvest, such as after the processing of sugar cane, but it becomes scarce during the growing season. Adequate planning is required in order to effect a continuous supply of the biomass and to assure a steady output from the power plant.

Biomass for energy will not play a significant role in oil substitution in the short term. Most developed countries have no immediate need and, consequently, only long-term interest in developing certain biomass technologies. Even so, some developed countries, although replete with abundant fossil fuel reserves, have already embarked on vigorous biomass production for energy use. Caribbean countries lack the financial resources to expend on biomass development and thus must prioritize biomass projects by using rigid criteria such as the energy contribution potential, risk, and pay-off time of each project. Assessment, development, and utilization of biomass resources should coexist with the optimization of oil usage and energy conservation. Integrated waste disposal/energy generating projects are of special interest. Positive benefits that are obtained from solving environmental problems can offset some of the costs of energy generation from wastes.

In the Caribbean, biomass sources include agricultural by-products, e.g., bagasse and sugar cane tops; agro-industrial waste, e.g., vinasse (dunder) from the sugar industry; municipal, domestic and animal waste, e.g., garbage, sewage, dung; aquatic biomass, e.g., spirulina, water hyacinth; wood and woody materials, including wood chips from the lumber industry.

Biomass stocks of garbage and vinasse, for instance, are sustainable but others must be continually regenerated. Research is necessary for increasing biomass productivity and energy crop management, harvesting, and storage. Availability of biomass for energy in Caribbean island states is also dependent on competition for food, given the limited available arable land.

Animal dung (from cattle, chickens, and pigs) and sewage are the resources for biogas. Mixed in a slurry of about 95 percent water they are fed into a specially built digester where digestion is allowed to take place for 2 to 8 weeks. The bacterial action generates heat and the ideal process temperature is at least 35°C. A well-run digester can produce 200 to 400 m^3 of biogas with a methane content of more than 50 percent for each dry tonne of input (Ramage and Scurlock, 1996). This is about 65 percent of the fuel energy of the original dung. Even at lower conversion efficiencies the process may be worthwhile in order to obtain a clean fuel and dispose of wastes. The remaining effluent is also useful as a fertilizer. The Scientific Research Council in Jamaica has carried out extensive research on biogas systems and the technology is well established there. Biogas technology in general is most widespread and best developed in China.

Biogas produced in landfills will have potential as an energy source in Caribbean states when the quantity of municipal solid waste in landfills is adequate for commercial production. The conditions are neither as wet nor as warm in a landfill compared to a biogas digester. Hence, the anaerobic digestion is slower, taking many years rather than weeks. The landfill gas produced is a mixture primarily of CH_2 and CO_2. Theoretically, the yield of a good site over time is of the order of 150 to 300 m^3 of gas per tonne of waste, with between 50 and 60 percent by volume of methane (Ramage and Scurlock, 1996). The landfill is usually lined with a layer of impermeable clay and covered with similar material after it is filled, producing an environment conducive to anaerobic digestion. The landfill gas is collected by a network of interconnected perforated pipes buried at depths of up to 20 metres in the solid waste. In planning new sites the pipe system is constructed before the solid waste is brought to the site. Landfill gas is increasingly used for power generation, with most plants using the gas to drive internal combustion engines. However, gas turbines that have better efficiencies are now coming into use. Wood fuels may also be integrated into landfill systems, allowing shared capital costs, increased security of supply, and increased overall power output (Harder and Freeman, 1996). Figure 6.16 shows a large-scale plant for generating process heat from wood chips (Ramage and Scurlock, 1996).

The major environmental concern with biomass is the need to grow the feedstock in a sustainable manner. Presently, wood by-products (including bagasse) are the major biomass feedstock used to generate electricity, and sugar cane (and corn) is used in the production of ethanol. If biomass is to contribute significantly to the Jamaican energy supply, then feedstocks grown specifically for biomass need to be developed. Moreover, the conversion of solar energy to biomass and then to electricity, heat, or transportation fuel is not very efficient, and large areas of land would need to be devoted to growing this feedstock. This can be part of a reforestation programme.

Required reductions in air pollution and the commitment to reducing oil imports will influence the contribution that gasolene will make to the transportation sector. In general, ethanol has fewer negative impacts on the environment than gasolene. By replacing pure gasolene with a gasolene/ethanol blend, nitrogen oxides may be increased slightly but atmospheric ozone formation and total carbon dioxide emissions are reduced. Tailpipe emissions of carbon monoxide are also reduced.

Table 6.6 shows the yields of ethanol obtainable from each tonne of raw material and each hectare of land for five crops. The energy loss in the fermentation process for ethanol is significant but is compensated for by the low cost of the technological process. Jamaica produces ethanol, which is presently exported to the U.S., where it is used as an octane enhancer in gasolene. In Brazil, ethanol is used as a gasolene extender and a 20 percent ethanol component is added to the gasolene, which is marketed as gasohol.

Although the growing of biomass crops consumes carbon dioxide and produces oxygen, the cultivation process requires manufactured equipment, fertilizers, and motor fuel. Biomass crops can contribute to the depletion of nutrients in the soil, to soil erosion if not properly managed, and to water quality problems.

One important positive environmental impact could come from the anaerobic treatment of distillery wastewater from sugar and citrus-based facilities. With treatment the average biological oxygen demand (BOD) reduction could be of the order of 90 percent. This

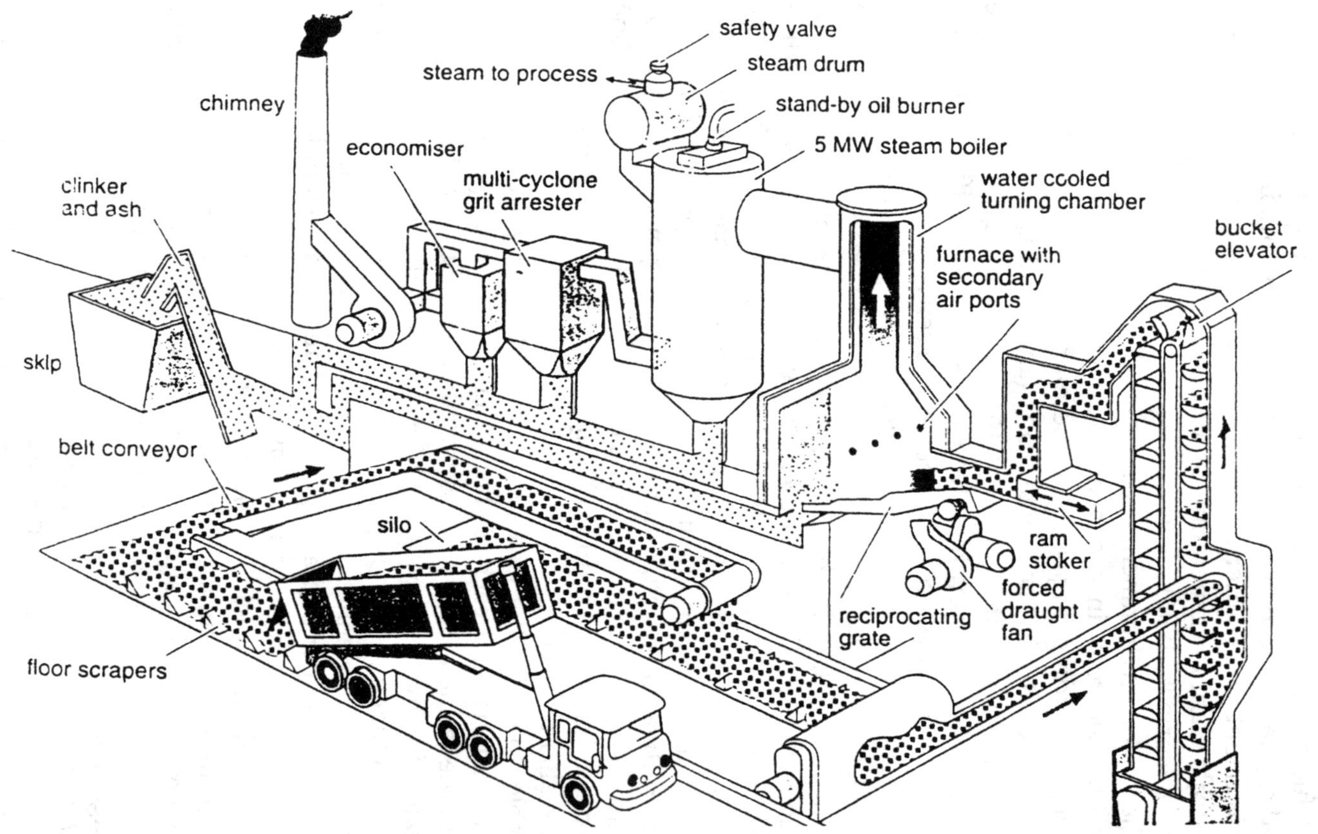

FIGURE 6.16 A large-scale plant for generating process heat from wood chips. (Adapted from Ramage and Scurlock, 1996.)

TABLE 6.6 Ethanol Yields from Various Crops

Raw Material	Litres per tonne	Litres per hectare per year
Sugar cane (harvested stalks)	70	400–12,000
Corn (maize, grain)	360	250–2,000
Cassava (roots)	180	500–4,000
Sweet potatoes (roots)	120	1,000–4,500
Wood	160	160–4,000

Data from Lou, 1994.

approach, where wastewater can be subjected to anaerobic digestion and converted to energy, not only solves an environmental waste disposal problem but also provides for the ancillary production of energy.

Bagasse (sugar cane residue) is an important biomass fuel in the Caribbean. Sugar factories in all Caribbean countries use bagasse as a heat source for raising steam, although it is burned inefficiently in order not to accumulate surplus wastes. Most Caribbean sugar factories also produce electricity from bagasse for their own needs but only a few (Cuba and Puerto Rico) are able to export electricity because of contractual and operational difficulties in selling power only during the one-crop per year growing season. Studies suggest that the "barbojo" (cane tops and leaves) could yield important amounts of electricity (Minott and Lewis, 1991). About 5.7 percent of the electricity produced in Jamaica comes from bagasse. This could be increased if the sugar cane industry had two crops per year. Among the problems in increasing the use of bagasse are:

- Inadequate or irregular cane supply
- Unreliable sugar mill operation caused by breakdowns, process bottlenecks, and unstable steam pressure
- Inadequate plant design, such as insufficient vapour bleeding, low system steam pressure, and no heat recovery from boiler flue gases

Whenever there is major rehabilitation of boilers or prime movers in a particular sugar mill, the economics of co-generation schemes of high efficiencies that permit electricity to be exported should be evaluated. Increased recovery of biomass material, coupled with improved efficiency of conversion to electricity, could result in up to

40 gigawatts (GW) of generating capacity being installed in association with the sugar industry worldwide.

Rice husks, although they have a high silica (ash) content compared with other biomass fuels, have a uniform texture that makes them suitable in gasification technologies. Rice husk gasifiers have been operated profitably in China and Indonesia.

Wood remains a major source of fuel. In Jamaica about 3.6 percent of energy needs comes from fuelwood and charcoal (Table 6.7). Wood can also be used for industrial energy. In Brazil, the steel industry uses over two million tonnes of charcoal per year. The end result of the unmanaged use of wood as fuel is deforestation. A solution being strongly encouraged in Jamaica and other Caribbean countries is the planting of fast-growing trees suitable for coppicing. This technique, which involves cutting the growth every few years and allowing the tree to sprout again, is the subject of trials in some Caribbean countries, including Jamaica, Cuba, and Costa Rica. An alternative is planting trees at high densities and thinning later, a practice followed in Sweden. Sweden expects biomass to satisfy an important part of its energy and transportation fuel demands in the next two decades (Johansson, 1996).

A strategy of biomass utilization should be developed that is congruent with the resources of the country. This will involve the introduction and adaptation of appropriate technologies for the production and consumption of firewood, charcoal, factory wastes, and biogas. It will also mean considering both forest and energy studies in conjunction with one another.

Because they use the mature generating technologies developed for fossil fuels, biomass for generating electricity is not expected to have major breakthroughs that would lead to marked reduction in production costs per kilowatt hour. In order for biomass to make important contributions to the electricity market two factors must be developed: a dedicated crop (feedstock) must be produced and the conversion technologies will have to be improved.

As a fuel supply, the dependence on waste material from the wood industry as well as agricultural residues must be removed. In the future, biomass for the electricity industry should depend on crops grown specifically for energy production even though crops dedicated to energy use may conflict with demands for the use of land for other purposes.

Most of biomass energy use at present occurs in developing countries – burning wood and charcoal for cooking and, in some

TABLE 6.7 Sources of Energy, Jamaica (1998)

Sources		
Petroleum		90.0%
Bagasse		4.1%
Fuelwood and coal		2.9%
Charcoal		1.0%
Hydropower		3.9%
Energy Imports		
Jamaica is approximately 90% dependent on foreign energy at an import cost of U.S.$ 688 million in 2000.		
Major Energy Importers (U.S.$)		
Petrojam refinery		(378 million)
Other oil markets		(130 million)
Bauxite/alumina companies		(180 million)
Electric Energy		
Jamaica Public Service Company Limited (JPSCo) had a net generation of 2,295.4 million kWh with peak demand of 498 MW in 2000.		
Installed Capacity – December 2000		
JPSCo installed capacity		510 MW
Steam	No. 6 HFO	292 MW
Diesel	No. 6 HFO	36 MW
Gas turbine	No. 2 Diesel	159 MW
Hydro		23 MW
Independent producers installed capacity		158 MW
Other Electricity Generators		
Bauxite/alumina companies		168 MW
Sugar factories		30 MW
Caribbean Cement Company		23 MW
Other		40 MW
Total:		**261 MW**
Energy consumption:		24.5 million barrels fuel oil equivalent
Per capita energy consumption:		9.1 barrels fuel oil equivalent

Data provided by the Petroleum Corporation of Jamaica, Kingston, Jamaica.

cases, for heating. In the Caribbean, biomass conversion systems have a role to play in reducing conventional energy demand and increasing energy supply. This role will be heightened as national policies encourage greater reliance on renewable energy, with its environmental and societal benefits.

Geothermal Energy

Geothermal resources can be found in areas of high volcanic activity in many parts of the world. Geothermal resources may be categorized as hydrothermal, geopressured, hot dry rock, and magma. Presently, all commercial operations are based on hydrothermal systems where wells are about 2000 metres deep with reservoir temperatures of 180 to 270°C (Hobbs, 1995).

Geothermal resources are utilized for power production in Guadeloupe and many other Caribbean islands, such as St Lucia, Dominica, and Montserrat, have potential. A total of 35 hot springs have been identified in Jamaica. However, a major drawback to the development of geothermal resources is capital. Enterprises in developing countries are usually not large or diversified enough to assume the investment risks associated with geothermal exploration. Thus, financial and technical assistance is crucial to enable countries to exploit their geothermal potential.

For geothermal resources to be productive there are three physical requirements – an aquifer containing geothermal water that can be reached by drilling, a cap rock to retain the geothermal heaters, and a heat source. The flow in the porous media that forms the aquifer is represented by Darcy's law, which states that the velocity (v) of a fluid moving through porous media is proportional to the pressure gradient causing the flow:

$$v = K_w H/L$$

Here K_w is the hydraulic conductivity of the rock (essentially the permeability), H is the effective head of water during the flow, and L is the distance along the flow direction. The volume of water, Q, flowing in unit time through a cross-sectional area A square metres is v times A. Hence, Darcy's law may also be written:

$$v = K_w A\, H/L$$

where K_w is regarded as the volume flowing through 1 square metre in a unit time under a unit hydraulic gradient. Table 6.8 shows that the highest porosities and permeabilities are in sand, gravels, and volcanic ash. Fracture-induced permeability is important in geothermal aquifers.

The importance of a cap rock is shown in Figure 6.17. Here the fluid pressure is high because mud rocks, clays, and unfractured lavas form a seal, preventing fluid escape upwards. The third requirement

TABLE 6.8 Typical Porosities and Permeabilities

Material	Porosity (%)	Permeability (Hydraulic Conductivity) (m day^{-1})
Unconsolidated sediments		
Clay	45–60	$<10^{-2}$
Silt	40–50	10^{-2}–1
Sand, volcanic ash	30–40	1–500
Gravel	25–35	500–10,000
Consolidated sedimentary rocks		
Mudrock	5–15	10^{-8}–10^{-6}
Sandstone	5–30	10^{-4}–10
Limestone	0.1–30	10^{-5}–10
Crystalline rocks		
Solidified lava	0.001–1	0.0003–3
Granite	0.0001–1	0.003–0.03
Slate	0.001–1	10^{-8}–10^{-5}

Data from Brown, 1996.

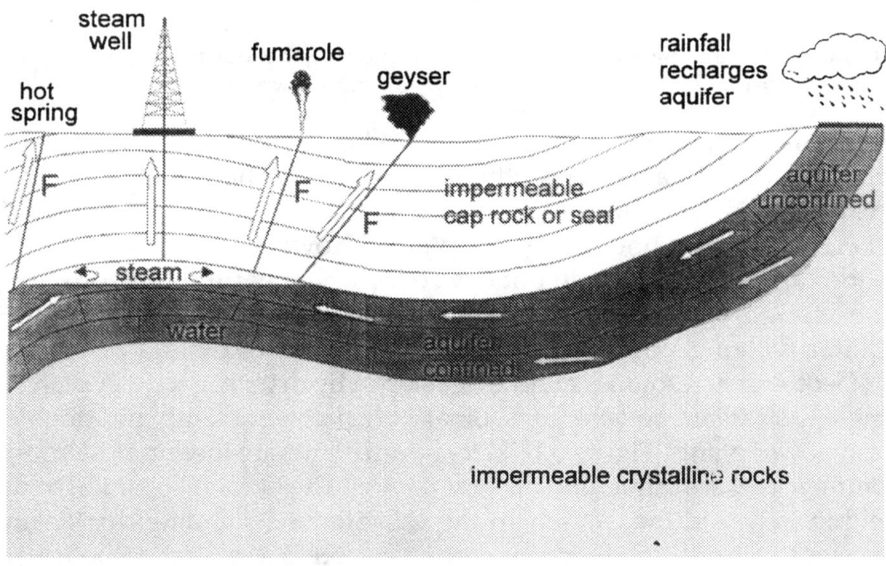

FIGURE 6.17 Schematic representation of a geothermal field. (Adapted from Brown, 1996.)

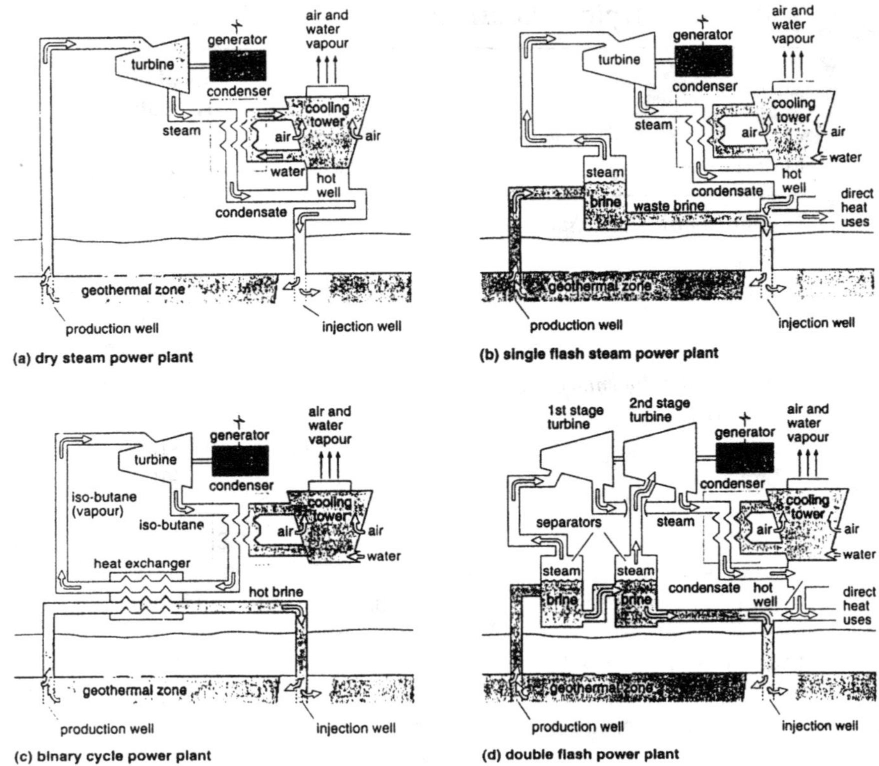

FIGURE 6.18 Simplified flow diagrams (a–d) showing the four main types of geothermal electrical energy production. (Adapted from Brown, 1996.)

for commercial geothermal resources is a heat source. In low-enthalpy areas such as Jamaica the geothermal resource, a heat source, can be created in a sedimentary basin where aquifers move water to depths where it becomes hot enough to exploit. However, the better possibilities are those located in hot dry rocks where natural heat production is high but the rocks must be fractured to create an artificial aquifer with a geothermal resource.

Geothermal resources may be developed by dry steam power plants, single flash steam power plants, binary cycle power plants, and double flash power plants (Figure 6.18). Dry steam plants are the simplest, most commercially attractive, and the best known. The Larderello geothermal field in Italy and the Geysers in the U.S. are long-standing dry steam developments. Falling fluid pressures have led to a reinjection policy at the Geysers to make the resource more sustainable.

In a single flash steam power plant the geothermal waters used at the surface may be wet steam, hot water at high pressure, or water that has flashed within the wall while moving to the surface. Flashing is often best avoided as dissolved minerals may cause a build-up of scale deposits. A conventional turbine is the heart of the plant. Reinjection wells must be available for fluid disposal of the unflashed brine.

In a binary cycle power plant a secondary working fluid such as butane or pentane is used. Such fluids have a lower boiling point than water and are vapourized and used to drive a turbine. This allows low-temperature resources to be used and thus is most applicable to Caribbean geothermal resources. Also, chemically impure fluids can be utilized if they are kept under pressure so that no flashing takes place. Higher efficiencies have been produced than in low-temperature steam flash plants but capital costs are high. Keeping the geothermal fluid under pressure and repressuring the secondary fluid consumes nearly 30 percent of the total power output of the system. Further, large volumes of geothermal fluids and large pumps are involved.

The double flash power plant is an attempt to improve flashing methods and an alternative to high-cost binary plants. Double flash can only be used where geothermal fluids have few impurities so that scaling and non-condensate gas problems are minimized. The procedure is that unflashed liquid remaining after the initial high-pressure flashing flows to a low-pressure tank where another drop in pressure provides more steam. This steam is mixed with the exhaust from the high-pressure turbine to drive another turbine or stage of the same turbine. Again, large volumes of fluid are needed, perhaps ten times more than for similar-sized dry steam plants. Variants on the binary and double flash systems are the main subject of present research.

The binary turbine is normally used in hot dry rock technology. Here, water is circulated down an injection well, through the fractured hot dry rock reservoir and up the production well where the mission is to provide thermal energy for generating electricity using a binary turbine and heat exchanger. In this closed-loop process, nothing is released to the environment except heat and no long-term wastes accumulate. Despite large investments in Germany, Japan, and the U.S., the hot dry rock technique has not been demonstrated on a large commercial scale. The hydrofracturing of the geothermal reservoir is a technique borrowed from the petroleum industry. Two boreholes are drilled, the second intersecting the fractured zone hundreds of metres above its base, and a closed circuit for water circulation through the system is put in place. The Los Alamos National Laboratory has a project of this type at Fenton Hill, New Mexico (Duchane,

1996). Among the problems encountered are high water loss, which, for economic reasons, should be kept at 10 percent or less. The system also maintains a higher resistance to flow than is desirable. There is optimism about the technical difficulties and European funding is also likely to develop a commercial prototype, probably on the fringes of the Larderello field in Italy, by the turn of the century.

The environmental effects of geothermal energy generation include induced seismicity, ground subsidence, and gaseous pollution. Induced seismicity is debatable and most fields are situated in areas already prone to earthquakes. On the other hand, fluid injection lubricates fractures, which increases pore pressure, leading to microseismicity. Ground subsidence is possible where there is a reduction of the higher pressures in primarily liquid systems, such as is caused by inadequate fluid reinjection. Non-condensable gases are created in geothermal energy production. They include carbon dioxide and lesser quantities of sulphur dioxide, hydrogen sulphide, methane, hydrogen, and nitrogen. Also, there may be heavy metals, dissolved silica, and sodium and potassium chlorides, depending on the rock body and water interaction at depth. The issue of hydrogen sulphide and other sulphur compounds being associated with geothermal systems has resulted in stricter environmental legislation. For example, this has delayed the completion and commissioning of the Miravalles plant in Northern Costa Rica, located on the margins of a rain forest. However, geothermal systems have a much less negative impact on the environment than conventional fuels. A geothermal plant produces less than 0.2 percent of the carbon dioxide produced by coal or oil-fired plant. Likewise, the comparable figures for sulphur dioxide (acid rain gas) and particulates is less than 1 percent. At the same time, geothermal plants are not particularly land intensive. Table 6.9 shows the worldwide generation and direct use of geothermal energy in 1994 (Friedleifsson, 1996).

Fuel Cells

Hydrogen is the fuel component of fuel cells. Most hydrogen is produced by conversion from natural gas using steam. This process, in which methane is re-formed into hydrogen, produces carbon dioxide, an undesirable gas.

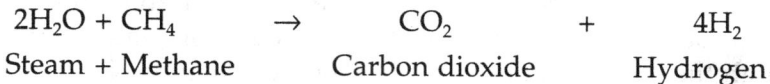

$$\underset{\text{Steam + Methane}}{2H_2O + CH_4} \rightarrow \underset{\text{Carbon dioxide}}{CO_2} + \underset{\text{Hydrogen}}{4H_2}$$

TABLE 6.9 Electricity Generation and Direct Use of Geothermal Energy in 1994

	Electricity Generation		Direct Utilization	
	Installed Capacity MW_e	Annual Output GWh	Installed Capacity MW_t	Annual Output GWh
China	28	98	2.143	5.527
Costa Rica	60	447	—	—
El Salvador	105	419	—	—
France	4	24	456	2.006
Georgia	—	—	245	2.136
Hungary	—	—	638	2.795
Iceland	50	265	1.443	5.878
Indonesia	309	1.048	—	—
Italy	626	3.417	308	1.008
Japan	299	1.722	319	1.928
Kenya	45	348	—	—
Macedonia	—	—	70	142
Mexico	753	5.877	28	74
New Zealand	286	2.193	264	1.837
Nicaragua	70	—	—	—
Philippines	1.051	5.470	—	—
Poland	—	—	63	206
Romania	2	—	137	765
Russian Fed.	11	25	210	673
Serbia	—	—	80	660
Slovakia	—	—	100	502
Switzerland	—	—	110	243
Tunisia	—	—	90	788
Turkey	20	68	140	552
U.S.	2.817	16.491	1.874	3.859
Others	7	40	329	1.935
Total	6.543	37.952	9.047	33.514

Adapted from Brown, 1996.

Hydrogen can be produced with a CO_2 by-product by the electrolysis of water and the thermal dissociation of water into hydrogen by concentrating solar collectors. Hydrogen can be used as a transport fuel, using metal hydride storage, and for electricity generation, using fuel cells. One major project now underway is a German–Saudi Arabian "Hysolar" project, in which a large PV array in the Saudi desert is being used to produce hydrogen for shipment by tanker to Germany for use

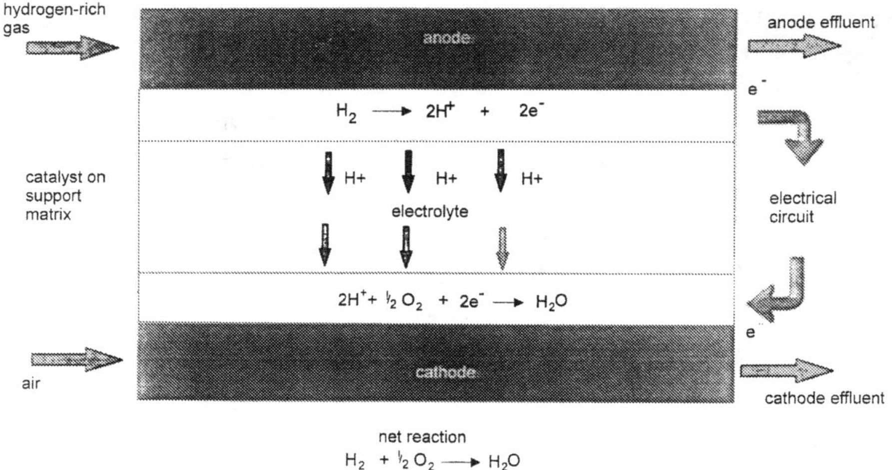

FIGURE 6.19 Operating principle of the phosphoric acid fuel cell (PAFC). (Adapted from Everett and Boyle, 1996.)

in transport vehicles (buses, cars) modified to burn hydrogen (Everett and Boyle, 1996). These vehicles are expected to use internal combustion engines initially but fuel cells will be used at a later stage.

Combustion engines are limited in the efficiency with which motive power is generated. Much of the energy ends up as waste heat. The fuel cell allows fuel to produce electricity at a much higher efficiency than an internal combustion engine. Fuel cells are similar to the conventional rechargeable lead acid battery used in cars, except that in a fuel cell the energy comes from recharging from a constant external fuel supply. Gases such as hydrogen and oxygen are brought in and DC electricity is the output. Water is the only by-product and there are no pollutants. There are no moving parts and much less waste heat than in combustion-based systems.

There are different types of fuel cells, perhaps five at present. The so-called alkaline fuel cells (AFCs), which run on pure hydrogen, can have electricity production efficiencies of about 60 percent. Most large systems are phosphoric acid fuel cells (PAFCs), with approximately 40 percent efficiency, which are designed to make their own hydrogen from natural gas by steam reforming (Figure 6.19). Most fuel cell designs require the utilization of small quantities of expensive metals as a catalyst. Platinum is the most commonly used example. Much of the metal in spent fuel cells can be recycled but with widespread use there could be catalyst supply problems (Everett and Boyle, 1996). Fortunately, some types of fuel cells presently being developed require little or no noble metals as catalysts. These include the molten carbonate fuel cell (MCFC), which operates at high temperature, the proton exchange membrane fuel cell (PEMFC), and the solid oxide fuel cell (SOFC).

Fuel cells are expected to compete in cost, efficiency, and reliability with internal combustion engines by about 2010, when they will also be used in motor cars. Electricity generated by fuel cells will be compatible and complementary to intermittent renewable energy supplies such as wind because their output can be increased or decreased in seconds.

INTEGRATING RENEWABLES WITH THE GRID

Utility companies are concerned about the problems of integrating renewable energy systems into grid networks designed to operate with conventional power plants. This problem will become more important in about 20 years when significant amounts of renewable energy have been brought on stream. Most power systems are designed to cope with substantial variation in demand. So, adding a variable source in small amounts has little effect because its variability is overshadowed by that of demand. Studies have suggested that supplying as much as 20 percent of demand from renewable sources will need no system modification. For large penetrations, the energy from renewables will become correspondingly less useful unless appropriate procedures are implemented to coordinate the output from a variety of renewables. With penetration higher than 20 percent problems may arise, including:

- *Cycling losses* due to increased start-up and shutdown of thermal plants
- *Discarded energy* when the available variable input exceeds the amount that can be safely absorbed while maintaining sufficient reserve and adequate dynamic control of the system
- *Reserve costs* accruing from the need to ensure that the system can respond properly to unpredicted changes

Most national electricity systems contain fossil fuel (and nuclear) plants that are *capacity limited.* On the other hand, most hydropower and biomass plants are *energy limited.* They are usually unable to generate continuously at maximum capacity because the energy source available is limited. *Variable power* sources, such as solar, wind, and OTEC plants form a third category of power sources characterized by high capital costs and particularly low operating costs so that they are excellent base plants. Their output should be accepted where possible if the initial economics are favourable. Most utility systems of the future will contain all three types of plants. The tendency will be to gradually reduce the use of capacity-limited plants and, by policy, optimize plants supporting variable power sources.

There are other issues summarized below which should be considered when integrating renewables into the energy network:

- Better use of system interconnection so that, spread over a wider area, variable sources become more reliable.
- Resources such as renewable energy can avoid uncertain future costs by substituting present capital investment for future fuel consumption. This will reduce risk and so require favourable discounting.
- Power injection nearer the grid reduces grid costs and losses.
- Smaller generating units reduce the needed reserve capacity.
- Dispersed electricity resources enhance reliability and through power–electronic interfaces generate reactive power at the point of use.
- In an energy system with significant dispersed renewables, it is likely that the mistakes made will be smaller and less consequential and that lessons learned can be implemented quicker and cheaper.
- Variable power sources are relatively small and use the economics of mass production. Production lines can take advantage of continuous improvement and innovation.
- Variable sources are well suited to load management.

When renewable sources of power reach a penetration of more than 20 percent a more flexible electricity supply system would need to be developed. It would require the increasing use of power plants such as gas turbines, which have rapid response times, together with demand management and, of course, energy storage (Grubb, 1991).

There are numerous methods of effecting storage of electrical energy, for example pumped storage in hydropower. In this approach electricity is used in times of low load to pump water from a low-level pond to a high-level one. At times of sudden peak demand the stored potential energy of the water can be used to generate electricity in less than a minute. Electronic metering and communication systems now being developed offer new possibilities for demand management over a short time span. These allow electrical loads to be switched off for a short time without causing significant problems. For example, refrigerators can be turned off for 5 minutes when a microwave oven or a coffee maker is being used. There are also flywheels that can be used for short-term storage, and yet to come are sophisticated techniques such as storage in superconducting electromagnets.

Finally, hydrogen produced from renewable energy sources could provide a means of storing energy for later use in electricity production and could provide a portable fuel for industrial use and for use in vehicles. Hydrogen has the advantage that when burned in air it does not produce carbon dioxide, carbon monoxide, or sulphur dioxide, unlike fossil fuels. The by-products of hydrogen combustion are water and small quantities of nitrogen oxides. Even these emissions can be eliminated if fuel cells are used instead of combustion.

TECHNOLOGY TRANSITION

It should be borne in mind that many decades are required for a significant transition from present conventional systems to future advanced energy systems. The history of changes in fuel patterns (wood – coal – oil) suggests that in a peaceful commercial environment four or five decades are needed to change the patterns of resource use. Four advanced sources hover on the horizon. They are:

- Integrated coal-gasification combined cycle (IGCC) coal conversion-based systems
- Natural gas-based liquid fuels and chemicals
- Direct production of liquid fuels from coal (transportation fuels)
- Molten carbonate fuel cell electricity

Syngas can be produced from both natural gas and coal and used as an input to advanced IGCC coal conversion systems or fuel cells. There is no doubt that coal-based IGCC plants will be commercially deployed after a development programme conducted during the decade of the 1980s.

Molten carbonate fuel cell technology in particular has just emerged from the research and development phase and small 200-kW units have been field-tested. The plan is for small units, in the early stage of this technology, to operate on natural gas or distillate fuels and be connected to the electricity grid system. Large systems (50 to 250 MW) based on synthesis of gas from coal gasification systems still require further development work. A feature of such plants is high efficiency (55 percent), low emissions of carbon dioxide, and no production of nitrogen oxides or sulphur (Starr et al., 1992). Perhaps 50 years will be required to install 100,000 MW of fuel cell equipment. To emphasize the long lead times required, we should recognize that catalytic cracking, which became commercially available in 1942, took approximately two decades to be generally used in oil refineries.

The long lead time needed for fuel source transitions has important implications for global energy strategies. Renewable energy also fits into this time scale – 30 to 50 years. However, by 2050 about 30 percent of the world's electricity generating capacity might be what today is considered advanced technology. In developed countries, the installation of advanced energy technologies is limited by the slow obsolescence of existing plants and by the pace at which additional capacity is required. With a long-term growth rate of 2 percent per annum, approximately 36 years is needed to double total capacity. In the case of the developing countries, scarcity of capital and avoidance of performance risk is more important than obsolescence. For this reason, developing countries are more interested in installing well-proven, reliable, conventional plants. Also, developing countries usually require small and dispersed power growth, providing a particular niche for solar and wind, as well as small conventional carbon-based units.

Energy conservation is often regarded as being equivalent to an energy resource because it extends the life of conventional resources. There are two main approaches: to change end-user habits to reduce energy consumption and to improve the efficiency of equipment and appliances.

Using public transportation rather than individual automobiles is an example of the former. Both strategies depend on cost savings. In the 1970s, U.S. industry invested in equipment to reduce energy use and the positive economic effect was important. On the other hand, the non-industrial end user is less influenced by long-term economics and usually waits for the normal obsolescence of equipment. Hence, the time for a shift to more efficient energy use is between 15 and 30 years in developed countries, depending on the incentives.

In modifying consumer habits to reduce energy demand we have to consider the cost of energy relative to consumer income. This is affected by the priorities of the consumer for various service, convenience, comfort, and timesaving factors. For instance, the driver of an automobile may find the time saved by travelling fast to be more valuable than the additional cost of the fuel used. The tendency will be to support low-cost energy, regardless of the "intangible" social costs of environmental damage. Without strong economic incentives, the implementation of pervasive global conservation programmes can be as long as the lead time for advance in technologies, that is, nearly 50 years.

ENVIRONMENTAL CONSTRAINTS

The effect of greenhouse gases, particularly CO_2, generated in large measure by fossil fuels, has been the subject of several studies for the past decade. The Intergovernmental Panel on Climate Change (2001) confirmed the ability of greenhouse gases to change the radiative balance of the atmosphere. This report cites sulphate aerosols as a secondary but potentially important influence on climate, although their radiative effect is less certain than that of greenhouse gases. For the first time also a General Circulation Model (GCM) has been able to replicate in broad terms the slow rise in global temperature since 1860 (Hadley Centre, 1995). Taking into account the sulphate aerosols, the model shows a rise in temperature close to the 0.5°C observed over the last century. This experiment was extended to 2050 and the model predicts a long-term increase in global temperatures of approximately 0.2°C per decade, which is twice the rate that some of the more sensitive ecosystems can tolerate. If the cooling effects of sulphate aerosols are removed the model predicts a warming of 0.3°C per decade.

GCM experiments such as the model above suggest a rise in average sea level globally of about 4 centimetres per decade; and an increased precipitation at mid and high altitudes, particularly in winter, and a reduction in precipitation in many subtropical areas. Some information on carbon dioxide and sulphur-dioxide should be given as background. CO_2 has an atmospheric lifetime of roughly 50 to 200 years and is nearly uniformly distributed in the atmosphere. Preindustrial atmospheric concentrations were about 280 parts per million (ppm); current values are about 355 ppm. It will take more than a decade for mankind to affect atmospheric concentrations of CO_2 upward or downward by 10 percent. Figure 6.20 shows different thresholds effected by global fossil fuel use while Figure 6.21 plots the average land surface temperatures from 1880 to 1995 and shows a general rise worldwide.

Sulphur dioxide, on the other hand, has an atmospheric lifetime of a few days, during which it forms aerosols. These aerosols have atmospheric lifetimes of approximately 10 days before they are removed by rain or settle under gravity. Hence, man-made aerosols are not well mixed in the atmosphere and have highest concentrations

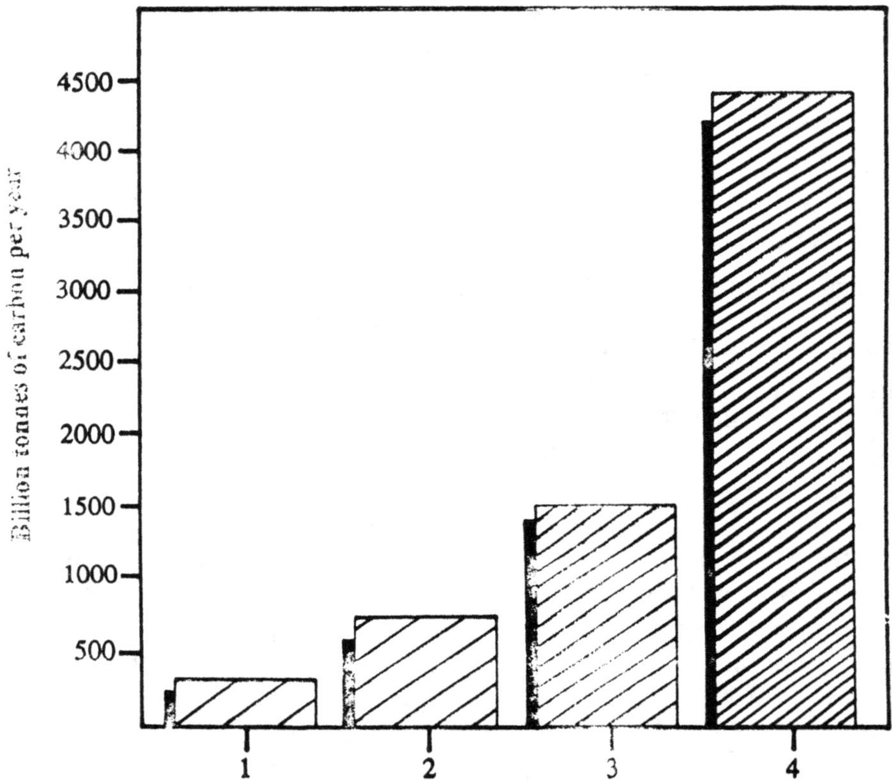

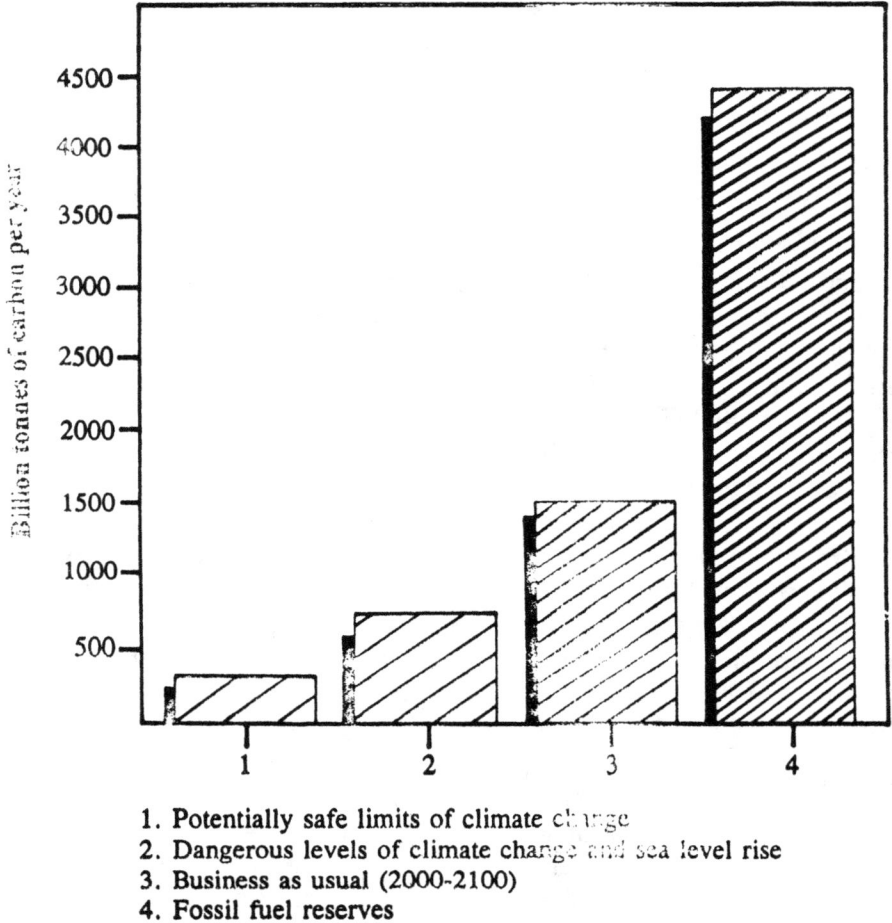

FIGURE 6.20 Thresholds of global fossil fuel use.

over and downwind of industrial areas. The regional variability and short lifetime of aerosol effects could increase the range of climatic extremes. Sulphate emissions, as aerosols, have a balancing effect in reducing greenhouse gas-induced climate change. This signals a future with greater reliance on renewable energy and emphasis on energy efficiency.

Economic growth that is compatible with reducing pollution can, in some measure, be accomplished by improving energy efficiency. The positive effects of energy efficiency are limited only by the additional capital that may be required to implement the most efficient systems. If the reduction of carbon emissions becomes a worldwide objective, a move to non-carbon fuel sources would be accelerated.

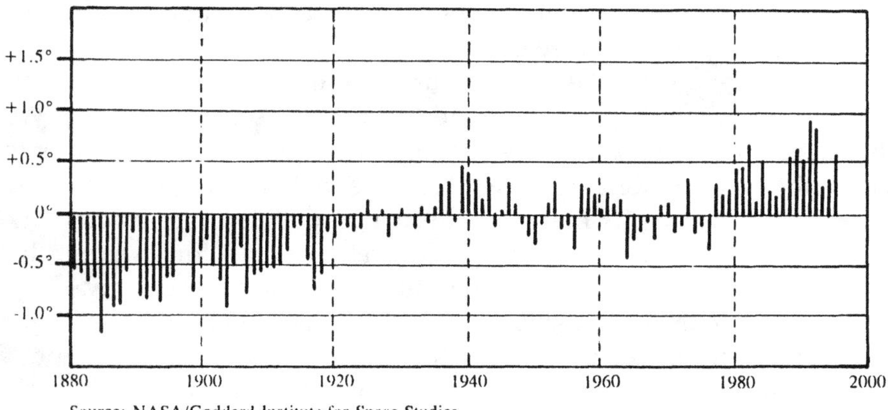

FIGURE 6.21 Rising temperature worldwide. The figure shows the average land surface temperature for each year compared with the average temperature for 1951 to 1980.

Perhaps a commercially viable fuel cell will offer a much used means of converting gasified fossil fuels to electricity, reducing polluting emissions by about 30 percent of current levels.

Only approximately 25 percent of the world's hydropower resources is now developed and more growth is expected in this sector, although there are ecological limits. The development of simpler, safer nuclear power plants may encourage an increase in the use of nuclear power. For solar and wind power, an increasing role would depend on the development of an efficient electricity storage system to overcome the question of intermediacy of supply.

With regard to end-use systems, there are evolving technologies that can reduce oil consumption and its attendant adverse environmental impact. Electric automobiles may become marginally competitive in some special situations, such as heavily polluted urban areas. Magnetically levitated versions of electric trains may benefit from new superconductivity developments. More efficient space heating and cooling equipment such as advanced heat pumps may move into common use.

POLICY

The future we face requires an array of flexible strategies in energy supply, energy efficiency, environmental sustainability, and economic growth. A balanced programme of energy development offers the best prospects of achieving the lowest social costs. The intention should be to encourage a range of technologies to move towards market viability, rather than to pick one or two winners in advance.

The energy policy maker has to utilize the forecasts that are available, even though they have the inevitable degree of uncertainty. We should rely less on accuracy of prediction and more on governments exhibiting a stable, long-term set of signals that encourage liberalized and competitive energy markets. This means developing a framework in which consumers and producers can respond – for example by removing monopolies on the generation and sale of electricity.

The knowledge that sustainable development requires the efficient use of resources in harmony with the environment will place emphasis on the development of renewable resources. Thus, an energy policy for countries in the Caribbean region should:

- Establish databases on energy supply, end use, and consumption, to serve as a strong basis for energy planning
- Require that energy prices to consumers fully reflect the economic cost, and that fiscal instruments such as taxes and duties effectively encourage energy efficiency
- Encourage electric utility companies to produce or purchase energy from renewable sources so that these resources can be brought on stream
- Require electric utility companies to evaluate the economic merit of energy efficiency in their least cost planning process
- Quantify, evaluate, and mitigate the environmental impacts of energy, both renewable and fossil-based, and seek to ensure that these impacts are included in project cost
- Reduce energy usage and exhaust emissions in the transportation sector
- Establish energy efficiency criteria in building codes and appliance standards

A general goal of energy policies for the region should be the fostering of economic development by reducing imports, creating employment, encouraging entrepreneurship, and reducing environmental impacts such as deforestation and air and water pollution.

Over the next two decades, the world will be focusing upon two major issues – energy and security of its supply, and energy and the environment. As Yergin (1991) put it, "a far-reaching clash between anxieties about energy security and economic well-being on the one side, and fears about the environment on the other, seems all but inevitable." The point of convergence of the two issues is energy conservation. Until there are significant technological breakthroughs in renewable energy technologies, there are but three primary clusters that will provide primary power, (1) oil, gas, and coal, (2) nuclear power, and (3) conservation in the form of technological improvements and increased efficiency in energy use.

National energy systems do not respond quickly to change because of intractable infrastructure (thermal power plants may function for 35 to 45 years) and long lead times (8 to 12 years) from concept to commissioning. Hence, we should carefully evaluate our choices for industrial fuels in the future, emphasizing clean fuels and indigenous renewable energy sources. It is important that global energy and environmental goals are aligned and work in association with each other. It will require not only policy but also practice.

Energy markets, as presently constituted, do not favour renewable energy sources. There is unequal access to investment capital, energy price distortions, and inadequate institutional capacity to commercialize immature technologies. Renewables usually cost more per kilowatt than fossil fuel power sources to install – even though low operating costs make them cost competitive on a lifecycle basis. Private power developers, whose discount rates are usually higher than those used by the public sector, try to minimize the initial investment to be financed. Also, because renewable energy projects are usually small, the transaction costs are high. Such costs include planning and developing projects, contracting with the utility, and assembling finance packages. Also, capital markets for conventional central station projects are better established than those for off-grid power equipment. In addition, some renewable energy technologies are classified as consumer goods and subject to a higher interest rate than that which utilities pay for capital.

Distortions in the price of energy are also barriers to renewable power development (Bates, 1993). Production and consumption subsidies lower the price of competing fossil fuels relative to renewable electricity generators that are grid connected. At the same time, they bias decisions away from off-grid applications of renewables that compete with diesel, kerosene, or power-line extensions. Some countries also subsidize fossil fuel consumption in markets where renewables can compete. Defined as the difference between consumer prices and world prices, 1995 world fuel subsidies exceed U.S.$ 212 billion. Of this total, coal and natural gas subsidies for power production totalled about U.S.$ 40 billion. Eastern Europe and republics of the former USSR have the highest fossil fuel subsidies. Instead of reducing subsidies on fossil fuels, some countries, such as India, have taken the more expensive approach of also subsidizing renewables. Some subsidies are also hidden. In India, for instance, the heavily subsidized railway system allocates 24 percent of its freight capacity to moving coal to power plants (Kozloff and Shobowale, 1994).

In the Caribbean, the institutional structure for commercializing renewable energy technologies is weak. This applies to scientific, engineering, manufacturing, and marketing capabilities. This is partly because the private sector is dominated by multinational companies that conduct little research and development through their local subsidies. Moreover, there is poor communication among stakeholders about new technologies and their applications.

Estimates for the cost of various technologies suggest that wind, solar thermal, and PVs offer the greatest cost-reduction opportunities. PV has the greatest potential for cost cutting, from about U.S.$ 0.21 per kilowatt hour to U.S.$ 0.06 per kilowatt hour. To achieve cost reductions of this magnitude will require larger production economies, and technical innovations. However, producers seem reluctant to invest the capital required to reduce cost when demand is low and uncertain. On the other hand, to a certain extent, demand stays low because at present costs for the technology it is not competitive in large markets.

Most countries now have policies and programmes to encourage the use of renewables by reducing their costs to competitive levels with conventional fossil fuel sources. Some of the newer sources such as wind, solar, and energy crops will need to expand their production and mature in commercial viability before they can replace established supply systems. Nevertheless, increasing market penetration is not only a matter of economic competitiveness but there are constraints such as a lack of familiarity as well as a reluctance to invest by financiers, manufacturers, and developers in what are regarded as immature technologies. Further, legal and administrative systems, which have accommodated large-scale conventional energy supply options, need modification in order to catalyse the development of small-scale, distributed energy sources. Renewables are now regarded as having the ability to provide energy in a sustainable way and as further constraints are imposed on emissions to the environment their development will be accelerated.

It is likely that the world population will stabilize at about three times present levels (10 to 15 billion) in the second half of this century. To cope with energy needs there will need to be a significant decrease in energy intensity, as a result of more energy-consuming transportation systems, buildings, and process industries (Lovejoy, 1996).

Also, fossil fuel consumption will be reduced not only because of resource depletion but also because of climate changes if the present consumption patterns are maintained. The transition to a stable, sustainable global economy with a high quality of life for all will be based on renewables and some increase in nuclear power while we await fuel cells. This has important implications for corporate and public sector planning, as well as for national and international policy making because effective action is required to stimulate development and market diffusion of renewable energy resources.

EPILOGUE

Energy plays a cardinal role in attaining the interrelated economic, social, and environmental objectives that lead to sustainable development. The delivery of energy services stimulates the development of income-generating opportunities and improves living standards. Accelerated application of clean energy technologies to fulfill the future need for energy services will play an important role in sustainable development.

Energy moves through a chain of development before it reaches the end user. The chain of conversions in energy systems is shown below.

Extraction	Primary Energy	Conversion Technologies	Distribution Technologies	Final Energy	End Use Technologies
Oil well	Oil	Refinery	Rail, sea, road pipeline	Gasolene	Transport
—	Sun	Photovoltaics	Electricity grid	Electricity	Lighting
Gas well	Natural gas	—	Pipeline grid	Natural gas	Oven, boiler
Coal mine	Coal	Power plant	Electricity grid	Electricity	Furnace
Uranium	Uranium	Power plant	Electricity grid	Electricity	Electricity
Agro-forestry	Biomass	Methanol plant	Road	Methanol	Engines

The end uses of energy are divided among transport, industry, agriculture, and others such as cooking, space cooling, and heating. From the viewpoint of the consumer, what is important is the level of service provided, rather than the amount of primary energy that goes into delivering the service. Because conserving a kilowatt hour of electricity is usually cheaper than producing an additional kilowatt hour, the most cost effective ways to deliver energy services often involve improving the efficiency of energy conversion to final energy or increasing the efficiency of end use devices.

Energy production and use are related to major issues such as poverty, rural development, food security, gender inequality, and the environment. Hence, the efficient use of energy intervenes positively in our social well-being. A major hurdle in improving energy efficiency lies in the way energy is perceived in the context of socio-economic development. Currently, energy consumption, rather than levels of energy service, is factored as the indicator of development. By using energy consumption as a major measure of development, economists are seemingly more concerned with increasing electricity and fuel supplies based on existing patterns of energy use, rather than seeking the appropriate level of energy services that would be required to provide the essential input for the full satisfaction of human needs. The need is to focus on how energy is used, its capacity for enhancing people's quality of life, and finding ways to increase access to energy services for the poor.

People at the lowest economic level cook with wood, dung, and charcoal. Those at the next level use coal and kerosene, while those at the highest levels use electricity and liquid propane gas (LPG). Interestingly, these levels are also related to energy efficiencies. For instance, the cook-stove efficiencies of firewood, kerosene, and LPG are roughly 15, 50, and 65 percent, respectively. Also, moving up the energy scale results in decreasing emissions of carbon dioxide, sulphur dioxide, and particulates. Further, the use of traditional fuels, when burned indoors, have a negative impact on the health of household members (Smith et al., 2000). Existing strategies for poverty alleviation that are concerned with macro-economic growth, human capital investment, and welfare programmes do not focus on the nexus between energy and poverty, bypassing opportunities for attention and improvement in this area (UNDP, 2000).

Gender-Sensitive Energy Planning

Women are important as activists and educators on energy and environmental issues. Women are influential to young people in the collection, management, and use of fuels and other natural resources, and influence how energy use patterns are replicated over time and passed on to future generations. Strengthening the role of energy in supporting sustainable development will require paying special attention to the participation of women in energy use.

Some energy projects to introduce new, fuel-efficient techniques or renewable technologies, particularly to developing countries, have failed partly because the projects and technologies have been designed by engineers without input from end users. End users, mainly women, should participate in the design of energy projects and the adaptation of technologies to suit local needs and preferences. Solar cooking is an example. In the Caribbean, women have rejected solar cookers because cooking in the middle of the day is considered to be too hot; and it is not convenient because the household eats its main meal in the evening.

Because they are familiar with the specific hardships other women experience due to lack of energy services, women as leaders and entrepreneurs are in a position to influence other women on the desirability of various energy alternatives.

Policies that give women choices of household energy sources and promote access to cleaner fuels, as well as more efficient cooking equipment, can have significant benefits for the health of women and children. Efforts are needed to make information available about technology options such as improved cook stoves, LPG, and electricity so that they are better able to make their own choices out of a range of possible options.

The Clean Development Mechanism (CDM)

The CDM is an instrument for promoting international cooperation on clean energy. Benefits to developing countries will obtain through investment in cleaner development strategies. Benefits to developed countries will relate to the ability to reduce emissions at a lower cost than would be the case through domestic action only.

The Kyoto Protocol of 1997 makes binding commitments for Annex 1 Parties (Industrialized Countries) to:

- Reduce total emissions of six key greenhouse gases by at least 5 percent for the post 2000 period
- Meet emission targets by the period 2008–2012

The potential operation of the CDM is based on an incentive structure directly linked to the fulfilment by Annex 1 Parties of their quantified commitments under the Protocol.

Developing countries do not have these commitments, but may participate through the CDM in the international effort aimed at combating global climate change. One way is through emissions trading. Emissions trading is a market tool that allows trading between countries that have accepted emission reduction commitments under the Kyoto Protocol. Emissions trading enables achievement of commitments, at least cost, by taking advantage of marginal cost differentials in emissions abatement among countries. For example, a 20-MW wind farm in Jamaica, a clean energy source, may save about 50,000 tonnes of carbon dioxide per annum. This could be traded to other countries as a credit towards meeting their commitments.

How Much More Oil?

Oil, and especially natural gas, will remain plentiful for many decades; oil for at least 40 years, and natural gas for 90 years. At the same time, the ways of converting those fuels into energy, such as internal combustion engines and combined-cycle gas turbines, are continually growing more efficient. Because of improvements in efficiency, reliance on oil in industrialized countries has diminished significantly.

Some optimists believe that hydrocarbons will remain the fuel of choice for the twenty-first century. Others argue that the predominance of oil in energy markets may soon start to weaken. The prospective scarcity of oil, coupled with the unstable politics of the Middle East, will cause a steep increase in oil prices by 2025. The high demand for oil in developing countries will also bolster oil prices.

Pessimists regard oil depletion as now close to the psychologically important halfway mark and they anticipate that there will be a decline in oil production before 2010. Most analysts, however, expect that the halfway mark will be reached closer to 2030. Most early forecasts (in the 1970s) did not consider that the power of technological advances in exploration and production and nontraditional oil such as tar sands and orimulsion would help to regulate the price of oil.

It is clear that oil will be replaced only by a fuel that is at least equally cheap, easy to use, efficient and has fewer emissions. Even if such a fuel comes on-stream in the next 5 years, oil will continue to prevail for many decades, because of the large investments that have been made in infrastructure, the large remaining deposits, the rapid advances in fossil fuel technology, and the resistant strength of incumbency.

However, prices are not likely to be as low as U.S.$ 10 per barrel again. This is because demand has increased and OPEC producers have failed to keep pace. Only Saudi Arabia has large spare capacity. If the world demand for oil is to be met, oil supply will have to increase by about 25 percent over the next 15 years, to about 100 million barrels per day.

Another factor is the bottlenecks in the pipeline and refining sector. Despite a strong growth in demand, no new refineries have been built in the U.S. for two decades. The industry opines that this is due to a combination of tougher environmental regulations, lower margins, and bureaucratic hurdles. Large energy companies are now switching emphasis away from refining and marketing to exploration and production.

The volatility of oil prices, combined with concerns about the adverse environmental impact of hydrocarbons, is stimulating the search for alternatives. Innovations will eventually eliminate the near-monopoly that oil has in the transport sector. Simply put, the stone age did not end because the world ran out of stones, and the oil age will end long before the world has run out of oil.

The biggest threat to the dominance that oil has in the transport sector is fuel cells. Fuel cells are quiet, produce energy from hydrogen and oxygen more efficiently than an internal combustion engine does from gasoline, and the only emission is benign water vapour. There are several types of fuel cells, all with three basic components:

1. A fuel processor that converts hydrocarbon fuel (e.g., natural gas or methanol) to a hydrogen-rich gas, which the fuel cell actually consumes.
2. A stack, in which the electrochemical reactions create the electrical energy.
3. A power conditioner that converts direct current (DC) from the stack to alternating current (AC) for use.

In principle, a fuel cell works much like a battery, only it does not run down. It creates electricity as long as it receives hydrogen.

Many automobile manufacturers are pursuing fuel cell technology diligently. DaimlerChrysler, General Motors, Honda, and Toyota expect to have fuel cell vehicles in production by 2005 and on the retail market during the period 2007–2008. Within the industry, there are people who predict that by 2025 approximately 20 percent of new passenger vehicles and about 80 percent of urban buses will be powered by fuel cells. The big problem in achieving this level of market penetration is the fuel infrastructure. The service station industry is simply not organized to deliver hydrogen on demand. Initially, the hydrogen may have to be derived from hydrocarbons.

Thus, in about two decades there will be severe competition between conventional vehicles and vehicles powered by fuel cells. However, the conventional internal combustion engine is a moving target, as improvements result in a conventional lowering of exhaust pollution, making it more competitive.

We are gradually moving towards the hydrogen age in energy. By 2050, hydrogen and natural gas will be more important fuels than oil and coal. By the turn of the century they will provide as much as 75 percent of the world's energy market. As such, there can be many visions for the future. For example, if technology can be developed to remove the carbon from hydrocarbons and sequester it, then oil and gas could be the major source of hydrogen. While we wait for this to happen, natural gas will be a clean and easily available transition fuel. This switch to hydrogen may occur in the last two decades of this century. Even if it does take that long, the energy market has begun to drift beyond the era of hydrocarbons and towards a hydrogen age, with increasing momentum. Thus, the twenty-first century may be as profoundly shaped by the move away from fossil fuels as the twentieth century was marked by the move towards them.

The Electricity Sector

Natural gas is on its way to becoming the most important fuel in electricity production. Gas is cleaner than oil or coal, and concerns about the health impacts of fuels have stimulated its use, as have recent technological trends in power generation. Combined cycle gas turbines are the standard bearers in power generation. Coming soon is distributed electricity by micropower units, such as microturbines and fuel cells, all of which now use natural gas as a primary source.

The gradual rise of micropower does not mean the end of power from large electricity grids. In most countries, a strong and robust grid network may become an important part of micropower in the future. However, in some developing countries an inadequate weak grid could be supplanted by distributed electricity. Advances in electronics and software will enhance micropower, allowing the flexibility of linking parts of electricity systems together. Micropower will enhance the ability of consumers to both buy and sell power more easily, through their electricity meters.

Micropower will also bring together the concept of microgrids that can link many micropower units together electronically, whether wind turbines, small-scale hydropower, solar energy, or fuel cells. In this scenario, the microchip will be both a consumer and supplier of electricity.

Sustainable Energy for the Caribbean

Regional cooperation in energy supply will be an important component of policy as the Caribbean faces its energy future, by meeting a dramatic increase in energy demand concomitant with economic growth. While we recognize the global nature of the energy problem, the approach will be to look first to our own neighbourhood – the energy-rich countries such as Venezuela, Trinidad and Tobago, Colombia, and Mexico.

Thus, most Caribbean countries will have a four-pronged energy strategy: first, to make energy security a priority of foreign policy; second, to encourage environmentally friendly exploration and production of indigenous hydrocarbon resources; third, to support the development of cost-effective alternative energy sources; and fourth, to promote the production of electricity, to keep pace with growing demands.

Many countries are now setting targets for the provision of electricity from renewable energy sources such as wind, solar, and hydropower. In Jamaica, the percentage of alternative energy installed (through hydropower) in the utility system presently stands at 4 percent. In 2001, the minimum targets set by the Jamaican government are:

Year	Period Target	Cumulative Target
2001	4% (present)	4% (present)
2005	2%	6%
2010	2%	8%
2020	4%	12%

Energy efficiency will see the growth of energy service companies (ESCOs). They not only provide traditional energy efficiency retrofits and management services, but work to incorporate higher value efficiency along with distributed renewable energy technologies. They are just beginning to make an impact on the market. However, high energy prices will move this industry into the mainstream, as a primary integrator of efficiency and renewable energy in commercial and industrial buildings and facilities.

Cheap energy will never return on a global scale. Perhaps the age of energy innocence is gone forever. Energy use has to work alongside energy efficiency and energy-saving measures. Success will come when we raise public interest in and knowledge of sustainable energy use, and increase public enthusiasm for sustainable energy applications, as efforts are made to ensure that energy supply matches demand.

REFERENCES AND FURTHER READING

Abbate, C. 1996. "Open public spaces and street furniture: The potential for increased use of photovoltaics in the built environment". *Progress in Photovoltaics* 4, no. 4: 269–277.

Abbate, C. 2001. "Power of design: The future of building-integrated PV". *Renewable Energy World* 4, no. 2: 59–65.

Bates, R. W. 1993. "The impact of economic policy on energy and the environment in developing countries". pp. 479–506, in R. H. Socolow, D. Anderson, and J. Harte, eds., *Annual Review of Energy and the Environment*. Annual Reviews, Inc., Palo Alto, California.

Boopsingh, T. M. 1990. *Oil, Gas and Development: A View from the South*. Longman, Trinidad.

Brown, G. 1996. "Geothermal energy". pp. 353–392, in G. Boyle, ed., *Renewable Energy*. Oxford University Press, Oxford, U.K.

Department of the Environment. 1993. *Renewable Energy, Annex on Wind Energy*, Planning Policy Guidance Note (PPG22). Her Majesty's Stationery Office, London.

Duchane, D. V. 1996. "Geothermal energy from hot dry rock: A renewable energy technology moving towards practical implementation". *Renewable Energy* 9, nos. 1–4: 1246–1249.

Duckers, L. 1995. "Water power – wave, tidal and low-head hydro technologies". *Power Engineering Journal* (August): 164–172.

Everett, R. and G. Boyle. 1996. "Integration". pp. 395–434, in G. Boyle, ed., *Renewable Energy*. Oxford University Press, Oxford, U.K.

Friedleifsson, I. B. 1996. "Present status and potential role of geothermal energy in the world". *Renewable Energy* 8, nos. 1–4: 34–39.

Goldenberg, J., L. C. Monaco, and I. C. Macedo. 1993. "The Brazilian fuel-alcohol program". In T. B. Johansson et al., eds., *Renewable Energy Sources for Fuels and Electricity*. Island Press, Washington, D.C.

Grubb, M. J. 1991. "The integration of renewable electricity sources". *Energy Policy* (September).

Hadley Centre. 1995. *Modelling Climate Change, 1860–2050*. The Meteorological Office, London.

Harder, M. K. and L. A. Freeman. 1996. "A study of an integrated land-fill and coppice power station". *Renewable Energy* 9, nos. 1–4: 989–992.

Headley, O. 1995. "Solar thermal systems for use in the Caribbean". Proceedings of the Caribbean High Level Workshop on Renewable Energy Technologies, December 5-9, 1994, St Lucia, UNESCO.

Hill, R. 1995. "Solar power". *Power Engineering Journal* (August): 175–180.

Hobbs, G. W. 1995. "Oil shale, coalbed gas, geothermal trends sized up". *Oil and Gas Journal* (September 11): 64–66.

Houghton, J. T. 1994. *Global Warming: The Complete Briefing*. Lion Publishing.

Infield, D. 1995. "Wind power – a major resource for the UK". *Power Engineering Journal* (August): 181–187.

Intergovernmental Panel on Climate Change. 2001. *The Third Assessment*. Cambridge University Press, Cambridge, U.K.

Jefferson, M. 1994. "Global prospects for renewable energy". *Renewable Energy* 5, pt. 1: 5–11.

Johansson, B. 1996. "Will Swedish biomass be sufficient for future transportation fuel demands?" *Energy* 21, no. 12: 1059–1069.

Kozloff, K. and O. Shobowale. 1994. *Rethinking Development Assistance for Renewable Electricity*. World Resources Institute, Washington, D.C.

Lennard, D. L. 1995. "The viability and best location for ocean thermal energy conversion systems around the world". *Renewable Energy* 6, no. 3: 359–365.

Lovejoy, D. 1996. "The necessity of solar energy". *Renewable Energy* 9, nos. 1–4: 1138–1143.

Lou, Y. 1994. "The engineering and economic evaluation for chemical utilization of biomass". *Renewable Energy* 5, pt. 11: 866–874.

May, J. 1990. *The Greenpeace Book of the Nuclear Age*. Pantheon Books, New York.

Mays, I. 1996. "The status and prospects for wind energy". *Renewable Energy* 8, nos. 1–4: 29–33.

McCallion, K. F. 1995. *Shoreham and the Rise and Fall of the Nuclear Power Industry*. Praeger Publishers, Westport, Connecticut.

Minott, D. A. and C. E. Lewis. 1991. "Imported coal or fuel gas from cane tops". *JBI Journal* 9: 84–91.

Ramage, J. 1996. "Hydroelectricity". pp. 183–226, in G. Boyle, ed., *Renewable Energy*. Oxford University Press, Oxford, U.K.

Ramage, J. and J. Scurlock. 1996. "Biomass". pp. 137–182, in G. Boyle, ed., *Renewable Energy*. Oxford University Press, Oxford, U.K.

Scheer, H. 2001. *A Solar Manifesto*. James and James (Science Publishers), London.

Simnad, M. T. 1996. "Has the nuclear power industry risen and fallen or will it rise again?" *Energy* 21, no. 12: 1095–1100.

Smith, K. R., J. M. Samet, I. Romieu, and N. Bruce. 2000. "Indoor air pollution in developing countries and ALRI in children". *Thorax* 55: 518–532.

Starr, C., M. F. Searl, and S. Alpert. 1992. "Energy sources: A realistic outlook". *Science* 256: 981.

Tanner, D. 1995. "Ocean thermal energy conversion: Current overview and future outlook". *Renewable Energy* 6, no. 3: 367–373.

Tavares, G. M. 1995. "Wind energy environmental considerations". *Environtech '95* (Abstracts), Rio de Janeiro, Brazil, pp. 71–72.

Taylor, D. 1996. "Wind energy". In G. Boyle, ed., *Renewable Energy*. Oxford University Press, Oxford, U.K.

UNDP (United Nations Development Program). 2000. "Energy and social issues". pp. 1–41, in *World Energy Assessment: Energy and the Challenge of Sustainability*. United Nations Development Program, New York.

Weightman, F. 1995. *Planning for Wind Power: Guidelines for Project Developers and Local Planners*. Friends of the Earth Limited, London.

World Energy Council. 1994. *New Renewable Energy Resources*. London: Kogan Page.

Wright, R. M. 1991. "Alternative energy prospects – with particular reference to Jamaica". *JBI Journal* 9: 37–70.

Wright, R. M. 1996. *Jamaica's Energy, Old Prospects, New Resources*. Petroleum Corporation of Jamaica, Kingston and Canoe Press, Mona.

Wright, R. M. 2001. "Wind energy development in the Caribbean". *Renewable Energy* 24: 439–444.

Yergin, D. 1991. *The Prize: The Epic Quest for Oil, Money and Power*. Simon and Schuster, New York.

7

Recreational Use of Natural Resources

Ivan Goodbody and David Smith

Contents

INTRODUCTION

In the context of this chapter, recreation is interpreted to mean the use of the natural environment for leisure, physical enjoyment, education, and intellectual stimulation. Historically, this type of activity took place in harmony with the environment, with few or no adverse effects. More recently, particularly over the past 30 years, the picture has changed, due largely to three things – an increase in disposable incomes making it possible to spend more on leisure activities, increased individual mobility through the use of automobiles or air travel, and improved communications, which have increased people's awareness of the global opportunities for leisure. As a consequence, whereas environmentally oriented leisure pursuits were hitherto relatively low key, with limited income-generating potential, they are now part of a worldwide and highly profitable commercial activity. Due to the profitability of the business, more and more "opportunities" are being opened up for leisure travelers to explore environments that had previously suffered little, if at all, from human impact. Whether it is walking tours in Tuscany, Land Rover safaris in the game parks of East Africa, cruise ship tours to Antarctica, guided tours to the summit of Mount Everest, or a submarine tour of a Caribbean coral reef, this new and massive use of the global environment for leisure has a significant impact on both the physical landscape and the biota living in these places. This in turn presents a challenge to both industry and managers of the environment to determine how the increasing demand can be met and sustained while maintaining the essential characteristics of the environment that travelers wish to enjoy. This chapter looks at this activity with special reference to the Caribbean and examines first the nature of the problem and second the economic and conservation issues involved.

RECREATIONAL USE AND IMPACT ON THE NATURAL ENVIRONMENT

It is impossible in this short chapter to encompass all forms of recreational activity in detail. Hence, in order to highlight the issues involved, we are using a simple classification of impacts into those arising from:

- Physical exercise
- Natural history interest
- Boating and fishing
- Swimming and SCUBA diving
- Hunting

Each of these types of activity has its own particular impact on the environment but there are linkages and problems common to them all which we will endeavour to address, while at the same time suggesting management practices through which recreational activity and environmental protection may be harmonized.

Physical Exercise

This type of activity varies from the simple "Sunday evening" walk to regular jogging, countryside hikes, hill-walking, climbing, and cycling. With the exception of rock climbing and cycling the impacts are similar and density dependent. Where an occasional visit by a few persons occurs, the impact is negligible, but when the environment is used regularly and by a large number of people, the impact quickly becomes injurious and management measures are required. Most urban areas in the world have places where people go for "a breath of air" and "to stretch their legs." Where the impact is low, natural paths can be allowed to develop. Just as sheep or cows on a hillside or animals in a forest find the most convenient routes from one feeding area to another or to water, so also humans find and make simple trails to follow. High density use in urban parks, however, can lead to compacted soils, erosion of grass and other vegetation and, in the absence of forward planning, this ultimately requires remedial action, usually ending in paved walkways and "Please keep off the grass" signs. The problem for management, therefore, is to anticipate these events and plan development of the area so as to permit high density usage along made trails coupled with minimum disturbance to the natural environment. Good examples of this type of management are to be seen in many provincial parks in Canada.

We introduce this topic through consideration of the urban park because historically damage due to walking is an old and universal activity in crowded cities and towns. Only recently has it impinged seriously on the wider rural landscape as a result of the increased mobility of people and their desire to enjoy the natural environment in whatever way pleases them. In the absence of management the impact is simple but deleterious; pathways are eroded and vegetation is cut or removed to widen trails, thus enhancing the opportunity for water to erode the trail further. The problem is most serious in moist hilly country where natural runoff of water tends to find and use steep trails as a water course. The problem is minimal on the packed ice of high latitudes or the hard lava rock of volcanic islands, such as those in the eastern Caribbean (for example, Dominica, St Lucia, and St Vincent) and the central Pacific (for example, Hawaii). The regulatory problem, however, is complex because on the one hand people should be encouraged to take an interest in and to enjoy the environment, while on the other hand their activities need to be managed in such a manner as to protect the environment. It is further complicated by the use of trail bikes, motorcycles, and four-wheel drive automobiles, all of which are destructive to underlying soils, especially in moist environments.

No matter how much one may respect the individual's right to enjoy the environment as he or she pleases, this philosophy can only be entertained if it is not detrimental to the interests of others. One must conclude, therefore, that, in the interests of the environment and of other users, countryside leisure activity has to be managed and regulated. Such management procedures should include the following:

- Sufficient trails and look-out points should be provided to permit users to move through and enjoy the environment with minimal disturbance. This effectively contains traffic without necessarily restricting those who need to or wish to explore more widely.
- There should be sign-posting at junctions and points of special interest.
- Trails should be carefully landscaped at points subject to special stress.
- Each park or system of trails should have its own set of user guidelines and regulations based on the nature of the environment and its anticipated usage and carrying capacity. This should include any desired restriction of access by trail bikes, motor cycles, and four-wheel drive automobiles.

Containment

There really is no issue about containment. The majority of hikers are willing and content to remain on designated trails, which provide comfort and security from getting lost. There are many excellent examples of such trails in action, such as the Appalachian Trail in the eastern U.S. and others found throughout the state and provincial parks of North America or through the forests and national parks in Europe. There are also excellent examples within the Caribbean, such as the Buccament Nature Trail in the Vermont Valley in St Vincent, the Blue Mountain Trail (Hodges, 1993) and Fairy Glade Trail in Jamaica, and the trails at Cockscomb and Chan Chich reserves in Belize (Perrottet, 1995). The process of containment on designated trails should not be seen as binding and restrictive (except in cases where elements of the biota need special protection). Instead, it is a management technique for channeling traffic in such a manner as to protect the attraction that visitors wish to enjoy.

Landscaping

Heavily used trails need to be managed. Proper sign-posting and markers to indicate trail limits (if necessary) and to guide hikers at junctions are critical. Other maintenance procedures include regular, careful bushing of margins delineating the trail to prevent overgrowth with lush vegetation, the inclusion of boardwalks or steps at critical areas of erosion so as to reduce the impact of human feet, surfacing paths on clay soils in wet areas, and training of water courses to reduce erosion. All of these management practices require the cost recovery procedures addressed below.

Visitor Information

A visitor's experience is enriched and the value of a trail is enhanced if visitors are provided with proper information about the trail before or during their walk. Visitors want to know what is special or interesting about the environment in question, what they are likely to see (biota and scenic points of interest), how long the trail is, and whether there are options for short walks or long walks. In an ideal situation, and especially in large parks, there will be a visitor centre where maps of the area and photographs of interesting features or elements of the biota can be displayed and guidebooks and souvenirs can be purchased. For the manager the visitor centre is also important because this is where cost recovery takes place through collection of user fees (if these are payable) and where he or she obtains information on who is using the trail at any given time and what numbers of people are using it at different periods of time (seasonal usage). Information for visitors that is available at a visitor centre needs to be supplemented by additional information provided by signs on the trail, whether simple number signs that refer the visitor to a guidebook or actual name tags on trees that are considered to be interesting.

Visitor centres are expensive to maintain and hence cost recovery has to be effective or more simple techniques used to provide visitor information. In some countries "honour boxes" are provided where visitors can drop a donation in a locked box and can pick up a small leaflet of information about the trail or other attraction. Alternatively signs at the beginning of a trail may direct visitors to a local shop or other outlet where they may purchase a guidebook. The provision of information is important and managers have to be innovative in how it is made available to visitors.

Regulation

It is impossible to manage any large public recreation area in the absence of certain rules of behaviour. To many people the very existence of regulation is confrontational and an invitation to rebel. While some regulations may have to exist it is probably more constructive to issue "guidelines for visitors", which advise them on how to behave and how they can assist in protecting the attraction. In this context some of the precautions that managers/regulators should ask visitors to take include the following:

- Visitors should stay on designated trails, both for individual safety and to protect the surrounding environment.
- Visitors should avoid damaging plants or picking wildflowers so that others may also enjoy them.
- Visitors should avoid disturbing nesting birds or animals with young.
- Visitors should respect other people's desire for quiet enjoyment of the countryside and hence not play radios or music systems.
- Visitors should take home all solid waste and not litter the countryside.
- Visitors should not light fires except at designated picnic or camp sites.

In certain circumstances (long forest walks or wilderness areas) it may be desirable, for safety reasons, for hikers to advise the visitor centre of their intended route and expected time of return.

Mechanical Vehicles

Trail bikes, motor cycles, and four-wheel drive automobiles are all potentially destructive to underlying soils and hence to the environment in general, especially where soils are moist and soft. In some parts of the world (for example, the Scottish Highlands) their uncontrolled use has become a matter of great concern to landowners and park managers and steps have had to be taken to regulate their activity. Except in special circumstances, therefore, their use needs to be restricted to dry environments, marled trails, or other made surfaces. In some places, such as large recreational parks, it is possible to set aside special trails for use by mechanical vehicles (especially trail bikes). This helps to protect the environment and, for reasons of safety, enforces a spatial separation between vehicles and hikers. Managers and regulators need to carefully examine methods of cost recovery to offset any damage incurred by mechanical vehicles.

Natural History Interest*

The explosion of interest in natural history has brought more and more people into rural areas to see plants and animals in their natural environment. Some of this is discrete and individualistic and does no harm to the environment. However, the socialization and commercialization of natural history has magnified the effect and, in some cases, imposes considerable stress on the environment and poses danger to the plants and animals concerned, so that regulation and management become of prime concern.

One of the outcomes of this escalation in interest is the development of a specialized form of tourism generally referred to as *ecotourism*. Ecotourism has been defined by the Caribbean Tourism Organisation (1993) as "the interaction between a visitor and the natural or cultural environment, which results in a learning experience while maintaining respect for the environment and culture and providing benefits for the local economy." Blommestein (1995), on the other hand recognizes two distinct activities, which he refers to as "nature tourism" and "ecotourism." He wrote:

> Perhaps the most significant difference between nature based mass tourism and ecotourism is that the latter should be based on the concepts of conservation, authenticity and economic development, while the former has economic

* Nature-based tourism in the sea is linked to SCUBA diving and snorkelling and is dealt with separately.

> development as its primary focus. While the two have economic development aspects in common the *modus operandi* differs. Ideally in ecotourism the focus is on community based development, whereby there is a broader distribution of benefits. (p. 196)

The word "ecotourism" is used far too loosely to denote a number of different concepts, including both heritage tourism and nature tourism. Indeed, this was recognized at the World Conservation Congress held by the World Conservation Union (IUCN) in Montreal in 1996 (IUCN, 1996). The delegates noted that "ecotourism is often used indiscriminately for all tourism in natural areas even when such activity provides no measurable benefits to the natural area or the people living close to the areas involved, and at times directly threatens those same areas" (IUCN, 1996, 32–33). Consequently, the Congress suggested that the definition of ecotourism should include the generation of tangible benefits for natural area conservation, allow protected areas to collect and retain revenue, support activities that benefit local communities, and develop partnerships among the private sector, the community, and the managers of the protected area.

The definition of ecotourism used by the Caribbean Tourism Organisation speaks only to "maintaining respect for the environment" without emphasizing the need for conservation. We believe that Blommestein's distinction between nature tourism and ecotourism is significant and should be borne in mind when planning for or regulating such activities. Whether the activity is by local groups or organized tours for visitors there are two main impacts to be considered: physical impact on the environment and disturbance to the biota.

Physical Impact

As previously mentioned, physical impact includes the compacting of soils and erosion along trails regularly used by hikers. Much of the land-based activity of nature tourism involves leading groups of people along trails to see wildlife, and unless these trails are periodically rested or properly managed by drainage, surfacing, and boardwalks where necessary, they will inevitably be degraded. The boardwalks through parts of the Everglades National Park in Florida are an excellent example of how this type of structure can be used to facilitate and control access with minimal disturbance to the biota. Where boardwalks prove impractical or too expensive and where human-induced stress is intense, managers need to consider the possibility of alternative trails so that trails may be periodically rested in the same way that farming practice sometimes calls for certain fields to be rested for a period.

The physical impacts in the marine environment are different to those on land and we return to them later.

Disturbance of the Biota

It is open to question as to how much the biota is actually disturbed by large numbers of interested tourists passing through any area, and naturally this must depend on local circumstances. Over 40,000 tourists walk through the nesting colonies of seabirds and haul up sites of sealions on the Galapagos Islands yearly and, seemingly, the animals are in no way disturbed (Jackson, 1994). Similarly, thousands of people drive through the game parks of East and South Africa with little noticeable harm to the wildlife, and similar conditions appear to prevail in Antarctica. However, all of these tourist locations are in open country where animals have a wide view of everything around them, and where "secrecy" is minimal. Conditions may not be the same in dense forest where human and animal encounters are more sudden and where the sense of smell for mammals may be more important than vision as a means of animal communication. Because of this over-riding element of secrecy in forests it is of special importance that nesting birds and mammals with young are not disturbed.

Tour companies and tour directors watch profits and have an interest in channeling as many people as possible through a particular attraction. It may not matter to them if the attraction is spoilt through overuse. They merely look for a new destination. In practice, conservation of the environment and the biota is far more important than profit and the responsibility for this and for sustainable development of the attraction belongs to local managers. To sustain the attraction on a long-term basis, a number of conditions are required of managers, including that they should:

- Be fully familiar with the ecology and the biota of the area under management
- Be conversant with the natural history of key fauna and flora
- Be conversant with the breeding activities of animals so that these activities are not unduly disturbed
- Know the carrying capacity of the area under management and control the flow of tourists so that this is not exceeded
- Make provision, where desirable, for "resting" certain areas of the attraction on a periodic basis

Many tourists are interested only in seeing birds and mammals. Among bird watchers in general there is a special activity which in some cases can lead to acute environmental stress; that is, the desire to see rarities and record that sighting in a life list of birds that the individual has seen. The activity is akin to stamp collecting rather than to serious natural history; the aim is to see and record as many species of bird as possible without necessarily understanding too much about the species and its way of life. This activity, termed "twitching", is described amusingly and in great detail by Oddie, who wrote:

> What distinguishes the real twitcher is his degree of emotional involvement in whether he succeeds in getting a new tick . . . If this kind of birder gets to hear that a bird has been sighted that would be a tick for him, he is so wracked with nervous anticipation . . . that he literally twitches . . . Perhaps the degree of involvement is conveyed [best] in the words of one young bird watcher who told me: *If I know that there is a new bird around, nothing will stop me – nothing*! (Oddie, 1980, 23)

In many of the instances described by Oddie the activities of twitchers are harmless – bird watchers rushing from place to place by car, train, airplane, and even helicopter in Britain, just to see rare migrant species. However, the activity is not always harmless and Oddie goes on to describe the damage to property and farmland and the social conflicts between visitors and local owners that sometimes arise.

This type of almost hysterical twitching barely exists in the Caribbean but the same set of emotions drives many nature tourists from country to country in search of new bird-watching experiences or in search of rare orchids, bromeliads, or other plants. The notion that equal or greater intellectual satisfaction might be achieved by staying in one place and studying in depth is foreign to most people but this emotional drive to see rarities is a factor to be considered by Caribbean conservationists and places increasing responsibility on managers. The ornithological tours of the endemic parrots of the Caribbean, especially those of St Vincent, St Lucia, and Dominica, are a case in point. They are a worldwide attraction for bird-watchers and this has both positive and negative effects. On the one hand, it has encouraged the setting aside of reserves for the protection of these birds. On the other hand, it increases environmental stress and disturbance of the birds in question. All of this is manageable but costs money. In both St Lucia and St Vincent visitors pay a fee to enter the trail on which parrots may be seen but no such charge appears to exist in Dominica. Once again, cost recovery in support of conservation and management in areas used for recreation is a central issue. With the increase in cruise ship tourism in the Caribbean and the possibility of many hundreds of persons wishing to visit a site on any one day the issue of carrying capacity will also be important and managers may have to limit the numbers who can visit.

The discussion so far has tended to centre on warm blooded animals, birds and mammals, but recreational use of the environment extends to other animals (butterflies, reptiles) and to plants. The underlying principles of conservation and management do not differ but, among plants, there are special considerations in respect of orchids and bromeliads because people all over the world grow them in private collections. Particularly in the case of orchids there is a high monetary value on some rare species and there are thriving businesses collecting and growing these plants. All orchids are listed in Appendix II of the Convention on International Trade in Endangered Species (CITES) and hence a license is required in order to import orchids into, or export them from, a country that is signatory to the Convention (Wijnstekers, 1992). This does not necessarily protect orchids from local or visiting collectors who are often prepared to go to any length to acquire rare orchids for their collections. In the same way that drugs can be smuggled from country to country so also can rare plants and animals, notwithstanding the rules of the Convention. This is not the place to expand on this issue and to discuss the measures for protection but we draw attention to it here as an issue related to recreational activity. For further information on the trade in endangered species the reader is referred to Wijnstekers (1992).

Aquatic Activities

Boating

The recreational use of power boats may at first appear to have little or no impact on the environment but the opposite is often the case. The principal problem is that power boats, when driven fast, create a laterally spreading bow wave or "wash", the size of which is related to both the size and speed of the boat, as well as its hull design. When this wash hits the shoreline it breaks as a series of heavy waves or a surge, impacting coastal structures. Marina operators are well aware of this effect and usually have speed limits within the marina in order to avoid damage to piers and other boats; but once outside the marina there are seldom any regulations to govern behaviour. For a full account of marinas and small craft harbours as they affect the environment the reader is referred to the Natural Resources Conservation Authority (1996).

Along rocky shores the impact of the wash from a boat is usually unimportant because the very existence of the rocky environment is an indication of a shoreline normally subjected to wave action. It is different when the wash impacts a beach where it will run up and down the shore, causing erosion and throwing sediments into short-term suspension. This becomes a serious issue if the beach is used by other people for recreational swimming and on more than one occasion we have seen small children knocked over by such a wash. The control of power boat activity around beaches used for recreation thus becomes an important managerial problem.

A special issue relating to power boats arises when they enter mangrove environments. Mangroves grow in sheltered environments and most mangrove lagoons are normally subjected to only minimal wave action. Around the margins of the lagoon the peripheral roots of the red mangrove (*Rhizophora mangle*) hang down into the water and are a substrate for the growth of communities of sessile organisms, notably sponges, oysters, and sea squirts (Rutzler and Feller, 1996). These organisms are an important part of the balanced ecosystem but are accustomed to surviving in sheltered environments. When the wash of a fast-moving boat hits the shoreline the roots are then thrown into motion, banging against each other and bouncing in the water, all of which damages and sometimes strips off the biotic community. A second impact is that the surge of water throws up soft bottom sediments into suspension and some of this resettles on the root biota, clogging their filtering mechanisms and killing or damaging the animals. It is important, therefore, that if mangrove areas are to be protected and under management, rules are enforced to control the speed of power boats through sensitive areas.

Another issue of importance in the Caribbean is that in many mangrove lagoons and river estuaries there are populations of manatees (*Trichecus manatus*). Manatees feed on seagrasses, especially *Thalassia testudinum*, and occasionally come to the surface to breathe but when they do so only the very tip of the snout emerges quickly and briefly and it is not easy for a boat operator to recognize that manatees are present. As a consequence, many manatees have been injured by impact with boats either by collision with the hull or, worse, by impact with the propeller. Some of these injuries will heal leaving the animal scarred but, in other cases, especially where impact is with the propeller, the animal dies. Manatees are an endangered species and it is particularly important that in areas they frequent, managers enforce rules for power boat operation. For further information the reader is referred to the Natural Resources Conservation Authority (1994).

The use of power boats is a major recreational activity throughout the Caribbean. However, there are significant management issues that need to be addressed to ensure safety for people and protection of the environment. These issues have to be addressed not only through regulation but also through education. We believe that many power boat operators are unaware of the risks to other people, the environment, and the biota arising from the manner in which they operate their boats. The following are issues managers must address:

- National regulations concerning issues of safety, for example speed control in harbours and beach environments, life support systems, distress signals, and fire protection.
- Special regulations relating to individually safeguarded areas which, through control of speed, anchoring, waste discharge, etc., ensure protection of the environment in general and the biota in particular.
- Installation of permanent moorings in heavily used areas (certain beaches, reefs, and marine parks) to which boats may tie up instead of anchoring. This prevents anchor damage to the environment.
- Implementation of regulations (swimming, boating, jet skiing) so that the safety of users is ensured. In certain cases there may be merit in designating safe swimming beaches where power boat activity is prohibited.
- Regulation and education to control waste discharge from boats (solid and liquid wastes and hydrocarbon spills). Under the MARPOL Convention the entire Caribbean is designated as a specially protected area and no wastes other than sewage should be discharged from boats.

Swimming

In general, recreational swimming along beaches has little environmental impact, except on the beach itself. Heavily used beaches become impacted, eroded, and frequently littered with solid waste. Two examples can be drawn from Jamaica. At Dunn's River Falls on the north coast about one million people visit the attraction every year. While the main attraction is to climb the falls, everyone who does so has to commence on a tiny bathing beach which is far too small to accommodate the number of people who pass across it or who remain to swim. It far exceeds its carrying capacity and this results in a highly compacted beach and visible signs of erosion. The second example is at Lime Cay in the Port Royal area of Jamaica. The cay is about one hectare in area, most of it covered by short mangrove bushes bordered by seaside mahoe (*Hibiscus tiliaceus*) and other plants. It has a fringing reef on its northern side and a sandy beach bordered by beach-rock along the southern and western margins. Formerly little used except by fishermen, this is now a focal point for recreation at weekends when, at busy times, many hundreds of people converge on the cay. Local fishermen provide transport for those who do not own boats, and entrepreneurs set up tables on Sundays, cook food, and serve drinks for visitors. At the time of writing, there is no formal management structure or regulatory system, so that the influx of people far exceeds the carrying capacity of the beach, litter is scattered,. and only half-hearted attempts are made to clear it up. Irresponsible power boat operators also clutter the beach with boats instead of anchoring offshore, and sometimes endanger swimmers with unnecessary wave wash. This sort of scenario is repeated in many other places and points to the following issues:

- The need to ensure that the populace in general, and not just tourists, has access to good swimming beaches and, in this way, spreads the impact more evenly instead of on a few small locations. In many Caribbean islands this already occurs. People by right have access to all coastal beaches (as, for example, in Antigua and Barbados) and no private individual or business can have exclusive use of a beach. In other islands the situation is different. In Jamaica, provision for exclusivity is written into the original Beach Control Law and the public is denied access to many of the best beaches. This results in the fact that those beaches to which the public does have access are heavily overused. A "beach policy" currently under discussion in Jamaica may, if implemented, go some way toward improving public access to the foreshore.
- The need to develop techniques for assessing the carrying capacity (optimal number of persons using a facility at any given time or over a period of time) of individual beaches and to use such assessments for management purposes in controlling access to and use of a particular facility.
- The need to avoid conflict between power boat operators and the necessity for safe bathing and swimming facilities at public beaches.
- The need for national policies relating to the foreshore which protect the public right of access to beaches but which also ensure that beaches are properly managed and that, where necessary, provision is made for cost recovery.

Snorkelling/SCUBA Diving

We have separated these activities from recreational swimming because snorkel swimming and SCUBA diving have become major recreational activities throughout the Caribbean, bringing thousands of people in contact with coral reef, mangrove swamps, and other environments every year. At first sight, both activities seem as if they might do little harm but unless carefully managed they can have serious effects. These include the following:

- Anchor damage to reefs. Most SCUBA dives are organized to take place on coral reefs and the surface cover boat has to be maintained stationary over the dive site. In most marine parks and protected areas (Hol Chan, Negril, Montego Bay, Netherlands Antilles) permanent moorings have been established to which boats can tie up, thus avoiding the necessity of dropping an anchor. Elsewhere, in many cases, anchors are dropped indiscriminately on the reef, breaking or damaging corals, and often, if there is wind, a dragging anchor will create additional damage. On several occasions large tour boats with as many as thirty divers on board have been observed dropping anchor in this way on pristine portions of the Belize barrier reef. This is a simple management problem requiring both regulation and education and ensuring that all major dive sites do have fixed moorings.
- Physical impact by boats. In an effort to provide surface cover for snorkellers boat handlers are sometimes careless in permitting the boat or even the propellers to scrape the tops of coral heads and inflict damage.
- Touching or handling corals. It is generally believed that corals are easily damaged if handled and once injured, fungus and other diseases get into the tissues and do further damage. There is little evidence to support this claim. Talge (1992), in a study of recreational divers in the Florida Keys, found that the average recreational diver had ten contacts, by hand or by fins, with corals on each (45 minute) dive. However, using gross morphological and histological studies of corals that had been experimentally touched in this way, she did not find evidence of damage to the polyps, or interference with their reproductive cycles. James Porter of the University of Georgia (personal communication) experimentally handled large numbers of corals in a feeding experiment and concluded that not a single polyp or coral

head showed signs of stress 4 weeks later. Notwithstanding the conclusions of these two researchers, and until much more is known about the effects of chronic long-term exposure of corals to impacts by divers, prudence indicates that the rule of not touching coral should be maintained by all divers and that dive operators should ensure that divers in their charge should respect the rule. Most dive operators are now apprised of this and take steps to advise divers of the need to be careful. Nevertheless, many inexperienced divers or snorkellers, when in any difficulty, are likely to grab the nearest solid structure as support and this is likely to be a coral head. For further information on the impact of SCUBA diving and snorkelling on coral reefs the reader is referred to Simmons and Associates (1994).

- Resuspension of sediments. This is a serious but little-appreciated issue and is more critical in mangrove lagoons than on coral reefs. The fringing roots around mangrove lagoons are a haven for numerous interesting and colourful organisms and are attracting increasing numbers of snorkellers. However, these roots hang over shallow water below which are soft sediments that are very easily resuspended in the water column. Swim fins carelessly used over these areas stir up and resuspend the sediments that, because of their low density, sink back very slowly and may settle on and partly smother some of the organisms on the roots. A worse scenario occurs when a snorkeller wishes to adjust his or her mask and, in order to do so, takes up a vertical position in the water, allowing the fins to sink into soft sediments. When the individual resumes a swimming position the fins literally drag sediments into suspension, creating a dense cloud of material in the water some of which inevitably settles on the root communities. The only way to control the problem is for snorkellers to wear a slightly inflated buoyancy vest. This gives sufficient support so that only minimal or no use of the fins is needed to maintain the position while they examine the roots. A further issue in the mangrove environment is the need to anchor boats far off the root system or to tie the boat instead to the mangrove trees and not drop any anchor at all; anchors close to the root system bring up dense clouds of sediment when they are hauled back to the boat. The problem of sediment resuspension on coral reefs is less critical because of the high density of the

> sediment material (mostly calcium carbonate) and its tendency to sink quickly. Nevertheless, swimmers have to be cautious with the use of their fins, especially in deep, calm water where fine sediments may accumulate. Careless swimming may still kick up sediments that subsequently settle on and damage living corals. In a study of divers and snorkellers in the Florida Cays, Talge (1991) reported that although snorkellers have fewer interactions with corals than SCUBA divers, they stir up large clouds of sediment when treading water and are more apt to stand on corals than SCUBA divers (Simmons and Associates, 1994).

SCUBA diving and snorkelling have considerable income-generating potential and, if properly managed, can be carried out with minimal impact on the environment. The principal management techniques required include:

- Educating dive operators to ensure that they are fully conversant with the environmental issues involved (for example, coral handling and sediment suspension) and are able and willing to instruct their dive parties accordingly.
- Ensuring that dive leaders do not conduct parties of divers numbering more than they can fully control underwater and hence reduce the risk of damage to the environment or biota.
- Establishing an optimal annual or daily carrying capacity for each dive site and seeing that these norms are not exceeded. In Bonaire this has been estimated to be between 4000 and 5000 dives per year at each dive site (Scura and Van't Hof, 1993).
- Installing fixed moorings at major dive sites to which boats may tie up, thus reducing anchor damage to the substratum.

Hunting

Hunting is a specialized form of recreational activity, which is expressly controlled by legislation in most countries. Such legislation, as a rule, specifies the season during which hunting may take place, the species that may be hunted, and the number of individuals (bag limit) that may be taken in any one period of time (usually a day). Hunting, particularly bird shooting, is often subject to much misplaced criticism. Most birds that are regularly hunted produce more young than the carrying capacity of the environment will permit. There is thus a surplus population that will either be culled by natural mortality factors or that will be available for sport shooting. Most gun clubs are responsible organizations that abide by bag limits and very often plant food trees to maintain the stock of birds in their area. Provided bag limits are set properly according to the best scientific advice available and are adhered to, and that endangered species are fully protected, bird shooting is usually no more harmful than sport fishing and, in some instances, has potential for income generation. However, there is room for concern in those countries where mammals are hunted, as in Trinidad and Guyana, and where legislation and monitoring may be inadequate to fully protect the populations.

Management issues related to hunting include the following:

- Obtaining and analysing scientific data on populations of hunted species so that this may be used in the decision-making process.
- Determining and gazetting the season for hunting, the times of day at which hunting may take place, and bag limits (numbers of individuals that may be killed in any one period).
- Issuing hunting licenses as a means of revenue generation and as a mechanism for monitoring the numbers of persons engaged in hunting.
- Monitoring and regulating hunting while it is in season.

MANAGEMENT

Tourism is not only the largest industry in the world but it is also the world's fastest growing industry. For small island developing states (SIDS) in the Caribbean, tourism is now the mainstay of the economic structure, replacing such traditional sources of revenue as bananas and sugar. The enjoyment of beaches and the coast contributes to 74 percent of gross domestic product in some Caribbean islands (Caribbean Development Bank, 1993). Within the industry, the development of ecotourism (including nature tourism and heritage tourism), which involves travel to sites of natural and cultural value, is the fastest growing segment. Revenue capture and the proper use of that revenue for developing facilities and improving infrastructure thus becomes an important issue in the growth and management of ecotourism. Revenue may be generated in several ways, indirectly through taxes and directly through user fees. No matter how it is generated it is through tourism that the private sector can also contribute to conservation and provide a means by which protected areas can generate revenue and help to support themselves outside of government subventions.

While tourism is good for income generation, the rapid expansion of the ecotourism market has often occurred too quickly for the associated infrastructure (roads, trails, visitor centres) to keep pace and for proper management structures to be put in place. Increases in visitor levels without a concomitant increase in facilities and institutional mechanisms for revenue capture to pay for these facilities mean that countries and local communities do not benefit from growth in tourism. Governments, non-governmental organizations (NGOs), and the private sector must work together to ensure that these revenues are set aside to pay for the development and maintenance of those sites that generate the income. We cannot stress too strongly that revenue generation and the proper use of those revenues is key to successful ecotourism development. Furthermore, unless countries have a proper policy framework and site managers have adequate resources, ecotourism will create the same problems that conventional tourism has in the past: resentment caused by the disruption of traditional living patterns and values without a full share in the associated benefits, loss of access to traditionally used sites, increase in crime, and migration of workers into tourism centres without the development of associated infrastructure and housing. Further, since ecotourism often takes visitors into previously unvisited and unspoiled areas, the potential for damage to natural systems is great. Consequently, managers of protected areas are often wary of ecotourism and such developments should be very carefully planned. Policy makers and developers must therefore learn from these experiences and ensure that in planning any ecotourism development it is not imposed on the local community but is developed with its involvement and participation so that the local community becomes a primary beneficiary of the development.

While ecotourism is often claimed to be the best way in which the private sector can become involved in conservation, the ecotourism experience in the Caribbean so far can best be described as mixed. There are no effective industry standards and ecotourism as practiced varies from good examples that protect the resource to others that cause as many problems as they solve. The subject has been extensively reviewed by Ceballos-Lascurain (1996) and is further briefly discussed by Blommestein (1995). To solve some of the problems, NGOs are beginning to work with tourism trade organizations and governments to develop guidelines and standards for the practice of ecotourism. At a minimum ecotourism should produce the following benefits:

- A measurable increase in conservation effectiveness
- A new source of net income for a protected area
- Employment for and benefits to local communities

A system of sites for ecotourism should have as its objectives the following:

- Conservation of the attraction
- Revenue generation
- Financial sustainability

Conservation of the Attraction

Managers of protected areas should bear in mind that the role of ecotourism is to generate money for biodiversity protection and to educate people to conserve valuable natural resources. Often, the infrastructure used to facilitate tourists affects the environment adversely and may encourage new human settlements in the area, which further exacerbates the situation. In certain critical cases, therefore, buffer zones may have to be created between physical development and the area to be protected. Regardless of the financial success of a tourism operation, it is not truly successful unless the resource is actually being protected. Therefore, managers need to have monitoring programmes in place that can objectively determine the quality of the resources they protect. This can range from a simple measure of tree or live coral cover to more complicated and meaningful indicators, such as the density and distribution of different feeding guilds of animals. The method used will depend on the management objectives of the protected area. In those reserves that are established to protect a single species, the density of that species is used as the indicator of environmental quality. In other areas the manager may be interested in watershed protection or protecting a particular type of ecosystem. To achieve these aims managers must be well informed about the biota and the ecology of the area that is being protected.

Revenue Generation

Governments around the world face a problem in financing protected areas. Few, if any protected areas outside the G7 countries are totally supported by national taxpayers; they rely mainly on ecotourism and foreign government assistance. Even in the U.S., the federal government is cutting back on its financing of national parks and national forests. Some states are responsible for supporting state-wide systems of protected areas but these also suffer from budget cutbacks. Even systems in richer states, such as the state park system in New Hampshire, may cover running costs by income generation but are not able to recover capital costs.

Belize has a significant part of its land area designated as protected areas and many attractions in Belize fall into the category of ecotourism. Expenditure by tourists accounts for only 25 percent of GDP (Caribbean Development Bank, 1993). Nevertheless, despite the diversity of the country's economy, ecotourism plays a significant role (Lindberg and Enriquez, 1995). Unfortunately, the benefits to the protected areas from ecotourism are not always clear. One exception to this is the Hol Chan Marine Park, where visitors are charged a fee that is used to support management and protection of the area.

Dominica is one of the most unspoiled Caribbean islands. It possesses great potential for nature tourism and the accessibility of some sites has meant that they have become an attraction for cruise ship visitors. However, steady increases in the number of visitors have brought problems so that there is an urgent need to put in place the infrastructural, management, institutional, and legal machinery to protect the integrity of attractions and develop their full income earning potential. If this is not done quickly, Dominica will lose some of its pristine areas. At the same time, the country needs to examine the possibility of cost recovery from persons using the more important natural attractions. Our experience suggests that this is not being done at present and that potential earnings are being lost.

SCUBA diving has traditionally been a sport with many opportunities for contributing to the conservation of marine areas. The Saba Marine Park in the Dutch Antilles is a good example of the private sector being tapped as the source of revenue to support a protected area. Divers pay a fee to get a diving permit and the revenues from this support the operational costs of the park. While all costs are not covered, the park is free of the need to seek continual external support in the form of grants. Other countries in the region where SCUBA diving is an important activity should learn from this experience.

It is important, however, that the need to pay bills does not become the only factor dictating recreational use. If this happens it may lead to deterioration of the attraction if the number of visitors is allowed to increase beyond the carrying capacity of the site. Since visitor numbers and activities may therefore have to be limited in any natural recreational area, other sources of funding have to be pursued in addition to tourism. Few natural areas can accommodate sufficient visitors to pay for all the costs of management and hence they have to finance protection through other means as well.

Financial Sustainability

It is clear that any natural area that is going to be used for tourism must make money and that the attraction has to be run as a business. While a single attraction may not have to pay all of its bills from tourism, the development must have sufficient basic amenities to provide the visitor with a satisfying experience for which he or she is prepared to pay. If this is not the case the attraction will not generate revenue and is not worth the cost of establishment. To be sustainable most protected areas have to have several sources of income. Charges for use, leases, licenses and concessions, subventions from government, trust funds, NGOs, and local communities may all be resources that the manager can use. Revenue generation at visitor centres from the sale of guidebooks and souvenirs are also significant sources of income. Sustainability comes from ensuring that there are sufficient sources to balance expenditure.

The Potential for Expansion

There is great potential for income generation within many protected areas in the Caribbean but this potential is seldom realized. While the best examples of this are found among marine parks, successful terrestrial areas have been set up in St Lucia and Dominica (Caribbean Development Bank, 1993). Similarly, the Conservation Trust of Puerto Rico has been able to generate a successful cost recovery programme on Las Cabezas de San Juan reserve (J. Blanco, Executive Director of the Puerto Rico Trust, personal communication).

There is no doubt that visitors to the Caribbean are interested in seeing examples of tropical forest as well as other attractions, including coral reefs and seagrass beds if the opportunity is made available. Particularly as visitors become more sophisticated and better educated, they want to do more than just lie on the beach. Surveys conducted among visitors to Jamaica indicate that the majority come to see the white sand beaches and waterfalls but would be interested in visiting the mountains (Bedasse, 1994). Of the 8 to 21 days spent in the island as many as 4 days might be spent on sightseeing tours. Nearly half of the visitors interviewed wanted to visit forest areas. However, at the time they left the island only 17 percent had actually done so. The majority of tourists wished to visit other inland attractions but were deterred from doing so mainly due to the lack of pre-booked tours and the similarity of the existing tours.

The survey in Jamaica concluded that it would be possible to attract some 2.6 percent or 25,000 visitors per annum to visit a single trail in the Blue Mountains. Those polled said that they would be willing to spend up to U.S.$ 10.00 in addition to the cost of transportation to visit a managed attraction in the Blue and John Crow Mountains National Park.

The potential therefore for adding nature and non-beach attractions to the Caribbean tourism product is enormous. Already Belize, Guyana, and Trinidad have visitor programmes centred solely on nature tourism, attracting mostly people who want to see birds or simply want to have the tropical forest experience. Cuba also has potential for similar developments but, for most of the smaller islands, attracting visitors solely for nature tourism can only be a small component of the tourism product. Nevertheless, adding natural attractions to the existing tourism product may increase the number of days a visitor will stay (G. Hilzward, 1991, personal communication). It would also increase spending and bring income inland. This in turn could reduce the amount of migration from rural areas to areas of high traditional tourism activity, along with its attendant problems.

Effects of Recreation on Resource Quality

The clear advantages of recreation must be balanced against the disadvantages. Recreation can be one of the most damaging activities in any natural area. In the marine environment, the impacts on coral reefs caused by careless snorkellers and by boats dropping anchor or scraping shallow reefs are often most important. Even deep reefs can be damaged if they are frequently used for recreational diving. Many dive operators do not caution or supervise divers sufficiently and even experienced recreational divers can be careless about dragging equipment or touching coral.

Trails through forests can also become damaged if they become pathways for invasive plants. Trails have markedly different vegetation from their surroundings. The plants that colonize trails in this way may also spread into the area through which the trail passes (Bates, 1935). On neglected trails trespassers or intrusion by domestic animals can also become a problem leading to damage to the resource, illegal logging, or theft of plants or animals by collectors (see Barker and Miller, 1997). Badly drained trails become watercourses, which then become sources of erosion and may cause landslides. Recreational trails that are not properly demarcated or drained inevitably get wider as more people walk on them. It is not uncommon for trails to start by being only 2 metres wide but in time and with overuse to expand to over 6 metres.

Managers of protected areas must therefore use a cost-benefit analysis type of approach to balance use against damage when planning for development and conservation. As in any development, before opening a recreational attraction it is appropriate to conduct an environmental impact assessment (EIA) to see if the project will be sustainable. If the development goes ahead, suitable monitoring should be put in place thereafter to ensure that management procedures are successful.

One of the issues that the EIA must address is the carrying capacity of the site. The carrying capacity relates to the number of people and amount of infrastructure that can be allowed in a recreational area within a predetermined time frame. It takes into account several effects of visitor numbers. The potential for damage to the resource is taken into account, as well as the potential for crowding as a factor likely to affect the visitor's enjoyment of the attraction. Social factors and the ability of management to cope with visitors in large numbers are also considered. Since there is no standard definition of carrying capacity, it will be set by the manager of the protected area in accordance with projections in the EIA. The primary considerations in making such calculations should be the purpose of the protected area and the need for proper management. The carrying capacity will vary according to the types of visitor activities that are available, the quality of the infrastructure, and the level of economic development of the surrounding community. (Carrying capacity is also discussed in Chapter 8; see also Clarke, 1977.)

Since all use will cause change to the resource, the concept of the "limits of acceptable change" has been developed to allow managers to determine the types of activities and number of visitors that will be allowed on a site. In this case, the manager considers the conditions that are desired within the natural area. Once this is determined, the manager must monitor the changes in the natural area caused by human activity. Activities and numbers of visitors are managed to keep the natural conditions within acceptable limits. Since the concept was first enunciated methods have been developed to ensure that limits of acceptable change can be applied to socio-economic conditions as well (Stankey, 1985).

Both carrying capacity and limits of acceptable change must be taken into account when an EIA is to be carried out. The assessment will evaluate the possible changes to the environment that may occur as a result of the development and then suggest ways in which any negative effects could be mitigated. Decision makers can then decide whether the development should go ahead, be modified, or be abandoned. Certain principles must guide this decision. For instance, virgin areas in general should not be developed and areas vital to a particular species should be closed off either totally or seasonally as appropriate to ensure survival.

Local Use Versus Tourism

Many nature tourist attractions are well known and used by local communities but are also marketed to overseas visitors. Usually, the two interest groups have different requirements and it is important to ensure that in catering for the foreign visitor the character of an attraction and its appeal or relevance to the local populace are not ignored. Local communities will resent changes to familiar attractions unless they perceive those changes as necessary and beneficial. It is critical, therefore, and we have already referred to this in a different context, that in any development there must be involvement of the local community from the earliest stages of planning. Furthermore, pricing should be based on a two-tiered system. Local people should pay less than tourists since their taxes have probably already helped to defray some of the costs of management and price levels should be adopted so that members of the immediate local community are not excluded from areas to which they are accustomed to having freedom of access.

RECREATION IN ACTION – THE JAMAICAN EXPERIENCE

In the previous sections the nature of recreational use of the environment and the problem of its management have been discussed. In this final section the Jamaican experience is used to highlight some practical aspects of environmentally based tourism. Space does not permit a more exhaustive look at the Caribbean in general.

Coastal Recreation

Jamaica plays host to some 1.5 million tourists every year, most of whom travel there with the intention of enjoying the beaches and the sea. Jamaica, however, has a serious problem due to the passing of the

Beach Control Act in 1956, which made provision for private property owners and hotels to obtain licenses for the exclusive use of the foreshore and floor of the sea. As a result, many of the finest beaches are closed to public access or have only very limited access on a paying basis, which in turn has other consequences. On the one hand, a growing population with more mobility and increasing disposable incomes comes to resent exclusion from prime beach land. This results in social tension. On the other hand, those beaches that are open to the public become overcrowded beyond their carrying capacity, which in turn leads to environmental degradation. The Beach Control Act was absorbed into the new Natural Resources Conservation Authority Act of 1991 but without significant change to its substance. The new responsible authority, the National Environment and Planning Agency (NEPA), is now developing a beach policy which, if passed into legislation, will address these issues and alleviate the tension, overcrowding, and degradation. This will include the opening up (for a fee) of some of the all inclusive beaches for a wider clientele, including local residents, the development of managed public beaches for use of which a fee is payable, and the provision of some open beaches at which facilities are minimal. Implementation of any such policy will, in itself, have difficulties that have to be faced and overcome if the resident population is to enjoy the benefits of the coastline. Some of these difficulties are already apparent at Negril, which is legally entirely and freely open to the public but where access is highly restricted by development and where intimidation is sometimes used as a tool for excluding local residents from selected parts of the foreshore. Negril could have been one of the finest coastal attractions in the Caribbean if development along the beach had been prohibited and instead restricted to the elevated areas at each end, preserving the beach strip as a national recreational park. That option was lost by decision makers in 1970. By the Beach Control Act of 1956 Jamaica also lost the opportunity for free and open access to all beaches, a freedom available and practiced in many other Caribbean islands.

Inland Recreation

Jamaica has huge potential for inland recreation, much of it poorly or underdeveloped. This includes:

- Hiking, particularly in the mountains
- Natural history activities, especially bird watching and nature photography
- Speleology – underground exploration of caves and sink holes

- River tours and rafting
- Pony trekking

The issue of hiking and hiking trails was referred to earlier but it is worth noting here that many of the old trails in the Blue Mountains are now overgrown or destroyed. Formerly kept open by the Colonial Forestry Department either for forest maintenance or as mule trails for bringing agricultural produce to market, they fell into disrepair partly because it became easier to bring produce by truck instead of by mule. As they fell into disuse they became overgrown and hard to find, while some were bulldozed to make roads and others were absorbed into coffee plantations and virtually lost. Some of these can be relocated and should be opened again to expand recreational opportunities, especially those around Newcastle in St Andrew and along the Grand Ridge of the Blue Mountains from Morce's Gap to Portland Gap.

Other Caribbean countries, endowed with greater biotic resources, have made excellent use of the potential of natural history for recreation. The best known of such resources are Cockscomb Reserve and Chan Chich Reserve in Belize and the Asa Wright Centre and Caroni Swamp in Trinidad. Jamaica has been slow to respond to the challenge in spite of the high level of endemism in its flora and fauna (Goodbody, 1994).

Speleology has potential as a recreational activity that has little or no impact on the natural environment. However, apart from a small group of local enthusiasts it does not seem to have attracted much attention as a marketable visitor attraction except at two commercial operations close to the north coast highway. The major cave systems of Jamaica have been documented by Fincham (1977).

Three types of recreational activity have been developed on Jamaica's rivers. On the Rio Grande, a 3-mile stretch of the lower reaches of the river is used for rafting down the river on bamboo rafts that carry two passengers each and are controlled by a captain. The operation carries visitors into a scenically dramatic area with virtually no negative impact on the environment. A similar type of activity on the Martha Brae in Trelawny occurs in less scenic surroundings but with greater potential for natural history observations.

A quite different river operation with potentially damaging consequences to the environment is carried out in the lower reaches of the Black River in St Elizabeth. This low lying swamp area is home to one of the largest populations of crocodiles (*Crocodilus americanus*) in Jamaica. Crocodiles and other wildlife present in this area are successfully exploited as part of recreational activities for local and overseas visitors. Groups of up to twenty-five persons are taken by boat along a 2-mile stretch of the river where they can view and photograph wildlife and learn about the local culture. In its formative stages, great care was taken by the developer to ensure that the environment was protected, that boats fitted with powerful slow revving engines traveled slowly so as to minimize disturbance to wildlife and prevent any wash from damaging or eroding the fragile river bank. This highly successful operation attracted large numbers of visitors, requiring additional boats, sometimes manned by less careful boat handlers and it also attracted another commercial operator. A subjective consideration of the outcome suggests the following:

- The environment is exceeding its carrying capacity
- Less careful handling of boats may cause erosion of the river bank and resuspension of sediments may interfere with commercially significant shrimp populations
- Wildlife may be unduly disturbed by the volume of traffic

This attraction at Black River is an excellent example of how an initially successful and carefully managed enterprise may grow to the point where it endangers the environment that supports the attraction. The entire Black River Morass (swamp area) is scheduled to become a national park but gazetting as a protected area and setting up the management structure is unlikely to be in place for several years and hence interim management of the activity in the lower reaches of the river may be necessary.

National Parks

Jamaica has two national parks. The Blue and John Crow Mountains National Park (BJCMNP) is a 79,000 hectare expanse of montane tropical wet forest, some of which has been cleared for agriculture, notably coffee growing (Muchoney et al., 1994). The Montego Bay Marine Park protects 15 square kilometres of the sea. Both parks were set up as outputs of the U.S. Agency for International Development (USAID)/Government of Jamaica-financed Protected Areas Resources Conservation (PARC) Project. The purpose of the parks is to ensure sustainable use while protecting biodiversity.

In order to ensure that the parks would survive after the project ended, the Jamaica National Parks Trust Fund was established to provide long-term funding. Initially funded with the proceeds of a debt for nature swap, the fund makes investments and pays salaries of park staff from the proceeds. Salaries for the majority of the staff within the parks have been paid in this way since 1993. This has allowed the park system to survive after USAID reduced its support to the two protected areas. In the future, the Trust Fund will become even more important to the protected areas system.

At the first Jamaican symposium on Protected Areas and Tourism in 1992 it was apparent that, in addition to attractions already in use, Jamaica has several other areas that could be developed for visitors. However, some natural attractions that are already open to tourists have already suffered deleterious effects, for instance, the attraction at Black River previously referred to. Another example is at Dunn's River Falls in St Ann, which is probably the single largest attraction in the Caribbean. These falls receive about one million visitors each year and despite the expansion of parking areas and the addition of garden areas and other activities for visitors, the majority of visitors is still concentrated on an extremely small area at the lower end of the falls. While the falls themselves can probably receive this impact with little damage, the sandy beach at the foot of the falls is severely impacted and stressed.

While much of the emphasis on recreational use of natural areas is organized for the overseas visitor, there is already considerable recreational use of natural environments by Jamaicans and even more use will be made of them as people become aware of the opportunities available.

Recreational Activity in the Blue and John Crow National Park

This park has four major areas of use: the trail to the peak, the Holywell Recreation Area, Clydesdale and the Cinchona Botanical Gardens, and the Rio Grande Valley. The Bath Fountain, which is near to the park, is also used for recreation but has no direct connection with it.

Blue Mountain Peak has an elevation of 2256 metres. The trail from Mavis Bank through Penlyne Castle to Portland Gap (1700 metres) and then to the peak is the most well-known part of the park. Hiking to the peak, Jamaica's highest point, is almost a rite of passage for Jamaicans (see Hodges, 1993). Overnight accommodation is available at Whitfield Hall and Wildflower Cottage, both at 1300 metres, and at Portland Gap. All of the accommodation is fairly rustic and camping sites are also available at Portland Gap. The area was operated by a community-owned and -managed tour group from 1992 to 1995 but is now managed by park rangers.

The peak trail is extensively used by Jamaicans and visitors. Visitors tend to use it during the week and Jamaicans are more likely to use it at weekends. On average, 200 persons use the trail each week, with sharp rises at holiday weekends. Park rangers have recorded up to 1500 visitors on a single weekend. The popularity of this trail leads to two serious environmental impacts. On the one hand, the density of traffic has led to serious erosion of the trail but much of this can be rectified by careful landscaping and control of water runoff. On the other hand, there is a serious solid waste problem, particularly at Portland Gap, and measures are needed to ensure that waste does not accumulate at this point and is either incinerated on site or taken down to Mavis Bank for disposal. It also calls for a greater effort to be made to ensure that visitors take home all their solid waste rather than leaving it on the mountainside.

Holywell is a recreational park within easy reach of Kingston, the capital city, which has a population in the region of one million. Most visitors to Holywell come from Kingston and the major activity is picnicking and walking on the nearby trails. A growing number of youth groups and camping clubs use the area for the whole weekend or longer periods in summer. The number of visitors to Holywell has increased from 5000 per annum in 1964 to 30,000 in 1994. This increase has not been concomitant with an increase in facilities. There are currently only three sleeping cabins and a few gazebos and picnic sites. The national park authorities would like to expand the facilities to provide additional sleeping cabins and camp sites but such expansion is constrained by a shortage of funds. While some maintenance and refurbishing has taken place, the facilities lag far behind the demand and there is need to revitalize some of the hiking trails in the vicinity to meet the demand for walking opportunities.

Recently, there has been considerable increase in the number of foreign visitors using the park on a daily basis. Most of these are brought by coach as part of a tour crossing the mountains from north to south and their stay at Holywell is brief. These tours are run five days per week and may bring as many as 300 persons in total. Additionally, there are two downhill bicycle tours offering a scenic ride through parts of the national park. These tours commence at Holywell, thus increasing the overall impact on the Holywell environment. Holywell Recreational Park and the nearby Fairy Glade Trail are suffering similar problems to those on the Blue Mountain Trail due to overuse. Both the picnic area, the surrounding recreation area, and the neighbouring trails have serious erosion problems and the picnic area has a perpetual solid waste problem because visitors will not take their waste home with them but instead choose to leave it lying around in the park. This is a problem throughout Jamaica and other parts of the Caribbean, which needs to be addressed through a campaign of public education.

Clydesdale is the site of a forest nursery maintained by the Forestry Department at an elevation of 1050 metres. There is a natural bathing pool in the river nearby and, until recently, it had a few picnic gazebos and a dormitory for youth groups. It has been a traditional recreation area for both hikers and motorists coming from Kingston. At the time of writing, the facility is in a state of disrepair (presumably for want of money) and is no longer suitable as a recreation site or as a dormitory for youth groups. Cinchona is an old botanical garden at an elevation of 1450 metres, immediately above Clydesdale. Formerly a magnificent mountain attraction with a holiday residence used by colonial governors and senior civil servants, it is now only a shadow of its former glory, suffering from neglect with some overgrown paths and some that have been eroded. Until about 1992, it was possible to drive a private motor car the entire way through Clydesdale and into Cinchona Gardens. Today it is barely possible to reach Clydesdale without a four-wheel drive vehicle and, even in such a vehicle, the journey to Cinchona is a perilous experience. We emphasize this state of degradation at Clydesdale and Cinchona (two of the great attractions of the Blue Mountains of Jamaica) because it underscores an important point about ecotourism development. Ecotourism visitors are usually sophisticated and discerning people. They are not interested in paying for second-rate attractions that are poorly maintained. Access is important. Therefore, roads and trails must be properly maintained so that the visitor is not exhausted by the journey before even reaching the attraction. Second, the attractions themselves must be maintained in a state that encourages relaxation and enjoyment. Cinchona and Clydesdale are good examples of how easily attractions will degenerate if not properly maintained. If Jamaica and other Caribbean countries are serious about ecotourism development they must pay attention to both the maintenance of the attractions and their access routes.

In the upper Rio Grande Valley, on the northern side of the national park in the vicinity of Millbank, a community tour group, Valley Hikes, conducts excursions to waterfalls and caves near to the national park. Also in this vicinity, the Rio Grande rafting trips are a well-known and popular attraction for visitors to the east end of the island. The development of recreation activities in this area is still in its infancy and park managers would be well advised to move swiftly to ensure that some of the environmental problems that have occurred elsewhere are not repeated in the Millbank area, which is a particularly sensitive environment containing one or more endangered species of animals. Due to the sensitivity of the Rio Grande valley, a programme of public education is required. In addition, regulations for the protection of the area should be drafted and implemented.

Despite all of these activities and the relatively high use of the national park and some of its trails, income generated by the park has been small. No entrance fee is charged. In any case, such an admission fee would be difficult to administer as there is a large population living within the park and several roads either cross through the park or penetrate far into it. There are a few facilities in the Blue and John Crow National Park for which visitors pay a fee but the fee is so small that the revenue generated is minimal. For example, a fee of J$ 150.00 (U.S.$ 4.28) is charged for the use of a cabin at Holywell for one night. Due to the low level of income generated, the cabins have been inadequately maintained. Cost recovery has to be addressed if the park is to succeed as a viable entity. Full realization of the potential for recreation in the protected areas of Jamaica will require the government to encourage more private sector participation. Either NGOs or private groups will need to be given access to land or facilities and allowed to operate them on behalf of the park. The park, in turn, needs to charge such operators for use of the facilities on a concession basis.

The Montego Bay Marine Park

The Montego Bay Marine Park protects 15.7 square kilometres of water from the coast to the 600 metre drop off. Montego Bay is a tourist city with a population of over 125,000 persons, an international airport, and numerous hotels. It is estimated that over 40 percent of the over 1.5 million tourists who visit the island each year stay in Montego Bay and enjoy the resources of the park. Consequently, the reefs, seagrass beds, and mangroves in the park are all under stress from a variety of causes.

Recreational use of the resource is very high. Swimming, SCUBA diving, snorkelling, glass-bottomed boat tours, semisubmersible tours, and a variety of water sports are carried out by the tourist visitors. All of these can cause physical damage to the reefs. Several Jamaicans make their living from fishing either with pots or with spears. Another source of stress on the environment is sewage because there is relatively poor treatment of sewage in the city. The major municipal plant, operated by the National Water Commission, is overstressed and is responsible for some two million gallons of sewage per day being placed into the Montego River when the effluent discharges into the Marine Park. The government has now received assistance to build a new sewage plant that will reduce the volume of sewage flowing into the river. There are also numerous point sources of pollution along the coast as well as non-point sources which are related to the limestone geology of the coastal strip. (For a fuller discussion of coastal pollution see Chapter 8.)

The park mandate provides it with powers to regulate and zone activities in the Marine Park. Regulations have thus made it possible to control some of the threats from fishing by determining the types of gear that may be used, as well as the locations where fishing is permitted. The recreational damage from boat moorings is being addressed by the use of mooring buoys. Additionally, there have been training courses for tourist operators, fishermen, and others who use the water.

Cost recovery in the park remains a serious problem. The park charges a fee for the use of its fixed moorings because these were installed by park staff and require periodic maintenance. The park is also considering requesting support from hotels based on a contribution per night per room. Unfortunately, at present, many of these ideas are still only proposals and have not yet been implemented, partly because the Natural Resources Conservation Authority (now NEPA) has delegated (in September 1996) the authority to collect fees to the Montego Bay Marine Park Trust (this did not take place for the Blue and John Crow Mountains National Park until December 1996). At this time, except for funds from foreign donors, very little money is available to put into infrastructure and maintenance. Consequently, the ability of the park managers to protect the natural resources within the park from recreational activity is severely compromised. Despite these difficulties, the Montego Bay Marine Park and its supporting NGO, the Marine Park Trust, have been successful in getting hotels and other tourism interests in Montego Bay to take an interest in the park and to support it in various ways. This is also the case in the protected area in Negril.

Although it cannot compare with other marine parks such as those in Bonaire, Hol Chan, and Saba, the Marine Park at Montego Bay is generally acknowledged as being successful. Consequently, NGOs in Negril, Port Antonio, and Ocho Rios are interested in protecting these areas by establishing marine parks that are managed along similar lines. Recreational use is high in all of these areas but pollution from sewage remains a problem. Successful management of the natural resources will depend on proper recreational management and a reduction in fishing.

CONCLUSION

It is clear that increased urbanization and improved living standards create a desire among people for leisure and recreation away from cities and engagement in activities that make extensive use of the natural environment. Such activity is beneficial not only as a form of relaxation but also as an educational experience for people whose contact with the natural environment is otherwise limited. Quite apart from any economic benefits, exploration of the natural environment by residents and tourists should be encouraged. However, in accepting that ecotourism and outdoor recreational activity is desirable, decision makers must also accept responsibility for ensuring that they are economically sustainable while at the same time preserving the basic character of the environment that people wish to enjoy. This does not preclude some modification of the natural environment, since it often can be improved, but it does demand that ecotourism development is not allowed to degrade it.

Future use of the natural environment for recreation and nature-based tourism, therefore, requires careful planning and expert management. Decision making must be based on good scientific information about the environment and properly conducted EIAs. It is incumbent on Caribbean governments, in collaboration with the scientific community, to ensure that research is conducted on all aspects of the environment, its geography, geology, and biology, so that comprehensive data bases may be created and made available for planners to make informed decisions. The existing process of employing environmental consultants on an *ad hoc* basis to conduct an EIA whenever needed is inadequate unless those consultants have access to good scientific data. Most consultants do not have either the expertise or the time to fully research the environmental background and obtain all the necessary data. Furthermore, EIAs involving large ecotourism or recreational developments (and indeed all developments) need careful review before being accepted by the regulatory agency. At present, many of these agencies do not have sufficient in-house expertise to evaluate environmental studies critically. In such cases, their staffing needs to be strengthened to ensure that they do have the capacity to review the EIAs that come to them for approval. Where adequate expertise is not present in-house, the agency should seek review from independent outside consultants.

The need to train environmental managers must be recognized. A complexity of skills is required based on both the natural and social sciences coupled with the relevant field experience. Such a need has already been recognized in Caribbean fisheries and the CARICOM Fisheries Resource Assessment and Management Program (CFRAMP) has initiated management training courses for senior fisheries officers. Complementary courses within the Caribbean should also be established to produce the management skills now needed for ecotourism development and recreational use of the natural environment. The management issues to which reference was made earlier in this chapter indicate the range of skills and expertise required. One of the points raised earlier is that nature tourism and heritage tourism attractions require that quality information be made available to the visitor either at visitor centres or elsewhere. In addition to this, decision makers and managers of ecotourism attractions should examine the need for well-trained guides. Too often, the Caribbean experience is of a "caretaker guide", a local individual briefed in the simplest aspects of the attraction but unable to engage in a serious dialogue about the site or its biota. This is inadequate for the well-informed tourist. Both nature-based attractions and heritage sites elsewhere in the world invariably employ guides, often university graduates, who are well trained and capable of sustained dialogue and questioning. If ecotourism is to succeed in the Caribbean, planners may also need to examine the need for this level of guided tour.

The third element in successful ecotourism is the user group, the visitors who come to make use of the attraction. Like decision makers and managers, the user group also has responsibilities: to take care of the attraction, to respect the regulations, and to ensure that it remains an attraction for those who follow. There has to be an interactive process between managers and users so that visitors are welcomed, stimulated, and educated and, in turn, feel that they have had value for money and that the attraction is worth preserving.

Finally, none of these processes can take place unless there is commitment and financial resources to develop and maintain the attraction. Financing has to be through direct cost recovery as well as through the use of taxpayer funds in government subventions. In the same way that visitors will pay to enter a cinema, use a golf course, or enter a bathing beach, it must also be accepted that there is a cost factor to using the natural environment, whether it be hiking trails, picnic parks, or dive sites, and the like. The mechanics of such cost recovery are often complex, particularly where there is more than one point of entry, as on many hiking trails. Nevertheless, the principle must be established and established early: in order to offer the use of the natural environment for recreation it has to be managed and conserved, management and conservation cost money and, therefore, users must pay. In this way, the burden of cost is placed squarely on those who make use of the attraction and not solely on the many taxpayers who may never have an opportunity to enjoy it.

Traditionally, the Caribbean has relied on its coastal resources and beaches as the primary basis for its tourism industry. While "sun, sea and sand" will continue to play a predominant role, the demand for alternatives, particularly in nature-based tourism, is steadily increasing. In the early development of coastal tourism little thought was given to environmental considerations so that many negative effects arose, such as beach erosion or sewage pollution. Most of these problems are now recognized and anticipated through EIAs prior to development. Decision makers must learn from this experience so as to ensure that in the rapid expansion of alternative nature-based tourism similar mistakes are not made. Furthermore the product must be competitive if it is to survive.

The need for competitiveness is well stated by Persaud and Douglas:

> Another impetus toward sustainability comes from increased global competition. Most of the new tourism destinations now being developed lie in the tropics, like Caribbean countries. They have similar climates, beaches, offshore waters, harbours, mountains, flora and fauna – in short similar ecologies. They thus compete directly with more traditional destinations such as the Caribbean. The result is that the region must pay close attention to the quality of the tourism product it offers, and therefore to environmental quality.

REFERENCES AND FURTHER READING

Bates, G. H. 1935. "The vegetation of footpaths, sidewalks, cart-tracks and gateways". *Journal of Animal Ecology* 23: 470–487.

Barker, D. and D. J. Miller. 1997. "Cockpits under attack". p. 11, in *Proceedings of the Third Conference of The Faculty of Pure and Applied Sciences*. University of the West Indies, Mona, Jamaica.

Bedasse, J. 1994. "Unpublished survey of incoming and outgoing tourists in Jamaica". Report to the Jamaica Conservation and Development Trust, Kingston, Jamaica.

Blommestein, E. 1995. "Sustainable tourism in the Caribbean". pp. 191–220, in M. Griffith and B. Persaud, eds., *Economic Policy and the Environment*. University of the West Indies Centre for Environment and Development, Mona, Jamaica.

Caribbean Development Bank. 1993. *Social and Economic Indicators (1991). Borrowing Member Countries*, Vol. IV. Bridgetown, Barbados.

Caribbean Tourism Organisation. 1993. "Ecotourism". Report of the Third Caribbean Conference on Ecotourism. Cayman Islands (May).

Ceballos-Lascurain, H. 1996. *Tourism, Ecotourism and Protected Areas: The State of Nature Based Tourism Around the World and Guidelines for its Development*. International Union for the Conservation of Nature, Gland, Switzerland.

Clarke, J. R. 1977. *Coastal Ecosystem Management*. John Wiley & Sons, New York.

Fincham, A. 1977. *Jamaica Underground*. Geological Society of Jamaica, Kingston, Jamaica.

Goodbody, I. 1994. "Avian refuges". *Jamaica Journal* 25, no. 2: 55–60.

Hilzward, G. 1992. "Unpublished report on the potential for ecotourism in Jamaica". Jamaica Tourist Board, Kingston, Jamaica.

Hodges, M. 1993. *Blue Mountain Guide*. Natural History Society of Jamaica, Kingston, Jamaica.

IUCN (International Union for the Conservation of Nature). 1996. *Report of The World Conservation Congress, 1st Session*. International Union for the Conservation of Nature. Montreal, Canada.

Jackson, M. H. 1994. *Galapagos – a Natural History*. University of Calgary Press, Calgary, Alberta.

Jenner, P. and C. Smith. 1992. *The Tourism Industry and the Environment*. The Economist Intelligence Unit, London.

Lawrence, K. 1992. "Sustainable tourism development". Unpublished paper presented at the World Parks Congress, Caracas, Venezuela.

Lindberg, K. and J. Enriquez. 1995. *An Analysis of Ecotourism's Contribution to Conservation and Development in Belize*. World Wide Fund for Nature, Sunderland, Massachusetts.

Muchoney, D. M., S. Iremonger, and R. Wright. 1994. *Blue and John Crow Mountains National Park, Jamaica*. The Nature Conservancy, Arlington, Virginia.

Natural Resources Conservation Authority. 1994. "Regional management plan for the West Indian manatee (*Trichechus manatus*)". Report of a Regional Workshop on the Conservation of the West Indian Manatee in the Wider Caribbean. Kingston, Jamaica (March).

Natural Resources Conservation Authority. 1996. "NRCA guidelines pertaining to marinas and small craft harbours". Final Draft (July).

Oddie, W. 1980. *Bill Oddie's Little Black Bird Book*. Methuen, London.

Perrottet, A. (ed.). 1995. *Insight Guide to Belize*. APA Publications, Hong Kong.

Primack, R. B. 1993. *Essentials of Conservation Biology*. Sinauer Associates Inc., Bridgetown, Barbados.

Rutzler, K. and I. C. Feller. 1996. "Caribbean mangrove swamps". *Scientific American* 274, no. 3: 94–99.

Scura, L. F. and T. Van't Hof. 1993. *The Ecology and Economics of the Bonaire Marine Park*. Divisional Paper No. 1993-44. The World Bank, Environment Department, Washington, D.C.

Simmons and Associates. 1994. *The Impact of Tourism on the Marine Environment of the Caribbean*. Caribbean Tourism Organisation.

Stankey, G. H. 1985. The Limits of Acceptable Change (LAC) System for Wilderness Planning. U.S. Department of Agriculture Forest Service General Technical Report INT-176. Intermountain Forest and Range Experimental Station, Ogden, Utah.

Talge, H. 1989. "Observations of recreational divers in the Florida Keys". Unpublished report. The Nature Conservancy, Key West, Florida.

Talge, H. 1992. "Impact of recreational divers on scleractinian corals at Looe Key, Florida". pp. 1077–1082, in *Proceedings of the 7th International Coral Reef Symposium, Guam*, Vol. 2.

Wijnstekers, W. 1992. *The Evolution of CITES*, 3rd edition. CITES Secretariat, Lausanne.

8

Coastal Zone Management

Barry A. Wade and Dale F. Webber

Contents

INTRODUCTION

The majority of Caribbean people live in the coastal zone, that is, in that relatively narrow strip of flat or gently sloping land next to the sea. Throughout Caribbean history, trade and commerce resulted in the development of settlements along the coast, with concomitant agricultural and recreational activities in that limited but highly productive space known as the coastal zone. Hence, it is not surprising that Caribbean capital cities, where most activity is concentrated, bear a striking resemblance to one another, whether it be Havana, Santo Domingo, Port au Prince, Kingston, Port of Spain, or Willemstad. Nor is it by chance that these cities are all nestled around partly enclosed deep-water bays where early seafarers found safe haven while promoting trade on the high seas. As commerce grew, so did the concentrations of people and, thus, the agricultural needs necessary to fill ships' holds and feed populations. Thus, huge sugar cane plantations, to produce sugar for export, and smaller farm holdings, to produce food staples, inevitably grew up near these centres, followed by the industries necessary for processing their outputs. Later, an interest in recreation as a business arose and tourism became another activity lured by the attractions of the coastal zone.

It is estimated that 75 percent of Caribbean populations are concentrated in the coastal zone, as are the island capital cities with their main commercial centres, seaports, airports, and resorts. All these activities have brought tremendous pressure to the coastal zone, resulting in the ever-increasing scarcity of resources and user conflicts. As a result, environmental quality has deteriorated. The resources of the coastal zone, their uses, and the approaches to managing them, therefore, are of considerable importance to the welfare of Caribbean states, as they are in other parts of the world, and deserve the most urgent and rigorous attention from persons interested in or involved with development.

Definition of the Coastal Zone

There are two approaches to defining the coastal zone. The first is a purely physical approach in which the coastal zone is defined in terms of the area it occupies. The second approach defines the coastal zone in terms of the relationships and interactions that make it a distinct and somewhat unique ecological entity. In this context, the concept of ecology is used in its broadest sense to include the relationships among all the living and nonliving components of the environment.

From a spatial point of view, the coastal zone includes all those areas that drain out to the sea and those that are either periodically inundated by the tides or are permanently covered by the sea down to the edge of the continental shelf where the sea bottom slopes rapidly to deep sea (Clarke, 1977). This definition embraces the coastal watersheds, plains, and shoreline; the rivers, estuaries, and wetlands that drain them; and the beaches, seagrass beds, reefs, and other marine formations occurring on the continental shelf. A schematic representation of these features is presented in Figure 8.1. The second definition of the coastal zone, which stresses relationships and interactions, refers to all the contiguous marine and land areas that are linked by direct physical, biological, or human interaction as a result of drainage, tides, currents, winds, storms, primary production, energy flows, migrations, resource utilization, and waste discharges. In this approach, the interactions and uses of the coastal zone, and therefore the human and management elements, take on more importance than the physical elements and the coastal zone is viewed as a dynamic resource base primarily fashioned and controlled by human uses (Brahtz, 1972).

Resource Utilization

Small islands are considered to be made up entirely of the coastal zone, since any activity carried on in one part of the island may have a direct impact on any other part. Thus, for example, trees cut down anywhere on the island may lead to erosion and soil loss which, in turn, could cause smothering and destruction of reefs, leading to beach erosion, loss of recreational space, a decline in tourism, and so on. In such a situation the interconnections are almost endless and cause and effect relationships become complex and even blurred as each part of the system affects and is affected by other parts. Such is the nature of small islands, and indeed the coastal zone in general, where physical space is limited but occupied by diverse ecosystems and where the demands on the resources are exacting due to high population concentrations and often conflicting interests.

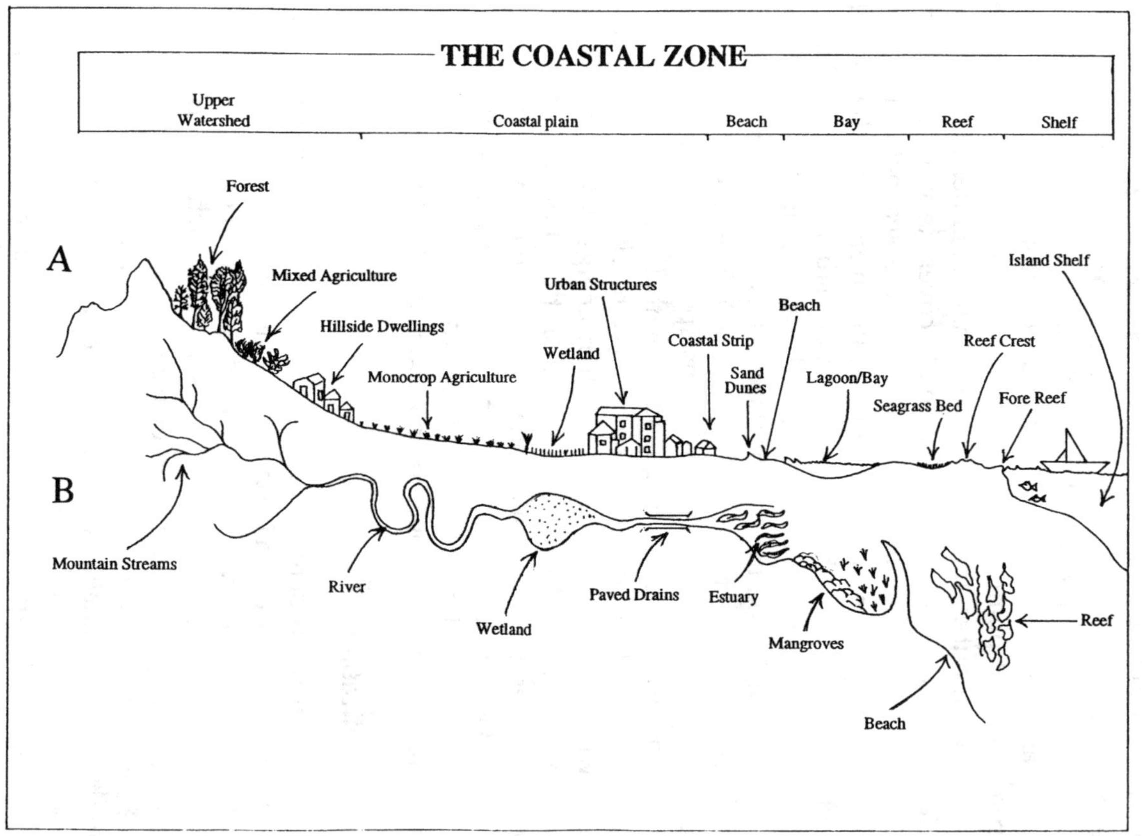

FIGURE 8.1 Schematic representation of the Caribbean coastal zone.

These conditions tend to be heightened by the fact that, in the coastal zone, there tends to be an absence of clear boundaries between one part of the system and another, thus leading to jurisdictional uncertainty and conflict. The conditions are also heightened by the existence of very rapid and effective natural transport mechanisms that move elements of the system from one place to another, thus achieving almost immediate and far-reaching effects. For example, the endless flow of rivers, tides, and currents in the coastal zone links all the aquatic elements in a seamless continuum, while sea and land breezes effectively modify the climate over the entire spectrum of environments. Similarly, and at times even more powerfully, human activities in the coastal zone have impacts that are felt immediately over wide areas. The case, for example, of building a water dam in the watershed or of disposing of solid waste in a coastal dump site are just two instances of activities that may have the most far-reaching effects.

Rodriquez (1981) described the environmental stresses in the Caribbean coastal zone brought on by human activity over the years. Most of the countries continue to depend on monocultural, export-oriented agriculture, with the use of fertilizers and chemical pesticides. Today, the effects of these chemicals are evident throughout the region, with ever increasing instances of fishkills and widespread nutrient enrichment of the coastal waters leading to ecological imbalances and coral reef destruction. Other impacts resulting from agriculture in the region have been deforestation and soil loss. Eyre (1991) estimated that Jamaican soil loss to the sea each year is close to the order of 54 tons per acre, while deforestation is rampant and is now regarded as the most rapid anywhere in the world, at 5 percent per annum (Eyre, 1996; World Resources Institute, 1994).

Although industrialization in the Caribbean is not widespread, certain local areas have been intensively industrialized for use as processing centres for indigenous or imported raw materials. Oil drilling and processing in Trinidad, Venezuela, and Curaçao, for example, or bauxite mining and processing in Jamaica, have created their own set of physical and social problems which seriously affect the coastal zone.

Parallel to the industrialization and intensification of agriculture, other sections of the economy, notably the tourism industry, have been developed to varying degrees in different countries, with overall positive impacts on the economy but with significant negative impacts on the environment. The result is that most of the Caribbean islands are grappling with the problem of how to expand and improve their tourism product while maintaining and even enhancing the quality of their environment. We will address this topic later in the chapter.

Brahtz (1972) discussed the manner and rate of utilization of coastal zone resources in a somewhat broader context and described the situation as follows:

> The many and diverse human activities involved in the use of the coastal zone constitute imposing, excessive, and competitive demands on the limited resources; consequently they often critically affect regional ecological systems. . . .
>
> The use of natural resources must modify the environment to some degree. It is therefore essential that we sufficiently understand the threatened ecology to determine what level of man's intervention can be tolerated without destabilising vital systems. Technology must supply tactical options for pursuing legitimate goals, and relative consequences of alterations must be well understood to modulate intelligently our activities in the coastal zone. Furthermore, the need for priority and decision criteria required for proper adjudication of goal conflicts along with the need to conserve resources to protect the natural environment compound and intensify the coastal management problem. Consequently, optional management of the coastal zone and the best skills and technology capabilities to support this management ideal are required. (p.2)

Brahtz concluded: "Excellence in management is an unmistakable requirement for handling the complexities of the coastal zone problem situation."

The Need for Management

These observations should lead to two sets of questions. The first is, "What are the vital resources of the coastal zone on which so much depends, and how are we utilizing them?" and the second, "How should we manage these resources for the optimum (and sustainable) good of all peoples?"

The coastal zone has been referred to as a place where several ecosystems meet, resulting in numerous and virtually continuous boundary interactions. It is these diverse ecosystems and interactions comprising geological, biological, meteorological, hydrological, and sociological elements that give to the coastal zone its richness and diversity. Thus, within the limited space of the coastal zone, one may find several, varied resources, such as forests, soils, rivers, wetlands, estuaries, harbours, beaches, reefs, fishes, minerals and petroleum, as well as cities, roads, ports, dams, buildings, and people. These resources are both natural and man-made and are exploited in extractive and nonextractive ways that may consume or degrade them. On the whole, nonextractive uses have less of an impact on resources, and activities such as swimming, boating, and sightseeing may cause little or no harm to the environment. On the other hand, some nonextractive activities, such as waste disposal, highway traffic, shipping, and industrial zoning, may have huge impacts.

With regard to extractive uses, the impacts are usually direct and may be quite severe. Petroleum production, sand mining, coastal dredging, lumber milling, fisheries, and the like all depend on extracting resources from the environment. In most cases, there is no replenishment of the resources although in some as, for example, fisheries and forestry, they may be renewable through natural processes. In such situations it is important that extraction does not exceed the maximum sustainable yield (MSY), a measure developed by natural resources managers to determine the maximum level at which such resources may be exploited without depleting or destroying them in the long run. (For a further discussion of MSY see Chapter 3.)

Extractive industries in the coastal zone are particularly damaging due to the general scarcity of resources and the limited spaces in which they occur and to the harm that is often inflicted on other nearby resources through accessing, processing, or transporting them. Oil drilling and lumber milling are two such examples. In some situations conscious decisions must be taken not to exploit valuable resources because of the possible harmful effects on the environment. The controversial decision made in Jamaica not to extract peat resources from the Negril wetlands is a good example (Wade and Reeson, 1985).

Just as much as the coastal zone is subject to man's exploitation and may be damaged to a great extent by these activities, so is it extremely vulnerable to the ravages of nature. In the Caribbean, we know full well the devastating effects of hurricanes, storms, floods, earthquakes, and volcanoes and, in other parts of the world, of tsunamis (tidal waves). Because of its exposure and low-lying form, the coastal zone is particularly vulnerable to all these perturbations and their effects on the natural and built environments, on the economy, livelihoods, and public health.

As if these hazards were not enough, there is another threat now looming that could have far more devastating effects on the coastal zone. This is the potential rising of the sea level as a result of global warming (Schneider, 1989; Nurse, 1990). While scientists do not all agree on the extent to which global warming may take place, they do agree that it will occur. In fact, the consensus now seems to be that global warming has already begun and that sea level rise is inevitable. Depending on whether the rise is only a few centimetres or perhaps a quarter to half a metre, Caribbean coastal zones will become inundated by the sea to varying degrees, resulting in the likely destruction of beaches, flooding of farmlands, more severe wave and storm damages to shoreline structures, and the loss of habitable areas. Indeed, by the year 2020, most of these effects could begin to manifest themselves.

Against this background, we may ask, how do we set about managing the resources of the coastal zone since it is prone to so much exploitation by people and such devastation by nature? How do we develop a rational approach to the management of small island systems, which are generally regarded as being all coastal zone? In Barbados in 1994, the United Nations sponsored a worldwide conference to address this problem. The Small Island Developing States (SIDS) Conference, as it was called, noted that SIDS have little margin for errors. They are characterized by a high degree of stress on the environment, both from the pressures of economic activity on limited land area and from a limited capacity to absorb or to recover quickly from disasters. Given these conditions, is it indeed possible to develop plans and programmes suitable for coastal zones and small islands to enable them to cope effectively, creatively, and in a sustainable manner? Is it possible to ensure the ability to meet essential human needs, maintain biodiversity, and improve the quality of life for everyone? These are some of the critical questions that need to be addressed.

DESCRIPTION OF THE COASTAL ZONE

Major Components, Resources, and Processes

The coastal zone is that portion of the Earth where land and sea influences encounter and interact with each other, resulting in diverse, delicate, and dynamic ecosystems. Coastal zones include gently sloping beaches with varying wave energies impacting the shoreline and steep rocky shores with extensive splash zones. Estuaries are found along coastlines where fresh river or stream water mixes with saline oceanic water. Extending inland from these or adjacent to them are wetlands. These range from salt or freshwater marshes to mangrove forests and swamps. Coastlines may be bordered by flat coastal plains, which extend landward and merge into the watersheds some distance from the coast itself but are still a part of the coastal zone. Seagrass meadows are found in the shallow near-shore waters of many coasts and provide both a habitat for marine organisms and a source of sediment. Finally, the coastal zone of warm tropical and subtropical waters often contains coral reefs consisting of calcium carbonate structures secreted by photosynthesizing algae and coral animals.

There are three major regions in the coastal zone: the terrestrial features, which are influenced by inland processes and the presence of the nearby sea; the littoral zone, which is the narrow area between low and high tide marks, extended to include the area that receives splash from waves; and the sublittoral zone, which comprises the shallow sea bottom extending from the lower part of the shore to the continental shelf edge, at about 200 metres deep (Boaden and Seed, 1993).

Coastal ecosystems are dynamic and interactive. Features and activities in any portion of the coastal zone impinge directly or indirectly on other portions of this ever-changing region. Coastlines may exist in one of two major forms: advanced or retreated. Advancing (also known as depositional or emerging) coasts may be formed either organically, for example by growth of mangroves or coral reefs (land accretion), or they can advance inorganically by deposition of silt from rivers. Retreated coasts (submerged or erosional) are eroded by wave action, glaciers, or rivers.

Tides and waves are important processes that affect the coastal zone, especially at the interface between land and sea. Tides are a complex phenomenon and are related to the gravitational and centrifugal forces of the Earth, moon, and sun (Gross 1990). Tides are created by the gravitational pull of the moon and the sun and result in a rise and fall in the level of the sea in relation to the coast once or twice per day. This rise and fall in the water level creates the intertidal zone or the area between the high and low tide marks. Thus, areas of the shoreline are subjected to cyclical immersion and emersion, either on a daily or monthly basis.

Waves are the result of the frictional drag of winds on the surface of the oceans (Gross, 1990). As waves approach the shore they are affected by the contours of the shore and sea bottom. There is a retarding effect and, as a wave enters shallow water and slows down, the bottom of the wave is slowed down more than the top and the wave breaks as surf. Waves help to shape the coastline and are critical in the formation and maintenance of beaches.

Land and sea breezes are generated by the difference in the specific heat capacity of the landmass and the sea. The land heats up at a faster rate than the sea and also cools at a faster rate. During the day the landmass gets hotter than the adjacent sea and heats the air above it. Hot air rises and the air over land is thus advected upward. This rising air mass is replaced by air over the sea, so that the direction of the wind is from the sea (sea breezes). At night, the land cools down faster than the sea. The air over the sea is therefore relatively warmer. It rises and is replaced by air from the land. At night the direction of the wind is from the land to sea (land breezes).

Beaches

Beaches are temporary land forms existing between the high- and low-water tide marks. They are comprised of unconsolidated sand particles of different sizes and from different sources. Sandy coastlines are dynamic intertidal environments where sand, water, and air are constantly in motion (Brown and McLachlan, 1990). Sand originates mainly from erosion of the land and may be transported to the sea from the upper reaches of the watershed by rivers. However, sand also originates from biogenic sources in the sea, such as the skeletal remains of animals, coral, and calcareous algae (for example the white sand beaches of Negril, Jamaica). Terrigenous sands may be quartz particles, which are formed by the erosion of sandstones; these tend to be white and coarse, as on Trinidad's north coast (Bacon, 1978). Alternatively, they may result from the erosion of volcanic rocks, which tend to form black sandy beaches, as, for example, Point Saline, Grenada.

Beaches occur where there is a gentle slope in the near-shore shelf, sufficient unconsolidated material and where tides, waves, and currents form, maintain, and sculpture the unconsolidated material. Softer material is removed from rocks to give rocky headlands their sculptured look. This material is moved along the shore by currents in a process called littoral transport or longshore drift and is deposited in low-energy places, forming beaches. Longshore drift is thought to have created the Palisadoes spit on the south coast of Jamaica with sand obtained from the large Hope, Yallahs, and Cane Rivers east of the area (Hendry, 1979). This sand movement is not always desirable, as it may result in beach erosion or unwanted deposition. Frequently, silting occurs offshore rather than longshore, resulting in berms and sills some distance from the shore. These, in turn, may affect beach nourishment, water circulation, and small vessel navigation.

Beaches are limited landward by a foredune, cliff, or some man-made construction. Being intertidal, sandy shores also experience changes in degree of wetness due to tides and waves. The level of exposure is also used to classify beaches as high- and low-energy beaches. Beaches with extremely high energy have steeper slopes, larger sand particles, and are more vulnerable to erosion and coastline changes, as seen at La Roselle beach on the south-east coast of Jamaica. Beaches with low energy are less steep and are made up of finer, more consolidated sand particles, with less possibility of erosion and coastline changes. As a result of the differing features displayed at high- and low-energy beaches, it is easy to understand why tourism is prevalent at low-energy beaches, which are often protected by coral reefs, while landing fish catches and boat building are more common at high-energy beaches.

Watersheds, Rivers, and Estuaries

As sandy shores become more protected from wave action they tend to become finer grained and accumulate more organic matter, thus becoming muddier. In extreme cases, mudflats are formed. These are more stable than sandy shores and have a very flat profile. In addition, water flow is minimal and anaerobic conditions prevail within the sediment. A muddy shore will only become established where there is an ample supply of fine-grained sediment particles and shelter. Fine silts and muds originate inland and are usually the product of deforestation and erosion in the hills some distance from the coastline (Guppy, 1984). The catchment basin or area of the nearby hills and plains, which is the physical limit of the watershed, is characterized by a network of rivers and tributaries that all eventually discharge into coastal waters. The watersheds that subtend coastal plains may be as much as ten times larger in surface area than the coastal plain itself. Thus, watersheds are possibly the dominant factor in determining the environmental status of the entire coastal zone (Brahtz, 1972).

Estuaries are of great importance as a coastal feature, since it is the muddy shores with mangrove stands in estuaries that receive the fluvial inputs. By spreading the flow of a river laterally, in a braided fashion, the fresh water in estuaries, with or without pollutants, is spread over a large surface area, allowing slow and gradual introduction into the coastal waters. Rivers usually discharge into embayments that may be somewhat protected. Thus, estuaries are usually associated with harbours, bays, and lagoons.

The interconnected nature of watersheds, rivers, estuaries, and the other coastal environments is very evident. Not only are the sediments from hillside erosion released into the rivers but so too are the wastes of riverside residential developments and the agricultural sector, including animal waste, fertilizers, pesticides, and herbicides. These products, along with the fresh water, may pose significant threats to most, if not all, of the other coastal zone environments (Benson, 1981).

Harbours, Bays, and Coastal Lagoons

Harbours, bays, and lagoons are coastal embayments that usually enjoy some form of protection from onshore waves and oceanic currents. Harbours and bays differ from lagoons in that these embayments may be protected by coral reefs, while lagoons may be protected by a sand bar, spit, or land mass. Harbours must be maintained at a prescribed water depth commensurate with the shipping and boating activities that are conducted within them. By the protection offered them from coral reefs and sand sills, bays have less energy and little circulation and are associated with tourism, recreation, and fishing activities. Urbanization is a frequent feature around harbours and bays.

A lagoon is a body of saline water with no connection, or a narrow restricted connection, to the sea (Barnes, 1980). Lagoon formation involves the development of a spit and eventually a bar across a depression in the coastline. The lagoon may be surrounded by mangroves, which assist with this process by accreting sediment along the shoreline, and, in some instances, on the bar. Ultimately, the lagoon may become filled in with sediment and a succession of mangrove vegetation follows. Lagoons are typically sheltered and are usually associated with estuaries since they receive fluvial inputs. Due to the narrow opening to the sea there is a high retention time, which results in lagoons frequently becoming stressed.

Wetlands, Marshes, and Swamps

The interface between terrestrial soils and marine sediments results in a saline, hydric environment known as a coastal wetland in which only specialized organisms can survive (Boaden and Seed, 1993). In temperate climates this region constitutes a saltmarsh, while in tropical climates this region is more frequently a swamp, mainly a mangrove swamp. Mangrove swamps (mangals) are found in tropical coastal wetlands (areas of land subjected to inundation) which support a peculiar type of emergent coastal vegetation (mangrove) belonging to different genera and possessing special adaptations. They occur in the intertidal areas where inundation may be daily or seasonal with either fresh or saline water. Mangroves occupy about 50 percent of coastlines in tropical areas and therefore constitute one of the most important coastal environments. The latitude limit is controlled by the occurrence of frost, which kills the young trees.

Mangroves are commonly associated with sheltered coasts, bays, lagoons, harbours (as in the Gulf of Paria, Trinidad and Kingston Harbour, Jamaica), on gently sloping accretional shores and in low-lying areas with extensive saline intrusion and large tidal amplitude. Mangrove trees are important for various ecological reasons. The elaborate rooting system of mangroves reduces water movement and traps and stabilizes especially fine terrigenous material so that the mangrove forest leads to land accretion. The prop roots that hang into the water provide a sheltered habitat for the juvenile stages of many marine animals which later move out to the coral reef environment. Mangroves also act as a sink (net accumulator) for various elements, including macronutrients (for example, nitrates and phosphates), trace elements, and heavy metals (Onuf and Teal, 1977). This reduces the possibility of eutrophication and other forms of coastal pollution.

Mangroves therefore act as "sponges", soaking up fresh water, nutrients, and mud so that riverine discharge is not dumped directly into the marine area and onto seagrass beds and coral reefs. Fresh water retained in the forest is lost to evaporation and the rest dissolves and dilutes excess salts accumulated in the inner portions of the mangrove forest during periods of drought. Thus, the volume of fresh water reaching the coast is reduced. Terrigenous sediments that cause temporary damage to seagrasses and permanent damage to coral reefs are trapped in the mangrove environment, thus reducing the impact on more delicate ecosystems. There is therefore a unique association among mangroves, seagrasses, and coral reefs.

It is interesting to note that, besides their ecological function, mangroves are important for other reasons. For example, they provide a renewable source of hardwood and dye in many parts of the world (Snedaker and Getter, 1985). This makes the mangroves a highly exploitable resource, frequently requiring protection by legislation.

Coral Reefs and Seagrass Beds

Coral reefs occur along shallow tropical coastlines in clear, clean, unpolluted marine waters. They are made up of calcium carbonate from colonies of animals called coral polyps and their skeletal remains. Within the polyps grow single-celled plants which photosynthesize by day and provide the polyp with energy (Weber et al., 1992). At night photosynthesis stops and the polyps are extended from their skeletal structure with tentacles surrounding a central mouth, capturing various floating microscopic plants and animals (Jones and Sefton, 1991). Corals require clear water with little or no sediments, full strength sea water (35 parts per thousand), warm temperatures, and bright light. Thus, the presence of rivers, which deliver fresh water, silt, and suspended matter, mitigates significantly against the success of coral reefs. Constant marine currents renew the supply of clean water and organic material necessary for the maintenance of the wide range of organisms associated with the reefs.

The coral reef ecosystem serves multiple roles in the coastal zone, chief among them that it provides habitats for marine organisms and protects beaches, wetlands, and estuaries from high wave energy, especially during storms. In some parts of the world there is a thriving trade in coral mining both for construction materials, ornaments, and jewels. However, perhaps the greatest value of the reefs is their role in fisheries in both large and small coastal communities. The alignment of coral reefs is such that they are usually parallel to the coastline and perpendicular to the oncoming waves. This, along with the projection of their calcareous structure above the sea floor, allows for maximum protection of the landward features of the coastal zone from wind-generated waves and surges. Without these protective measures wetlands become damaged by high-energy waves, erosion of beaches is exacerbated, urban coastal construction is threatened, and commercial ventures such as fisheries and shipping are affected.

In addition to a relatively close geographical relationship, there are also close ecological relationships among the coral reef, mangrove, and seagrass environments. Seagrasses and mangroves are highly dependent on hydrodynamic barriers, such as coral reefs, which dissipate wave energy and create low-energy environments on the leeward side. Coral reefs actively produce carbonate skeletal material at a high rate, which results in complex massive calcareous structures. The skeletal material produced is constantly being broken up by abrasion and ground into smaller fragments, forming sand, which is transported and deposited to the lower energy areas, forming beaches behind the reef. The calm areas that are found behind reefs are thus ideal to become colonized by seagrasses and mangroves.

Seagrasses trap and stabilize sediments. The subterranean roots provide anchorage and help to hold sediments together against erosion. The blades of the grass act as baffles which slow down water and encourage sediments to settle and accumulate in an area; this ensures the settling of material from the mangroves before it reaches the reef. The microorganisms living on the seagrass also contribute to the sediment as they die and fall off the blades. Seagrasses therefore encourage sediment build up and so either form beaches or allow the area to become shallow enough for mangroves to colonize (Thorhaug, 1981).

A large variety of marine organisms, many of commercial importance, live in seagrass beds. The weak currents prevent slow-moving animals from being washed away. Thus, many juvenile fish and shrimp find shelter and food in this habitat. Of the tremendous number of species found in seagrass beds only a few feed directly on the grass. Most do not possess the enzymes to digest the blades but feed on smaller epiphytic animals and plants. However, some important animals feed directly on the blades, including turtles, manatees, and sea urchins; the queen conch prefers broken blades. These commercially important species constitute the major resources in many Caribbean economies; however, fishing for turtles and manatee is now prohibited by law in most Caribbean countries.

ECONOMIC ACTIVITIES OF THE COASTAL ZONE

Urbanization

In order to meet the growing population needs of small island nations, coastal lands are constantly being developed for housing, recreation, industry, and other commercial uses. This gives rise to a new dimension to the coastal zone, which ranges from landfill activities, with the removal of mangrove forests, to overfishing and the introduction of industries that remove sediment aggregate, use sea water, and release toxins and hazardous waste.

The continuous construction of offices, factories, and residential complexes is complemented by roads, bridges, and railway lines, all of which become part of the newly constructed coastline. This is especially so around harbours that are sites of major port facilities, such as Port of Spain and Kingston. This is the urban portion of the coastal zone. Mangrove removal to create construction sites is common as, for example, at Hunts Bay, Jamaica. Also common is the training of waterways to direct flow (and overflow) to the desired area of the sea. This training usually involves changing natural river courses through the creation of concrete-lined gullies. The effect is a more rapid and violent release of land runoff into the sea with no possibility of the naturally occurring percolation and infiltration of river and stream water to recharge the aquifer. Deep water ports and high rise buildings are now common features of the coastal zone landscape, replacing beaches, mudflats, mangroves, and seagrasses. Urbanization is here to stay, stimulated by development and population increase as more individuals attempt to utilize the wide range of resources of the coastal zone.

An essential part of successful urbanization is also the provision of a network of communication by roads and bridges. The construction phase of roads and bridges results in removal of coastal vegetation, some of which is essential to coastline stability, and increased sedimentation in the marine environment. Occasionally, roads traverse wetlands and swamps, altering the circulation, tidal exchange, or surface runoff that characterizes some coastal areas, as in Negril and Portmore in Jamaica. Apart from the ecology of wetland removal (Goodbody, 1994), usage of the roadways inevitably results in automotive hydrocarbon release into the coastal zone.

The siting of industries in the coastal zone is primarily an economic consideration and is influenced mainly by easy access to shipping and port facilities. However, many industries desire access to sea water for cooling, as in power generation plants, with associated complications (Thorhaug et al., 1973) or are sited in the coastal zone to allow for easy disposal of wastewater. Commensurate with urbanization is also the need to treat and dispose of the domestic waste generated by the increased population. Coastal waters are therefore the most widely used recipient of domestic and industrial waste (Boaden and Seed, 1993). Waste disposal in the sea occurs because persons believe that the sea, with its large volume, can dilute any waste it receives. While this option is usually the most cost effective in the short term, the eventual damage and costs may far outweigh the earlier benefits. The costs involved in cleaning up Havana Bay (U.S.$ 210 million) and the estimate for doing the same job in Kingston Harbour (U.S.$ 350 million) serve to illustrate the point.

The bacterial component of domestic waste (sewage) introduces a range of microorganisms that cause numerous infectious diseases. Fortunately, many of the bacterial organisms that cause diseases in man do not survive for long periods in a saline environment (Webber, 1993). However, the presence of these microorganisms and other flora and fauna use up the oxygen available for respiration, resulting in a high biochemical oxygen demand, a typical condition of polluted coastal waters, which can lead to the death of other organisms through oxygen depletion.

The nutrient component of sewage when released into the marine environment results in excessive plant growth and major changes in the species composition, with the loss of some species and proliferation or bloom of others, as in Kingston Harbour (Wade, 1972; Grahame, 1977; Webber, 1993). These algal blooms are responsible for the phenomenon known as red tides commonly seen in Kingston Harbour (Steven, 1965; Webber 1994) prior to massive fishkills.

The potential problems associated with industrial waste release are determined by the nature of the industry and the types of operation employed. Energy generation companies and industries that use high-temperature kilns and furnaces often use continuously pumped sea water as a cooling medium. The intake of sea water by pumping often traps marine organisms of all sizes, impacting the flora and fauna. Antifouling chemicals are added to the system to prevent the fouling of equipment by marine organisms. These antifouling chemicals are then released into the environment with fatal effects on both sessile and planktonic organisms. Finally, the water, having provided its cooling effect, is returned to the marine environment at temperatures 10 to 15°C above ambient sea water temperatures. Heat shock, physiological breakdown, and death results in most marine organisms exposed to this dramatic temperature change over such a short time.

The wash water from the periodic cleaning of industry equipment, which is usually released into the sea, introduces chemicals that are sometimes toxic or very reactive. Specialized industries pose particular threats. For example, desalinization plants release hypersaline water and battery factories often have acidic and lead-contaminated effluents. Frequently, processing residues, oils, grease, and sediment are released, which either directly affect the flora and fauna or reduce the oxygen present in the water, indirectly killing organisms (Bate and Crafford, 1985).

Man by his interventions has created many shoreline problems. Erosion and accretion are natural processes which man attempts to change by the construction of coastal structures such as groynes and jetties (see shipping and ports). However, inland construction, such as a dam constructed on a river, affects the coastal zone by preventing sediments associated with the river from naturally nourishing the beaches. The same effect is caused by the mining of river sand for construction purposes, a practise that is widespread throughout the Caribbean. Good examples of this occur on the south coast of Jamaica where two large rivers (Hope and Yallahs) have lost their perennial flow and are being mined extensively. Consequently, the Palisadoes peninsula on which the Norman Manley International Airport sits is in danger of being starved of new sediment inflows.

Shipping and Ports

The importance of the oceans as a means of transport of personnel and cargo has created a vast economic enterprise in the form of cruise shipping, general cargo, oil tankers and container vessels. In order to receive, service, and attract more vessels, cities and towns at the coast have invested significantly in the establishment of ports with extensive berthing facilities, pleasure boat marinas, and dry dock facilities. New facilities have been constructed where none existed and major expansion has occurred where facilities existed before (Hershman et al., 1978). Developing these facilities as well as the shipping industry itself creates potential and actual problems that are both immediate and long term in nature. Other users, those based on military and fishing interests, pose similar problems, albeit on a less significant scale.

In most island states, the economic gain derived from the tourism cruise shipping industry is rivalled only by the economics associated with the operation of import/export activities and transhipment facilities, as in Jamaica. However, the Bahamas, Barbados, and islands of the lesser Antilles benefit far more from cruise ship port calls as a foreign exchange earner than from any other shipping activity (Hayward et al., 1981). Defense of coastal waters and fishing in these waters, while important, are of less tangible economic value and forge their way to the economic front in response to sovereignty disputes and the exploitation of exclusive economic zones.

The problems surrounding the shipping industry itself are many although apparently not as significant as those problems associated with port construction and expansion. These include the containment, treatment, and eventual disposal of shipboard waste. Regardless of international conventions and local legislation, without implementation and supervision ship waste is frequently disposed of within the 12-mile limit of countries, sometimes within the port of call itself. There is the ever present possibility of oil spills, commonly observed in Havana Harbour, spillage during the loading and unloading of vessels (especially where materials may be considered hazardous), and the introduction of foreign organisms from bilge washing. Finally, there is the potential for damage to benthic environments from navigational errors resulting in ships running aground.

Ports are usually sited in areas that offer natural protection, such as areas adjacent to headlands and behind spits and extensive and emergent fringing reefs. Changes in coastal dynamics and water quality usually accompany the extensive land-fills and wetland reclamation which are now common precursors to the upgrade or construction of port facilities as in Point Lisas, Trinidad (McShine and Siung-Chang, 1984). Wind and wave action further dictate the location of harbours that offer ports for large shipping vessels. Failure to consider these factors while constructing or expanding a port facility leads to more damaging effects on the environment.

Dynamite blasting of fringing coral reefs to make shipping channels is also common even though the detrimental ecological impacts are well known. Dredge and fill activities to keep shipping lanes clear to the prescribed depth cause constant threats to turbulence and reduce water clarity. Recently, while dredging Kingston Harbour, the vessel that should have taken the fill material 10 miles to sea was observed trailing a plume of sediment 200 metres long as its hull doors were accidentally lodged open. This resulted in a reduction of water quality, damage to habitats for marine organisms, and changes in the structure of the coastline inducing further siltation and deposition effects.

Harbours, by their protective requirements for ports, have greater water residence times and so retain sediments, pollutants, and enriched waters for long periods, as evidenced in Havana Bay and Kingston Harbour (Bigg and Webber, 2001). Sediment transport, erosion, and deposition, which are often affected by port installations such as jetties, groins, and seawalls, can have enormous effects on the presence and removal of beaches and other tourism-related concerns, as well as on the exposure of areas of coastline to strong oceanic waves and currents (Brown and McLachlan, 1990). Finally, the construction of a major port facility is likely to impact on the freshwater flow to the sea either by reducing flow as a result of the port infrastructure or increasing flow by introducing concrete spillways, gullies, and channels.

Recreation and Tourism

Increasingly island nations are depending more and more on tourism as the major revenue earner of their economies (Beekhuis, 1981). The coastal zones of countries with tourism as a major part of their financial base are characterized traditionally by coral reefs and beaches. Now though, nature trails, hiking, biking, and other nontraditional tourism activities are equally important, for example in the Caroni Swamp Reserve in Trinidad (Thelen and Faizool, 1980).

Considering the direct foreign exchange earning capacity of tourism, the number of jobs directly and indirectly involved, as well as the multiplier effect, especially through tourism-dependent coastal communities, tourism investments form a major part of all Caribbean state economies. Whether through all-inclusive seaside mega-hotel chain investments or small ecotourism ventures, the tourism service industry concept has become a major part of the social fabric of Caribbean communities. Reduction in or removal of the tourism market of these communities would have disastrous economic consequences (McElroy et al., 1990).

The phenomenon of "ribbon development", which intensifies the construction and establishment of resorts, accommodation, and tourism attractions along the narrow beachfront, places extreme stress on the coastal zone. Infrastructural needs such as airports, cruise shipping piers, and accommodation for tourists in the form of hotels, villas, and cottages impact the coastal zone in two ways. First, large numbers of persons in a relatively small area require large-scale investment in waste disposal systems. The old adage that dilution is the solution to pollution has often been tried and proven to be unwise and incorrect. The release of hotel waste into the marine environment results in a reduction of water quality, an increase in noxious algal growth, bacterial infections, and deterioration of the beach (Barnes, 1973; Paerl, 1988). Second, coastlines are affected by construction (landfill and port construction addressed above). This usually involves removal of seagrass from the sea floor and erection of groins to nourish beaches. This "improvement" of beach front property aesthetics and beach conditions often results in reef damage, irreversible deleterious changes in sedimentation, and changes in beach erosion patterns, as seen at Cornwall Beach, Montego Bay, Jamaica.

Recreational activities are concomitant with aspects of tourism development such as the presence of attractive beaches for water sports, swimming and leisure, glass bottom boat rides, and parasailing. While these activities present few environmental problems, others such as snorkelling, SCUBA diving, and leisure boating, if not conducted properly, may result in damage to coral reefs (as in the Montego Bay Marine Park, Jamaica), seagrass beds, and other marine environments (United Nations Environment Program, 1982).

Mining and Quarrying

The coastal and shallow water marine environment is a source of a wide variety of minerals and products that are mined and extracted with significant economic gain (Cronan, 1980). Among the more prominent of these resources are:

- Construction and fill material such as sand, rock, and coral, as well as sands for glass
- Gypsum, lime, and fertilizer components from marls and coral
- Jewellery from corals and shells
- Deposits of metals (tin, chromium, and manganese)
- Hydrocarbon deposits (oil, peat, and natural gas)
- Bauxite for aluminium

The mining and extraction processes vary from country to country and the value to each economy depends on the quantity of the resource, the method of mining and extraction, and the level of environmental concern since these are nonrenewable resources (Rees, 1980).

The sea floors of many coastal zones are areas of treasures waiting to be mined. However, the economic base, job creation, and investment opportunities in mining are finite since the mining of a nonrenewable resource must end at some time. Moreover, the deposits of oil, natural gas, and minerals are often too small or too difficult to access to make their commercial extraction a worthwhile venture. Still, for many countries, this mining forms a major foreign exchange earner or at least a foreign exchange saver as locally mined products may be used locally in place of imports.

The environmental consequences of marine mining are often profound. These include potential river pollution, threats to hydrology, wells, and groundwater, increased suspended sediment in the water column, the risk of blow outs and explosions, death of marine organisms, and alterations to the marine benthos, as well as the risk of oil spills from incomplete drilling, uncapped wells, and fires.

In the few instances where sea floor mining is feasible, environmental concern rather than lack of technology is a major consideration. For example, environmental fears were foremost in the minds of developers and policy regulators when the decision was taken to abort the mining of peat in the Jamaican coastal tourist resort of Negril. However, environmental and health disasters have occurred from other mining activities. A recent example was the 1995 river poisoning by the accidental release of toxic cyanide waste from the Omiah gold mining operation in Guyana, which resulted in massive river fishkills and constituted a threat to Caribbean coastal waters as the Orinoco River discharges into the Caribbean Sea.

Marine quarrying of sand for glass making and construction is becoming more widespread, resulting in changes in the bathymetry of coastal waters with changes in currents and perhaps wave action. The soft sediment that fills in the dredged areas remains uncolonized since seagrasses, marine algae, and corals are unable to re-establish themselves on this substrate. Mining of the sand that forms the beaches is also common place and has even greater impact on the environment. The presence of sand is an indication of a status of equilibrium, which is disturbed by mining, leading to further loss of sand offshore and changes in the coastal dynamics. Coastal erosion of valuable property, housing or recreational facilities is often the end result of these mining activities (Brown and McLachlan, 1990).

Agriculture and Agro-industry

After tourism, agriculture is perhaps the largest revenue earner for many countries, especially island states. Banana, sugar cane, coffee, coconuts, and citrus form the traditional agricultural exports and hence are major foreign exchange earners for most large Caribbean states. Smaller states also have agriculturally based economies, with crops such as pimento, ginger, ground provisions, and fruits as additional earners, albeit on a much smaller scale. Although fewer persons are now employed in the agricultural sector than 10 years ago, there are a large number of jobs dependent on the sector and, as a result, many communities are formed around this activity. Another issue that relates to agricultural activities is the change in the pattern of land use from forest to agriculture at an estimated cost of U.S.$ 1000 per hectare converted (Everitt et al., 1991). This economic estimate changes significantly if the new land usage is for subsistence and not export agriculture.

In order to expand the acreage and exploit the economic earning power of agriculture, many coastal areas considered to be marginal have been reclaimed for growing flat-land crops such as sugar cane. As the need for irrigation water has resulted in the overpumping of underground aquifers, an intrusion of saline water from the sea has occurred, causing an increase in the salinization of soils. This, along with coastal flooding, has turned many of these lands into coastal wetlands, but not before significant damage has been done to them (Turner, 1984).

By its monoculture and extensive nature, agriculture must impact the coastal environment since water flow from land to sea is interrupted by irrigation. The flow paths of these rivers, streams, and channels provide a perfect method of transporting nutrients and other chemicals (pesticides, herbicides, and fertilizers), as well as soil sediment, organic material, and fresh water into estuaries and eventually the marine coastal areas.

When nutrients and fertilizers are released into the waters of the coastal zone, eutrophication results. Eutrophication is the proliferation of aquatic plants (plankton blooms) due to high nutrient availability. Subsequent death and decay of these aquatic plants results in deoxygenation of the water and death of aquatic fauna. Furthermore, some marine phytoplankton that proliferate under these conditions produce toxins that result in fishkills and may lead to paralysis in humans who ingest fin or shell fish that have digested these plankton (Raymont, 1980).

Pesticides and herbicides used in agriculture inevitably end up in the coastal waters, hopefully after some time and in a diluted form.

However, the toxic nature of these chemicals renders them lethal to both the flora and fauna with which they come in contact (Kinne and Bulnheim, 1980). Sediment and silt from the soil erosion that often accompanies improper hillside farming practices damage the watershed and enter the rivers, as has been observed in Port Antonio on the north coast of Jamaica. These silt-laden rivers and other fluvial inputs to the coastal zone have a particularly detrimental effect on seagrasses and coral reefs, reducing light and covering and smothering these sensitive organisms (Thayer et al., 1975).

Aquaculture

Aquaculture is the technology that increases the yield of aquatic resources by various management methods. These management methods can take many forms and, as such, may be the source of a range of environmental problems depending on the organisms to be used, the type of technology to be employed, and the proximity of the activity to the coastline. A range of aquatic resources is found all across the Caribbean, from freshwater and marine fish in Jamaica and Martinique to lobsters and shrimp in Trinidad, conch, oysters, and turtles in Cuba, Jamaica, and Cayman, and seaweed in St Lucia. Aquaculture has provided a new and cheaper source of protein and has created new jobs. Beginning with hatcheries and grow-out ponds and ending with processing plants and factories, the aquaculture industry provides numerous jobs at various skill levels, as well as foreign exchange and a source of protein to many coastal communities (Pollnac and Weeks, 1992). There are some limitations though, such as land availability or change in land use and the lack of marketing necessary to sell a product that some consumers may consider inferior in taste and quality.

Grow out activities may take place either in ponds or raceways, or in cages suspended in the sea. Pond siting often involves the removal of mangroves, with associated problems, while cage siting raises potential eutrophication and land/sea use conflicts. The introduction of foreign species to stock the ponds may result in shifts in the food chain based on predator-prey interactions, as well as the introduction of potential new parasites. The nutrient enrichment that occurs as a result of the feeding of the organisms and the accumulation of their waste matter produces eutrophic conditions and harmful algal blooms, as described above (Pullin, 1993). This becomes a coastal problem when ponds must be emptied or when rainfall results in pond overflow, since proximity to the sea is a major determinant of the severity of the impact on the coastal zone (Pullin and Neal, 1984).

The construction of cages in the sea (mariculture) poses even greater potential problems, since nutrient enrichment from fish feeding and fish faecal matter occur right there in the coastal waters. The release or escape of exotic species from mariculture operations and the conservation of genetic diversity is also more significant since recapture is almost impossible.

Fisheries

Fisheries play an important role in Caribbean economies. Besides providing much-needed protein for diets, fisheries employ many individuals both directly and indirectly and exert a major influence on the culture of island peoples. In a number of countries, such as Belize and Guyana, fisheries exports contribute significantly to foreign exchange earnings. The fisheries industry is vast and involves a number of associated activities, such as the construction of boats, the sale of petrol, engines, and nets, the procurement and marketing of fish after landing, and the processing of fish for export. These and other issues are addressed in detail in Chapter 3.

With the introduction of exclusive economic zones (EEZs), many countries, especially island states, have expanded their fishing zones and more individuals are becoming involved in the fisheries industry. This has led to greater mechanization and greater exploitation of fin and shell fisheries. This, combined with the economic hardships in island states, has forced many jobless persons to turn to fishing, resulting, in some places, in overfishing. Fishermen now have to go further from the mainland with greater effort and still catch fewer fish.

The traditional methods used in reef fishing, trawling, and deep-sea line fishing have been supplemented by other less environmentally friendly practices. These include dynamiting of reefs, which kills organisms other than fish and results in at least half of the fish sinking to the bottom, and it destroys the reef structure. Uncontrolled spear fishing is another such activity in which inexperienced youth snorkel over the reef shooting any and everything, mature or juvenile, often missing the fish but damaging the reef as well as endangering unsuspecting swimmers. Mesh sizes in both traps and nets have been reduced in an attempt to increase the catch. However, the increasing proportion of juveniles present in the catch (robbing the population of next generation adults to breed) indicates that the problem of overfishing will persist as long as these practices continue (Munro and Williams, 1985).

The shellfish industry faces similar problems, although regulatory management measures, such as open and closed seasons and shell size and carapace length, have been implemented. The destruction of nursery grounds and habitat sites have impacted significantly on the populations and their distributions (Goodbody, 1994).

Scientific Research and National Parks

Caribbean coastal environments offer unique and varied opportunities for scientific research and the establishment of national parks. As far as tropical environmental research is concerned, the Caribbean has attracted the attention of world famous scientists for centuries. The first Caribbean botanical garden and the first Caribbean marine laboratory were established in the nineteenth century. Today, there are more than twenty marine laboratories throughout the Caribbean pursuing research on coral reefs, mangroves, seagrasses, and fisheries, as well as physical and biological oceanography. This provides the Caribbean with a pool of information and expertise that can be used for management of the coastal zone.

Several unique environments have been set aside as national parks, such as the Caroni Swamp Reserve, Montego Bay Marine Park, and Belize Hol Chan Marine Reserve. These attract many visitors and are prime tourism products in the regions where they have been developed. However, there are land conflicts and employment, zoning, and legislative considerations in identifying, establishing, and maintaining scientific stations and national parks.

While scientific research and academic development are important tools to be used in the preservation and enhancement of the coastal zone, there are components of these benign activities that result in potential problems. Genetic manipulations to produce disease resistant varieties of species and the introduction of new species to areas previously not inhabited by the introduced organisms are two examples of potentially detrimental research impacts. Furthermore, many experiments conducted in the field place the coastal environment at the mercy of the researchers and scientists. The nature of the experiments (oil spill contingencies or organisms' recovery rates after oil spills), while providing valuable information, may put entire fragile ecosystems at risk. Such experiments must therefore be carefully managed and monitored. Designating parks as protected areas is one regulatory mechanism that will prevent further destruction of parts of the coastal zone. However, considering the multiple uses of this valuable but delicate ecosystem, the coastal zone requires and demands an organized and methodical approach to management and development.

MANAGEMENT OF THE COASTAL ZONE

Environmental Setting

We have seen that the coastal zone is characterized by a number of distinctive features that make its management both necessary and difficult. First, its resources, while highly diverse, are generally sparse and they occur in very limited spaces under constraining conditions, which may make their use difficult and costly. Second, the major components of the coastal zone, with their juxtapositions and overlapping elements, have highly complex interactions and impacts on one another. The linkages between watersheds, coral reefs, and tourism, which have already been cited, are a case in point that is very relevant to Caribbean economies. Third, we have seen that the coastal zone is an area of intense economic activity and population growth and that the demands for use of its resources are heavy, frequently conflicting, and increasingly damaging, to the extent that their sustainability is seriously questioned. Caribbean mangrove swamps, for example, are under considerable threat of destruction and replacement by real estate fills, ports, and marinas, and even of farmlands. Finally, the ecology of the coastal zone, by its very nature, is fragile and vulnerable to perturbations from both man and nature.

Where several ecosystems meet, as exemplified in the coastal zone, a certain tension exists between the interacting components and there is a tendency for one or more ecosystems within the environment to dominate. However, since nature has its own checks and balances, these tensions are usually kept within limits and the ecological associations survive. With the impact of human activities or the occurrence of some extraordinary natural event, for example, a hurricane or earthquake, the checks and balances may be removed and the ecology become imbalanced. What follows is a succession of changes that may eventually lead to the elimination of a vital component of the coastal environment. This is taking place, for example, with respect to the coral reefs along Jamaica's north coast, where the combination of hurricane damage and sewage discharges, assisted by poor fishing practices and a sea egg disease, has served to destroy up to 80 percent of the shallow reef in some places (Hughes, 1994; Vogel, 1994; Goreau, 1995).

The fragility of coastal zone ecosystems is most pronounced in small island systems for two reasons. According to McEachern and Towle (1974):

> One reason for island vulnerability derives from the fact that the historical element of remoteness and "isolation" seeking to inhibit development is becoming inoperative. The revolution in transport and communications has spelled the end to this inhibitory factor . . . The barrier of isolation has further been transgressed by exogenous factors occurring far beyond the shores of the island itself. (p. 34)

These authors cite, for example, the means of modern transportation as contributors to the former and pollution of the high seas as a contributor to the latter.

> The second reason for island vulnerability arises from the fact that the traditional development barrier of resource scarcity – or its complete absence – is no longer of crucial import. Technology has overcome many of the constraints on development posed by physical resource deficiencies. (p. 35)

Principles of Environmental Management

As a result of these special conditions, coastal zones in general and small island systems in particular require an approach to their management that is sound in principle, practical in application, and sufficiently focused but flexible enough to meet the needs of specific situations. Let us examine first the sound principles upon which any sensible approach to a coastal zone management programme must be based. We recognize four:

1. *The maintenance of ecological integrity*: The management of the coastal zone, like that of any other natural resource, must recognize the need to maintain the environment in balance, free from excessive pollution, resource depletion, and ecological collapse. Boulding (1966) refers to this as maintenance of the capital stock, the total pool of resources on which life depends. McEachern and Towle (1974) maintain that, "acceptance of a conservation ethic is indispensable to the principle of maintaining the capital stock" (p. 49). They see the management imperative to conserve and preferably enhance the original endowment as of critical importance and the only means by which options for development may be kept open. In other words, maintenance of the total capital stock equates to maintenance of choice in the evaluation of development capital. Hence, to conserve is to manage wisely, thus allowing the possibility for more deliberate and directed development.

2. *The sustainability of production and growth*: If the coastal zone is to continue to support and enhance human activity, it must remain a viable resource base for production, growth, and development. Hence, agricultural production, resource extraction, industrial processing, and other vital economic endeavours must continue to be performed and, in some cases, increased within the coastal zone. At the same time, these must take place in ways that do not destroy the ecological integrity of the area. This requires a delicate balancing act between promoting growth on the one hand and recognizing the limits to growth on the other, a process that is not only technically complex and difficult, but also sociopolitically demanding and fraught with many dangers. Indeed, the challenge of accomplishing these ends now occupies the attention and effort of a wide variety of specialists committed to the attainment of sustainable development within the coastal zone.
3. *The equitable allocation of resources*: Any management plan for the coastal zone must be based on the principle of equal access for all to its total resource endowment. This certainly does not mean that resources are to be shared up and distributed to everyone for equal consumption (and exhaustion). What it does mean is that everyone's right to the use and enjoyment of all the resources must be recognized and accepted and means should be provided, whether by planning, legislation, or incentives, to ensure this. There are a number of considerations that bear upon this. The first is that the resources of the coastal zone are finite and may become exhausted or be destroyed. Therefore, wise use and restraint are called for. The second is that there are limits to growth based on the finite resources. Even though some resources may be imported into the system to make up for scarcity or lack, there are others that cannot be imported and therefore may always be in short supply. Clean air, for example, or the ability of the environment to receive and deal with waste (that is, its waste assimilative capacity) are critical factors. As a result, other components of the environment may play the somewhat dubious role of being the limiting factors, keeping growth within the limits that the environment can support. A third consideration arising from this is the recognition of carrying capacity as an essential

management concept (Clark, 1977). By carrying capacity we mean the level of population and activity that the environment can support over time, without its systems becoming exhausted and run down. Thus, for example, 2000 tourists using a 50-metre stretch of beach each day is, in all probability, exceeding its carrying capacity, whereas 100 tourists a day may well be within the limit. By applying the principle of carrying capacity, planners are able to determine just how far the resources are able to stretch without becoming consumed and, by this means also, arrive at decisions regarding uses, priorities, protection, and allocation. Furthermore, planners are able to avoid "the tragedy of the commons" which Hardin (1968) has described, based on the scenario of everyone having free access to, but no sense of responsibility for the care and management of, Earth's resources. According to Hardin, this equates to having so many grazing cows on an acre of pasture, the commons, that over time, if there is no restriction or intervention, tragedy will result not only to the commons, but also to all the cows grazing upon it. This striking analogy leads us to consideration of the fourth essential principle for managing the coastal zone.

4. *The proper accounting for resource use and depletion:* If the environment represents the total capital stock on which life depends and on which all development is based, then we should be able to ascribe value to it and, like all other capital, enter it into our accounting systems as capital invested, depreciated and, over time, enlarged. While this has been late in coming, economists are now paying considerable attention to it and are busily trying to set up national accounting systems that include the environment as a part of the quantifiable assets, thereby providing a sound economic basis for planning development, allocating costs, measuring returns, and determining viability (Lutz, 1993). As far as the coastal zone is concerned, this can provide a framework for sorting out some of the seemingly intractable problems that have plagued coastal zone management ever since it became recognized as a discipline; that is, how to choose the best options to pursue when faced with apparent conflicts between desirable outcomes, such as clean environment, public health, cultural satisfaction, agricultural production, industrial growth, and economic development.

> Since it is within the coastal zone that these conflicts are usually most intense, it is within this environment that natural resources accounting may prove to be most beneficial. In practical terms, this would help coastal zone managers to institute such economic instruments of resource management as the user and polluter pays principal (PPP) by which resource utilization and depletion are costed in direct proportion to the benefits derived or the damages inflicted. In this way, some sense of order and predictability can be brought to the process of coastal zone management and development.

All of the four management principles enunciated above have practical problem solving applications when it comes to tackling the issues of the coastal zone. For purposes of this chapter, we shall identify and deal with six of these. These are:

- The problems of population pressure
- Issues of land use allocation and conflict
- The need for sustainable production and growth
- The problem of waste management and pollution control
- The maintenance (and enhancement) of public health
- Issues of disaster preparedness and management

Population Pressures

We have already noted that 75 percent of Caribbean people live in the coastal zone. The reality is that that proportion is growing rapidly as more and more people migrate to the urban centres. For example, the capital cities of the Caribbean have growth rates (3 to 4 percent per annum) that double the national growth rates (1 to 1.5 percent per annum) due to the in-migration of rural people (Latin American and Caribbean Commission on Development and Environment, 1990) while, at the same time, satellite coastal settlements, such as Portmore and Ocho Rios in Jamaica, have experienced annual growth rates above 5 percent per annum at various times since the 1960s. Such data indicate a strong wave of urbanization, with most of the population pressures being exerted in the coastal zone. The results are seen in the following environmental problems:

- Unplanned and haphazard human settlements
- Poor land management
- Inadequate infrastructural services

- Substandard sanitation and public health
- Waste disposal and pollution generation

Arising from the haphazard settlements of the coastal zone is the problem of poor land management. This is seen in the clearing of land for houses and agriculture, the dredging and filling of wetland for infrastructural development, and the mining of beach sand for construction purposes. The results are far reaching as watersheds become damaged, soil is eroded, beaches are lost, and rivers and harbours become silted up. A very good example is to be found in Montego Bay, Jamaica, where flooding of this residential and tourist city is a frequent occurrence due to very poor land management practices caused primarily by unplanned squatter developments in the lower watershed areas.

Another consequence of unplanned development is the inadequacy of basic infrastructure, such as open green spaces, roads, utilities, and municipal services without which the maintenance of productive enterprises is virtually impossible. A problem that greatly impairs the quality of life in such situations is the absence of adequate sanitation and solid waste management systems, resulting in poor public health.

While the problems of urbanization are not unique to the coastal zone, it is within the coastal zone that they are the most pronounced in the Caribbean. The need for urban planning in the region is therefore closely linked with the need for integrated coastal zone management. The challenge for Caribbean planners is how to achieve this in a setting in which jurisdictional responsibility has been traditionally weak. Unfortunately, there are not many success stories in the Caribbean by which to model an approach and planners in the region must still work hard at establishing a truly successful methodology.

Land Use

Closely associated with the problems of population pressure is the use of land, as competing demands frequently result in lands being converted for very inappropriate and conflicting purposes. For example, critical watersheds are denuded for housing, steep lands are farmed for monocultural crops (for example, bananas and coffee), wetlands are drained for agriculture or dredged for ports and marinas, beaches are turned into resorts, and coastal flatlands are used for the dumping of wastes (Caribbean Construction Authority (CCA) and Island Resources Foundation (IRF), 1991). All of these result in the limited land and water resources on the coastal zone being used in ways that are wasteful and damaging. Several examples may be cited. In the Windward Islands, there is extensive banana cultivation on steep slopes resulting in increased erosion and runoff of soil, fertilizers, and pesticides to the sea (CCA and IRF, 1991). Should banana ever fail as an export crop, a future scenario that is not unlikely, these slopes would be left without any vegetation cover, resulting in possibly catastrophic consequences to the coastal and marine ecology.

The Point Lisas industrial complex in Trinidad and Tobago is a case in which huge tracts of mangrove wetlands are being used for industrial purposes (McShine and Siung-Chang, 1984). Another example is that in Jamaica, where the Falmouth freshwater wetlands were drained for agricultural purposes that were never successful. None of these wetlands is recoverable and their present value has been reduced as a result.

In Jamaica, dredge and fill operations to create waterfront real estate at Oracabessa have killed a good portion of a fringing reef, and much of the Portmore Housing Development, which has grown into a 100,000-resident satellite community of Kingston, is built on land "reclaimed" from extensive mangrove wetland. According to many observers, the ecology of Kingston Harbour is permanently altered as a result of this project (Goodbody, 1994). In Belize City, almost the entire population lives on land that was originally covered with mangroves. Today, there are areas where sinking of the land, and the destruction of houses, still occurs.

Failed projects, wasted resources, and chronic ecological problems due to poor land use practices in the coastal zone are to be found throughout the region. Lewsey (1990) is accurate in noting that:

> while the economies of most CARICOM nations are heavily dependent on their coastal environments and rely extensively on this zone to sustain economic growth and development, the national physical development plans of these countries do not reflect this phenomenon. These plans are usually traditional in scope and do not target the coastal area as a specialized sector for alternative development considerations. Furthermore, these plans lack functional elements to deal specifically with the coastal area. (p. 82, quoted in Cox and Embree, 1990)

In the Proceedings of a forum on resources management and sustainable development in the Caribbean, Cox and Embree (1990) report that:

> recommendations with respect to land use planning and zoning in the coastal zone included the need: to revise land use policies; to rationalise and exercise

> more effective control of physical development through the use of environmental impact assessment in the development process; enforce minimum building setback; maintain access to the coastal zone for residents; and assess the value of maintaining some areas/zones in their natural state. (p. 83)

The potential for reinforcing land use controls through such means as the transfer of development right to other zones and the judicious use of incentives and tax measures were also highlighted.

These are only some of the planning measures that may be applied. The important question is whether or not the governments and people of the Caribbean have the will to apply them.

After sugar cane processing, which dominated Caribbean industry for more than two centuries, the next big investment in industrial production in the Caribbean occurred following World War II. At the time, all industrial development was thought to be good because of the foreign currency and employment. Little attention was given to means of resource extraction, materials processing, and waste disposal as far as they impacted upon the environment. Consequently, the coastal zone has been damaged as valuable resources have been depleted (for example, fisheries), prime land has been blighted (for example, at Pointe Pierre in Trinidad), and aquatic and atmospheric environments have been polluted (for example, in Havana Bay and Kingston Harbour) (Phelps, 1995). It is only in recent years and as a result of these impacts that a new approach to industrial development is being fashioned in the region. Yet, many of the earlier impacts still continue and will have an effect for several years to come.

The tourism industry in the Caribbean has been built on the coastal resource base of fine weather, good beaches, and clean waters. The beaches and coastal waters have been exploited with little attention given to their sustainability in the long run (Bloomestein, 1995). Most Caribbean states have failed to develop national policies for the ownership, accessibility, and protection of their beaches and short-sighted and often greedy commercial interests have preyed upon this failure for their own short-term advantage (Nurse, 1990). As a consequence, prime beach lands have been allocated to a few, access by the wider public has been restricted, and no integrated management plan for their protection has been developed. Hence we find that throughout the Caribbean, the issues of responsibility for the management of beaches are of critical concern as beaches have become fouled or eroded and as waterfront structures have been undermined by advancing waves. Truly, the history of beaches in many parts of the Caribbean matches the tragedy of the commons. The same may be said for the coastal waters into which sewage effluents from the resort developments are discharged, as well as for the dumpsites used for the disposal of their solid wastes. In fact, for most components of the environment on which tourism depends, there has been little understanding of the need for their protection and for the kind of management programme that is necessary to achieve it. Furthermore, whose responsibility it should be to develop and implement the appropriate management programmes has been long debated. In the meantime, we have seen tourism assume the image of an extractive industry, depleting and/or fouling its resource base rather than conserving or enhancing it as it should.

Cox and Embree's report of the 1990 conference on sustainable development in the Caribbean referred to the issue of who should pay for environmental and resources management. There is a view that:

> the tourism industry does not contribute to environmental maintenance and waste management costs in proportion to its reliance for income on the natural resources base. As such the industry should be more protective in seeking ways to increase its contribution to effective environmental and resources management, protection and enhancement. (p. 80)

Suggested solutions included, "cost-sharing arrangements with governments for environmental management, charging a consistent and realistic user fee to all cruise ship passengers, soliciting international financial and technical assistance, and seeking ways to increase and retain in the region the net expenditure per tourist (Cox and Embree, 1990, 81).

Ivor Jackson, speaking at the same conference, pointed out that, "By and large tourism development strategies have been rigorously pursued without expending equivalent energy on managing the natural resources upon which tourism depends" (Jackson, 1990, 133). He concluded that:

> Environmental problems related to tourism may be quite alarming but sustainable tourism development does not imply the automatic curtailment of growth . . . This requires the integration of conservation and development policies, and a willingness to invest in the human and institutional capacity in order to improve management of the coastal and marine environments of the Caribbean. (p. 138)

Waste Management and Pollution Control

The air, the sea, the rivers, soils, and all living organisms have an inherent capacity to deal with waste. This ability is referred to as their waste assimilative capacity, an actual measure of the amount of waste they can absorb without destroying their ecological integrity. When waste assimilative capacities are exceeded, rivers become septic, the atmosphere becomes toxic, soils become poisonous, and coral reefs deteriorate and die. This is happening in the coastal zones of many countries. Examples are to be seen in Kingston Harbour in Jamaica, the Caroni River in Trinidad, and the north coast reefs of Jamaica (Wade, 1976; Bacon, 1978; Goreau, 1995). Other examples include oxygen depletion in many rivers and streams, nutrient enrichment in coastal waters, lead contamination in soils, sulphur dioxide and acid rain in the atmosphere, and pesticide build up in foods.

Consequently, waste management must be seen as a critical component of any coastal zone management plan, and there are several approaches to this. Since waste production is a function of inefficiency, it follows that any increase in efficiency should result in a reduction of waste. Therefore, any attempt at process improvement, such as total quality management (TQM), should contribute positively to a waste management programme (Wade and Forrest, 1993). Such a programme may be expressed in the "3Rs" of waste management – waste reduction, waste reuse, and waste recycling.

Once a particular waste has been reduced in volume and strength, it must still be disposed of. The higher the waste load, the greater the disposal problem, particularly in the coastal zone, where space is limited and waste assimilative capacities tend to be low. Therefore, the best conditions for waste disposal must be found to reduce the likelihood of pollution. In the case of liquid wastes, this almost invariably includes eventual disposal in the sea where, it is hoped, oceanographic conditions will favour maximum dilution of the effluent and its dispersion by water currents further out to sea.

By applying appropriate waste management and pollution control measures in the Caribbean, we can solve most if not all of the pollution problems that now plague our coastal zones. Hence, for example, the contamination of our beaches by sewage, a widespread and chronic problem, can be stopped. The deterioration of our ground- and surface waters, which impairs our use of them as domestic water supplies, can be reversed. Nutrient enrichment of the coastal waters leading to the proliferation of algae and nuisance species (eutrophication) with consequent damage to our coral reefs need not be tolerated. Smoke, foul air, and acid rain in our cities and industrial areas are uncalled for. Why then should these problems persist? For that answer, we must question our planning and management systems, systems that seem to be failing us.

Sanitation and Public Health

Sanitation and public health are important considerations in the coastal zone, particularly in situations of rapid population growth and unplanned development. In a study in Port Antonio, Jamaica, where tourism and agriculture have much potential for development but have been constrained by lack of infrastructure, the close interrelatedness of water supply, sewerage, drainage, solid waste management, and public health has been highlighted (Environmental Solutions Ltd., 1996). The reliability of the water supply (both quantity and quality) is inadequate and only about half of the population is served by a piped supply. There is no central sewerage system and disposal is made into the ground by various types of soakaways. The drainage system is undersized and is blocked by sediment, vegetation, and solid waste, leading to frequent flooding, with significant damage to structures and major inconveniences to the public. Solid waste management, too, is inadequate and only about 58 percent of the garbage generated is collected and disposed of in a legal manner. Consequently, there is much litter, scavenging, and proliferation of pests, notably rats. As a result of all these conditions, public health is substandard and is further threatened by potentially devastating diseases and epidemics.

Current and future health problems in Port Antonio and their associated causes include:

- Gastroenteritis (water supply, sewage, and solid waste disposal)
- Typhoid (water supply and sewage disposal)
- Leptospirosis (solid waste and rats)
- Dengue (flooding and mosquitoes)
- Ear aches, skin rashes, etc. (sewage-contaminated bathing waters)
- Threat of cholera (water supply and sewage)

In order to deal with these problems, an integrated sanitation waste plan has been proposed since it has been determined that none of the sanitation systems can function effectively without the others. Hence, an improved water supply without a proper sewage disposal system would lead to more widespread contamination and therefore be counterproductive, while an improved drainage system without better solid waste management would most likely result in further drainage blockages and impairment by illicitly disposed of garbage. However, while these synergies are recognized, problems arise in financing truly integrated and comprehensive sanitation systems and in maintaining them in good condition. Due to the scale of such needs, international agencies like the World Bank, the World Health Organization, and the Inter American Development Bank have become closely involved in funding sanitation infrastructural development throughout the Caribbean. In Jamaica alone, in 1995, there were four such projects in Negril, Montego Bay, Ocho Rios, and Port Antonio. All of these included substantial sewerage improvements, one of the two sectors that lag furthest behind. The other is solid waste management, for which a comprehensive study for the entire island was begun in 1995.

While the technical and environmental aspects of these improvements are relatively easy to deal with, the financial and socio-economic aspects are much more difficult. In the first place, international funding sources are now requiring that financial feasibility be clearly demonstrated for all investments in the sanitation sectors. This means that a reasonable rate of return has to be shown after all costs and benefits have been taken into account (Serageldin, 1994). This includes such hard-to-value benefits as better sanitary conditions, reduced risk of diseases and epidemics, more amenable aesthetics, and overall improved public health and quality of life. In the case of the Port Antonio project (population 30,000), the proposed improvements were costed at more than U.S.$ 20 million with an internal rate of return (IRR) over 25 years of 12 percent. In actual fact, several improvements had to be eliminated from the project because they could not generate the required IRR.

Other questions, such as who should pay in the long run for these investments, and how, remain. Should it be the entire country or just the direct beneficiaries and users of the services? In a willingness-to-pay survey among potential users of the improved garbage collection system in Port Antonio, very few residents were willing to pay anything at all, much less the economic cost of providing the service. In such a case, should the project be abandoned because only few are willing to pay or should the government pick up the costs? And should payment be by means of a direct cess on households according to the volume of garbage collected or by a flat tax on all the community?

These are very difficult questions indeed which poorer countries are grappling with. Meanwhile, the funding bodies are laying down their own conditions for pay back, which are often contrary to the economic and social norms of recipient countries. This means that significant shifts have to be made in how people appreciate and value good sanitation and public health. This, in turn, requires effective public education and participation programmes and this is where the whole web of interactions frequently and finally breaks down.

Within the coastal zone, the problems are more pronounced than in most other environments and many solutions need to be provided. Throughout the Caribbean, the problems are the same. It is surprising therefore, that problems posed, for example, by the inadequate sewerage collection and disposal systems that plague all our coastal areas have not been more comprehensively and successfully tackled.

Disaster Management

Caribbean states are vulnerable to a large number of natural hazards, including hurricanes, earthquakes, volcanic eruptions, floods, and landslides. These have frequently led to wide-scale disaster resulting in loss of life, personal injury, damage to structures, and damage to or loss of crops. In addition, there has been considerable disruption to daily living and, in extreme cases, severe dislocation of people, businesses, and the entire economy (Collymore, 1992; Brown, 1994). Ahmad has argued that the distribution, frequency, and severity of disasters in the Caribbean is a result of the characteristic physical features (geographic–tectonic–geophysical) which are common to many of the island nations and, by extension, their coastal zones. However, even more important, as Ahmad points out, "are the decisions made, activities undertaken and technologies utilized during the process of development" (Ahmad, 1992).

Flooding is the most common natural hazard affecting Caribbean states. It may be riverine, coastal (due to storm surge), or flash floods induced by intense rains in the watersheds. In most cases, the flood-prone areas are well known due to past events and an understanding of the physical elements in the area. However, this has not prevented people from establishing settlements and carrying out their daily lives in some of the most hazardous areas. In Belize, for example, the entire Belize City is built up in an extremely high flood-prone area and it was not until about 30 years ago that the government decided to relocate the capital inland because of the high risk to the entire country of running the government from such a vulnerable area. Nevertheless, Belize's largest population remains in Belize City and the new capital, Belmopan, has failed to attract the population as intended.

In simple terms, Caribbean people have learned to live with flooding but this has been at a great cost and carries with it chronic risks. In a sense, a decision seems to have been made to take the chance and pay the price. This might be far too simplistic an explanation though. What about the government whose responsibility it is to establish a framework for safe and secure living and what about poor people who really do not have much of a choice about where they live? Can Caribbean people really be satisfied with the continued acceptance of flooding as a "normal" life experience? After all, technology exists to counter most flooding events, appropriate planning can reduce exposure to risk, and learned behaviour (for example, early warning and evacuation) can be used to mitigate impacts. While it is true that all of these strategies have been employed in one place or another throughout the Caribbean, it is equally true to say that they have not been widely and comprehensively applied, either in our already built-up areas or in new developments. Thus, in Greater Portmore, Jamaica, for example, a major satellite town that has been developing next to Kingston for the past 30 years (population more than 100,000), early warning and evacuation is the only strategy that operates. Even today, as new settlements are created within this complex, common strategies to prevent flooding are being ignored and the same is true for many other new developments in the region. For lack of adequate planning and management, therefore, Caribbean people continue to be exposed to the risks of flooding in the coastal zone.

Hurricanes, volcanic eruptions, and earthquakes have been described as three of the worst kinds of natural disaster, and the Caribbean is prone to all three (Tomblin, 1981). The evidence indicates that almost every city in the region has been devastated in the last 300 years (Collymore, 1992).

The costs in direct damages of recent hurricanes in the eastern Caribbean have been considerable. In Montserrat, for example, with a population of only 12,000, damages from Hurricane Hugo in 1989 amounted to approximately U.S.$ 100 million, that is U.S.$ 8300 per person. In Dominica, following Hurricane David in 1979, the gross domestic product (GDP) per capita fell approximately 20 percent below the 1978 level in that year. By any standards, these economic effects were devastating.

Collymore (1992) stressed that if Caribbean islands in general, and coastal zones in particular, are to be spared the ravages of nature, a brand new approach to disaster management must be developed.

DEVELOPING A COASTAL ZONE MANAGEMENT PROGRAMME

Methodologies

Ali and Armstrong (1976) have described coastal zone management as a process involving the setting forth of objectives, policies, and standards to guide and regulate private and public uses of the lands and waters of the coastal zone. This, they regard as a complex problem requiring that a nation view its coastal zone as a complete system of interconnected natural, social, and economic elements.

In developing coastal resource management programmes countries need to carry out a number of tasks:

- Develop basic goals and objectives for use of the coastal resources
- Develop and utilize procedures and plans for evaluating the coastal resources
- Formulate basic policies by which various proposed uses of coastal resources can be assessed
- Adopt necessary rules, regulations, and organizational arrangements to implement policy

The framework for establishing the basic goals and objectives of coastal zone management has been discussed in detail above. This section examines the means of developing appropriate procedures, plans, and policies necessary for achieving these goals and objectives and ends with a discussion of the institutional arrangements required for implementing truly effective programmes. Three sets of activities embrace the necessary methodologies. These are resources evaluation, impact assessment, and natural resources accounting.

Resources Evaluation

If the resources of the coastal zone are to be managed, they must first be defined, described, quantified, and mapped. It may be surprising, therefore, to learn that many coastal states have no such inventory of resources on which to base even the rudiments of a management programme. For example, only a few Caribbean countries have sought to carry out comprehensive coastal zone survey programmes, including their watersheds, wetlands, beaches, reefs, and fisheries, while others have only initiated such surveys within the last decade. As a result, the Caribbean data base is still quite meagre and is one of the limitations coastal zone managers have to face in the region.

To be fair, though, these survey programmes can be quite complex and costly, requiring several specialist skills and input. It should be noted, however, that both the technologies and our access to them have improved by leaps and bounds. For example, it was not too long ago that aerial photography was the only means available for obtaining an overview picture of what resources existed and where. Today, satellite photography and other remote imaging devices are common place and easily accessible from international networks. Furthermore, they allow quite accurate inventories down to minute detail (habitat types, soils, water availability, species lists, etc.), and may even show up patterns and degrees of interaction, exploitation, and depletion. By these means, information can be made available to anyone wishing to evaluate coastal resources, even if they do not hold jurisdictional responsibilities for them. Of course, distance imaging can and should be supported by other available on-the-ground techniques and any serious coastal zone management programme should include the necessary traditional methodologies, such as surface and subsurface surveys, testing, and analysis.

The results of all these surveys usually generate huge data bases that can only be managed effectively by computer programmes specifically designed for the purpose. However, several such programmes now exist that can facilitate attempts at resource evaluation. Some of the most popular are those that convert data sets into absolute and relational maps, thus allowing for visual outputs that significantly aid the evaluation process. At its most developed level, this is represented by geographic information systems (GISs), which facilitate complex manipulation and map overlays, thus allowing for significant interrelationships to be readily identified and assessed. These include all the natural, social, and economic elements that comprise the coastal zone. Because of their power and versatility, GIS systems are being used in a wide range of management situations that find ready application within the coastal zone. For example, watershed management, highway planning, and tourism development, all of which depend on multisectoral inputs, are greatly assisted by GIS systems that enable planners and managers to effectively compile and analyse complex data sets as a prelude to decision making. Of particular value too is the facility which GIS affords to apply "what if" scenario planning to the decision making process.

Resource evaluation is most useful when the environment is treated as a composite of dynamic systems whose components, interactions, and outputs are constantly changing. However, this is a difficult end to achieve when the essential processes are not fully understood and inventories capture only instant snapshots. For this reason, on-going research on how the coastal environment is comprised and what processes make it function the way it does is absolutely critical to an accurate evaluation of its resources.

Impact Assessment

Coastal zone management requires making choices between different actions, the outcomes of which may be neither likely nor apparent. Furthermore, the choices may not be between right and wrong or even between good and better. Frequently, the choices are between equally attractive options or options in which conservation values have to be weighed against social and/or economic values. In order to facilitate such choices, the coastal zone manager has a number of techniques available to the process that may make it a great deal more scientific, logical, and accurate. These all fall within the category of impact assessment and include such proven methodologies as environmental audits, risk analyses, environmental impact assessments, and cost/benefit analyses. A discussion of each follows.

An environmental audit is a systematic and thorough review of the processes and practices of an on-going operation to identify current or potential environmental problems and to recommend solutions. It covers a wide range of analyses:

- It reviews performance against regulations
- It evaluates environmental management systems
- It assesses environmental impacts
- It assesses environmental risk and liability

Environmental audits are most useful when they are conducted for the purpose of determining the effectiveness of operations already in place and for identifying where improvements can be made. Frequently too, environmental audits will help to reveal what opportunities exist for more environmentally beneficial practices and products as, for example, how to treat, dispose of, and/or reuse waste.

The greatest benefits of environmental audits result when individuals learn that processes can be operated more efficiently, raw materials can be utilized more effectively, and waste generation can be reduced significantly. In other words, when persons accept that waste and pollution need not be inevitable consequences of their operations. Of course, this has very significant implications for the profit line, which makes the environmental audit a powerful management tool for businesses.

One specific objective of an environmental audit is to assess the level of risk that an operation or set of operations may be exposed to as a result of environmental factors. These may be natural factors such as hurricanes, earthquakes, or floods, or human-induced factors such as the handling of hazardous materials, changes in zoning laws, or new environmental requirements for international trading. These, in one way or another, may threaten the stability and continuance of any operation or business. As a result, assessment of the level of environmental risk is of critical importance to businesses as they reveal vulnerability to new or unusual circumstances and the liabilities contingent on their occurrence.

There are many ways in which levels of risk may be assessed and the methodologies connected with environmental risk assessment are not fundamentally different from any other. What is new, however, is the identification of the nature of the risks and the conditions that may generate them. For example, liabilities that now result as a consequence of the polluter pays principle have caught many industries by surprise and have placed some in dire financial circumstances since, traditionally, they have always enjoyed the "privilege" of polluting the environment without bearing any of the costs. Similarly, vendors of real estate in certain parts of the world have been discovering, to their dismay, that they are being held liable for land remediation costs in cases where wastes have been improperly disposed of in the ground, over decades, sometimes hundreds of years, even when they were not the culprits.

Some of the "hidden" environmental risks to businesses may come from location, zoning laws, site condition, land transfer regulations, the source and nature of raw materials, management of hazardous materials, disposal of wastes, product life cycle impacts, and so on. Furthermore, a new and added risk is the exposure to prosecution that individual managers may face as a result of the environmental violations of their businesses. In the U.S., for example, company directors are now being imprisoned for violations and, in most parts of the world, insurance costs have soared as a result of these new kinds of exposure. For all these reasons, environmental risk analysis has become a critical component of business and resources management, so much so that it is employed in both environmental audits and environmental impact assessments (EIAs).

Whereas environmental audits are concerned with assessing ongoing operations, EIAs deal with proposed developments and attempt to predict their impacts on the environment. They include an evaluation of the environmental resources base and an identification of the opportunities and threats that the environment provides and is exposed to as a result of the proposed development. They assess potential impacts and recommend how they may be mitigated or eliminated altogether. They also examine alternative development strategies, including cost benefit analyses, and should always present guidelines along which development should proceed. Finally, a monitoring programme for determining the real versus the predicted impacts should also be a feature of an EIA.

EIAs are now mandatory in a number of Caribbean countries and are meant to protect the environment from inappropriate development. At the same time, if properly conducted, they should not only enhance the development, but also make them more cost effective (Smith, 1993). In fact, according to Smith, "a good EIA can indicate to the developer many positive ways in which the environment can benefit the development." For these reasons, an EIA, like an environmental audit, should be viewed as an effective management tool and should therefore be conducted with sensitivity and with the fullest cooperation between the EIA practitioners, the developers, and the regulatory agencies. An excellent example of this occurred recently in Jamaica where a hotel developer wanted to develop a new resort in a greenfield area where there had been no previous tourism activity. As an essential component of the development concept, the developer wished to build the resort along architectural and operational lines that had proven extremely successful in other locations. Furthermore, in order to seed tourism development in the area, he had sought for and received certain concessions and other encouragement from the government. As part of his early planning, the developer contracted an environmental consultancy firm to conduct an EIA of the proposed development with a view to proceeding as quickly as possible to receive all the necessary permits and to complete construction within 2 years. However, he had no idea what the EIA would reveal. Briefly, it was that the site was completely unsuitable for the kind of development proposed, for several reasons:

- The site was heavily flood prone
- Wetlands on the site were critical to its hydrological and ecological balance and needed to be preserved
- The beach was prone to erosion and instability
- Wildlife, including protected species, had their major habitats on the site
- Water supply and other infrastructure could not be supplied as expected

Faced with this evidence, the developer quickly recognized that he had been going down an unsustainable path with his desire to import an otherwise successful concept into an environment that could not support this type of development. Consequently, and wisely, he decided to have the resort redesigned according to the environmental imperatives and thereby to come up with a new resort concept in harmony with the features of the site. In this case, not only did the environment benefit but also the developer and other tourism interests who would otherwise have been faced with a major development failure in an enterprise meant to promote the industry in a new area. Furthermore, this was achieved at minimum cost because the EIA process had been employed at an early stage in the development.

In many cases, the decision such as that taken above to amend or abort a project is not as easily taken because data on the relative costs and benefits are neither readily available nor understood. In particular, the valuation of costs and benefits associated with environmental damage and enhancement are most often lacking. Fortunately, that is now being overcome as economists learn to place dollar values on environmental variables.

In the long run, sustainable development can only be achieved if development decisions are based on really effective cost/benefit analyses. The way we have looked at development in the past has been to value our goods and services (for example gross domestic product, GDP) without taking into account the costs of natural resources depletion and environmental degradation. The clear lesson is that we can no longer do this, as the World Bank and other funding bodies are now emphasizing in their projects criteria.

Natural Resources Accounting

What is the value of a tree, a beach, a river, or a reef and can we account for these in any financial evaluation the way we do a building, a road, or a bridge? These are questions that have gone unanswered for many years, with the result that national accounts in general and project feasibility studies in particular have not factored in their value into any determination of economic success and growth. Unfortunately too, underlying this lack has been an assumption that natural resources are so abundant that they have only marginal value and, further, that these are "free gifts of nature" which, as investment costs, can be written off (Repetto, 1989). Hence, in managing national economies, the costs of depleting natural resources or of polluting the environment have not been accounted for.

In a well-documented case study of the Indonesian economy, it was discovered that when environmental costs were actually factored in, the GDP was reduced by more than 3 percent per annum over a period of 12 years (World Resources Institute, 1991). This figure has been found to be a fairly conservative estimate for economies in other developing countries. Hence, in countries such as those in the Caribbean that report GDPs anywhere from 0 to 3 percent per annum, real growth could in fact be zero or even a minus quantity when environmental decline is taken into account. As the World Resources Institute report has concluded, "In resource-dependent countries, failure to extend the concept of depreciation to the capital stock embodied in natural resources, which are such a significant source of income and consumption, overstates the level and growth of income."

As far as the economies of the coastal zone, which are heavily resource-dependent, are concerned, the same can be said. Indeed, much of what has been hailed as development in the coastal zone has been at such expense to the environment that a case may be argued for having left certain of these developments undone. For example, the draining of certain wetlands for agriculture is a good case in point.

As a result of the new awareness, the United Nations has endorsed and promoted the accounting for natural resources in what they have termed the United Nations System of National Accounts (SNA). With improved measurement of economic performance resulting from adequately capturing the value of natural resources, better economic decision making should occur. Indeed, this has been accepted by several nations as well as by multilateral institutions such as the World Bank and the International Monetary Fund (Munasinghe, 1993). The practical outcome of this may be seen in the fact that for most new development projects being funded by these institutions, potential environmental costs and their impacts on the economic indicators must be demonstrated before approval is given. This in turn has forced many countries to begin to seriously evaluate their resources and to determine the costs of poor environmental management to their economies. This has had a profound effect in the Caribbean where, for the first time, the "free gifts" of sun, sand, and sea, for example, to name just a few of our resources, are being regarded the way they should. It is also reflected in the Port of Spain Accord on the Management and Conservation of the Caribbean Environment (1989) issued by the First CARICOM Ministerial Conference on the Environment:

> In conclusion, we reiterate our firm and unswerving commitment to the rational use and conservation of our environmental resources. We call upon all Caribbean peoples to exercise the respect and reverence for the environment which will ensure its protection for the benefit of future generations.

As a postscript, it should be noted that the methodologies used by economists to value natural resources have not been described in this account. For literature on that, the reader is referred to several World Bank publications on the subject which have emerged in recent years. One of the most recent and comprehensive of these is *Valuing the Environment*, edited by Serageldin and Steer (1994).

The Institutional Framework

The techniques of coastal zone management that we have outlined above can only be fully utilized when they are employed in the context of a well thought out and ordered policy administered by competent and responsible organizations. This, in turn, requires that there be a suitable legal and institutional framework in place that is known and accepted by the public at large.

Within the last decade we have seen attempts in the Caribbean to establish a modern legal framework for environmental management which embodies former legislation but which also brings a fresh approach to the matter of compliance, not merely through command and control measures but also through incentives and rewards schemes (Carnegie, 1995; McCalla, 1995). Such legislation includes the National Conservation and Environmental Protection Act, 1987 (St Kitts and Nevis); the Natural Resources Conservation Authority Act, 1991 (Jamaica); the Environmental Protection Act, 1992 (Belize); and the Environmental Management Authority Act, 1994 (Trinidad and Tobago). The basic tenet of these Acts is the achievement of sustainable development through the active participation of the entire community, and the common vehicle is through jurisdiction by a central overriding regulatory authority, such as the Natural Resources Conservation Authority in Jamaica or the Environmental Management Authority in Trinidad and Tobago. Of critical importance to these bodies is the power given to them to bind the government to any and all regulations established by them for proper management of the environment.

In all the modern legislation, the coastal zone is given special consideration, not only because its resources are recognized as important to Caribbean development but also because its management difficulties are clearly understood. Indeed, in a number of these countries, there is a special unit established within the government structure to develop and oversee management programmes for the coastal zone. Thus, Barbados has its Coastal Conservation Unit and Belize its Coastal Zone Management Programme. There is also a Coastal Zone Division within Trinidad and Tobago's Institute of Marine Affairs and a Coastal Zone Project within Jamaica's Natural Resources Conservation Authority. These all testify to the prominence of the coastal zone as a very special component of the Caribbean environment.

Ali and Armstrong (1976) have outlined the purposes that coastal zone policies administered by a coastal zone unit should serve, as follows:

1. They may help guide the selection of coastal uses that a nation wishes to pursue.
2. They may assist the nation in establishing priority of potential uses by clarifying the preference ranking of the various uses.
3. They can determine the degree to which the adopted coastal objectives can be met.
4. They can help in the design of the organizational structure necessary to implement the policies by determining the types of manpower and resources required.
5. They can help identify those coastal areas requiring special attention by determining impacts or resource protection issues in specific geographical areas.

An outline of the programme by which these purposes may be fulfilled has been provided by Goodman (1976) and is presented in Figure 8.2. From this, a number of points emerge:

- The development of a coastal zone management programme is a multistep process that is strongly dependent upon human relations as well as technical information.
- The techniques available for handling the programme development process are varied and range over several disciplines.
- There are a series of actions and decision points that require multisectoral cooperation and agreement.
- Policies and procedures are closely integrated at all stages.

These highlight the fact that the development of a coastal zone management programme is a complex, demanding, and integrating exercise which can only be achieved through national policy and commitment. However, Caribbean countries that have embarked on such programmes have discovered that, despite the difficulties, these are far outweighed by the benefits. In small island systems, there appears to be no real choice but to approach development in this way.

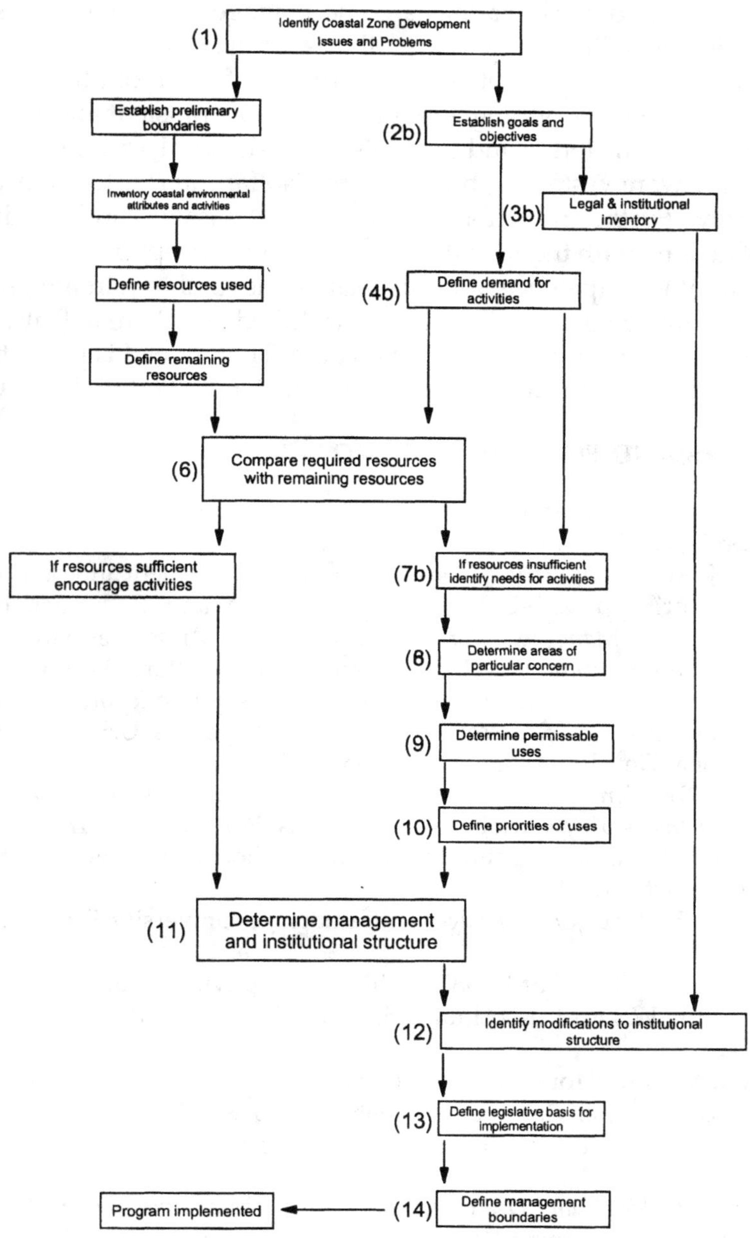

FIGURE 8.2 Outline of a coastal zone management programme development process. (From Goodman, 1976.)

CONCLUSION

In closing, we return to an earlier quote from Ali and Armstrong (1976): "It is instructive to consider coastal zone management as a process." Indeed it is and will always be just that – a never ending process, a journey without end, yet not without purpose; for although the purpose may be fixed, everything about the means is transient and imperfect. What we know today and the tools at our disposal are far superior to what they were yesterday, but they are also far inferior to what will be tomorrow. Furthermore, the complexity of the issues, and the difficulties of dealing with them, will never completely disappear, no matter the level of our competence. For this reason, the total requirements for coastal zone management will remain unfulfilled and there will always be a wide range of problems to be overcome. That indeed is the nature of the discipline and the lot of all who pursue it, now and in the future.

REFERENCES AND FURTHER READING

Ahmad, R. (ed.). 1992. Natural Hazards in the Environment – Preface. *Journal of the Geological Society of Jamaica* Special issue, no. 12.

Ali, R., and J. Armstrong. 1976. "Coastal resource management and economic development". pp. 257–289, in K.-H. Szekielda and B. Breuer, eds., *Development and Management of Resources of Coastal Areas*. German Foundation for International Development and United Nations, Berlin.

Auer, M. R. 1991. *Urban Impacts of the Coastal Zones of Developing Countries: Problem Identifications and Recommendations for Mitigations*. U.S. Agency for International Development, Washington, D.C.

Bacon, P. R. 1978. *Flora and Fauna of the Caribbean. An Introduction to the Ecology of the West Indies*. Key Caribbean Publications, Port of Spain, Trinidad.

Barnes, E. S. 1973. "Sewage pollution from tourist hotels in Jamaica". *Marine Pollution Bulletin* 4: 102–105.

Barnes, R. S. K. 1980. *Coastal Lagoons*. Cambridge University Press, Cambridge.

Bate, G. C., and S. D Crafford. 1985. "Inhibition of phytoplankton photosynthesis by the W.S.F. of used lubricating oil". *Marine Pollution Bulletin* 16: 401–404.

Beekhuis, J. V. 1981. "Tourism in the Caribbean: Impacts on the economic, social and natural environments". *Ambio* 10, no. 6: 325–331.

Benson, N. G. 1981. "The fresh water-inflow-to-estuaries issue". *Fisheries* 6, no. 5: 8–10.

Bernstein, J. D. 1994. *Land Use Consideration in Urban Environment Management*. Urban Management Program. World Bank, Washington, D.C.

Bigg, G., and D. Webber. 2001. "The impact of development and coastline changes on the flushing time of Kingston Harbour Jamaica". *Jamaica Journal of Science and Technology* 11: 1–21.

Blommestein, E. 1995. "Sustainable tourism in the Caribbean: An enigma". pp. 191–220, in M. D. Griffith and B. Persaud, eds., *Economic Policy and the Environment*. University of the West Indies Centre for Environment and Development, Mona, Jamaica.

Boaden, P., and R. Seed. 1993. *An Introduction to Coastal Ecology.* Blackie Academic, Glasgow.

Boulding, K. 1966. "The economics of the coming Spaceship Earth". pp. 307–319, in H. Jarrett, ed., *Environmental Quality in a Growing Economy.* Johns Hopkins University Press, Baltimore, Maryland.

Brahtz, J. F. (ed.). 1972. *Coastal Zone Management: Multiple Use with Conservation.* John Wiley & Sons, New York.

Brown, A. C., and A. McLachlan. 1990. *Ecology of Sandy Shores*. Elsevier, New York.

Brown, H. A. 1994. *Economics of Disasters with Special Reference to the Jamaican Experience*. Working Paper no. 2. University of the West Indies Centre for Environment and Development, Mona, Jamaica.

Caribbean Conservation Association (CCA) and Island Resources Foundation (IRF). 1991. *Environmental Agenda for the 1990's: A Synthesis of the Eastern Caribbean Country Environment Profile Series*. CCA, St Michael, Barbados and IRF, St Thomas, U.S. Virgin Islands.

CARICOM. 1989. The Port of Spain Accord on the Management and Preservation of the Caribbean Environment. Issued by the First CARICOM Ministerial Conference on the Environment, June.

Carnegie, A. R. 1995. "Governmental institutional organization and legislature requirements for sustainable development policies". pp. 105–119, in M. D. Griffith and B. Persaud, eds., *Economic Policy and the Environment.* University of the West Indies Centre for Environment and Development, Mona, Jamaica.

Clarke, J. R. 1977. *Coastal Ecosystem Management*. John Wiley & Sons, New York.

Collymore, J. McA. 1992. "Planning to reduce the socio-economic impacts of natural hazards on Caribbean society". *Journal of the Geological Society of Jamaica* Special Issue 12: 88–96.

Country Environmental Profile of Jamaica. 1987. Environmental Hazards. International Institute for Environment and Development and Government of Jamaica, Kingston, Jamaica. pp. 329–347.

Cox, J., and C. Embree, 1990. *Sustainable Development in the Caribbean: A Report on the Public Policy Implications of Sustainable Development in the Caribbean Region Conference, May 28–30, 1990*. Institute for Research on Public Policy, Halifax, Nova Scotia.

Cronan, D. S. 1980. *Underwater Minerals*. Academic Press, London.

Davis, C., and Balleyram. 1995. "Challenges to integrating economic and environmental policies into the Anglo-Caribbean sustainable development agenda: The case of agriculture". pp. 167–189, in M. D. Griffith and B. Persaud, eds., *Economic Policy and the Environment*. University of the West Indies Centre for Environment and Development, Mona, Jamaica.

Environmental Solutions Limited. 1996. "Environmental assessment, Port Antonio sanitation project". Report submitted to the Urban Development Corporation, Kingston, Jamaica.

Everitt, R. E., B. von Rabenau, C. Walters, and J. J. Zimmermann. 1991. "A sustainable ecological economic development model". In N. P. Girvan and D. A. Simmons, eds., *Caribbean Ecology and Economics*. Caribbean Conservation Association, St Michael, Barbados.

Eyre, A. L. 1991. "Jamaica's crisis in forestry and watershed management". *Jamaica Journal* 21, no. 1: 27–35.

Eyre, A. L. 1996. "The tropical rainforests of Jamaica". *Jamaica Journal* 26, no. 1: 26–37.

Goodbody, I. 1994. "Issues in the conservation of the marine environment". *Jamaica Naturalist* 4: 21–26.

Goodman, J. M. 1976. "Management techniques". pp. 317–338, in K.-H. Szekielda and B. Breuer, eds., *Development and Management of Resources of Coastal Areas*. German Foundation for International Development and United Nations, Berlin.

Goreau, T. J. 1995. "Coral reefs, sewage, and quality standards". pp. 98–116, in *Proceedings of the Caribbean Water and Wastewater Association 3rd Annual Conference*, Kingston, Jamaica.

Grahame, S. E. 1977. "The ecology of plankton in Kingston Harbour, Jamaica. II. The phytoplankton". *Research Report from the Zoology Department*, no. 4. University of the West Indies, Mona, Jamaica.

Gross, M. G. 1990. *Oceanography*. Merril Publishing, Columbus, Ohio.

Gumbs, F. 1981. "Agriculture in the wider Caribbean". *Ambio* 10, no. 6: 335–339.

Guppy, N. 1984. "Tropical deforestation: A global view". *Foreign Affairs* 62, no. 4: 928–965.

Hardin, G. 1968. "The tragedy of the commons". *Science* 162: 1243–1248.

Hayward, S. J., V. H. Gomez, and W. Sterrer (eds.). 1981. *Bermuda's Delicate Balance. People and Environment*. Bermuda National Trust, Hamilton.

Hendry, M. 1979. "A study of coastline evolution and sedimentology: The Palisadoes, Jamaica". PhD thesis. Geology Department, University of the West Indies, Mona, Jamaica.

Hershman, M., R. Goodwin, A. Ruotsala, M. McCrea, and Y. Hayuth. 1978. *Under New Management: Port Growth and Emerging Coastal Management Problems*. University of Washington Press, Seattle.

Hughes, T. B. 1994. "Catastrophes, phase shifts, and large-scale degradation of a Caribbean coral reef". *Science* 265: 1547–1551.

Jackson, I. 1990. "Tourism and sustainable development in the Caribbean". pp. 127–138, in J. Cox and C. Embree, eds., *Sustainable Development in the Caribbean*. Institute for Research on Public Policy, Halifax, Nova Scotia.

Jones, A., and N. Sefton. 1991. *Marine Life of the Caribbean*. Macmillan Caribbean, London.

Kinne, O., and H. P. Bulnheim (eds.). 1980. "Protection of life in the sea. 14th European Marine Biology Symposium. Helgol". *Wissenschaftliche Meeresunters* 33: 1–72.

Latin American and Caribbean Commission on Development and Environment. 1990. *Our Own Agenda.* Inter American Development Bank, Washington, D.C. and United Nations Development Programme, New York.

Levy, R., and M. Jones. 1993. "The Jamaica Broilers experience". pp. 35–38, in *The Environment as Good Business: Managing Waste for Profit.* Workshop Proceedings, Earth Day, 1993. Environmental Solutions Ltd., Kingston, Jamaica.

Lutz, E. (ed.). 1993. *Toward Improved Accounting for the Environment.* World Bank, Washington, D.C.

McCalla, W. 1995. *Compendium on Environmental Protection and Natural Resource Management in Belize.* Government of Belize, Belmopan.

McEachern, J., and E. Towle. 1974. "Resource management programs for oceanic islands". pp. 31-56, in C. Frankenhoff, ed., *Environmental Planning and Development in the Caribbean.* University of Puerto Rico, San Pedro, Puerto Rico.

McElroy, J., B. Potter, and E. Towle. 1990. " Challenges for sustainable development in small Caribbean islands". pp. 43–55, in W. Beller et al., eds., *Sustainable Development and Environmental Management of Small Islands.* Paris: UNESCO.

McShine, H., and A. Siung-Chang. 1984. "Point Lisas Environmental Protection Project". *Naturalist* 5, no. 3: 13–26.

Munasinghe, M. (ed.). 1993. *Environmental Economics and Natural Resource Management in Developing Countries.* World Bank, Washington, D.C.

Munro, J. L., and D. M. Williams. 1985. "Assessment and management of coral reef fisheries: Biological, environmental and socio-economic aspects". pp. 545–581, in *Proceedings of the 5th International Coral Reef Congress,* volume 4.

Nurse, L. 1990. "The deterioration of Caribbean coastal zones: A recurring issue in regional development". pp. 117–125, in J. Cox and C. Embree, eds., *Sustainable Development in the Caribbean.* Institute for Research on Public Policy, Halifax, Nova Scotia.

Onuf, C. P., and J. Teal. 1977. "Interaction of nutrients, plant growth and herbivory in a mangrove ecosystem". *Ecology* 58: 514–526.

Paerl, H. W. 1988. "Nuisance phytoplankton blooms in coastal, estuarine and inland waters". *Limnology and Oceanography* 33: 823–847.

Phelps, H. O. 1995. "Manufacturing and urban waste management". pp. 221–242, in M. D. Griffith and B. Persaud, eds., *Economic Policy and the Environment.* University of the West Indies Centre for Environment and Development, Mona, Jamaica.

Pollnac, R. B., and P. Weeks (eds.). 1992. *Coastal Aquaculture in Developing Countries: Problems and Perspectives.* International Centre for Marine Resources Development Publications (ICMRD). University of Rhode Island, Providence, Rhode Island.

Pullin, R. S. V. 1993. "An overview of environmental issues in developing country aquaculture". pp. 1–19, in R. S. V. Pullin, H. Rosenthal, and J. C. Maclean, eds., *Environment and Aquaculture in Developing Countries.* ICLARM Conference Proceedings 31.

Pullin, R. S. V., and R. A. Neal. 1984. "Tropical aquaculture. Need for a strong research base". *Marine Policy* 8: 217–228.

Raymont, J. E. G. 1980. *Plankton and Productivity in the Ocean*. Volume 1, *Phytoplankton*. Pergamon Press, Oxford.

Rees, C. P. 1980. "Environmental impacts of dredging operations". pp. 373–381, in *Third International Symposium on Dredging Technology.* Bordeaux, France.

Reid, R. 1981. "Environment and public health in the Caribbean". *Ambio* 10, no. 6: 312–317.

Repetto, R. 1989. *Wasting Assets: Natural Resources in the National Income Accounts*. World Resources Institute, Washington, D.C.

Rodriguez, A. 1981. "Marine and coastal environmental stress in the wider Caribbean region". *Ambio* 10, no. 6: 283–294.

Schneider, S. H. 1989. "The changing climate". *Scientific American* 261, no. 3: 70–79.

Serageldin, I. 1994. *Water Supply, Sanitation and Environmental Sustainability: The Financing Challenge*. World Bank, Washington, D.C.

Serageldin, I., and A. Steer (eds.). 1994. *Valuing the Environment. Proceedings of the 5th Annual International Conference on Environmentally Sustainable Development*. World Bank, Washington, D.C.

Smith, D. 1993. "Harmonizing development with the environment: Environmental impact assessments". *Money Index* (May 25): 20–21.

Snedaker, S. C., and C. D. Getter. 1985. *Coasts: Coastal Resources Management Guidelines*. Coastal Publication no. 2, Renewable Resources Information Series. Research Planning Institute, Columbia, South Carolina.

Steven, D. M. 1965. "Productivity of inshore waters off Jamaica, a comparative study at four stations". pp. 64–87, in *Primary Productivity in the Tropical North Atlantic off Barbados and the Caribbean Sea off Jamaica, Bermuda Biological Station*. Final report submitted to Biology Branch, Office of Naval Research. N.O.N.R. 1135 (05).

Thayer, G. W., D. A.Wolfe, and R. B. Williams. 1975. "The impact of man on seagrass systems". *American Scientist* 63: 288–296.

Thelen, K. D., and S. Faizool. 1980. "Plan for a system of national parks and other protected areas in Trinidad and Tobago". Technical Document, Forestry Division/Organization of American States Project, Trinidad.

Thorhaug, A. 1981. "Biological management of seagrass in the Caribbean". *Ambio* 10, no. 6: 295–298.

Thorhaug, A., D. H. Segar, and M. H. Roessler. 1973. "Impact of a power plant on a subtropical estuarine environment". *Marine Pollution Bulletin* 4: 166–169.

Tomblin, J. 1981. "Earthquakes, volcanoes and hurricanes: A review of natural hazards and vulnerability in the West Indies". *Ambio* 10, no. 6: 340–345.

Turner, R. E. 1984. *Coastal Fisheries, Agriculture, and Management in Indonesia: Case Studies for the Future*. Coastal Case Studies, Coastal Publication no. 2, Renewable Resources Information Series. Research Planning Institute, Columbia, South Carolina.

United Nations Environment Program. 1982. "Tourism". pp. 546–559, in M. W. Holgate, M. Kassas, and G. F. White, eds., *The World Environment, 1972–1982*. Natural Resources and the Environment Series, no. 8. Tycooly International Publishing, Dublin.

Vogel, P. 1994. "Jamaica's coral reefs have collapsed". *Jamaica Naturalist* 4: 27.

Wade, B. 1972. "A description of a highly diverse soft bottom community in Kingston Harbour, Jamaica". *Marine Pollution Bulletin* 3: 106–110.

Wade, B. A. 1976. "The pollution ecology of Kingston Harbour, Jamaica". Research Report, Zoology Department, University of the West Indies, Mona, Jamaica.

Wade, B. A., and D. Forrest. 1993. "Use environmental audits to improve profitability and public image". *Investors Choice* (June): 26–28.

Wade, B. A., and P. H. Reeson. 1985. "Jamaican peat resources: An approach to their development, use and management". pp. 47–70, in *Tropical Peat Resources: Prospects and Potential. Proceedings of the International Peat Society Symposium, February 25–March 1.*

Webber, D. F. 1993. "A rapid assessment of Kingston Harbour. Phase I Report. Harbour condition assessment". Prepared for SENTAR Consultants and National Water Commission, Kingston, Jamaica.

Webber, D. F. 1994. "The water quality of Kingston Harbour, some sources and solutions". *Proceedings of the Scientific Research Council, 7th Annual National Conference on Science and Technology.* Scientific Research Council, Kingston, Jamaica.

Weber, M., R. T. Townsend, and R. Bierce. 1992. *Environmental Quality in the Gulf of Mexico. A Citizen's Guide.* Centre for Marine Conservation.

Wilson, M. 1990. *The Caribbean Environment. Geography for CXC.* Oxford University Press, Oxford.

World Resources Institute. 1991. "Policies and institutions: Natural resources accounting". pp. 231–239. in *World Resources 1990–1991*. World Resources Institute, Washington, D.C.

World Resources Institute. 1994. *World Resources 1994–1995*. World Resources Institute, Washington, D.C.

Contributors

William S. Chalmers is an environmental forestry consultant in Norfolk, England.

Lester Forde is a consultant in water supply, sanitation and environmental engineering at Forde Engineering Consultants, St Augustine, Trinidad.

Garry W. Garcia is lecturer in the Department of Food Production, University of the West Indies, St Augustine, Trinidad.

Ivan Goodbody is Professor Emeritus of Zoology in the Department of Life Sciences, University of the West Indies, Mona, Jamaica.

Anthony Greenaway is senior lecturer in the Department of Chemistry, University of the West Indies, Mona, Jamaica.

Ayuh Khan is lecturer in the Department of Food Production, University of the West Indies, St Augustine, Trinidad.

Robin Mahon is a fisheries and environmental consultant, Bridgetown, Barbados.

Carlisle A. Pemberton is senior lecturer and head of the Department of Agricultural Economics, University of the West Indies, St Augustine, Trinidad.

David Smith is an environmental management consultant and the managing director of Business and Environment Management Services Ltd Jamaica, and former executive director of the Jamaica Conservation and Development Trust.

Elizabeth Thomas-Hope is the James Seivright Moss-Solomon (Snr.) Professor of Environmental Management and head of the Department of Geography and Geology, University of the West Indies, Mona, Jamaica.

Barry A. Wade is chairman and consulting principal, Environmental Solutions Ltd., Kingston, Jamaica.

Dale F. Webber is lecturer in the Department of Life Sciences, University of the West Indies, Mona, Jamaica.

Lawrence A. Wilson is Professor Emeritus of Crop Science in the Department of Food Production, University of the West Indies, St Augustine, Trinidad.

Raymond M. Wright is group managing director of the Petroleum Corporation of Jamaica, Kingston, Jamaica.

Index

C

G

H

M

N

Q

R

S

T

U

V

W

Y

www.ingramcontent.com/pod-product-compliance
Lightning Source LLC
Chambersburg PA
CBHW060948280326
41935CB00009B/660

* 9 7 8 9 7 6 8 1 2 5 7 6 7 *